T0202924

Lecture Notes in Computer Science

Lecture Notes in Artificial Intelligence   14118

Founding Editor

Jörg Siekmann

Series Editors

Randy Goebel, *University of Alberta, Edmonton, Canada*
Wolfgang Wahlster, *DFKI, Berlin, Germany*
Zhi-Hua Zhou, *Nanjing University, Nanjing, China*

The series Lecture Notes in Artificial Intelligence (LNAI) was established in 1988 as a topical subseries of LNCS devoted to artificial intelligence.

The series publishes state-of-the-art research results at a high level. As with the LNCS mother series, the mission of the series is to serve the international R & D community by providing an invaluable service, mainly focused on the publication of conference and workshop proceedings and postproceedings.

Zhi Jin · Yuncheng Jiang ·
Robert Andrei Buchmann · Yaxin Bi ·
Ana-Maria Ghiran · Wenjun Ma
Editors

Knowledge Science, Engineering and Management

16th International Conference, KSEM 2023
Guangzhou, China, August 16–18, 2023
Proceedings, Part II

 Springer

Editors
Zhi Jin ⓘ
Peking University
Beijing, China

Robert Andrei Buchmann ⓘ
Babeş-Bolyai University
Cluj-Napoca, Romania

Ana-Maria Ghiran ⓘ
Babeş-Bolyai University
Cluj-Napoca, Romania

Yuncheng Jiang ⓘ
South China Normal University
Guangzhou, China

Yaxin Bi ⓘ
Ulster University
Belfast, UK

Wenjun Ma ⓘ
South China Normal University
Guangzhou, China

ISSN 0302-9743   ISSN 1611-3349 (electronic)
Lecture Notes in Artificial Intelligence
ISBN 978-3-031-40285-2   ISBN 978-3-031-40286-9 (eBook)
https://doi.org/10.1007/978-3-031-40286-9

LNCS Sublibrary: SL7 – Artificial Intelligence

© The Editor(s) (if applicable) and The Author(s), under exclusive license
to Springer Nature Switzerland AG 2023

This work is subject to copyright. All rights are reserved by the Publisher, whether the whole or part of
the material is concerned, specifically the rights of translation, reprinting, reuse of illustrations, recitation,
broadcasting, reproduction on microfilms or in any other physical way, and transmission or information
storage and retrieval, electronic adaptation, computer software, or by similar or dissimilar methodology now
known or hereafter developed.
The use of general descriptive names, registered names, trademarks, service marks, etc. in this publication
does not imply, even in the absence of a specific statement, that such names are exempt from the relevant
protective laws and regulations and therefore free for general use.
The publisher, the authors, and the editors are safe to assume that the advice and information in this book
are believed to be true and accurate at the date of publication. Neither the publisher nor the authors or the
editors give a warranty, expressed or implied, with respect to the material contained herein or for any errors
or omissions that may have been made. The publisher remains neutral with regard to jurisdictional claims in
published maps and institutional affiliations.

This Springer imprint is published by the registered company Springer Nature Switzerland AG
The registered company address is: Gewerbestrasse 11, 6330 Cham, Switzerland

Preface

We are extremely pleased to introduce the Proceedings of the 16th International Conference on Knowledge Science, Engineering and Management (KSEM 2023), this is a four-volume set containing the papers accepted for this year's conference, which was organized by and hosted at the South China Normal University, Guangzhou, China during August 16–18, 2023.

Since its inaugural conference back in 2006, KSEM has accumulated great success under the immense efforts from each year's organizing committee and beyond. Previous years' events were held in Guilin, China (KSEM 2006); Melbourne, Australia (KSEM 2007); Vienna, Austria (KSEM 2009); Belfast, UK (KSEM 2010); Irvine, USA (KSEM 2011), Dalian, China (KSEM 2013); Sibiu, Romania (KSEM 2014); Chongqing, China (KSEM 2015); Passau, Germany (KSEM 2016); Melbourne, Australia (KSEM 2017); Changchun, China (KSEM 2018); Athens, Greece (KSEM 2019). Even during the COVID pandemic, KSEM was continued and held in Hangzhou, China (KSEM 2020); Tokyo, Japan (KSEM 2021) and Singapore (KSEM 2022), respectively.

The objective of KSEM is to create a forum that gathers researchers and practitioners from academia, industry, and government around the globe to present advancements in theories and state-of-the-art technologies in the field of knowledge science, engineering, and management. Attendees were encouraged to present prototypes and deploy knowledge-based systems, discuss and debate practical challenges as well as opportunities for the research community. With its interdisciplinary nature, KSEM 2023 focused on four broad areas: Knowledge Science with Learning and AI (KSLA), Knowledge Engineering Research and Applications (KERA), Knowledge Management Systems (KMS), and Emerging Technologies for Knowledge Science, Engineering and Management (ETKS).

In this year's conference, we received 395 submissions. Single-blind review was adopted for the conference review process. Each submission was peer reviewed by 2 to 4 reviewers from the program committee members and external reviewers. Among them, 114 regular papers (28.8% acceptance rate) and 30 short papers were selected, giving a total of 144 papers. We have separated the proceedings into four volumes: LNCS 14117, 14118, 14119, and 14120. The collection of papers represents a wide range of research activities, covering knowledge representation and reasoning, knowledge extraction, knowledge integration, data mining and knowledge discovery, and beyond.

In addition to the regular sessions, this year's event featured the following keynote speakers:

- Witold Pedrycz, University of Alberta, Canada, with the presentation titled *Credibility of Machine Learning Through Information Granularity*;
- Zhi-Hua Zhou, Nanjing University, China, with the presentation titled *A New Paradigm to Leverage Formalized Knowledge and Machine Learning*;

- Geoff Webb, Monash University, Australia, with the presentation titled *Recent Advances in Assessing Time Series Similarity Through Dynamic Time Warping*;
- Jie Tang, Tsinghua University, China, with the presentation titled *ChatGLM: Run Your Own "ChatGPT" on a Laptop.*

We would like to express our sincere gratitude to the many contributors who were steadfast supporters and made KSEM 2023 a great success. First of all, we would like to thank the KSEM 2023 Organizing Committee, the School of Computer Science at South China Normal University, Sun Yat-sen University, and our publisher Springer, without their crucial support the conference would not have been possible. Secondly, we would like to thank the members of our Steering Committee (Honorary General Chairs), Ruqian Lu from the Chinese Academy of Sciences, and Dimitris Karagiannis from the University of Vienna, Austria, for their invaluable guidance throughout the event; the General Co-chairs, Zhi Jin from Peking University, Christos Douligeris from the University of Piraeus, Daniel Neagu from the University of Bradford, and Weihua Ma from South China Normal University. They were involved in the whole process of the organization efforts, and provided various critical resources, including but not limited to connections to external reviewers and professional advice. Last but not least, we would like to thank the authors who submitted their papers to this year's conference, the Program Committee and the external reviewers, without whom the daunting tasks of paper reviews would not have been accomplished in time.

We hope that the reader finds the results of the conference program valuable and thought-provoking, and we hope attendees had a valuable opportunity to share ideas with other researchers and practitioners from institutions around the world.

August 2023

Zhi Jin
Yuncheng Jiang
Robert Andrei Buchmann
Yaxin Bi
Ana-Maria Ghiran
Wenjun Ma

Organization

Honorary General Chairs

Ruqian Lu	Chinese Academy of Sciences, China
Dimitris Karagiannis	University of Vienna, Austria

General Chairs

Zhi Jin	Peking University, China
Christos Douligeris	University of Piraeus, Greece
Daniel Neagu	University of Bradford, UK
Weihua Ma	South China Normal University, China

Program Chairs

Yuncheng Jiang	South China Normal University, China
Robert Buchmann	Babeș-Bolyai University, Romania
Yaxin Bi	Ulster University, UK

Publication Chairs

Ana-Maria Ghiran	Babeș-Bolyai University, Romania
Wenjun Ma	South China Normal University, China

Publicity Chairs

Ye Zhu	Deakin University, Australia
Jieyu Zhan	South China Normal University, China

Steering Committee

Ruqian Lu (Honorary Chair)	Chinese Academy of Sciences, China
Dimitris Karagiannis (Chair)	University of Vienna, Austria

Bo Yang	Jilin University, China
Chengqi Zhang	University of Technology, Sydney, Australia
Christos Douligeris	University of Piraeus, Greece
Claudiu Kifor	Lucian Blaga University of Sibiu, Romania
Gang Li	Deakin University, Australia
Hui Xiong	State University of New Jersey, USA
Jörg Siekmann	German Research Centre of Artificial Intelligence, Germany
Martin Wirsing	Ludwig-Maximilians-Universität München, Germany
Meikang Qiu	Texas A&M University-Commerce, USA
Xiaoyang Wang	Zhejiang Gongshang University, China
Yaxin Bi	Ulster University, UK
Yoshiteru Nakamori	Japan Advanced Institute of Science and Technology, Japan
Zhi Jin	Peking University, China
Zili Zhang	Southwest University, China

Technical Program Committee

Achim D. Brucker	University of Exeter, UK
Achim Hoffmann	University of New South Wales, Australia
Agostino Cortesi	Universita' Ca' Foscari di Venezia, Italy
Andrea Polini	University of Camerino, Italy
Ben Roelens	Open Universiteit, Netherlands
Bo Luo	University of Kansas, USA
Bowen Zhao	Singapore Management University, Singapore
Chaobo He	South China Normal University, China
Chenyou Fan	South China Normal University, China
Cheng Huang	Sichuan University, China
Chunxia Zhang	Beijing Institute of Technology, China
Claudiu Kifor	Lucian Blaga University of Sibiu, Romania
Cungen Cao	Chinese Academy of Sciences, Beijing, China
Dan Oleary	University of Southern California, USA
Daniel Volovici	Lucian Blaga University of Sibiu, Romania
Dantong Ouyang	Jilin University, China
Dimitris Apostolou	University of Piraeus, Greece
Dongning Liu	Guangdong University of Technology, China
Florin Leon	Gheorghe Asachi Technical University of Iasi, Romania
Haibo Zhang	University of Otago, New Zealand

Hans Friedrich Witschel	Fachhochschule Nordwestschweiz, Switzerland
Hansi Jiang	SAS Institute, USA
Hao Tang	City University of New York, USA
Hechang Chen	Jilin University, China
Jiahao Cao	Tsinghua University, China
Jan Vanthienen	KU Leuven, Belgium
Jia-Huai You	University of Alberta, Canada
Jianfei Sun	University of Science and Technology of China, China
Jiangning Wu	Dalian University of Technology, China
Jianquan Ouyang	Xiangtan University, China
Jianting Ning	Singapore Management University, Singapore
Jiaqi Zhu	Chinese Academy of Sciences, China
Juan Manuel Vara	University Rey Juan Carlos, Spain
Jue Wang	Chinese Academy of Sciences, China
Jun Zheng	New Mexico Institute of Mining and Technology, USA
Junwei Zhang	Xidian University, China
Krzysztof Kluza	AGH University of Science and Technology, Poland
Leilei Sun	Beihang University, China
Lihua Cai	South China Normal University, China
Liang Chang	Guilin University of Electronic Science and Technology, China
Luca Cernuzzi	Universidad Católica, Chile
Man Zhou	Huazhong University of Science and Technology, China
Marite Kirikova	Riga Technical University, Latvia
Md Ali	Rider University, USA
Meiyong Liu	Sun Yat-sen University, China
Meng Li	Hefei University of Technology, China
Mengchi Liu	South China Normal University, China
Naveed Khan	Ulster University, UK
Nick Bassiliades	Aristotle University of Thessaloniki, Greece
Norbert Pataki	Eötvös Loránd University, Hungary
Pengfei Wu	National University of Singapore, Singapore
Pietro Ferrara	Ca' Foscari University of Venice, Italy
Priscila Cedillo	Universidad de Cuenca, Ecuador
Qiang Gao	Southwestern University of Finance and Economics, China
Qianli Ma	South China University of Technology, China
Qingtian Zeng	Shandong University of Science and Technology, China

Qingzhen Xu	South China Normal University, China
Radu Tudor Ionescu	University of Bucharest, Romania
Remus Brad	Lucian Blaga University of Sibiu, Romania
Ruisheng Shi	Beijing University of Posts & Telecommunications, China
Shaojing Fu	National University of Defense Technology, China
Songmao Zhang	Chinese Academy of Sciences, China
Suqin Tang	Guangxi Normal University, China
Takeshi Morita	Aoyama Gakuin University, Japan
Wei Luo	Deakin University, Australia
Weina Niu	UESTC, China
Weipeng Cao	Guangdong Laboratory of Artificial Intelligence and Digital Economy (Shenzhen), China
Xiang Zhao	National University of Defense Technology, China
Xiangyu Wang	Xidian University, China
Xiangru Li	South China Normal University, China
Xingfu Wu	Argonne National Laboratory, USA
Ye Zhu	Deakin University, Australia
Yiming Li	Tsinghua University, China
Yong Tang	South China Normal University, China
Yongmei Liu	Sun Yat-sen University, China
Yuxin Ye	Jilin University, China
Zehua Guo	Beijing Institute of Technology, China
Zengpeng Li	Lancaster University, UK
Zheng Wang	Northwestern Polytechnical University, China
Zhiping Shi	Capital Normal University, China
Zhiwen Yu	South China University of Technology, China
Zili Zhang	Deakin University, Australia
Zongming Fei	University of Kentucky, USA

Keynotes Abstracts

Credibility of Machine Learning Through Information Granularity

Witold Pedrycz📵

Department of Electrical and Computer Engineering, University of Alberta,
Edmonton, Canada
wpedrycz@ualberta.ca

Abstract. Over the recent years, we have been witnessing numerous and far-reaching developments and applications of Machine Learning (ML). Efficient and systematic design of their architectures is important. Equally important are comprehensive evaluation mechanisms aimed at the assessment of the quality of the obtained results. The credibility of ML models is also of concern to any application, especially the one exhibiting a high level of criticality commonly encountered in autonomous systems and critical processes of decision-making. With this regard, there are a number of burning questions: how to quantify the quality of a result produced by the ML model? What is its credibility? How to equip the models with some self-awareness mechanism so careful guidance for additional supportive experimental evidence could be triggered?

Proceeding with a conceptual and algorithmic pursuits, we advocate that these problems could be formalized in the settings of Granular Computing (GrC). We show that any numeric result be augmented by the associated information granules being viewed as an essential vehicle to quantify credibility. A number of key formalisms explored in GrC are explored, namely those involving probabilistic, interval, and fuzzy information granules. Depending on the formal settings, confidence levels and confidence intervals or coverage and specificity criteria are discussed in depth and we show their role as descriptors of credibility measures.

The general proposals of granular embedding and granular Gaussian Process models are discussed along with their ensemble architectures. In the sequel, several representative and direct applications arising in the realm of transfer learning, knowledge distillation, and federated learning are discussed.

A New Paradigm to Leverage Formalized Knowledge and Machine Learning

Zhi-Hua Zhou

Department of Computer Science and Technology, School of Artificial Intelligence,
Nanjing University, China
zhouzh@nju.edu.cn

Abstract. To develop a unified framework which accommodates and enables machine learning and logical knowledge reasoning to work together effectively is a well-known holy grail problem in artificial intelligence. It is often claimed that advanced intelligent technologies can emerge when machine learning and logical knowledge reasoning can be seamlessly integrated as human beings generally perform problem-solving based on the leverage of perception and reasoning, where perception corresponds to a data-driven process that can be realized by machine learning whereas reasoning corresponds to a knowledge-driven process that can be realized by formalized reasoning. This talk ill present a recent study in this line.

Recent Advances in Assessing Time Series Similarity Through Dynamic Time Warping

Geoff Webb

Department of Data Science and Artificial Intelligence, Monash Data Futures Institute,
Monash University, Australia
Geoff.Webb@monash.edu

Abstract. Time series are a ubiquitous data type that capture information as it evolves over time. Dynamic Time Warping is the classic technique for quantifying similarity between time series. This talk outlines our impactful program of research that has transformed the state of the art in practical application of Dynamic Time Warping to big data tasks. These include fast and effective lower bounds, fast dynamic programming methods for calculating Dynamic Time Warping, and intuitive and effective variants of Dynamic Time Warping that moderate its sometimes-excessive flexibility.

ChatGLM: Run Your Own "ChatGPT" on a Laptop

Jie Tang

Department of Computer Science, Tsinghua University, China
jietang@tsinghua.edu.cn

Abstract. Large language models have substantially advanced the state of the art in various AI tasks, such as natural language understanding and text generation, and image processing, multimodal modeling. In this talk, I am going to talk about how we build GLM-130B, a bilingual (English and Chinese) pre-trained language model with 130 billion parameters. It is an attempt to open-source a 100B-scale model at least as good as GPT-3 and unveil how models of such a scale can be successfully pre-trained. Based on GLM-130B, we have developed ChatGLM, an alternative to ChatGPT. A small version, ChatGLM-6B, is opened with weights and codes. It can be deployed with one RTX 2080 Ti (11G) GPU, which makes it possible for everyone to deploy a ChatGPT! It has attracted over 2,000,000 downloads on Hugging Face in one month, and won the trending #1 model for two weeks.

GLM-130B: https://github.com/THUDM/GLM-130B.
ChatGLM: https://github.com/THUDM/ChatGLM-6B.

Contents – Part II

Knowledge Engineering Research and Applications

Knowing Before Seeing: Incorporating Post-retrieval Information into Pre-retrieval Query Intention Classification

Xueqing Ma[1,2], Xiaochi Wei[3], Yixing Gao[1,2(✉)], Runyang Feng[1,2], Dawei Yin[3], and Yi Chang[1,2(✉)]

[1] Jilin University, Changchun, China
{maxq21,fengry22}@mails.jlu.edu.cn, {gaoyixing,yichang}@jlu.edu.cn
[2] Engineering Research Center of Knowledge-Driven Human-Machine Intelligence, Ministry of Education, Changchun, China
[3] Baidu inc., Beijing, China

Abstract. Query intention classification is crucial for modern search engine, which explicitly limits the search range to the suggested leaf categories where related search results can be retrieved accurately. Recent studies in the field of query intention classification mainly rely on various post-retrieval information, e.g., click-graphs, document categories and click-through logs. However, despite the promising results of such methods, they are not always valid when applied to real search engines. This mainly can be attributed to the unavailability of the post-retrieval information especially for 1) the pre-retrieval scenario and 2) processing the massive long-tail data that have never appeared. To address the problems , we introduce a unique **Post**-retrieval **I**nformation **F**usion (**PostIF**) framework to incorporate post-retrieval information into a pre-retrieval model during training, instead of directly leveraging a straightforward post-retrieval model in both training and inference. The PostIF framework consists of two parts: an imitation module and an integration module. The imitation module learns to transform existing pre-retrieval information into pseudo post-retrieval information under the guidance of real post-retrieval information, and the integration module predicts the final result by integrating the pre-retrieval and the pseudo post-retrieval representation. We further design two specific methods (i.e., detective method, generative method) to implement the imitation module. Extensive experiments on real-world search logs have validated the proposed method in the pre-retrieval query intention classification task.

Keywords: Query Intention Classification · Transfer Learning · Mask Language Model · Information Retrieval · Deep Learning

Supported by the National Natural Science Foundation of China (No. 61976102, No. U19A2065 and No. 62203184).

© The Author(s), under exclusive license to Springer Nature Switzerland AG 2023
Z. Jin et al. (Eds.): KSEM 2023, LNAI 14118, pp. 3–15, 2023.
https://doi.org/10.1007/978-3-031-40286-9_1

1   Introduction

Query intention classifier is a key component of modern search engines [9]. With the help of the query intention, search engines are able to understand users' needs accurately and further provide reliable search results accordingly. Great efforts have been dedicated to query intention classification [15,25,26]. Most recently, more and more classifiers try to improve performance by involving more informative post-retrieval information as input features, such as click graphs [11], document category [2] and click-through logs [1,7].

Despite the effectiveness of the post-retrieval-based query intention classification methods, the post-retrieval information required by them is not always available. The reasons are **twofolds. 1.Pre-Retrieval Scenario.** In a well-designed search engine system [9], as illustrated in Fig. 1(a), the pre-retrieval query classifier is usually the first component that the input query goes through. This means that the post-retrieval information has not yet been generated when the pre-retrieval classifier begins to work, and the classification algorithms cannot observe this useful information in the inference procedure. **2.The Long-Tail Data.** We made statistics on the search frequency of 10 million queries which are randomly sampled from the commercial search engine, Baidu[1]. According to the power-law distribution, as illustrated in Fig. 1(b), most queries have rarely been met before by the search engine. As a result, it is difficult for these queries to obtain their sufficient post-retrieval information due to rare user feedback caused by low presence frequency. Therefore, how to involve post-retrieval information in the query intention classification in a restricted pre-retrieval scenario is a vital but nontrivial problem.

In contrast to the previous work that fully explores the post-retrieval information in both the training and the inference stage, we take into account the unavailability of the post-retrieval information in inference and accordingly present a novel **Post**-retrieval Information **F**usion Framework (**PostIF**). PostIF consists of an imitation module and an integration module. To avoid explicitly using the post-retrieval information in the inference stage, the framework introduces an imitation part to generate the pseudo post-retrieval representation according to the given pre-retrieval representation, and the imitation part is optimized by enforcing the pseudo post-retrieval information to imitate the real counterpart. In the integration module, we fuse the pre-retrieval information and the pseudo post-retrieval information to obtain the final representations for the final query intention classification task.

Within the PostIF framework, we further propose two methods, i.e., a detective method and a generative method, to implement the imitation module. More specifically, the detective method directly tries to minimize the disagreement between the pseudo post-retrieval representation and the real one. While the generative method tries to generate the post-retrieval representation from the pre-retrieval information via a sequence-to-sequence architecture.

The main contributions of this paper are summarized as follows:

- This is the first work that considers the unavailability of the post-retrieval information in inference.

---

[1] Baidu is the largest Chinese commercial search engine. https://www.baidu.com/.

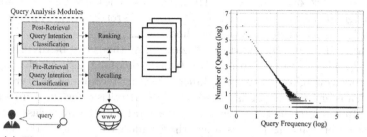

(a) The process of a search engine   (b) The statistics of query frequency

Fig. 1. The illustration of problems in query intention classification methods.

- We propose a novel PostIF framework that is composed of two modules, i.e., the imitation module and the integration module. Based on the PostIF, we introduce a detective method and a generative method to implement the imitation module.
- Extensive experiments on the real search log dataset validated the effectiveness of the proposed framework.

2   Related Work

2.1   Query Intention Classification

Query intention classification plays an irreplaceable role in search engines [15, 25, 26]. Earlier query intention classification technologies include traditional classification approaches, such as Naive Bayes classifier [23], Random Forest [10] and Conditional Random Field [3]. Along with the enormous development of neural networks in recent years, query intention classification approaches can also be further improved. Zhang et al. predicted query category utilizing convolutional neural networks [25]. Shi et al. worked for query features involving deep long-short-term-memory based feature mapping [14]. Sreelakshmi et al. utilized bi-directional long-short-term-memory for query intention [15].

Apart from the work focused on the model structure, a great number of studies tried to incorporate external information to enrich the original input queries. There are two kinds of external information, i.e., pre-retrieval information and post-retrieval information. Pre-retrieval query intention classification relies on the information before searching, such as Wikipedia information [8], external probabilistic knowledge base [20] and session context queries reflecting user preference [26]. In contrast, post-retrieval query intention classfication depends on recalling results after searching, such as retrieved titles and documents of the queries [2], query logs [1] and queries-URLs click graphs [11].

2.2   Transfer Learning

The aim of transfer learning is to improve the performance of the model on target domains through transferring the knowledge contained in the related source domains. In this work, our proposed PostIF framework tries to transfer the abundant knowledge of post-retrieval information into pre-retrieval classifier, which can be regarded as a transfer learning method.

According to transfer objects, transfer learning methods can be divided into four cases [12]. The first refers to instance transfer learning [22], which mainly utilizes instance reweighting and importance sampling techniques. Feature representation transfer learning [24] is the second case. It transforms the source feature representation into the target feature representation. The third case, called parameter transfer learning [19], assumes that a model trained for the source domain could encode some common knowledge for the target domain. Relation transfer learning [5] is the last case, aiming at mining the relational knowledge between the source and target domain. The proposed PostIF framework belongs to the second case, which learns to generate plausible post-retrieval representation based on the pre-retrieval information for query classification enhancement.

3 Methodology

3.1 Problem Definition and Notations

The task of this paper is to fuse the post-retrieval information into the pre-retrieval query intention classification model. Specifically, the pre-retrieval model means that only the pre-retrieval information can be utilized in the inference stage. Thereinto, we use the original query as the pre-retrieval information, while for convenience and reliability, we use the titles of the top retrieval documents as the post-retrieval information in this paper [2].

Therefore, our task can be formalized as follows. We provide a query set $\mathcal{Q} = \{Q_1, Q_2, \cdots, Q_N\}$ and for each query Q_i, a set of titles corresponding to the top retrieved documents are also provided as $\mathcal{T}_i = \{T_1^i, T_2^i, \cdots, T_M^i\}$, where T_j^i denotes the title of the j-th document under the i-th query Q_i. The label is provided as $\mathcal{Y} = \{Y_1, Y_2, \cdots, Y_N\}$, where Y_i represents the category that the query Q_i belongs to. In the task of our work, $\mathcal{Q}$, $\mathcal{T}$, and $\mathcal{Y}$ are all provided in the training stage, while in the inference stage, only $\mathcal{Q}$ is observable to infer $\mathcal{Y}$.

3.2 PostIF Framework

As the post-retrieval information cannot be observed in the inference stage, we find that the post-retrieval information, i.e. titles has a strong relation to the pre-retrieval information, i.e. queries, so that the most important knowledge contained by the titles can be inferred via the queries [2]. Followed this fact, we propose the PostIF framework, and the overall structure is displayed in Fig. 2(a), which consists of two components: the imitation module and the integration module. Next, we will describe the two components in detail.

3.3 Imitation Module

As we cannot observe the titles in the inference stage, the imitation module tries to learn the vital information of both queries and titles, as well as the

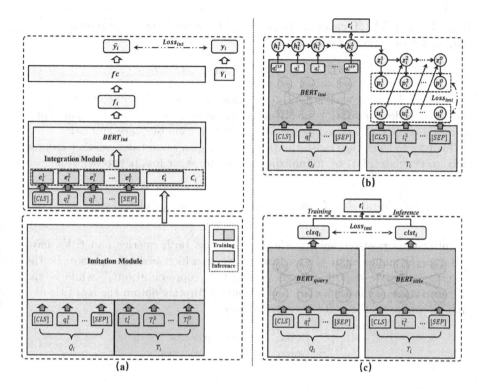

Fig. 2. The overall structure of the PostIF framework.

transformation between them in the training stage. In the inference stage, the imitation module serves as a generator, which re-constructs the representation of titles from the observed queries according to the transformation learned in the training stage. As the re-constructed title representation is generated via the query and different from the real one, we names it "pseudo title", and contrarily the title representation generated by the original title is named as "real title". We propose two kinds of specific methods, i.e., the **detective method** and the **generative method**, to achieve this transformation. The validity of the "pseudo title" has been proven by experiments in Sect. 4.5.

Detective Method. The detective method is shown in Fig. 2(b). Given a query Q_i and a title set T_i, it learns the transformation between them by making the real title representation and the query representation as similar as possible.

In the training stage, we first obtain the representation of each query and its corresponding titles. Since the BERT model has been shown to be outstanding in language representation learning [6], we use the BERT model as the query encoder and the title encoder. In the beginning, two special tokens, "[CLS]" and "[SEP]", are added to the beginning and the end of the query and title sentence, respectively. "[CLS]" is used as the representation of the whole sentence and "[SEP]" denotes the end of the query. For each token, we sum its token, position and segmentation embedding up following the input structure of BERT to obtain the initial embedding. Then the initial embedding of a query Q_i and a title set

$\mathcal{T}_i$ are fed into BERT encoders respectively to obtain the query representation $\textbf{clsq}_i$ and title representation $\textbf{clst}_i$:

$$\textbf{clsq}_i = BERT_{query}(Q_i), \quad \textbf{clst}_i = BERT_{title}(T_i). \tag{1}$$

where $BERT_{query}(\cdot)$ and $BERT_{title}(\cdot)$ stand for the BERT encoder for query and the encoder for titles, respectively. In these two encoders, the output representation of "[CLS]" is used as the final representation of query and title.

In order to learn the transformation between query and titles, we then enforce $\textbf{clsq}_i$ to simulate $\textbf{clst}_i$ by minimizing the square error loss between them:

$$minimize \ Loss_{imitation} = \frac{1}{N} \sum_{i=1}^{N} \|\textbf{clsq}_i - \textbf{clst}_i\|^2. \tag{2}$$

Intuitively, post-retrieval methods which use both queries and titles have better performance than pre-retrieval methods which just use queries. In the training stage, we regard $\textbf{clst}_i$ as pseudo title representation t_i', while in the inference stage, we use the $\textbf{clsq}_i$, as we cannot directly obtain the real title and $\textbf{clsq}_i$ is similar to the real title representation:

$$t_i' = \begin{cases} \textbf{clst}_i, & training\,process, \\ \textbf{clsq}_i, & inference\,process. \end{cases} \tag{3}$$

Generative Method. As the name suggests, the generative method achieves the transformation by directly generating the pseudo title from the query with the guidance of the real titles. As illustrated in Fig. 2(c), this structure follows the "Encoder-Decoder" framework [4], which is widely used in sequence to sequence tasks. Specifically, given a query Q_i, the embedding is generated by a BERT model. Contrary to the above detective method, we make use of the sequence representation $\textbf{SEQ}_i \in \mathbb{R}^{K*L}$ of a BERT model here:

$$\textbf{SEQ}_i = BERT_{imitation}(Q_i), \tag{4}$$

where $BERT_{imitation}(\cdot)$ stands for a BERT model with the sequence representation as the output, where K represents the number of the queries and L represents the length of the query. We feed $\textbf{SEQ}_i$ into a standard LSTM network and use the output of the final state $\textbf{h}_i^L$ as the representation.

The decoder mechanism is also carried out on LSTM. According to $\textbf{h}_i^L$, the previous word in title sequence $\textbf{u}_i^l$ and the previous hidden state $\textbf{z}_i^{l-1}$, we calculate the current hidden state $\textbf{z}_i^l$ and finally predict the probability distribution of the l-th words $\textbf{p}_i^l$ by a fully connected layer with a softmax activation function.

We choose cross entropy to describe the distance between the distribution of decoded pseudo title words p_i^i and the distribution of real title words u_n^i [4]:

$$minimize \ Loss_{imitation} = \sum_{i=1}^{N} H(\textbf{u}_i, \textbf{p}_i) = -\sum_{i=1}^{N} \sum_{l=1}^{L} \textbf{u}_i^l \log \textbf{p}_i^l. \tag{5}$$

Because real titles are used as labels in this method, the pseudo title representations in both training and inference stages are generated title:

$$\mathbf{t}_i{}' = \mathbf{h}_i^L \tag{6}$$

3.4   Integration Module

This module is used to integrate the information of both queries from the input and the pseudo title information served from the imitation module. Given a query Q_i and the pseudo title $\mathbf{t}_i{}'$, the initial embedding $\mathbf{e}_i^j$ for each token q_i^j in Q_i and $\mathbf{t}_i{}'$ are concatenated as $\mathbf{C}_i = [\mathbf{e}_i^1, \cdots, \mathbf{e}_i^L, \mathbf{t}_i{}']$, which is fed into BERT:

$$\mathbf{f}_i = BERT_{integration}\left(\mathbf{C}_i\right) \tag{7}$$

where $BERT_{integration}\left(\cdot\right)$ is a BERT structure with the utilization of "[CLS]" representation among the output as $\mathbf{f}_i$ due to its efficiency in representing the whole sequence. Then $\mathbf{f}_i$ is fed into a fully connected layer with an activation function to obtain the final prediction $\hat{\mathbf{y}}_i \in \mathbf{R}^G$, where G is the number of labels:

$$\hat{\mathbf{y}}_i = softmax\left(\mathbf{W}\mathbf{f}_i + \mathbf{b}\right). \tag{8}$$

where $\mathbf{W}$ and $\mathbf{b}$ represent the learnable weight matrix and bias vector.

We minimize the cross entropy between the prediction $\hat{\mathbf{y}}_i$ and the real label $\mathbf{y}$ to optimize the integration module, and the loss is formulated as:

$$minimize\ Loss_{integration} = \sum_{i=1}^{N} H(\mathbf{y}_i, \hat{\mathbf{y}}_i) = -\sum_{i=1}^{N}\sum_{j=1}^{G} \mathbf{y}_i^j \log \hat{\mathbf{y}}_i^j. \tag{9}$$

3.5   Loss Function

We combine the loss functions of two modules with a hyper-parameter α:

$$minimize\ Loss = Loss_{integration} + \alpha Loss_{imitation}, \tag{10}$$

4   Experiment

4.1   Dataset and Evaluation Metrics

We construct dataset from real search logs of Baidu[2]. Specifically, we randomly select 1 million queries, together with the titles of the top5-searched documents. These queries are classified into 31 first-level categories and 204 second-level categories. For example, we have *"Medicine"* as the first-level category, while the second-level categories are classified in more detail, e.g., *"Disease"*, *"Maternal and Child"*, and *"Cosmetic Medicine"*. These category labels are generated with

---

[2] Baidu is the largest Chinese search engine in the world. http://www.baidu.com.

Table 1. The overall results of different methods. The performances of our proposed methods are in bold and the best performances except BERT-Title are underlined.

Category	Method	Metrics			
		Accuracy	Precision	Recall	F1-score
First leve	BERT	71.62%	71.91%	72.55%	71.88%
	ERNIE	75.50%	74.12%	76.06%	74.53%
	BM25	71.20%	72.00%	73.04%	72.01%
	BERT-Ft	71.87%	71.91%	73.29%	72.31%
	PFD	71.73%	71.44%	73.05%	71.87%
	PostIF-D	**76.24%**	**76.51%**	**76.09%**	**76.59%**
	PostIF-G	**76.05%**	**75.76%**	**76.26%**	**76.67%**
	BERT-Title	78.23%	77.59%	77.28%	77.08%
Second level	BERT	76.17%	74.40%	75.13%	74.70%
	ERNIE	80.63%	79.11%	79.28%	79.08%
	BM25	76.52%	75.26%	76.02%	75.42%
	BERT-Ft	76.29%	74.29%	75.93%	74.98%
	PFD	76.27%	73.98%	75.35%	74.55%
	PostIF-D	**81.50%**	**80.54%**	**79.87%**	**0.15%**
	PostIF-G	**81.37%**	**79.42%**	**80.52%**	**79.82%**
	BERT-Title	83.31%	81.44%	81.44%	81.22%

crowd-sourcing[3]. When labeling, each query is first labeled by two people, and if their labels are different, the third person will make a judgment.

In experiments, all queries are divided into training set, validation set, and testing set, with ratios of 90%, 5%, and 5%. It is worth mentioned that all queries in the validation set and testing set are "long-tail" queries that have not appeared in the training set.

We evaluate our work with traditional evaluation metrics of classification tasks: accuracy, precision, recall and F1. It should be noted that each query can only belong to one category whether in the first-level or the second-level dataset, then the Precision, Recall and F1 we use are macro values.

4.2 Baseline

In order to demonstrate the effectiveness of the proposed approach PostIF, we compare the performance of various baseline methods:

- **BERT** [6]: A six-layer BERT structure model is utilized as the text encoder. In both the training and the inference stage, only the queries are used.
- **ERNIE** [16]: ERNIE is an enhanced pretrained language model with Chinese-adaptive pretrained tasks. Similar to BERT, only queries are observed.
- **BERT-Finetune:** BERT-Finetune uses the same structure as BERT. But it is first pretrained by titles then finetuned by queries. In the inference stage, only queries are observed. This is the basic method to involve post-retrieval information.

---

[3] The data is labeled on Baidu Test platform, http://test.baidu.com/.

– **PFD** [21]: This method trains a teacher model and a student model. The teacher model processes both queries and titles, while the student model distills information from the teacher model with the soft labels, and only the queries are used for the student model.

– **BERT-Title:** This method is the variant of the PostIF and the difference is that both queries and titles are observed in the training and inference stages.

– **BM25** [18]: BM25 is an effective method to find the most relative title of the given query. In order to show the problem of long-tail data, we use BM25 to find the most similar titles from title vocabulary with the restriction of pre-retrieval scenario. Then fed the original query and retrieved title into PostIF to get the final result.

4.3 Overall Performance

The overall results are shown in Table 1, which are statistically significant using a one-tailed Student's t-test with a p-value < 0.05. We make the following observations:

(1) Out of all the methods, BERT-Title method achieves the best performance. The structure of BERT-Title is the same as PostIF, which demonstrates the PostIF framework is able to incorporate post-retrieval information effectively. Because this method utilizes the post-retrieval information, titles, in the inference stage, this performance can be regarded as the ceiling of the PostIF.

(2) BM25 method selected titles from title vocabulary. However, long-tail queries cannot always find suitable titles, which leads to uncertain noise. Therefore, the BM25 method gets an oddly uneven performance: outperforms BERT in the first level but gets contradictory results in the second level. Besides, it takes a major expenditure of time and effort to select titles, which is unfavourable for the pre-retrieval query intention classification.

(3) Other BERT with title information methods, i.e., BERT-Finetune and PFD outperform a single BERT method. These two methods transfer the title information in the BERT model from different angles, which shows that introducing title information can further enhance accuracy.

(4) Two methods of PostIF framework outperform other baselines except BERT-title. The proposed method can utilize title information into the model more effectively without titles in the inference process. Compared with BERT-Title, the performance gap between the PostIF-based method is relatively narrow. This is because the proposed PostIF framework can better incorporate post-retrieval information into the pre-retrieval model with the help of the imitation module and the pseudo title.

(5) The performances of PostIF-Detective and PostIF-Generative shows that both fitting the real title and directly generating the pseudo title can effectively transfer post-retrieval information into the pre-retrieval model.

(6) The above conclusions are quite similar in the first- and second-category datasets. The performance of methods is stable when applied to different datasets.

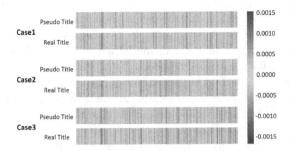

Fig. 3. Visualization of normalized embedding of real title and pseudo title of 3 cases.

Query	True title	Generated title	Predicted label
五年不唯一什么意思 (What's the meaning of five years and not the only one)	现在房产上所说的满五 不唯一是什么意思?税费 是怎么算的? (What's the meaning of more than five and not the only one in real estate? How to calculate the tax？)	现在房产上所说的满五 不唯一是什么意思?税费 是怎么算的? (What's the meaning of more than five and not the only one in real estate? How to calculate the tax？)	生活和情感 (Life and emotion)
微信我想你了星星 (WeChart I miss you Star)	总结7种微信表情雨 (The summary of 7 kinds of Wechat emoji rain)	总结7种微信表情雨 (The summary of 7 kinds of Wechat emoji rain)	信息技术与社交网络 (Information technology and Social network)
成绩没考好的作文 (Composition about poor performance in exam)	写期末考试没考好的作 文,500字 (Composition about poor performance in final exam, 500 words)	写期末考试没考好的作 文,短字 (Composition about poor performance in final exam, short words)	教育培训 (Education)

Fig. 4. The real titles, generated titles and predicted labels of three queries.

4.4   Parameter Tuning

The proposed PostIF introduces a vital hyper-parameter α in Eq.(10). The optimal value of α is carefully tuned on the validation set by grid search. Based on the experiments, we choose $\alpha = 100$ and $\alpha = 10$ for the second-level the first-level dataset in the detective method. As for the generative method, we choose $\alpha = 0.00001$ and $\alpha = 0.01$ for the second-level and the first-level, respectively.

4.5   Pseudo Title Analysis

We compare the pseudo title to the real one in order to analyze its effectiveness.

Detective Method. In the detective method, the pseudo title is constructed by minimizing the disagreement between the representation of the pseudo title and the real one. Therefore, we visualized the pseudo title representation generated by the $BERT_{query}$ and the real title representation inferred by the $BERT_{title}$, respectively. This experiment was conducted on the testing set. We measured the similarity with cosine distance, and the statistical average distance value is 0.0115 with the variance $1.7e-05$. This value is quite small and the performance is stable. Besides, We randomly selected three cases and visualized them in Fig. 3. The representation of both the real and the pseudo title look remarkably similar. These results demonstrates that the pseudo title can imitate the real title using the detective method.

Generative Method. As for the generative method, we compared the corresponding real titles and pseudo titles generated by the generator $G(\cdot)$, which utilize the Beam Search algorithm [17]. We used the BLEU score [13] to evaluate the quality of the generated pseudo titles. The average BLEU score of all testing data is 0.818 with a variance of 0.055. We randomly selected three queries and showed the generated pseudo titles in Fig. 4. We can find that the real titles and the pseudo titles of the first two queries are exactly the same. Although the generated pseudo title is different from the real one, the different terms "500" and "short" have little semantic difference. Therefore, the pseudo titles in the generative method have learned the information in real titles already.

5 Conclusion

In this paper, we propose PostIF framework to incorporate post-retrieval information into the pre-retrieval query intention classification model. Specifically, PostIF trains an imitation module to learn the transformation from the queries to the titles. In the inference stage, the imitation module generates pseudo titles based on the query while the further classifier makes the final decision according to the query and the pseudo titles. Under this framework, two specific methods, the detective and the generative method, are proposed. The experimental results on the real search log dataset demonstrate the outperformance of the proposed PostIF framework. In the future, we consider improving PostIF from the following aspects: Richer Information, User preference and Transfer Method.

References

1. Ashkan, A., Clarke, C.L.A., Agichtein, E., Guo, Q.: Classifying and characterizing query intent. In: Boughanem, M., Berrut, C., Mothe, J., Soule-Dupuy, C. (eds.) ECIR 2009. LNCS, vol. 5478, pp. 578–586. Springer, Heidelberg (2009). https://doi.org/10.1007/978-3-642-00958-7_53
2. Broder, A.Z., Fontoura, M., Gabrilovich, E., Joshi, A., Josifovski, V., Zhang, T.: Robust classification of rare queries using web knowledge. In: Proceedings of SIGIR 2007, pp. 231–238. ACM, Amsterdam (2007)
3. Cao, H., et al.: Context-aware query classification. In: Proceedings of SIGIR 2009, pp. 3–10. ACM, Pairs (2009)
4. Cho, K., et al.: Learning phrase representations using RNN encoder-decoder for statistical machine translation. In: Proceedings of EMNLP 2014, pp. 1724–1734. ACL, Doha (2014)
5. Davis, J., Domingos, P.M.: Deep transfer via second-order markov logic. In: Proceedings of ICML 2009. ACM International Conference Proceeding Series, vol. 382, pp. 217–224. ACM, Montreal (2009)

6. Devlin, J., Chang, M., Lee, K., Toutanova, K.: Bert: Pre-training of deep bidirectional transformers for language understanding. In: Proceedings NAACL HLT 2019, pp. 4171–4186. Association for Computational Linguistics, Minneapolis (2019)

7. Guo, S., et al.: Enhanced doubly robust learning for debiasing post-click conversion rate estimation. In: Proceedings of SIGIR 2021, pp. 275–284. ACM (2021)

8. Hu, J., Wang, G., Lochovsky, F.H., Sun, J., Chen, Z.: Understanding user's query intent with wikipedia. In: Proceedings of WWW 2009, pp. 471–480. ACM, Madrid (2009)

9. Kayhan, V.O., Warkentin, M.: Seeking information using search engines: The impact of negation on judgments. Commun. Assoc. Inf. Syst. **52**, 5 (2022)

10. Khabsa, M., Wu, Z., Giles, C.L.: Towards better understanding of academic search. In: Proceedings of JCDL 2016, pp. 111–114. ACM, Newark (2016)

11. Li, X., Wang, Y., Acero, A.: Learning query intent from regularized click graphs. In: Proceedings of SIGIR 2008, pp. 339–346. ACM, Singapore (2008)

12. Pan, S.J., Yang, Q.: A survey on transfer learning. IEEE Trans. Knowl. Data Eng. **22**(10), 1345–1359 (2010)

13. Papineni, K., Roukos, S., Ward, T., Zhu, W.: Bleu: a method for automatic evaluation of machine translation. In: Proceedings of ACL 2002, pp. 311–318. ACL, Philadelphia (2002)

14. Shi, Y., Yao, K., Tian, L., Jiang, D.: Deep LSTM based feature mapping for query classification. In: Proceedings of NAACL HLT 2016, pp. 1501–1511. The Association for Computational Linguistics, San Diego (2016)

15. Sreelakshmi, K., Rafeeque, P., Sreetha, S., Gayathri, E.: Deep bi-directional lstm network for query intent detection. Proc. Comput. Sci. **143**, 939–946 (2018)

16. Sun, Y., et al.: ERNIE 2.0: A continual pre-training framework for language understanding. In: Proceedings of AAAI 2020, pp. 8968–8975. AAAI Press, New York (2020)

17. Sutskever, I., Vinyals, O., Le, Q.V.: Sequence to sequence learning with neural networks. In: Advances in NIPS 2014, pp. 3104–3112. Montreal (2014)

18. Trotman, A., Puurula, A., Burgess, B.: Improvements to BM25 and language models examined. In: Culpepper, J.S., Park, L.A.F., Zuccon, G. (eds.) Proceedings of the 2014 Australasian Document Computing Symposium, ADCS 2014, Melbourne, VIC, Australia, 27–28 November 2014. p. 58. ACM, Melbourne (2014)

19. Wang, D., et al.: Softly associative transfer learning for cross-domain classification. IEEE Trans. Cybern. **50**(11), 4709–4721 (2020)

20. Wang, Z., Zhao, K., Wang, H., Meng, X., Wen, J.: Query understanding through knowledge-based conceptualization. In: Proceedings of IJCAI 2015, pp. 3264–3270. AAAI Press, Buenos Aires (2015)

21. Xu, C., et al.: Privileged features distillation at taobao recommendations. In: Proceedings of KDD 2020, pp. 2590–2598. ACM, Virtual Event (2020)

22. Yang, C., Xie, L., Qiao, S., Yuille, A.L.: Training deep neural networks in generations: A more tolerant teacher educates better students. In: Proceedings of AAAI 2019, pp. 5628–5635. AAAI Press, Honolulu (2019)

23. Yoshida, M., Matsushima, S., Ono, S., Sato, I., Nakagawa, H.: ITC-UT: tweet categorization by query categorization for on-line reputation management. In: CLEF (Notebook Papers/LABs/Workshops). CEUR Workshop Proceedings, vol. 1176. CEUR-WS.org, Padua (2010)

24. Yu, J., et al.: Modelling domain relationships for transfer learning on retrieval-based question answering systems in e-commerce. In: Proceedings of WSDM 2018, pp. 682–690. ACM, Marina Del Rey (2018)

25. Zhang, H., Song, W., Liu, L., Du, C., Zhao, X.: Query classification using convolutional neural networks. In: ISCID 2017, pp. 441–444. IEEE, Hangzhou (2017)
26. Zhao, J., Chen, H., Yin, D.: A dynamic product-aware learning model for e-commerce query intent understanding. In: Proceedings of CIKM 2019, pp. 1843–1852. ACM, Beijing (2019)

Live-Stream Identification Based on Reasoning Network with Core Traffic Set

Yingshuo Bao[1,3], Shuaili Liu[1,3], Zhongfeng Qu[2], and Lizhi Peng[1,3(✉)]

[1] Shandong Provincial Key Laboratory of Network Based Intelligent Computing, University of Jinan, Jinan 250022, China
[2] School of Mathematical Sciences, University of Jinan, Jinan 250022, China
[3] Quancheng Laboratory, Jinan, China
`plz@ujn.edu.com`

Abstract. The proportion of live-stream traffic in network traffic has been boosting rapidly in recent years, which brings severe challenges to network management. Particularly, some game lives transmit harmful information, which poses great potential harm to adolescents. Therefore, how to effectively identify live-stream traffic becomes an urgent issue to be solved. However, traditional works based on machine learning (ML) methods do not consider many important causalities between flows and video in a live-stream session, lacking interpretability, which inspires us to propose a novel reasoning method to identify different live-stream scenarios. Firstly, we first propose a new technical concept namely core traffic set to contain the most important and significant flows in a live-stream session, and then analyzed the relationship between video flow and other related flows to construct the core traffic set for each session. Then the features related to the live-stream content will be extracted, and a Live-Stream Reasoning Network (LSRN) is designed to infer the corresponding type of live-stream. To evaluate the effectiveness of the proposed approach, a set of experiments are conducted on the dataset collected from the three platforms. In addition, compared with state-of-the-art (SOTA) methods and ensemble classifiers, the results also show that LSRN can significantly contribute to identifying the live video.

Keywords: Live-stream · Reasoning Network · Network Management

1 Introduction

With the development of streaming media technology, online live streaming has become more popular. By 2022, video traffic represented by live streaming will account for 82% of global IP traffic, posing a severe challenge to network management [1]. For example, live streaming requires enormous bandwidth, and some game lives spread harmful information to adolescents. Therefore, identifying different types of live video traffic, especially game live streaming, has become an urgent problem to be solved.

© The Author(s), under exclusive license to Springer Nature Switzerland AG 2023
Z. Jin et al. (Eds.): KSEM 2023, LNAI 14118, pp. 16–26, 2023.
https://doi.org/10.1007/978-3-031-40286-9_2

At present, streaming media platforms use HTTP-based adaptive bit rate streaming (ABS), leading to varied traffic patterns. This provides a possible solution for scholars to extract traffic fingerprints for side channel identification. However, identification methods based on fingerprint matching have apparent limitations: scalability issues, inability to infer video categories and focus only on video flows rather than multimodal traffic. Therefore, to solve the above problems, this paper proposes a live video traffic identification method. Our method is oriented to multi-modal video traffic in real network environments and aims to analyze the relationship between flows and extract traffic features on this basis. Then, we proposed LSRN to analyze the causality between traffic features and live streaming labels, realizing more interpretable live scenario identification.

This paper has the following contributions: (1). A weight measurement is proposed to analyse the similarity of flows in the time domain. (2). A new concept namely *core traffic set* is introduced to describe flows most relevant to the content of the session and uses kernel-based conditional independence (KCI) test to extract it. (3). A live-stream reasoning network (LSRN) is proposed to reason the live-stream scenario.

The rest of the paper is as follows: Sect. 2 reviews the related work. Sect. 3 describes the detail of the method. Sect. 4 shows the experiment and Sect. 5 concludes the paper.

2   Related Work

Most works for video traffic identification aim to extract effective features from encrypted traffic, which can be roughly divided into statistical flow features, bytes per second (BPS) features, burst features, and ADU features. Statistical flow features can directly reflect the variation of encrypted video traffic. Li et al. [2] set change points from the time series to divide traffic and extracted the mean, variance, skewness, and kurtosis of packet-level features to recognize and cluster basic daily behaviours. To extract high-level semantic information, Khan et al. [3] extracted BPS from video flows to train ML models, including support vector machines and CNN. However, it is not enough to represent the variation of video. Therefore, Schuster R et al. [4] propose that the burst pattern of a video flow caused by a video segment can be used as a unique fingerprint. Unfortunately, burst patterns should be easy to distinguish with a stable network environment. Hence, some scholars have focused on studying transmitted video ADUs. Li et al. [5] used coarse ADU size and other flow features as thresholds to identify video flows. To obtain more reliable fingerprints, Wu et al. [6] used the HTTP header and TLS segment features as the ADU length fitting features and proposed an accurate recovery method for encrypted ADU fingerprints. Overall, current studies aim to use an ML algorithm to identify known video titles based on various feature fingerprints, but this approach cannot give interpretable results.

To address the above problems, some researchers devote to the application of causality in the network field, Cheng et al. [7] used BN to explore causality between context and QoS metrics, and deployed the model in real multimedia conference systems to achieve context-aware cognitive QoS management.

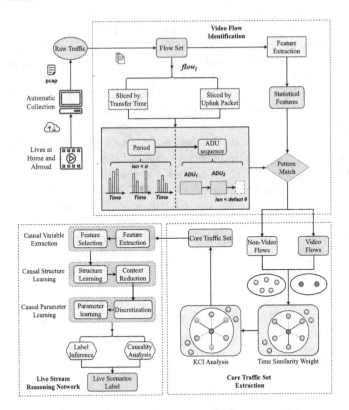

Fig. 1. The overview of the live streaming identification. **Video flow identification** identifies video flow from raw traffic. **Core traffic set identification** focuses on the relationship between flows. **Live Stream Reasoning Network** aims to analyse the causality between features and live scenario labels.

3   Methodology

3.1   Video Flow Identification

Video flow is the base of video behaviour analysis which inspires us to identify video flow from the mixed raw traffic. Firstly, we use five tuples(src IP, dst IP, src port, dst port, protocol) to filter out irrelevant flows to obtain a collection of TCP flows. Due to the live video mostly transmitted by elephant flow, this section uses the duration to filter the rat flows as Eq. 1:

$$f(t_i) = \begin{cases} 1 & t_i < \beta T \\ 0 & t_i > \beta T \end{cases} \tag{1}$$

where T denotes the total time of the live session, t_i denotes the duration of each flow, and β is a filter parameter used to distinguish elephant from rat flows.

As we know, most platforms divide the video into ADUs with different lengths, which inspires us to use ADU to design a general identification method for multiple platforms. As Fig. 1 shows, we extracted a BPS sequence $a = (a_1, a_2, ..., a_m)$, where a_i represents the sum of the packet payload in the ith second for the downlink of flow. After that, the BPS sequence would be sliced by transfer time or uplink packet according to their traffic pattern. If the uplink of flow doesn't have a non-empty packet, a time interval σ would be used to divide the BPS sequence. Otherwise, two consecutive uplink packets with the same payload would be used as a slice flag whose payload usually exceeds the fixed threshold ϵ. Based on this, the period larger than the default ADU size would be selected to get the final ADU sequence $P = (p_1, p_2, ..., p_{l-1}, p_l)$, where l represents the number of ADUs. The number of ADUs is an important identifying feature for video flows. In addition, other traditional flow-level features are also used for video flow identification. It will be marked as video flow if a flow meets the following threshold conditions in Table 1.

Table 1. The details of threshold conditions

Thresh.	Description	Defaults
T_v	segment length threshold for video ADU	100 KB
R_v	rate threshold for video	300 Kb/s
R_a	rate threshold for non-video	192 Kb/s
L_v	pkt length threshold for video	900 B
L_a	pkt length threshold for non-video	450 B
S_v	segment for Live ADU	3
σ	time interval for Live ADU	2 s
ϵ	fixed uplink payload for Live ADU	89 B

3.2 Core Traffic Set Identification

Core traffic set identification aims to remove irrelevant flows and identify video-related flows from video sessions. After video flow identification, we take video flows as Y and other flows as X. Then we extract the trend of segments to uniquely represent each flow, which is relatively stable in various resolutions.

First, the weight w is introduced to measure the similarity of the flow in the time domain, which can be calculated as follows:

$$w = (\mid t^1_{start} - t^2_{start} \mid) \times (\mid \tau^1_{mean} - \tau^2_{mean} \mid) \tag{2}$$

where t^1_{start} and t^2_{start} correspond to the start time of Y and X, τ^1_{mean} and τ^2_{mean} present the average arrival time interval of them at flow level respectively. if the weight is smaller, the similarity between the two flow patterns is higher.

Afterwards, the KCI test [9] is used to analyze the nonlinear relationship between X and Y. To meet the requirement of consistent variable length, we zero-padded variables for the length of X smaller than Y to obtain the same length. Under the null hypothesis, the statistics between them as Eq. 3 shows.

$$T_{UI} \triangleq \frac{1}{n} Tr (\tilde{K}_X \tilde{K}_Y) \triangleq \frac{1}{n^2} \sum_{i,j=1}^{n} \lambda_{x,i} * \lambda_{y,j} * z^2_{ij} \tag{3}$$

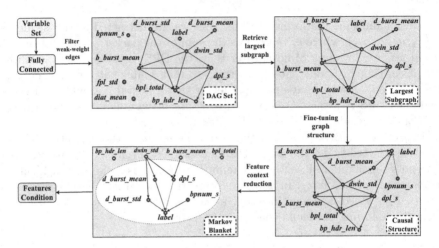

Fig. 2. Causal structure learning framework, including structure learning based on Notears, filtering weak weight edge, retrieving the largest subgraph, fine-tuning graph structure and feature context reduction. In the figure, blue nodes are irrelevant features, orange nodes are interrelated features, yellow nodes are isolated labels, and white nodes are features that are indirectly related to labels. (Color figure online)

3.3 Causal Inference

Based on the core traffic set, we propose LSRN to analyze the causality between features and live labels, which is based on causal Bayesian networks including causal variable extraction, causal structure and causal parameter learning.

Causal Variables Extraction. This part selects the most relevant features from the core traffic set and constructs the causal variable set together with the live label. To remove redundant features and reduce training time, XGBOOST is used to select the most important 10 related features. After that, we propose important feature constraints to ensure the connection between labels and features. If it does not exist edges between labels and features in structure learning, we will select some related features to create connections according to feature constraints, including statistics of bursts, data rates, and packet rates.

Causal Structure Learning. This part introduces the Notears algorithm [10] to learn the causal structure between features and label variables. From the perspective of training objectives, the Notears algorithm formulates the DAG learning problem as a pure continuous optimization problem on a real matrix, avoiding heuristic combination constraints, as shown in the following.

$$\begin{array}{ll} \min\limits_{W \in \mathbb{R}^{d \times d}} & F(W) \\ C \quad s.t. \quad G(W) \in DAGs \end{array} \iff \begin{array}{ll} \min\limits_{W \in \mathbb{R}^{d \times d}} & F(W) \\ C \quad s.t. \quad h(W) = 0 \end{array} \qquad (4)$$

where $G(W)$ is a d-node graph represented by the weighted adjacency matrix W, $F : \mathbb{R}^{d \times d} \to \mathbb{R}$ is a scoring function, and $h : \mathbb{R}^{d \times d} \to \mathbb{R}$ is a smoothing function for setting constraints, whose level set at 0 means DAGs have been learned.

Causal Parameters Learning. This part introduces Maximum a Posterior (MAP) to calculate the label probability of samples under different feature conditions. Suppose $C = (C_1, C_2, ...C_i, ..., C_n)$ is a sample containing n features determined by structure learning. To quantize the feature value C_i, we use linear regularization to normalize it to $[0-1]$, then map it to different intervals by equidistant discretization (default 3 intervals). Afterwards, the probability of labels can be easily expressed as Eq. 5.

$$P\left(S = s | CC_1 = cc_1, ..., CC_n = cc_n \right) = p \tag{5}$$

where S is a label variable, $(CC_1, CC_2, ..., CC_n)$ is n discrete feature variables.

Since S is a multinomial distribution with three parameters, a Dirichlet distribution is introduced as a conjugate distribution to calculate the posterior probability p, whose parameters are $\alpha = (\alpha_1, \alpha_2, \alpha_3)$, where α_i represents the ith parameter. Based on this, the prior probability of the label can be expressed as $\theta = (\theta_1, \theta_2, \theta_3)$, where θ_i represents the ith label probability. Under the condition of the prior probability, assuming there are n experiments, denote x_i as the occurrences numbers of ith label during identification. Then the posterior probability of the θ can be calculated as Eq. 6.

$$
\begin{aligned}
p\left(\theta | D \right) &= \frac{\Gamma\left(\sum_{i=1}^{3} \alpha_i + n \right)}{\prod_{i=1}^{3} \Gamma\left(\sum_{i=1}^{3} \alpha_i + x_i \right)} \prod_{i=1}^{3} \theta_i^{\alpha_i + x_i - 1} \\
&= \frac{1}{Beta\left(\alpha' \right)} \prod_{i=1}^{3} \theta_i^{\alpha_i' - 1}
\end{aligned}
\tag{6}
$$

where $Beta\left(\alpha \right) = \frac{\prod_{i=1}^{3} \Gamma(\alpha_i)}{\Gamma(\sum_{i=1}^{3} \alpha_i)}$, $a' = (a_1 + x_1, a_2 + x_2, a_3 + a_3)$ and D represents the condition set that m features sample during n experiments. Finally, we can infer the label type with maximum posterior probability based on feature conditions.

4 Experiment

4.1 Data Collection

During the collection, we use laptops to play live video on the Edge browser and use Wireshark to collect multimodal traffic. The video resolutions include 720p and 1080p, and video scenes include online games, video chat, and outdoor activities. We regard distinguishing game and non-game live as coarse-grained tasks and further infer game, chat, and outdoor lives as fine-grained tasks. Due to different experimental purposes, data collection is divided into four groups as shown in Table 2. The training and test set of all experiments is split at a ratio of 8:2. To enhance the credibility of experiments, the public data set CRAWDAD [11] is used to evaluate the effect of the core traffic set, which is traffic generated by video applications including HotStar, StarSports, TED, and TimesNow.

Table 2. The description of all experimental data. **Video.** is the video flow identification, **Core.** stands the core traffic set experiment, **LSRN.** indicates the LSRN evaluation, **Multi.** indicates the application on multiple platforms.

Experiment	Types	Sources	Resolutions.	Groups	Numbers	Size
Video.	Collected	BiliBili	1080 p	100 s	6	1.00 GB
				200 s	6	1.42 GB
				300 s	6	1.97 GB
Core.	Public	CRAWDAD	uncertain	HotStar	7	0.75 GB
				StarSports	6	0.67 GB
				TED	10	0.34 GB
				TimesNow	3	0.16 GB
	Collected	BiliBili	720p	No-Div	154	4.47 GB
LSRN.	Collected	BiliBili	1080 p	Game	100	4.92 GB
				Chat	50	2.24 GB
				Outdoor	50	2.12 GB
	Collected	Multi.	1080 p	BiliBili	200	13.67 GB
				Douyu	200	26.17 GB
				Huya	200	11.95 GB

4.2   Video Flow Identification

To evaluate the ACC of encrypted video flow identification, we introduce server name indication (SNI) which can easily indicate each flow. Our experiment collected multi-modal traffic from BiliBili 720p live video, which we divided into three groups (100s, 200s, and 300s) as shown in Table 3. The ACC of all *video* is 100%, and *nonvideo* is above 98.5%. Among the flows marked as *maybe*, the actual video flow ratios are 13.14%, 12.20% and 20.00% respectively, suggesting that we should explore it further. In summary, the identification results are consistent with the actual situation, and the longer the detection time, the more accurate the result where the ACC of the 300s group can reach 98.5%.

Table 3. The details of video identification.

Data Set.	Flow type	Predicted Flows	Fact Flows	Accurate
100s * 6	video	15	15	100%
	nonvideo	719	709	98.60%
	maybe	82	11	13.41%
	All	816	735	**90.07%**
200s * 6	video	6	6	100%
	nonvideo	632	627	99.21%
	maybe	41	5	12.20%
	All	679	316	**93.96%**
300s * 6	video	13	13	100%
	nonvideo	594	591	99.49%
	maybe	10	2	20.00%
	All	617	606	**98.22%**

4.3   Evaluation of the Core Traffic Set

To evaluate different core traffic sets, we used RF, Adaboost, GBDT, and Cat-Boost as identification models. The experiments were divided into five groups based on the extraction method. *Elephant* filters out rat flow whose transmission time is less than 10 s and less than 10 packets. *Weighted* filters out the flow whose time similarity weight is below 15. *DTW*, *Pearson*, and *KCI* are the comparison groups based on elephant flows, which use dynamic time warping, linear correlation and KCI test to extract the core traffic set respectively. As shown in Fig. 3, applying weights is more effective than simply filtering rat flows. All three methods for extracting core traffic sets significantly improved identification accuracy, and the proposed KCI method performed best relatively.

Additionally, we also evaluated the performance of KCI combined weight on LSRN using traffic collected from BiliBili 720p live video. As shown in Fig. 4, using KCI weighted (KCIs) significantly improved the result, especially for fine-grained tasks where the ACC increased by 5% and the AUC of both coarse and fine-grained tasks improved by 3%. These results show that the proposed method is effective for live-streaming traffic inference.

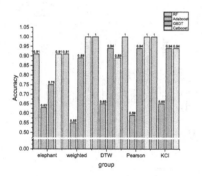 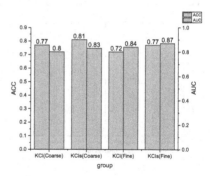

Fig. 3. Comparison of Core Flow Sets.   **Fig. 4.** Comparison of KCI and KCIs

Table 4. The comparisons of three methods on different tasks

Model	DTW		Person		KCI		DTW		Person		KCI		KCI	
Task	coarse		coarse		coarse		fine		fine		fine		other	
Index	Acc	AUC	Acc	AUC	Acc	AUC	Acc	AUC	Acc	AUC	Acc	AUC	Time	Num
LSRN	81.25	0.83	**81.25**	**0.83**	81.81	0.83	75.00	0.84	72.91	0.82	**77.08**	0.87	0.331	**10**
CatBoost	78.00	0.77	**81.25**	0.81	81.25	0.80	68.75	0.74	68.75	0.74	68.75	0.74	0.307	87
RF	75.00	0.75	68.75	0.69	81.25	0.81	**78.12**	0.89	**75.00**	0.87	71.88	0.90	0.129	87
AdaBoost	75.00	0.75	77.50	0.78	80.00	0.80	77.50	**0.91**	65.00	0.84	70.00	0.85	**0.095**	87
Bagging	**85.00**	**0.85**	78.00	0.77	80.00	0.80	70.00	0.89	70.00	**0.89**	75.00	**0.91**	0.132	87

4.4   Evaluation of Live Scenario Reasoning Network

LSRN is a classification model used for label inference. We use DTW, Pearson, and KCI to conduct experiments on BiliBili's 1080p live video traffic to extract core traffic sets and use five classification models of RF, Catboost, GBDT, Adaboost, and Bagging as the control group.

As Table 4 shows, coarse-grained performance is better than fine-grained tasks, especially for the Person and KCI groups. Meanwhile, the ACC of LSRN achieves the highest in the KCI group for fine-grained tasks, indicating that our method is effective. Although LSRN's execution time is slightly higher than other models, it achieves high accuracy with only 10 traffic features, making it a worthwhile trade-off compared to models that require a large number of features.

Lastly, we also compare LSRN with ET-BERT[12], a transformer-based state-of-art (SOTA) approach for large-scale unlabeled encrypted traffic classification. The results are shown in Fig. 5, the performance of LSRN is better than ET-BERT, which shows that LSRN is more suitable for the identification of live video traffic than ET-BERT under the same amount of data.

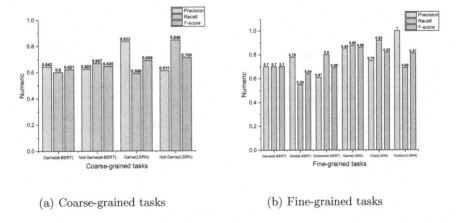

(a) Coarse-grained tasks   (b) Fine-grained tasks

Fig. 5. The comparison of LSRN and ET-BERT on the different grained tasks.

Table 5. Comparison of discretization at three scales on the three platforms

Platform	BiliBili		DouYu		HuYa		BiliBili		DouYu		HuYa	
Task	coarse		coarse		coarse		fine		fine		fine	
Index	Acc	AUC	Acc	AUC	Acc	AUC	Acc	AUC	Acc	AUC	Acc	AUC
Binary	**82.50**	0.82	60.86	0.63	61.36	0.69	**72.50**	0.80	54.34	0.75	59.10	0.79
Ternary	77.50	0.79	71.39	0.84	70.45	0.77	70.00	0.79	71.73	0.92	**72.72**	0.87
Quaternary	80.00	**0.83**	**76.08**	**0.91**	**72.72**	**0.82**	70.00	**0.81**	**76.08**	**0.94**	**72.72**	**0.90**

To explore the sensitivity of each platform, we also discretized continuous traffic features into three groups: Binary, Ternary, and Quaternary. As shown in Table 6, the results of platforms increase with feature discretization.

5 Conclusion

This paper successfully combines a weight measure and KCI to construct core traffic set for a live video session. Based on this, we propose LSRN to analyze the causality between live scenes and traffic features, which improves identification performance. Overall, it shows that LSRN is an effective and lightweight model.

Acknowledgement. This research was partially supported by the National Natural Science Foundation of China under Grant No.61972176, Shandong Provincial Natural Science Foundation, China under Grant No. ZR2021LZH002, Jinan Scientific Research Leader Studio, China under Grant No.202228114, Shandong Provincial key projects of basic research, China under Grant No.ZR2022ZD01, Shandong Provincial Key R&D Program, China under Grant No.2021SFGC0401, and Science and Technology Program of University of Jinan (XKY1802)).

References

1. Barnett, T., Jain, S., Andra, U., Khurana, T.: Cisco visual networking index (vni) complete forecast update, 2017–2022. Americas/EMEAR Cisco Knowledge Network (CKN) Presentation, pp. 1–30 (2018)
2. Li, H., He, Y., Sun, L., Cheng, X., Yu, J.: Side-channel information leakage of encrypted video stream in video surveillance systems. In: IEEE INFOCOM 2016-The 35th Annual IEEE International Conference on Computer Communications, pp. 1–9. IEEE (2016)
3. Khan, M.U., Bukhari, S.M., Khan, S.A., Maqsood, T.: Isp can identify youtube videos that you just watched. In: 2021 International Conference on Frontiers of Information Technology (FIT), pp. 1–6. IEEE (2021)
4. Schuster, R., Shmatikov, V., Tromer, E.: Beauty and the burst: Remote identification of encrypted video streams. In: 26th USENIX Security Symposium (USENIX Security 17), pp. 1357–1374 (2017)
5. Li, F., Chung, J.W., Claypool, M.: Silhouette: Identifying youtube video flows from encrypted traffic. In: Proceedings of the 28th ACM SIGMM Workshop on Network and Operating Systems Support for Digital Audio and Video, pp. 19–24 (2018)
6. Wu, H., Yu, Z., Cheng, G., Guo, S.: Identification of encrypted video streaming based on differential fingerprints. In: IEEE INFOCOM 2020- IEEE Conference on Computer Communications Workshops (INFOCOM WKSHPS), pp. 74–79. IEEE (2020)
7. Cheng, B., Wang, M., Lin, X., Chen, J.: Context-aware cognitive QoS management for networking video transmission. IEEE/ACM Trans. Network. 29(3), 1422–1434 (2021)
8. Zhang, K., Peters, J., Janzing, D., Scholkopf, B.: Kernel-based conditional independence test and application in causal discovery. arXiv preprint arXiv:1202.3775 (2012)

9. Zheng, X., Aragam, B., Ravikumar, P.K., Xing, E.P.: Dags with no tears: Continuous optimization for structure learning. In: Advances in Neural Information Processing Systems 31 (2018)
10. Fu, S., Desmarais, M.C.: Markov blanket-based feature selection: a review of past decade. In: Proceedings of the world congress on Engineering, vol. 1, pp. 321–328. Newswood Ltd., Hong Kong, China (2010)
11. Sengupta, S., Gupta, H., Ganguly, N., Mitra, B., De, P., Chakraborty, S.: CRAW-DAD dataset iitkgp/apptraffic (v. 2015–11-26). Downloaded from https://crawdad. org/iitkgp/apptraffic/20151126/apptraffictraces (Nov 2015). https://doi.org/10. 15783/C77S3W
12. Lin, X., Xiong, G., Gou, G., Li, Z., Shi, J., Yu, J.: Et-bert: A contextualized datagram representation with pre-training transformers for encrypted traffic classification. In: Proceedings of the ACM Web Conference 2022, pp. 633–642 (2022)

Implicit Offensive Speech Detection Based on Multi-feature Fusion

Tengda Guo(iD), Lianxin Lin(iD), Hang Liu(iD), Chengping Zheng(iD), Zhijian Tu(iD), and Haizhou Wang(✉)(iD)

School of Cyber Science and Engineering, Sichuan University, Chengdu 610207, China
{guotengda,linlianxin,liuhang,zhengchengping,tuzhijian}@stu.scu.edu.cn,
whzh.nc@scu.edu.cn

Abstract. As social media platforms become increasingly strict in censorship of user posts, aggressive and insulting language has gradually shifted to implicit expressions using homophones, metaphors, and other forms of camouflage. This not only intensifies the satirical attacks of negative posts but also leads to a significant decrease in the effectiveness of models designed to detect offensive speech. This paper aims to achieve high accurate detection of implicit offensive speech. We conducted targeted investigations on the speech characteristics on Weibo, which is one of the largest social media platform in China. Based on the identified features of implicit offensive speech, including semantic, emotional, metaphorical, and fallacy characteristics, this paper constructs a BERT-based Multi-Task learning model named BMA (BERT-Mate-Ambiguity) to accurately detect the implicit offensive speech in the real world. Additionally, this paper establishes a dataset based on posts of Weibo that contain implicit offensive speech and conducts various comparative, robustness, and ablation experiments. The effectiveness of the model is demonstrated by comparing it to existing models that perform well in this field. Finally, this paper discusses some of its limitations and proposes future research work.

Keywords: Implicit Offensive Speech · Classification · Deep Learning · Natural Language Processing · Weibo

1 Introduction

1.1 Background

In the era of rapid development of information technology, social media have infiltrated every aspect of human life and become an important means of communication and interaction among people. With the rapid development of social networks represented by Twitter, TikTok, and Weibo, communication among people has become more convenient. And the anonymity of the Internet has reduced moral constraints, leading to a significant increase in online bullying.

© The Author(s), under exclusive license to Springer Nature Switzerland AG 2023
Z. Jin et al. (Eds.): KSEM 2023, LNAI 14118, pp. 27–38, 2023.
https://doi.org/10.1007/978-3-031-40286-9_3

Currently, research on detecting offensive speech in social media mainly focuses on processing some relatively obvious offensive text. However, on social networking platforms, a large amount of offensive speech often evade detection by deliberately misspelling or using metaphors, and the same sentence may show completely opposite meanings in different contexts, which makes the existing detection methods ineffective. Therefore, there are still significant challenges in the field of detecting implicit offensive speech on social networking platforms.

Social media offensive speech may involve targeted hate speech, abusive language, and threats to individuals or communities in terms of race, ethnicity, sexual orientation, religion, political stance, etc. [1]. In this paper, we define offensive speech on social media as a medium to target individuals or groups. It aims to attack, harm, provoke, or intimidate others, with the intent to belittle, insult, or tarnish them. Implicit offensive speech refers to language that has features that are not easily detected by social platforms based on offensive speech.

1.2   Challenges

The main challenges in detecting implicit offensive speech on social media include two aspects: (1) current research mostly focuses on explicit offensive speech, and there is less research on detecting implicit offensive speech; (2) there is currently no dataset for implicit offensive speech, and there is no consensus on the definition and features of implicit offensive speech. Due to the lack of Chinese language corpora, such problems in natural language processing have become more challenging [2]. To address the existing challenges, this paper uses pre-trained language model and multi-task learning theory to detect implicit offensive speech on social platforms. By utilizing the powerful semantic analysis ability of BERT (Bidirectional Encoder Representations for Transformers) to extract deep features and adopting multi-task learning to reduce model complexity, which have achieved significant results.

1.3   Contributions

The main contributions of this paper are as follows:

(1) Collecting explicit and implicit offensive speech posted by users on Weibo and constructing the first Chinese implicit offensive speech dataset.
(2) Proposing a multi-feature fusion implicit offensive speech detection model based on the pre-training self-supervised BERT model and Multi-Task learning method, which efficiently detects implicit offensive speech through features such as metaphors and ambiguity.

1.4   Organization of the Paper

The first part of this paper mainly describes the research background, challenges, and contributions of this paper to the problem. The second part analyzes the main methods and their advantages and disadvantages for detecting offensive speech. The third part elaborates on the dataset and the BMA model construction method. The fourth part describes the experimental settings, relevant experimental methods, and results visualization. The fifth part presents the conclusion of this paper.

2 Related Work

The methods for detecting offensive speech can be classified into three categories: machine learning-based, deep learning-based, and other methods.

2.1 Machine Learning-based Offensive Speech Detection

In the early stages of offensive speech detection, the primary methods used were machine learning-based methods. For example, Davidson et al. [3] used a multi-class classifier trained on a tweet sample containing hate speech, offensive speech, and neutral language to distinguish them. George Kennedy's research, based on N-Gram features and sentiment polarity features, used random forests to learn the features and achieved excellent results [4]. However, machine learning-based methods is generally based on shallow models, which are effective for linearly separable or simple nonlinear data, but the performance of machine learning declines sharply when there is a highly complex, difficult-to-understand nonlinear relationship between input and output.

2.2 Deep Learning-Based Offensive Speech Detection

Compared to traditional machine learning methods, deep learning-based methods performs better for complex real-world tasks. For example, The research by Chatzakou et al. [20] demonstrate that combining multiple types of features can effectively improve the classification performance. Mishra et al. [5] proposed a graph convolutional network that incorporated more related information such as user personal information and social information to better capture features. However, using deep learning methods for offensive speech detection still has some limitations, and different algorithms may be suitable for data with different labels under different data balance conditions. By analyzing the results of multiple tests on offensive speech detection, many algorithms still need to improve their accuracy.

2.3 Other Offensive Speech Detection Methods

Other offensive speech detection methods mainly use BERT to improve detection accuracy. Kumar et al. [6] conducted an approximate investigation of several methods for detecting hate content and found that the BERT model far exceeded other methods. Shukla et al. [7] proposed a method that uses BERT and convolutional neural networks to detect the offensive speech in Hindi, which achieved good results. However, these methods did not specifically focus on effective detection of implicit offensive speech.

3 Research Methodology

3.1 Data Set Construction

Existing datasets of offensive speech doesn't contain specific labeling of implicit offensive speech. Therefore, we constructed our own offensive speech dataset, namely WIOS-Dataset (Weibo Implicit Offensive Speech Dataset), which includes one part of the data we crawled from Weibo, the largest Chinese social media platform, and another part from the COLData[1] and ITD[2] (Illegal Text Detection) datasets. In the data crawling process, we filtered out a large number of duplicate or invalid data to ensure the validity and timeliness of the data. The COLData and Illegal Text Detection datasets are recognized as the most reliable Chinese datasets for offensive speech detection research. However, they do not differentiate between explicit offensive speech and implicit offensive speech, thus we have re-annotated the data we used in this paper.

Table 1. Overall composition of the WIOS-Dataset

	Weibo Data	COLData[*a]	ITD[*a]
Normal Speech	35,139	5928	3,165
Explicit Offensive Speech	479	649	3,220
Implicit Offensive Speech	1,392	1,934	2,808

[a]The data in COLData and ITD has been labeled again as we need

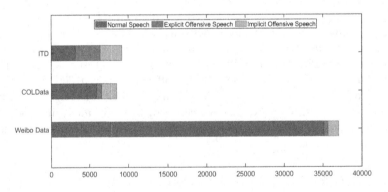

Fig. 1. Overall composition of the WIOS-Dataset

We selected 7,000 normal speech and 5,000 implicit offensive speech for model training and testing.

---

[1] https://github.com/thu-coai/COLDataset.
[2] https://github.com/wjx-git/IllegalTextDetection.

3.2   BMA Model Construction

The BMA model consists of three modules: Semantic Module based on BERT, Multi-Feature Extraction Module, and Feature Fusion Module. The model structure is shown in Fig. 2.

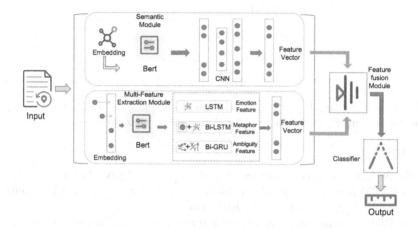

Fig. 2. Model Architecture

At the input layer, the data is vectorized using BERT's tokenizer. The input text is processed into tokens, mapped to indices in the pre-training word table of BERT, and converted into the same format as the markers used in the pre-training process of BERT. BERT's tokenizer uses the WordPiece algorithm, which splits words into smaller subwords, allowing for better handling of unknown words.

Semantic Module. Semantic features are extracted using the BERT+CNN (Convolutional Neural Networks) module. The input text sequence is encoded using the pre-trained deep learning model BERT, and its semantic features are extracted, which are further processed using CNN to obtain its deep features.

Multi-feature Extraction Module. The Multi-Feature Extraction Module is responsible for extracting sentiment, metaphor, and ambiguity features [9]. This module first performs embedding on the input, and then passes the resulting vectors to the feature extractors for extracting corresponding feature vectors, which will be used for the subsequent detection:

1) Extraction of Emotion Features:

First, a pre-trained model is used to represent the input text as a feature vector R. The output of the last time step of this feature representation is used as the input of the LSTM (Long Short Term Memory Networks) . Then, the input is encoded using the LSTM to obtain the hidden state. For bidirectional LSTM, the forward and backward hidden states are concatenated to obtain the vector H. Equations (1)–(4) show the operations performed by the Bi-LSTM (Bidirectional Long Short-Term Memory Network) layer at time step t:

$$C_t = f_t * C_{t-1} + i_t * C_{t-1} \tag{1}$$

$$o_t = \sigma \left(W_o \left[h_{t-1}, x_t \right] + b_o \right) \tag{2}$$

$$h_t = o_t * \tanh \left(C_t \right) \tag{3}$$

$$H = \{ h_1, h_2, \ldots, h_n \} \tag{4}$$

Here, f_t i_t o_t are the forget, input, and output gates' values at time step t, respectively, and C_t represents the hidden state at time step t.

2) Extraction of Metaphor Features:

In this module, metaphor features are extracted using a combination of BERT and Bi-LSTM models.Firstly, the input data is transformed into a BERT output vector R by calling a pre-trained BERT model.

The BERT output vector is then passed through an LSTM layer to obtain the output sequence H and the state vector L at the last time step. The operations of Bi-LSTM at time t are shown in Eqs. (1)–(4) above.

Maping the encoding vector through a fully connected layer and an activation function to obtain the final output metaphor feature vector mp_f.

3) Extraction of Ambiguity Features:

This feature extraction model uses a bidirectional GRU (Gate Recurrent Unit) as a detector, which takes an embedding sequence as input and outputs the error probability P for each position, as shown in Eq. (5):

$$P = \{ p_1, p_2, \ldots, p_n \} \tag{5}$$

Positions with higher error probabilities will be subject to greater penalties (smaller weights) in the subsequent models, while positions with lower error probabilities will be subject to smaller penalties (larger weights). The resulting sum vector E is then passed through an encoder structure, and finally through a linear layer and Softmax activation function to obtain the final fd_f.

Feature Fusion Module The feature vectors extracted by the two feature extraction modules are concatenated and processed through a fully connected layer, where each neuron provides feedback based on its own weight. The output is the result of classification, which is obtained by adjusting the weights and network.

The extracted semantic, emotional, metaphorical, and phonetic-orthographic features are concatenated to obtain the final 256-dimensional feature vector, which is then processed through a fully connected layer. The softmax output result is denoted as 'out', and the specific operations are shown in Eqs. (6)–(8):

$$feature = md\_f \& mn\_f \& mpp\_f \& fd\_f \qquad (6)$$

$$X = feature * W + b \qquad (7)$$

$$Result = Softmax(X) \qquad (8)$$

Here, '&' denotes feature concatenation, 'W' is a weight matrix of size (256, 2) , 'b' is a bias vector of size 2, and '*' denotes matrix multiplication.

4 Experiments

4.1 Experimental Design

In this section, we will comprehensively validate the effectiveness of our proposed BMA model. Firstly, we conducted comparative experiments between BMA and various machine learning and deep learning models. In addition, we combined the various features we used and conducted ablation experiments to explore the contribution of each feature to the performance of model. To test the robustness of model, we added noise to the labels. Finally, we visualized the model's output results to show its performance more intuitively.

4.2 Comparative Experiment

To evaluate the effectiveness of our proposed BMA model and demonstrate its superior performance, we surveyed SOTA (State-Of-The-Art) models in the field of offensive speech detection published in recent years and reproduced them. The models involved in the comparative experiments are as follows:

BERT: A large-scale language pre-training model based on the Transformer architecture. The research in [6] shows that BERT model exceed another method in offensive speech detection.

LSTM: Long Short-Term Memory structure, a variant of the traditional Recurrent Neural Network model which capable of learning long-term dependencies. It was applied in [10] for the classification of hate speech.

Bi-LSTM: Bidirectional Long Short-Term Memory model, a combination of forward LSTM and backward LSTM. It was used in [11] to capture the context information and represent the comment vectors.

Bi-GRU: A Bidirectional Gated Recurrent Unit structure. It works well in extract the relevant indicator texts and images [12].

TextCNN: A convolutional neural network in [13], trained on top of pre-trained word vectors for sentence-level classification tasks.

SVM: A binary classification model based on discriminative machine mearning mlassification algorithm. It was a method to identify online harassment in social media and comment streams in [4].

Logistic: A nonlinear regression model with a logistic function form. Being used to identify online harassment in social media in [4].

BERT Mate Sentiment: Adding a sentiment feature extraction module based on the BERT pre-training model. It a way to do text classification in [15].

Distil-BERT+SVM: A lightweight BERT model using knowledge distillation and SVM for classification to detect hate speech in social media networks in [16].

BERT+Blend-CNN: A model that combines BERT with the Blend-CNN module to do text classification in [15].

Transformer: A transduction model relying entirely on self-attention to compute representations of its input and output.It was applied in [14] as a method for sentiment analysis.

The experiment mainly compared the Accuracy, Precision, Recall, and F1-score. We trained and tested each model on our dataset and used 10-fold cross-validation to ensure the accuracy and reliability of the experimental results [17]. The results are as follows:

Table 2. Comparison of experimental results

Models	Accuracy	Precision	Recall	F1-score
BERT [6]	90.21	89.70	89.45	89.40
LSTM [10]	85.01	87.00	79.00	83.09
Bi-LSTM [11]	86.30	84.24	87.70	85.40
Bi-GRU [12]	86.05	81.00	92.03	86.00
TextCNN [13]	81.00	83.08	77.00	80.02
SVM [4]	65.21	64.97	44.23	52.63
Logistic [4]	64.29	71.89	30.00	42.33
BERT Mate Sentiment [15]	91.01	89.40	91.30	90.30
Distil-BERT+SVM [16]	76.29	74.85	73.23	74.14
BERT+Blend-CNN [15]	90.50	90.10	89.50	89.60
Transformer [14]	86.00	79.02	95.00	86.09
BMA(ours)	**93.90**	**93.01**	**94.02**	**93.50**

It can be observed that our model in this paper outperforms other models in all metrics, demonstrating the feasibility and superiority of the BMA model.

4.3   Experimental Study on Feature Ablation

The proposed BMA model combines semantic, emotional, metaphorical, and ambiguity features to achieve better detection performance for implicit offensive speech. To investigate the contribution of each feature to the detection performance, we keep the model structure unchanged and combine the semantic features extracted by BERT with other features for training and testing, and compare their F1-scores and Accuracy results [18].

In this experiment, each model is trained and tested with different feature combinations. The corresponding relationship is as follows. The S, M, E and A respectively represent semantic feature, metaphor feature, emotion feature and ambiguity feature:

Table 3. The description of different variants

Feature set	Features categories
BMA\(A+E)	Memantic, Metaphor
BMA\(A+M)	Memantic, Emotional
BMA\(M+E)	Memantic, Ambiguity
BMA\A	Memantic, Emotional, Metaphor
BMA\E	Memantic, Ambiguity, Metaphor
BMA\M	Memantic, Emotional, Ambiguity
BMA	Metaphor, Emotional, Ambiguity, Metaphor

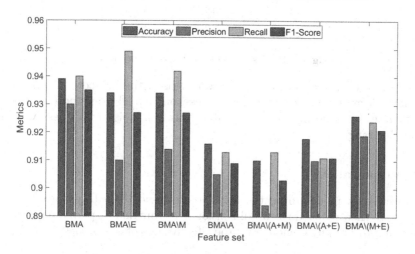

Fig. 3. Results of ablation experiment among different variants

Among the features, ambiguity features make the largest contribution to the model's performance, while emotional features contribute the least. This highlights the crucial role of ambiguity features in detecting implicit offensive speech. In conclusion, the feature combination in the BMA fusion model leads to improved detection performance and accuracy.

4.4   Robustness Experiment

We verify the training effectiveness of our proposed BMA model in different noisy environments by adding different proportions of mislabeled data to the training dataset [12]. We selected seven representative models from the baseline for comparison with our model and discussed their effectiveness in terms of F1-score and Accuracy. As the noise level increases, both the F1 score and accuracy gradually decrease. However, compared to other models, our BMA model still maintains satisfactory performance and has a greater advantage. The experimental results are shown in the Fig. 4:

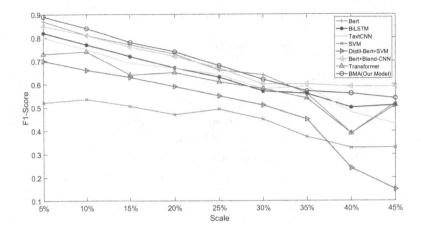

Fig. 4. Results of the robustness experiment

It can be observed that as the noise increases, the F1-score and Accuracy gradually decrease. Throughout this process, our model consistently maintains a high level of performance and exhibits the best noise robustness within a reasonable range.

4.5 Visualization

We selected six models from the baseline and used them to extract features, which were then reduced to two-dimensional vectors and displayed on a coordinate graph to visually demonstrate the effectiveness of our model.

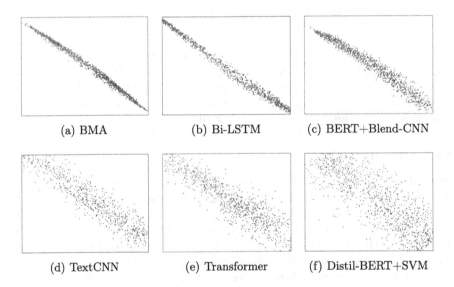

(a) BMA   (b) Bi-LSTM   (c) BERT+Blend-CNN

(d) TextCNN   (e) Transformer   (f) Distil-BERT+SVM

Fig. 5. Visualization

It can be observed that in this task of implicit offensive speech classification, our model achieved better separation and more concentrated feature extraction results compared to other models.

5 Conclusion

In this paper, we collected data from Weibo and public datasets to establish a dataset containing normal language, explicit offensive speech, and implicit offensive speech. We summarized the characteristics and definitions of implicit and explicit offensive speech. Based on this, we designed a BMA model for detecting implicit offensive speech, which extracts semantic, emotional, metaphorical, and fallacious features of natural language and integrates four detection modules: fallacy detection module, semantic detection module, metaphor detection module, and emotion detection module. By fusing these features, we achieved higher accuracy in detecting implicit offensive speech. Additionally, we conducted model comparison experiments, robustness experiments, and ablation experiments, and visualized the effectiveness of the model using representation learning through ten-fold cross-validation. Our designed BMA model achieved satisfactory results in all aspects, including accuracy and robustness.

Acknowledgment. This work is supported by the Key Research and Development Program of Science and Technology Department of Sichuan Province under grant No. 2023YFG0145. In addition, this work is also partially supported by the National Key Research and Development Program of China under grant No. 2022YFC3303101, the Key Research and Development Program of Science and Technology Department of Sichuan Province (nos. 2020YFS0575, 2021YFG0159, 2021KJT0012-2021YFS0067), Sichuan University and Yibin Municipal People's Government University and City Strategic Cooperation Special Fund Project (No. 2020CDYB-29), and Science and Technology Plan Transfer Payment Project of Sichuan Province (No. 2021ZYSF007).

References

1. Suciu, P.: Cyberbullying remains rampant on social media. Forbes (2022)
2. Dhanya, L., Balakrishn, K.: Hate speech detection in asian languages: a survey. In: Proceedings of 1st IEEE International Conference on Communication, Control and Information Sciences, pp. 1–5 (2021)
3. Davidson, T., Warmsley, D., Macy, M., et al.: Automated hate speech detection and the problem of offensive speech. In: Proceedings of 11th AAAI International Conference on Web and Social Media, pp. 512–515 (2017)
4. Kennedy, G., McCollough, A., Dixon, E., et al.: Technology solutions to combat online harassment. In: Proceedings of 1st ACL Workshop on Abusive Language Online, pp. 73–77 (2017)
5. Mishra, P., Del Tredici, M., Yannakoudakis, H., et al.: Abusive language detection with graph convolutional networks. arXiv preprint arXiv:1904.04073 (2019)
6. Kumar, A.: A Study: Hate speech and offensive speech detection in textual data by using RNN, CNN, LSTM and BERT model. In: Proceedings of 6th IEEE International Conference on Intelligent Computing and Control Systems, pp. 1–6 (2022)

7. Shukla, S., Nagpal, S., Sabharwal, S.: Hate speech detection in hindi language using BERT and convolution neural network. In: Proceedings of 3rd IEEE International Conference on Computing, Communication, and Intelligent Systems, pp. 642–647 (2022)
8. Deng, J., Zhou, J., Sun, H., et al.: Cold: A benchmark for chinese offensive speech detection. arXiv preprint arXiv:2201.06025 (2022)
9. Zhang, S., Huang, H., Liu, J., et al.: Spelling error correction with soft-masked BERT. arXiv preprint arXiv:2005.07421 (2020)
10. Ma, Y., Peng, H., Khan, T., et al.: Sentic LSTM: a hybrid network for targeted aspect-based sentiment analysis. Cogn. Comput. **10**, 639–650 (2018)
11. Xu, G., Meng, Y., Qi, X., et al.: Sentiment analysis of comment texts based on BiLSTM. IEEE Access **7**, 51522–51532 (2019)
12. Gui, T., Zhu, L., Zhang, Q., et al.: Cooperative multimodal approach to depression detection in twitter. In: Proceedings of 33th AAAI Conference on Artificial Intelligence, pp. 110–117 (2019)
13. Chen, Y.: Convolutional neural network for sentence classification. University of Waterloo (2015)
14. Naseem, U., Razzak, I., Musial, K., et al.: Transformer based deep intelligent contextual embedding for twitter sentiment analysis. Futur. Gener. Comput. Syst. **113**, 58–69 (2020)
15. Lu, D.: daminglu123 at semeval-2022 task 2: Using bert and lstm to do text classification. In: Proceedings of 16th International Workshop on Semantic Evaluation, pp. 186–189 (2022)
16. Kavatagi, S., Rachh, R.: A context aware embedding for the detection of hate speech in social media networks. In: Proceedings of 1st IEEE International Conference on Smart Generation Computing, Communication and Networking, pp. 1–4 (2021)
17. Yang, X., Lyu, Y., Tian, T., et al.: Rumor detection on social media with graph structured adversarial learning. In: Proceedings of 29th International Conference on International joint Conferences on Artificial Intelligence, pp. 1417–1423 (2021)
18. Wu, Y., Fang, Y., Shang, S., et al.: A novel framework for detecting social bots with deep neural networks and active learning [J]. Knowl.-Based Syst. **211**, 106525 (2021)
19. Miao, Z., Chen, X., Wang, H., et al.: Detecting offensive speech based on graph attention networks and fusion features. IEEE Trans. Comput. Soc. Syst., 1–13 (2023)
20. Chatzakou, D., Kourtellis, N., Blackburn, J., et al.: Mean birds: detecting aggression and bullying on twitter. In: Proceedings of 9th ACM on Web Science Conference, pp. 13–22 (2017)

SIE-YOLOv5: Improved YOLOv5 for Small Object Detection in Drone-Captured-Scenarios

Zonghui Wen[✉], Jia Su, and Yongxiang Zhang

Capital Normal University, Beijing, China
wenzonghui@gmail.com

Abstract. With the widespread application of unmanned aerial vehicles (UAVs), object detection from the perspective of UAVs has received increasing attention from scholars. The high image density and small objects in images captured by UAVs pose significant challenges for detection. To address this problem, we propose a detection algorithm for UAV images, called SIE-YOLOv5. Based on YOLOv5, we fully explore the downsampling process and propose the Spatial Information Extraction (SIE) structure to fully utilize the information in feature maps, and better detect small objects in images. Then, we improve the feature pyramid pooling structure and propose a new LeakySPPF module, which achieves faster speed while maintaining comparable performance. To better locate attention regions, we incorporate the attention mechanism CBAM [1] into the model. Finally, we also improve the IoU calculation method of the baseline model by introducing Wise-IoU [2] to address calculation issues. Through extensive experiments, we demonstrate that our proposed SIE-YOLOv5 has better small object detection capabilities in UAV-captured scenes. On the VisDrone2021 dataset, the mAP is improved by 6.6%.

Keywords: Small Object Detection · UAVs · SIE · YOLOv5 · VisDrone

1 Introduction

Object detection has practical value in many fields, and in this paper, we focus on small object detection in images captured by unmanned aerial vehicles (UAVs). Object detection technology based on UAV images has been widely used in scenarios where manpower is limited, such as animal conservation [3] and plant protection [4]. In this paper, we mainly study how to improve the level of object detection in UAV image scenes.

Since the advent of deep learning, convolutional neural networks (CNNs) have been widely applied. Current object detection mainly focuses on the detection of medium to large objects, and related datasets such as MS COCO [5] and PASCAL VOC [6] mainly contain medium to large objects, which are not friendly for small object detection. Directly applying these models to detect objects in

© The Author(s), under exclusive license to Springer Nature Switzerland AG 2023
Z. Jin et al. (Eds.): KSEM 2023, LNAI 14118, pp. 39–46, 2023.
https://doi.org/10.1007/978-3-031-40286-9_4

drone-captured scenes poses various challenges, such as shooting angle problems and low pixel resolution issues, which result in poor detection performance. These difficulties make object detection in drone-captured scenes very challenging.

In object detection tasks, the YOLO series [7,8] is a well-known single-stage detector. In this study, we propose an improved model, SIE-YOLOv5, based on YOLOv5 to enhance small object detection in the context of unmanned aerial vehicle (UAV) captured scenes. In the backbone, we use the newly proposed SIE module to extract spatial position information from feature maps and introduce the faster LeakySPPF feature pyramid pooling. In the network's neck part, the CBAM structure is added to focus on detecting objects in the extensive background of the images. Additionally, the latest Wise-IoU algorithm is adopted to calculate IoU during the process. Compared with YOLOv5, our improved SIE-YOLOv5 performs better in processing images captured by UAVs.

The contributions of this paper can be summarized as follows:

- We propose a small object detection algorithm, SIE-YOLOv5, for UAV-captured scenes, which demonstrates better small object detection capabilities compared to the baseline.
- We propose the Spatial Information Extraction module to effectively leverage the spatial position information in feature maps.
- We propose a new, faster spatial pyramid pooling structure called LeakySPPF.

2   Proposed Method

YOLOv5 offers four different scales in their model - S, M, L, and X. We conducted experiments on different versions of the models, and YOLOv5s demonstrated promising results with a smaller model size. We chose to improve upon YOLOv5s and used the unmodified official version as the baseline for comparison analysis.

2.1   SIE-YOLOv5

YOLOv5 is a single-stage object detection network that uses multi-scale feature maps to deliver high accuracy and detection speed, which has made it a popular choice in industry applications. This paper aims to enhance the baseline YOLOv5 model to better handle small object detection in drone-captured scenarios by incorporating advanced network structures. Specifically, we propose the SIE module to preserve feature map information and fully leverage spatial information during the downsampling process. To improve the network's ability to locate attention regions in complex drone scenes, we introduce the CBAM attention mechanism at the end of the backbone. In addition, we introduce the Wise-IoU Loss to address shortcomings in the calculation of the CIoU Loss. Lastly, we propose a new spatial pyramid pooling module, LeakySPPF, to replace the original SPP module, offering faster speed. The complete model structure is showed in Fig. 1.

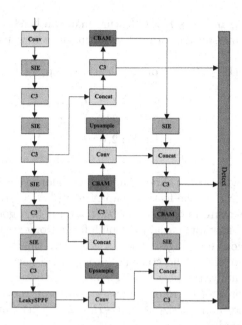

Fig. 1. The architecture of the SIE-YOLOv5.

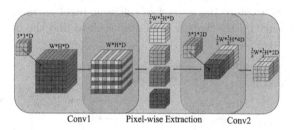

Fig. 2. The overall structure of the SIE.

Spatial Information Extraction (SIE). In our experiments, we found that the downsampling used in the CNN network architecture can result in the loss of fine-grained information in the feature map, which in turn affects the detection performance. To address this issue, we proposed an innovative Spatial Information Extraction (SIE) module to avoid such a problem. The SIE module is capable of extracting spatial position information while reducing the feature map size, thus achieving downsampling without sacrificing fine-grained information in the feature map.

The SIE module is composed of one Pixel-wise Extraction layer and two non-strided convolution blocks. The convolution blocks utilize non-strided convolutions to minimize feature information loss and retain as much image features as possible, while obtaining the location information of the image, which is necessary for subsequent feature map pixel-wise extraction. For feature map pixel-wise extraction, any $W \times H \times C$ feature map can be sliced and aggregated according to the folow specific formula, resulting in a new feature map of size $\frac{1}{2}W \times \frac{1}{2}H \times 4C$.

For each layer $x(W \times H \times 1)$ on any feature map $X(W \times H \times C)$, we can obtain:

$$
\begin{aligned}
x1 &= [0 : W : 2, 0 : H : 2] \\
x2 &= [0 : W : 2, 1 : H : 2] \\
x3 &= [1 : W : 2, 0 : H : 2] \\
x4 &= [1 : W : 2, 1 : H : 2]
\end{aligned}
\tag{1}
$$

Then, these sub-layers $x1$, $x2$, $x3$ and $x4$ are stacked along the channel dimension, the final output layer x' of the feature map X is $x'(\frac{1}{2}W \times \frac{1}{2}H \times 4)$.

For an original feature map of size $W \times H \times C$, it first goes through a non-strided convolution block for spatial position information extraction, keeping the feature map dimensions unchanged. Then, it is fed into the Pixel-wise Extraction layer for feature map slicing and stacking, producing a new feature map of size $\frac{1}{2}W \times \frac{1}{2}H \times 4C$. Finally, the new feature map is sent into another non-strided convolution block for another round of spatial position information extraction, resulting in a feature map of size $\frac{1}{2}W \times \frac{1}{2}H \times 2C$. This completes the entire process of the SIE module.

The inspiration for the SIE model was derived from YOLOv5. In the future, we will continue to explore the impact of different pixel extraction methods on network performance on the feature map, and seek to find the optimal solution.

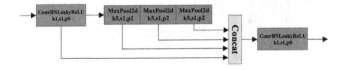

Fig. 3. The overall structure of the LeakySPPF.

LeakySPPF. Spatial Pyramid Pooling is a Feature Pyramid Pooling technique proposed by Kaiming He et al. in 2015, designed to address the issue of scale variance resulting from varying object sizes in object detection. The SPP architecture partitions the input feature map into numerous subregions of diverse sizes, followed by pooling operations being executed on each subregion to extract the feature information within the region. Manipulation of the stride and size of the pooling layer can achieve various subregion sizes. This enables the SPP structure to effectively solve the scale variance problem, thereby enhancing the performance of object detection models.

In this paper, we propose a new feature pyramid pooling structure called LeakySPPF, which is faster than the commonly used Spatial Pyramid Pooling (SPP) method. LeakySPPF unifies the pooling operations with kernel sizes of

3, 5, and 9 used in SPP to a single pooling operation with a kernel size of 5. Furthermore, we change the three parallel pooling operations in SPP to a serial structure, where the output of each pooling operation becomes the input for the next pooling operation. Additionally, we replace the SiLU activation function with Leaky-ReLU to save computation time from exponential operations. These changes not only improve the overall speed of the network but also enhance its efficiency.

CBAM. The CBAM module comprises a channel attention module (CAM) and a spatial attention module (SAM), which enable attention operations to be performed on both channel and spatial dimensions. The CAM enables the network to pay more attention to the foreground and meaningful regions of the image, while the SAM allows the network to focus on positions that contain rich contextual information across the entire image. In drone-captured images, large coverage areas often contain many non-relevant environmental factors. By utilizing the CBAM module, attention areas can be extracted to aid our SIE-YOLOv5 in disregarding distracting information and focusing on useful target objects.

Wise-IoU. In recent years, most studies have assumed that the examples in the training data have high quality and have focused on enhancing the fitting ability of the bounding box loss. However, in drone-captured scenes, there are often many low-quality examples. Overfitting the bounding box to low-quality examples can harm the improvement of detection performance. Focal-EIoU [9] was proposed to address this problem, but its static focusing mechanism did not fully exploit the potential of non-monotonic focusing mechanisms. Based on this observation, Tong et al. proposed a dynamic non-monotonic focusing mechanism and designed Wise-IoU (WIoU). In YOLOv5, the default loss function used is CIoU [10], which also suffers from the aforementioned problem. We have incorporated the latest research on WIoU into YOLOv5, which can effectively alleviate the problem of limited detection performance caused by excessive regression on low-quality examples in the training data.

3   Experiments and Analysis

To verify the model's validity further, we performed a series of ablation experiments in this section. We used an SGD optimizer for training purposes; the batch size was set to 8, the initial learning rate was 0.01. We chose the VisDrone2021 dataset to train and evaluate our model, which contains multiple views in drone-captured scenes and has a large number of small objects, making detection very challenging.

3.1   Performance Comparison of Different YOLOv5models

As demonstrated in Table 1, we conducted a comparative analysis among various YOLOv5 models. With an increase in the number of model parameters, the detection performance of the model also improves considerably. Among YOLOv5s, YOLOv5m, and YOLOv5l, YOLOv5s exhibits superior accuracy while requiring fewer parameters and computations. Hence, we selected it as the baseline model for our study.

Table 1. Performance comparison of different YOLOv5 models.

Model	Params(M)	AP50(%)	mAP(%)
YOLOv5s	7.2	41.9	24.1
YOLOv5m	19.9	45.1	26.6
YOLOv5l	44.1	46.2	27.7

3.2 Comparison of Different Feature Pyramid Pooling Structures

In addition, to intuitively demonstrate the speed of several different feature pyramid pooling structures, we designed a simple experiment to verify their performance. We input an image with a dimension of $640 \times 640 \times 3$ and require an output dimension of $640 \times 640 \times 64$, and perform 1000 calculations on a single Tesla P100 GPU. The average time (s) for every 10 calculations is recorded and presented in Table 2. From the experimental results, it can be observed that our proposed LeakySPPF is 15% faster than SPP, which represents a significant improvement in speed.

Table 2. Comparison of different feature pyramid pooling structures.

Structure	SPP	SPPF	SimSPPF	SPPCSPC	LeakySPPF
Params(K)	0.4	0.4	0.4	100	**0.4**
FLOPs(G)	0.2	0.2	0.2	43	**0.2**
Time(s)	1.79	1.62	1.57	23.92	**1.53**

3.3 Comparison of Different Methods

After conducting ablation experiments, we compared all of the improved methods and summarized the results in Table 3. It can be observed that the SIE structure has a significant impact on improving the results, while CBAM and Wise-IoU also have positive effects on the final accuracy. However, the addition of LeakySPPF resulted in a slight decrease in accuracy. Nevertheless, considering the speed advantage brought by this structure, we decided to retain it.

In addition, we conducted comparison experiments with several well-known object detectors. Training and testing were performed with input sizes of 1536 $\times$ 1536, and the results are presented in Table 4. It can be observed that our proposed SIE-YOLOv5 exhibits superior detection performance compared to other mainstream detectors, achieving a 6.6% higher mAP than YOLOv5.

Table 3. Comparison of different methods.

SIE	LeakySPPF	CBAM	Wise-IoU	mAP(%)
✔	✘	✘	✘	25.3
✔	✔	✘	✘	25.0
✔	✔	✔	✘	25.4
✔	✔	✔	✔	25.7

Table 4. Comparison of different models.

Model	AP50(%)	mAP(%)
RetinaNet	21.4	11.8
RefineDet	28.8	14.9
DetNet59	29.2	15.3
FPN	32.2	16.5
CornetNet	34.1	17.4
YOLOv5s	41.9	24.1
SIE-YOLOv5s	**43.9 (4.8%↑)**	**25.7 (6.6%↑)**

We present the detection results of specific categories on the VisDrone2021 dataset in Table 5. Compared with the original network, our method achieves significant performance improvements in each category. The categories with lower detection accuracy showed more significant performance improvements. Across all categories, the highest mAP improvement was 15.7%, the lowest was 3.4%, and the average improvement was 6.6%, which is an encouraging result.

Table 5. Performance comparison of YOLOv5 and SIE-YOLOv5.

Class	YOLOv5		SIE-YOLOv5	
	AP50(%)	mAP(%)	AP50(%)	mAP(%)
car	81.9	53.5	82.6	55.3
bus	63.0	44.2	65.1	46.5
van	47.2	32.4	49.2	34.3
truck	46.9	29.5	52.3	33.5
pedestrian	44.9	18.4	45.5	19.1
motor	42.3	17.7	43.0	18.3
tricycle	25.4	14.0	28.6	16.2
people	25.6	9.3	26.4	9.7
awning-tricycle	23.8	13.7	26.9	15.7
bicycle	18.4	7.8	19.3	8.3
all	41.9	24.1	**43.9**	**25.7**

4   Conclusion

In this study, we chose the well-engineered YOLOv5 as the baseline and propose a novel network structure named SIE-YOLOv5. It incorporates two new methods we propose, SIE and LeakySPPF, and add some cutting-edge techniques Wise-IoU and CBAM to YOLOv5. The results show that SIE-YOLOv5 significantly improves the detection of small objects captured by drones. We conducted extensive experiments to validate the reliability of our proposed methods and the remarkable performance of the new network. We hope that our research will provide a new perspective for object detection in the field.

References

1. Woo, S., Park, J., Lee, J.-Y., Kweon, I.S.: CBAM: convolutional block attention module, CoRR, vol. abs/ arXiv: 1807.06521 (2018)
2. Tong, Z., Chen, Y., Xu, Z., Yu, R.: Wise-iou: Bounding box regression loss with dynamic focusing mechanism (2023)
3. Kellenberger, B., Marcos, D., Tuia, D.: Detecting mammals in uav images: Best practices to address a substantially imbalanced dataset with deep learning. Remote Sens. Environ. **216**, 139–153 (2018)
4. Hird, J.N.: Use of unmanned aerial vehicles for monitoring recovery of forest vegetation on petroleum well sites. Remote Sens. **9**, 413 (2017)
5. Lin, T.-Y., et al.: Microsoft COCO: common objects in context, CoRR, vol. abs/ arXiv: 1405.0312 (2014)
6. Everingham, M., Gool, L.V., Williams, C.K.I., Winn, J.M., Zisserman, A.: The pascal visual object classes (voc) challenge. Int. J. Comput. Vis. **88**, 303–338 (2010)
7. Bochkovskiy, A., Wang, C.-Y., Liao, H.-Y.M.: Yolov4: Optimal speed and accuracy of object detection, CoRR, vol. abs/ arXiv: 2004.10934 (2020)
8. Wang, C.-Y., Bochkovskiy, A., Liao, H.-Y.M.: Yolov7: Trainable bag-of-freebies sets new state-of-the-art for real-time object detectors (2022)
9. Zhang, Y.-F., Ren, W., Zhang, Z., Jia, Z., Wang, L., Tan, T.: Focal and efficient iou loss for accurate bounding box regression (2022)
10. Zheng, Z., et al.: Enhancing geometric factors in model learning and inference for object detection and instance segmentation. IEEE Trans. Cybern. **52**(8), 8574–8586 (2022)

Learning-Based Dichotomy Graph Sketch for Summarizing Graph Streams with High Accuracy

Ding Li[ID], Wenzhong Li[(✉)][ID], Yizhou Chen, Xu Zhong, Mingkai Lin,
and Sanglu Lu

State Key Laboratory for Novel Software Technology, Nanjing University,
Nanjing 210023, China
{liding,mf20330010,xuzhong,mingkai}@smail.nju.edu.cn,
{lwz,sanglu}@nju.edu.cn

Abstract. Graph stream data is widely applied to describe the relationships in networks such as social networks, computer networks and hyperlink networks. Due to the large volume and high dynamicity of graph streams, several graph sketches were proposed to summarize them for fast queries. However, the existing graph sketches suffer from low performance on graph query tasks due to hash collisions between heavy and light edges. In this paper, we propose a novel learning-based Dichotomy Graph Sketch (DGS) mechanism, which adopts two separate graph sketches, a *heavy sketch* and a *light sketch*, to store heavy edges and light edges respectively. DGS periodically obtains heavy edges and light edges in a session of a graph stream, and use them as training samples to train a deep neural network (DNN) based binary classifier. The DNN-based classifier is then utilized to decide whether the upcoming edges are heavy or not, and store them in different graph sketches accordingly. With the learnable classifier and the dichotomy graph sketches, the proposed mechanism can resolve the hashing collision problem and significantly improve the accuracy for graph query tasks. We conducted extensive experiments on three real-world graph stream datasets, which show that DGS outperforms the state-of-the-art graph sketches in a variety of graph query tasks.

Keywords: Sketch · Graph sketch · Deep learning · Graph stream

1 Introduction

In many data stream applications, the connections are indispensable to describe the relationships in networks such as social networks, computer networks and communication networks. In these applications, data are organized as *graph*

This work was partially supported by the Natural Science Foundation of Jiangsu Province (Grant No. BK20222003), the National Natural Science Foundation of China (Grant Nos. 61972196, 61832008, 61832005), the Collaborative Innovation Center of Novel Software Technology and Industrialization, and the Sino-German Institutes of Social Computing.

© The Author(s), under exclusive license to Springer Nature Switzerland AG 2023
Z. Jin et al. (Eds.): KSEM 2023, LNAI 14118, pp. 47–59, 2023.
https://doi.org/10.1007/978-3-031-40286-9_5

streams [15] [4] which are different from traditional data streams that are modeled as isolated items. A graph stream can form a dynamic graph that changes with every arrival of an edge. For example, network traffic can be seen as a graph stream, where each item in the stream represents the communication between two IP addresses. The network traffic graph will change if a new packet arrives. For another example, interactions between users in a social network can also be seen as a graph stream, and these interactions forms a dynamic graph. The social network graph will dynamically change when new interactions occur. Formally, a graph stream is a consecutive sequence of items, where each item represents a graph edge usually denoted by a tuple consisting of two endpoints and a weight.

With the increase of graph sizes, it is necessary to build an accurate but small representation of the original graph for more efficient analytics. To achieve this goal, researchers studied the *graph summarization* problem to concisely preserve overall graph structure while reducing its size. For example, Hajiabadi et al. designed a utility-driven graph summarization method G-SCIS [6] that produced optimal compression with zero loss of utility. However, graph summarization focused on summarizing static graphs, which was unable to handle dynamic graphs that are formed by graph streams. To summarize graph streams, some researchers proposed *graph sketch*. For example, Tang et al. proposed a novel graph sketch called TCM [15]. TCM summarized a graph stream by a matrix where each edge was mapped to a bucket of the matrix using a hash function, and the edge weight was recorded in the corresponding bucket. TCM supported not only edge query but also node query since it kept the topology information of the graph. More recently, Gou et al. desinged GSS [4] which combined a matrix and an adjacency list buffer to improve the accuracy of edge query. The adjacency list buffer stored the edge when a hash collision happened in the matrix. In their follow-up work [5], they partitioned the matrix of GSS into multiple blocks, and accelerated the query with bitmaps and FPGA (Field Programmable Gate Array).

Typically, conventional graph sketches use a random hash function to map each edge to a bucket of a matrix, and then record the edge weight in the corresponding bucket, which works as illustrated in Fig. 1. However, due to the randomness of hash function, hash collisions may occur in querying an edge or a node with the graph sketch. Especially when a heavy edge (an edge with large

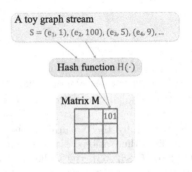

Fig. 1. Conventional graph sketch stores all edges in a single matrix.

weight) is collided with a light edge (an edge with small weight), it will cause severe performance degradation on query tasks. As shown in Fig. 1, a toy graph stream consists of a heavy edge (edge e_2) whose weight is 100 and several light edges (edge e_1, e_3, and e_4). The conventional graph sketches may map a heavy edge e_2 and a light edge e_1 to the same bucket of the matrix due to a hash collision. In graph sketch, the bucket stores the sum of the edge weights (see Sect. 3 for details), and thus the value recorded in this bucket is $1 + 100 = 101$. In this case, if we query the weight of edge e_1, the graph sketch will return the value 101, and the relative error of this query is $(101 - 1)/1 = 100$, which is exceptionally high for a light edge.

To address this issue, it is desirable to design a new graph sketch mechanism to resolve the high query error caused by hash collisions. In this paper, we propose a novel Dichotomy Graph Sketch (DGS) approach, which is able to differentiate heavy edges and light edges during the sketch updating process and respectively store them in two separate matrices to avoid hash collisions. When a new edge arrives, DGS first decides whether it is a heavy edge or not by an *edge classifier*. If the edge is classified as a heavy edge, it will be stored in a *heavy sketch*; otherwise, it will be stored in a *light sketch*. To train the edge classifier, we set a *sample generator* which consists of a temporal graph sketch and two min-heaps to generate training samples. The edges in each session are also fed into the sample generator to obtain the heavy edges (see Sect. 4 for details) to train the edge classifier. In this way, hash collision can be avoided and the query performance will be improved.

The main results and contributions of this paper are summarized as follows.

- We propose dichotomy graph sketch (DGS), a novel mechanism for graph stream summarization. It is able to differentiate heavy edges from light edges during the edge updating process.
- We introduce deep learning techniques into the design of graph sketch mechanism. Specifically, we design a novel deep neural network architecture to detect heavy edges during the edge updating process, which helps to store heavy edges and light edges in separate matrices to avoid hash collision.
- We conduct extensive experiments on three real-world graph streams to evaluate the performance of the proposed DGS. The experimental results show that DGS outperforms the state-of-the-art graph sketches in a variety of graph query tasks.

2 Related Work

2.1 Data Stream Sketches

Data stream sketches are designed for data stream summarization. C-sketch [1] utilized several hash tables to record data streams, but suffered from both overestimation and underestimation in frequency estimation task. Estan et al. designed CU-sketch [3] which improved query accuracy at the cost of not supporting item deletions. SF-sketch [14] used both a large sketch and a small sketch to upgrade the query accuracy. Li et al. designed WavingSketch [13] which was a generic and unbiased algorithm for finding top-k items. Zhang et al. proposed On-Off sketch [16] which focused on the problem of persistence estimation and finding persistent items by a technique to separate persistent and non-persistent items. Stingy Sketch [12] was a sketch framework which designed bit-pinching counter tree and prophet queue to optimize both the accuracy and speed for frequency estimation task.

2.2 Graph Stream Sketch

In contrast to data stream sketches, graph sketches are specially designed for graph stream summarization, keeping the topology of a graph and thus simultaneously supporting several queries such as edge query and node query. Tang et al. proposed TCM [15] which adopted several adjacency matrices with irreversible hash functions to store a graph stream. Different from TCM, gMatrix [8] used reversible hash functions to generate graph sketches. Gou et al. proposed GSS [4] which consisted of not only an adjacency matrix but also an adjacency list buffer. Adjacency list buffer was used to store the edge when an edge collision happened to improve the query accuracy. In their follow-up work [5], they proposed an improved version called blocked GSS, and designed two directions of accelerating query: GSS with node bitmaps and GSS implemented with FPGA. In [11], Li et al. proposed Dynamic Graph Sketch which was able to adaptively extend graph sketch size to mitigate the performance degradation caused by memory overload.

In summary, all the existing graph sketches use a single matrix to store both heavy edges and light edges and thus suffer from low query accuracy (especially for light edge query task) due to hash collisions.

3 Preliminaries

In this section, we provide formal definitions and introduce the preliminary of summarizing a graph stream with graph sketches.

Definition 1 (Graph stream). *A graph stream is a consecutive sequence of items $S = \{e_1, e_2, \ldots, e_n\}$, where each item $e_i = (s, d, t, w)$ denotes a directed edge from node s to node d arriving at timestamp t with weight w.*

It is worth noting that an edge e_i may appear multiple times at different timestamps. Thus, the final weight of e_i is computed by an *aggregation function* based on all edge weights of e_i. Common aggregation functions include $min(\cdot)$, $max(\cdot)$, $average(\cdot)$, $sum(\cdot)$, etc. Among them, $sum(\cdot)$ is mostly adpoted [15] [4], and thus we also use $sum(\cdot)$ as the aggregation function in the rest of this paper.

Since the edges in a graph stream arrive one by one, a graph stream $S = \{e_1, e_2, \ldots, e_n\}$ can form a dynamic graph which changes with every arrival of an edge (both edge weight and graph architecture may change).

Definition 2 (Session). *A session $C = \{e_i, e_{i+1}, \ldots, e_j\}(1 \le i < j \le n)$ is defined as a continuous subsequence of a graph stream $S = \{e_1, e_2, \ldots, e_n\}$.*

Definition 3 (Heavy edge). *A heavy edge refers to the edge whose final weight is ranked in the top k percentage among all the unique edges in a graph stream S.*

Definition 4 (Light edge). *Except heavy edges, all the other edges are regarded as light edges in a graph stream S.*

Definition 5 (Graph sketch [15]). *Supposing that a graph $G = (V, E)$ is formed by a given graph stream S, graph sketch $\mathcal{K}$ is defined as a graph $\mathcal{K} = (V_\mathcal{K}, E_\mathcal{K})$ whose size is smaller than G, i.e., $|V_\mathcal{K}| \leq |V|$ and $|E_\mathcal{K}| \leq |E|$, where a hash function $H(\cdot)$ is associated to map each node in V to a node in $V_\mathcal{K}$. Correspondingly, an edge (s, d) in E will be mapped to the edge $(H(s), H(d))$ in $E_\mathcal{K}$.*

To reduce the query error caused by hash collisions, a common method is to simultaneously use a set of graph sketches $\{\mathcal{K}_1, \mathcal{K}_2, \ldots, \mathcal{K}_m\}$ with different hash functions $\{H_1(\cdot), H_2(\cdot), \ldots, H_m(\cdot)\}$ to summarize a graph stream.

Definition 6 (Graph compression ratio[15]). *Compression ratio r in graph summarization means that a graph sketch uses $|E| \times r$ space to store a graph $G = (V, E)$. For example, if a graph stream contains $500,000$ edges, compression ratio $1/50$ indicates that the graph sketch takes $500,000 \times 1/50 = 10,000$ space units, which is a $\sqrt{10,000} \times \sqrt{10,000}$ (i.e. 100×100) matrix. In practice, adjacency matrix is usually adopted to implement a graph sketch. We call $\alpha = \sqrt{|E| \times r}$ the* width *of graph sketch.*

Assuming that two graph sketches with different hash functions are utilized to summarize a graph stream S, at the beginning, all values in the two adjacency matrices are initialized with 0. When an edge arrives, both graph sketches conduct an *edge update* operation as follows.

Edge Update: To record an edge $e = (s, d, t, w)$ from graph stream S, each graph sketch $\mathcal{K}_i$ calculates the hash values $(H_i(s), H_i(d))$. Then, it locates the corresponding position $M_i[H_i(s)][H_i(d)]$ in the adjacency matrix, and adds the value in that position by w.

After the graph sketches process all edge updates in the graph stream, they can be used to fastly answer edge query and node query in linear time, which can be described as follows.

Edge Query: Given an edge $e = (s, d)$, edge query is to return the weight of e estimated by the graph sketch. To answer the query, we first query the weight of e in all the graph sketches. Specifically, for each graph sketch $\mathcal{K}_i$, we locate the corresponding position $M_i[H_i(s)][H_i(d)]$ and return the value in the position as the estimated weight. In this way, we can obtain a set of weights $\{w_1, w_2, \ldots, w_m\}$. According to the principle of count-min sketch [2], the minimal value of the set of sketches is used to estimate the value of the accumulative count, therefore we return $min\{w_1, w_2, \ldots, w_m\}$ for the edge query.

Node Query: Given a node n, node query is to return the aggregated edge weight *from* node n. To answer the query, for each graph sketch $\mathcal{K}_i$, we can first locate the row corresponding to node n (i.e. the $H_i(n)$th row) in the adjacency matrix M_i, and then sum up the values in that row to obtain a set of sums $\{sum_1, sum_2, \ldots, sum_m\}$. Similarly, we return $min\{sum_1, sum_2, \ldots, sum_m\}$ for the node query.

Top-K Node Query: Top-k node query is to return the list of top-k nodes with the highest aggregated weights in graph stream S. To answer this query, we additionally maintain a min-heap with size k to store the top-k nodes. Specifically, after updating each edge $e = (s, d)$, we conduct a node query for node s, and obtain its aggregated weight w_s. Then, we push the tuple (s, w_s) into the min-heap. If the min-heap is full, it will pop out the tuple with the lowest weight. After all edge updates, we return the set of nodes in the min-heap as the answer of top-k node query.

4   Dichotomy Graph Sketch Mechanism

In this section, we detailly introduce the proposed Dichotomy Graph Sketch (DGS) mechanism which is able to mitigate the performance problem caused by hash collisions between heavy edges and light edges. The proposed framework is illustrated in Fig. 2. Firstly, all edges in the current session are represented by a sub-graph stream $C = \{e_i, e_{i+1}, \ldots, e_j\}$. These edges are sequentially fed into an *edge classifier*. If an edge is classified as a heavy edge, it will be stored in the *heavy sketch* ($\mathcal{K}_h$); otherwise it will be stored in the *light sketch* ($\mathcal{K}_l$). In the first session, since the edge classifier has not been trained, all edges will be stored in the light sketch. In the subsequent sessions, a *sample generator* is applied to generate the training samples for the edge classifier. It obtains heavy edges in the current session by querying all heavy edges from the min-heap, and chooses the same amount of light edges in the current session with random sampling. The heavy edges together with the chosen light edges are used as training samples to train the edge classifier, which is used to construct dichotomy sketches. After each session, all values in the sample generator are reset to null, and DGS continues to process the next session to construct the graph sketches incrementally.

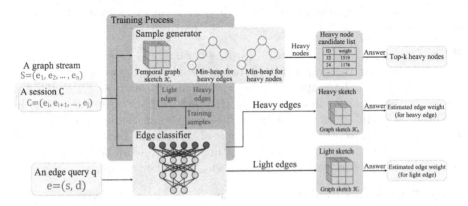

Fig. 2. The framework of our proposed dichotomy graph sketch.

The major components of DGS, i.e., the heavy sketch, the light sketch, the sample generator and the edge classifier, are introduced as follows.

4.1 Heavy Sketch and Light Sketch

Heavy sketch and light sketch both work exactly as a basic graph sketch (see definition 5 for details). When an edge in the graph stream arrives, it will first be fed into the edge classifier. If the edge is classified as a heavy edge, it will be stored in the heavy sketch; otherwise it will be stored in the light sketch.

Since the number of heavy edges is usually much smaller than the number of light edges in a graph stream, we set the size of heavy sketch smaller than that of the light sketch in practice.

4.2 Sample Generator

To obtain the heavy edges and the heavy nodes in each session, we design a sample generator which consists of a temporal graph sketch and two min-heaps. The temporal graph works exactly the same as a basic graph sketch, and the two min-heaps are maintained for obtaining heavy edges and heavy nodes, respectively. After the sample generator finishes all edge updates of the current session, the heavy edges in the min-heap will be used as training samples to train the edge classifier, and heavy nodes together with their aggregated weights will be recorded in the *heavy node candidate list* (which is a hash table that maps the node ID to its aggregated weight as shown in Fig. 2) as the candidates for top-k nodes query. If a node is already in the heavy node candidate list, we simply update its aggregated weight by adding up the old weight and the new weight. Finally, before processing the edges in the next session, sample generator resets all the values of the temporal graph sketch to null, and clear the min-heaps.

4.3 Edge Classifier

To differentiate heavy edges from light edges during the edge updating process, we build a binary probabilistic classification model. The basic idea is to learn a model f that can predict if an edge $e_i = (n_a, n_b)$ is a heavy edge or not. In other words, we can train a deep neural network classifier based on dataset $\mathcal{D} = \{(e_i = (n_a, n_b), y_i = 1 | e_i \in \mathcal{H}\} \cup \{(e_i = (n_a, n_b), y_i = 0 | e_i \in \mathcal{L}\}$ where $\mathcal{H}$ denotes the set of heavy edges, and $\mathcal{L}$ denotes the set of light edges (from the sample generator). According to the discussion in Sect. 4.3, we find that *node embeddings* are very recognizable features to differentiate between heavy edges and light edges. Therefore the node embeddings are included in the input feature vector to train the DNN.

Node embeddings using a graph auto-encoder In graph representation learning, it is common to obtain node embeddings which are essentially feature representations to help accomplish downstream tasks. Thus, to help the classifier accurately classify heavy edges and light edges, we obtain node embeddings using a graph auto-encoder (GAE) [9] model.

Formally, given a graph $G = (V, E)$ with $|V| = N$, we denote its degree matrix as $\mathbf{D}$, and its adjacency matrix as $\mathbf{A}$. In addition, node features are summarized in an $N \times M$ feature matrix $\mathbf{X}$.

GAE utilizes a two-layer graph convolutional network (GCN) [10] as the encoder to form the node embeddings of a graph. Formally, the node embeddings are denoted by $\mathbf{Z} = GCN(\mathbf{X}, \mathbf{A})$ where $GCN(\cdot)$ denotes the two-layer graph convolutional network. The two-layer GCN is defined as

$$GCN(\mathbf{X}, \mathbf{A}) = \tilde{\mathbf{A}} ReLU(\tilde{\mathbf{A}} \mathbf{X} \mathbf{W_0}) \mathbf{W_1}, \tag{1}$$

where $ReLU(\cdot) = max(0, \cdot)$, and $\tilde{\mathbf{A}} = \mathbf{D}^{-\frac{1}{2}} \mathbf{A} \mathbf{D}^{-\frac{1}{2}}$ is the symmetrically normalized adjacency matrix. To reconstruct the graph, GAE adopts $\hat{\mathbf{A}} = \sigma(\mathbf{Z}\mathbf{Z}^{\mathbf{T}})$ as the decoder where $\hat{\mathbf{A}}$ denotes the adjacency matrix of the reconstructed graph G'.

To train a GAE for a graph G, we can feed the G's adjacency matrix $\mathbf{A}$ together with its node feature matrix $\mathbf{X}$ into the GAE, and obtain the adjacency matrix $\hat{\mathbf{A}}$ of the reconstructed graph G'. Then, we minimize the following cross entropy loss:

$$\mathcal{L} = \frac{1}{n} \sum y log \hat{y} + (1 - y) log(1 - \hat{y}), \tag{2}$$

where y denotes the element in $\mathbf{A}$, and $\hat{y}$ denotes the element in $\hat{\mathbf{A}}$. After the GAE is well trained, we can obtain the current node embeddings $\mathbf{Z} = GCN(\mathbf{X}, \mathbf{A})$.

Note that it is time-consuming and space-expensive to construct a lossless graph G for each session of the graph stream. To reduce the complexity, we use the temporal graph sketch $\mathcal{K}_s$ in the sample generator as input to train the GAE, since a graph sketch can be regarded as the compression of the original graph.

Structure of the Edge Classifier. The structure of the proposed deep neural network classifier is presented in Fig. 3. As mentioned previously, the input consists of two nodes (source node and destination node of an edge) and their corresponding node embeddings. The input first respectively goes through two fully-connected layers. Then, the output of the fully-connected layer is fed into a softmax layer, which outputs a probability distribution representing the probability that the input edge is a heavy edge. The details of the edge classifier is illustrated in Fig. 3.

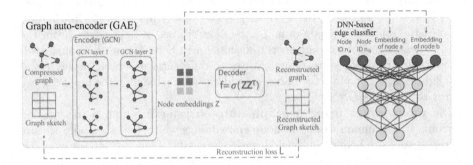

Fig. 3. The details of the proposed edge classifier.

4.4 Implementation of Graph Query Tasks

In this section, we introduce how DGS answers different kinds of queries.

Dealing with Edge Query and Node Query. Given an edge $e_i = (s, d)$, we first feed node s, node d, and their node embeddings into the trained edge classifier to predict whether e_i is a heavy edge. If e_i is classified as a heavy edge, the heavy sketch will answer the weight of e_i (the method to answer the weight is exactly the same as that introduced in Sect. 3); otherwise the light sketch will answer the weight of e_i. As for node query for node n, we first locate the row corresponding to node n in the graph sketch, sum up the values in that row, and then return the minimum value among all the sums.

Dealing with Top-K Node Query. Since we store the heavy nodes of each session in the heavy node candidate list, to answer the top-k heavy node query, we can simply return the top-k heavy nodes with the highest weight in the heavy node candidate list.

5 Performance Evaluation

To validate the effectiveness of the proposed Dichotomy Graph Sketch (DGS), we conducted extensive experiments on three real-world graph stream datasets. We compare our method with two state-of-the-art graph sketches: **TCM** [15] and **GSS** [4]. All experiments were performed on a laptop with Intel Core i5-9300H processors (4 cores, 8 threads), 8 GB of memory, and NVIDIA GeForce RTX 2060 GPU. All sketches except GSS were implemented in Python. For GSS, we used the C++ source code provided on the Github[1].

5.1 Datasets

We use three real-world graph stream datasets, which are described as follows.

Wiki_talk_cy [2]: The first dataset is the communication network of the Welsh Wikipedia. Nodes represent users, and an edge from user A to user B denotes that user A wrote a message on the talk page of user B at a certain timestamp. It contains 2,233 users (nodes) and 10,740 messages (edges).

Subelj_jung [3]: The second dataset is the software class dependency network of the JUNG 2.0.1 and javax 1.6.0.7 libraries, namespaces edu.uci.ics.jung and java/javax. Nodes represent classes, and an edge between them indicates that there exists a dependency between two classes. It contains 6,210 classes (nodes) and 138,706 dependencies (edges).

---

[1] https://github.com/Puppy95/Graph-Stream-Sketch.
[2] http://konect.cc/networks/wiki_talk_cy/.
[3] http://konect.cc/networks/subelj_jung-j/.

Facebook-wosn-wall [4]: The third dataset is the directed network of a small subset of posts to other user's wall on Facebook. The nodes of the network are Facebook users, and each directed edge represents one post, linking the users writing a post to the users whose wall the post is written on. It contains 46,952 users (nodes) and 876,993 posts (edges).

5.2   Performance Metrics

We adopt the following metrics for performance evaluation in our experiments.
Average relative error (ARE) [15]: it measures the accuracy of the weights that are estimated by a graph sketch in the edge query task.
Intersection accuracy (IA) [15]: it measures the accuracy of the top-k heavy nodes reported by a graph sketch.
Normalized discounted cumulative gain (NDCG) [7]: it is a measure of ranking quality representing the usefulness (also called gain) of a node based on its position in the ranking list. Normally $NDCG \in [0,1]$, and the higher NDCG means the stronger ability to find the top-k nodes.

5.3   Numerical Results

We analyze the numerical results for edge query and node query of different sketches. *For a fair comparison, the memory usages of TCM, GSS, and our proposed DGS are equal in both edge query task and node query task.* Note that the DGS framework refers to two hyperparameters: compression ratio (set to 1/10 by default), and the input size of the edge classifier (set to 32 by default).

Edge Query. To evaluate the ability to answer edge query on the baseline methods and our proposed DGS, for each dataset, we query all the edges and calculate the average relative error (ARE). Table 1, 2 and 3 show the ARE of edge query task achieved by TCM, GSS and our proposed DGS. Besides calculating the total ARE by querying all edges, we also separately calculate the ARE of querying heavy edges and that of querying light edges. As can be seen, DGS achieves the lowest ARE among all three methods. Specifically, in TCM and GSS, the ARE of edge queries on dataset *subelj_jung* is 22.359 and 39.386, respectively. In contrast, our proposed DGS outperforms the other algorithms significantly, and its ARE is only 17.264. Moreover, both the ARE of querying light edges (17.295) and that of querying heavy edges (1.433) achieved by DGS are the lowest compared with the baseline methods. Similarly, DGS also achieves the lowest ARE on the other two datasets.

---

[4] http://konect.cc/networks/facebook-wosn-wall/.

Table 1. The ARE of edge query (wiki_talk_cy)

Method	Total ARE	ARE of light edges	ARE of heavy edges
TCM	10.388	10.436	0.274
GSS	10.038	10.083	0.622
DGS	**7.875**	**7.909**	**0.202**

Table 2. The ARE of edge query (subelj_jung)

Method	Total ARE	ARE of light edges	ARE of heavy edges
TCM	22.359	22.399	2.079
GSS	39.386	39.458	3.320
DGS	**17.264**	**17.295**	**1.433**

Table 3. The ARE of edge query (facebook-wosn-wall)

Method	Total ARE	ARE of light edges	ARE of heavy edges
TCM	2.261	2.262	**0.015**
GSS	5.256	5.258	0.340
DGS	**2.056**	**2.057**	0.212

Top-K Heavy Node Query. We evaluate the ability to find top-k heavy nodes of DGS as well as TCM. We do not conduct this experiment with GSS since GSS does not support heavy node query. The results are shown in Fig. 4 and Fig. 5. As shown in Fig. 4, DGS outperforms TCM on all three datasets. Specifically, in the task of finding top-20 heavy nodes, DGS achieves an IA of 95%, 85% and 90% on dataset *wiki_talk_cy*, *subelj_jung*, and *facebook-wosn-wall*, respectively. In contrast, TCM only achieves an IA of 80%, 25%, and 45%. In the task of finding top-50 and top-100 heavy nodes, DGS also outperforms TCM significantly. This illustrates that DGS has strong ability to find heavy nodes accurately.

We also calculate the NDCG based on the result list of top-k heavy node query. The results are shown in Fig. 5. Similarly, the NDCG achieved by DGS is much higher than that of TCM.

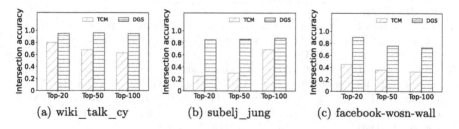

(a) wiki_talk_cy   (b) subelj_jung   (c) facebook-wosn-wall

Fig. 4. Heavy node query (intersection accuracy)

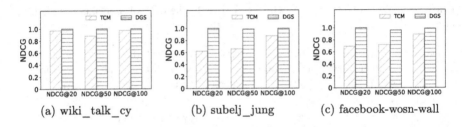

Fig. 5. Heavy node query (NDCG)

6   Conclusion

This paper proposed a novel framework for large-scale graph stream summarization called DGS. Different from conventional graph sketches that store all edges in a single matrix, DGS adopts two separate matrices, the heavy sketch and the light sketch, to respectively store heavy edges and light edges to avoid the serious performance drop caused by hash collisions. DGS designs a DNN-based binary classifier to decide whether an edge is heavy or not before storing it. If the edge is classified as a heavy edge, it will be stored in the heavy sketch; otherwise it will be stored in the light sketch. Extensive experiments based on three real-world graph streams showed that the proposed method is able to achieve high accuracy for graph queries compared to the state-of-the-arts.

References

1. Charikar, M., Chen, K.C., Farach-Colton, M.: Finding frequent items in data streams. In: 29th International Colloquium on Automata, Languages and Programming, pp. 693–703 (2002)
2. Cormode, G., Muthukrishnan, S.: An improved data stream summary: the count-min sketch and its applications. J. Algorithm. **55**(1), 58–75 (2005)
3. Estan, C., Varghese, G.: New directions in traffic measurement and accounting: focusing on the elephants, ignoring the mice. ACM Trans. Comput. Syst. **21**(3), 270–313 (2003)
4. Gou, X., Zou, L., Zhao, C., Yang, T.: Fast and accurate graph stream summarization. In: The 35th IEEE International Conference on Data Engineering (ICDE 2019), pp. 1118–1129 (2019)
5. Gou, X., Zou, L., Zhao, C., Yang, T.: Graph stream sketch: summarizing graph streams with high speed and accuracy. IEEE Trans. Knowl. Data Eng. (2022)
6. Hajiabadi, M., Singh, J., Srinivasan, V., Thomo, A.: Graph summarization with controlled utility loss. In: The 27th ACM SIGKDD Conference on Knowledge Discovery and Data Mining, Singapore, pp. 536–546 (2021)
7. Järvelin, K., Kekäläinen, J.: Cumulated gain-based evaluation of IR techniques. ACM Trans. Inform. Syst. **20**(4), 422–446 (2002)
8. Khan, A., Aggarwal, C.C.: Query-friendly compression of graph streams. In: 2016 IEEE/ACM International Conference on Advances in Social Networks Analysis and Mining (ASONAM 2016), pp. 130–137 (2016)

9. Kipf, T.N., Welling, M.: Variational graph auto-encoders (2016). arxiv.org/abs/1611.07308

10. Kipf, T.N., Welling, M.: Semi-supervised classification with graph convolutional networks. In: 5th International Conference on Learning Representations (ICLR 2017), Toulon, France (2017)

11. Li, D., Li, W., Chen, Y., Lin, M., Lu, S.: Learning-based dynamic graph stream sketch. In: Advances in Knowledge Discovery and Data Mining - 25th Pacific-Asia Conference, Virtual Event (PAKDD 2021), vol. 12712, pp. 383–394 (2021)

12. Li, H., Chen, Q., Zhang, Y., Yang, T., Cui, B.: Stingy sketch: a sketch framework for accurate and fast frequency estimation. Proc. VLDB Endowm. **15**(7), 1426–1438 (2022)

13. Li, J., et al.: Wavingsketch: An unbiased and generic sketch for finding top-k items in data streams. In: The 26th ACM SIGKDD Conference on Knowledge Discovery and Data Mining, Virtual Event (KDD 2020), pp. 1574–1584 (2020)

14. Liu, L., et al.: SF-sketch: A two-stage sketch for data streams. IEEE Trans. Parallel Distrib. Syst. **31**(10), 2263–2276 (2020)

15. Tang, N., Chen, Q., Mitra, P.: Graph stream summarization: From big bang to big crunch. In: The 2016 International Conference on Management of Data (SIGMOD 2016), pp. 1481–1496 (2016)

16. Zhang, Y., et al.: On-off sketch: a fast and accurate sketch on persistence. Proc. VLDB Endowm. **14**(2), 128–140 (2020)

SNAFA-Net: Squared Normalization Attention and Feature Alignment for Visible-Infrared Person Re-Identification

Jiahao Wu, Qiang Chen, and Guoqiang Xiao[✉]

College of Computer and Information Science, Southwest University,
Chongqing, China
{a948246605,cq0907}@email.swu.edu.cn, gqxiao@swu.edu.cn

Abstract. Visible-infrared person re-identification (VI-ReID) aims to match images of the same individual across visible and infrared image sets. Due to the modality discrepancy between different modalities and the inter-modality discrepancy caused by occlusions and postures, make this a challenge task. In this paper, we propose a novel network, called SNAFA-Net, that uses innovative techniques to address the key challenges in VI-ReID. The squared normalization attention (SNA) module addresses the modality disparity by attending to the invariant features of pedestrians in each modality. The feature alignment-enriched part-based convolutional block (FA-PCB) module allows us to partition the human body image into multiple parts and extract corresponding features for each part of the body. These features are then aligned using the shortest path method, reducing the impact of posture and viewpoint changes. This alignment process ultimately reduces feature redundancy and improves the feature representation and discrimination accuracy. The experiments performed on the SYSU-MM01 [18] and RegDB [14] datasets demonstrate that the proposed approach achieves state-of-the-art performance.

Keywords: Visible-infrared person re-identification · SNA · Invariant feature · FA-PCB · Modality discrepancy · SNAFA-Net

1 Introduction

Person re-identification (ReID) is a challenging task in computer vision, aimed at searching for the same person in given images or video sequences. It plays a crucial role in intelligent monitoring and security fields. During the day, traditional visible-visible re-identification (VV-ReID) typically involves matching RGB images captured by intelligent cameras. However, due to the excessive reliance on lighting, the performance of VV-ReID significantly decreases during low-visibility nights. Intelligent cameras at night switch to infrared (IR) mode to capture IR images, but the inherent modality differences between RGB and

© The Author(s), under exclusive license to Springer Nature Switzerland AG 2023
Z. Jin et al. (Eds.): KSEM 2023, LNAI 14118, pp. 60–69, 2023.
https://doi.org/10.1007/978-3-031-40286-9_6

IR images cause significant performance degradation of VV-ReID techniques. To achieve real-time monitoring, Wu *et al.* [18] proposed the definition of visible-infrared person re-identification (VI-ReID), which aims to match images from different modalities (RGB and IR) within the same individual.

The main challenges of VI-ReID are twofold. Firstly, there are traditional challenges such as posture, occlusion, and viewpoint changes within each modality. Secondly, there are color and texture differences between the visible and infrared modalities. To alleviate these differences, an intuitive approach is to use the ResNet [5] network to extract pedestrian features from both visible and infrared images, and map them to a common feature space for similarity measurement.

Generally speaking, two main categories of VI-ReID approaches have been proposed: feature-based methods and image generation methods.

Image generation methods attempt to convert between modalities to reduce the modality discrepancy between RGB and IR images. Therefore, some GAN-based methods [1,17,24] have been proposed to perform style transfer between cross-modal images with consistent identities. However, the quality of generated images is generally low due to the interference of background information and the lack of data.

Feature-based methods aim to reduce the distance between shared and specific features in the same feature space. Therefore, Lu *et al.* [13] tries to perform mutual transfer between shared and specific features of samples to minimize the distance between modalities. Liu *et al.* [8] proposes to constraint the distance between samples by using the center distance of different modality samples' features. Wu *et al.* [18] proposes amodal module to remove irrelevant information from the extracted feature map. However, due to the large gap between RGB and IR images, it is difficult to directly project cross-modality images into public spaces. ·

Most existing work [7,22] focuses on extracting modality-shared features, but fails to consider the invariant features that are independent of the modality. For alleviating the modality discrepancy, the invariant features that are independent of the modality are extremely important. MSO [3] regarded the outline of a person as an invariant feature independent of modalities and proposed an edge feature enhancement module to enhance the modality-shared features in each single-modal space. However, MSO does not consider the deformation of the human outline caused by occlusion. In order to reduce the impact of occlusion, a widely used ReID method utilizes part-based convolutional block (PCB) [16] to divide the global features into multiple local features, extracting fine-grained information from each local feature. Liu *et al.* [8] first adopts PCB in VI-ReID and achieves excellent performance. However, these local features contain redundant background information and have no correspondence.

Therefore, this paper proposes a squared normalization attention (SNA) module to encourage the network to adapt to the invariant features of pedestrians. Additionally, to address the impact of occlusion, we design a Feature Alignment-enriched PCB (FA-PCB) module, which utilizes the shortest path algorithm to achieve cross-modal alignment of local features and adapts the corresponding relationships between local features.

The main contributions of this paper can be summarized as follows:

1. We propose a novel squared normalization attention (SNA) module, which greatly improves the representation ability of pedestrian features by enables the network to focus more on important parts and invariant features of pedestrians;
2. The FA-PCB module incorporates both global and Part-level features as person feature representations, and achieves cross-modal local feature alignment through optimizing the shortest path. This approach effectively addresses challenges such as occlusion and posture changes in cross-modal person re-identification;
3. We conducted a series of experiments on the SYSU-MM01 and RegDB datasets and achieved state-of-the-art result. Our proposed model outperforms baseline methods such as CAJ [20], showing a significant improvement in performance.

2   The Proposed Method

CAJ [20] has achieved excellent performance in VI-ReID, it randomly selects one of the three channels of the visible image to generate a new three-channel intermediate modality image. This modality serves as a bridge, extracting modality-specific features through the non-sharing stage. The feature extractor inputs the specific features and outputs modality-shared features. Finally, the shared features are mapped to the feature space for similarity measurement.

Our proposed SNAFA-Net is shown in Fig. 1. Based on CAJ, we add a squared normalization attention module and a feature embedding module based on feature alignment-rich PCB at the end of the feature extractor. The feature extractor generates global features shared by the modalities, and then the FA-PCB divides the global features into part-level features and constructs an Euclidean distance matrix of local features. Finally, the part-level features are mapped to the same space, and the shortest distance is optimized to achieve feature alignment. Finally, the part-level features are mapped to the same feature space, and the shortest path in the distance matrix is optimized to achieve feature alignment. In addition, we set identity loss (L_{id}), heterogeneous center triplet loss (L_{HcTri}), and feature alignment loss (L_{fa}) to help model training and effective convergence.

2.1   Squared Normalization Attention

There is no doubt that the global features shared by multiple modalities play an important role in person re-identification. We have designed a squared normalization attention (SNA) module to further enhance the ability to learn invariant features that are modality-independent from the global features of heterogeneous

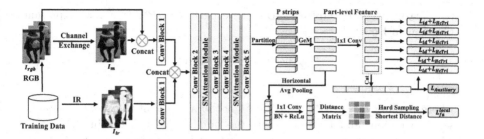

Fig. 1. Framework of our SNAFA-Net, which is based on a baseline CAJ [20].

modalities. Simply, we perform squared normalization on the feature map's information distribution to enhance the importance of modality-specific information in the distribution. The specific process is as follows:

1. Firstly, we subtract the mean value μ of each feature channel and perform the square, then divide the variance σ^2 to obtain fine-tuned features x_i^{fine}. The process can be represented by Eq. 1:

$$x_i^{fine} = \frac{(x_i - \mu)^2}{\sigma^2 + \lambda} + \delta \qquad (1)$$

where $\mu = \frac{1}{N}\sum_{i=1}^{N} x_i$, $\sigma^2 = \frac{1}{N}\sum_{i=1}^{N}(x_i - \mu)^2$, N is the total number of features in the feature map, and we set $\lambda = 10^{-12}$ to ensure that the values are effective. Additionally, $\delta = 0.5$ provides an initial value for x_i^{fine}.

2. Finally, the fine-tuned feature x_i^{fine} is passed through sigmoid activation function and element-wise multiplied by the original feature map to obtain the enhanced feature x_i^{SNA}, which can be described as Eq. 2:

$$x_i^{SNA} = x_i \cdot Simgoid(x_i^{fine}) \qquad (2)$$

2.2 Feature Alignment-Enriched PCB Module

To address pedestrian occlusion, we propose feature alignment-enriched part-based convolutional block (FA-PCB), which incorporates multiple local features to represent pedestrians and aligns local features between different images. Given a person's image (visible or infrared), the feature extractor generates a 3D feature map. Based on the 3D feature map, part-level features are extracted and aligned in the following steps:

1. We divide the 3D feature map into p strips evenly, generating body part feature maps as shown in Fig. 1, where $p = 6$.
2. Instead of using widely-used maximum or mean pooling, we use generalized-mean (**GeM**) pooling layer to convert the body part feature maps into 1D

part feature vectors. Given a 3D feature part $X \in R^{C \times H \times W}$, we represent **GeM** as in Eq. 3:

$$x^{gem} = \left(\frac{1}{|X|} \sum_{x_i \in X} x_i^{\mathrm{p}}\right)^{\frac{1}{\mathrm{p}}}, \tag{3}$$

where pooling result $x^{gem} \in R^{C \times 1 \times 1}$ is the average of the elements in the selected region, and $|\cdot|$ represents the number of elements in the region. The pooling hyper-parameter p can be set statically or learned through back-propagation.

3. Furthermore, we use 1×1 convolution blocks to reduce the dimension of part-level features. By concatenating part-level features, we generate the final person feature.

4. Finally, we calculate the distance matrix between local features in different modalities and mine the shortest distance between hardest positive and negative samples using L_{fa}^{local} for learning and optimization.

In addition, we use L_{HcTri} for metric learning of the Part-level features and final person features. We also set p classifiers to perform softmax L_{id} for identifying the Part-level features. During testing, we use the final person feature for similarity measurement.

2.3   Loss Function

Classification loss is commonly used in the ReID task and is calculated through cross-entropy loss using pedestrian identity labels, also known as id loss. We define the global and the local classification loss as $L_{id}^{g,l}$, which can be described by Eq. 4:

$$L_{id}^{g,l} = \sum_{i=1}^{N} -q_i \log(p_i^{g,l}) \tag{4}$$

where N is the total number of categories in the training dataset, q_i is the true probability distribution of the samples, and $p_i^{g,l}$ are the predicted probability distributions.

For each batch of training, we randomly select P pedestrians and sample K visible images and K thermal images for each pedestrian, for a total of $2 \times P \times K$ images. For each image, we use the same P pedestrians as positive samples, and use the remaining pedestrians as negative samples. We use heterogeneous center triplet loss (L_{HcTri}) to optimize the sample center distance of each person rather than the distance between each person's samples. We define the the modality feature center and L_{HcTri} as Eq. 5 and Eq. 6:

$$c_v^i = \frac{1}{K} \sum_{j=1}^{K} v_j^i, c_t^i = \frac{1}{K} \sum_{j=1}^{K} t_j^i \tag{5}$$

$$L_{HcTri} = \sum_{i=1}^{P} \left[\gamma_{tri} + \|c_v^i - c_t^i\|_2 - \min_{\substack{n \in \{v,t\} \\ j \neq i}} \|c_v^i - c_n^j\|_2 \right]_+ \qquad (6)$$

$$+ \sum_{i=1}^{P} \left[\gamma_{tri} + \|c_t^i - c_v^i\|_2 - \min_{\substack{n \in \{v,t\} \\ j \neq i}} \|c_t^i - c_n^j\|_2 \right]_+,$$

where γ_{tri} is a hyper-parameter. L_{HcTri} concentrates on only one cross-modality positive pair and the mined hardest negative pair in both the intra- and inter-modality. We use the euclidean distance between the sample's feature centers instead of all features.

Furthermore, we design feature alignment loss L_{fa}^{local} to constraint the short-est distance between hardest positive and negative samples, improving the net-work's generalization ability and achieving alignment. The L_{fa}^{local} is defined as Eq. 7:

$$L_{fa}^{local} = \sum_{i=1}^{P} \sum_{a=1}^{2K} \sum_{j=2}^{p} \left[\gamma_{fa} + \max_{k \in \{v,t\}} d_{i,j}^{kap} - \min_{k \in \{v,t\}} d_{i,j}^{kan} \right]_+ \qquad (7)$$

where γ_{fa} is a hyper-parameter, k represents different modalities, and $d_{i,j}^{kap}$ is the distance between all positive samples of visible/infrared modality local features, while $d_{i,j}^{kan}$ is the distance between all negative samples.

Additionally, we set the auxiliary loss $L_{Auxiliary}$ to reduce the discrepancy between the visible and infrared modalities, which can expressed as Eq. 8:

$$L_{Auxiliary} = \frac{1}{N} \sum_{i=1}^{N} mean\left(\|f_{v_i} - f_{t_i}\|_2\right) \qquad (8)$$

The total number of images is denoted as N, and f_{v_i} and f_{t_i} represent the features of the visible and infrared modalities, respectively.

In this paper, the total loss function L_{total} is defined as Eq. 9:

$$L_{total} = L_{id}^g + L_{id}^l + L_{HcTri} + L_{Auxiliary} + L_{fa}^{local} \qquad (9)$$

3 Experiments

3.1 Experiments Setting

Dataset and Evaluation Metrics. We evaluate our cross-modal person re-identification method on the widely used SYSU-MM01 and RegDB datasets. The SYSU-MM01 dataset contains RGB and infrared images of 491 pedestrians from 4 RGB and 2 infrared cameras. We use 22,258 RGB and 11,909 infrared images with 395 pedestrians for training, and 3,803 infrared images with 96 pedestrian identities for testing. The SYSU-MM01 dataset includes both indoor-search (lim-ited to four cameras) and all-search modes, while the RegDB dataset contains 412 different pedestrian identities, each with 10 visible and 10 infrared images, for a total of 8,240 images. We randomly split the RegDB dataset into 2,060 identities for training and testing ten times to ensure robustness, and take the average accuracy as the final evaluation metric. We evaluated our model's performance on SYSU-MM01 and RegDB using the rank-k matching accuracy, mean inverse negative penalty (mINP), and mean average precision (mAP) metrics.

Implementation Details. Each model used in our experiments is was implemented with Pytorch framework, based on a dual-stream network with SNA module, which employs ResNet-50 as the backbone, pre-trained on ImageNet. During training, we first apply zero-padding and random cropping to the input image to obtain a size of 288×144, and then use techniques such as random erasing and flipping for data augmentation. We use stochastic gradient descent (SGD) for optimization, with a starting learning rate of 0.1, which decreases 10 times every 10 epochs. The model was trained for a total of 100 epochs, with each training step randomly selecting 8 identities, consisting of 4 visible and 4 infrared images to form a batch.

3.2   Experiment Results

We compare the proposed SNAFA-Net with the existing works that have attained reputable performance for the cross-modal person Re-ID task, on SYSU-MM01 and RegDB in Table 1.

Table 1. Comparison with the state-of-the-art methods on the SYSU-MM01 and RegDB datasets.

Datasets		SYSU-MM01						RegDB			
Settings		All-search			Indoor-search			Visible-Thermal		Thermal-Visible	
Method	Times	rank-1	mAP	mINP	rank-1	mAP	mINP	rank-1	mAP	rank-1	mAP
AlignGAN [17]	2019	42.41	40.70	-	45.90	54.30	-	57.90	53.60	56.30	53.40
HcT [8]	2020	61.68	57.51	39.54	63.41	68.10	64.26	91.05	83.28	89.30	81.46
AGW [21]	2021	56.52	57.47	38.75	68.72	75.11	64.22	78.30	70.37	75.22	67.28
MSO [3]	2021	58.70	56.42	-	63.09	70.31	-	73.62	66.91	74.60	67.50
CM-NAS [2]	2021	61.99	60.02	-	67.01	72.95	-	84.54	80.32	82.57	78.31
SFANet [9]	2021	65.74	60.83	-	71.60	80.05	-	76.31	68.00	70.15	63.77
MCLNet [4]	2021	65.40	61.98	47.39	72.56	76.58	72.10	80.31	73.07	75.93	69.49
MPANet [19]	2021	70.58	68.24	-	76.74	80.95	-	83.70	80.90	82.80	80.70
CMTR [6]	2021	62.58	61.33	-	67.02	73.78	-	80.62	74.42	81.60	73.75
PMT [12]	2022	67.53	64.98	51.86	71.66	76.52	72.74	84.83	76.55	84.16	75.13
FMCNet [23]	2022	66.34	62.51	-	68.15	74.09	-	89.12	84.43	88.38	83.36
MAUM [11]	2022	71.68	68.79	-	76.97	**81.94**	-	87.87	85.09	86.95	85.34
AGM [10]	2023	69.63	66.11	-	74.67	78.30	-	88.40	81.45	85.34	81.19
CAJ(baseline) [20]	2021	69.88	66.89	53.61	76.26	80.37	76.79	85.03	79.14	84.80	77.80
Ours-SNA	-	70.83	67.66	53.88	76.01	79.66	75.89	89.71	83.35	87.32	80.62
Ours-FAPCB	-	71.92	68.31	54.41	76.20	80.30	76.58	92.32	85.35	90.16	83.43
Ours-SNAFA	-	**73.01**	**69.64**	**56.14**	**77.64**	81.32	**77.73**	**93.06**	**86.50**	**92.01**	**85.37**

Results on SYSU-MM01. We evaluated our proposed cross-modal person Re-ID method on SYSU-MM01 dataset with All-search and Indoor-search methods. Our approach achieved strong results with rank-1 accuracy of 73.01% and 77.64%, mAP of 69.64% and 81.32%, and mINP of 56.14% and 77.73%.

Results on RegDB. A quantitative evaluation results are presented in Table 1. we present a novel approach, referred to as Ours-SNAFA, that simultaneously leverages the effectiveness of SNA and FA-PCB. Our method achieved a rank-1 accuracy of 93.06% and 92.01% and mAP of 86.50% and 85.37% in the Visible-Thermal and Thermal-Visible tests, respectively.

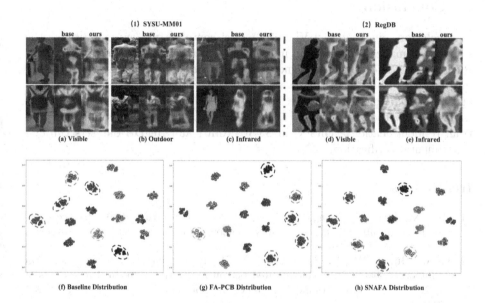

Fig. 2. (a-e) are visualizations of the feature activations obtained using Grad-CAM [15], it can be observed that SNAFA-Net focuses primarily on consistently relevant features, such as the head, arms, and legs, of pedestrians cross different sensory modalities. (f-h) show the distribution of feature embeddings in the 2D feature space is shown by different-colored circles and triangles, indicating the visible and infrared modalities. A total of 16 persons were selected from the test set. Images with the same color originate from the same person. "circle" and "triangle" represent images from the visible and infrared modalities, respectively.

3.3 Evaluation

We visualize the feature distribution of SNAFA-Net in a 2D feature space using t-SNE. As shown in Fig 2, this indicates that the SNAFA-Net is effective in discriminating and aggregating feature embeddings of the same person while reducing the modality discrepancy. And we evaluate squared normalization attention (**SNA**) and feature alignment-enriched part-based block (**FA-PCB**).

Effectiveness of FA-PCB. In VI-ReID model, the use of FA-PCB modules has multiple benefits. By aligning different parts of the person image based on body structure, the accuracy and efficiency of feature embedding are improved.

Effectiveness of SNA. To evaluate the effectiveness of the proposed squared normalization attention module for VI-ReID, we visualize the global features of RGB and infrared images from different datasets. As shown in Fig. 2 (a-e), the proposed method enhances the representation power of pedestrians by attending to invariant features.

4 Conclusion

In conclusion, our proposed VI-ReID model contains two key innovations: the squared normalization attention mechanism and the feature alignment-enriched PCB module. The model is designed to extract shared invariant features that are independent of both pedestrians and modalities, which contain unique and recognizable visual clues that render it more stable and effective in challenging scenarios. Our method has achieved significant improvements in cross-modal pedestrian re-identification accuracy on SYSU-MM01 and RegDB datasets through experimental verification.

References

1. Fan, X., Luo, H., Zhang, C., Jiang, W.: Cross-spectrum dual-subspace pairing for rgb-infrared cross-modality person re-identification. arXiv preprint arXiv:2003.00213 (2020)
2. Fu, C., Hu, Y., Wu, X., Shi, H., Mei, T., He, R.: Cm-nas: Cross-modality neural architecture search for visible-infrared person re-identification. In: Proceedings of the IEEE/CVF International Conference on Computer Vision, pp. 11823–11832 (2021)
3. Gao, Y., et al.: Mso: Multi-feature space joint optimization network for rgb-infrared person re-identification. In: Proceedings of the 29th ACM International Conference on Multimedia, pp. 5257–5265 (2021)
4. Hao, X., Zhao, S., Ye, M., Shen, J.: Cross-modality person re-identification via modality confusion and center aggregation. In: Proceedings of the IEEE/CVF International Conference On Computer Vision, pp. 16403–16412 (2021)
5. He, K., Zhang, X., Ren, S., Sun, J.: Deep residual learning for image recognition. In: Proceedings of the IEEE Conference On Computer Vision And Pattern Recognition, pp. 770–778 (2016)
6. Liang, T., et al.: Cmtr: Cross-modality transformer for visible-infrared person re-identification. arXiv preprint arXiv:2110.08994 (2021)
7. Liu, H., Chai, Y., Tan, X., Li, D., Zhou, X.: Strong but simple baseline with dual-granularity triplet loss for visible-thermal person re-identification. IEEE Signal Process. Lett. **28**, 653–657 (2021)
8. Liu, H., Tan, X., Zhou, X.: Parameter sharing exploration and hetero-center triplet loss for visible-thermal person re-identification. IEEE Trans. Multimedia **23**, 4414–4425 (2020)

9. Liu, H., Ma, S., Xia, D., Li, S.: Sfanet: A spectrum-aware feature augmentation network for visible-infrared person reidentification. IEEE Trans. Neural Netw. Learn. Syst. (2021)
10. Liu, H., Xia, D., Jiang, W.: Towards homogeneous modality learning and multi-granularity information exploration for visible-infrared person re-identification. IEEE J. Selected Topics Signal Process. (2023)
11. Liu, J., Sun, Y., Zhu, F., Pei, H., Yang, Y., Li, W.: Learning memory-augmented unidirectional metrics for cross-modality person re-identification. In: Proceedings of the IEEE/CVF Conference on Computer Vision and Pattern Recognition, pp. 19366–19375 (2022)
12. Lu, H., Zou, X., Zhang, P.: Learning progressive modality-shared transformers for effective visible-infrared person re-identification. arXiv preprint arXiv:2212.00226 (2022)
13. Lu, Y., et al.: Cross-modality person re-identification with shared-specific feature transfer. In: Proceedings of the IEEE/CVF Conference on Computer Vision and Pattern Recognition, pp. 13379–13389 (2020)
14. Nguyen, D.T., Hong, H.G., Kim, K.W., Park, K.R.: Person recognition system based on a combination of body images from visible light and thermal cameras. Sensors **17**(3), 605 (2017)
15. Selvaraju, R.R., Cogswell, M., Das, A., Vedantam, R., Parikh, D., Batra, D.: Gradcam: Visual explanations from deep networks via gradient-based localization. In: Proceedings of the IEEE International Conference on Computer Vision, pp. 618–626 (2017)
16. Sun, Y., Zheng, L., Yang, Y., Tian, Q., Wang, S.: Beyond part models: Person retrieval with refined part pooling (and a strong convolutional baseline). In: Proceedings of the European Conference On Computer Vision (ECCV), pp. 480–496 (2018)
17. Wang, G., Zhang, T., Cheng, J., Liu, S., Yang, Y., Hou, Z.: Rgb-infrared cross-modality person re-identification via joint pixel and feature alignment. In: Proceedings of the IEEE/CVF International Conference on Computer Vision, pp. 3623–3632 (2019)
18. Wu, A., Zheng, W.S., Yu, H.X., Gong, S., Lai, J.: Rgb-infrared cross-modality person re-identification. In: Proceedings of the IEEE International Conference on Computer Vision, pp. 5380–5389 (2017)
19. Wu, Q., et al.: Discover cross-modality nuances for visible-infrared person re-identification. In: Proceedings of the IEEE/CVF Conference on Computer Vision and Pattern Recognition, pp. 4330–4339 (2021)
20. Ye, M., Ruan, W., Du, B., Shou, M.Z.: Channel augmented joint learning for visible-infrared recognition. In: Proceedings of the IEEE/CVF International Conference on Computer Vision, pp. 13567–13576 (2021)
21. Ye, M., Shen, J., Lin, G., Xiang, T., Shao, L., Hoi, S.C.: Deep learning for person re-identification: a survey and outlook. IEEE Trans. Pattern Anal. Mach. Intell. **44**(6), 2872–2893 (2021)
22. Ye, M., Wang, Z., Lan, X., Yuen, P.C.: Visible thermal person re-identification via dual-constrained top-ranking. In: IJCAI. vol. 1, p. 2 (2018)
23. Zhang, Q., Lai, C., Liu, J., Huang, N., Han, J.: Fmcnet: Feature-level modality compensation for visible-infrared person re-identification. In: Proceedings of the IEEE/CVF Conference on Computer Vision and Pattern Recognition, pp. 7349–7358 (2022)
24. Zhang, Z., Jiang, S., Huang, C., Li, Y., Da, Xu., R.Y.: Rgb-ir cross-modality person reid based on teacher-student gan model. Patt. Recogn. Lette. **150**, 155–161 (2021)

A Comparative Study of Chatbot Response Generation: Traditional Approaches Versus Large Language Models

Michael McTear[ID], Sheen Varghese Marokkie, and Yaxin Bi[✉][ID]

Ulster University, Belfast BT15 1ED, Northern Ireland, UK
{mf.mctear,Varghese_Marokkie-S,y.bi}@ulster.ac.uk
https://www.ulster.ac.uk/

Abstract. Chatbot responses can be generated using traditional rule-based conversation design or through the use of large language models (LLMs). In this paper we compare the quality of responses provided by LLM-based chatbots with those provided by traditional conversation design. The results suggest that in some cases the use of LLMs could improve the quality of chatbot responses. The paper concludes by suggesting that a combination of approaches is the best way forward and suggests some directions for future work.

Keywords: Conversational AI · Large Language Models · Conversation design · ChatGPT · Bard · Rasa

1 Introduction

Traditionally chatbots (also known as conversational assistants, virtual companions, digital personal assistants, dialogue systems, etc.) have been designed and developed by conversation designers using best practice guidelines that have been developed over several decades [1–3]. In this tradition chatbot responses are hand-crafted by conversation designers, whereas with LLMs the responses are generated automatically [4]. Considering the impressive capabilities of LLMs, we can ask whether they pose a potential threat to conversation designers or provide an opportunity for increased productivity. With this in mind, in this paper we conduct a comparative analysis, examining responses generated by a rule-based system and comparing them with responses generated by LLMs in order to address the following research question:

Can LLMs produce better responses than responses that are hand-crafted by conversation designers?

The remainder of the paper is structured as follows. In the next section we provide a brief overview of related work. Following this we describe two approaches to the generation of chatbot responses: traditional hand-crafting and

© The Author(s), under exclusive license to Springer Nature Switzerland AG 2023
Z. Jin et al. (Eds.): KSEM 2023, LNAI 14118, pp. 70–79, 2023.
https://doi.org/10.1007/978-3-031-40286-9_7

using LLMs. The main part of the paper then compares the quality of hand-crafted responses with those generated by LLMs in a number of use cases taken from the e-VITA project [5] in which a virtual coach is being developed in Europe and Japan to support active and healthy ageing.[1] The paper concludes with a brief discussion of the limitations of the work and some suggestions for future research.

2 Related Work

Large language models are being increasingly integrated into conversational AI products with many providers announcing that their platforms are "LLM enabled" in a race to differentiate themselves from their competitors [6]. Indeed, LLMs are revolutionizing the chatbot design landscape to the extent that the role of designers is changing from hand-crafting chatbot responses and conversation flows to refining the conversational abilities of the chatbot [7].

Several studies have investigated the use of LLMs in chatbot design and, in particular, in response generation. [8] examined how ChatGPT could perform various chatbot design tasks including generating personas and simulating interviews with fictional users. The results showed that ChatGPT was able to effectively perform these design tasks and generally provide appropriate responses. [9] presented examples showing how various types of text can be generated from user prompts, while [10] compared ChatGPT with a number of chatbot development platforms, including Rasa, finding that, in terms of response generation, ChatGPT is more versatile in that it is able to generate human-like responses automatically, thus saving time and resources for developers. Similarly, [11] showed how LLMs can provide more natural responses compared with knowledge base actions.

In a comparative study questions about movies were submitted to a Rasa-based chatbot trained on an extensive movie dataset and to GPT-3 [12]. It was found that the Rasa-based chatbot answered 6 out of 7 questions correctly while GPT-3 got 5 correct, although it improved with a more careful prompt design. A comparison of the two systems indicated that Rasa can be trained with specialized and current data but in this application took 4 months to develop, while GPT-3 was trained on data that was current only up to October 2019 but on the other hand was able to match the performance of the Rasa-based chatbot almost out of the box and was also able to tackle a wide range of additional topics while the Rasa chatbot could only answer questions about movies.

Some limitations of LLM-powered chatbots include forgotten information, partial responses, and a lack of output diversity [8]; failure in unexpected ways [12]; the fact that designers cannot easily control the output of the LLM and that it has the potential to hallucinate facts and is potentially vulnerable

---

[1] The e-VITA project has received funding from the European Union H2020 Programme under grant agreement no. 101016453. The Japanese consortium received funding from the Japanese Ministry of Internal Affairs and Communication (MIC), Grant no. JPJ000595.

to prompt injection attacks [11]. In the next section we compare responses by a Rasa-based and two LLM-based chatbots to user inputs in five different use cases.

3   Response Generation in Chatbots

Tradition ally chatbot responses have been hand-crafted by conversation designers using a conversational development framework such as Rasa [13]. In Rasa the system's actions include responses which can be defined directly in the system's domain file, for example:

```
responses:
    utter_greet:
        - text: "Hey there!"
```

Responses can include rich content such as buttons and attachments as well as content retrieved from external sources, and they can vary according to predefined conditions.

LLMs generate responses using a process known as *autoregressive generation* in which the text to be output is generated one word at a time by predicting the most probable word to output given the preceding words.

In order to compare these two approaches, the following use cases were selected:

- Remembering and using information about the user.
- Helping the user send an email.
- Monitoring the user's emotional state.
- Obtaining information from an external API.
- Accessing a knowledge source.

Prompts were submitted to ChatGPT and Bard and the results were compared with those obtained in a Rasa-based chatbot described in [14]. The version of ChatGPT used in the study was based on the GPT-4 LLM [15]. Bard is an experimental system developed by Google based on the LaMDA (Language Model for Dialogue Applications) technology [16].

4   Results

The following sub-sections compare how responses were generated in the Rasa system and by ChatGPT and Bard.

4.1   Remembering and Using Information About the User

Storing information about the user enables a chatbot to provide a more personalised experience. As a simple example the current study explored how the chatbot could remember and use the user's name.

The Rasa-based chatbot explicitly asked for the user's name using a form in which there were required slots to store the user's first and last names. Using forms and slots in this way enabled the chatbot to make use of this information subsequently in the conversation. Forms could also be used for more complex use cases to request and store useful details about a user, such as next-of-kin, carer, preferences, hobbies, etc. that could be useful in future conversations.

As LLMs respond to prompts rather than pro-actively initiating a topic, in order to explore this use case we prompted with a name, as in *Hi, my name is John Philips*. ChatGPT and Bard made similar responses, greeting the user and making use of the first name. For example, ChatGPT responded *Hello John! It's nice to meet you. How can I assist you today?*

In order to test whether the LLM-powered chatbots could remember the user's name later in the conversation, the following prompt was issued about two hours after the user had introduced himself: *Do you remember my name?* ChatGPT responded positively, while Bard responded: *You haven't told me your name yet. Can you please tell me so I can remember it?* Currently Bard's ability to maintain context is limited, as described in an FAQ [17]:

> *Bard's ability to hold context is purposefully limited for now. As Bard continues to learn, its ability to hold context during longer conversations will improve.*

4.2   Helping the User Perform a Task

Helping the user accomplish a task consisting of a well-defined sequence of steps, such as sending an email or text message, making a phone call, or accessing a music API, requires the chatbot to elicit the required information to carry out the task and then to submit this information to an external API. Here we focus on acquiring the required information.

In the Rasa-based chatbot this was achieved using a custom action involving an email form with slots for the recipient's email address, the subject of the email, and the text of the message. The form contained questions to elicit the values for these slots and then called a method to submit the values to an email API.

ChatGPT and Bard were prompted with *I want to send an email to a friend*. ChatGTP first checked some details about the user's email account and then listed the steps required to send the email. Bard also listed the steps and additionally composed a short sample email that could be sent to a friend. In this respect Rasa and the LLMs provide similar support. However, it is also possible to ask the LLMs to generate text on any given topic, as shown in Fig. 1 in response to a request for an email inviting a friend to a party on Friday.

ChatGPT produced a similar draft email. Generating arbitrary text in this way is one of the strengths of LLMs. This would not be possible using a traditional chatbot development framework in which the chatbot's responses are pre-defined at design time.

Hi [Friend's name],
I hope this email finds you well. I'm writing to invite you to a party I'm having next Friday at my place. It's going to be a casual get-together with some friends, food, drinks, and music.
The party will start at 7pm and go until late. I'd love to see you there!
Please RSVP by Wednesday so I can get a headcount.
Can't wait to see you!

Best,
[Your name]

Fig. 1. Bard's response to a prompt asking for a draft of an email inviting a friend to a party on Friday

4.3   Monitoring the User's Emotional State

Analysing the user's sentiments and emotions is an important use case in the e-VITA project. In the Rasa-based chatbot **spaCy NLP** sentiment analysis was used to analyse the user's sentiments using the **TextBlob** library [18]. However, there were a few situations where this approach did not work very well. For example, for statements like *I don't feel so good* or *not bad*, the system was unable to classify the correct sentiments and responded with confusing statements. More work is needed using more sophisticated NLU analysis to train the system on inputs such as these.

In its response to the input *I am feeling sad*, ChatGPT began with some words of empathy:

I'm sorry to hear that you're not feeling very happy. Is there something specific that's causing you to feel this way, or is it a general feeling? It's important to take care of yourself when you're not feeling happy.

However, ChatGPT did not allow the user to respond to its questions and continued to make a list of suggestions of things to do to help feel better, finishing with:

Remember that it's okay to not feel happy all the time, and that it's important to take care of yourself when you don't. If you need someone to talk to, don't hesitate to reach out.

Although responses such as this are helpful, in terms of conversational quality they are deficient as they do not allow the user to engage in a conversation about their problem. While ChatGPT asks *Is there anything specific that's causing you to feel this way, or is it a general feeling?* it does not allow the user to respond, but instead continues with a long list of things to do.

ChatGPT and Bard were both able to identify utterances containing a negative, such as *I am not very happy*, as expressing sadness and then proceeded to give similar responses about how to deal with this emotion.

4.4   Obtaining Information from an External API

Obtaining information such as weather updates, news, or sports results was achieved in the Rasa-based chatbot using a story that is triggered by recognising the relevant intent. For example, the user's input *what is the weather like in Belfast?* was classified as a **weather_intent** that triggered a **weather** story that included an action to extract the city if it was not specified in the user's utterance and then submitted this value to a weather API using a custom action. A response was then created showing the maximum and minimum temperature and the overall weather status of the city.

ChatGPT and Bard differed in how they handled this query. ChatGPT stated that it did not have access to weather information and then went on to provide helpful suggestions for how to obtain the information. Bard produced the following response:

> *The weather in Belfast is currently 11° C and clear. The humidity is 75% and the wind is blowing from the east at 10 mph. The forecast for the rest of the day is for mostly sunny skies with a high of 14° C and a low of 7° C.*

In such a situation it is not clear whether the LLM is hallucinating, i.e., generating content that is not factually correct. However, Bard provides a button that can trigger a Google search to verify the response.

4.5   Accessing a Knowledge Source

External knowledge can be stored in a database, knowledge base, or knowledge graph, and can be accessed by the system using a custom action [19]. The chatbot described in [14] made use of an **in-memory knowledge base** in the form of a **json** file that was developed in the e-VITA project to store information about illnesses. Figure 2 shows a small extract from this knowledge base.

```
"name": "Diabetes",
"cause": "Overweight, obesity, and physical inactivity",
"precaution": "Reduce your total carb intake, Exercise regularly, Quit
smoking",
"cure": "There are some medicines that can help with diabetes. But there is
no long term cure",
```

Fig. 2. Extract from Json file for diseases

The following are examples of possible user inputs that would be classified as the intent **query_knowledge_base** in the Rasa-based chatbot, invoking an action within a story to access the knowledge base and retrieve a response:

- what is the cause of diabetes?
- how can I prevent diabetes?
- can diabetes be cured?

If an attribute of the disease, such as cause, prevention, and cure, is identified in the user's utterance, the associated response is output by the chatbot.

Similar prompts were put to ChatGPT and Bard. The following shows Bard's response to the prompt *what is the cause of diabetes?*

> *There are two main types of diabetes: type 1 and type 2.*
> - ***Type 1 diabetes:*** *Type 1 diabetes is an autoimmune disease. This means that the body's immune system attacks and destroys the cells in the pancreas that produce insulin. Insulin is a hormone that helps the body use glucose for energy. Without insulin, glucose builds up in the blood, leading to high blood sugar levels.*
> - ***Type 2 diabetes:*** *Type 2 diabetes is the most common form of diabetes. It occurs when the body becomes resistant to insulin or doesn't produce enough insulin. As a result, glucose builds up in the blood, leading to high blood sugar levels.*
>
> *There is no cure for diabetes, but it can be managed with medication, diet, and exercise. If you have diabetes, it is important to work with your doctor to develop a treatment plan that is right for you.*

5   Discussion

In the previous section we have seen how the Rasa-based chatbot was able to handle well-defined interactions, such as storing information about the user, performing tasks with specific steps, obtaining information from an external API, and accessing a knowledge source using constructs such as intents, entities, slots, responses, stories, forms, and actions. The conversation designer can control the behaviour of the chatbot by specifying how the NLU component classifies user inputs and provides appropriate responses, how the conversation should flow, and what actions should be taken in response to the user's utterances.

On the downside, defining intents and providing training examples is time-consuming and error-prone, especially in systems with a large number of intents, as there is a possibility of overlapping intents resulting in inaccurate classification. There is also the problem of utterances that appear to be 'out-of-scope' as they cannot be mapped to one of the pre-defined intents. Creating stories is also problematic as the conversation designer has to anticipate all possible deviations from the 'happy path' defined in a basic story. More generally, because the behaviours of the system are pre-determined, there is no possibility of more open-ended responses requiring the generation of new content, as shown in the example of the drafting of an email by the chatbot Bard.

Chatbots using LLMs can address some of these issues. They are able to understand virtually any input from the user compared to chatbots trained on a limited number of training examples. They can also generate more varied content, as seen in the responses to queries about topics such as diabetes. Although they are able to store some of the context of a conversation, it is not obvious to what extent. For example, it is not clear whether they can reliably store and remember specific details about the user. ChatGPT and Bard were able to remember the user's name for some time during a conversation but after a certain length of time, in this case two hours, Bard no longer knew the user's name. Such data would also not be remembered in a later conversation.

Accessing external knowledge is also an issue with LLM-powered chatbots. It is important to realize that LLMs do not have a specific representation of knowledge, such as is contained in a knowledge graph or database. In this respect they are different from search engines which find and return a ranked list of web pages in response to a user's query. In contrast, LLMs use the patterns and structures in the data they were trained on to generate responses based on the content of the prompts they receive. While search engines can return results from any web page that is indexed by the search engine, LLMs are limited to the patterns and statistical relationships between words that they acquired during training and do not have the ability to browse the internet or access new information. Because of this an LLM will always generate a response based on its prediction of the most probable next word in a sequence but with the danger of hallucinating, i.e., producing content that is potentially not factually correct. In the use case involving a request for information about the weather, ChatGPT made clear that it did not have access to external APIs. Bard appears to have been able to access external information and produced a weather report that could be verified against a Google search.

The LLM-powered chatbots performed particularly well when they were required to generate content, such as drafting an email for a situation that had not been defined in advance. They also provided relevant responses to user input, displaying sentiment, showing empathy, and providing useful advice. In the use case involving queries about diabetes, the Rasa-based chatbot was only able to answer queries and produce responses that had been pre-programmed in its knowledge base, whereas the LLM-powered chatbots were able to answer a range of queries and produce original responses. Future work is needed to investigate whether content generated in this way is factually accurate, or whether the LLM-powered chatbot is 'hallucinating'. Relative to this question it is interesting to note that in a recent study ChatGPT was able to respond accurately to all 24 questions in the diabetes knowledge questionnaire (24-DKQ) and was also able to expand and provide useful explanations [20].

One area where the content generated by LLM-powered chatbots is deficient is in the conversational nature of the responses. As can be seen from some of the examples in the previous section, responses were often lengthy and did not give the user the opportunity to reply. Moreover, the responses were more suitable as text to be read by the user and would not be suitable as output in a voice-based chatbot where the content needs to be more concise and more conversational [21].

6   Limitations of the Present Work

The current study is small scale and it would be important to investigate a wider range of use cases to make more detailed comparisons between chatbots developed using traditional methods and those powered by LLMs. Simple measures were taken to assess the quality of the chatbot's outputs. Future work should make use of more precise measures, such as those used in the LaMDA study [16], and there should be user studies to determine user satisfaction and acceptance.

7   Concluding Remarks

This paper has compared conversations with chatbots developed using traditional rule-based conversation design and those using LLMs. It was found that both approaches have their advantages and disadvantages, suggesting that a combination of approaches may be required. Indeed, this is the direction that is being taken by several providers of chatbot development frameworks. For example, LLMs can be used to handle user inputs that were not part of the training of the NLU component and would otherwise be treated as 'out-of-scope'. Also, as has been shown, an LLM is able to generate content on the fly whereas traditional chatbots are restricted to the content provided by the conversation designer.

The field of LLM-powered chatbots is developing rapidly and some of the issues discussed here are currently being addressed. For example, OpenAI is developing plugins to connect ChatGPT to third-party applications to perform tasks such as retrieving real-time information and performing transactions such as booking a flight [22]. There is also a lot of attention being paid to prompt design and prompt engineering as well as to problems such as hallucinations and, more generally, issues related to ethical and responsible AI.

Acknowledgements. Michael McTear received support from the e-VITA project (https://www.e-vita.coach/) (accessed on 23 April 2023). Sheen Varghese Marokkie and Yaxin Bi received support from the School of Computing, Ulster University (https://www.ulster.ac.uk/faculties/computing-engineering-and-the-built-environment/computing).

References

1. Cohen, M.H., Giangola, J.P., Balogh, J.: Voice User Interface Design. CA., USA, Addison-Wesley Professional, Redwood City (2004)
2. Pearl, C.: Designing Voice User Interfaces: Principles of Conversational Experiences. O'Reilly Media Inc, Sebastapol, USA (2016)
3. Deibel, D., Evanhoe, R.: Conversations with Things: UX Design for Chat and Voice. Rosenfeld Media, Brooklyn, New York, USA (2021)
4. Lizhou, F., Lingyao, L., Ma, Z., Lee, S., Yu, H., Hemphill, L: A Bibliometric Review of Large Language Models Research from 2017 to 2023. https://arxiv.org/abs/2304.02020. Accessed 3 Jun 2023 (2023)
5. e-VITA coach Homepage. https://www.e-vita.coach/. Accessed 3 Jun 2023
6. Greyling, C. Large language models are forcing conversational AI frameworks to look outward, https://cobusgreyling.medium.com/large-language-models-are-forcing-conversational-ai-frameworks-to-look-outward-54a1ad49ce63. Accessed 3 Jun 2023

7. Agbai, C. Chatbot design in the era of large language models (LLMs). https://azumo.com/insights/chatbot-design-in-the-era-of-large-language-models-llms. Accessed 3 Jun 2023
8. Kocaballi, A.B.: Conversational AI-powered design: ChatGPT as designer, user, and product. https://arxiv.org/abs/2302.07406. Accessed 3 Jun 2023 (2023)
9. Alto, V.: Modern Generative AI with ChatGPT and OpenAI models: leverage the capabilities of OpenAI's LLM for productivity and innovation with GPT3 and GPT4. Packt Publishing, Birmingham (2023)
10. Moonash. ChatGPT vs other chatbot tools: a comprehensive comparison. https://everythingaboutchatgpt.com/chatgpt-comparison/#ChatGPT_vs_Rasa. Accessed 3 Jun 2023
11. Nichol, A.: Answering questions about structured data with Rasa Open Source and ChatGPT. https://rasa.com/blog/answering-questions-about-structured-data-with-rasa-open-source-and-chatgpt/. Accessed 3 Jun 2023
12. Ryan, M.: GPT-3 vs. Rasa chatbots. https://towardsdatascience.com/gpt-3-vs-rasa-chatbots-8b3041daf91d. Accessed 3 Jun 2023
13. Rasa Homepage. https://rasa.com/docs/rasa/. Accessed 3 Jun 2023
14. Marokkie, S.-V., McTear, M., Bi, Y.: A virtual companion for older adults using the Rasa Conversational AI framework. In: CONVERSATIONS 2022–the 6th International Workshop on Chatbot Research, Applications, and Design. https://conversations2022.files.wordpress.com/2022/11/conversations_2022_positionpaper_10_mctear.pdf. Accessed 3 Jun 2023 (2022)
15. ChatGPT Homepage. https://openai.com/blog/chatgpt. Accessed 3 Jun 2023
16. Thoppilan, R., De Freitas, D., Hall, D., et al.: LaMDA: Language Models for Dialog Applications. https://arxiv.org/abs/2201.08239. Accessed 3 Jun 2023
17. Bard FAQ. https://bard.google.com/faq. Accessed 3 Jun 2023
18. spacytextblob: A TextBlob sentiment analysis pipeline component for spaCy. https://spacytextblob.netlify.app. Accessed 3 Jun 2023
19. Wilcock, G., Jokinen, K.: Conversational AI and Knowledge Graphs for Social Robot Interaction. Late-Breaking Reports. In: The 17th ACM/IEEE International Conference on Human-Robot Interaction (HRI-2022) (2022)
20. Nakhleh, A., Spitzer, S., Shehadeh, N.: ChatGPT's response to the Diabetes Knowledge Questionnaire: Implications for diabetes education. Diabetes Technology & Therapeutics. https://doi.org/10.1089/dia.2023.0134 Accessed 3 Jun 2023 (2023)
21. So, P.: Voice Content and Usability. https://abookapart.com/products/voice-content-and-usability Accessed 3 Jun 2023 (2021)
22. ChatGPT Plugins. https://platform.openai.com/docs/plugins/introduction. Accessed 3 Jun 2023

Investigating the Impact of Product Contours on User Perception of Product Attributes

Huizhen Ding[1]([✉])([iD]) and Zuyao Zhang[1,2]([iD])

[1] Art and Design Institute, Zhejiang Sci-Tech University, Hangzhou 310018, China
202131004045@mails.zstu.edu.cn
[2] Design Intelligence Innovation Center, China Academy of Art, Hangzhou 310024, China

Abstract. Perceptual engineering research has examined product contours as a crucial component of product design. The research, however, mostly focuses on the contours of particular products, and it is not yet obvious what the general relationship is between product contours and perceived product qualities. In order to create a three-level model of perceived product attributes, this paper classifies product qualities into categories based on Norman's dimensions. The exterior contour of the mouse product is used as the research object, and web crawler technology is used to extract the impression keywords. After that, the eye-tracking method is employed to investigate how the product contours influence consumers' eye movements in relation to certain impression keywords. The findings demonstrate how users' particular perceptions of a particular product attribute can be improved by the matching product contour features. The study illustrates the connection between product contours and perceived product qualities, providing product designers with a reference point during the initial sketching stage.

Keywords: Product contours · Perceived product attributes · Eye-tracking technology

1 Introduction

As customer-centricity becomes paramount in the evolving market, successful companies cater to varied consumer needs [1], contributing to the growth of perceptual engineering-a field that focuses on consumer perceptions of product design [2].

Research indicates that consumers use visual design to assess a product's hidden attributes [3], with the product's outline playing a critical role. Various studies have explored how product contours affect visual impressions and user perceptions. For instance, aesthetic geometric features embedded in product contours can significantly influence perceptions; curves and round shapes are often linked to softness and warmth, while angles and straight lines suggest speed [4].

While the impact of product contour shapes on user preferences has been examined, few studies have aimed to refine these preferences, which are shaped by

© The Author(s), under exclusive license to Springer Nature Switzerland AG 2023
Z. Jin et al. (Eds.): KSEM 2023, LNAI 14118, pp. 80–88, 2023.
https://doi.org/10.1007/978-3-031-40286-9_8

both product attributes and emotional feedback. This research seeks to comprehend the relationship between these features and attribute perceptions, thereby uncovering detailed mapping relationships that can serve as methodological references for designers in the early stages of product design.

2 Theoretical Study of Perceived Product Attributes

Technological advancements have made markets more competitive, leading to the rise of emotional design as a tool to forge durable relationships between users and products.

According to Jordan, people purchase items for the pleasure derived from interacting with admirable, desirable products. Products can provide practical, emotional, and hedonic benefits [5]. Desmet suggests that unconscious evaluations categorize products as potentially beneficial or detrimental, explaining diverse emotional responses to the same product. Three types of evaluations include usefulness, pleasantness, and justification [6]. Norman's emotional design model classifies user reactions into three levels: Visceral, Behavioral, and Reflective [7].

Each method explains product-consumer interaction differently but shares a common perspective on distinguishing emotional, practical, and aesthetic effects. Drawing from these theories, we propose the perceptual product attribute model, targeting users' visual perception and divided into emotional, usage, and appearance attributes. This model suggests that users' developed visual perception enables them to infer not just appearance attributes but also usage and emotional attributes from product shape.

- Appearance attributes: Users assess a product's shape to evaluate if it aligns with their aesthetics.
- Usage attributes: Users infer the product's usage qualities, such as its comfort level, through its appearance. This pertains to the user-experience that the product delivers.
- Emotional attributes: Users observe a product's appearance and experience the emotions it elicits, including feelings of pleasure, nostalgia.

3 Research Hypotheses

After extensive literature research, the following hypotheses are proposed.

H1. Users use a longer average gaze time when evaluating unobservable attributes.

H2. Users form product impressions through product local contour features.

H3a. Product shapes with symmetrical outer contours are more attractive when the impression of appearance attributes is assessed.

H3b. Product shapes with curved contours are more attractive when emotional attribute impressions are assessed.

H3c. Product shapes with complex contours are more appealing when evaluated emotional attribute impressions.

We use three scales—symmetrical vs. asymmetrical, complex vs. simple, and rounded vs. hard—to categorize product outlines. Experiments then examine how different product outlines impact users' product attribute impressions.

4   Methods and Processes

4.1   User Comment Data Acquisition and Processing Technology

Online user reviews reveal authentic feelings about products, including evaluations and expectations. Analyzing this data provides insights into user demands. Despite certain limitations, web crawlers are commonly used to collect this internet data.

Preprocessing is required due to the unstructured nature of comment data. This includes data cleaning, sentence separation, lexical annotation, word deactivation, and text representation, leading to word expressions for product reviews.

4.2   Eye-Tracking Technology

Eye-tracking techniques employ infrared and image capture devices to track subtle eye changes in real time. This non-intrusive method records various data during eye movement, offering an objective assessment of design solutions [8]. The Area of Interest (AOI) method is commonly used to visualize eye-tracking data, extracting precise metrics during the experiment and analyzing visual search and information processing [9]. These eye movement metrics are outlined in Table 1.

Table 1. Detail of eye-tracking measures.

Measures	Detail
ATD	Average fixation duration: the average value of all fixation durations
TFD	Total fixation duration: the summed duration of all fixations to an AOI
FC	Fixation count: the number of fixation points within the AOI
RC	Regression count: number of times to return to an area of interest after leaving it
FFD	First fixation duration: the duration of the first fixation on an object
TTFF	Time to first fixation: the time it takes for a subject to view a specific AOI from stimulus onset
TVD	Total visit duration: the summed duration of all visits to an AOI

For this study, four highly correlated eye-tracking metrics were selected: Average fixation duration, Total fixation duration, Fixation counts, and Time to first fixation. Generally, a longer fixation duration suggests more interest in an area, higher fixation counts indicate greater satisfaction with a contour, and a shorter time to first fixation shows a higher likelihood of attraction to an area.

5   Implementation and Results

This study uses the outer contour of a mouse product as a case study to investigate how it influences user's eye movements and perception. The mouse, a common office item, provides an accurate representation of overall shape via its top view contour.

5.1   User Comment Data Acquisition and Processing Technology

We gathered data from Taobao's mouse product reviews using Anaconda Navigator 2.1.1 and PyCharm 2022.2.2. After pre-processing, notable keywords, corresponding to different attributes, were extracted from the reviews and converted into word clouds via Python. The word clouds maps are shown in Fig. 1. "Beautiful" pertains to appearance, "sensitive" and "comfortable" to usage, and "satisfied" to emotional attributes.

Fig. 1. Word cloud map of mouse product user evaluations.

5.2   Eye-Tracking Experimental Design

Twelve students, 7 females and 5 males, with vision under 300° and no color deficiencies, participated in a randomized experiment using Tobii Pro Glasses 2 for eye-tracking. Data collected was transferred to Tobii Pro Lab software. The experiment was conducted in a controlled laboratory environment.

Determination of the Experimental Samples

Stimulation Materials. The stimuli consisted of various frontal images of mouse contours categorized into three dimensions: roundness, symmetry, and complexity. Eight orthogonal combinations of these dimensions resulted in 24 stimulus samples, contoured using Photoshop and displayed against a white background, as is shown in Fig. 2.

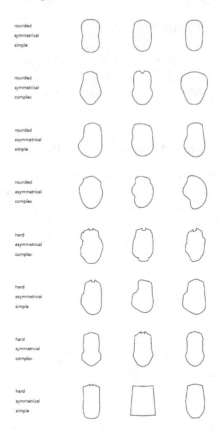

Fig. 2. Eye movement samples of the extracted contour mouse product.

Aesthetic Evaluation Scales. The semantic differential method, developed by Osgood et al., interprets sentence meanings to reveal consumption psychology [10]. In this study, we extracted keywords from user evaluations of mouse products using web crawlers. Products were assessed on appearance, usage, and emotional attributes using a semantic differential scale. Each attribute was rated on a seven-level scale, with "+3" and "−3" indicating extreme levels of comfort or discomfort, respectively.

Experimental Data Collection

Experimental Procedure. Participants were informed, consented, and tested individually prior to the experiment. Positioned 65 cm from the screen, their gaze data was collected and calibrated. The trial involved evaluating tasks based on virtual impression keywords and visual stimuli. Verbal responses were recorded for product profile preferences.

The formal experiment followed a similar procedure with equipment calibration and randomized keywords. Participants assessed a product silhouette and verbally indicated their choice.

Data Analysis. Data was collected with Tobii Pro Lab and analyzed with SPSS. The gaze behavior was segmented using custom events in Tobii Pro Lab. Experimental samples were partitioned into three segments using the AOI method: global, left, and right.

Test Methods. Nonparametric tests.

Nonparametric tests were utilized when overall variance was unknown or undefined, providing conclusions about the distribution shape. The test for multiple independent samples was used to discern significant median or distribution differences in multiple groups.

The Kruskal-Wallis test evaluated if multiple samples came from the same probability distribution, specifically used to assess H1 data. Comparisons of two aggregate properties were made to detect significant differences, with the test statistic choice depending on factors like sample size and known status of the overall standard deviation.

Tests for two overall parameters.

Comparisons of two aggregate properties were made to detect significant differences, with the test statistic choice depending on factors like sample size and known status of the overall standard deviation.

The Z-test was used for overall mean differences when the sample size was 30 or larger, with different test statistics expressions for known and unknown variances.

In this paper, using the test of independent large samples, let the two samples be independent random large samples, then the sampling distribution of the difference between the means of the two samples $(\bar{x}_1 - \bar{x}_2)$ approximately obeys Normal distribution.

When σ_1^2 and σ_2^2 are known, the test statistic is:

$$z = \frac{(\bar{x}_1 - \bar{x}_2) - (\mu_1 - \mu_2)}{\sqrt{\frac{\sigma_1^2}{n_1} + \frac{\sigma_2^2}{n_2}}} \tag{1}$$

When σ_1^2 and σ_2^2 are not known, the test statistic is:

$$z = \frac{(\bar{x}_1 - \bar{x}_2) - (\mu_1 - \mu_2)}{\sqrt{\frac{s_1^2}{n_1} + \frac{s_2^2}{n_2}}} \tag{2}$$

Results. SPSS normal test revealed skewed results, so a nonparametric Kruskal-Wallis test was used. No significant difference was found among eye movement events matching impression keywords (Table 2, p>0.05), rejecting H1.

Table 2. Non-parametric test for "beautiful", "sensitive", "comfortable", and "satisfied".

Null hypothesis	Test method	Statistical significance	Decision
The general distribution is the same across all of the sample's categories	Kruskal-Wallis test	0.782	Accept the null hypothesis

Null Hypothesis: Time to first fixation on the left side of the image is equal to the time to first fixation on the right side of the image.

Alternative Hypothesis: Time to first fixation on the left side of the image is smaller than it on the right side of the image.

H2 was tested using a Z-test, revealing no significant difference in initial fixation times between picture sides ($z = -1.922696879, z > -z_\alpha(-1.96)$). However, protruding contours generated pleasant impressions ($z = -3.031909196$, $z < -z_\alpha(-1.96)$), and also supported by high comfort ratings in user scores, validating H2.

For H3, the experimental participants' score data were assessed using the test of the difference between the means of two overall values in separate big samples. Table 3 displays the outcomes.

Table 3. Z-test of user scoring data.

Title	Average	Variance	Z-score
Beautiful_rounded	4.236	2.736	*6.445
Beautiful_hard	3.042	2.207	
Beautiful_symmetrical	3.597	2.852	−0.424
Beautiful_asymmetrical	3.681	2.801	
Beautiful_simple	4.090	2.860	*4.725
Beautiful_complex	3.188	2.388	
comfortable_rounded	4.278	2.603	*4.729
comfortable_hard	3.396	2.406	
comfortable_symmetrical	3.479	2.541	*−3.784
comfortable_asymmetrical	4.194	2.601	
comfortable_simple	4.306	2.865	*5.055
comfortable_complex	3.368	2.094	
sensitive_rounded	4.201	2.341	1.464
sensitive_hard	3.938	2.309	
sensitive_symmetrical	4.167	2.500	1.083
sensitive_asymmetrical	3.972	2.166	
sensitive_simple	4.194	2.615	1.391
sensitive_complex	3.944	2.039	
satisfied_rounded	4.521	2.138	*7.916
satisfied_hard	3.174	2.032	
satisfied_symmetrical	3.792	2.637	−0.591
satisfied_asymmetrical	3.903	2.435	
satisfied_simple	4.278	2.715	*4.762
satisfied_complex	3.417	1.993	

Testing the difference between means of large independent samples showed no significant difference in assessing appearance attributes between symmetrical and asymmetrical contours ($z = -0.424$), rejecting H3a. Rounded and simple contours scored significantly higher than hard and complex ones ($z = 6.445, z = 4.725$).

Usage attributes favored asymmetric, rounded, and simple contours under "comfortable", with no significant difference under "sensitive".

In emotional attributes, rounded contours outperformed rigid ones, supporting H3b, but no significant difference was found between simple and complex contours, rejecting H3c. Appearance and emotional attributes showed similar trends.

6 Discussion

This study confirmed hypotheses H2 and H3b, while rejecting H1, H3a, and H3c. Findings diverged from past research, indicating no significant gaze time difference between observable and unobservable features (H1) and no distinct visual appeal between symmetrical and asymmetrical outlines (H3a).

Contrary to expectations (H3c), complex product outlines weren't more appealing, suggesting "satisfaction" involves broader emotional factors. Results differed between "comfort" and "sensitive" attributes; while all "comfort" groups showed significant differences, "sensitive" groups did not, potentially due to diverse user perceptions of sensitivity.

The research confirms local product contour features significantly impact perception (H2), underlining the need for designers to consider these features early on.

The study involved classifying product attributes per Norman's model, and collecting and analyzing user reviews of mouse product outlines. The resultant data yielded a perception space, with eye-tracking used to study gaze behavior related to product contours and impression keywords. The analysis provides a partial support to our hypotheses, helping designers incorporate features into product outlines that influence perception. This insight bridges the gap between user-designer perceptions, providing an invaluable early-stage design reference.

Acknowledgments. The authors extend their gratitude to the Zhejiang Sci-Tech University Laboratory for providing essential facilities for the eye-tracking experiments.

References

1. Liu, P.: An aesthetic measurement approach for evaluating product appearance design. Math. Probl. Eng. **2020**, 1–15 (2020)
2. Bloch, P.H.: Seeking the ideal form: product design and consumer response. J. Mark. **59**(3), 16–29 (1995)
3. Du, P.: A test of the rapid formation of design cues for product body shapes and features. J. Mech. Des. **140**(7) (2018)

4. Westerman, S.J.: Product design: preference for rounded versus angular design elements. Psychol. Market. **29**(8), 595–605 (2012)
5. Jordan, P.W.: Designing Pleasurable Products: An Introduction to the New Human Factors. CRC Press (2000)
6. Desmet, P.M.A.: Three levels of product emotion. In: Proceedings of the International Conference on Kansei Engineering and Emotion Research, pp. 236–246, Paris (2010)
7. Norman, D.A.: Emotional Design: Why We Love (or Hate) Everyday Things. Civitas Books (2004)
8. Tian, S.X.: Research on color emotion based on eye tracking technology. Mod. Commun. J. Commun. Univ. China **6**, 70–76 (2015)
9. Cheng, S.W.: A survey on visualization for eye tracking data. J. Comput.-Aided Des. Comput. Graph. **26**(5), 698–707 (2014)
10. Osgood, C.E., Suci, G.J., Tannenbaum, P.H.: The Measurement of Meaning. University of Illinois Press (1957)

Conf-UNet: A Model for Speculation on Unknown Oracle Bone Characters

Yuanxiang Xu, Yuan Feng$^{(\boxtimes)}$, Jiahao Liu, Shengyu Song, Zhongwei Xu, and Lan Zhang

Faculty of Information Science and Engineering, Ocean University of China, Qingdao, China
{xuyuanxiang,liujiahao6266,songshengyu,xzw}@stu.ouc.edu.cn, fengyuan@ouc.edu.cn

Abstract. Oracle Bone Characters (OBC) are the oldest developed pictographs in China, having been created over 3000 years ago. As a result of their antiquity and the scarcity of relevant historical sources, identifying and interpreting OBC has been an ongoing challenge for scholars of oracle bone characters. Large Seal Script evolved from OBC, and retains many of its features, making the linking of these two scripts an urgent task. The traditional method of textual study and interpretation can be time-consuming, requires a high degree of professionalism, and demands significant material and human resources. To address these issues, we propose the Conf-UNet model, a deep learning approach that incorporates a U-net combined with a multi-head self-attention mechanism. This model was used to link Large Seal Script with unidentified oracle bone characters to reduce the workload and provide linguists with a reliable method to speculate the sealed characters that correlate with unidentified OBC. The proposed model also enables linguists to use deep learning to research the evolution of pictographs. Experiments on the HWOBC-A dataset demonstrate that our model outperforms other models on this task of identifying oracle bone characters.

Keywords: Deep learning · Transformer · Semantic speculation · Image recognition · Oracle bone characters

1 Introduction

The interpretation of Oracle Bone Characters (OBCs) is essential in comprehending the Shang Dynasty. The complexity in writing and intricate typefaces of OBCs has limited their dissemination. Moreover, several oracle bone characters have been lost due to various reasons, including conflicts. More than 150,000 OBCs have been excavated from different sites in China, representing over 4,000 distinct characters. Nevertheless, approximately 2,200 of these characters have been decoded, implying that almost half of the OBCs still require interpretation.

The analysis of OBCs is hard. Researchers need to confirm the meaning of a word several times. Traditional OBCs are interpreted using the three approaches

© The Author(s), under exclusive license to Springer Nature Switzerland AG 2023
Z. Jin et al. (Eds.): KSEM 2023, LNAI 14118, pp. 89–103, 2023.
https://doi.org/10.1007/978-3-031-40286-9_9

most utilized by researchers today: glyphs, radicals, and historical documents. But, all three methods need a significant amount of manpower, and the meaning of a word may only be confirmed after a lengthy period of verification. Furthermore, due to the variety and intricacy of oracle bone characters, some oracle bone characters have many variants, making their identification harder.

Computer vision technologies such as image classification, semantic segmentation, and object identification continue to evolve, improving the state-of-the-art in a variety of tasks. An example of this progress is CoCa, which has achieved 91.0% Top1 accuracy in image classification on the ImageNet dataset [25]. Similarly, YOLO-v7-E6E is currently the top performer in object detection, achieving an average precision of 56.8 [23]. While computer technology has made significant contributions in these fields, in the realm of Oracle Bone Characters, the majority of progress has been centered around the creation and improvement of oracle bone character databases, as well as font recognition research. The transformation of oracle bone characters to large seal script can be likened to the change from one style of painting to another. In this way, we can appreciate the technological advancements of computer vision in a new context.

As a result, in response to the above issues, the contributions of this paper might be described as follows:

- The unique aspect of our study is the proposal of a model that links OBCs with large seal scripts. By connecting OBCs with large seal scripts, the proposed model aids researchers in determining the sequence of large seal scripts for unidentified oracle bone characters, reducing their workload. To speculate on unknown oracles, we utilize Conf-UNet, a model that combines U-net and the multi-head self-attention mechanism. Conf-UNet outperformed other models used in the research.
- Our proposed encoder model utilizes a Merger Block, which combines both local detail features extracted by the ResNetV2 module and global relationship features extracted by the Transformer module between multiple sections. By leveraging these features, our model enhances its capacity to extract features for improved performance.
- The speculation block is used to weight the output prediction image and the original Oracle image. From this, major seal scripts the most closely related to the oracle bone characters are inferred.

2   Related Works

2.1   Advances in the Oracle Field

Many technologies have been implemented in the field of Oracle due to the constant advancements and developments in computer technologies. Li et al. [15] initially proposed a methodology for analyzing Oracle bone characters as an undirected graph, utilizing graph theory to extract Oracle bone inscription properties. The development of the Oracle Bone Inscription library and database serves as a fundamental basis for promoting research on Oracle Bone Characters

(OBCs) in the field of computer science [12,17]. Gao et al. [4] have further refined the Oracle bone character database and established a comprehensive semantic knowledge base that integrates Chinese and Oracle script. It is evident that the focus of research during this stage is primarily on the establishment of the Oracle database and the optimization of various methods.

The researchers then utilized machine learning techniques to identify oracle bone characters. Gao et al. [3] suggested employing the Hopfield network to recognize oracle bone characters with high matching degrees that correspond to the same category. Guo et al. [7] introduced a multi-level model that incorporated convolutional neural networks to classify oracle bone characters. They utilized Gabor for low-level feature representation and sparse autoencoders for mid-level feature representation. The proposed method can recognize the Oracle Bone Inscription Sketch Text dataset with remarkable precision. Zhang et al. [26] transformed oracle bone character images into Euclidean space and computed image similarity employing the distance between varying text images. Gao et al. [5] applied the VGG16 model to detect Oracle variants. In another study, Zhang et al. [27] achieved the cross-modal recognition of oracle bone inscriptions by applying nearest neighbor classification and shared space modeling to rubbing and copying. Moreover, Tu et al. [19] employed transfer learning and the InceptionV3 model to classify oracle bone inscriptions with a 77.3% accuracy rate. They also predicted the part of speech of unrecognized characters after combining image and corpus. In addition, Liu et al. [16] optimized and improved oracle bone inscription classification accuracy using the Mask R-CNN, the three-tuple loss function, and the rotation angle regression technique. Lastly, Huang et al. [11] published the OBC306 oracle bone character rubbing database, the first accessible database with a large collection of single-character rubbings. This database serves as a link for integrating computer vision technology into oracle bone inscription research.

2.2 Advances in the Deep Learning Field

U-Net: The initial application of the U-net model was aimed at tackling the challenge of biomedical image analysis [18]. Nonetheless, owing to its remarkable segmentation capabilities, the U-net is now being widely used for an array of semantic segmentation tasks, including remote sensing image segmentation and road crack detection. As an illustration, Wang et al. [21] introduced UNetFormer, a model that can segment urban scenes in real-time utilizing a decoder that models both local and global information. Similarly, Han et al. [8] fused the DenseNet structure with the U-net model for identifying cracks on roads.

Transformer: The original Transformer model devised by [20] was initially proposed for Natural Language Processing (NLP) applications, where it has been instrumental in achieving state-of-the-art results in numerous works. Subsequently, the vision of Alex et al. [2] paved the way for introducing Transformer architecture in computer vision tasks. The proposed Vision Transformer (VIT) model segments the input image into a set of small patches, and then each patch is projected into a fixed-length vector, which is subsequently inputted to the Transformer block.

CNN Combined with Global Self-attention: Numerous studies have attempted to establish relationships between global features in a CNN using self-attention mechanisms. For example, Zhang et al. [28] proposed a Relation-Aware Global Attention (RGA) module that captures global feature relationships. In order to incorporate all spatially global contextual data for each pixel, Jin et al. [13] proposed the Global Spatial Context Attention (GSCA) module.

3   Method

This part of the paper introduces the proposed OBC speculation model. Section 3.1 discusses the model's architecture. Section 3.2 describes the encoder structure, which is based on convolution operation and transformers. The structure of the decoder is described in depth in Sect. 3.3. In Sect. 3.4, the role of the CBAM in the whole model is introduced in detail. Section 3.5 illustrates the mapping process that maps oracle bone characters to large seal scripts.

3.1   Model Architecture

The proposed model architecture is illustrated in Fig. 1. The architecture of our model is based on the encoder-decoder paradigm. The ResNetV2-Transformer Encoder is employed to encode features of various dimensions. Subsequently, the CBAM module performs spatial and channel attention on the skip-connected features. To generate trained seal images, the decoder combines multi-dimensional features. Using both the original oracle image and the trained seal image, the speculating block searches for the most similar seal in the seal database.

The ResNetV2-Transformer Encoder receives the Oracle image $\mathbb{R}^{(C \times H \times W)}$ as its input during training. Convolutional Neural Network (CNN) is employed to extract local details from an input image. The multi-head self-attention mechanism is used to establish the relationships between features of distinct parts in the high-dimensional space. The Merger Block is applied to fuse local and global features to form the input of the decoder. During decoding, the fused features are up-sampled and combined with the output of the ResnetV2 feature in a high-to-low manner based on their respective dimensions. The generated image is utilized for further analysis.

3.2   Encoder

The backbone of our encoder is composed of ResnetV2 and Transformer. As shown in Fig. 1(a), the structure is depicted. ResnetV2 improves the generalization performance over Resnet by redesigning a residual unit [10]. As the oracle

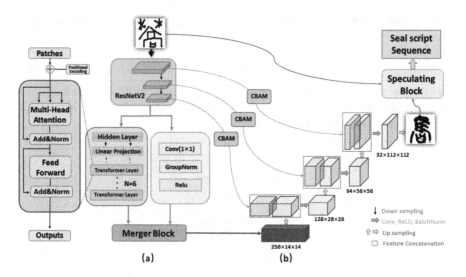

Fig. 1. The overall architecture of the model.

bone character is characterized by continuous strokes, we employ Transformer to model the interdependence among the various elements of the image. Unlike TransUNet [1], our approach combines the ResnetV2 and Transformer outputs to effectively capture the interdependence of local and global features.

In the spatial dimension, we partition and vectorize the feature information x_P. Next, a trainable linear projection layer maps x_P into a D-dimensional latent feature space. Additionally, to preserve the positional information of the patch embedding, a learnable positional embedding is added to it. This process is mathematically represented in Eq. 1.

$$z_0 = [x_P^1 E; x_P^2 E; \ldots; x_P^N E] + E_{pos} \tag{1}$$

The vectorized patch is represented as x_P^1 to x_P^N, where N is the number of patches included. $\mathbb{R}^{(P^2 \times C) \times D}$ denotes linear projection features as E, where P refers to size and C refers to the number of projected feature channels. The position feature $E_{pos} \in \mathbb{R}^{N \times D}$ is learnable.

The initial step of the feature fusion process is the transmission of patch features through multi-head self-attention blocks and multi-layer perception modules before being conveyed to the Merger Block for fusion with local features. Before embarking on the feature fusion, reshaping is carried out to transform the dimension of X_T from $\mathbb{R}^{384 \times 196}$ to $\mathbb{R}^{384 \times 14 \times 14}$, followed by down-sampling to decrease the number of channels to $\mathbb{R}^{256 \times 14 \times 14}$. The feature fusion itself happens by executing the process with $X_R = \mathbb{R}^{256 \times 14 \times 14}$, and the output follows with Convolution, Group Normalization, and Activation Function. Figure 2 illustrates the entire procedure. The Feature Fusion can be formulated with the following equation:

$$X_M = \phi[(X_T \downarrow) \oplus X_R] \qquad (2)$$

where $\oplus$ denotes the feature concatenation; $\downarrow$ represents the down-sampling operation; ϕ represents the combined operation of Convolution, Group Normalization, and Activation Function.

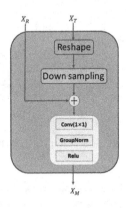

Fig. 2. Internal structure of Merger Block.

3.3 Decoder

The decoder of the model is composed of multiple up-sampling components, which output the inferred seal image by decoding the high-dimensional hidden features. Figure 1 (b) illustrates the structure of the decoder. After going through the CBAM module, the low-level features that the encoder outputs are combined layer-by-layer with the up-sampled features. This up-sampled feature map contains additional low-level semantic information, which preserves the features of the Oracle. Each up-sampling block is comprised of a bilinear interpolation layer, a convolutional layer, and a Relu layer, and its learned parameters make it superior to the pure, simple bilinear interpolation method in terms of decoding and image restoration for modeling the seal. Moreover, this method is able to minimize the occurrence of Checkerboard Artifacts.

3.4 CBAM Module

The CBAM module is a lightweight attention module that can be seamlessly integrated into any CNN architecture [22]. Notably, the module has a small computational cost while also improving the overall performance of the model. As the model outputs features of varying dimensions through downsampling, the CBAM module applies attention to the spatial and channel-wise features connected by skip connections. Through this process of attention, the model's expressive power is improved as it emphasizes or suppresses the content and position of the features.

3.5   Speculation Stage

At this stage, we proceed with identifying the seal scripts that correspond to the unidentified oracle bone inscriptions via the use of Mean Absolute Error (MAE) technique as the loss function during the training process. The MAE loss function was determined to be more robust and less sensitive to outliers than other prevalent loss functions [6]. To begin the process of speculation, we calculated $Loss_O^{i,j}$ of image i and seal j in an oracle bone character category. Next, the encoder generated a predicted image, and $Loss_P^{i,j}$ was calculated between the speculated image and seal j. Equation 3 expresses the total Loss of seal j and N oracle bone character images within a category. $Loss_O$ was finally added to $Loss_P$ and sorted. The first 100 minimum loss values were then selected following Eq. 4. Table 1 depicts the speculative process in detail, and Fig. 3 shows the flowchart.

Table 1. The table describes the procedure for speculating large seal scripts from oracle bone characters.

Find the seal that most resemble the oracle

Input: oracle sequence $\{O_i\}_{i=1}^N$, speculated seal sequence $\{P_i\}_{i=1}^N$, seal sequence $\{S_j\}_{j=1}^M$.
Step 1: For each j $(1 \le j \le M)$
  For each i $(1 \le i \le N)$
    Calculate $Loss_j$ using Eq. 3
Step 2: $Sort\{Loss_j\}_{j=1}^M$ was done from small to large, taking the first 100 smallest values, and finding the corresponding seal scripts in the seal dataset.
This is shown in Eq. 4.
Output: The result of the speculation process is a list Y of speculated seal scripts consisting of 100 identified scripts.

$$Loss_j = \sum_{i=1}^{N} \left(Loss_O^{i,j} + Loss_P^{i,j} \right) \tag{3}$$

$$Y = Sort_{min}^{100} \{Loss_1, Loss_2 \cdots Loss_M\} \tag{4}$$

Sort means selecting the top 100 minima from the list. N is the number of images representing an Oracle character, and M is the total number of images representing seal scripts.

Through the above process, we will get 100 seal scripts most related to oracle bone characters.

Sort involves selecting the top 100 minima from a list. The variable N represents the number of images that correspond to an Oracle character, and the variable M represents the total number of images that correspond to seal scripts. The above process will yield the 100 seal scripts that are most related to oracle bone characters.

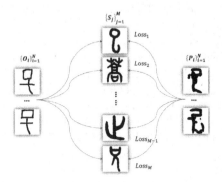

Fig. 3. The representation of calculating Loss for N images of an oracle bone character and M big seal images.

Fig. 4. (a) enumerates the seal scripts, (b) documents the corresponding Oracle characters, and (c) presents a catalog of the various characters corresponding to the Oracle characters.

4   Experiments

This section discusses the dataset, its pre-processing, the experimental settings, the contrasting methods, the experimental results, and the analysis.

4.1   Dataset and Preprocessing

Oracle bone script in this study is based on the HWOBC-A handwritten oracle bone character recognition database [14], while the seal character library used is the *Regular Version 1.00 November 1, 2007, initial release*. As shown in Fig. 4, the HWOBC-A dataset is intended for offline recognition training of handwritten oracle bone characters. The characters in the seal character library were transformed into 400×400 PNG images comprising the seal database. One hundred large seal scripts were randomly selected along with their corresponding oracle bone characters to form the test set, and the remaining large seal scripts and matching oracle bone characters were used as our training set.

The distribution of images across character categories in the HWOBC-A dataset is uneven. To address this data imbalance, we standardized the number of images across each Oracle category to 20. Note that the position and scale of glyphs in each image vary significantly. To ensure pixel-level correspondence, we employ a cropping and scaling mechanism that preserves the glyph aspect ratio (see Fig. 5). The font size in each modified image remains largely uniform.

Fig. 5. (a) displays the raw input image, (b) shows the output of preprocessing steps applied to the input.

4.2 Experimental Settings

PyTorch was employed for the model construction and experiments in this study. The GeForce RTX2080 Super served as the platform for training and evaluation. The input images were resized to 224 × 224, and the models were trained for 300 epochs with the Adam optimizer. The learning rate was initially set to 0.0001, increased to a maximum of 0.01, and reset after every 100 epochs. The batch size used was 40.

4.3 Contrasting Methods

In this part, we compare our proposed method with three other state-of-the-art models: Resnet, Res-Unet, and TransUNet.

1. Resnet [9]: Resnet is an end-to-end residual neural network that learns key features for categorization. The residual structure of Resnet enables deeper model layers without compromising performance. It has a significant impact on image classification. We employed an up-sampling block with a residual block as a decoder
2. Res-Unet [24]: Res-Unet extends U-net by including a residual module and an attention mechanism. Additionally, it deepens the network and uses feature fusion through concatenation. Despite its simplicity, Res-Unet shows considerable effectiveness.
3. TransUNet: TransUNet leverages the advantages of both Transformer and U-net by encoding image features as sequences, thereby enhancing contextual information. It not only achieves pixel-level localization but also connects the features of different image regions.

4.4 Evaluation

In this study, we extracted a list of potential seal scripts from each oracle bone character. Subsequently, we analyzed and determined whether the correct seal script was present in the respective lists and at what position. For each oracle bone character, we recorded the accuracy of Top10, Top20, Top50, and Top100 results.

4.5　Results and Analysis

Table 2 presents the TopN accuracy results. Figure 6 compares the different models. Based on U-net and multi-head self-attention mechanism, our proposed method outperforms the other three models.

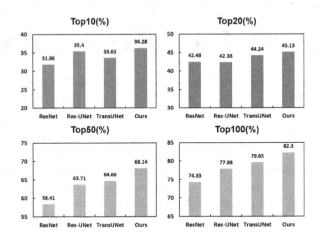

Fig. 6. The representation of calculating Loss for N images of an oracle bone character and M big seal images.

Res-UNet utilizes skip connections, in contrast to ResNet, which does not transfer low-level semantic information to deeper layers, as it solely focuses on learning high-dimensional feature relationships. Therefore, Res-Net achieves relatively superior TopN accuracy. On the other hand, the TransUNet decoder exploits the multi-head self-attention mechanism that logically exhibits the relationships between the high-level feature outputs and the convolutional layers. Our model integrates the advantages of TransUNet and introduces an exclusive Merger Block that merges both local and global high-dimensional features, resulting in detailed and global information extraction. Moreover, we apply the Convolutional Block Attention Module (CBAM) within the skip connection to facilitate the application of channel and spatial attention when propagating feature information into deeper layers. The feature fusion diagram, illustrated in Fig. 7, reveals that the Merger Block flawlessly fuses the features produced by the Transformer layer and ResNetV2, thereby amplifying the model's representation capability of the features. In addition, our Conf-UNet model outperforms the aforementioned models in terms of TopN accuracy.

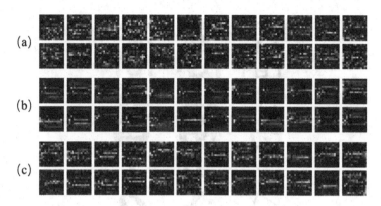

Fig. 7. (a) is the feature map output by Transformer Block, (b) denotes the feature map output by ResNetV2, and (c) shows the feature map after fusion.

Our proposed model achieved an accuracy of 68.14% in the Top50 results, outperforming the other three models, all of which scored above 50%. This suggests that our model could be a useful tool in the field of oracle, enabling workers to narrow down the scope when deciphering oracle bone characters. The suggested model's accuracy rate in the Top100 results was a substantial 82.30%, which was 2.65% higher than the second-ranked TransUNet.

Table 2 reveals only slight variances in the top-performing models' performance at the Top10 and Top20. Regrettably, all models exhibit suboptimal accuracy due to several factors:

1. Oracle comprises numerous variant characters, all with distinctive glyphs, that have a mutual substitution relationship but lack common evolution.
2. There may be a difference in the image style of fonts between the seal and the Oracle datasets. The thick large seal scripts and thin oracle bone characters in Fig. 4 illustrate this problem.
3. Notably, significant differences exist between oracle bone characters and large seal scripts, with simplification taking place during evolution, and some radicals typically removed, resulting in a profound disparity between the two.

As seen in Fig. 8, a comparison between the actual seal and the one generated by Conf-UNet reveals that the model's glyph outline closely resembles the true outline. However, the character's internal structure appears to be somewhat imprecise. While the speculation module in oracle bone characters can successfully predict the corresponding seal characters, for more complex characters without evolutionary connections, Conf-UNet's ability to generalize may be limited.

In order to demonstrate the effectiveness of the suggested module, we conducted ablation experiments. Table 3 presents the quantitative results. The findings in the table demonstrate that our proposed modules have a positive impact on the TopN accuracy. Therefore, our suggested module is capable of efficiently extracting and concatenating Oracle features.

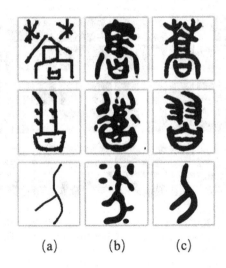

(a)   (b)   (c)

Fig. 8. (a) enumerates the seal scripts, (b) documents the corresponding Oracle characters, and (c) presents a catalog of the various characters corresponding to the Oracle characters.

Table 2. TopN results of each model on the HWOBC dataset.

Model	Top10	Top20	Top50	Top100
ResNet	31.86	42.48	58.41	74.33
Res-UNet	35.40	43.36	63.71	77.88
TransUNet	33.63	44.24	64.60	79.65
Ours	**36.68**	**45.13**	**68.14**	**82.30**

Table 3. Ablation experiments on the HWOBC-A dataset.

Transformer Block	Merger Block	CBAM	Top10	Top20	Top50	Top100
✗	✗	✗	32.74	41.60	61.95	75.22
✓	✗	✗	33.63	44.24	64.60	79.65
✓	✓	✗	34.51	43.36	66.37	81.41
✓	✓	✓	35.68	45.13	68.14	82.30

5   Conclusion

1. In this paper, we present a novel model that facilitates linguists in predicting the corresponding large seal scripts of unidentified oracle bone characters. Our proposed model combines the multi-head self-attention mechanism with U-net and employs ResNetV2 and Transformer as the backbone of the encoder. Furthermore, we incorporate a Merger Block for feature fusion and integrate a skip-connection module with CBAM to propagate shallow semantic infor-

mation into deep layers. The up-sampling module of our model is followed by a speculation module that outputs the speculated seal list. Our experimental results demonstrate that our proposed model outperforms all other methods. Specifically, Conf-UNet achieves an average improvement of 2.43% over the second-ranking TransUNet in the TopN results. Moreover, it attains an impressive accuracy of 82.30% in the Top100 results, which enables linguists to narrow down the scope of an unknown oracle bone character to 100 characters. As a consequence, it reduces their workload in deciphering the characters.

2. The present study proposes a methodology that employs deep learning techniques for analyzing the evolution of pictographs. Specifically, we investigate the evolutionary patterns between oracles and seals as a case study. Using this approach, we assign weights to the original OBC images and the model-generated output images to deduce the correct seal sequence. The significance of this approach extends beyond this specific case as it can be potentially applied to similar studies exploring the evolution of pictographs.

The Top10 accuracy of the four models is suboptimal. The suboptimal performance can be attributed to the incomplete dataset and the models' inadequacy in extracting glyph features. A suitable performance metric for quantitatively analyzing the results is yet to be identified, given that this is pioneering work.

Our future research will focus on investigating the evolution process from oracle bone script to seal script and improving the algorithm's performance. Additionally, we aim to identify a suitable performance metric that will quantitatively evaluate the models' performance. We also plan to improve the Oracle bone script database as another objective. Besides, we intend to augment the model's generalization capability to enable its application in the evolution process of other pictographic scripts.

References

1. Chen, J., et al.: TransUNet: transformers make strong encoders for medical image segmentation (2021)
2. Dosovitskiy, A., et al.: An image is worth 16×16 words: transformers for image recognition at scale. In: 9th International Conference on Learning Representations, ICLR 2021, Virtual Event, Austria, 3–7 May 2021. OpenReview.net (2021). https://openreview.net/forum?id=YicbFdNTTy
3. Gao, F., Qinxia, W., Liu, Y., Xiong, J.: Recognition of fuzzy character based on component for bones or tortoise shells. Sci. Technol. Eng. (67–70+86) (2014)
4. Gao, F., Xiong, J., Liu, Y.: Research on the extenics of Oracle bone inscriptions interpretation based on how net. Data Anal. Knowl. Discov. **Z1**, 58–64 (2015)
5. Gao, J., Liang, X.: Distinguishing Oracle variants based on the isomorphism and symmetry invariances of Oracle-bone inscriptions. IEEE Access **8**, 152258–152275 (2020). https://doi.org/10.1109/ACCESS.2020.3017533
6. Ghosh, A., Kumar, H., Sastry, P.S.: Robust loss functions under label noise for deep neural networks. In: Proceedings of the AAAI Conference on Artificial Intelligence, vol. 31 (2017)

7. Guo, J., Wang, C., Roman-Rangel, E., Chao, H., Rui, Y.: Building hierarchical representations for Oracle character and sketch recognition. IEEE Trans. Image Process. **25**(1), 104–118 (2016). https://doi.org/10.1109/TIP.2015.2500019

8. Han, C., Ma, T., Huyan, J., Huang, X., Zhang, Y.: CrackW-Net: a novel pavement crack image segmentation convolutional neural network. IEEE Trans. Intell. Transp. Syst. **23**(11), 22135–22144 (2022). https://doi.org/10.1109/TITS.2021.3095507

9. He, K., Zhang, X., Ren, S., Sun, J.: Deep residual learning for image recognition. In: 2016 IEEE Conference on Computer Vision and Pattern Recognition, CVPR 2016, Las Vegas, NV, USA, 27–30 June 2016, pp. 770–778. IEEE Computer Society (2016). https://doi.org/10.1109/CVPR.2016.90

10. He, K., Zhang, X., Ren, S., Sun, J.: Identity mappings in deep residual networks. In: Leibe, B., Matas, J., Sebe, N., Welling, M. (eds.) Computer Vision - ECCV 2016–14th European Conference, Amsterdam, The Netherlands, 11–14 October 2016, Proceedings, Part IV. LNCS, vol. 9908, pp. 630–645. Springer, Cham (2016). https://doi.org/10.1007/978-3-319-46493-0_38

11. Huang, S., Wang, H., Liu, Y., Shi, X., Jin, L.: OBC306: a large-scale Oracle Bone character recognition dataset. In: 2019 International Conference on Document Analysis and Recognition (ICDAR), pp. 681–688 (2019)

12. Jiang, M., Deng, B., Liao, P., Zhang, B., Yan, J., Ding, Y.: Construction on wordbase of Oracle-Bone inscriptions and its intelligent repository. Comput. Eng. Appl. (04), 45–47+60 (2004)

13. Jin, Y., Xu, W., Hu, Z., Jia, H., Luo, X., Shao, D.: GSCA-UNet: towards automatic shadow detection in urban aerial imagery with global-spatial-context attention module. Remote Sens. **12**(17) (2020)

14. Li, B., Dai, Q., Gao, F., Zhu, W., Li, Q., Liu, Y.: HWOBC-a handwriting oracle bone character recognition database. J. Phys. Conf. Ser. **1651**(1), 012050 (2020). https://doi.org/10.1088/1742-6596/1651/1/012050

15. Li, F., Zhou, X.: Graph theory method for automatic oracle recognition. J. Electron. Inf. Technol. **S1**, 41–47 (1996)

16. Liu, F., Li, S., Ma, J., Yan, S., Jin, P.: Automatic detection and recognition of Oracle rubbings based on mask R-CNN. Data Anal. Knowl. Discov. **5**(12), 88–97 (2021). https://kns.cnki.net/kcms/detail/10.1478.G2.20210906.1332.002.html

17. Liu, Y., Li, Q.: Design and implementation of visual input method of oracular inscriptions on tortoise shells and bones. Comput. Eng. Appl. **17**, 139–140 (2004)

18. Ronneberger, O., Fischer, P., Brox, T.: U-Net: convolutional networks for biomedical image segmentation. In: 18th International Conference on Medical Image Computing and Computer-Assisted Intervention, MICCAI 2015, 5–9 October 2015. LNCS (Including Subseries Lecture Notes in Artificial Intelligence and Lecture Notes in Bioinformatics), vol. 9351, pp. 234–241. Springer, Cham (2015). https://doi.org/10.1007/978-3-319-24574-4_28

19. Tu, C., Wang, G., Tian, J., Li, H., Li, T.: Research on Oracle Bone inscriptions classification algorithm based on deep learning. Mod. Comput. **27**(26), 67–72 (2021)

20. Vaswani, A., et al: Attention is all you need. In: Guyon, I., et al. (eds.) Advances in Neural Information Processing Systems: Annual Conference on Neural Information Processing Systems 2017, 4–9 December 2017, Long Beach, CA, USA, vol. 30, pp. 5998–6008 (2017). https://proceedings.neurips.cc/paper/2017/hash/3f5ee243547dee91fbd053c1c4a845aa-Abstract.html

21. Wang, L., et al.: UNetFormer: a UNet-like transformer for efficient semantic segmentation of remote sensing urban scene imagery. ISPRS J. Photogramm. Remote Sens. **190**, 196–214 (2022). https://doi.org/10.1016/j.isprsjprs.2022.06.008

22. Woo, S., Park, J., Lee, J.-Y., Kweon, I.S.: CBAM: convolutional block attention module. In: Ferrari, V., Hebert, M., Sminchisescu, C., Weiss, Y. (eds.) ECCV 2018. LNCS, vol. 11211, pp. 3–19. Springer, Cham (2018). https://doi.org/10.1007/978-3-030-01234-2_1

23. Wortsman, M., et al.: Model soups: averaging weights of multiple fine-tuned models improves accuracy without increasing inference time (2022). https://doi.org/10.48550/arXiv.2203.05482

24. Xiao, X., Lian, S., Luo, Z., Li, S.: Weighted Res-UNet for high-quality retina vessel segmentation. In: 2018 9th International Conference on Information Technology in Medicine and Education (ITME) (2018)

25. Yu, J., Wang, Z., Vasudevan, V., Yeung, L., Seyedhosseini, M., Wu, Y.: CoCa: contrastive captioners are image-text foundation models. CoRR abs/2205.01917 (2022). https://doi.org/10.48550/arXiv.2205.01917

26. Zhang, Y.K., Zhang, H., Liu, Y.G., Yang, Q., Liu, C.L.: Oracle character recognition by nearest neighbor classification with deep metric learning. In: 15th IAPR International Conference on Document Analysis and Recognition, ICDAR 2019, 20–25 September 2019, pp. 309–314. Proceedings of the International Conference on Document Analysis and Recognition, ICDAR. IEEE Computer Society (2019). https://doi.org/10.1109/ICDAR.2019.00057

27. Zhang, Y., Zhang, H., Liu, Y., Liu, C.: Oracle character recognition based on cross-modal deep metric learning. Acta Automatica Sinica **47**(4), 791–800 (2021). https://dx.doi.org/10.16383/j.aas.c200443

28. Zhang, Z., Lan, C., Zeng, W., Jin, X., Chen, Z.: Relation-aware global attention for person re-identification. In: 2020 IEEE/CVF Conference on Computer Vision and Pattern Recognition, CVPR 2020, Proceedings of the IEEE Computer Society Conference on Computer Vision and Pattern Recognition, 14–19 June 2020, pp. 3183–3192. IEEE Computer Society (2020). https://doi.org/10.1109/CVPR42600.2020.00325

An Efficient One-Shot Network and Robust Data Associations in Multi-pedestrian Tracking

Fuxiao He and Guoqiang Xiao(✉)

College of Computer and Information Science, Southwest University, Chongqin, China
kylekyle@email.swu.edu.cn, gqxiao@swu.edu.cn

Abstract. Recently, one-shot trackers, which integrate multi-tasks into a unified network, achieve good performances in multi-object video tracking and successfully handle the core challenge of multi-object tracking, that is, how to realize the trade-off between the high accuracy and real-time performance. In this paper, we abandon the traditional approach of redundant backbones and feature fusion networks commonly used by one-shot trackers, and propose a new one-shot model that is faster and lighter. We propose a new channel-spatial attention module to improve the detection and re-identification performance of the one-shot model for more robust tracking. Furthermore, in order to deal with complex video tracking scenarios more robust, we have made innovations in data association and proposed a new robust association method, which combines the advantages of the motion, appearance and the detection information to associate. On the MOT20 testing set, our proposed one-shot model with robust associations termed as BFMOT reduces the number of ID switches by 52.1% and improves the tracking accuracy (i.e. MOTA) by 6.7% compared with the state-of-the-art tracker. BFMOT runs close to 30 FPS on MOT16,17 testing sets, which is more oriented to real-time tracking.

Keywords: Multi-object tracking · One-shot · Detection · Re-identification · Data association

1 Introduction

1.1 The Proposed Light-Weight and Efficient One-Shot Network

The one-shot method usually refers to joint learning of multiple tasks in multi-object tracking (i.e. MOT) tasks. Compared to the previous tracking mode under the TBD (Tracking by Detection) paradigm, which involves separately and independently completing detection task and re-ID task, our proposed one-shot model can unify detection task and re-ID task into a single network for simultaneous processing, greatly improving the tracking speed.

We find that previous one-shot trackers habitually use DLA-34 [1] as the default backbone, e.g., CenterTrack, FairMOT, TraDeS, GSDT and LMOT [2–6]. It seems that DLA-34 is the best choice for joint detection and re-ID framework,

© The Author(s), under exclusive license to Springer Nature Switzerland AG 2023
Z. Jin et al. (Eds.): KSEM 2023, LNAI 14118, pp. 104–120, 2023.
https://doi.org/10.1007/978-3-031-40286-9_10

but its shortcomings are also obvious. DLA-34, which adds multi-layer feature fusion over ResNet-34, replaces each convolutional layer with the deformable convolution. Such a structure can fully integrate the features of all layers, but a large amount of computation is also a major disadvantage. LMOT [6] seems to solve this problem, so it uses the simplified DLA-34 as the backbone, but this destroys the original structure of the DLA-34, resulting in a significant decline in the final detection and tracking results. Therefore, the improvement of backbone needs to be treated with caution. More importantly, each upsampling operation of DLA-34 will be performed with a corresponding multi-layer feature fusion, which also brings the problem of the large number of repetitive feature fusion operations, but more efficient and concise feature fusion methods should be more pursued in real-time tracking. Based on the above problems, we design a more efficient feature fusion module, and propose a new, faster and more accurate one-shot model for MOT.

1.2 The Proposed Channel-Spatial Attention Module

Currently, MOT tasks largely rely on the quality of the detection. Improving the performance of the detector is also one of the main approaches to improve the accuracy of multi-object tracking. Previous works (e.g., SE [10] and CBAM [11]) show that channel attentions focus on the objects in the image, while spatial attentions focus on the locations of the objects in the image. The combination of the two can reduce the interference of the background to the objects. We design a new channel-spatial attention module to improve the one-shot model's object localization capabilities.

On the base of CBAM attention, we make improvements and propose a lightweight CS attention module suitable for tracking tasks. It is noted that the CS attention module has a plug and play characteristic, and its scope of use is not limited to detection and tracking tasks.

1.3 The Proposed Robust Data Associations

Data association is the core of multi-object tracking, in each frame, which first computes the similarity between existing tracklets and detection boxes of the current frame to match them and then assigns identities of the tracklets to the matched detected objects. The process of the tracklet generation is shown in Fig. 1. Location, motion, and appearance are major similarities of associations.

Our association process integrates the advantages of MOTDT's [8] two-stage association strategy and ByteTrack's [9] detection boxes classification matching strategy. Specifically, We first use the extracted re-ID features from the high confidence detected objects to calculate the appearance similarity (by re-ID metric) with historical re-ID objects features kept by existing tracklets in the first association stage, and use Kalman Filtering [12] to predict tracklets' locations and tracking boxes in the following frames and then calculate the motion similarity (by IoU metric) with low confidence detection boxes in the second association stage. However, we find that previous works [8,9] only use a single similarity for

Fig. 1. The process of the association and the tracklet generation. (a) shows the detection boxes with their confidence scores. (b) shows the tracklets obtained by previous methods which associate detection boxes by single similarity. The solid boxes of different colors represent object instances with different IDs. The dashed box represents the predicted tracking box of the tracklet in a new frame predicted by Kalman Filtering.

each matching, which is limited to deal with the complex video scenes. We will elaborate on the limitations of single similarity for matching in *method* section.

We propose a more robust association method to further improve the ability of our one-shot model to handle complex video scenes by combining the advantages of the motion, appearance and the detection information to associate. We believe that even if the predicted tracklet and the real tracklet can be 100% coincident, but the ID of the predicted tracklet changes frequently in the tracking process, which is also a failure of tracking, and the root cause of ID switch (IDsw) is that tracklets and detections are mismatched. Furthermore, our algorithm is committed to reducing the number of such mismatches for more robust tracking.

2   Related Work

2.1   One-Shot Trackers

RetinaTrack [13], JDE [14], and FairMOT [3] all append re-ID branch to detectors. The difference is that the formers use anchor-based detectors, while FairMOT [3] selects anchor-free detectors to mitigate the incompatibility between anchor-based detection and re-ID tasks. DLA-34 is selected as the backbone and feature fusion network to solve the feature conflict between the two tasks. In particular, CSTrack [15] separately extracts features more suitable for detection and re-ID tasks by adding attention module on the basis of JDE [14] to alleviate the feature conflict of the two tasks, but the speed is significantly reduced compared with FairMOT [3]. The above are all one-shot baseline models. More extension work is based on them. OMC [16] adds a re-check network on the basis of CSTrack [15] to try to handle the occlusion of the objects, but the speed is further reduced. CorrTracker [17] enhances the current features by spatiotemporal relational modeling that exploits previous frames on the basis of FairMOT [3], but the speed is also significantly reduced.

2.2 Online Data Association

SORT [18] realizes associations by using location and motion similarities, that is, first using Kalman Filter [12] to predict the location of the tracklets in the new frame, and then calculating IoU between the detection boxes and the predicted tracking boxes as the similarity. For short-term tracking tasks, the location and motion similarities are reliable. In order to handle long-term tracking, Deep-SORT [7] uses an independent re-ID model to extract appearance features from the detection boxes as the primary similarity metric, which has achieved better results, due to the appearance information that can recover the identities of long-term occluded objects. MOTDT [8] uses a hierarchical association strategy, which first uses appearance similarity to match, and then use motion similarity to match the unmatched tracklets. ByteTrack [9], on the other hand, proposes a two-stage association strategy of the detections classification matching, which achieves the best matching results. However, We find that the previous association similarity (i.e. location, motion and appearance) is used singly, but in fact, each similarity has its own adaptive scenes. We hope to integrate multiple cues as a new similarity to handle more complex scenes.

3   Method

In this section, we will elaborate on three parts. The first part is the network structure of the proposed one-shot model for MOT, as shown in Fig. 2. We will respectively introduce the backbone, neck, detection branch and re-ID branch of the one-shot network. Furthermore, We will introduce the network structure of the proposed CS attention module. Finally, we will introduce limitations of the single similarity association method and extend the process of our proposed fusion similarity association algorithm in detail.

3.1   The One-Shot Model for MOT

Backbone and Neck Network. Common one-shot trackers often use the DLA-34 as the backbone of the joint detection and re-ID framework, such as Center-Track, FairMOT, TraDeS, GSDT and LMOT [2–6]. We believe that DLA-34 is indeed suitable for both detection and re-ID tasks, but its computation cost is so high, which is the most time-consuming part for the entire network. In order

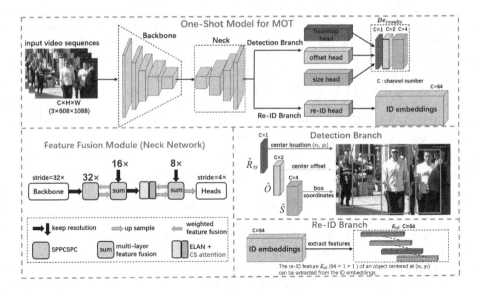

Fig. 2. Overview of the proposed efficient one-shot model. The heads generate detection results and ID embeddings. It is noted that we extract the re-ID feature E_{id} only at the object center (x_c, y_c) to represent the object appearance feature. Detection results and extracting re-ID features are used for data association.

to develop the real-time advantage of the one-shot tracker, it is necessary to simplify the backbone. We choose to use the backbones of the more lightweight YOLO series detectors. Here, we use YOLOv7's [19] backbone as the default backbone of our one-shot efficient network.

As shown in Fig. 2, we first build the neck network based on the Feature Pyramid Network (FPN) [20]. In order to solve the image distortion caused by downsamplings, we add SPPCSPC module [19] at the input of neck network to increase receptive field and help to adapt to images with different resolutions. Furthermore, in the FPN network, we add the weighted feature fusion (BiFPN) [21] each time when we perform the multi-layer feature fusion. In this way, features can be fused in both two directions, and features of different layers can be further integrated.

We resize the original video sequence to 608 * 1088 (H × W) as the input of backbone and the neck network outputs the feature map with the shape of H/4 × W/4 (stride = 4).

Detection Branch. We use the detection heads of the anchor-free detector CenterNet [1] as the detection branch. After the neck network, we append three parallel heads to estimate the heatmap, the object center offset, and the bounding box coordinates. For each head including re-ID head, the feature maps from the neck network then separately pass through heads which are constructed of a 3 × 3 convolution, SiLu( ), and another 1 × 1 convolution.

Heatmap Head. We use the heatmap head to predict the center point location of the object in the input frame. $\hat{R}_{xy}$ is the predicted heatmap response at a location (x, y) in the heatmap. When $\hat{R}_{xy} = 1$, it corresponds to a detected object center keypoint. The heatmap head is to output the predicted heatmap response $\hat{R}_{xy} \in [0,1]^{1 \times \frac{H}{4} \times \frac{W}{4}}$.

We train this head using a pixel-wise logistic regression loss function, L_H, with focal loss [24], as illustrated in Eq. (1), where R_{xy} is the real heatmap response of the ground-truth corresponding object center point at location (x, y) in the heatmap. Further more, α, β are focal loss hyper-parameters. We set $\alpha = 2$ and $\beta = 4$ following CenterNet [1], and the N is the number of detected objects in the image.

$$
L_H = -\frac{1}{N} \sum_{xy} \begin{cases} \left(1 - \hat{R}_{xy}\right)^{\alpha} \log\left(\hat{R}_{xy}\right), & R_{xy} = 1; \\ \left(1 - R_{xy}\right)^{\beta} \left(\hat{R}_{xy}\right)^{\alpha} \log\left(1 - \hat{R}_{xy}\right) & \text{otherwise,} \end{cases} \tag{1}
$$

Box Offset and Size Heads. To recover the discretization error caused by the output stride, we predict a local offset $\hat{O} \in R^{2 \times \frac{H}{4} \times \frac{W}{4}}$ relative to the object center for each pixel and the $\hat{O}_i$ is the estimated offset at the object center point. Different from the regression method of CenterNet [1], we do not directly regress the weight (W) and height (H) of the bounding box, but predict the two coordinates $\hat{S} \in R^{4 \times \frac{H}{4} \times \frac{W}{4}}$ of the upper left and lower right corners of the box, and then calculate the box size as $\hat{S}_i = (\hat{W}_i, \hat{H}_i)$ from the predicted coordinates at the object center location.

Denote that the O_i and S_i are computed with given ground-truth boxes. Then we enforce L1 loss for the two heads in Eq. (2), where the λ_O and λ_S are weighting parameters set as 1 and 0.1.

$$
L_B = \sum_{n=1}^{N} \frac{\lambda_O |\hat{O}_i - O_i| + \lambda_S |\hat{S}_i - S_i|}{N} \tag{2}
$$

Re-ID Branch. We can obtain the output ID embeddings $\in R^{64 \times \frac{H}{4} \times \frac{W}{4}}$ from the re-ID head and the re-ID feature E_{id} of a predicted object center location can be extracted from ID embeddings. We learn re-ID features through a classification task. We treat each object ID as a class. All object instances with the same ID are of the same class. For vector E_{id}, it performs a fully connected layer and a softmax operation mapped into a class distribution vector $V = \{p(i), i \in [1, max]\}$, where the max is the maximum identity number contained in a batch of training data, and we set it to 500. Denote the one-hot representation of the GT class label as L(i). We compute the re-ID loss with cross entropy loss as

$$
L_R = -\sum_{n=1}^{N} \sum_{i=1}^{max} L(i) \log(p(i)) \tag{3}
$$

The Loss for the One-Shot Model. The loss of the one-shot model for MOT is the weighted sum of the detection branch loss and the re-ID branch loss. To

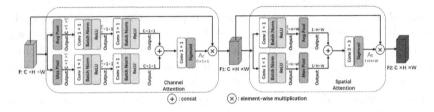

Fig. 3. Overview of the proposed CS attention module, including the channel and spatial attention module. We set the channel dimension compression ratio r to 16.

balance each task, we assign weighting parameters λ regulated to the loss of each branch. The proposed one-shot model's loss is computed as

$$L_{\text{Model}} = \lambda_H \cdot L_{\text{H}} + \lambda_B \cdot L_B + \lambda_R \cdot L_R \tag{4}$$

3.2   The CS Attention Module

On the base of CBAM [11] attention, we make improvements and propose a lightweight CS attention module suitable for tracking tasks, as shown in Fig. 3. We have mainly made three improvements. One is to *concat* the channel attention's pooling results to double the original dimension, and then performs a 1×1 convolution to get the final channel attention map $A_c \in R^{C \times 1 \times 1}$. Compared with the simple *add* operation of CBAM, the output information of the original pooling results can be better retained. The second improvement is that each branch of our spatial attention first performs a 1×1 convolution. The purpose of 1×1 convolution is to reduce the dimension of the feature map by half while keeping the width and height of the feature map unchanged. The feature map with half dimension has less parameters, and then compute the maximum pooling and average pooling respectively. While CBAM uses the method of directly compressing the feature maps to obtain the results of maximum pooling and average pooling, it will lead to the loss of some texture information in the feature maps. Finally, in spatial attention, we use small convolutional kernels (3×3) to reduce the computation caused by large kernels and obtain the final spatial attention map $A_s \in R^{1 \times H \times W}$. In addition, we add a *batch normalization* operation before each activation function and experiments show that during the training process it is conducive to the convergence of detection and re-ID tasks.

In order not to affect the loading of pretrained weights for YOLOV7's backbone, we place the CS attention module in the neck network, as shown in Fig. 2. Specifically, we place the CS attention after the convolutional model ELAN [19], which is closer to the detection branch. CS attention refines the feature map after multi-layer feature fusions. Specifically, proposed channel attention is used to enhance object features of interest in the original feature map and suppress background features. Proposed spatial attention enhances the attention to the spatial location information. The combination of the two can improve the object localization ability, which is important for both detection and re-ID tasks of our one-shot model. For the specific input feature map $F \in R^{C \times H \times W}$, the process of obtained final refined feature map $F_2 \in R^{C \times H \times W}$ through our proposed CS attention module is summarized in Eq. (5) and Eq. (6).

$$F_1 = A_c(F) \otimes F \tag{5}$$

$$F_2 = A_s(F_1) \otimes F_1 \tag{6}$$

3.3 Limitations of Single Similarity Association

Previous association algorithms [7–9] seem to ignore some specific scenarios, which are more prone to mismatches between tracklets and detections. We enumerate several scenarios to illustrate limitations of using the single similarity for associating and extend our fusion similarity association strategy.

In the scene of large flow of people, several small objects with similar appearances will appear, or especially we track objects that are in the process of occlusion, which may cause appearance changes. As shown in Fig. 1 (b) and Frame t3, it is possible that the extracted appearance features undergo the change, resulting in an identity switch for the object with ID = 4. All of the above will make the results of the first association stage unreliable by single appearance similarity (re-ID metric).

We reserve all the low confidence detection boxes due to the possibility of occluded objects and use them to associate with the tracklets which are not matched in the first association stage following ByteTrack [9]. However, the reserved low confidence detections also include the false background detections. In particular, when the object occlusion occurs, it is very possible to cause false detections (FP) with very low confidence scores [9]. In the second association stage, when the IoU distances between the tracking box predicted by Kalman Filter and several current low confidence detection boxes are all close, the tracklet's predicted tracking box may be incorrectly matched with the false background detection, as shown in Fig. 1 (b) and Frame t2. In this way, results of the second association stage will become unreliable by single motion similarity (IoU metric).

Due to limitations of single appearance similarity, our fusion strategy is to use the appearance similarity (by calculating cosine distance between currently extracted re-ID features from detection objects and historical objects features kept by the tracklets) to combine the motion similarity (by calculating GIoU distance between the detection boxes and the predicted tracking boxes of tracklets by Kalman Filter) as the fusion similarity metric of the first association stage, which can eliminate the mismatches that candidate tracklets are farther from the detections but have close cosine distances. Due to limitations of single motion similarity, our fusion strategy is to use the IoU metric to combine the detection confidence score as the fusion similarity metric of the second association stage. We tend to match the detection with higher confidence, which can reduce the probability of mismatches with background detections.

3.4   Fusion Similarity Association

We first classify detection boxes based on the detection confidence, which are divided into high and low confidence detection boxes following ByteTrack [9]. It is noted that in the first frame, we will initialize a number of tracklets based on the detected boxes. Then in the subsequent frames, we associate the detected boxes to the existing tracklets using a two-stage association strategy following MOTDT [8]. We set the high confidence threshold τ_{high} as 0.4. The high confidence detection boxes are used in the first association stage, while the reserved low confidence detection boxes are used in the second association stage.

In the first association stage, we combine motion and appearance information as the fusion similarity metric *similarity1*. We use Kalman Filtering to predict the locations and boxes of tracklets in the new frame based on previous tracks, and calculate GIoU distance D_g with the high confidence detection boxes of the new frame. In addition, we still calculate the cosine distance D_c between the re-ID features extracted from the high confidence detection objects and the historical re-ID objects features kept by tracklets. Therefore, the fusion distance of *similarity1* for the first association stage is

$$D_{S1} = aD_g + bD_c \tag{7}$$

where we take weighting parameters a and b as 0.35 and 0.65 respectively, and we adopt Hungarian algorithm [25] with a matching threshold $\tau_1 = 0.45$ to assign tracklets' identities to the matched detected objects based on the D_{S1}. Furthermore, we use the exponential moving average (EMA) strategy to update the historical objects features kept by tracklets that match detection boxes.

After the first association stage, there will be some unmatched tracklets left, which will be associated with low confidence detection boxes we divided in the second association stage. We use the predicted tracking box of the unmatched tracklet to calculate the IoU distance D_i with low confidence detection boxes. Moreover, we use IoU metric to combine the confidence score De_{conf} of the low confidence detection box as a new similarity metric *similarity2*. The fusion distance of *similarity2* used for the second association stage is calculated as

$$D_{S2} = 1 - [(1 - D_i) \times De_{\text{conf}}] \tag{8}$$

where we use Hungarian algorithm with a matching threshold $\tau_2 = 0.85$ to assign identities to the objects based on the D_{S2} and finish the matching. We delete all the unmatched low confidence detection boxes after the second association.

Finally, we initialize the unmatched high confidence detections after the first association as new tracks and save the remaining unmatched tracklets after the second association for 30 frames in case they reappear in the future.

4   Experiments

4.1   Datasets and Metrics

We mix seven public data sets to train our model. Specifically, the composition of the mixed dataset is as follows: CityPerson [26], ETH [27], MOT17 [22], CalTech

Table 1. Performance of different combinations of backbones and necks. All the models shown in the table adopt the same association algorithm (i.e. MOTDT [8]).

Backbone	Neck	MOTA↑	IDF1↑	FPS↑
DLA-34 [1]	-	73.2	71.9	24.8
YOLOv5s [37]	FPN	69.3	68.8	35.7
YOLOv5s	BiFPN	69.6	69.0	33.6
YOLOv7 [19]	FPN	74.0	73.4	32.6
YOLOv7	BiFPN	74.4	73.6	30.8

[29], CUHK-SYSU [30], PRW [31] and CrowdHuman [32] dataset. We extensively evaluate our model on the testing sets of three benchmarks: MOT16 [22], MOT17 and MOT20 [33]. We use the CLEAR metrics [34], including MOTA [22], IDF1 [23] and the recently released HOTA [35] to evaluate the tracking accuracy. We also use IDF1 and IDsw [22] to measure the stability of the tracklet's ID.

4.2 Implementation Details

We use YOLOv7's [19] backbone as our default backbone, and we load the YOLOv7's parameters pretrained on the coco dataset [36] to initialize our model. We use Adam optimizer to train our one-shot base model for 30 epochs, that is, the first 20 epochs with a learning rate of 5e−4 and the last 10 epochs with a rate of 5e−5. We train our model on the single Tesla V100 for about 28 h.

4.3 Ablation Experiments

We obtain ablation experiments results evaluated on MOT16, 17 testing sets to prove series of conclusions.

Backbone and Neck Network. We take YOLO series detectors' backbones as the default backbones of our model and directly compare with the DLA-34 on the MOT16 testing set. As shown in Table 1, YOLOv7, as the backbone, can achieve the best indicator results in MOTA and IDF1 (MOTA = 74.0, IDF1 = 73.4), which measure the accuracy of MOT. As for the indicator FPS, which measures the speed of tracking, YOLOv5 can obtain the best result (FPS = 35.7). All of the above show that lightweight YOLO series detectors' backbones are more suitable for the one-shot model. Further more, on the basis of YOLOv5 and YOLOv7 as backbones, we replace the original feature fusion structure of FPN [20] with BiFPN [21], as shown in Table 1. Using BiFPN as the feature fusion network can achieve better MOT results (MOTA, IDF1) due to integrating multi-layer features in both two directions.

CS Attention Module. Whether the anchor-free detector can accurately predict the center location of the object is the premise of the detection and re-ID tasks, because we base the predicted center location to regress the detection box, and also base it to extract the re-ID feature of the object. The CS attention we proposed can make the network more focus on the object and its location in the

Table 2. Results Of the CS attention module appended on our one-shot model evaluated on the MOT17 testing set. All the models shown in the table adopt the same association algorithm (i.e. MOTDT [8]).

Attention	Detection		MOT			Speed
	FN↓	Recall↑	MOTA↑	Frag↓	IDsw↓	FPS↑
✗	117639	79.2	73.6	8649	3681	31.0
CS (Ours)	112782	80.0	73.9	8379	3324	27.9

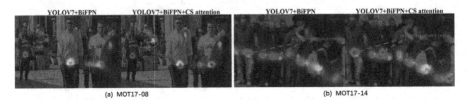

(a) MOT17-08   (b) MOT17-14

Fig. 4. Visualization of heatmaps from the heatmap head of the detection branch.

image, which improves the object localization ability. As shown in Table 2, on the MOT17 testing set results, compared with the proposed one-shot model without CS attention, the model with CS attention is significantly reduced by nearly 5000 times FN [22] (missed detections) and further improves the detection performance (+0.8 Recall), so the tracklets fragments (Frag) decrease due to less missed detections. Accurately predicting the object center location also helps the re-ID branch to extract more accurate features of the object, so ID switches (IDsw) reduce by 9.7% because of the more reliable appearance similarity. All of those make the final tracking accuracy improve (+0.3 MOTA).

The visualization of heatmaps can further illustrate the impact of the CS attention. We randomly selected two frames from MOT17-08 and MOT17-14 testing set videos for heatmaps visualization. As shown in Fig. 4 (a), the CS attention makes up for the previously undetected object center points, which directly shows that adding CS attention alleviates the occurrence of missed detections. As shown in Fig. 4 (b), the CS attention improves the model's object localization ability and helps to predict the object center location more accurately, which is important for both detection and re-ID tasks.

Fusion Similarity. We use the one-shot model proposed by us to verify the performance of different fusion methods evaluated on MOT16 testing set. The *similarity1* and *similarity2* are used for the first and the second data association stage respectively. As shown in Table 3, keep the similarity2 metric as IoU distance, when the similarity1 metric becomes the fusion distance *fusion1* of the cosine distance with the GIoU distance, which can eliminate the mismatches that candidate tracklets are farther from the detections but have close cosine distances, so the stability of the tracklet's ID of our algorithm has improved significantly (+0.8 IDF1, −22.7% IDsw). Furthermore, when the similarity2 metric becomes the fusion distance *fusion2* of the IoU distance with the detection con-

Table 3. Performance of different fusion methods of similarity.

Association	Similarity1	Similarity2	IDF1↑	IDsw↓	MOTA↑
Ours	Re-ID	IoU	74.5	890	74.7
Ours	Fusion1	IoU	75.3	688	75.0
Ours	Fusion1	Fusion2	75.6	676	75.0
BoT-SORT [28]	Fusion1*	IoU	74.9	802	74.7

fidence score, which can reduce the probability of mismatches with background detections, the stability of our algorithm is further enhanced.

Bot-SORT [28] proposes another fusion method for combining the appearance and motion similarity as *fusion1**. Equation (9) redefines the cosine distance $\hat{d}_{i,j}^{\cos}$ between the i-th tracklet and the j-th detection box. Thresholds θ_{emb} and θ_{iou} are used to reject unlikely pairs of tracklets and detections, namely low cosine similarity or far away candidates. The fusion method of BoT-SORT is in Eq. (10).

$$\hat{d}_{i,j}^{\cos} = \begin{cases} 0.5 \cdot d_{i,j}^{\cos}, \left(d_{i,j}^{\cos} < \theta_{emb}\right) \wedge \left(d_{i,j}^{iou} < \theta_{iou}\right) \\ 1, \text{ otherwise} \end{cases} \quad (9)$$

$$Fusion1^* = min\left\{\hat{d}_{i,j}^{\cos}, d_{i,j}^{iou}\right\} \quad (10)$$

However, the *fusion1** of this method still comes from a single similarity metric, namely the re-ID or IoU metric, which leads to some matching pairs only using IoU distance as the final matching distance. However, in fact, in the first association stage, we should rely more on the matching results of appearance similarity based on deep learning.

4.4   Comparing with SOTA MOT Methods

We have extensively evaluated the proposed models and algorithms on the MOT16, MOT17, and MOT20 testing sets, and compare them with the state-of-the-art (SOTA) methods.

Comparing with SOTA Association Methods. We adopt the one-shot model proposed by us and continue to train on the main state-of-the-art association algorithms, and finally get the key indicators results on the MOT17 testing

Table 4. Comparison with the SOTA association algorithms

Association	Published	IDF1↑	IDsw↓	MOTA↑
DeepSORT [7]	ICIP2017	72.1	3822	73.3
MOTDT [8]	ICME2018	73.0	3681	73.6
ByteTrack [9]	ECCV2022	73.9	2757	74.3
Ours	Ours	**74.9**	**2127**	**74.5**

Table 5. Results Of CSTrack and FairMOT are all derived from original papers. Our proposed base one-shot model with fusion similarity association is termed as BFMOT. BFMOT-L is the larger version of the BFMOT appended the CS attention module.

Dataset	Baseline	MOTA↑	IDsw↓	FPS↑
MOT16	CSTrack [15]	70.7	1071	15.8
	BFMOT (Ours)	75.0	**676**	**29.7**
	BFMOT-L (Ours)	**75.4**	680	26.5
MOT17	FairMOT [3]	73.7	3303	25.9
	BFMOT (Ours)	74.5	2127	**29.9**
	BFMOT-L (Ours)	**74.7**	**2106**	26.6

set. As shown in Table 4, our fusion similarity association algorithm can greatly improve the tracklet's stability (IDF1, IDsw) and achieves more robust association results (IDF1, MOTA). Particularly, compared with the most popular association algorithm ByteTrack [9], our algorithm still has a great advantage in the stability of tracklet's ID. Specifically, IDF1 has increased by 1%, while IDsw has significantly decreased by 22.9%.

Comparing with SOTA One-Shot Baselines. The final performance of BFMOT (our one-shot model with proposed fusion similarity association termed as BFMOT) on the MOT16,17 testing set is shown in Table 5. Furthermore, two

Table 6. Comparison of the state-of-the-art one-shot trackers. It is noteworthy that FPS considers both detection and association time. The best results of each dataset are shown in bold. The values not provided are filled by "-".

Dataset	Tracker	Published	IDF1↑	IDsw↓	HOTA↑	MOTA↑	FPS↑
MOT16	GSDT [5]	ICRA2021	68.1	1229	56.6	74.5	<10
	MeMOT [38]	CVPR2022	69.7	845	57.4	72.6	-
	FairMOT [3]	IJCV2021	72.8	1074	-	74.9	25.9
	CorrTracker [17]	CVPR2021	74.3	979	61.0	**76.6**	14.8
	BFMOT	**Ours**	**75.6**	**676**	**61.1**	75.0	**29.7**
MOT17	TrackFormer [39]	CVPR2022	68.0	2829	57.3	74.1	<10
	GTR [40]	CVPR2022	71.5	2859	59.1	75.3	19.6
	FairMOT [3]	IJCV2021	72.3	3303	59.3	73.7	25.9
	SGT [41]	WACV2023	72.8	4101	-	76.4	-
	MO3TR [42]	TPAMI2022	72.9	2847	60.3	**77.6**	-
	CorrTracker [17]	CVPR2021	73.6	3369	**60.7**	76.5	14.8
	OMC [16]	AAAI2022	73.8	-	-	76.3	12.8
	BFMOT	**Ours**	**74.9**	**2127**	**60.7**	74.5	**29.9**
MOT20	FairMOT [3]	IJCV2021	67.3	5243	54.6	61.8	13.2
	BFMOT	**Ours**	**70.8**	**2512**	**56.4**	**68.5**	**14.4**

versions of BFMOT both outperform CSTrack [15] and FairMOT [3], which also join the detection and re-ID tasks for MOT.

Comparing with SOTA One-Shot Trackers. Furthermore, the BFMOT tracker and other SOTA online one-shot trackers (private detection) are widely compared on MOT16, MOT17, and MOT20 testing sets. All the following one-shot trackers' results are derived from the original papers and from the official MOT challenge evaluation server. Note that all of the results of the BFMOT tracker are directly obtained from the official MOT challenge evaluation server. As shown in Table 6, BFMOT tracker achieves the best results in the stability of tracklet's ID (IDF1, IDsw) and tracking accuracy (HOTA, IDF1).

Compared with other one-shot trackers, BFMOT tracker's real-time performance (FPS) can be further highlighted. In particular, on the MOT20 testing set with the most complex scenes, BFMOT has great advantages than the SOTA tracker FairMOT [3] (-52.1% IDsw), which shows BFMOT's excellent robustness to handle complex scenarios.

5 Conclusion

In this paper, we propose a new efficient one-shot model of joint detection and re-ID paradigm for MOT. We also propose a new channel-spatial attention to enhance the detection and tracking performances. In addition, we design a fusion similarity association algorithm to further improve the ability of proposed model for more robust tracking. We visualized the tracking results of BFMOT tracker processing MOT17-14 and MOT20-04, the two most complex video scenes in their respective testing sets, as shown in Fig. 5. The challenges of the MOT17-14 scene are the small objects with low resolution, while the challenges of the MOT20-04 scene are that the flow of people is large and a lot of objects occlusion occurs in each frame. BFMOT is able to cope with the tough challenges of all.

Fig. 5. Visualization of tracking results of BFMOT on the testing set. Each row shows the results of sampled frames in chronological order of a video sequence. Bounding boxes with different colors represent different identities.

References

1. Zhou, X., Wang, D., Krähenbühl, P.: Objects as points. arXiv preprint arXiv:1904.07850 (2019)
2. Zhou, X., Koltun, V., Krähenbühl, P.: Tracking objects as points. In: Vedaldi, A., Bischof, H., Brox, T., Frahm, J.-M. (eds.) ECCV 2020. LNCS, vol. 12349, pp. 474–490. Springer, Cham (2020). https://doi.org/10.1007/978-3-030-58548-8_28
3. Zhang, Y., et al.: FairMOT: on the fairness of detection and re-identification in multiple object tracking. Int. J. Comput. Vis. **129**(11), 3069–3087 (2021)
4. Wu, J., et al.: Track to detect and segment: an online multi-object tracker. In: Proceedings of the IEEE/CVF Conference on Computer Vision and Pattern Recognition, pp. 12352–12361 (2021)
5. Wang, Y., Kitani, K., Weng, X.: Joint object detection and multi-object tracking with graph neural networks. In: 2021 IEEE International Conference on Robotics and Automation (ICRA), pp. 13708–13715 (2021)
6. Mostafa, R., Baraka, H., Bayoumi, A.: LMOT: efficient light-weight detection and tracking in crowds. IEEE Access **10**, 83085–83095 (2022)
7. Wojke, N., Bewley, A., Paulus, P.: Simple online and realtime tracking with a deep association metric. In: 2017 IEEE International Conference on Image Processing (ICIP), pp. 3645–3649 (2017)
8. Chen, L., et al.: Real-time multiple people tracking with deeply learned candidate selection and person re-identification. In: 2018 IEEE International Conference on Multimedia and Expo (ICME), pp. 1–6 (2018)
9. Zhang, Y., et al.: ByteTrack: multi-object tracking by associating every detection box. In: Avidan, S., Brostow, G., Cissé, M., Farinella, G.M., Hassner, T. (eds.) Computer Vision – ECCV 2022. LNCS, vol. 13682, pp. 1–21. Springer, Cham (2022). https://doi.org/10.1007/978-3-031-20047-2_1
10. Hu, J., Li S., Sun, G.: Squeeze-and-excitation networks. In: Proceedings of 2018 IEEE/CVF Conference on Computer Vision and Pattern Recognition, pp. 7132–7141 (2018)
11. Woo, S., Park, J., Lee, J.-Y., Kweon, I.S.: CBAM: convolutional block attention module. In: Ferrari, V., Hebert, M., Sminchisescu, C., Weiss, Y. (eds.) ECCV 2018. LNCS, vol. 11211, pp. 3–19. Springer, Cham (2018). https://doi.org/10.1007/978-3-030-01234-2_1
12. Kalman, R.E.: A new approach to linear filtering and prediction problems, pp. 35–45 (1960)
13. Lu, Z., et al.: RetinaTrack: online single stage joint detection and tracking. In: Proceedings of the IEEE/CVF Conference on Computer Vision and Pattern Recognition, pp. 14668–14678 (2020)
14. Wang, Z., Zheng, L., Liu, Y., Li, Y., Wang, S.: Towards real-time multi-object tracking. In: Vedaldi, A., Bischof, H., Brox, T., Frahm, J.-M. (eds.) ECCV 2020. LNCS, vol. 12356, pp. 107–122. Springer, Cham (2020). https://doi.org/10.1007/978-3-030-58621-8_7
15. Liang, C., et al.: Rethinking the competition between detection and Re-ID in Multi-Object Tracking. arXiv preprint arXiv:2010.12138v2 (2020)
16. Liang, C., et al.: One more check: making "fake background" be tracked again. In: Proceedings of the AAAI Conference on Artificial Intelligence, vol. 36, no. 2, pp. 1546–1554 (2022)
17. Wang, Q., et al.: Multiple object tracking with correlation learning. In: Proceedings of the IEEE/CVF Conference on Computer Vision and Pattern Recognition, pp. 3876–3886 (2021)

18. Bewley, A., et al.: Simple online and realtime tracking. In: 2016 IEEE International Conference on Image Processing (ICIP), pp. 3464–3468 (2016)
19. Wang, C., Alexey, B., Liao, H.: YOLOv7: trainable bag-of-freebies sets new state-of-the-art for real-time object detectors. Preprint arXiv:2207.02696 (2022)
20. Lin, T., et al.: Feature pyramid networks for object detection. In: Proceedings of the IEEE/CVF Conference on Computer Vision and Pattern Recognition, pp. 2117–2125 (2017)
21. Tan, M., Pang, R., Le, Q.: EfficientDet: scalable and efficient object detection. In: Proceedings of the IEEE/CVF Conference on Computer Vision and Pattern Recognition, pp. 10781–10790 (2020)
22. Milan, A., Leal-Taixé, L., Reid, I., Roth, S., Schindler, K.: MOT16: a benchmark for multi-object tracking. arXiv preprint arXiv:1603.00831 (2016)
23. Dendorfer, P., et al.: MOTChallenge: a benchmark for single-camera multiple target tracking. Int. J. Comput. Vis. **129**(4), 845–881 (2021)
24. Lin, T., et al.: Focal loss for dense object detection. In: Proceedings of the IEEE/CVF International Conference on Computer Vision, pp. 2980–2988 (2017)
25. Kuhn, H.: The Hungarian method for the assignment problem. Naval Res. Logistics Q. **2.1-2**, 83–97 (1955)
26. Zhang, S., Benenson, R., Schiele, B.: CityPersons: a diverse dataset for pedestrian detection. In: Proceedings of the IEEE/CVF Conference on Computer Vision and Pattern Recognition, pp. 3213–3221 (2017)
27. Ess, A., et al.: A mobile vision system for robust multi-person tracking. In: 2008 IEEE Conference on Computer Vision and Pattern Recognition, pp. 1–8 (2008)
28. Aharon, N., Orfaig R., Bobrovsky B.: BoT-SORT: robust associations multi-pedestrian tracking. arXiv preprint arXiv:2206.14651v2 (2022)
29. Dollár, P., et al.: Pedestrian detection: a benchmark. In: 2009 IEEE Conference on Computer Vision and Pattern Recognition, pp. 304–311 (2009)
30. Xiao, T., et al.: Joint detection and identification feature learning for person search. In: Proceedings of the IEEE/CVF Conference on Computer Vision and Pattern Recognition, pp. 3415–3424 (2017)
31. Zheng, L., et al.: Person re-identification in the wild. In: Proceedings of the IEEE/CVF Conference on Computer Vision and Pattern Recognition, pp. 1367–1376 (2017)
32. Shao, S., et al.: CrowdHuman: a benchmark for detecting human in a crowd. arXiv preprint arXiv:1805.00123 (2018)
33. Dendorfer, P., et al.: MOT20: a benchmark for multi object tracking in crowded scenes. arXiv preprint arXiv:2003.09003 (2020)
34. Bernardin, K., Stiefelhagen, R.: Evaluating multiple object tracking performance: the clear MOT metrics. EURASIP J. Image Video Process. 1–10 (2008)
35. Luiten, J., et al.: HOTA: a higher order metric for evaluating multi-object tracking. Int. J. Comput. Vis. **129**(2), 548–578 (2021)
36. Lin, T.-Y., et al.: Microsoft COCO: common objects in context. In: Fleet, D., Pajdla, T., Schiele, B., Tuytelaars, T. (eds.) ECCV 2014. LNCS, vol. 8693, pp. 740–755. Springer, Cham (2014). https://doi.org/10.1007/978-3-319-10602-1_48
37. Glenn, J.: https://github.com/ultralytics/yolov5/releases/tag/v6.1
38. Cai, J., et al.: MeMOT: multi-object tracking with memory. In: Proceedings of the IEEE/CVF Conference on Computer Vision and Pattern Recognition, pp. 8090–8100 (2022)
39. Meinhardt, T., et al.: TrackFormer: multi-object tracking with transformers. In: Proceedings of the IEEE/CVF Conference on Computer Vision and Pattern Recognition, pp. 8844–8854 (2022)

40. Zhou, X., et al.: Global tracking transformers. In: Proceedings of the IEEE/CVF Conference on Computer Vision and Pattern Recognition, pp. 8771–8780 (2022)
41. Hyun, J., et al.: Detection recovery in online multi-object tracking with Sparse Graph Tracker. arXiv preprint arXiv:2205.00968 (2022)
42. Zhu, T., et al.: Looking beyond two frames: end-to-end multi-object tracking using spatial and temporal transformers. IEEE Trans. Pattern Anal. Mach. Intell. (2022)

Sampling Spatial-Temporal Attention Network for Traffic Forecasting

Mao Chen[1] , Yi Xu[2](✉) , Liangzhe Han[2] , and Leilei Sun[2]

[1] Beihang University, Beijing 100191, China
chenmao@buaa.edu.cn
[2] State Key Laboratory of Software Development Environment, Beihang University,
Beijing 100191, China
{xuyee,liangzhehan,leileisun}@buaa.edu.cn

Abstract. Spatial-temporal graph learning has been a critical approach to modeling complex dependencies between variables in multivariate time series such as traffic series. However, when modeling the spatial dependencies between traffic nodes, most existing approaches regard the predefined or adaptive graphs as static, overlooking the dynamic nature of realistic graphs that change over time. In addition, due to limitations in model complexity and information density, most models only consider short-term historical series for future series forecasting, failing to account for the periodicity of long-term series. Furthermore, spatial-temporal indistinguishability is also a challenge for many approaches. Aiming to address these problems, we propose a novel neural network framework **S**ampling **S**patial-**T**emporal **A**ttention **N**etwork (**SSTAN**) to effectively capture latent spatial and temporal dependencies. Firstly, a spatial encoder is proposed to learn multi-level dynamic graph structures. Secondly, a temporal encoding framework with long-term sampling and temporal encoders is designed to capture long-term periodic features that contain high-density information. Thirdly, with the global information of the entire graph and long-term series, our model overcomes the challenge of spatial-temporal indistinguishability to distinguish similar series with different latent patterns. Finally, experimental results on three real-world datasets not only demonstrate the superiority of our model over baselines on traffic forecasting but also illustrate our model's effectiveness in spatial-temporal dependencies learning.

Keywords: traffic forecasting · dynamic graph · long-term learning · discrete sampling · pattern identification

1 Introduction

In recent years, the development of data collection and computation has greatly promoted the research of traffic forecasting. And the advancement of traffic forecasting has been crucial for the development of Intelligent Transportation Systems (ITS) [16] which aim to improve the efficiency, safety, and sustainability of

© The Author(s), under exclusive license to Springer Nature Switzerland AG 2023
Z. Jin et al. (Eds.): KSEM 2023, LNAI 14118, pp. 121–136, 2023.
https://doi.org/10.1007/978-3-031-40286-9_11

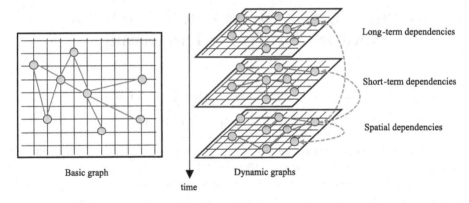

Fig. 1. Dynamic graph structures and temporal-spatial temporal dependencies in traffic series.

transportation. As a representative example of multivariate time series, traffic series data exhibits both temporal and spatial dependencies between variables such as sensors, as demonstrated in Fig. 1. The intricate dependencies of traffic series have instigated numerous studies to explore the identification of time patterns and relationships between variables for more accurate forecasting.

With the development of deep learning techniques, many neural-network-based models have exhibited promising performance in traffic forecasting. Among these technologies, spatial-temporal graph modeling [18] has been regarded as one of the most effective methods, which combines Graph Neural Networks (GNNs) [10] with sequential models such as Recurrent Neural Networks (RNNs) to extract spatial-temporal dependencies. Initially, spatial-temporal graph modeling mainly relied on a predefined graph to learn the spatial dependencies [11,15,20]. However, considering that the predefined graph can be inaccurate, recent studies have shifted their focus towards self-adaptive graphs learned from data without prior knowledge [3,4,8,18]. Despite the encouraging performance of these models, there are still three main shortcomings that can be further improved.

Firstly, the spatial dependencies between nodes in most predefined and self-adaptive graphs are regarded as static, since constructing different graphs for each time step leads to excessive model complexity. As a result, the relationships between nodes are considered to be unchanging, whereas they are variable over time. An illustrated example is the traffic tide phenomenon between nodes. The absence of spatial dynamics makes it challenging to fully capture the interactions between nodes. Secondly, most models only use short-term historical series for forecasting, which is susceptible to random disturbances and incapable of learning long-term periodic patterns. The main challenges of learning long-term historical series are high computation costs and a low density of relevant information due to the presence of many unrelated patches. Neglecting long-term periodicity undermines the ability of these models to achieve more satisfactory performance in long-term prediction tasks. Thirdly, the issue of spatial-temporal indistinguishability [14] poses a significant challenge to accurate prediction in these models. Two comparable historical series sampled from distinct nodes or at different time steps may lead to different future series, making it difficult to distinguish the differences and make the corresponding prediction.

To address these challenges, a novel framework called Sampling Spatial-Temporal Attention Network (SSTAN) is proposed in this paper. To learn a dynamic graph structure with low complexity, we introduce a spatial encoder based on self-attention mechanism [17] to extract the dynamic spatial dependencies between nodes based on the current and historical traffic states. This approach obviates the need to construct different graphs for each time step, and the attention of one node towards another is directly linked to its state, thus reflecting the dynamics of the graph and enabling easy computation. Furthermore, to address the low information density and high computation costs in long-term series learning, a discrete periodic long-term sampling method is employed in our work. Each sampled series with a small size is encoded by a temporal encoder separately to neglect the impact of unrelated series and ensure high-density information. The separate temporal features are linearly aggregated into a low-dimensional representation that contains both long-term periodic and short-term information. By combining the spatial dependencies of the entire graph and long short-term temporal features, our model is capable of capturing the global information to address the issue of spatial and temporal indistinguishability that is limited by local information.

In summary, the main contribution of our work lies in the following aspects:

- A discrete sampling method and a temporal features encoding framework are designed. The long-term sampling and temporal encoding enable the model to capture both long-term periodic time patterns and short-term temporal impacts from high-density aggregated information efficiently and strengthen the model's ability to distinguish similar series with distinct latent time patterns.
- A spatial encoder for dynamic graph structure learning is proposed. Instead of constructing different graphs for each time step, based on self-attention, our model generates a dynamic graph that is related to history and current traffic states with low computation complexity.
- Experiment results on three real-world datasets demonstrate the effectiveness of our model in capturing latent spatial and long-term temporal dependencies. Our spatial-temporal encoding framework can be widely applied to other downstream tasks.

2   Related Work

2.1   Traffic Forecasting

As one significant field of multivariate time series prediction, traffic forecasting has drawn increasing attention [12]. Many models, such as ARMA [2] and VAR

[22], were proposed based on statistical methods to analyze interrelated patterns and random disturbance. With the development of deep learning technologies in recent years, various models have emerged and displayed strong ability in sequence prediction. Long-Short Term Memory (LSTM) [9] introduces a memory cell with several gates that control the flow of information to capture long-term dependencies. Additionally, one-dimensional CNN is also commonly used for analyzing time series. However, spatial dependencies and the graph structure of traffic have been ignored in sequential models, leading researchers to pay attention to spatial-temporal correlation. Based on the view that there is a stronger correlation between adjacent nodes than distant nodes, Graph Convolution Network (GCN) is used to capture local spatial dependencies. To compensate for GCN's shortcomings in learning distant spatial dependencies, graph diffusion convolution is employed to reconstruct complicated graph structures [11]. More recently, with the development of deep learning in other fields, many new methods such as self-attention and Transformer [17] have been adopted in both spatial and temporal dependencies learning.

2.2 Spatial-Temporal Graph Neural Network

Based on graph neural networks and seq2seq models, Spatial-Temporal Graph Neural Networks (STGNNs) are capable of learning spatial-temporal dependencies simultaneously and have demonstrated remarkable performances. Constructing a graph structure that reflects the hidden interactions between nodes is one of the major tasks of STGNNs. Based on a pre-defined graph, STGCN [19], DCRNN [11] and T-GCN [20] combine Graph Convolution Networks with other technologies including Gated Convolutional Networks, diffusion convolution and GRU [6] to capture spatial-temporal dependencies. However, the pre-defined graph is always missing or inaccurate, as it fails to fully represent the dynamic interactions and deep spatial dependencies between nodes. Therefore, some recent works have focused on learning an adaptive graph structure without prior knowledge. Graph WaveNet [18] uses a Self-Adaptive Adjacent Matrix to describe the hidden diffusion process and capture hidden spatial dependencies. AGCRN [3] adopts Node Adaptive Parameter Learning (NAPL) to learn the unique pattern of each node, and Data Adaptive Graph Generation (DAGG) to improve the learning of adaptive graphs. In addition, self-attention mechanism [17] is utilized in GMAN [21] to extract the spatial features and StemGNN [4] combines GRU [6] with self-attention as Latent Correlation Layer to generate an adaptive adjacent matrix. In line with the approach of learning adaptive graphs, we employ a spatial encoder to construct a dynamic adaptive graph based on the current and historical traffic states.

3   Preliminaries

In this section, we present the definitions of traffic series and dynamic graph and then formalize the problem of traffic forecasting that we address in this paper.

Definition 1. Traffic Series. *Traffic series is one type of multivariate time series, which consists of multi variables that are interrelated. The variables in traffic series typically represent traffic features such as traffic speed or volume measured by different sensors. In this paper, we denote the traffic series as a tensor $\mathcal{X}_{t+1:t+T} \in \mathbb{R}^{T \times N \times C_{in}}$, where T is the number of time steps, N is the number of traffic sensors and C_{in} is the number of input channels. In addition, we denote the series measured by sensor i as $X_{t+1:t+T}^{i} \in \mathbb{R}^{T \times C_{in}}$.*

Definition 2. Dynamic Graph. *The dynamic dependencies between sensors in traffic series can be described as a graph $\mathcal{G}_t = (V, E_t)$, where V is the set of nodes and E_t is the set of dynamic edges that vary over time. Each node represents a sensor, and the edge $e_{t,i,j} \in E_t$ corresponds to the dependencies between node i and j at time step t. Furthermore, the dynamic graph is also denoted as a matrix $A_t \in \mathbb{R}^{N \times N}$ where $A_{t,i,j}$ is the weight of dependencies between node i and j at time step t.*

Definition 3. Traffic Forecasting. *The objective of traffic forecasting is to predict $\mathcal{Y}_{t+1:t+T_f} \in \mathbb{R}^{T_f \times N \times C_{out}}$ for the subsequent T_f time steps based on a given short-term history traffic series $\mathcal{X}_{t+1-T_h:t} \in \mathbb{R}^{T_h \times N \times C_{in}}$ for the past T_h history time steps. Considering the periodicity of traffic series, the long-term historical series $\mathcal{X}_{t+1-jT_d:t+T_f-jT_d} \in \mathbb{R}^{T_f \times N \times C_{in}}$ is also included as input series in this paper, where T_d is the number of time steps each day.*

4 Methodology

In this section, the detailed framework and mathematical definition of our proposed model will be discussed. As is shown in Fig. 2, there are three main components in SSTAN: time series sampling, temporal encoding, and spatial encoding.

4.1 Time Series Sampling

Given the presence of clear periodicity in traffic flow and speed, it is crucial for the model to learn the underlying periodic patterns. One general approach is to sample long continuous historical series. However, this method suffers from two major issues: low information density of many unrelated series and significant complexity, which can result in limited benefits but high computation costs. To address these challenges and enable the model to capture long-term periodic features with lower complexity, we propose to sample several discrete long-term historical series which are most relevant to the target series, rather than sampling a continuous long series. Specifically, to forecast node i's future series $Y_{t+1:t+T_f}^{i} \in \mathbb{R}^{T_f \times C_{out}}$, long-term historical series $X_{t+1-jT_d:t+T_f-jT_d}^{i} \in \mathbb{R}^{T_f \times C_{in}}$ are sampled discretely with an interval of T_d, where T_f is the number of future time steps, T_d is the number of time steps of each day, C_{in} is the number of input channels, $j \in [1, N_s]$ and N_s is the number of long-term samples. In addition to long-term historical series, the recent one also has a significant effect on future series. Therefore, the short-term series $X_{t+1-T_h:t}^i \in \mathbb{R}^{T_h \times C_{in}}$ is sampled as well, where T_h is the number of recent history time steps. By combining long-term sampling with short-term sampling, each sampled series is closely related to the target series and contains high-density temporal information.

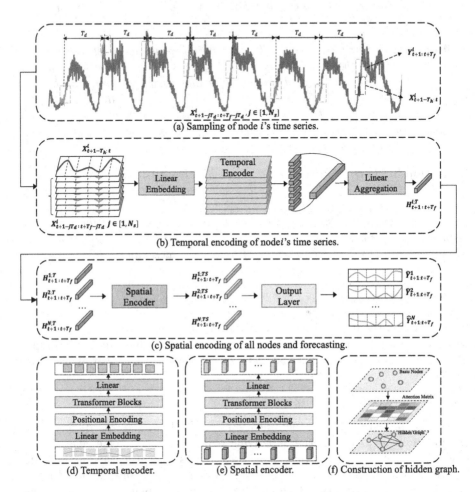

Fig. 2. Architecture of SSTAN. (a) The combination of long-term and short-term sampling of time series. (b) Temporal encoding of long-term and short-term sampled series separately and linear aggregation of separate temporal features. (c) Spatial encoding of all nodes to construct spatial dependencies based on temporal features without a pre-defined graph, and forecasting with a simple output layer. (d) The architecture of temporal encoder, which captures the temporal dependencies in single sampled series. (e) The architecture of spatial encoder, which captures the spatial dependencies of all nodes. (f) Construction of hidden graph based on spatial-temporal encoded features with self-attention.

4.2   Temporal Encoding

In temporal encoding, each sampled series is embedded linearly and encoded by one temporal encoder. Then encoded representations are linearly aggregated into a one-dimensional tensor of temporal representation of a single node.

Linear Embedding. The sampled series are first linearly projected into latent space:

$$H^i_{t+1-T_h:t} = X^i_{t+1-T_h:t}W + b \tag{1}$$

$$H^i_{t+1-jT_d:t+T_f-jT_d} = X^i_{t+1-jT_d:t+T_f-jT_d}W + b \tag{2}$$

where $W \in \mathbb{R}^{C_{in} \times d}$ and $b \in \mathbb{R}^d$ are learnable parameters shared by all sampled series, $H^i_{t+1-T_h:t} \in \mathbb{R}^{T_h \times d}$ and $H^i_{t+1-jT_d:t+T_f-jT_d} \in \mathbb{R}^{T_f \times d}$ are the latent representations of sampled series, and d is the hidden dimension.

Temporal Encoder. N_s+1 latent representations of sampled series are encoded by $N_s + 1$ temporal encoders separately. Assume k-th temporal encoder's input representation as $H_k \in \mathbb{R}^{T \times d}$, where $T \in \{T_h, T_f\}$. H_k is transformed by a fully connected layer and a positional encoding layer:

$$E^{(0)}_k = H_k W^I_k + b^I_k + P_k \tag{3}$$

where $W_{kI} \in \mathbb{R}^{d \times d}$, $b_{kI} \in \mathbb{R}^d$ and $P_k \in \mathbb{R}^{T \times d}$ are learnable parameters. It is worth noting that P_k attaches additional positional information to series representation. Then N_b transformer blocks [17] are used to capture the relation between different time steps in single sampled series:

$$E^{(l)}_k = \text{TransformerBlock}(E^{(l-1)}_k) \quad l = 1, 2, \cdots, N_b \tag{4}$$

where $E^{(l)}_k \in \mathbb{R}^{T \times d}$. Specifically, with an input tensor $E^{(l-1)}_k$, the calculation of each transformer block with N_h attention heads can be described as [17]:

$$Q = E^{(l-1)}_k W^Q_k + b^Q_k \tag{5}$$

$$K = E^{(l-1)}_k W^K_k + b^K_k \tag{6}$$

$$V = E^{(l-1)}_k W^V_k + b^V_k \tag{7}$$

$$A_h = \text{softmax}(\frac{Q_h K^T_h}{\sqrt{d_h}})V_h \quad h = 1, 2, \cdots, N_h \tag{8}$$

$$A = \text{Concat}(A_1, A_2, \cdots, A_{N_h})W^A_k + b^A_k \tag{9}$$

$$E^{(l-1)'}_k = \text{LayerNorm}(E^{(l-1)}_k + A) \tag{10}$$

$$E^{(l)}_k = \text{LayerNorm}(E^{(l-1)'}_k + \text{FeedForward}(E^{(l-1)'}_k)) \tag{11}$$

where $W^Q_k, W^K_k, W^V_k, W^A_k \in \mathbb{R}^{d \times d}$ and $b^Q_k, b^K_k, b^V_k, b^A_k \in \mathbb{R}^d$ are learnable parameters, $Q, K, V \in \mathbb{R}^{T \times d}$ are the query, key, and value in Multi-head Attention, $d_h = d/N_h$ is the dimension of hth head, $Q_h, K_h, V_h, A_h \in \mathbb{R}^{T \times d_h}$ are the query, key, value, and attention output of hth head, and $\boldsymbol{A} \in \mathbb{R}^{T \times d}$ is the output of Multi-head Attention. Finally, a linear transformation is performed:

$$\boldsymbol{H}_k^{'} = \boldsymbol{E}_k^{(N_b)} \boldsymbol{W}_k^O + \boldsymbol{b}_k^O \tag{12}$$

where $\boldsymbol{W}_k^O \in \mathbb{R}^{d \times d}$ and $\boldsymbol{b}_k^O \in \mathbb{R}^d$ are learnable parameters, $\boldsymbol{H}_k^{'} \in \mathbb{R}^{T \times d}$ is the output of kth temporal encoder.

Linear Aggregation. The latent representations of sampled series are encoded by temporal encoders separately and linearly aggregated together:

$$\boldsymbol{H}_{t+1-T_h:t}^{i'} = \text{TemporalEncoder}(\boldsymbol{H}_{t+1-T_h:t}^i) \tag{13}$$

$$\boldsymbol{H}_{t+1-jT_d:t+T_f-jT_d}^{i'} = \text{TemporalEncoder}(\boldsymbol{H}_{t+1-jT_d:t+T_f-jT_d}^i) \tag{14}$$

$$\boldsymbol{H}_{t+1:t+T_f}^{i;T} = \text{Flatten}(\text{Concat}(\boldsymbol{H}_{t+1-T_h:t}^{i'}, \boldsymbol{H}_{t+1-T_d:t+T_f-T_d}^{i'},$$
$$\cdots, \boldsymbol{H}_{t+1-N_sT_d:t+T_f-N_sT_d}^{i'}))\boldsymbol{W}^{Agg} + \boldsymbol{b}^{Agg} \tag{15}$$

where $\boldsymbol{W}^{Agg} \in \mathbb{R}^{(T_h+N_sT_f)d \times T_f d}$, $\boldsymbol{b}^{Agg} \in \mathbb{R}^{T_f d}$ are learnable parameters, and $\boldsymbol{H}_{t+1:t+T_f}^{i;T} \in \mathbb{R}^{T_f d}$ is the encoded temporal representation of node i to forecast future series $\boldsymbol{Y}_{t+1:t+T_f}^i$.

4.3 Spatial Encoding

To capture the dynamic spatial dependencies, a dynamic latent graph is constructed by a spatial encoder based on self-attention mechanism, and the temporal representation of each node is further encoded in the spatial dimension, considering the effects of other nodes. The spatial encoder has almost the same architecture as the temporal encoder, but the input tensor of the spatial encoder is composed of all nodes' temporal representations:

$$\boldsymbol{H}_{t+1:t+T_f}^T = \text{Concat}(\boldsymbol{H}_{t+1:t+T_f}^{1;T}, \cdots, \boldsymbol{H}_{t+1:t+T_f}^{N;T}) \tag{16}$$

where $\boldsymbol{H}_{t+1:t+T_f}^T \in \mathbb{R}^{N \times T_f d}$ and N is the number of nodes. The input representation is first transformed by a fully connected layer and a positional encoding layer as well:

$$\boldsymbol{E}^{(0)} = \boldsymbol{H}_{t+1:t+T_f}^T \boldsymbol{W}^I + \boldsymbol{b}^I + \boldsymbol{P} \tag{17}$$

where $\boldsymbol{W}^I \in \mathbb{R}^{T_f d \times T_f d}$, $\boldsymbol{b}^I \in \mathbb{R}^{T_f d}$ and $\boldsymbol{P} \in \mathbb{R}^{N \times T_f d}$ are learnable parameters, and $\boldsymbol{E}^{(0)} \in \mathbb{R}^{N \times T_f d}$. Then N_b transformer blocks are employed to effectively capture spatial dependencies:

$$\boldsymbol{E}^{(l)} = \text{TransformerBlock}(\boldsymbol{E}^{(l-1)}) \quad l = 1, 2, \cdots, N_b \tag{18}$$

where $\boldsymbol{E}^{(l)} \in \mathbb{R}^{N \times T_f d}$ and the computation of the transformer block can be described as equations (5) to (11). Finally, a linear transformation is performed:

$$\boldsymbol{H}_{t+1:t+T_f}^{TS} = \boldsymbol{E}^{(N_b)} \boldsymbol{W}^O + \boldsymbol{b}^O \tag{19}$$

where $\boldsymbol{W}^O \in \mathbb{R}^{T_f d \times T_f d}$ and $\boldsymbol{b}^O \in \mathbb{R}^{T_f d}$ are learnable parameters, $\boldsymbol{H}_{t+1:t+T_f}^{TS} \in \mathbb{R}^{N \times T_f d}$ is the output of spatial encoder which contains rich information in both temporal and spatial dimensions.

4.4   Forecasting

In the forecasting stage, we use a simple Multilayer Perceptron (MLP) as the output layer to construct forecasting series based on temporal-spatial representation $\boldsymbol{H}_{t+1:t+T_f}^{TS}$:

$$\boldsymbol{\mathcal{H}}_{t+1:t+T_f}^{TS'} = \text{reshape}(\boldsymbol{H}_{t+1:t+T_f}^{TS}, (N, T_f, d)) \tag{20}$$

$$\boldsymbol{\mathcal{H}}_{t+1:t+T_f}^{TS''} = \text{ELU}(\boldsymbol{\mathcal{H}}_{t+1:t+T_f}^{TS'}\boldsymbol{W}_1 + \boldsymbol{b}_1) \tag{21}$$

$$\hat{\boldsymbol{\mathcal{y}}}_{t+1:t+T_f} = \boldsymbol{\mathcal{H}}_{t+1:t+T_f}^{TS''}\boldsymbol{W}_2 + \boldsymbol{b}_2 \tag{22}$$

where $\boldsymbol{W}_1 \in \mathbb{R}^{d \times d}$, $\boldsymbol{b}_1 \in \mathbb{R}^d$, $\boldsymbol{W}_2 \in \mathbb{R}^{d \times C_{out}}$, $\boldsymbol{b}_2 \in \mathbb{R}^{C_{out}}$ are learnable parameters, and $\hat{\boldsymbol{\mathcal{y}}}_{t+1:t+T_f} \in \mathbb{R}^{N \times T_f \times C_{out}}$ is the forecasting result.

5   Experiments

In this section, we present experimental results that validate the effectiveness of the proposed SSTAN on three real-world datasets. As SSTAN comprises modules with different functions, we conduct comprehensive experiments to analyze the impact of each module on the overall performance of the model. In addition, detailed experiments are performed to investigate the specific functions of the modules in SSTAN.

5.1   Datasets

Our experiments are conducted on three real-world multivariate time series datasets: PEMS04, PEMS08, and PEMS-BAY.

- **PEMS04** is a traffic flow dataset collected by Caltrans Performance Measurement System (PEMS) [5] during the period spanning January 1st 2018 to February 28th 2018 [7,15]. The dataset comprises data collected by 307 sensors, with measurements taken every 5 min, resulting in a total of 16,992 time slices.
- **PEMS08** is a traffic flow dataset collected by PEMS during the period spanning July 1st 2018 to August 31st 2018 [15]. The dataset comprises data collected by 170 sensors, with measurements taken every 5 min, resulting in a total of 17856 time slices.
- **PEMS-BAY** is a traffic speed dataset collected by PEMS during the period spanning January 1st 2017 to March 31st 2017 [11]. The dataset comprises data collected by 325 sensors, with measurements taken every 5 min, resulting in a total of 52116 time slices.

The summary statistics of the three datasets are presented in Table 1.

Table 1. Summary statistics of experiment datasets.

Datasets	#Nodes	#Time Steps	#Sample Rate
PEMS04	307	16992	5 mins
PEMS08	170	17856	5 mins
PEMS-BAY	325	52116	5 mins

5.2 Baselines

We compare SSTAN with the following models to demonstrate its effectiveness.

- **FC-LSTM** [11]: a model based on Long Short-Term Memory (LSTM) [9] network consisting of fully connected units.
- **DCRNN** [11]: a model based on diffusion convolution and recurrent neural networks, where the diffusion convolutional layers are used to learn the dependencies between nodes, and the RNN layers are used to process time-series information.
- **Graph WaveNet** [18]: a model based on graph convolutional neural networks (GCN) to process the dependency relationships between nodes and the WaveNet structure to effectively extract features of time-series data.
- **GMAN** [21]: an encoder-decoder model, composed of multiple ST-Attention Blocks, which employ time attention mechanism to extract temporal dependencies, and spatial attention mechanism to extract spatial dependencies.
- **STID** [14]: a model incorporating Spatial-Temporal Identity (STID) to the data to address the spatial-temporal indistinguishability issue, while employing a simple Multilayer Perceptron (MLP) as the underlying model for forecasting.

5.3 Experimental Setup

In our model, we sample the $N_s = 7$ long-term history time series at an interval of 1 day for a week to predict $T_f = 12$ next time steps. The temporal encoders and spatial encoder both use $N_b = 4$ layers of transformer block with 4 attention heads. The hidden dimension d of each history time step is set to 4. A batch size of 32 is employed for model training, with the Adam optimizer utilizing a learning rate of 0.001. Dropout with p=0.5 is applied in transformer blocks. Regarding the dataset splits, for PEMS04 and PEMS08, we use 60% of data for training, 20% of data for testing, and 20% of data for validation; for PEMS-BAY, we use 70% of data for training, 20% of data for testing, and 10% of data for validation. The evaluation of model performance is measured using three metrics: Mean Absolute Error (MAE), Mean Absolute Percentage Error (MAPE), and Root Mean Square Error (RMSE).

5.4 Main Result

The results of the comparison of SSTAN with baselines in predicting the next 15, 30, and 60 min on PEMS04, PEMS08, and PEMS-BAY are presented in Table 2.

Table 2. Performance comparison of Sampling Spatial-Temporal Attention Network with baselines on PEMS04, PEMS08, and PEMS-BAY datasets. We keep the same dataset splits with previous works [14,18], and the results of baselines are cited from [14].

Datasets	Models	Horizon 3			Horizon 6			Horizon 12		
		MAE	RMSE	MAPE	MAE	RMSE	MAPE	MAE	RMSE	MAPE
PEMS04	FC-LSTM	21.37	33.31	15.21%	23.72	36.58	18.02%	26.76	40.28	20.94%
	DCRNN	18.53	29.61	12.71%	19.65	31.37	13.45%	21.67	34.19	15.03%
	GWNet	18.00	28.83	13.64%	18.96	30.33	14.23%	20.53	32.54	15.41%
	GMAN	18.27	29.35	12.66%	18.81	30.85	13.25%	20.01	**31.32**	13.40%
	STID	**17.51**	**28.48**	12.00%	18.29	29.86	12.46%	19.58	31.79	13.38%
	SSTAN	17.53	28.50	**11.96%**	**18.27**	**29.80**	**12.37%**	**19.41**	31.49	**13.32%**
PEMS08	FC-LSTM	17.38	26.27	12.63%	21.22	31.97	17.32%	30.69	43.96	25.72%
	DCRNN	14.16	22.20	9.31%	15.24	24.26	9.90%	17.70	27.14	11.13%
	GWNet	13.72	21.71	8.80%	14.67	23.50	9.49%	16.15	25.95	10.74%
	GMAN	13.80	22.88	9.41%	14.62	24.12	9.57%	15.72	26.47	10.56%
	STID	13.28	21.66	8.62%	14.21	23.57	9.24%	15.58	25.89	10.33%
	SSTAN	**13.16**	**21.36**	**8.34%**	**13.73**	**22.76**	**8.77%**	**14.33**	**24.16**	**9.46%**
PEMS-BAY	FC-LSTM	2.05	4.19	4.80%	2.20	4.55	5.20%	2.37	4.96	5.70%
	DCRNN	1.31	2.80	2.73%	1.67	3.81	3.75%	1.99	4.66	4.73%
	GWNet	1.30	2.78	**2.71%**	1.63	3.73	3.66%	1.95	4.52	4.63%
	GMAN	1.34	2.92	2.88%	1.65	3.81	3.71%	1.89	4.38	4.51%
	STID	1.30	2.81	2.73%	1.62	3.72	3.68%	1.89	4.40	4.47%
	SSTAN	**1.29**	**2.75**	**2.71%**	**1.56**	**3.57**	**3.54%**	**1.79**	**4.17**	**4.30%**

On all datasets, SSTAN demonstrates superior performance in horizons 6 and 12, indicating that it is more effective and stable in long-term prediction. Furthermore, SSTAN's performance in short-term prediction still remains competitive. FC-LSTM fails to perform well in all horizons due to its lack of consideration of spatial dependencies. DCRNN overcomes this limitation by using a predefined graph to extract basic spatial features. However, some crucial spatial dependencies may not be captured from the pre-defined graph. In contrast, Graph WaveNet can capture the hidden spatial dependencies better by generating an adaptive adjacent matrix without relying on a predefined graph, leading to better performance. GMAN adopts a multi-head attention mechanism, including spatial, temporal, and transform attention, which allows it to effectively handle long-term prediction tasks. STID introduces spatial and temporal identity into the data, achieving promising performance with a simple network architecture. The remarkable performance demonstrated by Graph WaveNet and GMAN highlights the crucial importance of adaptive graph modeling. The spatial encoder of our proposed model employs global attention on the entire graph to capture the interdependence among nodes and effectively extracts the time-varying dynamic spatial features. In addition, our model achieves remarkable performance in long-term prediction by utilizing stacked layers of temporal encoders to learn periodic temporal features separately and aggregating them as long-short-term temporal features. Finally, by combining global spatial features and long-short-term temporal features, our model is able to differentiate similar series, which are hard to identify solely based on local information.

5.5   Ablation Study

SSTAN consists of three primary components with different functionalities: the long-term series sampling for identifying periodic features, temporal encoders for extracting short-term temporal features, and a spatial encoder for learning the deep dependencies among nodes. To have a better insight into the contributions of each component, an ablation study is conducted on PEMS04 with three variants:

- **SSTAN w/o long-term sampling**: without long-term series sampling, the input series only contain $X^i_{t+1-T_h:t}$. Therefore, only one temporal encoder is required to process short-term series rather than the originally proposed 8 layers of the temporal encoder.
- **SSTAN w/o temporal encoders**: all temporal encoders are removed from the model to demonstrate the effectiveness of short-term temporal feature extraction.
- **SSTAN w/o spatial encoder**: the spatial encoder is eliminated so that the processing of the series of different nodes is separate and independent.

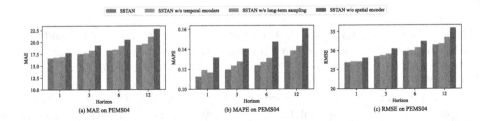

Fig. 3. Ablation Study on PEMS04

As is shown in Fig. 3, SSTAN consistently outperforms other variants, especially in the long-term prediction, which suggests that all three main components have a positive effect on SSTAN. Meanwhile, SSTAN w/o spatial encoder exhibits the poorest performance, indicating the critical significance of dynamic graph learning. Furthermore, the superiority of SSTAN over SSTAN w/o temporal encoders demonstrates that short-term temporal feature extraction and aggregation play a positive role in forecasting. Lastly, it is noticeable that SSTAN w/o long-term sampling is competitive in short-term prediction, but fails to attain equally excellent performance in long-term prediction. This shows the fact that the periodic temporal features learned from sampled series enable SSTAN to forecast more stably.

5.6   Study of Spatial Encoder

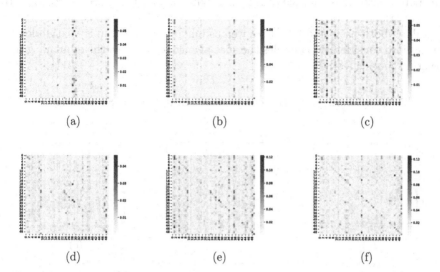

(a)   (b)   (c)

(d)   (e)   (f)

Fig. 4. The heatmaps of attention scores for the first 50 nodes of PEMS04. (a)(b)(c)(d) Attention scores of first, second, third, and fourth transformer blocks for the first series. (e)(f) The sum of attention scores for the first and second series.

In this subsection, we aim to explore the dynamic graph structure that the spatial encoder learns. To investigate the dynamic graph structures learned by different transformer blocks, we randomly choose two historical series from the PEMS04 dataset and visualize the attention scores of 4 transformer blocks for the first 50 nodes as shown in Fig. 4.

Basic Graph Structure. It is noticeable that the first and second transformer blocks primarily learn the graph structure of the nodes that are highly influenced by others as shown in Fig. 4(a)(b). This means that the basic graph structure is captured in the shallow transformer block layers.

Latent Spatial Dependencies. Conversely, the graph structures learned by the third and fourth transformer blocks are considerably complicated, with a larger number of nodes exhibiting strong interactions with others in Fig. 4(c)(d). This demonstrates that the deeper transformer blocks focus on the latent spatial dependencies between nodes.

Inherent Individual Spatial Features . The third and fourth transformer blocks' attention in Fig. 4(c)(d) are mainly self-directed, suggesting that they also extract inherent and independent features of individual nodes.

Dynamic Graph Structure. The significant difference between the sum of attention scores for two different series illustrated in Fig. 4(e)(f) indicates that the spatial encoder is capable of learning dynamic graph structure according to different traffic states.

Taking both basic and latent, as well as inherent and dynamic spatial dependencies into consideration enables the spatial encoder to learn the dynamic graph structure more effectively.

5.7   Study of Temporal Encoders with Long-Term Sampling

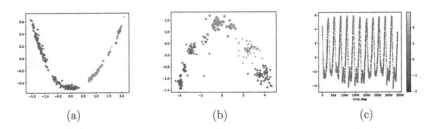

(a)   (b)   (c)

Fig. 5. Temporal features extracted by temporal encoders. (a) Clustering of 260 series with 5 different patterns based on short-term features. Shapes represent different time patterns. Colors represent the clustering results. (b) Clustering of 260 series with 5 different patterns based on both long-term and short-term features. (c) Temporal features for each time step.

In this subsection, two experiments are conducted on the PEMS04 dataset to explore what temporal encoders have learned from sampled series.

Different Time Patterns. Firstly, to determine whether temporal encoders can discern various time patterns and whether long-term sampling can enhance spatial-temporal distinguishability, we randomly select 260 input series with five distinct patterns. We then process the temporal features outputted by temporal encoders to two-dimensional points using Principal Component Analysis (PCA) [1] and cluster these 260 points using the KMeans method [13]. As illustrated in Fig. 5(a)(b), points with the same shape belong to the same time pattern, and the colors represent the clustering results. Our results demonstrate that with short-term features, 75 out of 260 points are clustered incorrectly as is shown in Fig. 5(a), while only 4 out of 260 points are clustered into wrong time patterns when considering long-term features as in Fig. 5(b). This indicates that temporal encoders effectively differentiate distinct time patterns with the global information captured from short-term and long-term series.

Long-term Periodicity. As traffic sequences exhibit clear periodicity, we aim to investigate whether temporal encoders have acquired the knowledge of recurring patterns. As is shown in Fig. 5(c), the temporal features extracted by temporal encoders at each time step are transformed into two-dimensional points using

PCA and plotted on the y-coordinate with varying colors. The result shows that the temporal features obtained by temporal encoders are also periodic, indicating that temporal encoders can learn the long-term periodic pattern.

The results of the two aforementioned experiments demonstrate that temporal encoders are capable of extracting long-term periodic temporal features while also distinguishing between different time patterns, which enables temporal encoders to provide characteristics of both history and the future.

6 Conclusion

In this paper, we proposed an innovative and effective model SSTAN to tackle the challenges of long-term periodic time pattern learning, dynamic spatial dependencies reconstruction, and spatial-temporal indistinguishability in traffic forecasting. The model employs discrete long-term sampling to enable temporal encoders to extract long-term periodic temporal features with low complexity. In addition, a spatial encoder is used to reconstruct the dynamic graph that contains both basic, latent, and inherent spatial dependencies. The proposed framework of temporal encoders and the spatial encoder can be applied to other downstream tasks, considering their effectiveness in encoding deep spatial-temporal representations. The results of experiments conducted on three real-world datasets demonstrate the superiority of SSTAN in spatial-temporal dependencies learning.

Acknowledgement. This work was supported by the National Natural Science Foundation of China (62272023, 51991391, 51991395).

References

1. Abdi, H., Williams, L.J.: Principal component analysis. Wiley Interdiscip. Rev.: Comput. Stat. **2**(4), 433–459 (2010)
2. Akaike, H.: Maximum likelihood identification of gaussian autoregressive moving average models. Biometrika **60**(2), 255–265 (1973)
3. Bai, L., Yao, L., Li, C., Wang, X., Wang, C.: Adaptive graph convolutional recurrent network for traffic forecasting. Adv. Neural. Inf. Process. Syst. **33**, 17804–17815 (2020)
4. Cao, D., et al.: Spectral temporal graph neural network for multivariate time-series forecasting. Adv. Neural. Inf. Process. Syst. **33**, 17766–17778 (2020)
5. Chen, C., Petty, K., Skabardonis, A., Varaiya, P., Jia, Z.: Freeway performance measurement system: mining loop detector data. Transp. Res. Rec. **1748**(1), 96–102 (2001)
6. Cho, K., Van Merriënboer, B., Bahdanau, D., Bengio, Y.: On the properties of neural machine translation: Encoder-decoder approaches. arXiv preprint arXiv:1409.1259 (2014)
7. Guo, S., Lin, Y., Feng, N., Song, C., Wan, H.: Attention based spatial-temporal graph convolutional networks for traffic flow forecasting. In: Proceedings of the AAAI Conference On Artificial Intelligence. vol. 33, pp. 922–929 (2019)

8. Han, L., Du, B., Sun, L., Fu, Y., Lv, Y., Xiong, H.: Dynamic and multi-faceted spatio-temporal deep learning for traffic speed forecasting. In: Proceedings of the 27th ACM SIGKDD Conference on Knowledge Discovery and Data Mining, pp. 547–555 (2021)
9. Hochreiter, S., Schmidhuber, J.: Long short-term memory. Neural Comput. **9**(8), 1735–1780 (1997)
10. Kipf, T.N., Welling, M.: Semi-supervised classification with graph convolutional networks. arXiv preprint arXiv:1609.02907 (2016)
11. Li, Y., Yu, R., Shahabi, C., Liu, Y.: Diffusion convolutional recurrent neural network: Data-driven traffic forecasting. arXiv preprint arXiv:1707.01926 (2017)
12. Lv, Y., Duan, Y., Kang, W., Li, Z., Wang, F.Y.: Traffic flow prediction with big data: a deep learning approach. IEEE Trans. Intell. Transp. Syst. **16**(2), 865–873 (2014)
13. MacQueen, J.: Classification and analysis of multivariate observations. In: 5th Berkeley Symp. Math. Statist. Probability, pp. 281–297. University of California Los Angeles LA USA (1967)
14. Shao, Z., Zhang, Z., Wang, F., Wei, W., Xu, Y.: Spatial-temporal identity: A simple yet effective baseline for multivariate time series forecasting. In: Proceedings of the 31st ACM International Conference on Information and Knowledge Management, pp. 4454–4458 (2022)
15. Song, C., Lin, Y., Guo, S., Wan, H.: Spatial-temporal synchronous graph convolutional networks: A new framework for spatial-temporal network data forecasting. In: Proceedings of the AAAI Conference on Artificial Intelligence. vol. 34, pp. 914–921 (2020)
16. Stathopoulos, A., Karlaftis, M.G.: A multivariate state space approach for urban traffic flow modeling and prediction. Transp. Res. Part C: Emerg. Technol. **11**(2), 121–135 (2003)
17. Vaswani, A., et al.: Attention is all you need. In: Advances in Neural Information Processing Systems, vol. 30 (2017)
18. Wu, Z., Pan, S., Long, G., Jiang, J., Zhang, C.: Graph wavenet for deep spatial-temporal graph modeling. arXiv preprint arXiv:1906.00121 (2019)
19. Yu, B., Yin, H., Zhu, Z.: Spatio-temporal graph convolutional networks: A deep learning framework for traffic forecasting. arXiv preprint arXiv:1709.04875 (2017)
20. Zhao, L., et al.: T-gcn: a temporal graph convolutional network for traffic prediction. IEEE Trans. Intell. Transp. Syst. **21**(9), 3848–3858 (2019)
21. Zheng, C., Fan, X., Wang, C., Qi, J.: Gman: A graph multi-attention network for traffic prediction. In: Proceedings of the AAAI Conference on Artificial Intelligence. vol. 34, pp. 1234–1241 (2020)
22. Zivot, E., Wang, J.: Vector autoregressive models for multivariate time series. Modeling financial time series with S-PLUS®, pp. 385–429 (2006)

ST-MAN: Spatio-Temporal Multimodal Attention Network for Traffic Prediction

Ruozhou He[1]📷, Liting Li[1]📷, Bei Hua[1(✉)]📷, Jianjun Tong[2], and Chang Tan[2]

[1] School of Computer Science and Technology, University of Science and Technology of China, Hefei 230027, Anhui, China
{fward,ltli}@mail.ustc.edu.cn, bhua@ustc.edu.cn
[2] iFLYTEK CO., LTD., Hefei 230088, Anhui, China
{jjtong,changtan2}@iflytek.com

Abstract. Traffic prediction is an essential part of Intelligent Transportation System (ITS). Existing work typically use unimodal traffic data, combining with road network graph or external factors (e.g., weather, POIs) for prediction. However, in real traffic systems multimodal traffic data are collected from one or more co-located sensors, and data of non-target modality are not fully utilized by existing work. To overcome this limitation, we utilize multimodal traffic data to improve target prediction tasks. We propose a novel Spatio-Temporal Multimodal Attention Network (ST-MAN) for traffic prediction. Firstly, we design a cross-modal attention mechanism to learn dynamic inter-modal correlations. Secondly, we propose a compact yet effective multimodal fusion framework to exploit both the inter-modal and intra-modal correlations. Thirdly, a refined spatio-temporal embedding mechanism is designed to feed in more implicit information. Extensive experiments on three real-world datasets show that ST-MAN not only outperforms state-of-the-art methods in all aspects, but also has high computational efficiency. Moreover, the framework is easily generalized to include more data modalities.

Keywords: Spatio-temporal prediction · Traffic prediction · Multimodal · Attention Mechanism · Intelligent Transportation Systems

1 Introduction

Traffic prediction aims to predict future traffic conditions (e.g., traffic volume, vehicle speed, or occupancy rate) in road network based on historical observations. Accurate prediction can assist route planning, guide vehicle dispatching, mitigate traffic congestion, etc.

In recent years researchers resort to deep neural networks to capture spatial and temporal correlations in traffic data [4, 11, 17, 19–21, 23]. However, most

---

L. Li—The majority of this work was done during their internship in iFLYTEK CO., LTD.

© The Author(s), under exclusive license to Springer Nature Switzerland AG 2023
Z. Jin et al. (Eds.): KSEM 2023, LNAI 14118, pp. 137–152, 2023.
https://doi.org/10.1007/978-3-031-40286-9_12

existing works use only one traffic condition to do the prediction work, e.g., using historical vehicle speeds to predict future vehicle speeds, and some of them may combine external factors such as weather, dates, and POIs to improve prediction accuracy. In real traffic systems, different kinds of sensors (e.g., loop detectors and cameras) are deployed at observation points, and different traffic conditions (e.g., traffic volume, vehicle speed, and occupancy rate) are collected simultaneously by these sensors. In the rest of this paper, each traffic condition is called a data modality.

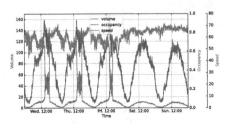 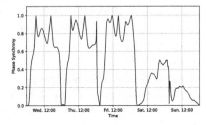

(a) A data fragment in the Seattle Loop Dataset [2], shows certain correlations between volume, occupancy, and speed.

(b) Instantaneous phase synchronization between volume and speed. The phase of the signal is obtained by the Hilbert transform.

Fig. 1. Phenomenon of cross-modal data correlations

There are correlations between these different data modalities (inter-modal correlations), as they characterize the situation of the same traffic system from different aspects. Figure 1(a) shows a data fragment in the Seattle Loop Dataset [2] that displays the traffic volume, vehicle speed, and occupancy rate across five days. It is obvious that on weekdays a surge in traffic volume is accompanied by a sharp drop in vehicle speed and a rapid increase in occupancy rate, showing strong inter-modal correlations. Such strong correlations would be helpful to improve the prediction accuracy of the target modality. However, the correlation strength varies over time, e.g., on weekends a rapid rise in traffic volume is not accompanied by an apparent decrease in vehicle speed or a significant increase in occupancy rate. Such weak correlations or even irrelevant information between modalities could be detrimental to prediction accuracy. Figure 1(b) shows the instantaneous phase synchronization between traffic volume and vehicle speed in Fig. 1(a). It is clear that phase synchronization between them is stronger on weekdays than on weekends, validating the existence of changing inter-modal correlation strengths.

More recently, some researchers have noticed that additional data modality may help to improve traffic prediction accuracy. Huang et al. [7] and Han et al. [5] fuse traffic modalities like traffic volume, vehicle speed, and occupancy rate to predict traffic speed. However, these works neglect the fact that inter-modal correlations change over time and thus fail to use them properly, i.e., did not make good use of strong correlations and meanwhile ignore weak correlations or irrelevant information. This limits the benefits of using multimodal information. How to exploit the dynamically changing inter-modal correlations is a challenge.

In addition to complex inter-modal correlations, there are also complex spatio-temporal correlations within a data modality (intra-modal correlations). A lot of works have explored this issue and revealed that spatial correlations exist between sensor nodes due to road network and POI distributions, and temporal correlations exist between time steps due to people's daily lifestyles. Actually, spatial correlations also change with time, e.g., correlations between nodes located in residential areas and work areas are stronger on weekday mornings, and correlations between nodes located in residential areas and business districts are stronger on weekends. How to deal with dynamic inter-modal and intra-modal correlations in an effective and comprehensive way is another challenge.

In this paper, we propose a multimodal traffic prediction network, called Spatio-Temporal Multimodal Attention Network (ST-MAN). Unlike existing methods, ST-MAN exploits multiple spatio-temporally correlated traffic conditions to predict one of them. To address the first challenge, a cross-modal attention mechanism is designed that first learns dynamic inter-modal correlations based on feature representations of all modalities through a cross-modal attention module, and then extracts salient correlations through max-pooling fusion. To address the second challenge, a multimodal fusion framework is proposed that connects inter-modal learning with intra-modal learning to form a linear backbone, and uses well-designed spatio-temporal attention blocks to mine intra-modal correlations.

The main contributions of this paper are summarized as follows:

- We design a distinctive cross-modal attention mechanism that can automatically extract strong correlations while suppressing weak correlations or irrelevant information between modalities.
- We propose a compact yet effective multimodal fusion framework that can comprehensively introduce inter-modal and intra-modal correlations in a natural way; moreover, it can be easily generalized to use more data modalities without modifying the backbone architecture.
- We conduct extensive experiments on three real-world large-scale datasets. Experimental results show that ST-MAN consistently outperforms all the baselines to achieve state-of-the-art prediction accuracy. Moreover, it achieves the highest computation efficiency. ST-MAN is easily reproducible, and source code is available at https://github.com/HowardZorn/ST-MAN.

2 Related Works

2.1 Traffic Prediction

Traffic prediction is a spatio-temporal prediction task that has been studied for decades. As traditional machine learning methods like Auto-Regressive Integrated Moving Average (ARIMA) [16] are not adequate to handle time series with complicated and long-term dependencies, Long Short-Term Memory

(LSTM) networks [14] originally proposed for sequence transduction is applied to traffic series to learn dynamic temporal correlations [11]. To model spatial correlations, Zhang et al. [20] introduce CNN to model spatial correlations in Euclidean space, and later Yu et al. [19] adopt spectral-based GCN to model non-Euclidean spatial correlations in the road network. Li et al. [11] apply Diffusion Convolution to model the spatial dependency as diffusion processes on the directed graph. Based on Yu et al. [19], Guo et al. [4] introduce spatial and temporal attention mechanisms to better capture the spatio-temporal correlations in traffic series. STFGNN learns hidden spatio-temporal dependencies by a novel graph fusion operation that fuses spatial graphs with multiple temporal graphs based on time series analysis [10]. Recently, self-attention is popular and several traffic prediction models based on Transformer are proposed [18,23].

2.2 Fusion Methods in Traffic Prediction

Information fusion methods used in traffic prediction can be divided into two main categories: feature fusion and multi-graph fusion. Feature fusion is the most common method that extracts features from different aspects and incorporates them in the prediction network. Li et al. [12] propose a structure called MFFB that fuses temporal features, spatial features and external features (e.g., weather, events, etc.) using softmax attention. Zhao et al. [22] adopt feature transformer to map low-level additional features to a high level feature, which is then combined with spatio-temporal features directly. Multi-graph fusion usually constructs multiple network graphs from different aspects, and combines them to mine more correlations in the data. Jin et al. [8] integrate graph information from grid-based map and network topology, thus obtaining spatial correlations related to Euclidean distance and road network structure. Li et al. [10] fuse various spatial and temporal graphs to learn hidden dependencies. However, few current methods are about multimodal fusion in the field of traffic prediction. Huang et al. [7] model the multimodal traffic data through attention mechanism, but only use simple concatenation to fuse multimodal features. Han et al. [5] handle primary modality and auxiliary modality through Primary Block and Auxiliary Block respectively, and fuse unaligned traffic volume and vehicle speed data by dimensional transformation. None of them took into account dynamically changed inter-modal correlations.

3 Preliminaries

We define a road network as a directed graph $\mathcal{G} = (\mathcal{V}, \mathcal{E}, \mathcal{A})$, where $\mathcal{V}$ is a set of nodes representing all the sensors in the network ($|\mathcal{V}| = N$), $\mathcal{E}$ is a set of edges representing the connectivity between nodes; and $\mathcal{A} \in \mathbb{R}^{N \times N}$ is an adjacency matrix where each element represents the proximity (calculated from road network distance) between a pair of nodes.

The number of time steps contained in a given dataset is denoted as L. At a certain time step t, the traffic conditions of the road network are denoted as

$X^t \in \mathbb{R}^{N \times C}$, where C is the number of traffic conditions (e.g., traffic volume, vehicle speed, occupancy rate, etc.); the traffic condition that we need to predict for future time step t' is denoted as $\hat{X}^{t'} \in \mathbb{R}^{N \times 1}$. In addition, we use D to denote the dimension of the hidden space of the model.

Given the historical traffic conditions on graph $\mathcal{G}$ at the previous T time steps, the goal is to predict the traffic condition at the next T' time steps on $\mathcal{G}$. In general, traffic prediction is to learn a mapping function f:

$$[X^{(t-T+1)}, \cdots, X^t; \mathcal{G}] \xrightarrow{f} [\hat{X}^{(t+1)}, \cdots, \hat{X}^{(t+T')}].$$

4   Model Architecture

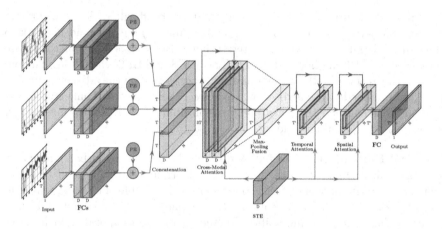

Fig. 2. The overall architecture of ST-MAN. As an example, we use three traffic modalities to predict one target modality. In this figure, the green directed lines represent the data flow, and the blue directed lines represent residual connections [6]. To facilitate these residual connections, all modules in the model produce their outputs in the same D-dimensional space. (Color figure online)

The framework of our traffic prediction model, called Spatio-Temporal Multimodal Attention Network(ST-MAN), is illustrated in Fig. 2. Multimodal inputs are first transformed into a D-dimensional space through two fully connected layers, then Positional Encoding [15] is applied to inject the temporal position information of T time steps. Hidden space representations of all modalities are concatenated. Then a Cross-Modal Attention is applied to extract intra-modal and inter-modal spatio-temporal correlations for each modality, and after that, a Max-Pooling Fusion Layer is used to obtain the salient correlations from them. The spatio-temporal correlations learned for the previous T time steps are transformed by a Spatio-Temporal Attention Block, consisting of a Temporal Attention followed by a Spatial Attention, into representations for the future T' time steps. At last, the predicted traffic condition is obtained through a fully connected layer. To feed more useful information into the model, mainly the road network structure (spatial information) and the periodic patterns of traffic data (temporal information), a Spatio-Temporal Embedding (STE) is used to encode and provide the information for attention modules.

The main details of the framework are introduced as follows.

4.1 Spatio-Temporal Embedding

In order for the attention mechanisms to learn more about the spatio-temporal information contained in the traffic data, we propose a well-designed Spatio-Temporal Embedding block that consists of a Spatial Embedding module and a Temporal Embedding module.

Spatial Embedding. As the adjacency matrix is difficult to be used directly by attention networks, we adopt graph embedding to map the road network to a low-dimensional hidden space. After trying various embedding methods, we choose *node2vec* [3] method as it can balance DFS and BFS when doing random walks on the graph. Firstly, a random walk is performed on the adjacency matrix A to get an embedding matrix using *node2vec*, then two fully connected layers are used to strengthen the feature expression ability of the embedding matrix and output the spatial embedding SE.

Temporal Embedding. Affected by people's daily lifestyles, urban traffic flow exhibits cyclical characteristics, such as the daytime peak hours and the late-night troughs. Although the attention mechanism is capable of learning temporal correlations in traffic data, we consider that explicit use of periodicity information can enhance its learning ability. Therefore, we use temporal embedding to exploit the periodic patterns in traffic data.

Fast Fourier Transform (FFT) can convert time-domain sampling into frequency-domain sampling to study the spectral structure of the signal efficiently [1]. We apply FFT to Seattle-Loop dataset and get the results in Fig. 3, where the horizontal axis is harmonic frequency, and the vertical axis is amplitude. As the sampling period of traffic data is 5 min (i.e., 300 s), the fundamental frequency is $1/300$ Hz. After converting frequency into period, the six peaks in Fig. 3 represent periods of 1-week, 1-day, 12-h, 8-h, 6-h, and 4-h from left to right. Then we use one-hot encoding to encode the above periodic information and further integrate it into the model through fully connected layers. At last, we get the corresponding temporal embedding TE.

Spatio-Temporal Embedding. We add spatial embedding SE and temporal embedding TE to form Spatio-Temporal Embedding E, which will further provide spatial-temporal information for attention modules.

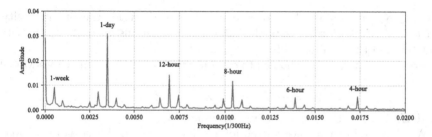

Fig. 3. Result of FFT on Seattle-Loop dataset. The 6 peaks from left to right correspond to periods of 1-week, 1-day, 12-h, 8-h, 6-h, and 4-h, respectively.

4.2 Cross-Modal Attention Module

Based on self-attention mechanism [15], we propose Cross-Modal Attention to extract inter-modal correlations between modalities. Actually, Cross-Modal Attention also extracts intra-modal correlations simultaneously. The key idea is to assign proper attention weights indicating different correlation strengths between different modalities.

As shown in Fig. 2, the Cross-Modal Attention module consists of a Concatenation layer and a Cross-Modal Attention layer. Let $Z_1, Z_2, \ldots, Z_i, \ldots, Z_n$ denote the input of the Cross-Modal Attention module, where $Z_i \in \mathbb{R}^{N \times T \times D}$ corresponds to the features of the i-th modality.

Firstly, all the Z_i's are concatenated to obtain $\mathbf{Z} = (Z_1, Z_2, \ldots, Z_i, \ldots, Z_n)^T \in \mathbb{R}^{N \times nT \times D}$. Please note that we concatenate all the features in the time dimension instead of in the hidden space dimension. This enables the dynamic correlations between multimodal data at different time steps to be learned and processed by the subsequent Cross-Modal Attention layer, and thus the time-varying inter-modal correlations can be exploited. Secondly, we concatenate Z with E to obtain $\mathbf{I}$ as the input of the Cross-Modal Attention layer, which allows the prior spatio-temporal knowledge to be fully utilized.

The queries Q, keys K and values V are formed with the following equations:

$$
\begin{aligned}
Q &= \mathrm{ReLU}(\mathbf{I}W_Q + b_Q) = (Q_1, Q_2, \ldots, Q_n)^T, \\
K &= \mathrm{ReLU}(\mathbf{I}W_K + b_K) = (K_1, K_2, \ldots, K_n)^T, \\
V &= \mathrm{ReLU}(\mathbf{I}W_V + b_V) = (V_1, V_2, \ldots, V_n)^T,
\end{aligned}
\tag{1}
$$

where W and b are learnable parameters. Then the attention matrix A is computed as:

$$
\begin{aligned}
A &= \mathrm{softmax}\left(\frac{Q \cdot K^{\mathrm{T}}}{\sqrt{d}}\right) \\
&= \mathrm{softmax}\left(\frac{1}{\sqrt{d}}
\begin{bmatrix}
Q_1 K_1^T & Q_1 K_2^T & \ldots & Q_1 K_n^T \\
Q_2 K_1^T & Q_2 K_2^T & \ldots & Q_2 K_n^T \\
\vdots & \vdots & \ddots & \vdots \\
Q_n K_1^T & Q_n K_2^T & \ldots & Q_n K_n^T
\end{bmatrix}\right),
\end{aligned}
\tag{2}
$$

where $Q_i K_i{}^T$ represents the intra-modal relationship inside the i-th modality, and $Q_i K_j{}^T$ $(i \neq j)$ represents the inter-modal relationship between the i-th modality and the j-th modality.

After that, values V are joined to compute the output $\mathbf{Z}'$ of the Cross-Modal Attention:

$$\mathbf{Z}' = A \cdot V = \left(Z_1{}', Z_2{}', \ldots, Z_n{}' \right)^T, \tag{3}$$

where $Z_i{}'$ denotes the output of the i-th modality.

We also employ multi-head attention mechanism [15] and Feed-Forward Networks(FFN) to further exploit the information from different subspaces. For brevity, we will cover the details of multi-head attention in Sect. 4.4.

4.3 Max-Pooling Fusion Layer

After getting the feature representations containing inter-modal correlations for each modality, how to aggregate this information to benefit our target prediction task is a problem. To get a more stable prediction performance, We use a Max-Pooling Fusion Layer to extract salient correlations for downstream tasks and suppress non-salient correlations to prevent negative effects.

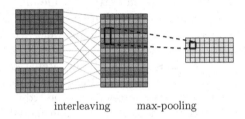

interleaving   max-pooling

Fig. 4. The max-pooling fusion layer. Feature representations of different modalities are aggregated to serve downstream tasks.

Figure 4 shows the processing method of max-pooling fusion. The input feature tensors of all modalities $(Z_1, Z_2, \ldots, Z_n)$ are first interleaved to form a new tensor as described in the middle part of Fig. 4, then a $n \times 1$ max-pooling is performed on the interleaved tensor to extract the most salient correlations, as shown in the right part of Fig. 4. The output Z' of the max-pooling layer is denoted as:

$$Z' = \text{MaxPooling}(\text{Interleaving}(Z_1, Z_2, \ldots, Z_n)). \tag{4}$$

4.4 Spatio-Temporal Attention Block

With the feature representations output by Max-pooling Fusion Layer, we have obtained consistent characterizations of the traffic system from all modalities. To deeply mine the spatio-temporal correlations hidden in the traffic data, the feature representations are further input into a Spatio-Temporal Attention Block composed of a Temporal Attention module followed by a Spatial Attention module. Each Attention module consists of a self-attention layer and an FFN.

Temporal Attention. We apply multi-head attention mechanism [15] to improve the representation of multiple subspaces. Assuming the number of attention heads is H, then the dimension of each head is $d = D/H$, and the superscript (h) represents the h-th head.

Equation 5 shows how temporal correlations between time steps are calculated for a given node ν, in the form of element-level operations:

$$
\begin{aligned}
s_{\nu,t_i,t_j}^{(h)} &= \frac{\mathbf{q}_{\nu,t_i}^{(h)} \cdot \mathbf{k}_{\nu,t_j}^{(h)}}{\sqrt{d}}, \\
\alpha_{\nu,t_i,t_j}^{(h)} &= \frac{\exp(s_{\nu,t_i,t_j}^{(h)})}{\sum_{t \in T} \exp(s_{\nu,t_i,t}^{(h)})},
\end{aligned}
\tag{5}
$$

where $\mathbf{q}_{\nu,t_i}^{(h)} \in \mathbb{R}^d$ is a vector which represents the query value for node ν at time step t_i, $\mathbf{k}_{\nu,t_j}^{(h)} \in \mathbb{R}^d$ is a vector which represents the key value for node ν at time step t_j, s_{ν,t_i,t_j} indicates the relevance between time steps t_i and t_j for node ν, and α_{ν,t_i,t_j} is the attention score indicating the importance of time step t_i to t_j for node ν.

Spatial Attention. Multi-head self-attention mechanism is also used to design the spatial attention, with the same number of heads. The main difference from Temporal Attention is that the relevance between time steps is computed in Temporal Attention, while the relevance between nodes needs to be computed in Spatial Attention.

Specifically, Eq. 6 shows how spatial correlations between nodes are calculated at a certain time step τ, in the form of element-level operations:

$$
\begin{aligned}
s_{\tau,v_i,v_j}^{(h)} &= \frac{\mathbf{q}_{\tau,v_i}^{(h)} \cdot \mathbf{k}_{\tau,v_j}^{(h)}}{\sqrt{d}}, \\
\alpha_{\tau,v_i,v_j}^{(h)} &= \frac{\exp(s_{\tau,v_i,v_j}^{(h)})}{\sum_{v \in V} \exp(s_{\tau,v_i,v}^{(h)})},
\end{aligned}
\tag{6}
$$

where $\mathbf{q}_{\tau,v_i}^{(h)}$ is a vector representing the query value for node v_i at time step τ, $\mathbf{k}_{\tau,v_j}^{(h)}$ is a vector representing the key value for node v_j at time step τ, s_{τ,v_i,v_j} indicates the relevance between nodes v_i and v_j at time step τ, and α_{τ,v_i,v_j} is the attention weight indicating the importance of node v_i to v_j at time step τ.

5   Experiments

5.1   Experimental Settings

Experimental Environment. The hardware platform is a server equipped with Intel Xeon E5-2650 v3/2.30 GHz CPUs and an NVIDIA GeForce RTX 2080 Ti/12 GB GPU. The deep learning framework we use is PyTorch.

Datasets. We evaluate ST-MAN on three real-world large-scale datasets.

- **Seattle Inductive Loop Detector Dataset (Loop)** contains 2 months (7/1/2015 – 8/31/2015) of traffic volume, speed, and occupancy rate data collected from 323 inductive loop detectors on freeways in the Seattle area.[1]
- **PeMS04** contains 2 months (01/01/2018–02/28/2018) of traffic volume, speed, and occupancy rate data collected from 307 sensors in the Bay Area;
- **PeMS08** contains 2 months (7/1/2016–8/31/2016) of traffic volume, speed, and occupancy rate data collected from 170 sensors in the San Bernardino Area[2];

All data are aggregated into 5-min windows. ST-MAN makes use of all three modalities to make predictions.

Data Preprocessing. We normalize the traffic data using Z-Score, same as the previous work [11]. Each dataset is divided in chronological order into a training set, a validation set and a test set. To be consistent with the previous work [10], PeMS04 and PeMS08 are divided according to the ratio of 6:2:2. For the Loop dataset, we follow the common division ratio of 7:1:2.

Hyperparameters. ST-MAN uses the traffic conditions at the previous 12 time steps (1 h) to predict the traffic states at the future 12 time steps (1 h), i.e., $T = T' = 12$. The following hyperparameters are tuned on the validation set to achieve the highest prediction accuracy. The batch size for training is set to 16, and an early stop is set to avoid overfitting (patience = 7). The model is trained using Adam optimizer [9] with an initial learning rate of 0.001. As training progresses, we use a decay rate of 0.97 to reduce the learning rate gradually. As for multi-head attention, we set the number of attention heads to $H = 8$ and the dimension of each head to $d = 8$.

Baselines

1. Diffusion Convolutional Recurrent Neural Network (DCRNN) [11] that models the traffic flow as a diffusion process on a directed graph;
2. Attention Based Spatial-Temporal Graph Convolutional Networks (AST-GCN) [4] that uses attention and graph convolution for traffic prediction;
3. Graph WaveNet [17], a graph neural network model with self-adaptive adjacency matrix that captures spatio-temporal dependencies efficiently by combining graph convolution with dilated casual convolution;
4. Spatial-Temporal Synchronous Graph Convolutional Networks (STSGCN) [13] that utilizes localized spatio-temporal subgraph module to capture the complex localized spatio-temporal correlations;
5. Spatial-Temporal Fusion Graph Neural Networks (STFGNN) [10] that captures spatio-temporal dependencies using a novel fusion operation and achieves excellent results on PeMS04 and PeMS08 datasets;

---

[1] This dataset is released by Cui et al. [2].
[2] These two datasets are released by Guo et al. [4].

6. Multi-relational Synchronous Graph Attention Network (MS-GAT) [7] that models channel, temporal, and spatial relations based on graph attention scheme;
7. Dynamic and Multi-faceted Spatio-Temporal Graph Convolution Network (DMSTGCN) [5] that explores the dynamic and multimodal spatio-temporal correlations of traffic data.

For each comparative experiment, we run ST-MAN and each other model three times and average the experimental results.

Loss. We use MAE (Mean Absolute Error) to estimate the loss of ST-MAN, as shown in Eq. 7, and the model parameters Θ are updated via back-propagation:

$$\mathcal{L}(\hat{X}^{(t+1):(t+T')}; \Theta) = \sum_{i=1}^{T'} \left| \hat{X}^{(t+i)} - X^{(t+i)} \right|. \tag{7}$$

Metrics. We evaluate these models with three widely used metrics in traffic prediction: Mean Absolute Error (MAE), Root Mean Squared Error (RMSE), and Mean Absolute Percentage Error (MAPE). Missing values are not calculated.

5.2   Experimental Results

Table 1. Performance comparison of different models for traffic flow prediction on Loop

Dataset-Target	T	Metric	Graph WaveNet	STSGCN	STFGNN	MS-GAT	DMSTGCN	ST-MAN
Loop-Volume	15 min	MAE	5.64	6.38	6.10	6.21	5.72	**5.46**
		RMSE	8.35	9.43	9.03	9.38	8.53	**8.27**
		MAPE(%)	11.00	12.22	11.65	11.80	11.00	**10.79**
	30 min	MAE	6.09	7.07	6.69	6.84	6.18	**5.84**
		RMSE	9.17	10.60	10.07	10.67	9.40	**8.88**
		MAPE(%)	11.63	13.59	12.81	12.59	11.92	**11.41**
	1 h	MAE	6.74	8.38	7.80	7.68	6.86	**6.28**
		RMSE	10.20	12.59	11.80	12.35	10.49	**9.61**
		MAPE(%)	13.08	16.26	15.08	13.88	13.41	**12.45**
	average	MAE	6.08	7.12	6.73	6.81	6.18	**5.82**
		RMSE	9.10	10.72	10.15	10.70	9.35	**8.83**
		MAPE(%)	11.70	13.75	12.94	12.60	11.93	**11.45**
Loop-Speed	average	MAE	3.25	3.54	3.49	3.59	3.24	**3.16**
		RMSE	5.83	6.49	6.45	5.88	5.80	**5.71**
		MAPE(%)	9.62	10.61	10.37	10.01	9.33	**9.00**
Loop-Occupancy*	average	MAE	1.52	1.76	1.71	1.94	1.75	**1.40**
		RMSE	4.16	4.89	4.92	4.86	4.88	**3.97**
		MAPE(%)	19.04	23.79	21.60	28.71	25.52	**17.65**

*: Since the range of occupancy rate is small ($0 \sim 1$), we multiply the original occupancy rate by 100 before the experiments for better comparison.

Table 2. Performance comparison of different models for traffic flow prediction on PeMS04 and PeMS08

Dataset	Metric	DCRNN*	ASTGCN*	Graph WaveNet*	STSGCN*	STFGNN*	MS-GAT*	DMSTGCN	ST-MAN
PeMS04	MAE	24.70	22.93	25.45	21.19	19.83	19.54	18.94	**18.21**
	RMSE	38.12	35.22	39.70	33.65	31.88	31.69	30.42	**30.29**
	MAPE(%)	17.12	16.56	17.29	13.90	13.02	13.44	13.06	**12.06**
PeMS08	MAE	17.86	18.61	19.13	17.13	16.64	14.78	14.49	**13.64**
	RMSE	27.83	28.16	31.05	26.80	26.22	24.15	23.54	**23.22**
	MAPE(%)	11.45	13.08	12.68	10.96	10.60	10.07	9.43	**8.93**

*: Data for these baselines is taken from [7,10].

Prediction Performance Comparison. Table 1 shows the performance of ST-MAN and four excellent baseline models on the Loop dataset on 15 min ahead, 30 min ahead, and 1 h ahead traffic volume prediction. Table 2 shows the performance on 1 h ahead traffic volume predictions on the PeMS04 and PeMS08 datasets. We can observe that ST-MAN surpasses all the baselines on all metrics. Compared with the current SOTA model – DMSTGCN, ST-MAN improves MAE by 5.8% on Loop-Volume, 3.9% on PeMS04, and 5.9% on PeMS08.

We observe that: (1) some models that perform well on PeMS datasets are inferior on the Loop dataset (e.g., STFGNN, MS-GAT and DMSTGCN), while some models that perform badly on PeMS datasets are superior on the Loop dataset (e.g., Graph-WaveNet). This shows that these models have poor adaptability to different datasets, while ST-MAN can well adapt to different datasets; (2) though MS-GAT utilizes modalities of traffic volume, speed, and occupancy, its prediction performance is not satisfactory; (3) DMSTGCN performs well in predicting speed and volume, but poorly in predicting occupancy rate. The main reason is that DMSTGCN uses all the auxiliary data indiscriminately without filtering out irrelevant relations in multimodal data. This also limits DMSTGCN to utilize more modalities to improve performance.

Table 1 and Table 2 show that ST-MAN outperforms all baselines on all three metrics, on all three real-world datasets, and all three prediction tasks, exhibiting excellent versatility.

Impact of Multimodal Fusion. To investigate the effectiveness of multimodal fusion, we measure the impact of other modalities on traffic volume prediction task. We construct three variants of ST-MAN, i.e., ST-MAN without speed, ST-MAN without occupancy rate, and ST-MAN without speed and occupancy rate (i.e. degenerated into the unimodal case), and use ST-MAN as the base model.

Figure 5 plots the prediction accuracy of ST-MAN and its three variants in terms of MAE values. We can observe that ST-MAN outperforms all its three variants, which means that information from other modalities (speed and occupancy rate) is beneficial to the target prediction task (volume prediction).

This set of experiments demonstrates that relevant data modalities help to improve the target prediction task, and ST-MAN effectively extracts the cross-modal correlations and utilizes them in the prediction task.

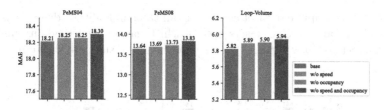

Fig. 5. Study on the impact of multimodal fusion on traffic volume prediction.

Ablation Experiments. We conduct ablation experiments to analyze the effect of Cross-Modal Attention (CMA), Spatial Embedding (SE), Temporal Embedding (TE), Spatial Attention (SA), and Temporal Attention (TA). We compare ST-MAN with its five variants, i.e., ST-MAN without CMA, ST-MAN without SE, ST-MAN without TE, ST-MAN without SA, and ST-MAN without TA. The experimental results on the PeMS04 dataset are shown in Table 3, with ST-MAN as the base model. We have the following observations: (1) all five components play a role in improving prediction accuracy; (2) Spatial Embedding and Temporal Embedding make the greatest contributions, as they explicitly embed the road network structure and periodicities of traffic conditions in the prediction network; (3) Spatial Attention, Temporal Attention, and Cross-Modal Attention have similar effects, only differ in the aspects from which the spatio-temporal correlations are mined.

Table 3. Ablation study on PeMS04

Dataset	Metrics	Models					
		w/o CMA	w/o SE	w/o TE	w/o SA	w/o TA	base
PeMS04	MAE	18.30	20.55	19.03	18.33	18.26	**18.21**
	RMSE	30.38	33.54	30.94	30.38	30.32	**30.29**
	MAPE(%)	12.08	13.61	12.57	12.18	12.09	**12.06**

Robust to Data Missing. In a real traffic network, temporary data missing often occurs due to various kinds of reasons, such as equipment failure or collection errors. Neural networks that rely on single modal data usually cannot work properly if the input data is missing. However, when the target data modality is missing, ST-MAN can still work by using other correlated traffic modality(s) to output relatively good prediction results.

To cope with possible data missing during operation, we adjust the training process as follows. We randomly choose a modality and remove its data from the training dataset in each epoch, so that the model can learn to adapt to incomplete data input. We test the performance of the randomly trained model with four datasets, i.e., a complete dataset containing all three modalities (denoted as ST-MAN random), and three datasets each of which has a target modality missing (denoted as ST-MAN w/o target). The experimental results are shown in Fig. 6.

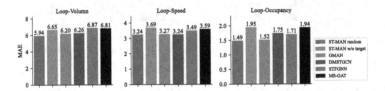

Fig. 6. Prediction accuracy of randomly trained ST-MAN and some superior baselines on the Loop dataset, with volume, speed and occupancy rate taken as the target modality respectively.

We can see that the randomly trained ST-MAN outperforms all the baselines when there is no data missing, and the performance is only slightly worse even when the target modality is missing. These experiments demonstrate ST-MAN's robustness to data missing, which greatly improves its practical value.

Computational Efficiency. To evaluate the computational efficiency of ST-MAN, we compare the number of parameters and computation time of ST-MAN, DMSTGCN, MS-GAT, STFGNN, STSGCN, and Graph WaveNet for traffic volume prediction task on Loop dataset, as shown in Table 4. It is clear that ST-MAN uses the least number of parameters. For computation time, we can see that the training speed and inference speed of ST-MAN are in the first tier, much faster than MS-GAT and DMSTGCN. In consideration of the highest prediction accuracy, the least memory consumption, and fast computing speed, ST-MAN undoubtedly achieves the highest computational efficiency.

Table 4. Computational efficiency study on Loop-Volume

Models	#parameters	Inference(s)	Training(s/epoch)
STFGNN	4,199,212	4.31	102.48
STSGCN	3,058,222	4.37	109.31
DMSTGCN	2,717,708	19.09	226.20
MS-GAT	800,460	18.55	306.84
Graph WaveNet	311,720	5.98	163.70
ST-MAN	125,505	4.27	101.14

6   Conclusion

In this paper, we propose ST-MAN, a spatio-temporal multimodal attention network that utilizes multimodal traffic data for traffic prediction. Important inter-modal correlations are learned by the cross-modal attention mechanism and used to assist the target prediction task. Knowledge about road network structure and periodicities of traffic flow are used by Spatial Attention, Temporal Attention, and Cross-Modal Attention through a refined Spatio-Temporal Embedding block. Extensive experiments show that ST-MAN not only achieves state-of-the-art performance but also has very high computational efficiency. In addition, the framework is generic and extensible, providing a paradigm for making good use of multimodal traffic data to improve prediction. In the future, we will explore more fusion methods in this area and investigate multimodal fusion learning in other spatio-temporal prediction fields.

Acknowledgment. This work was supported by the National Key R&D Program of China under Grant No. 2018AAA0101200.

References

1. Brigham, E.O., Morrow, R.: The fast fourier transform. IEEE Spect. **4**(12), 63–70 (1967)
2. Cui, Z., Ke, R., Wang, Y.: Deep bidirectional and unidirectional LSTM recurrent neural network for network-wide traffic speed prediction. CoRR abs/1801.02143 (2018)
3. Grover, A., Leskovec, J.: node2vec: scalable feature learning for networks. In: Krishnapuram, B., Shah, M., Smola, A.J., Aggarwal, C.C., Shen, D., Rastogi, R. (eds.) Proceedings of the 22nd ACM SIGKDD International Conference on Knowledge Discovery and Data Mining, 2016, pp. 855–864. ACM (2016)
4. Guo, S., Lin, Y., Feng, N., Song, C., Wan, H.: Attention based spatial-temporal graph convolutional networks for traffic flow forecasting. In: The Thirty-Third AAAI Conference on Artificial Intelligence, 2019, pp. 922–929. AAAI Press (2019)
5. Han, L., Du, B., Sun, L., Fu, Y., Lv, Y., Xiong, H.: Dynamic and multi-faceted spatio-temporal deep learning for traffic speed forecasting. In: Zhu, F., Ooi, B.C., Miao, C. (eds.) KDD 2021: The 27th ACM SIGKDD Conference on Knowledge Discovery and Data Mining, 2021, pp. 547–555. ACM (2021)
6. He, K., Zhang, X., Ren, S., Sun, J.: Deep residual learning for image recognition. In: 2016 IEEE Conference on Computer Vision and Pattern Recognition, CVPR 2016, pp. 770–778. IEEE Computer Society (2016)
7. Huang, J., Luo, K., Cao, L., Wen, Y., Zhong, S.: Learning multiaspect traffic couplings by multirelational graph attention networks for traffic prediction. IEEE Trans. Intell. Transp. Syst. **23**(11), 20681–20695 (2022)
8. Jin, G., Cui, Y., Zeng, L., Tang, H., Feng, Y., Huang, J.: Urban ride-hailing demand prediction with multiple spatio-temporal information fusion network. Transp. Res. Part C: Emerg. Technol. **117**, 102665 (2020)
9. Kingma, D.P., Ba, J.: Adam: a method for stochastic optimization. In: Bengio, Y., LeCun, Y. (eds.) 3rd International Conference on Learning Representations, ICLR 2015, San Diego, CA, USA, 7–9 May 2015, Conference Track Proceedings (2015)

10. Li, M., Zhu, Z.: Spatial-temporal fusion graph neural networks for traffic flow forecasting. In: Thirty-Fifth AAAI Conference on Artificial Intelligence, AAAI 2021, pp. 4189–4196. AAAI Press (2021)
11. Li, Y., Yu, R., Shahabi, C., Liu, Y.: Diffusion convolutional recurrent neural network: Data-driven traffic forecasting. In: International Conference on Learning Representations (2018)
12. Li, Z., et al.: A multi-stream feature fusion approach for traffic prediction. IEEE Trans. Intell. Transp. Syst. **23**(2), 1456–1466 (2022)
13. Song, C., Lin, Y., Guo, S., Wan, H.: Spatial-temporal synchronous graph convolutional networks: a new framework for spatial-temporal network data forecasting. In: The Thirty-Fourth AAAI Conference on Artificial Intelligence, 2020, pp. 914–921 (2020)
14. Sutskever, I., Vinyals, O., Le, Q.V.: Sequence to sequence learning with neural networks. In: Ghahramani, Z., Welling, M., Cortes, C., Lawrence, N., Weinberger, K.Q. (eds.) Advances in Neural Information Processing Systems, vol. 27. Curran Associates, Inc. (2014)
15. Vaswani, A., et al.: Attention is all you need. In: NIPS, pp. 6000–6010 (2017)
16. Williams, B.M., Hoel, L.A.: Modeling and forecasting vehicular traffic flow as a seasonal arima process: theoretical basis and empirical results. J. Transp. Eng. **129**(6), 664–672 (2003)
17. Wu, Z., Pan, S., Long, G., Jiang, J., Zhang, C.: Graph wavenet for deep spatial-temporal graph modeling. In: IJCAI, pp. 1907–1913 (2019)
18. Xu, M., et al.: Spatial-temporal transformer networks for traffic flow forecasting. CoRR abs/2001.02908 (2020)
19. Yu, B., Yin, H., Zhu, Z.: Spatio-temporal graph convolutional networks: a deep learning framework for traffic forecasting. In: IJCAI, pp. 3634–3640 (2018)
20. Zhang, J., Zheng, Y., Qi, D.: Deep spatio-temporal residual networks for city-wide crowd flows prediction. In: Proceedings of the AAAI Conference on Artificial Intelligence, vol. 31 (2017)
21. Zhang, X., et al.: Traffic flow forecasting with spatial-temporal graph diffusion network. In: Thirty-Fifth AAAI Conference on Artificial Intelligence, 2021, pp. 15008–15015 (2021)
22. Zhao, B., Gao, X., Liu, J., Zhao, J., Xu, C.: Spatiotemporal data fusion in graph convolutional networks for traffic prediction. IEEE Access **8**, 76632–76641 (2020)
23. Zheng, C., Fan, X., Wang, C., Qi, J.: GMAN: a graph multi-attention network for traffic prediction. In: The Thirty-Fourth AAAI Conference on Artificial Intelligence, AAAI 2020, pp. 1234–1241. AAAI Press (2020)

Sparse-View CT Reconstruction via Implicit Neural Intensity Functions

Qiang Chen🆔 and Guoqiang Xiao$^{(\boxtimes)}$🆔

College of Computer and Information Science, Southwest University, Chongqing, China
cq0907@email.swu.edu.cn, gqxiao@swu.edu.cn

Abstract. Sparse-view CT (SVCT) reconstruction is an inverse problem that solves for unknown CT images of an object by sparse sampling-based projections. Many efforts are contributing to SVCT reconstruction, but it is still a challenging task for reconstructing high-quality CT images from high sparse-view level. In this paper, we proposed Implicit Neural Intensity Functions (INIF) representation to improve reconstruction quality. Our proposed method represents an image using multi-layer perceptron (MLP), whose input is a 4D area coordinate (centroid location (x, y) and the width (w) and height (h) of local area) and whose output is the intensity value at that spatial area, where w and h are adjustable and thereby achieving multiresolution sampling. Compared to other CT reconstruction algorithms, INIF has two advantages: 1) Different from the traditional methods, INIF learns a continuous implicit function, which can effectively reduce artifacts and recover details without complex hyperparameter settings; 2) Distinguishing from data-driven deep learning-based methods, large-scale data is not required to train the INIF except for sparsely sampled projections. In addition, the quantitative and qualitative results on two public AAPM Challenge datasets demonstrate the effectiveness of INIF compared to other CT reconstruction approaches. Code: https://github.com/cq0907/INIF.

Keywords: Inverse problem · Sparse-view CT reconstruction · Implicit neural representation · Multiresolution

1 Introduction

X-ray computed tomography (CT) aims to non-invasively visualize the internal structures of objects. In practice, given the potential harm that x-ray can cause to objects, it is highly desirable to achieve the lowest level of radiation dose without compromising the diagnostic value of a CT scan. Thus, many efforts are contributing to sparse-view CT (SVCT) reconstruction that is an inverse problem [1,6,15] by taking a limited number of projection data for CT image reconstruction. To address this challenging problem, the algorithms of SVCT reconstruction can be grouped into three categories: 1) Pre-processing methods; 2) Iterative reconstruction (IR) methods; and 3) Deep learning-based methods.

© The Author(s), under exclusive license to Springer Nature Switzerland AG 2023
Z. Jin et al. (Eds.): KSEM 2023, LNAI 14118, pp. 153–161, 2023.
https://doi.org/10.1007/978-3-031-40286-9_13

Pre-processing methods are adopted to alleviate the information loss in the projection domain. Li *et al.* [9] proposed a dictionary learning method, which applied the learned dictionary to inpaint the missing projections and then improve reconstruction quality. Zhang *et al.* [19] proposed a directional projection interpolation (DSI) method by optimizing double-orientation estimation in the projection domain. However, the reconstructions may suffer from secondary artifacts due to the errors of interpolation-based methods in the projection domain.

To further improve the reconstruction quality, numerous IR methods have been developed for SVCT reconstruction, where most well-known IR constraint was total variation (TV) minimization [14] for artifact suppression. Afterward, Liu *et al.* [10] proposed an adaptive-weighted TV (AwTV) minimization algorithm to alleviate over-smoothing edges by the anisotropic edge property. Sequentially, a new AwTV [18] (NAWTV) was proposed to boost performance in artifact suppression and edge preservation. Although IR methods benefit SVCT reconstruction in artifact removal and detail preservation, the quality of images reconstructed by IR methods highly relied on the appropriate hyperparameter settings, otherwise over-smoothing or over-sharpening may occur.

The deep learning-based methods aim to learn the mapping from raw measurement data to the reconstructed image by training the convolutional neural networks [5] (CNNs) with large-scale training data. Chen *et al.* [2] proposed a novel residual encoder-decoder neural network for low-dose CT imaging and performed well in noise suppression and structural preservation. To enhance the expression of the network for SVCT artifact removal, Zhang *et al.* [20] proposed a method based on a combination of DenseNet and deconvolution, which achieved competitive performance in terms of artifact removal and structure preservation. In addition, Lee *et al.* [8] applied U-Net to interpolate the missing projection data by combining with residual learning for better convergence. Assisted by large-scale data, CNN-based methods achieve encouraging performance with the end-to-end optimization strategy. However, these methods have also exposed some limitations: 1) The acquisition of large-scale training datasets can be a bottleneck; 2) The reconstruction can be unstable with subtle yet significant structural changes, for example tumor growth.

To overcome the drawbacks of above methods, we propose Implicit Neural Intensity Functions (INIF) representation, which is a case-by-case representation method. Different from traditional methods, including pre-processing methods and IR methods, INIF aims to learn continuous implicit functions, which can effectively reduce artifacts and recover details without complex hyperparameter settings. Additionally, distinguishing from data-driven deep learning-based methods, INIF learns the multi-layer perceptron (MLP) to map the 4D area coordinate (centroid location (x, y) and the width (w) and height (h) of local area) of image to the corresponding intensity values, instead of learning large-scale image features. Specifically, INIF encodes the full image spatial field into the weights of MLP network and then achieves reconstruction by querying the intensity values corresponding to the area coordinate of all pixels. To improve robustness, we adopt multiresolution sampling strategy to dynamically adjust

(w, h). In short, we transform the ill-posed inverse problem into a MLP weights optimization problem, which finds an optimal solution through gradient descent.

The main contribution of our work can be summarized as follows: 1) A new Implicit Neural Intensity Functions (INIF) representation is proposed, which transforms the SVCT reconstruction problem into a case-by-case weights optimization problem; 2) We introduce area intensity learning with multiresolution sampling strategy, which is beneficial to SVCT reconstruction due to it represents the intensity value from a larger area range; 3) Our proposed method achieves competitive performance compared to traditional and deep learning-based methods on two public AAPM Challenge datasets.

2   The Proposed Method

In this section, we first make a problem formulation about our task (Sect. 3.1), and then describe the forward process of the proposed Implicit Neural Intensity Functions (INIF) representation (Sect. 3.2).

2.1   Problem Formulation

Sparse-view CT (SVCT) reconstruction is typically formulated as an inverse problem, which in its prototypical form reads as follows:

$$\left\{ \begin{array}{c} Given\ a\ linear\ forward\ operator\ \mathcal{A} \in \mathbb{R}^{k \times m} \\ and\ sparsely\ sampled\ projections\ \boldsymbol{y} = \mathcal{A}\boldsymbol{x} + \boldsymbol{e} \\ with\ the\ acquisition\ noise\ \boldsymbol{e},\ reconstruct\ the\ unknown\ image\ \boldsymbol{x} \end{array} \right\}, \quad (1)$$

where $k \ll m$. This restriction turns SVCT reconstruction into an ill-posed inverse problem, which does not possess a unique solution. To address this problem, some works take account of transforming it into an optimization problem with regularization:

$$\varepsilon = \underset{x}{argmin}\ f(Ax, y) + \Phi(x) \quad (2)$$

where $f(\cdot, \cdot)$ represents distance metric function, such as L_1 or L_2 norm, which estimates the errors between inputs. $\Phi(\cdot)$ is the regularizer term, which is used to capture the various characteristics of image and then augment image.

2.2   Implicit Neural Intensity Functions Representation

In implicit neural representation learning, the unknown image is represented by a neural network as a continuous function, as illustrated in Fig. 1. The network F_θ with parameters θ can be defined as:

$$F_\theta : c \to v; \ c \in [0, 1]^n \ and \ v \in \mathbb{R}, \quad (3)$$

where the input c is the normalized coordinate (x, y) in the image spatial field, and the output v is the corresponding intensity value at the coordinate. The network function F_θ achieves the mapping from spatial coordinate to the intensity.

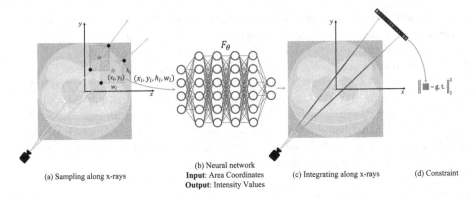

(a) Sampling along x-rays

(b) Neural network
Input: Area Coordinates
Output: Intensity Values

(c) Integrating along x-rays

(d) Constraint

Fig. 1. An overview of our proposed Implicit Neural Intensity Functions (INIF) representation and differentiable projection procedure. We first sample 4D area coordinates (centroid location (x, y) and the width (w) and height (h) of local area) along x-rays (a), feeding those area coordinates into an MLP to produce the intensity values (b), and using line integral techniques to composite these values into projections (c). Due to the whole process is differentiable, we can optimize the MLP by minimizing the errors between prediction projections and GT projections (d).

However, due to the limited expressive power of point coordinates, it is impossible for us to traverse all points in the continuous field. Therefore, we change the point coordinate into an area coordinate, which can be redefined as:

$$F_\theta : a \to v; \ a \in [0, 1]^t \ and \ v \in \mathbb{R}, \qquad (4)$$

where a is the normalized local area, which consists of centroid coordinate (x, y) and the width (w) and height (h) of local area. Based on the area coordinate, we will now introduce the specific framework used in our method.

Multiresolution Area Sampling. Inspired by the principle of CT system [7], we sample $N + 1$ points uniformly along each x-ray, and then obtain N local areas by taking adjacent two points (black points) as the diagonal, as shown in Fig. 1(a). Accordingly, we represent a local area by the midpoints (centroid) of adjacent points, width and height, denoted by $\{(x_i, y_i, w_i, h_i)|i = 1, \cdots, N\}$. In addition, for each iteration, we set N to be adjustable within a certain range, and dynamically change the resolution of local areas accordingly, which is beneficial for improve the robustness of network.

Positional Encoding. Current some works [11,13,17] find that deep networks are biased towards learning lower frequency functions. They additionally show that mapping the inputs to a higher dimensional space using high frequency functions before passing them to the network enables better fitting of data that contains high frequency variation. Following these works, we use a Fourier encoding function γ to encode the area coordinates a into a higher dimensional space.

Hence, the encoded area coordinates are:

$$\gamma(a) = \left\{ sin(2^i \pi a), cos(2^i \pi a) | i = 0, \ldots, L \right\}. \tag{5}$$

Note that (x, y) and (w, h) are separately encoded by function $\gamma(\cdot)$. In our experiments, we set $L=10$ to encode (x, y) and $L=4$ to encode (w, h).

Network Training and Loss. Given the encoded coordinates $\gamma(a)$ and sparsely sampled projections y, we first fed $\gamma(a)$ into MLP F_θ to learning corresponding intensity value. Based on the formulation in Eq. 4, the mathematical form is denoted by:

$$v = F_\theta \circ \gamma(a). \tag{6}$$

With the intensity values v, we can integrate along x-rays r to obtain the prediction projection $\hat{y}$. Afterward, we adopt the total squared error to estimate the errors between prediction projections and GT projections, formulated as:

$$\hat{y}(r) = \sum_{i=1}^{N} v_i \delta_i, \tag{7}$$

$$\mathcal{L} = \sum_{r \in \mathcal{R}} \|\hat{y}(r) - y(r)\|_2^2, \tag{8}$$

where N is the number of local areas along each x-ray. δ_i refers to the diagonal length of ith local area. $\mathcal{R}$ is the set of x-rays in each mini-batch. To keep the gradient consistency between adjacent local areas, we introduce the gradient L_1 norm regularization term, which enforces the gradient of v along the x-axis and y-axis direction as close to zero as possible. In short, we design the following overall objective function:

$$\mathcal{L} = \sum_{r \in \mathcal{R}} \|\hat{y}(r) - y(r)\|_2^2 + \bigtriangledown F_\theta, \quad \bigtriangledown F_\theta = \left| \frac{\partial v}{\partial x} \right| + \left| \frac{\partial v}{\partial y} \right|, \tag{9}$$

where F_θ represents the MLP with parameters θ. Because above process is naturally differentiable, we can use gradient descent to optimize the parameters θ of MLP by minimizing the $\mathcal{L}$, i.e., minimizing the errors between prediction projections and GT projections.

3 Experiments

3.1 Implementation Details

In the multiresolution sampling phase, we set the number of sampling points between 450 and 512, denoted by $N \in [450, 512]$. For the network architecture, we construct an 8-layers MLP network, where each FC layer is followed by the *softplus* activation function [3] except for the output layer. Following [12], we insert a skip connection that concatenates the input to the fifth layer's activation. Based on the idea of gradient descent, we use Adam optimizer with a initialized learning rate of 5×10^{-4} to find the optimal parametric solution. The number of training epochs is 500. In addition, we implement the proposed method with PyTorch and use single Geforce RTX 3090 GPU for acceleration.

158   Q. Chen and G. Xiao

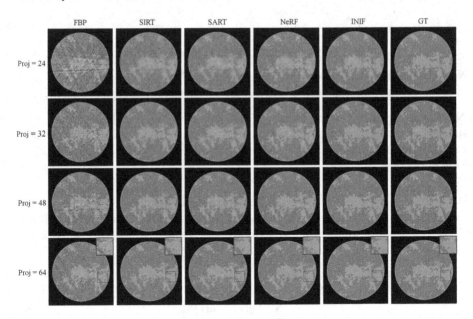

Fig. 2. Results of sparse-view reconstruction using 24/32/48/64 projections on DL-sparse-view dataset.

3.2 Datasets and Evaluation Metrics

Datasets. In our experiments, we validate our method on two public datasets: DL-sparse-view CT Challenge dataset and TrueCT Reconstruction Challenge dataset. Both can be freely downloaded from the official website of AAPM Grand Challenge (https://www.aapm.org/GrandChallenge/). The former is from a breast phantom simulation that has complex random structure modeling fibroglandular tissue in circular cross-section of a breast model, it contains a total of 4000 phantom images and corresponding 128-view fan-beam beam projection data (sinogram). The latter includes 200 unique computational phantoms and sinograms from varied patients. Moreover, the size of each phantom is 512×512 and each sinogram is 128×1024.

Evaluation Metrics. We evaluate the reconstruction quality of our method not only through qualitative evaluation by visualization, but also through quantitative evaluation using root mean square error (RMSE) and structural similarity (SSIM). Note that the RMSE values can be easily transformed into PSNR values through a logarithmic function.

3.3 Experiments on Sparse-View CT Reconstruction

We compare our proposed INIF with several popular CT reconstruction algorithms on two public datasets, including filtered back projection [7] (FBP), simul-

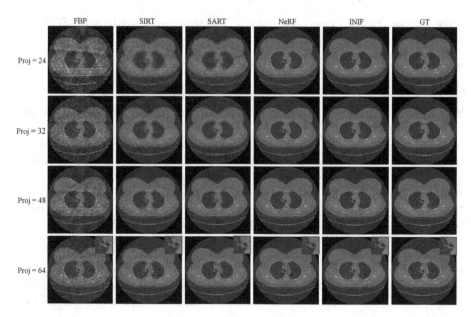

Fig. 3. Results of sparse-view reconstruction using 24/32/48/64 projections on TrueCT dataset.

taneous iterative reconstruction technique [16] (SIRT), simultaneous algebraic reconstruction technique [4] (SART) and neural radiance fields [11] (NeRF).

Qualitative Comparisons . In the Fig. 2 and Fig. 3, we show the sparse-view reconstruction results using the proposed INIF and other algorithms on two public dataset. Note that we set the iterations for each algorithm to be 500. By qualitatively comparing the reconstruction results obtained by various algorithms based on 24, 32, 48, and 64 projections, INIF achieves better performance than other methods in terms of artifact removal and detail recovery. Compared to traditional methods including FBP, SIRT, and SART, our approach learns a continuous implicit intensity function, which is the main reason why INIF is advantageous for artifact removal. Additionally, compared to deep learning-based method, such as NeRF, INIF learns the intensity values of local areas through multiresolution sampling, instead of learning the intensity value of a single point, which is conducive to compensate for information loss from the sparse-view projection process.

Quantitative Comparisons . From the Table 1, we can see that INIF outperforms other algorithms comprehensively under 24, 32, 48, and 64 projections, which demonstrates that INIF can achieve better quality reconstruction compared to other algorithms. Note that quantitative results shown in Table 1 are obtained by randomly selecting 64 samples and calculating the average RMSE and SSIM values of these samples.

Table 1. Quantitative comparisons between INIF and other algorithms. RMSE/SSIM values are reported.

Porjections = 24					
Dataset	FBP	SIRT	SART	NeRF	**NeAR (ours)**
DL-sparse-view CT	0.0191/0.6565	0.0072/0.9138	0.0067/0.9186	0.0074/0.8817	**0.0062/0.9371**
TrueCT	0.0301/0.4398	0.0132/0.7989	0.0116/0.8132	0.0101/0.8520	**0.0084/0.8969**
Porjections = 32					
Dataset	FBP	SIRT	SART	NeRF	**NeAR (ours)**
DL-sparse-view CT	0.0140/0.7113	0.0053/0.9302	0.0051/0.9337	0.0075/0.9051	**0.0046/0.9693**
TrueCT	0.0230/0.4836	0.0113/0.8071	0.0103/0.8197	0.0079/0.8915	**0.0067/0.9192**
Porjections = 48					
Dataset	FBP	SIRT	SART	NeRF	**NeAR (ours)**
DL-sparse-view CT	0.0113/0.7713	0.0044/0.9439	0.0042/0.9470	0.0025/0.9847	**0.0023/0.9899**
TrueCT	0.0189/0.5542	0.0097/0.8256	0.0086/0.8385	0.0046/0.9431	**0.0042/0.9555**
Porjections = 64					
Dataset	FBP	SIRT	SART	NeRF	**NeAR (ours)**
DL-sparse-view CT	0.0079/0.8217	0.0035/0.9558	0.0033/0.9582	0.0020/0.9873	**0.0018/0.9951**
TrueCT	0.0155/0.6045	0.0090/0.8392	0.0081/0.8502	0.0038/0.9575	**0.0036/0.9640**

4   Conclusion

In this paper, we proposed Implicit Neural Intensity Functions (INIF) representation for sparse-view CT (SVCT) reconstruction, which transforms the ill-pose reconstruction problem into a case-by-case MLP's parameters optimization problem. In addition, INIF replaces point coordinates with area coordinates of multiresolution sampling to further improve the reconstruction quality and robustness of network. In summary, the advantages of INIF can be summarized in two-fold: 1) INIF learns a continuous implicit function which is beneficial for artifact removal and detail preservation; 2) INIF requires no large-scale training data except for sparsely sampled projections. The experimental results on two public datasets have demonstrated the effectiveness of INIF.

References

1. Arridge, S.R.: Optical tomography in medical imaging. Inver. Prob. **15**(2), R41 (1999)
2. Chen, H., et al.: Low-dose ct with a residual encoder-decoder convolutional neural network. IEEE Trans. Med. Imaging **36**(12), 2524–2535 (2017)
3. Glorot, X., Bordes, A., Bengio, Y.: Deep sparse rectifier neural networks. In: Proceedings of the Fourteenth International Conference on Artificial Intelligence and Statistics, pp. 315–323. JMLR Workshop and Conference Proceedings (2011)
4. Gordon, R., Bender, R., Herman, G.T.: Algebraic reconstruction techniques (art) for three-dimensional electron microscopy and x-ray photography. J. Theor. Biol. **29**(3), 471–481 (1970)

5. He, K., Zhang, X., Ren, S., Sun, J.: Deep residual learning for image recognition. In: Proceedings of the IEEE Conference on Computer Vision and Pattern Recognition, pp. 770–778 (2016)
6. Herman, G.T., Lent, A.: Iterative reconstruction algorithms. Comput. Biol. Med. **6**(4), 273–294 (1976)
7. Kak, A.C., Slaney, M.: Principles of Computerized Tomographic Imaging. SIAM (2001)
8. Lee, H., Lee, J., Kim, H., Cho, B., Cho, S.: Deep-neural-network-based sinogram synthesis for sparse-view CT image reconstruction. IEEE Trans. Radiat. Plasma Med. Sci. **3**(2), 109–119 (2018)
9. Li, S., Cao, Q., Chen, Y., Hu, Y., Luo, L., Toumoulin, C.: Dictionary learning based sinogram inpainting for CT sparse reconstruction. Optik **125**(12), 2862–2867 (2014)
10. Liu, Y., Ma, J., Fan, Y., Liang, Z.: Adaptive-weighted total variation minimization for sparse data toward low-dose x-ray computed tomography image reconstruction. Phys. Med. Biol. **57**(23), 7923 (2012)
11. Mildenhall, B., Srinivasan, P.P., Tancik, M., Barron, J.T., Ramamoorthi, R., Ng, R.: Nerf: Representing scenes as neural radiance fields for view synthesis. Commun. ACM **65**(1), 99–106 (2021)
12. Park, J.J., Florence, P., Straub, J., Newcombe, R., Lovegrove, S.: Deepsdf: learning continuous signed distance functions for shape representation. In: Proceedings of the IEEE/CVF Conference on Computer Vision and Pattern Recognition, pp. 165–174 (2019)
13. Rahaman, N., et al.: On the spectral bias of neural networks. In: International Conference on Machine Learning, pp. 5301–5310. PMLR (2019)
14. Rudin, L.I., Osher, S., Fatemi, E.: Nonlinear total variation based noise removal algorithms. Physica D: Nonlinear Phenomena **60**(1–4), 259–268 (1992)
15. Tarantola, A.: Inverse Problem Theory and Methods for Model Parameter Estimation. SIAM (2005)
16. Trampert, J., Leveque, J.J.: Simultaneous iterative reconstruction technique: physical interpretation based on the generalized least squares solution. J. Geophys. Res. Solid Earth **95**(B8), 12553–12559 (1990)
17. Vaswani, A., et al.: Attention is all you need. Adv. Neural Inf. Process. Syst. **30** (2017)
18. Wang, Y., Qi, Z.: A new adaptive-weighted total variation sparse-view computed tomography image reconstruction with local improved gradient information. J. X-ray Sci. Technol. **26**(6), 957–975 (2018)
19. Zhang, H., Sonke, J.J.: Directional sinogram interpolation for sparse angular acquisition in cone-beam computed tomography. J. X-ray Sci. Technol. **21**(4), 481–496 (2013)
20. Zhang, Z., Liang, X., Dong, X., Xie, Y., Cao, G.: A sparse-view CT reconstruction method based on combination of densenet and deconvolution. IEEE Trans. Med. Imaging **37**(6), 1407–1417 (2018)

Tennis Action Recognition Based on Multi-Branch Mixed Attention

Xianwei Zhou, Weitao Chen, Zhenfeng Li, Yuan Li, Jiale Lei,
and Songsen Yu$^{(\boxtimes)}$

School of Software, South China Normal University, Foshan 528225, China
zhouxianwei@m.scnu.edu.cn, yss8109@163.com

Abstract. Tennis action recognition is a challenging problem due to its inherent characteristics such as high speed and large amplitude of actions. In this paper, an end-to-end, Multi-Branch Mixed Attention-based network model (MBMA-Net) is proposed to tackle those challenges. Specifically, the model is designed to: (a) capture the inter-dependencies between channel features using channel attention; (b) improve the spatial receptive field to better filter spatial features by spatial attention;and (c) model the actions between consecutive frames using motion excitation to improve the accuracy of action feature extraction and recognition. The experimental results on dataset THETIS show that MBMA-Net achieves an accuracy of 0.8698, 5.35% higher than other baseline models for tennis action recognition and the model is further validated through various ablation experiments.

Keywords: Tennis · Action recognition · Mixed attention · Deep learning

1 Introduction

Sports video analysis attracts lots of academic attention recently, and action recognition is a prerequisite for further analysis such as action analysis, action quality assessment and tactics decision. Much efforts have been made in such sports as skating [1], golf [2], and gymnastics [3]. Among them, tennis is a racket sport with such characteristics as high speed and large amplitude of actions. Its complex technical actions requires the synergy of muscles from multiple parts of the neck, shoulders, back, chest and legs. Therefore, it's quite a challenge for tennis action recognition due to the difficulty of capturing the correlation information among actions.

The three main types of mainstream tennis action recognition methods are based on LSTM [4], ST-GCN [5] and 3DCNN [6]. The first two methods suffer from the problem of non-end-to-end manner, i.e., it's not able to train the model in a whole and require an additional feature extraction process, which can lead to the loss of some information. In addition, the ST-GCN-based methods rely on accurate skeleton information. As shown in Fig. 1(a), when the actual extracted

ⓒ The Author(s), under exclusive license to Springer Nature Switzerland AG 2023
Z. Jin et al. (Eds.): KSEM 2023, LNAI 14118, pp. 162–175, 2023.
https://doi.org/10.1007/978-3-031-40286-9_14

skeleton differs significantly from the expected skeleton, it leads to difficulty in learning action features. And the LSTM-based method performs spatial feature extraction by general 2DCNNs and then uses LSTM for temporal processing, as shown in the ResNet34 feature map in Fig. 1, the 2DCNNs cannot capture the information of temporal evolution. In contrast, the general 3DCNNs approach (as shown in the Inception-v1 feature map in Fig. 1) can learn the correlation of spatial-temporal features, but suffers from the problems of large computational effort and redundancy of feature information.

In order to address the above problems, to enhance the attention to the channel information such as the technical tennis action power part, to focus on the useful spatial information as well as to improve the attention to the key frames, this paper proposes a multi-branch mixed attention tennis action recognition method based on the 3DCNN method. The method performs feature extraction and classification prediction in an end-to-end model, modeling the interdependencies between channel features in the channel dimension; generating spatial attention maps to focus on useful features in the spatial dimension; and capturing the associations between action information in the temporal dimension. And the above features are fused to improve the accuracy of action feature extraction and the accuracy of classification. In this paper, experiments are conducted on the publicly available THETIS [7] tennis dataset, and the experimental results validate the effectiveness of the proposed method. The main contributions of this paper are as follows:

1. For the high speed and large amplitude of actions characteristics of tennis, a multi-branch mixed attention module is proposed, which considers the dependencies between different dimensions of channel, spatial and temporal, and improves the accuracy of action feature extraction by modeling the dependencies between channel features, responses between spatial features and action features between adjacent frames.
2. Based on the multi-branch mixed attention module, an end-to-end model of tennis action recognition method called MBMA-Net is proposed; compared with 3DCNNs, this method can not only simplify the model and hence reduce the computational cost, but also improve the accuracy of action recognition.
3. By conducting various experiments on the THETIS dataset, this paper verifies that the MBMA module can effectively fuse information in channel, spatial and temporal dimensions. Moreover, the results of the comparison experiments show that the proposed method outperforms the state-of-the-art baseline of tennis action recognition using only RGB video on the THETIS dataset.

The rest of the paper is organized as follows: Sect. 2 gives a brief review of related works. In Sect. 3, a MBMA-Net model is proposed for tennis action recognition. Experimental results and analysis are given in Sect. 4. Finally, Sect. 5 concludes with a discussion.

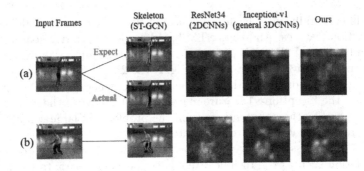

Fig. 1. Feature visualization of current mainstream tennis action recognition methods, including Skeleton (ST-GCN), ResNet34 (2DCNNs), Inception-v1 (general 3DCNNs) and Ours (the proposed method).

2   Related Work

This section first summarizes related work on the field of tennis sports action recognition, followed by a description of the research progress on the attention mechanism used in this paper.

2.1   Tennis Action Recognition

Current mainstream deep models for tennis action recognition are mainly based on LSTM [4,8–10],ST-GCN [5],and 3DCNN [6].

For the first time,Mora [4] et al. propose a deep learning model for tennis action classification based on LSTM and Inception network [11]. Specifically, the Inception neural network is pre-trained on the ImageNet dataset for frame feature extraction; subsequently, a 3-layer LSTM network is jointly trained to capture the temporal information for classification on the THETIS dataset. Faulkner [8] et al. constructed a dataset TenniSet on tennis match videos for the problems of event recognition and localization, and used RNNs to capture temporal information for action recognition.Subsequently Cai [9] et al. proposed a Historical LSTM model, which uses the output state at time t and the historical update features at time t-1 to generate an overall feature vector that truly achieves the classification of 12 tennis actions with an average accuracy of 74%. Scholar Maria [5] first used spatio-temporal graph convolution ST-GCN to solve the classification task of forehand hitting, backhand hitting and non-hitting in tennis, and the experimental results showed that ST-GCN can perform better when using fuzzy input graphs. Recently, Sen [10] et al. used InceptionResNetV2 [12], ResNet152V2 [13] and Xception [14] as feature extractors and trained LSTM networks for classification, which has achieved 75.25% with only 15 frames in the THETIS dataset. Rasmussen [6] et al. applied Tucker decomposition to the video and performed experiments on a modified THETIS dataset. The results showed that the memory of the compressed network was reduced by a factor of nearly 51 and comparable accuracy was maintained.

The numerous approaches mentioned above for tennis motion recognition almost all extract spatial features first and then process the temporal information using LSTM. This approach considers only the image features at the individual frame level during feature extraction and tends to ignore the motion information on consecutive frames of the video. The approach using ST-GCN, on the other hand, relies on accurate skeleton information, which often leads to large deviations in the obtained skeleton information due to body self-obscuring or motion blurring for tennis sports with high speed and large amplitude of actions features [15,16]. And the general 3DCNNs method may not perform as well as other models [17] when dealing with complex 3D data because it does not consider the feature relationship and weight assignment within the data. Therefore, this paper considers the learning of channel, spatial and motion information simultaneously on the basis of 3DCNNs, focusing on which feature channels are more important, which spatial regions are more important and which frames are more critical to achieve highly accurate tennis action recognition.

2.2 Attention Mechanism in Computer Vision

Attention mechanism in computer vision is an important component of neural networks, which enables the network to focus on the key information in the image/video and suppress irrelevant information, thus improving the performance of the network. To deal with the problem of invariance of spatial transformation, Jaderberg [18] et al. proposed a spatial attention mechanism to improve network robustness and generalization to geometric transformations such as rotation, scaling and translation by introducing differentiable spatial transformers. For the "information redundancy" problem in convolutional neural networks, Hu [19] et al. proposed a channel attention network SENet, which learns the importance of different channel features by modeling the inter-dependencies between channel features of the input feature map. For the temporal modeling problem in video recognition, Liu [20] et al. proposed a temporal adaptive module (TAM) that considers both local and global information in order to capture complex temporal relationships efficiently and flexibly. Among them, 2 Conv1D of kernel size 3 are used in the local branch to learn importance feature map solely based on a local temporal window. And in the global branch, the adaptive kernel with the global receptive field is learned by leveraging the long-term information.

In this paper, a multi-branch mixed attention method for tennis action recognition is proposed inspired by the above research. Since tennis is a sport with high speed and large amplitude of actions, as well as the more complex channel features in the middle layer of the network and the presence of a large amount of redundant information in its videos, these reasons can make tennis action recognition very challenging. To address these challenges and improve the accuracy of tennis action recognition, this method combines channel attention mechanism, spatial attention mechanism and action motivation mechanism, focusing on the dependencies between channel, spatial and temporal dimensions of video features, as described in Sect. 3.

3   Method

In this section, the architecture of the proposed MBMA-Net together with technical detail of MBMA module is introduced.

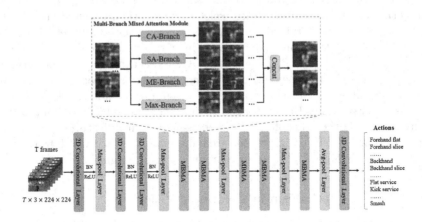

Fig. 2. The architecture of MBMA-Net.

3.1   Multi-Branch Mixed Attention Network

Multi-Branch Mixed Attention Network (MBMA-Net) is an end-to-end 3D convolutional neural network built based on MBMA modules, as shown in Fig. 2. The network mainly consists of one 2D convolutional layer, three 3D convolutional layers, five MBMA modules, four maximum pooling layers and one average pooling layer. The initial 2D convolutional layer and the maximum pooling layer are used for downsampling and spatial feature dimensionality reduction to reduce the computational cost of the model. 3D convolutional layers perform convolutional operations to extract deeper features. The average pooling layer is used for global averaging of features to obtain the final output.

The MBMA module, which forms the backbone of MBMA-Net, is based on an improved version of the Inception-v1 module, as shown in Fig. 3. The performance of Inception-v1 is competitive for general human action recognition. However, it still has some shortcomings in tennis action recognition as follows:

1. Firstly, tennis contains a variety of technical actions, and the subtle differences between them are often reflected in specific channels, such as a channel representing the moving part of the body and a channel for the direction of the body motion. Therefore, it is very important to model the channel features. Inception-v1 module has the ability to extract the channel feature information and retain the significant features, but the ability to model between channels is lacking. Therefore, in this paper, the channel attention module is

added before the feature extraction operation of the $3 \times 3 \times 3$ convolutional branch, which is used to model the dependencies between different channels to emphasize the useful feature channels and suppress the useless ones, so as to improve the ability of feature extraction and performance of the network.

2. Secondly, there is a large amount of redundant and distracting information in tennis sports videos, such as the net and background, which can greatly affect the effectiveness of action recognition. Therefore, it is important for the filtering of spatial features. the Inception-v1 module is similar to the channel dimension for processing information in the spatial dimension. To solve this problem, in this paper, a spatial attention module is added before the feature extraction operation in another $3 \times 3 \times 3$ convolutional branch, which aims to improve the network's attention to different spatial locations in the input data and thus filter out the important spatial features.

3. Finally, due to the high speed and large amplitude of actions characteristics of tennis, the same action may take different forms in different situations, so the modeling of information between actions is very important. In response to the deficiency that the Inception-v1 module lacks action information modeling, in this paper, a motion excitation module is added to it, which improves the focus on features with large changes by modeling the action information between adjacent frames.

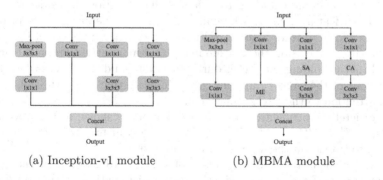

(a) Inception-v1 module   (b) MBMA module

Fig. 3. The structure of Inception-v1 module and MBMA module.

In summary, the MBMA module adds the ability to model information between actions, the ability to actively filter spatial features, and the ability to model dependencies between different channels while retaining the multi-scale information fusion, as shown in the specific feature heat map in Fig. 5. The channel attention module, spatial attention module and motion excitation module will be described in detail in the subsequent Subsects. 3.2 to 3.4.

3.2 Channel Attention

Inspired by Lee [21] that the combination of global average pooling (GAP) and global standard pooling (GSTDP) can better extract channel information. Thus,

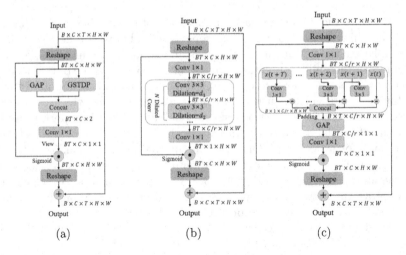

Fig. 4. The MBMA module consists of three main sub-modules:(a) Channel Attention module, (b) Spatial Attention module and (c) Motion Excitation module.

in this paper, a residual Channel Attention (CA) is constructed using a dynamic combination of GAP and GSTDP, aiming to solve the problem of interdependence among different channels to enhance the attention of model to tennis action-related features, such as human body's force-generating parts in tennis actions. As shown in rows 2 and 3 of Fig. 5, the contrasting effect of the purple boxes indicates that using the CA module places more attention on the area of the hand that is holding the racket during the "forehand slice" action, while the other regions of the same comparing group indicate that using the CA module reduces attention to the background area.

The concrete implementation of the CA module is shown in Fig. 4(a). For a given input $F \in \mathbb{R}^{B \times C \times T \times H \times W}$, the CA module will first perform a *reshape* operation to transform the input feature map into $F' \in \mathbb{R}^{BT\ timesC \times H \times W}$. Subsequently, global average pooling and global standard pooling in the spatial dimension are performed to obtain the global distribution of channel feature responses. Then, a dynamic combination of the learnable parameters $f_\theta(x)$ is performed using the 1×1 convolution of the adaptive convolution kernel for local cross-channel interaction without dimensionality reduction, and finally the channel mask is obtained by the *sigmoid* activation function. This can be specifically expressed as Eqs. (1)–(5).

$$G = \frac{1}{H \times W} \sum_{i=1}^{H} \sum_{j=1}^{W} F'[:,:,i,j] \tag{1}$$

$$STD = \sqrt{\frac{1}{N} \sum_{i=1}^{N} (F' - \overline{F'})^2} \tag{2}$$

$$\sigma(x) = \frac{1}{1 + e^{-x}} \tag{3}$$

$$M = \sigma(K_{1\times1} * f_\theta(x) * concat(G, STD, dim = C)) \tag{4}$$

$$Y = F + reshape(F' \odot M) \tag{5}$$

where $\sigma(\cdot)$ is the *sigmoid* activation function. G is the global average pooled feature, STD is the global standard pooled feature, $concat(G, STD, dim = C)$ is the fused feature by channel connectivity. $M \in \mathbb{R}^{BT\times C\ times1\times1}$ is the channel mask, $\odot$ is element-wise multiplying, and $Y \in \mathbb{R}^{B\times C\times T\times H\times W}$ is the output feature map of the channel attention module.

3.3 Spatial Attention

Cheng [22] et al. demonstrated that the dilation convolution can effectively increase the spatial receptive field. In this paper, N dilation convolutions with increasing dilation factors are used to construct a residual Spatial Attention (SA) module, which aims to generate spatial attention maps to enhance players and relevant features in tennis sports videos while suppressing irrelevant features. As shown in rows 4 and 5 of Fig. 5, the contrast effect in the blue box demonstrates the ability of the SA module to enhance the human body and racket features in "forehand slice" action while reducing the attention to redundant information such as the vicinity of the racket.

The specific implementation of the SA module is shown in Fig. 4(b). For a given input $F \in \mathbb{R}^{B\times C\times T\times H\times W}$, the SA module will first perform a *reshape* operation to transform the input feature map into $F' \in \mathbb{R}^{BT\ times C\times H\times W}$. Then a 1×1 2D convolutional layer is used to perform channel compression in the ratio of $1 : r$ to reduce the computational cost of model. Subsequently, N 3×3 2D dilated convolutions with incremental dilation factors are used to obtain a more efficient spatial attention map than the standard convolution. Finally, channel compression and spatial mask acquisition are performed using a 2D convolutional layer with 1×1 and a *sigmoid* activation function. This can be specifically expressed as Eqs. (6)–(8).

$$y_{m_{i,j}} = DC_{d_m}^{k_m}(x_{i,j}) = \sum_{c,l} x_{i+d_m\cdot c, j+d_m\cdot l} \cdot k_{m_{c,l}} \tag{6}$$

$$S = DC_{d_N}^{k_N}(DC_{d_{N-1}}^{k_{N-1}}(\cdots DC_{d_1}^{k_1}(F^*)))$$
$$= DC_{d_N}^{k_N} \circ DC_{d_{N-1}}^{k_{N-1}} \circ \cdots \circ DC_{d_1}^{k_1}(K_{1\times1} * F') \tag{7}$$

$$M = \sigma(K_{1\times1} * S) \tag{8}$$

where $DC_{d_m}^{k_m}$ in Eq. (6) denotes the dilation convolution operator, k_m denotes the size of the m-th convolution kernel, d_m denotes the dilation factor of the m-th convolution kernel. $x_{i,j}$ denotes the value of the i-th row and j-th column of the input feature map, $y_{m_{i,j}}$ denotes the result after the dilation convolution operation. $x_{i+d_m\cdot c, j+d_m\cdot l}$ has a similar meaning to $x_{i,j}$. $k_{m_{c,l}}$ denotes the weight value of the c-th row and l-th column of the convolution kernel. The $S \in \mathbb{R}^{BT \times C/r \times H \times W}$ in Eq. (7) is the spatial attention map after N dilated convolution processing, $K_{1 \times 1}$ represents the 2D convolution of 1×1, and $\sigma(\cdot)$ in Eq. (8) is the *sigmoid* activation function, $M \in \mathbb{R}^{BT \times 1 \times H \times W}$ is the spatial mask. The output of the final spatial attention module is similar to Eq. (5).

3.4   Motion Excitation

Inspired by the research of Jiang [23] et al., optical flow method can effectively obtain motion information. Thus, the optical flow calculation method is draw upon in this paper, RGB frame information are used as input to construct a residual Motion Excitation (ME) module. This module aims to model the motion information between adjacent frames of tennis motion, so as to improve the focus on features with large variations. As shown in rows 6 and 7 of Fig. 5, the comparison effect in the red box shows that the ME module can effectively improve the attention to the "swinging" sub-action of "forehand slice".

The concrete implementation of the ME module is shown in Fig. 4(c). For a given input $F \in \mathbb{R}^{B \times C \times T \times H \times W}$, a *reshape* operation is first performed to transform the input feature map into $F' \in \mathbb{R}^{BT \times C \times H \times W}$. Subsequently, the channel compression is performed by a 1×1 2D convolution layer in the ratio of $1 : r$ to obtain the compressed feature map $F^* \in \mathbb{R}^{BT \times C/r \times H \times W}$. Immediately after that, the features are extracted for the later $T - 1$ frames using a 3×3 convolutional layer and the difference features ΔF of the previous $T - 1$ frames are obtained using subtraction operation. Then, similar to Eq. (1), spatial average pooling is performed on ΔF, and finally a 2D convolutional layer of 1×1 is used for channel unsqueezing and fed to the *sigmoid* activation function to obtain the channel mask. The specific representation is shown in Eqs. (9)–(11).

$$\Delta F = \sum_{t=2}^{T} K_{3 \times 3} * F^*[:, t, :, :, :] - F^*[:, t - 1, :, :, :] \tag{9}$$

$$G = \frac{1}{H \times W} \sum_{i=1}^{H} \sum_{j=1}^{W} \Delta F[:, :, i, j] \tag{10}$$

$$M = \sigma(K_{1 \times 1} * G) \tag{11}$$

where $K_{3 \times 3}$ is the 2D convolution layer of 3×3 and $\Delta F \in \mathbb{R}^{B \times T-1 \times C/r \times H \times W}$ is the motion information difference between the later $T - 1$ frames and the previous $T - 1$ frames. Since the motion information difference of the T-th frame requires the information of the $(T + 1)$-th frame, The size of ΔF will be padded by *padding* operation to $B \times T \times C/r \times H \times W$, G is the features after spatial average pooling. $K_{1 \times 1}$ is a 1×1 2D convolution layer, $M \in \mathbb{R}^{BT \times C \times 1 \times 1}$ is the channel mask, and finally the output of the motion excitation module is similar to Eq. (5).

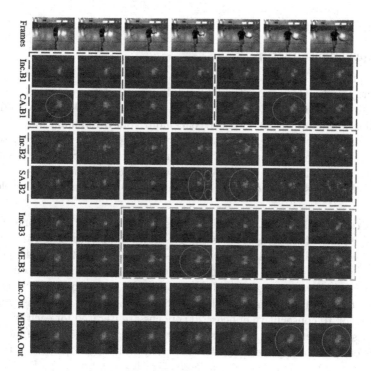

Fig. 5. Comparison of mid-level feature maps of Inception-v1 and MBMA modules. Inc is the abbreviation of Inception-v1. Line 1 is the input frames, lines 2, 4, 6, and 8 are the branches and total features of Inc, and lines 3, 5, 7, and 9 are the features of the CA branch, SA branch, ME branch, and MBMA.Note: The red circles represent places where attention has increased, and the orange circles represent places where attention has weakened. (Color figure online)

3.5 Summary

In this paper, the feature fusion of CA-Branch features Y_{CA}, SA-Branch features Y_{SA}, ME-Branch features Y_{ME} and Max-Branch features Y_{Max} is adopted the method of concatenating to each other according to the channel dimension, as shown in Eq. (12). The CA module, the SA module and the ME module are effectively integrated in MBMA module. The purpose of this is to add channel relationship modeling capabilities that can highlight the differences between different tennis actions, the ability to actively filter useful spatial features, and the ability to model inter-frame sub-actions under the premise of retaining multi-scale information fusion, thereby improving the accuracy of tennis action recognition. As shown in lines 8 and 9 of Fig. 5, the middle-level feature map in line 9 is more obvious than the feature map in line 8 in the feature heat map of the hand parts, footsteps, and player's body.

$$Y = concat(Y_{CA}, Y_{SA}, Y_{ME}, Y_{Max}, dim = C) \tag{12}$$

4   Experiment

4.1   Experimental Setup

Dataset. The THETIS dataset is a publicly available, high-quality tennis sports dataset proposed by Gourgari et al. in 2013. It uses Kinect to capture 12 types of technical actions for 55 players, as shown in Fig. 6(a), including backhand with two hands, backhand, backhand slice, backhand volley, forehand flat, forehand open stands, forehand slice, forehand volley, service flat, service kick, service slick, and smash. There are a total of 1980 samples in THETIS, with 165 samples for each type of action, and each sample provides five data modalities, as shown in Fig. 6(b): RGB, silhouette, depth information, 2D skeleton and 3D skeleton.

Implementation Details. Experiments is conducted in the Pytorch framework, and Kinetics400 [24] is used as the pre-training dataset. The video data is pre-processed as follows: the size of its frames were resized to 224×224, and were enhanced by random horizontal flipping. In the training process, 16 consecutive frames are used for training, and the Dropout rate is set to 0.2. The learning rate is set to 3×10^{-3} initially, and decaying exponentially if the loss remains unchanged for 10 consecutive epochs. 200 epochs are iterated for each train, and the batch size is set to 12. ReLU is mainly used as the activation function in MBMA-Net, and the cross-entropy loss function and Adam optimizer are used.

(a)   (b)

Fig. 6. The contents of THETIS dataset: (a) the examples of 12 tennis actions and (b) 5 data modalities.

4.2   Comparison with Other Methods

In this paper, MBMA-Net is compared with other advanced models in Table 1, including Inception+LSTM [9], Xception+LSTM [10], ResNet50+VTN [25], R(2+1)D-50 [26], S3D [27] and I3D [24]. The experimental results show that the MBMA-Net model is able to achieve an accuracy of 0.8698 using only simple RGB data, which is much better than other models (more than 5.35% higher). In addition, the proposed model contains only 7.56 MB of parameters, which is almost equal to S3D model and much less than any other models, and hence the computation efficiency is also competitive.

Table 1. Comparison of our method with existing methods on THETIS dataset.

Method	Type	Pre-trained	Accuracy	Params.(MB)	Flops.(GB)
Inception+LSTM	CNN+LSTM	ImageNet	0.74	–	–
Xception+LSTM	CNN+LSTM	ImageNet	0.7525	–	–
Resnet50+VTN	CNN+VTN	ImageNet	0.6122	128.17	**7.23**
R(2+1)D-50	3DCNN	Kinetics	0.4518	46.50	39.29
S3D	3DCNN	Kinetics	0.8163	**7.55**	16.95
I3D	3DCNN	Kinetics	0.7738	12.11	25.98
MBMA-Net(Ours)	3DCNN	Kinetics	**0.8698**	7.56	30.23

Table 2. Ablation experiment results of each module on THETIS dataset.(Note: "BS = 4" means the batch size is 4)

No	ME	CA	SA	Accuracy	Diff.(%)	Params.(MB)	Flops.(GB)	Flops.(GB), BS = 4
1	–	–	–	0.8239	0	7.53	30.21	120.83
2	✓	–	–	0.8265	0.26	7.55	30.23	120.90
3	–	✓	–	0.8418	1.79	7.54	30.21	120.83
4	–	–	✓	0.8316	0.77	7.54	30.21	120.85
5	✓	✓	–	0.8520	2.81	7.56	30.23	120.90
6	✓	-	✓	0.8443	2.04	7.55	30.23	120.92
7	–	✓	✓	0.8545	3.06	7.54	30.21	120.85
8	✓	✓	✓	**0.8698**	**4.59**	7.56	30.23	120.92

4.3 Ablation Experiment

In order to further investigate whether the MBMA module is able to effectively improve the accuracy of action recognition, ablation experiments are conducted in this paper. Under the condition that the fixed the size of input is $4 \times 3 \times 16 \times 224 \times 224$, this paper compares the effect of different combinations of the three modules, ME, CA and SA, as shown in Table 2. The experimental results show that the performance is 0.8239 when no module is added (i.e., No. 1, in which the MBMA module is replaced by the Inception-v1 module in the MBMA-Net network architecture). Then, this paper adds ME, CA, and SA modules in the subsequent No. 2, No. 3, and No. 4, respectively. The results show that the addition of each module has a certain improvement, and in particular, the performance improvement is the largest when only the CA module is added, which indicates that the interdependence between channels can more directly improve the accuracy of feature extraction. Subsequently, in No. 5–8, the ME, CA and SA modules are combined in this paper. These four sets of experiments show that inter-channel dependency modeling, expanding spatial receptive field and modeling of action information can promote each other to improve the performance in action feature extraction.

5 Conclusion

In this article, we present a multi-branch mixed attention (MBMA) model for tennis action recognition, which combines information from three dimensions: channel, spatial, and temporal. Our model outperforms state-of-the-art baseline models by 5.35% in terms of accuracy on the THETIS dataset. Various ablation experiments confirm that the model is capable of (a) enhancing the perception of subtle feature differences among different yet similar actions through channel attention; (b) filtering key spatial features using spatial attention; (c) improving the accuracy of action recognition by using a motion excitation mechanism to increase the attention to the features of tennis actions with high speed and large amplitude of actions. For future work, we plan to lighten the MBMA-Net model and extend the model to similar sports video analysis such as badminton.

References

1. Liu, S., et al.: Temporal segmentation of fine-gained semantic action: a motion-centered figure skating dataset. In: Proceedings of the AAAI Conference on Artificial Intelligence, vol. 35, pp. 2163–2171 (2021)
2. McNally, W., Vats, K., Pinto, T., Dulhanty, C., McPhee, J., Wong, A.: Golfdb: a video database for golf swing sequencing. In: Proceedings of the IEEE/CVF Conference on Computer Vision and Pattern Recognition Workshops (2019)
3. Shao, D., Zhao, Y., Dai, B., Lin, D.: Finegym: a hierarchical video dataset for fine-grained action understanding. In: Proceedings of the IEEE/CVF Conference on Computer Vision and Pattern Recognition, pp. 2616–2625 (2020)
4. Vinyes Mora, S., Knottenbelt, W.J.: Deep learning for domain-specific action recognition in tennis. In: Proceedings of the IEEE Conference on Computer Vision and Pattern Recognition Workshops, pp. 114–122 (2017)
5. Skublewska-Paszkowska, M., Powroznik, P., Lukasik, E.: Learning three dimensional tennis shots using graph convolutional networks. Sensors 20(21), 6094 (2020)
6. Rasmussen, T.E., Clemmensen, L.H., Baum, A.: Compressing cnn kernels for videos using tucker decompositions: towards lightweight cnn applications. arXiv preprint arXiv:2203.07033 (2022)
7. Gourgari, S., Goudelis, G., Karpouzis, K., Kollias, S.: Thetis: three dimensional tennis shots a human action dataset. In: Proceedings of the IEEE Conference on Computer Vision and Pattern Recognition Workshops, pp. 676–681 (2013)
8. Faulkner, H., Dick, A.: Tenniset: a dataset for dense fine-grained event recognition, localisation and description. In: 2017 International Conference on Digital Image Computing: Techniques and Applications (DICTA), pp. 1–8. IEEE (2017)
9. Cai, J., Tang, X.: Rgb video based tennis action recognition using a deep historical long short-term memory. arXiv preprint arXiv:1808.00845 (2018)
10. Sen, A., Hossain, S.M.M., Uddin, R., Deb, K., Jo, K.H.: Sequence recognition of indoor tennis actions using transfer learning and long short-term memory. In: Frontiers of Computer Vision: 28th International Workshop, IW-FCV 2022, Hiroshima, Japan, 21–22 February 2022, Revised Selected Papers, pp. 312–324. Springer, Heidelberg (2022). https://doi.org/10.1007/978-3-031-06381-7_22
11. Szegedy, C., et al.: Going deeper with convolutions. In: Proceedings of the IEEE Conference on Computer Vision and Pattern Recognition, pp. 1–9 (2015)

12. Szegedy, C., Ioffe, S., Vanhoucke, V., Alemi, A.: Inception-v4, inception-resnet and the impact of residual connections on learning. In: Proceedings of the AAAI Conference on Artificial Intelligence, vol. 31 (2017)
13. He, K., Zhang, X., Ren, S., Sun, J.: Identity mappings in deep residual networks. In: Leibe, B., Matas, J., Sebe, N., Welling, M. (eds.) ECCV 2016. LNCS, vol. 9908, pp. 630–645. Springer, Cham (2016). https://doi.org/10.1007/978-3-319-46493-0_38
14. Chollet, F.: Xception: deep learning with depthwise separable convolutions. In: Proceedings of the IEEE Conference on Computer Vision and Pattern Recognition, pp. 1251–1258 (2017)
15. Tölgyessy, M., Dekan, M., Chovanec, L.: Skeleton tracking accuracy and precision evaluation of kinect v1, kinect v2, and the azure kinect. Appl. Sci. 11(12), 5756 (2021)
16. Hu, T., Meng, W., Li, S.: Extract accurate 3D human skeleton from video. In: 2019 International Conference on Virtual Reality and Visualization (ICVRV), pp. 100–107. IEEE (2019)
17. Le, V.T., Tran-Trung, K., Hoang, V.T.: A comprehensive review of recent deep learning techniques for human activity recognition. Comput. Intell. Neurosci. 2022 (2022)
18. Jaderberg, M., Simonyan, K., Zisserman, A., et al.: Spatial transformer networks. Adv. Neural Inf. Process. Syst. 28 (2015)
19. Hu, J., Shen, L., Sun, G.: Squeeze-and-excitation networks. In: Proceedings of the IEEE Conference on Computer Vision and Pattern Recognition, pp. 7132–7141 (2018)
20. Liu, Z., Wang, L., Wu, W., Qian, C., Lu, T.: Tam: temporal adaptive module for video recognition. In: Proceedings of the IEEE/CVF International Conference on Computer Vision, pp. 13708–13718 (2021)
21. Lee, H., Kim, H.E., Nam, H.: Srm: a style-based recalibration module for convolutional neural networks. In: Proceedings of the IEEE/CVF International Conference on Computer Vision, pp. 1854–1862 (2019)
22. Cheng, L., Khalitov, R., Yu, T., Zhang, J., Yang, Z.: Classification of long sequential data using circular dilated convolutional neural networks. Neurocomputing 518, 50–59 (2023)
23. Jiang, B., Wang, M., Gan, W., Wu, W., Yan, J.: Stm: spatiotemporal and motion encoding for action recognition. In: Proceedings of the IEEE/CVF International Conference on Computer Vision, pp. 2000–2009 (2019)
24. Carreira, J., Zisserman, A.: Quo vadis, action recognition? a new model and the kinetics dataset. In: proceedings of the IEEE Conference on Computer Vision and Pattern Recognition, pp. 6299–6308 (2017)
25. Neimark, D., Bar, O., Zohar, M., Asselmann, D.: Video transformer network. In: Proceedings of the IEEE/CVF International Conference on Computer Vision, pp. 3163–3172 (2021)
26. Tran, D., Wang, H., Torresani, L., Ray, J., LeCun, Y., Paluri, M.: A closer look at spatiotemporal convolutions for action recognition. In: Proceedings of the IEEE Conference on Computer Vision and Pattern Recognition, pp. 6450–6459 (2018)
27. Xie, S., Sun, C., Huang, J., Tu, Z., Murphy, K.: Rethinking spatiotemporal feature learning for video understanding, vol. 1, no. 2, p. 5. arXiv preprint arXiv:1712.04851 (2017)

Cascade Sampling via Dual Uncertainty for Active Entity Alignment

Jiye Xie[1,2], Jiaxin Li[1,2], Jiawei Tan[1,2], and Hongxing Wang[1,2(✉)]

[1] Key Laboratory of Dependable Service Computing in Cyber Physical Society
(Chongqing University), Ministry of Education, Chongqing, China
{xiejiye,jiaxin_li,jwtan,ihxwang}@cqu.edu.cn
[2] School of Big Data and Software Engineering, Chongqing University,
Chongqing, China

Abstract. Entity Alignment (EA) aims to find and unite equivalent entities across different knowledge graphs for knowledge fusion. It requires pre-aligned entity pairs as seed alignments to train an EA model. Recent effort has employed active learning (AL) to query more informative seed alignments for effective EA modeling at a lower cost. However, it still challenges existing AL methods to find and diversify seed alignments since true alignments themselves are sparse and unavailable before getting annotated. To address this issue, we manipulate seed alignment query based on entity selection on a single knowledge graph and deploy active learning on the EA task by querying entities that behave with (i) Matching Uncertainty determined by the EA model in training and (ii) Novelty-oriented Uncertainty estimated through diverse entity identification. To adapt the query set to changes in the EA model and aligned entities during AL iterations, we propose a dynamic cascade sampling strategy by trading-off between matching uncertainty and novelty-oriented uncertainty in a two-stage manner. Experiments on real-world benchmark datasets show the effectiveness of the proposed approach in comparison with state-of-the-art methods.

Keywords: Entity Alignment · Active Learning · Dual Uncertainty · Cascade Sampling · Knowledge Graph

1 Introduction

A Knowledge Graph (KG) symbolizes the entity concepts and their relationships in the real world, which is fundamental to plenty of downstream applications such as recommendation systems [27] and semantic search [23]. The last decade has witnessed the rapid emergence of open-source and large-scale KGs, such as DBpedia [10], YAGO-3 [12], and Wikidata [21]. However, KGs are usually developed independently by multiple organizations who may phrase the same entity from different concepts according to their specific needs, leading to gaps

© The Author(s), under exclusive license to Springer Nature Switzerland AG 2023
Z. Jin et al. (Eds.): KSEM 2023, LNAI 14118, pp. 176–187, 2023.
https://doi.org/10.1007/978-3-031-40286-9_15

in knowledge sharing. To produce a single and comprehensive KG, Entity Alignment (EA) is needed to integrate various KGs by aligning equivalent entities in different KGs.

Learning a model for EA cannot do without a collection of a training set of seed alignments, which is made up by pre-aligned entities across different KGs. However, manual annotation of seed alignments could be labor-intensive and time-consuming. To mitigate the annotation burden, it is of vital importance to guarantee the quality of seed alignments, which exactly meets the goal of active learning [1]. Surprisingly, active learning has rarely been explored in the EA task. The major challenge lies in true alignments themselves are sparse and unavailable before getting annotated, and traditional active learning may exhaust itself on querying and annotating entity pairs that have no alignment relationship. To avoid missed queries, recent effort has shifted the attention towards entity-induced active alignment, where each query is from entities of a single KG, and the annotation is to match those queries to the right entities from the other KG. Its potential has been partially shown by [2,11] when combined with some heuristics like node centrality [3,6], graph coverage [15], and prediction margin [16]. Despite these advances, considerable entities triggering heuristic conditions may be homogeneous to those already aligned. Not only is annotation redundant if querying such entities, but the EA performance may degrade when trained on the annotated data of bias.

In this study, we propose to address the pitfall of annotating similar entities by jointly considering model and sample states during AL iteration loops. From a model state perspective, in each active learning loop, we start with catching those entities that encounter uncertain (*i.e.*, seemingly random) alignments inferred from the current EA model, which we call matching uncertainty sampling. To further ensure more distinct information participating in EA modeling, we force a second stage sampling on previously sampled entities, which selects entities different from those already aligned. In light of such a sample state perspective, we propose to train a novel entity detector to rank sampling candidates by their novelty-oriented uncertainty. After the two-stage Cascade Sampling via Dual Uncertainty (CSDU), the top-ranked entities will be annotated with their alignments for training data update and EA model retraining. In addition, considering that there may exist sampling bias, we propose to dynamically trade-off sampling between matching uncertainty and novelty-oriented uncertainty, for which we make the sampling adaptive to the size of misaligned data.

The main contributions of this paper are summarized as:

- We propose an entity sampling strategy, Cascade Sampling via Dual Uncertainty (CSDU), which dynamically holds the trade-off between matching uncertainty and sample diversity in a two-stage manner.
- We rely on CSDU to realize an entity-induced alignment annotation scheme and build a cascade active learning framework to facilitate training entity alignment models with limited alignment annotations.

- We conduct extensive experiments and ablation studies on three benchmark datasets. Experimental results show the superiority of our proposed approach when compared with existing methods.

2   Related Work

2.1   Entity Alignment

In recent years, significant research effort has been dedicated to Entity Alignment (EA) tasks. Most of the existing work [5,8,13,17–19,22] is devoted to learning better entity representations using KG embedding techniques such as TransE [18] and GNN [22]. Specifically, some work [9,18] models relations to help guide the alignment of entities, and some others [17,19] capture neighbor information to learn entity representations. These methods all rely on a collection of seed alignments to train an EA model, but obtaining seed alignments is a labor-intensive job. As a result, EA training has a strong demand for data-efficient algorithms. Active learning, as a representative efficient annotation paradigm, received attention from the research community [2,11].

2.2   Active Learning

Active learning is an approach that iteratively selects the most informative samples from unlabeled data for annotation so that one can train a model with high accuracy using fewer labeled data [1]. The most mainstream AL framework is pool-based sampling [1,2,4,11,24–26], which has a basic pool of unlabeled instances to query. In the general domain, entropy-defined uncertainty sampling has been proven to be effective and easy to implement [1,14,26], while some researchers have gone as far as designing a discriminator to predict sample uncertainty for selection purposes [4,26]. Recently, several attempts [2,11] have explored active learning in EA tasks. Current methods primarily focus on identifying valuable data for alignment labeling during the evaluation of the alignment model but few take into account the uncertainty about the entities themselves, resulting in selected entities with poor sample coverage and diversity. Nevertheless, the diversity of data is an important factor that impacts label redundancy. In light of this, we propose in this study a cascade active entity alignment method that can simultaneously consider both the uncertain state of the alignment model and the misaligned data.

3   Method

3.1   Problem Formulation

A Knowledge Graph (KG) can be expressed as $\mathcal{G} = (\mathcal{E}, \mathcal{R})$, where $\mathcal{E}$ is the set of entities, and $\mathcal{R}$ is the set of relations. In the Entity Alignment (EA) task, we have two KGs: $\mathcal{G}^1 = \{\mathcal{E}^1, \mathcal{R}^1\}$, $\mathcal{G}^2 = \{\mathcal{E}^2, \mathcal{R}^2\}$. EA is to find the set of equivalent entity pairs $\mathcal{A} = \{(e^1, e^2) | e^1 \in \mathcal{E}^1, e^2 \in \mathcal{E}^2, e^1 \sim e^2\}$, where $\sim$

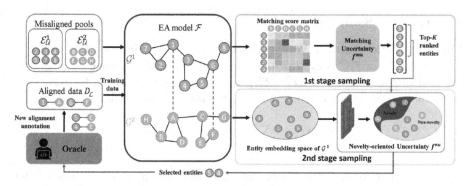

Fig. 1. Overview of our proposed CSDU for active entity alignment. In the first sampling stage, entities in $\mathcal{G}^1$ with the top-K matching uncertainty scores are extracted and form a candidate set $\mathcal{E}_c^1$. In the second sampling stage, we find entities of high novelty score from $\mathcal{E}_c^1$ for subsequent alignment annotation.

denotes the alignment relationship. For ease of reference, we split entity sets as $\mathcal{E}^1 = \mathcal{E}_\mathcal{U}^1 \cup \mathcal{E}_\mathcal{L}^1$ and $\mathcal{E}^2 = \mathcal{E}_\mathcal{U}^2 \cup \mathcal{E}_\mathcal{L}^2$, where subscript $\mathcal{U}$ suggests entities in the set are misaligned, and subscript $\mathcal{L}$ suggests aligned. An EA model can be learned when fed with a set of manually annotated training data $D_\mathcal{L} = \{(e^1, e^2)|e^1 \in \mathcal{E}_\mathcal{L}^1, e^2 \in \mathcal{E}_\mathcal{L}^2, e^1 \sim e^2\}$. In this work, we set active learning as iterative loops among entity selection, alignment annotation, and EA model training, by which we can gradually expand $D_\mathcal{L}$ and improve the EA model until the annotation budget is exhausted. Without loss of generality, we iteratively select informative entities from misaligned pool $\mathcal{E}_\mathcal{U}^1$ of $\mathcal{G}^1$ and manually match them with corresponding aligned entities from misaligned pool $\mathcal{E}_\mathcal{U}^2$ of $\mathcal{G}^2$.

3.2 Framework Overview

Our proposed active entity alignment features two sampling stages, which we coin as Cascade Sampling via Dual Uncertainty (CSDU). We illustrate the idea in Fig. 1. During each iteration, we rely on present training data $D_\mathcal{L}$ to retrain an EA model which targets at matching any pair of entities from different KGs in the same embedding space. In the first sampling stage, we run EA between $\mathcal{G}^1$ and $\mathcal{G}^2$ so that we can evaluate the matching uncertainty of each entity in $\mathcal{E}_\mathcal{U}^1$ and put top-K ranked entities in an annotation candidate set $\mathcal{E}_c^1$, where the second stage takes further sampling. We intend to retain entities that are distinct from those in $\mathcal{E}_\mathcal{L}^1$. To this end, we devise a novelty-oriented uncertainty to distinguish between novelty and non-novelty of entities relative to all $e \in \mathcal{E}_\mathcal{L}^1$. Upon annotating alignments from finally selected entities to their counterparts in $\mathcal{E}_\mathcal{U}^2$, we update the training data $D_\mathcal{L}$ and the alignment state for all the entities from both $\mathcal{G}^1$ and $\mathcal{G}^2$. It is worth noting that we will in the following allow our CSDU for a balanced selection of entities in terms of matching uncertainty and novelty-oriented uncertainty.

3.3 Cascade Sampling

Matching Uncertainty. We view each $e_j^2 \in \mathcal{E}_\mathcal{U}^2$ as an independent category so that EA from $\mathcal{E}_\mathcal{U}^1$ to $\mathcal{E}_\mathcal{U}^2$ can be compared to classifying each $e_i^1 \in \mathcal{E}_\mathcal{U}^1$ by different category labels $\{e^2 : e^2 \in \mathcal{E}_\mathcal{U}^2\}$. In such a case, we measure the matching uncertainty of e_i^1 as the entropy of its categorization distribution:

$$f^{mu}(e_i^1) = -\sum_{j \in I_t} s(e_i^1, e_j^2) \log_2 s(e_i^1, e_j^2), \tag{1}$$

where $s(*, *)$ represents the cosine similarity between involved entities in the feature embedding space and I_t indexes the first t matching scores between e_i^1 and all $e^2 \in \mathcal{E}_\mathcal{U}^2$. By using Eq. 1, we can select the top-K entities with high matching uncertainty and have an annotation candidate set $\mathcal{E}_c^1$. The size of K will vary dynamically and we will cover the details in a follow-up.

Novelty-Oriented Uncertainty. After matching uncertainty sampling, to further spot novel entities that are distinct from those in $\mathcal{E}_\mathcal{L}^1$, we need to divide $\mathcal{E}_c^1$ into two parts, where one collects novel entities and the other not novel. We then in the entity embedding feature space train a three-layer MLP classifier, f_M, on entity set $\mathcal{E}_1$ of $\mathcal{G}_1$ so that f_M can distinguish between aligned and misaligned entities. Therefore, we define the loss by

$$\ell = -\frac{1}{|\mathcal{E}_\mathcal{L}^1|} \sum_{e_i^1 \in \mathcal{E}_\mathcal{L}^1} \log(f_M(e_i^1)) - \frac{\lambda}{|\mathcal{E}_\mathcal{U}^1|} \sum_{e_j^1 \in \mathcal{E}_\mathcal{U}^1} \log(1 - f_M(e_j^1)), \tag{2}$$

where $|\cdot|$ returns the number of its input set, and λ is a weighting factor in our loss function to balance the contribution of aligned and misaligned cross-entropy to the loss. Once the training is completed, we can evaluate each $e \in \mathcal{E}_c^1$ by $f_M(e)$ which returns the possibility of being similar for e to aligned entities. Considering that novel entities should be dissimilar to those already aligned, we define Novelty-oriented Uncertainty of entity e as

$$f^{nu}(e) = 1 - |\tau - f_M(e)|, \tag{3}$$

where $f_M(e) \in [0, 1]$, and τ anchors the decision reference for novel entities. To select diverse entities, τ should be close to 0. Equation 3 enables us to score entities in $\mathcal{E}_c^1$ and take a subset $\mathcal{E}_s^1$ that is composed of top-b entities for alignment annotation. According to the new annotation, we update the training data $D_\mathcal{L}$, and move newfound aligned entities from the misaligned pools $\mathcal{E}_\mathcal{U}^1, \mathcal{E}_\mathcal{U}^2$ to corresponding aligned pools $\mathcal{E}_\mathcal{L}^1, \mathcal{E}_\mathcal{L}^2$. This process is repeated until the entire budget is exhausted.

Dynamic Mechanism. In the early AL stages, training data are scarce, but EA modeling favors diverse training data. We need to set a larger K (which equals $|\mathcal{E}_c^1|$) to provide a wider range of matching uncertainty sampled entities

---

Algorithm 1. Active entity alignment with CSDU

Input: Two knowledge graphs with initial aligned data $D_{\mathcal{L}}$ and misaligned entity pools $\mathcal{E}_{\mathcal{U}}^1$, $\mathcal{E}_{\mathcal{U}}^2$
Output: Entity alignment model $\mathcal{F}$
1: **repeat**
2:     Train $\mathcal{F}$ on $D_{\mathcal{L}}$;
3:     Calculate matching uncertainty $f^{mu}(e)$ for each $e \in \mathcal{E}_{\mathcal{U}}^1$ in the $\mathcal{F}$ derived feature embedding space by Eq. 1;
4:     Calculate K by Eq. 4;
5:     Select top-K entities from $\mathcal{E}_{\mathcal{U}}^1$ based on f^{mu} scores to form the annotation candidate set $\mathcal{E}_c^1$;
6:     Train entity novelty detector f_M by minimizing loss Eq. 2;
7:     Calculate novelty-oriented uncertainty $f^{nu}(e)$ for each $e \in \mathcal{E}_c^1$ by Eq. 3;
8:     Select top-b entities from $\mathcal{E}_c^1$ based on f^{nu} scores and annotate them with their aligned entities in $\mathcal{E}_{\mathcal{U}}^2$;
9:     Add new annotated alignments into $D_{\mathcal{L}}$;
10:    Remove aligned entities from $\mathcal{E}_{\mathcal{U}}^1$ and $\mathcal{E}_{\mathcal{U}}^2$;
11: **until** Annotation budget is consumed

---

for sampling with novelty-oriented uncertainty so that entities selected for annotation are significantly diverse within iterations. As training progresses and the EA model performance improves, our focus shifts to highly matching uncertain entities and K should decrease. We can achieve the above purpose by simply making K proportional to $|\mathcal{E}_{\mathcal{U}}^1|$:

$$K = |\mathcal{E}_{\mathcal{U}}^1| \times p, \tag{4}$$

where p is a pre-set ratio for sampling with matching uncertainty.

For the complete process of our active entity alignment with CSDU, we provide a summary in Algorithm 1.

4   Experiments

4.1   Experimental Setup

Datasets. We adopt three popular EA datasets for evaluation: D-W-15K-V1, D-Y-15K-V1 and EN-FR-15K-V1. These datasets are all from OpenEA [20], but different in terms of KG sources and languages. Each dataset has two KGs and 15,000 equivalent entity pairs. All the involved KGs are from widely used real graphs in the EA community: DBpdiea [10], Wikidata [21] and YAGO [12].

Evaluation Metrics. Following the convention [5,7,19], we evaluate the EA performance using Hit@1 and MRR as the primary metrics. Hits@1 measures the percentage of correctly aligned entities that are ranked first by the alignment model, while MRR calculates the average rank of the correctly aligned entities.

Table 1. Hit@1 and MRR performance comparison against all AL sampling baselines on the datasets D-W-15K-V1, D-Y-15K-V1, and EN-FR-15K-V1. The annotation proportion is 30% for all the participants.

methods	D-W-15K-V1		D-Y-15K-V1		EN-FR-15K-V1	
	Hits@1	MRR	Hits@1	MRR	Hits@1	MRR
random	44.19	0.54	55.41	0.63	33.29	0.46
betweenness [2]	40.77	0.51	45.71	0.54	30.88	0.44
degree [6]	36.81	0.48	43.03	0.51	27.83	0.40
pagerank [3]	44.25	0.56	54.91	0.64	34.05	0.48
vanilla margin [16]	50.55	0.60	59.78	0.69	37.81	0.51
struct-margin [11]	50.12	0.62	61.81	0.72	37.81	0.52
CSDU	**51.96**	**0.63**	**63.91**	**0.73**	**39.46**	**0.53**

To assess the overall performance of our AL strategy and compare it with other strategies, we plot the performance curve of the EA model against the proportion of annotated entities and calculate the area under the curve (AUC).

Sampling Strategies. We conduct a comparative analysis of the proposed CSDU with various sampling methods in active learning, including (i) Random sampling, (ii) Topology-based sampling that utilizes graph topology to select entities with betweenness centrality [2], degree centrality [6], and pagerank centrality [3] for annotation, as well as (iii) Margin-based sampling with vanilla margin[16] and struct-margin [11] that are designed around the measurement on the margin between the highest and second entity matching. We run the baseline sampling strategies using their officially released code or replicate them if not provided. During evaluation, these methods are tested against the same EA model, Alinet [19].

Parameter Settings. We initialize the aligned data $D_{\mathcal{L}}$ by using the pagerank centrality algorithm [3] to select and annotate 10% of the entities from the entire dataset, while the remaining 90% constitute the initial misaligned pool. Then we iteratively select 5% of the data from the misaligned pool in each active learning loop, until the number of aligned entities reaches 40%. For the matching uncertainty sampling, we set $p = 15\%$, $t = 10$ and $\lambda = 1.2$, for the novelty-oriented sampling, we set $\tau = 0.1$.

4.2   Experimental Results

Based on the two evaluation metrics, Hits@1, and MRR, Table 1 compares the performance of various methods at a 30% annotation level. The results reveal that the proposed method has a significant advantage, thereby confirming the effectiveness of cascade sampling in entity alignment tasks. For a more comprehensive comparison between these methods, we plotted the performance curves of each method at different annotation levels using the Hits@1 metric, as depicted in Fig. 2. Additionally, Table 2 reports the AUC values of each curve.

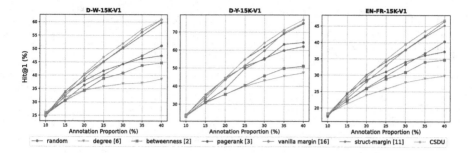

Fig. 2. Hit@1 performance curves of different AL sampling strategies on the datasets D-W-15K-V1, D-Y-15K-V1, and EN-FR-15K-V1.

Table 2. Overall AUC(%) value of Hit@1 curve (Fig. 2) for each AL sampling strategy on the datasets D-W-15K-V1, D-Y-15K-V1, and EN-FR-15K-V1.

methods	D-W-15K-V1	D-Y-15K-V1	EN-FR-15K-V1
random	11.86	13.87	8.86
betweenness [2]	11.15	11.99	8.41
degree [6]	10.41	11.52	7.60
pagerank [3]	11.98	14.60	9.08
vanilla margin [16]	13.29	15.32	9.80
struct-margin [11]	13.34	15.73	9.99
CSDU	**13.63**	**15.96**	**10.16**

Random Sampling. Random sampling is generally not effective when the proportion of annotations is small, especially less than 20%, but it becomes more competitive as the number of annotations increases, outperforming many topology-based sampling methods. However, for most annotation scales, random sampling falls significantly behind the best methods in terms of performance.

Topology-Based Sampling. Previous literature [2,11] suggests that topology-based sampling strategies, betweenness [2], degree [6], and pagerank [3], have advantages when dealing with small amounts of annotation. But as the amount of annotations increases (e.g., greater than 15%), the impact of the bias between the training set and the test set can affect the performance of these strategies, causing them to lose competitiveness.

Margin-Based Sampling. Margin-based sampling strategies, vanilla margin [16], and struct-margin [11] select entities that the current EA model lacks confidence in predicting. When the amount of available annotations is limited, an inaccurate EA model may not be able to induce a well-ordered margin, which makes vanilla margin sampling less effective. As the number of annotations increases, vanilla margin sampling gets performance improved. On the other hand, struct-margin introduces graph propagation into margin sampling, making

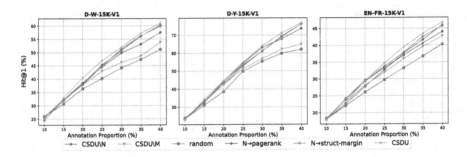

Fig. 3. Ablation study on the two sampling modules of our proposed CSDU.

margin estimates more accurate. As shown in Fig. 2, struct-margin also becomes highly competitive even if the annotation proportion is less than 20%.

CSDU. The proposed CSDU sampling places great importance on both sample uncertainty and diversity by introducing its matching uncertainty sampling and novelty-oriented uncertainty sampling. The matching uncertainty sampling uses alignment information between different KGs, while the novelty-oriented uncertainty sampling exploits the affinity information within a single KG. As a result, structural information between and within knowledge graphs are both accounted for. From the results in Fig. 2 and Table 1, we can observe that CSDU performs well in most annotation cases, particularly when the volume of annotation is equal to or greater than 20%.

4.3   Ablation Studies

To evaluate the impact of different modules in our method, we conduct ablation experiments. As the novelty-oriented uncertainty sampling is a crucial component of our work, we run tests if without it (denoted as CSDU\N) or having it replaced with competitive (*c.f.* the results in Sect. 4.2) pagerank centrality sampling (denoted as N→pagerank) or struct-margin sampling (denoted as N→struct-margin). Ablation also has been conducted by removing matching uncertainty sampling from our CSDU (denoted as CSDU\M). Moreover, as a control group, we eliminate both sampling modules and replace them with random sampling (devoted as random).

Figure 3 shows the outcomes of the ablation experiments. The complete CSDU method consistently outperforms all ablations, while random sampling in the place of our two sampling modules exhibits the lowest performance. This phenomenon indicates that both the matching uncertainty and novelty-oriented uncertainty sampling are beneficial in enhancing the performance of active entity alignment.

4.4   Hyperparameter Sensitivity

As mentioned in Sect. 3.3, determining the appropriate value for the hyperparameter p is critical to the trade-off between matching uncertainty and sample diversity. In this section, we test several values for p, including 10%, 15%, 20%, and 30%.

Figure 4 shows the results on the used benchmark datasets. As can be seen, when p is equal to 15%, the proposed CSDU performs the best. If p is too small, our cascade sampling almost degenerates into matching uncertainty sampling, which results in insufficient diversity in sampling and weak competitiveness especially when the annotation quantity is limited. Conversely, if p is too large, our cascade sampling may pay less attention to matching uncertainty, resulting in limited improvement to the current EA model by selecting entities when annotation increases.

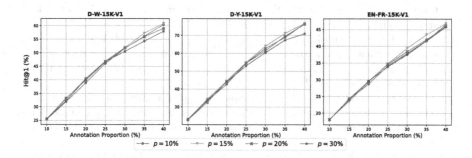

Fig. 4. Impact of hyperparameter p that Eq. 4 defines

5   Conclusion

In this paper, we proposed a novel entity sampling strategy, Cascaded Sampling with Dual Uncertainty (CSDU), which dynamically balances matching uncertainty and sample diversity in a two-stage manner to select high quality entities for alignment annotation. Based on the proposed CSDU, we build a cascade active learning framework that is able to effectively address the challenges of entity alignment with limited annotations. Through extensive experiments and ablation studies, we demonstrate that our proposed active learning approach on entity alignment achieves state-of-the-art performance on multiple benchmarks when compared with existing methods.

Acknowledgment. The work was supported in part by the Major Project of New Generation Artificial Intelligence of the Ministry of Science and Technology of China under Grant 2021ZD0113402 and the National Natural Science Foundation of China under Grant 61976029.

References

1. Aggarwal, C.C., Kong, X., Gu, Q., Han, J., Philip, S.Y.: Active learning: a survey. In: Data Classification, pp. 599–634. Chapman and Hall/CRC, Boca Raton (2014)
2. Berrendorf, M., Faerman, E., Tresp, V.: Active learning for entity alignment. In: Hiemstra, D., Moens, M.-F., Mothe, J., Perego, R., Potthast, M., Sebastiani, F. (eds.) ECIR 2021. LNCS, vol. 12656, pp. 48–62. Springer, Cham (2021). https://doi.org/10.1007/978-3-030-72113-8_4
3. Brin, S., Page, L.: The anatomy of a large-scale hypertextual web search engine. Comput. Netw. ISDN Syst. **30**(1–7), 107–117 (1998)
4. Caramalau, R., Bhattarai, B., Kim, T.K.: Sequential graph convolutional network for active learning. In: Proceedings of the IEEE/CVF International Conference on Computer Vision, pp. 9583–9592 (2021)
5. Chen, M., Tian, Y., Yang, M., Zaniolo, C.: Multilingual knowledge graph embeddings for cross-lingual knowledge alignment. arXiv preprint arXiv:1611.03954 (2016)
6. Das, K., Samanta, S., Pal, M.: Study on centrality measures in social networks: a survey. Social Netw. Anal. Min. **8**, 1–11 (2018)
7. Gao, Y., Liu, X., Wu, J., Li, T., Wang, P., Chen, L.: ClusterEA: scalable entity alignment with stochastic training and normalized mini-batch similarities. In: Proceedings of the ACM SIGKDD Conference on Knowledge Discovery and Data Mining, pp. 421–431 (2022)
8. Ge, C., Liu, X., Chen, L., Zheng, B., Gao, Y.: Make it easy: an effective end-to-end entity alignment framework. In: Proceedings of the International ACM SIGIR Conference on Research and Development in Information Retrieval, pp. 777–786 (2021)
9. Guo, L., Sun, Z., Hu, W.: Learning to exploit long-term relational dependencies in knowledge graphs. In: International Conference on Machine Learning, pp. 2505–2514. PMLR (2019)
10. Lehmann, J., et al.: Dbpedia-a large-scale, multilingual knowledge base extracted from wikipedia. Semant. Web **6**(2), 167–195 (2015)
11. Liu, B., Scells, H., Zuccon, G., Hua, W., Zhao, G.: ActiveEA: active learning for neural entity alignment. arXiv preprint arXiv:2110.06474 (2021)
12. Mahdisoltani, F., Biega, J., Suchanek, F.: Yago3: a knowledge base from multilingual wikipedias. In: Biennial Conference on Innovative Data Systems Research (2014)
13. Mao, X., Wang, W., Xu, H., Lan, M., Wu, Y.: MRAEA: an efficient and robust entity alignment approach for cross-lingual knowledge graph. In: Proceedings of the International Conference on Web Search and Data Mining, pp. 420–428 (2020)
14. Ostapuk, N., Yang, J., Cudré-Mauroux, P.: ActiveLink: deep active learning for link prediction in knowledge graphs. In: The World Wide Web Conference, pp. 1398–1408 (2019)
15. Puthal, D., Nepal, S., Paris, C., Ranjan, R., Chen, J.: Efficient algorithms for social network coverage and reach. In: IEEE International Congress on Big Data, pp. 467–474. IEEE (2015)
16. Scheffer, T., Decomain, C., Wrobel, S.: Active hidden Markov models for information extraction. In: Hoffmann, F., Hand, D.J., Adams, N., Fisher, D., Guimaraes, G. (eds.) IDA 2001. LNCS, vol. 2189, pp. 309–318. Springer, Heidelberg (2001). https://doi.org/10.1007/3-540-44816-0_31

17. Sun, Z., Hu, W., Zhang, Q., Qu, Y.: Bootstrapping entity alignment with knowledge graph embedding. In: Proceedings of the International Joint Conference on Artificial Intelligence (IJCAI) (2018)
18. Sun, Z., Huang, J., Hu, W., Chen, M., Guo, L., Qu, Y.: TransEdge: translating relation-contextualized embeddings for knowledge graphs. In: Ghidini, C., et al. (eds.) ISWC 2019. LNCS, vol. 11778, pp. 612–629. Springer, Cham (2019). https://doi.org/10.1007/978-3-030-30793-6_35
19. Sun, Z., et al.: Knowledge graph alignment network with gated multi-hop neighborhood aggregation. In: Proceedings of the AAAI Conference on Artificial Intelligence, pp. 222–229 (2020)
20. Sun, Z., et al.: A benchmarking study of embedding-based entity alignment for knowledge graphs. arXiv preprint arXiv:2003.07743 (2020)
21. Vrandečić, D., Krötzsch, M.: Wikidata: a free collaborative knowledgebase. Commun. ACM 57(10), 78–85 (2014)
22. Wang, Z., Lv, Q., Lan, X., Zhang, Y.: Cross-lingual knowledge graph alignment via graph convolutional networks. In: Proceedings of the Conference on Empirical Methods in Natural Language Processing, pp. 349–357 (2018)
23. Xiong, C., Power, R., Callan, J.: Explicit semantic ranking for academic search via knowledge graph embedding. In: Proceedings of the International Conference on World Wide Web, pp. 1271–1279 (2017)
24. Yang, L., Zhang, Y., Chen, J., Zhang, S., Chen, D.Z.: Suggestive annotation: a deep active learning framework for biomedical image segmentation. In: Descoteaux, M., Maier-Hein, L., Franz, A., Jannin, P., Collins, D.L., Duchesne, S. (eds.) MICCAI 2017. LNCS, vol. 10435, pp. 399–407. Springer, Cham (2017). https://doi.org/10.1007/978-3-319-66179-7_46
25. Zeng, W., Zhao, X., Tang, J., Fan, C.: Reinforced active entity alignment. In: Proceedings of the ACM International Conference on Information & Knowledge Management, pp. 2477–2486 (2021)
26. Zhang, B., Li, L., Yang, S., Wang, S., Zha, Z.J., Huang, Q.: State-relabeling adversarial active learning. In: Proceedings of the IEEE/CVF International Conference on Computer Vision, pp. 8756–8765 (2020)
27. Zhang, F., Yuan, N.J., Lian, D., Xie, X., Ma, W.Y.: Collaborative knowledge base embedding for recommender systems. In: Proceedings of the ACM SIGKDD International Conference on Knowledge Discovery and Data Mining, pp. 353–362 (2016)

Template Shift and Background Suppression for Visual Object Tracking

Yiwei Wu[1], Ke Qi[1(✉)], Wenbin Chen[1], Jingdong Zhang[2], and Yutao Qi[3]

[1] School of Computer Science and Cyber Engineer, Guangzhou University,
Guangzhou 510000, China
`2112106060@e.gzhu.edu.cn`
[2] South China Normal University, Guangzhou 510000, China
[3] School of Computer and Information Engineering, Guangzhou Huali College,
Guangzhou 510000, China

Abstract. In recent years, transformer-based object tracking methods have demonstrated strong potential for development and outperformed traditional convolutional neural networks (CNN)-based models. However, most transformer-based trackers ignored the contradiction between the position of the target appearance and the window partitioning of the template, which breaks the integrity of the object. In this paper, we propose a more effective way of performing cross-correlation between the template and search region. Furthermore, we also design a method to suppress the impact of background factors in the template. We conducted a series of ablation experiments to evaluate the effectiveness of our design choices. Our method greatly improves the performance of the model. Because our method can be easily ported to other models, which indicates the potential for further improvement and development.

Keywords: Visul · Object Tracking · Transformer · Swin-Transformer

1 Introduction

Object tracking is a highly important research topic in the field of computer vision and has great practical value in video surveillance, autonomous driving, UAV autopilot, sports broadcasting, and other areas. Its main purpose is to extract reliable visual features from the given initial frame and corresponding tracked target, and based on this information, to locate the correct target and its position in subsequent video frames.

In recent years, the success of Vision Transformer (ViT) [1] in the field of computer vision has greatly promoted the development of transformer-based object tracking models. Since the feature extraction of transformers is based on attention calculation using windows, most transformer-based trackers cut the search area and template into several windows for feature embedding during the initial process, and a series of subsequent operations are performed based on these windows. SwinTransformer [2] is based on the transformer architecture. Its

ⓒ The Author(s), under exclusive license to Springer Nature Switzerland AG 2023
Z. Jin et al. (Eds.): KSEM 2023, LNAI 14118, pp. 188–200, 2023.
https://doi.org/10.1007/978-3-031-40286-9_16

main feature is the use of a feature pyramid structure based on local receptive fields to replace the traditional global attention mechanism. This enables the capture of local features at a lower computational cost. Although this approach improves the efficiency of object recognition, it has some drawbacks for the task of object tracking. The reason is that object tracking is of better matching the features between the template and the search region.

As shown in Fig. 1, when the target appears in the middle of a divided window, the window partitioning separates the key parts of the target into several individual windows, which undermines the integrity of the target. This results in the target not being well-matched with the target in the search area. Therefore, this article proposes a method of Template Shift, which recombines the windows and moves the target that was originally located in the middle of several windows to the center of a single window. This allows for more effective correlation calculations in subsequent operations.

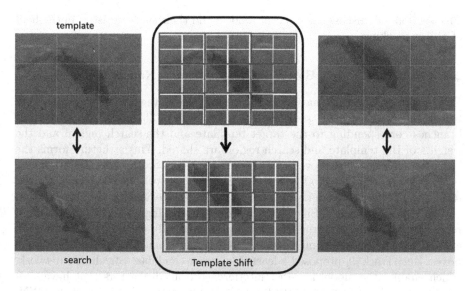

Fig. 1. The effect of template shift. The top left corner shows the template and the bottom left corner shows the search area. The black box represents the template shift module. After passing through the template shift module, the template is better matched with the target in the search area.

In addition, most models directly embed all images in the template region for feature extraction, and then all windows of template will participate in the subsequent calculation. This approach adds the background feature vector of the tracked object in the first frame to the subsequent calculation, but the background inevitably changes during the motion of the object. In this case, continuing to involve background features in correlation calculation will interfere with the tracking results. To minimize the impact of background features in the template on the tracking results, this paper proposes a method that can effectively suppress the influence of background in the template. In the computation process, we eliminate the tokens belonging to the background, so that they do not participate in the cross-correlation operation with the search region. Therefore, the model will pay more attention to the tracked object itself during the detection process and reduce the interference of excessive background factors.

Overall, this paper proposes a new model and makes the following contributions:

1. A new Swintransformer-based object tracking model.

2. A more effective and portable template feature extraction and cross-correlation operation method.

3. A structure that effectively suppresses template background information.

2 Related Work

This section will discuss some recent models and their characteristics in the field of object tracking.

2.1 Tracking Models Based on Convolutional Neural Networks

CNN-based architectures have been the mainstream in the field of object tracking before the emergence of transformers. The SiamFC [3] model has two input branches corresponding to the target template and the search region, and the weights of the template and search region are shared. This structure forms the basis for subsequent improvements in the Siamese network series. After that, a series of target tracking models based on Siamese network structure were derived [4–6]. The Ocean [7] adopts different sampling strategies for the classification and regression branches. SiamBAN [8] regards tracking as a classification and regression problem using the expression ability of fully convolutional networks, eliminating the need for multi-scale search patterns and pre-defined candidate boxes. KeepTrack [9] proposed a learnable target candidate correlation network, which enables the model to resist interference from distractors that have very similar appearance features to the tracked object. In summary, most of the CNN-based models use the Siamese network structure, which is also followed by our model. Our model uses two branches to extract features from the template and search regions, and they share weights.

2.2 Tracking Models Based on Transformer

In 2021, [10] combine transformer and tracking for the first time, and introduced a model structure similar to the Siamese network, using the encoder and decoder structures in the transformer, and achieving significant improvement in performance. Similarly, models such as STARK [11], AIT [12], SwinTrack [13], etc. also use encoder-decoder structures. In STARK [11], the encoder enables the model to learn global temporal and spatial features, while the decoder learns the query's embedding to predict the temporal and spatial position of the target. AIT [12] proposed a multi-head co-attention (MCA) module to explore the correlation of features, and used this information to optimize the target feature map. SwinTrack [13] uses Swin Transformer for feature extraction, followed by encoder and decoder for transformer-based feature fusion. It comprehensively studies different strategies for feature fusion, position encoding, and training loss, making it a simple yet powerful model.

[14] uses transformer to extract features of the template and search region, and proposes a network called Feature Fusion Network to fuse features, which effectively combines the template and search region. The model achieves very promising results. SparseTT [15] model uses a novel sparse Transformer tracker to enhance Transformer-based visual tracking and achieve more accurate tracking. CSWinTT [16] proposed a new Multi-Scale Cyclic Shifting Window Attention structure for visual object tracking models, which elevates attention from pixel-level to window-level. It has the advantage of aggregating attention across different scales and producing the best fine-scale matching for the target object. Our difference with [16] is that the window shift in CSWinTT [16] is to improve the accuracy of similarity and is based on the shift of the search region, changing and expanding the features of the search region. While the window shift proposed in this paper is an operation aimed at improving the completeness of the target for the template feature map.

3 Our Method

3.1 Model Overview

This section mainly describes our proposed model and method: Template Shift and Background Suppression Network (TSBS) for visual tracking. As shown in Fig. 2, the model consists of four parts: feature extraction, encoder, decoder, and prediction head.

Feature Extraction: Our model is based on the Siamese network architecture, with two branches using Swin Transformer to extract the feature maps of the template and search region, and the feature extraction network shares weights between the branches. Compared to VIT, Swin Transformer has a slightly smaller computation cost. Compared to traditional CNN networks, Swin Transformer has better global features and richer semantic information, allowing for more effective extraction of target features for matching.

Encoder: The template and search region features extracted by the first part are concatenated and inputted into the encoder. The encoder consists of the template shift module. The specific steps of template shift are as follows. First, the features of the template and search region are concatenated and passed through an attention layer. Then the template features will be separated and undergo a reverse window operation, which will split the original window into four small windows, perform window shifting operations, and then recombine them.

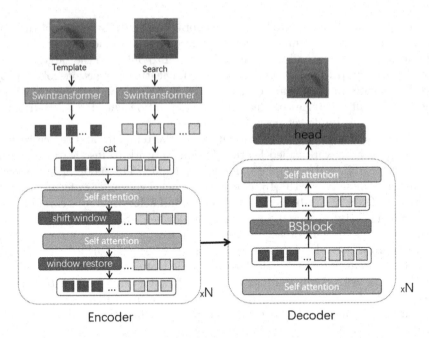

Fig. 2. The construct of our model.

Decoder: The decoder is composed of several background suppression modules. After the feature vectors obtained by the encoder are inputted into the decoder, the decoder performs self-attention calculation and uses attention weights to sort the template window. The feature of the window with low weight is removed and does not participate in subsequent attention calculations, suppressing the background while reducing the computational cost.

Head: Similar to traditional Siamese networks, the prediction head of our model consists of classification and regression branches. The feature vector obtained from the decoder is inputted into the prediction head to obtain the final response map and prediction results.

3.2 Template Shift Module

The template shift module consists of three components: the attention layer, the window shift layer, and the marginal mask layer. Assuming the dimensions of the template feature Z are $(B \times H_Z \times W_Z \times C)$ and the search area feature X are $(B \times H_x \times W_x \times C)$. (B represents batch size for each epoch, H_Z, H_x represents the number of windows per column in the feature map, W_Z, W_x represents the number of windows per row in the feature map) The template and search region will be processed by the feature extraction module, they will obtain a feature map U(Z,X), which is composed of the template feature Z and the search region feature X.

As show in the bottom left corner of Fig. 2, the specific steps of the Template shift operation are as follows: 1) separate the features of the template and the search region. 2) Perform inverse window operation on the template feature Z to make its dimension become $(B \times 2 * H_Z \times 2 * W_Z \times \frac{C}{4})$. 3) Cyclically shift the template feature towards the upper left corner. 4) Merge the feature vectors to obtain Z $(B \times H_Z \times W_Z \times C)$. Then concatenate Z and X to get a new feature vector U.

Due to the leftward and upward shift of the template feature during window decomposition, the window at the bottom-right corner of the feature map after merging will contain information from windows that were not originally adjacent. If this information is also included in the attention mechanism calculation, it may have a negative impact on the feature of the search region. Therefore, the paper proposes a marginal mask method. The specific approach is to directly save the last row and last column windows of the feature map, so that they do not participate in the initial attention calculation after window shifting, thereby reducing the impact on the generated feature map. They are later concatenated back after the next attention calculation is completed.

Window restoration: after the attention calculation, the template feature is restored by a window restoration operation. The feature vector with marginal mask is concatenated back, and the window is restored to its original shape.

3.3   Background Suppression Module

Inspired by SparseTT [15] and pnp [17], we propose a Background Suppression Module to suppress the background information in the template that may affect the subsequent tracking. Due to the computational characteristics of the attention mechanism, the feature of each window in the template is multiplied with the feature of each window in the search region, resulting in a vector inner product operation to obtain the attention weights W. The process can be represented by the following formula (d_k is the vector dimension of each head in the multi-head attention mechanism.):

$$W = Softmax\left(\frac{UU^T}{\sqrt{d_k}}\right) = Softmax\left(\frac{[Z;X][Z;X]^T}{\sqrt{d_k}}\right) \tag{1}$$

Assuming that batchsize is 1, each sample has L_z windows in the template and L_x window in the search region. According to the formula (1), we can obtained U$[L_Z + L_X, C]$, W$[L_Z + L_X, L_Z + L_X]$. We select matrix $W_1[L_z, L_x]$ from W ranging from W$[0, L_z]$ to W$[L_z, L_z + L_x]$. By taking the average of each row of $W_1[L_z, L_x]$, we obtain a similarity weight sequence $W_z[L_z, 1]$ that represents the similarity of each window in the template. Then, sort the windows according to the similarity weight sequence W_z, and calculate the TOP-K windows with the highest weights based on the keep rate k (The final settings in this paper are 0.9 and 0.8).

3.4   Head and Loss

Head: Similar to traditional Siamese network-based models, the model's classification head has two branches. One is the classification branch responsible for identifying foreground and background in the feature response map, while the other is the regression branch responsible for regressing the final predicted box. Each branch consists of a three-layer perceptron that receives feature response maps from the decoder output and generates the classification response map and bounding box regression map, respectively.

Classification Loss: We follow SwinTrack [13] employ the IoU-aware classification score as the training target and the varifocal loss [18] as classification loss function. The classification loss can be formulated as:

$$L_{cls} = L_{VFL}(p, IoU(b, \hat{b})) \qquad (2)$$

where p denotes the predicted IACS, (This concept is mentioned in [18] which is named the IoU-aware classification score) b denotes the predicted bounding box, and $\hat{b}$ denotes the ground-truth bounding box.

Regression Loss: For bounding box regression, we employ the generalized IoU loss [19]. The regression loss function can be formulated as:

$$L_{reg} = \sum_j \mathbb{1}_{\{IoU(b_j,\hat{b})>0\}} \left[pL_{GIoU} \left(b_j, \hat{b} \right) \right] \qquad (3)$$

The GIoU loss is weighted by p to emphasize the high classification score samples. The training signals from the negative samples are ignored.

4   Experiments

4.1   Implementation

We train TSBS using training splits of LaSOT [20], TrackingNet [21], GOT-10k [22] (1,000 videos are removed for fair comparisons with other trackers) and COCO 2017 [23]. Besides, we also report the performance of our model with GOT-10k training split only to follow the protocol described in [22].

The model is optimized with AdamW [24], with a learning rate of 4e−4, and a weight decay of 1e−4. The learning rate of the backbone is set to 5e−5. We train the network on 4 NVIDIA Tesla t4 GPUs for 300 epochs with 131,072 samples per epoch. The learning rate is dropped by a factor of 10 after 210 epochs. A 3-epoch linear warmup is applied to stabilize the training process. DropPath [25] is applied on the backbone and the encoder with a rate of 0.1.

Model Details: We use SwinTransformer-Tiny as the backbone network for the feature extraction. In the encoder and decoder, we set the number of heads of multi-headed attention to 8. The number of layers of the encoder is 1 and the number of layers of the decoder is 5. The background suppression module is in the first and third layers of the decoder, respectively, and the keep rate K is 0.9 and 0.8, respectively.

4.2   Ablations Study and Analysis

The Number of Encoder Layers. In our model, the role of the encoder is to better extract information about the interaction features of the template and the search region. So the number of encoder layers is also very important. Table 1 represents the ablation experiments in our model for the number of encoder layers on the GOT10K dataset. It can be seen that the model has some improvement compared to no encoder, but it slowly decreases as the number of encoder layers increases. We believe it is possible that our encoder is different from the encoder of the general model. One layer in our encoder will be computed twice by the attention mechanism, while one layer in the general model is computed only once, so too many layers of encoder in our model will be more likely to lead to overfitting. The encoder is set to 1 in the final model.

Table 1. The performance of our method on the test split of GOT10k when setting the number of encoder layers to 0, 1, 2, and 3

N	AO	$SR_{0.5}$	$SR_{0.75}$	FPS
0	0.689	0.784	0.626	**34.9**
1	**0.695**	**0.786**	**0.786**	32.91
2	0.692	0.783	0.635	32.9
3	0.677	0.766	0.618	27.2

The Number of Decoder Layers. The role of the decoder is to better suppress the background information of the template, so that the model can track more focused on the tracked object rather than the background. Table 2 represents the ablation experiments of our decoder. It can be seen that as the number of layers increases, the performance of the model continues to improve, but after exceeding 5 layers, the model starts to show a trend of effective performance decline. Therefore, we ultimately chose 5 layers for the decoder.

Table 2. The performance of our method on the test split of GOT10k when setting the number of Decoder layers to 2, 3, 4, 5 and 6

N	AO	$SR_{0.5}$	$SR_{0.75}$	FPS
2	0.666	0.750	0.599	**35.21**
3	0.680	0.775	0.621	34.97
4	0.692	0.783	0.635	33.6
5	**0.695**	**0.786**	**0.642**	32.91
6	0.661	0.754	0.610	30.1

Template Shift and Background Suppression. We utilized template drift method (TS) and background suppression (BS) method in our model. In order to test the effectiveness of these methods, we designed ablation experiments on the GOT10k dataset, where the encoder was set to 1 layer and the decoder was set to 5 layers. The experimental results are shown in Table 3.

Table 3. The performance of our method on the test split of GOT10k. (Base means using only attention mechanism for computation. TS means Template shift, BS means Background Suppression)

N	AO	$SR_{0.5}$	$SR_{0.75}$	FPS
Base	0.679	0.722	0.611	**36.62**
Base+TS	0.693	**0.810**	0.636	32.21
Base+TS+BS	**0.695**	0.786	**0.642**	32.91

The Keep Rate in the Background Suppression Module. To further explore the template background suppression module, we designed ablation experiments on the template background suppression rate. The encoder was set to 1 layer and the decoder was set to 5 layers. Background suppression modules were used in the second and fourth layers, with template background retention rates of K1 and K2, respectively. The experimental results are shown in Table 4.

Table 4. The performance of our method on the test split of GOT10k when setting different keep rate

K1, K2	AO	$SR_{0.5}$	$SR_{0.75}$	FPS
0.9,0.9	0.692	0.793	0.646	32.89
0.9,0.8	**0.695**	0.786	0.642	32.91
0.9,0.7	0.694	**0.788**	**0.651**	**33.21**
0.8,0.9	0.691	0.784	0.645	31.88
0.7,0.9	0.692	0.784	0.645	31.88

4.3   Comparison with the State-of-the-Art

LaSOT [20] is a large-scale long-term dataset with high-quality annotations. Its test split consists of 280 sequences, the average length of which exceeds 2500 frames. We evaluate our method on the test split of LaSOT and compare it with other competitive methods. As shown in Table 5, our method achieves the best performance in terms of success, precision, and normalized precision metrics.

TrackingNet [21] is a large-scale dataset whose test split includes 511 sequences covering various object classes and tracking scenes. We report the performance of our method on the test split of TrackingNet. As shown in Table 6, our method achieves the best mAO of 0.695,

GOT10k [22] provides 180 sequences for testing and it requires trackers to be trained using GOT-10k train split only. The results and comparisons are displayed in Table 7, we see that our model achieves the best mAO of 0.695, outperforming other Transformer based counterparts.

Table 5. Performance comparison on LaSOT

Tracker	SUC	PRE	NPRE
SiamRPN++ [6]	49.6	-	56.9
DiMP [26]	56.9	53.4	65.0
SiamR-CNN [27]	64.8	-	72.2
TrSiam [10]	62.4	60.0	-
TrDiMP [10]	63.9	61.4	-
STMTrack [28]	60.6	63.3	69.3
TransT [10]	64.9	69.0	73.8
STARK-ST50 [11]	66.4	-	-
STARK-ST101 [11]	67.1	-	77.0
KeepTrack [9]	67.1	70.2	77.2
SwinTrack-T [13]	66.7	70.6	75.8
SparseTT [15]	66.0	70.1	74.8
Ours	**67.2**	**71.1**	**76.2**

Table 6. Performance comparison on Trackingnet

Tracker	SUC	PRE	NPRE
PrDimp [29]	74.8	70.4	81.6
SiamFC++ [4]	75.4	70.5	80.0
KYS [30]	74.0	68.8	80.0
TrSiam [10]	78.1	72.7	82.9
TrDiMP [10]	78.4	73.1	83.3
STMTrack [28]	80.3	76.7	85.1
TransT [10]	81.4	80.3	86.7
STARK-ST50 [11]	81.3	-	86.1
STARK-ST101 [11]	82.0	-	86.9
SiamR-CNN [27]	81.2	80.0	85.4
SwinTrack-T [13]	80.8	77.9	85.5
SparseTT [15]	81.7	**79.5**	86.6
Ours	**81.9**	78.3	**86.8**

Table 7. Performance comparison on GOT10k

Tracker	AO	$SR_{0.5}$	$SR_{0.75}$
SiamRPN++ [6]	51.7	61.6	32.5
DiMP [26]	61.1	71.7	49.2
SiamR-CNN [27]	64.9	72.8	59.7
TrSiam [10]	66.0	76.6	57.1
TrDiMP [10]	67.1	77.7	58.3
STMTrack [28]	64.2	73.7	57.5
TransT [10]	67.1	76.8	60.9
STARK-ST50 [11]	68.0	77.7	62.3
STARK-ST101 [11]	68.8	78.1	64.1
SwinTrack-T [13]	69.0	78.1	62.1
SwinTrack-B [13]	69.4	78.0	64.3
SparseTT [15]	69.3	79.1	63.8
Ours	**69.5**	**78.6**	**64.2**

5   Conclusions

This paper presents a template shift and background suppression network model based on attention mechanism, which consists of a feature extraction part composed of Swin-Transformer, an encoder composed of template drift module, a decoder composed of background suppression module, and a classification and regression head composed of two three-layer perceptrons. Furthermore, the effectiveness of the proposed method is demonstrated through ablation experiments, which effectively improve the performance of the tracker. Importantly, our approach is very simple and can be transferred to other target tracking models. Overall, it is a new method for further study.

Acknowledgements. This work is supported by the research project of Guangzhou University under Grant No. YK2022048 and the innovation training program for college students of Guangzhou University (202111078028), and the Science and Technology Projects in Guangzhou (202102010412).

References

1. Dosovitskiy, A., Beyer, L., Kolesnikov, A., et al.: An image is worth 16x16 words: transformers for image recognition at scale. arXiv preprint arXiv:2010.11929 (2020)
2. Liu, Z., et al.: Swin transformer: hierarchical vision transformer using shifted windows. IN: Proceedings of the IEEE/CVF International Conference on Computer Vision (2021)

3. Bertinetto, L., Valmadre, J., Henriques, J.F., Vedaldi, A., Torr, P.H.S.: Fully-convolutional Siamese networks for object tracking. In: Hua, G., Jégou, H. (eds.) ECCV 2016. LNCS, vol. 9914, pp. 850–865. Springer, Cham (2016). https://doi.org/10.1007/978-3-319-48881-3_56

4. Xu, Y., et al.: SiamFC++: towards robust and accurate visual tracking with target estimation guidelines. In: Proceedings of the AAAI Conference on Artificial Intelligence, vol. 34. no. 07 (2020)

5. Li, B., et al.: High performance visual tracking with Siamese region proposal network. In: Proceedings of the IEEE Conference on Computer Vision and Pattern Recognition (2018)

6. Li, B., et al.: SiamRPN++: evolution of Siamese visual tracking with very deep networks. In: Proceedings of the IEEE/CVF Conference on Computer Vision and Pattern Recognition (2019)

7. Zhang, Z., Peng, H., Fu, J., Li, B., Hu, W.: Ocean: object-aware anchor-free tracking. In: Vedaldi, A., Bischof, H., Brox, T., Frahm, J.-M. (eds.) ECCV 2020. LNCS, vol. 12366, pp. 771–787. Springer, Cham (2020). https://doi.org/10.1007/978-3-030-58589-1_46

8. Chen, Z., et al.: Siamese box adaptive network for visual tracking. In: Proceedings of the IEEE/CVF Conference on Computer Vision and Pattern Recognition (2020)

9. Mayer, C., et al.: Learning target candidate association to keep track of what not to track. In: Proceedings of the IEEE/CVF International Conference on Computer Vision (2021)

10. Wang, N., et al.: Transformer meets tracker: exploiting temporal context for robust visual tracking. In: Proceedings of the IEEE/CVF Conference on Computer Vision and Pattern Recognition (2021)

11. Yan, B., et al.: Learning spatio-temporal transformer for visual tracking. In: Proceedings of the IEEE/CVF International Conference on Computer Vision (2021)

12. Chen, D.-J., Hsieh, H.-Y., Liu, T.-L.: Adaptive image transformer for one-shot object detection. In: Proceedings of the IEEE/CVF Conference on Computer Vision and Pattern Recognition (2021)

13. Lin, L., et al.: SwinTrack: a simple and strong baseline for transformer tracking. In: Advances in Neural Information Processing Systems vol. 35, pp. 16743–16754 (2022)

14. Chen, X., et al.: Transformer tracking. In: Proceedings of the IEEE/CVF Conference on Computer Vision and Pattern Recognition (2021)

15. Fu, Z., et al.: SparseTT: visual tracking with sparse transformers. arXiv preprint arXiv:2205.03776 (2022)

16. Song, Z., et al.: Transformer tracking with cyclic shifting window attention. In: Proceedings of the IEEE/CVF Conference on Computer Vision and Pattern Recognition (2022)

17. Wang, T., et al.: PnP-DETR: towards efficient visual analysis with transformers. In: Proceedings of the IEEE/CVF International Conference on Computer Vision (2021)

18. Zhang, H., et al.: VarifocalNet: an IoU-aware dense object detector. In: Proceedings of the IEEE/CVF Conference on Computer Vision and Pattern Recognition (2021)

19. Rezatofighi, H., Tsoi, N., Gwak, J., Sadeghian, A., Reid, I., Savarese, S.: Generalized intersection over union (2019)

20. Fan, H., et al.: LaSOT: a high-quality benchmark for large-scale single object tracking. In: Proceedings of the IEEE/CVF Conference on Computer Vision and Pattern Recognition (2019)

21. Müller, M., Bibi, A., Giancola, S., Alsubaihi, S., Ghanem, B.: TrackingNet: a large-scale dataset and benchmark for object tracking in the wild. In: Ferrari, V., Hebert, M., Sminchisescu, C., Weiss, Y. (eds.) ECCV 2018. LNCS, vol. 11205, pp. 310–327. Springer, Cham (2018). https://doi.org/10.1007/978-3-030-01246-5_19

22. Huang, L., Zhao, X., Huang, K.: Got-10k: a large high-diversity benchmark for generic object tracking in the wild. IEEE Trans. Pattern Anal. Mach. Intell. **43**(5), 1562–1577 (2019)

23. Lin, T.-Y., et al.: Microsoft COCO: common objects in context. In: Fleet, D., Pajdla, T., Schiele, B., Tuytelaars, T. (eds.) ECCV 2014. LNCS, vol. 8693, pp. 740–755. Springer, Cham (2014). https://doi.org/10.1007/978-3-319-10602-1_48

24. Loshchilov, I., Hutter, F.: Decoupled weight decay regularization. In: ICLR (2019)

25. Larsson, G., Maire, M., Shakhnarovich, G.: FractalNet: ultra-deep neural networks without residuals. In: ICLR (2016)

26. Bhat, G., Danelljan, M., Van Gool, L., Timofte, R.: Learning discriminative model prediction for tracking. In: ICCV (2019)

27. Voigtlaender, P., Luiten, J., Torr, P.H.S., Leibe, B.: Siam R-CNN: visual tracking by re-detection. In: CVPR (2020)

28. Zhihong, F., Liu, Q., Zehua, F., Wang, Y.: Stmtrack: template-free visual tracking with space-time memory networks. In: CVPR (2021)

29. Gool, L.V., Timofte, R.: Probabilistic regression for visual tracking. In: CVPR (2020)

30. Bhat, G., Danelljan, M., Van Gool, L., Timofte, R.: Know your surroundings: exploiting scene information for object tracking. In: Vedaldi, A., Bischof, H., Brox, T., Frahm, J.-M. (eds.) ECCV 2020. LNCS, vol. 12368, pp. 205–221. Springer, Cham (2020). https://doi.org/10.1007/978-3-030-58592-1_13

Reversible Data Hiding in Encrypted Images Based on a Multi-Granularity Adaptive Classification Mechanism

Yaling Zhang, Yicheng Zou, Chao Wang, Chengcheng Huang, and Shiqun Yin$^{(\boxtimes)}$

College of Computer and Information Science, Southwest University, Chongqing 400715, China

ruby0110@email.swu.edu.cn, qqqq-qiong@163.com

Abstract. In the era of cloud computing, many people pay attention to privacy protection issues while transferring data to the cloud, leading to the emergence of Reversible Data Hiding in Encrypted Images (RDHEI). The main difficulty in RDHEI is how to fully use the redundant room in the image to improve the Embedding Rate (ER). To solve this problem, an efficient RDHEI method based on Multi-Granularity Adaptive Classification (MGAC) mechanism is proposed in this paper. In image encryption, a block-based image encryption algorithm based on Cellular Neural Networks (CNN) hyper-chaotic system is utilized, including confusion and diffusion. The room reservation part uses the MGAC mechanism based on the block's global correlation and local correlation. Specifically, each block is classified according to the quantitative characteristics of the same bit plane in this block. Afterward, different room reservation strategies are applied to different types of blocks adaptively. The multi-granularity is reflected in each block's rough reservation and refined reservation operations. The image decryption part realizes the separability of data extraction and image recovery. Extensive experimental results show that the average ER of the proposed method on the datasets BOSSbase, BOWS-2, and UCID is about 0.16bpp higher than that of the baseline method on average. Meanwhile, the image security performance of the proposed method has also been improved.

Keywords: Reversible Data Hiding · The Encrypted Image · Adaptive Classification Mechanism · Intra-block Correlation · Cloud Computing

1 Introduction

Reversible Data Hiding (RDH) is a technology that aims at reversibly embedding secret data into plaintext images [11]. The secret data must be extracted entirely after embedding, and the image can also be wholly recovered [17]. Due to its reversibility, RDH technology was initially applied in some sensitive fields such as medical [19], military [16], and law. Barton [2] first proposed the concept of embedding information into digital data streams. Moreover, Tian [18] first defined what RDH is. Subsequently, numerous RDH methods have been

© The Author(s), under exclusive license to Springer Nature Switzerland AG 2023
Z. Jin et al. (Eds.): KSEM 2023, LNAI 14118, pp. 201–213, 2023.
https://doi.org/10.1007/978-3-031-40286-9_17

proposed, which can be roughly divided into three categories: (1) RDH based on lossless compression [7]; (2) RDH based on difference expansion [1]; (3) RDH based on histogram shifting [15].

In the era of big data, due to the wide application of cloud computing, people transfer data to the cloud more and more frequently for processing and storage [6]. While technology brings convenience to people, it also leads to many data security problems, such as enterprise information leakage and personal portrait infringement. Therefore, people tend to encrypt images before transferring them to the cloud [25]. As an information security technology, Reversible Data Hiding in Encrypted Images (RDHEI) can ensure not only the security of the secret data embedded in the image but also the privacy of the information in the original image. Nowadays, RDHEI has been applied in many fields, such as copyright protection, privacy protection, confidential information management, and content integrity authentication [12]. Hence, RDHEI has important practical significance in contemporary society. The existing RDHEI methods have a good performance in various aspects, but they still have great potential in improving the utilization rate of redundancy room and the security of ciphertext images.

In this paper, an improved high-capacity RDHEI method is proposed, which is based on the Multi-Granularity Adaptive Classification (MGAC) mechanism. This classification mechanism ensures that the redundant room of blocks with different global and local correlations can be well utilized. In addition, the proposed method introduces an image encryption algorithm based on Cellular Neural Network (CNN) hyper-chaotic system to encrypt the image. The image encryption stage is based on a block, which can preserve more correlation features within one block. In image decryption, the separability of data extraction and image recovery is realized.

The main contributions are presented as follows:

- Traditional encryption algorithms use a single key for image encryption, so the key may be cracked during image transmission, leading to image leakage. The proposed method in this paper introduces a hyper-chaotic encryption algorithm to relieve this problem. The experiment verifies the improvement of image security through a variety of indicators.
- The proposed room reservation scheme performs a rough reservation operation according to the global correlation of the block and a refined reservation operation according to the local correlation of the block. It can fully reuse the low-level planes with low redundancy in the image by using the adaptive classification mechanism.
- Compared with the state-of-the-art methods, the proposed RDHEI method has significant embedding performance improvements on several classic gray images and three open image datasets BOSSbase, BOWS-2, and UCID.

In the rest of this paper, Sect. 2 introduces the related work of this study. Sect. 3 describes the proposed method in detail. It mainly includes three parts: (1) image encryption; (2) room reservation and data embedding; (3) data extraction and image recovery. The experimental results and analyses of the proposed method are given in Sect. 4. Finally, the conclusion is presented in Sect. 5.

2   Related Work

RDHEI involves image encryption technology and room reservation technology. Image encryption technology [10, 28] aims to transform the plaintext image into a ciphertext image through several operations with pseudo randomness, such as confusion and diffusion. Room reservation technology aims to compress the redundant room of the image as much as possible to embed the secret data, which can be classified into two methods: Reserving Room Before Encrypted (RRBE) and Vacating Room After Encrypted (VRAE). Ma et al. [13] first proposed an RRBE method. To be specific, they reserved a continuous room at a particular location to embed secret data before image encryption. Subsequently, many other RRBE methods [3, 4, 23, 24] were proposed by researchers to get better embedding performance, but they ignored the security of encrypted images. Zhang [26], who first proposed a VRAE method, embedded the data into the image by modifying part of the encrypted pixel values. He first achieved the separability of data extraction and image recovery, which became the standard of RDHEI. Although the researchers have proposed various VRAE methods [5, 20–22] to achieve relatively better performance, they do not make good use of the redundant room of the low-level planes in the image. Combining the RRBE and VRAE methods, an improved VRBE method that can enhance not only the image security but also the embedding performance is elaborated next.

3   Proposed Method

The framework of our proposed method is shown in Fig. 1. It can be divided into three parts: (1) The image owner uses an image encryption algorithm based on a six-dimensional CNN chaotic system to generate the ciphertext image. (2) The data hider uses a room reservation scheme based on the MGAC mechanism to vacate the room for embedding secret data in the encrypted image, including rough reservation and refined reservation. (3) The receiver can perform data extraction and image recovery operations according to the type of key they have. In this section, Sect. 3.1 introduces the process of image encryption. Section 3.2 describes room reservation and data embedding in detail. Section 3.3 involves data extraction and image recovery.

3.1   Image Encryption

In the proposed method, an image encryption algorithm based on CNN hyper-chaotic system is used to encrypt the original image, as shown in Fig. 2. An original image I sized $M \times N$ is divided into m blocks sized $n \times n$. Specifically, $n = 4$ is taken as an example in this paper. In the process of confusion, the hyper-chaotic sequence generated by a six-dimensional CNN chaotic system is used as the key [9] to scramble these blocks. In the process of diffusion, the modified hyper-chaotic sequence is utilized to perform block-based XOR operation on the image. After that, the encrypted image can be obtained.

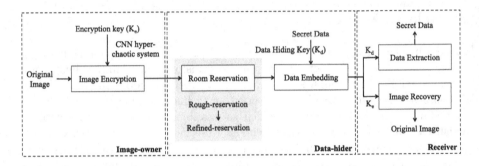

Fig. 1. The framework of our proposed method.

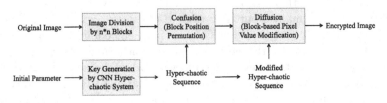

Fig. 2. Illustration of image encryption.

Block-Based Confusion. Considering each pixel of each block as a cell $C_{i,j}$. The dynamic equation for cellular $C_{i,j}$ can be represented as follows:

$$G\frac{dx_{i,j}(t)}{dt} = -\frac{x_{i,j}(t)}{R_x} + \sum_{k,l \in N_{i,j}(r)} A_{k,l}\, y_{k,l}(t) + \sum_{k,l \in N_{i,j}(r)} B_{k,l}\, u_{k,l} + I_{i,j}, \quad (1)$$

where $x_{i,j}$, $u_{k,l}$, and $y_{k,l}$ correspond to the state variable, input variable, and output variable. G and R_x are system constants, while $I_{i,j}$ is the threshold. $A_{k,l}$ and $B_{k,l}$ is the feedback and control coefficient matrix, respectively. Assume that the system constants are all 1, the initial step size is 0.005, and the initial state variable is (0.1, 0.2, 0.2, 0.2, 0.2, 0.2). Plug them into Eq. (1) to obtain the six-dimensional chaotic sequence. By applying this sequence to the block position matrix of the original image, the confusion of blocks can be accomplished.

Block-Based Diffusion. Both forward and backward diffusion are used in block-based diffusion to increase the complexity of the encryption. Each number in the six-dimensional chaotic sequence is converted into an 8-bit binary number to generate the modified hyper-chaotic bit stream R. And then, using R to perform the XOR operation on pixels of each block in the image, the formula is as follows:

$$E_{i,j,k} = R_i \oplus P_{i,j,k} \quad (1 \le i \le M,\ 1 \le j \le N^2,\ 1 \le k \le 8), \quad (2)$$

where $E_{i,j,k}$ is block i, pixel j, bit plane k of the encrypted image. $\oplus$ is the XOR operation. Finally, the encrypted image I_e is generated.

3.2   Room Reservation and Data Embedding

The proposed method uses the MGAC mechanism for room reservation in encrypted images. This mechanism is divided into two stages: (1) rough reservation according to the global correlation; (2) refined reservation according to local correlation. After reserving the room, the auxiliary information and secret data are embedded in order. Then, the marked encrypted image can be obtained.

Rough Reservation. The encrypted image I_e sized $M \times N$ is divided into m blocks sized $n \times n$, with the same n in Sect. 3.1. The pixels in each block generate a corresponding sequence. The maximum value in the sequence is denoted by E_{max}, and the minimum value is denoted by E_{min}. Equation (3) is to get the sequence tag X_i of the i-th block in the image.

$$X_i = E_{max} \oplus E_{min}. \tag{3}$$

The number of consecutive "0" from left to right in binary X_i is denoted by num_i ($0 \leq num_i \leq 7$), indicating the number of consecutive identical bit planes starting from the high-level bit plane in each block [8]. In brief, in the former num_i layers of the i-th block, the pixel values in each layer are all "0" or "1". Blocks with the same num_i are grouped into the same type, and the following operations are performed on blocks of different types: (1) $num_i = 1\sim7$: The num_i is converted into a 3-bit binary number as auxiliary information and stored in the Least Significant Bit (LSB) plane of the current block. Meanwhile, the primitive values in the LSB plane are stored in the sequence A. In the former num_i layers, the last pixel of each layer called the reference pixel, which cannot be changed, is utilized to restore the current layer during the image recovery. The remaining pixels in the former num_i layers constitute the embeddable room where sequence A is stored. Finally, each block can be reserved ($4 \times 4 \times num_i$-num_i-3) bits through the rough reservation method. (2) $num_i = 8$: Treat it as if $num_i = 7$ because the LSB plane will be used to store auxiliary information. So there is no real $num_i = 8$ block. (3) $num_i = 0$: will be explained in detail later.

Refined Reservation. After making the rough reservation on each block, a second reservation called the refined reservation should be carried out. It involves four methods for different kinds of blocks and how each of these methods works is shown as follows. A description of how to use them is given at the end.

(1) Special Method (SM)

This method is suitable for blocks with $num_i = 0$. This kind of block may be the edge of the object in the image, so its Most Significant Bit (MSB) plane may manifest apparent features. In this case, whether to compress the MSB plane is the first thing to be considered. Vertically scan the MSB plane of the encrypted block, and the scanning results are denoted as c_1, c_2, c_3, c_4. Horizontally scan the MSB plane of the encrypted block, and the scanning results are denoted as d_1, d_2, d_3, d_4. The scanning mode is shown in Fig. 3.

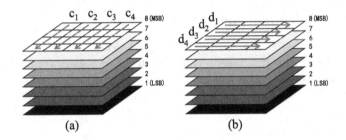

Fig. 3. Scanning mode: (a) longitudinal scanning; (b) transversal scanning.

The auxiliary information S_2 indicates whether the MSB plane is compressed, S_3 indicates how the MSB plane is compressed, and t indicates the compressed sequence. If $c_1 = c_2 = c_3 = c_4$ or $d_1 = d_2 = d_3 = d_4$, then $S_2 = 1$. Otherwise, $S_2 = 0$. If $c_1 = c_2 = c_3 = c_4$, then $S_3 = 1$ and $t = c_1$. If $d_1 = d_2 = d_3 = d_4$, then $S_3 = 0$ and $t = d_1$.

In one block, the pixels great than or equal to 128 are classified into set SH, and the rest are classified into set SL. Calculate the num_i of SH and SL, denoted as num_{SH} and num_{SL} respectively. Both of the sets use the rough reservation method to reserve the room. If the length of the reserved room is less than the length of overall auxiliary information, then $S_1 = 1$, denoting that this block is reserved the room by the SM successfully. Otherwise, $S_1 = 0$, denoting that this block no longer has other auxiliary information and reservation operations.

The auxiliary information of this method includes num_i, S_1, S_2, S_3, t, num_{SH} and num_{SL}. The composition is shown in Fig. 4(a). The auxiliary information is stored in the LSB plane of the current block, and the primitive values in the LSB plane are stored in the sequence A. If $S_1 = 1$, A will be stored in the reserved room. If $S_1 = 0$, A will be stored in sequence B. Denote the number of blocks with $S_1 = 0$ as U and the length of sequence B as L, the formula is shown below:

$$L = 4U. \qquad (4)$$

(2) Four-layer Correlation Method (FCM)

This method is suitable for blocks with $num_i = 1 \sim 2$. Take the block with $num_i = 1$ as an example. The 7th, 6th, 5th, and 4th layers of the block are taken out, and the remaining layers are filled with "0" to generate a new block. The bit plane of the pixel is denoted as $e_{i,j,k}$, representing block i, pixel j, bit plane k of the image. When $num_i = 2$, the 6th, 5th, 4th, and 3rd layers are taken out, and the subsequent operations are shifted down one layer accordingly. The bit plane used for identifying categories is called the Identification Layer (IL), and the bit plane used for reserving the room is called the Reservation Layer (RL). The 7th layer of the block with $num_i = 1$ is IL, which should not be changed. Let $t_1 = (e_{i,j,7}, e_{i,j,6})$, $t_2 = (e_{i,j,7}, e_{i,j,6}, e_{i,j,5})$, $t_3 = (e_{i,j,7}, e_{i,j,6}, e_{i,j,5}, e_{i,j,4})$.

There exist five cases: (1) Compare the t_3 of all pixels in a block. If there are only two types of t_3, then the auxiliary information $T_1 = 1$, $T_2 = 11$, M_1 is the last three bits of t_3 beginning with "0", M_2 is the last three bits of t_3 beginning with "1". The 6th, 5th, and 4th layers are RL. (2) If there are three or more types of t_3, then compare t_2. If there are two types of t_2, then $T_1 = 1$, $T_2 = 10$, M_1 is the last two bits of t_2 beginning with "0", M_2 is the last two bits of t_2 beginning with "1". The 6th and 5th layers are RL. (3) If there are three or more types of t_3 and three types of t_2, then compare t_1. If there are two types of t_1, then $T_1 = 1$, $T_2 = 01$, M_1 is the first two bits of the two different t_2 with the same t_1, M_2 is the third t_2. The 6th, 5th (, and 4th) layers are RL. (4) If there are three or more types of t_3 and four types of t_2, then compare t_1. If there are two types of t_1, then $T_1 = 1$, $T_2 = 00$, M_1 is the last bit of t_1 beginning with "0", M_2 is the last bit of t_1 beginning with "1". The 6th layer is RL. (5) In other cases, $T_1 = 0$, indicating that this block can no longer be reserved. And there is no other auxiliary information for this block.

The auxiliary information of this method includes T_1, T_2, M_1, and M_2. The composition is shown in Fig. 4(b). The auxiliary information is stored in the LSB plane of the current block, and the primitive values in the LSB plane are stored in the sequence A. If $T_1 = 1$, then A will be stored in the room reserved by this method. If $T_1 = 0$, then A only has one bit and will be stored in the room reserved by the rough reservation method.

(3) Three-layer Correlation Method (ThCM)

This method is suitable for blocks with $num_i = 1 \sim 4$. Take an example of a block with $num_i = 2$. The 6th, 5th, and 4th layers of the block are taken out, and the remaining layers are filled with "0" to generate a new block. The rest operations are the same as the FCM. The 6th layer of the block with $num_i = 2$ is IL. Let $t_1 = (e_{i,j,6}, e_{i,j,5})$, $t_2 = (e_{i,j,6}, e_{i,j,5}, e_{i,j,4})$.

There exist three cases: (1) Compare the t_2 of all pixels in a block. If there are only two types of t_2, then the auxiliary information $T_1 = 1$, $T_2 = 0$, M_1 is the last two bits of t_2 beginning with "0", M_2 is the last two bits of t_2 beginning with "1". The 5th and 4th layers are RL. (2) If there are three or more types of t_3, then compare t_1. If there are only two types of t_1, then $T_1 = 1$, $T_2 = 1$, M_1 is the last bit of t_1 beginning with "0", M_2 is the last bit of t_1 beginning with "1". The 5th layer is RL. (3) Other cases are the same as the FCM.

The auxiliary information of this method includes T_1, T_2, M_1, and M_2. The composition is shown in Fig. 4(c). The rest operations are the same as the FCM.

(4) Two-layer Correlation Method (TwCM)

This method is suitable for blocks with $num_i = 3 \sim 4$. Take a block with $num_i = 3$ as an example. The 5th and 4th layers of the block are taken out, and the remaining layers are filled with "0" to generate a new block. The remaining operations are the same as above. The 5th layer of the block with $num_i = 2$ is IL. Let $t_1 = (e_{i,j,5}, e_{i,j,4})$.

There exist two cases: (1) Compare the t_1 of all pixels in a block. If there are only two types of t_1, then auxiliary information $T_1 = 1$, M_1 is the last bit of t_1 beginning with "0", M_2 is the last bit of t_1 beginning with "1". The 4th layer is RL. (2) Other cases are the same as the FCM.

The auxiliary information of this method includes T_1, M_1, and M_2. The composition is shown in Fig. 4(d). The rest operations are the same as above.

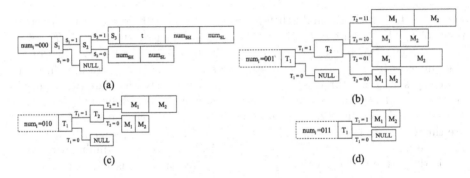

Fig. 4. The composition of the auxiliary information: (a) SM; (b) FCM; (3) ThCM; (4) TwCM.

The processes of using these four methods adaptively are shown below: (1) $num_i = 0$: Use the SM to reserve the room. (2) $num_i = 1\sim2$: Decide whether to use the FCM or the ThCM. Choose one which reserves more room. If the length of the reserved room using two methods is both less than 0, then the auxiliary information $C = 0$, representing that all blocks of this kind are not reserved by the refined reservation method. Otherwise, $C = 1$. If the FCM is used, then the auxiliary information $D = 1$. If the ThCM is used, then $D = 0$. (4) $num_i = 3\sim4$: Decide whether to use the ThCM or the TwCM. Choose one which reserves more room. The remaining operations are the same as above. (5) $num_i = 5\sim7$: No refined reservation operation is performed.

The length of C and D are both 4. C records whether each type of block uses the refined reservation method and is embedded in the last 4 bits of the 7th layer of the last block of the image. D records which method each type of block uses and is embedded in the last 4 bits of the 7th layer of the penultimate block of the image. The primitive values are stored at the front of the sequence B. Therefore, $L = 8+4U$ at last. Finally, B and the secret data are embedded in the overall reserved room. The marked encrypted image I_{me} can be obtained.

3.3   Data Extraction and Image Recovery

After receiving the marked encrypted image, the receiver can execute corresponding operations based on the key he has: (1) The embedded plaintext data can be correctly obtained if the receiver has the data embedding key K_d. Firstly, the first three bits of the LSB plane of each block are obtained to determine the num_i. Next, identify which kind of room reservation operation is performed on different types of blocks according to their auxiliary information. Finally, the secret data can be extracted from the $(9+4U)$th bit of the overall reserved room. (2) In a similar way, the original image can be correctly recovered if the receiver has the image encryption key K_e.

4   Experiment and Analysis

In this section, the experimental results of the proposed method, compared with the most advanced existing methods [5, 8, 14, 27], are presented. Eight classic gray images sized 512×512 are used as the test images. They are "Lena", "Boat", "Jetplane", "Man", "Airplane", "Peppers", "Baboon", and "Tiffany", as shown in Fig. 5. In addition, three open classic datasets, BOSSBase, BOWS-2, and UCID, are used to further demonstrate the performance of the proposed method. All experiments are accomplished on a computer with 16GB of memory and a six-core 2.6 GHz CPU.

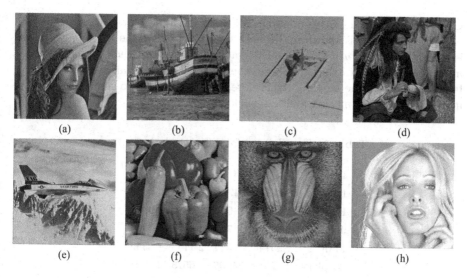

Fig. 5. Gray images: (a) 'Lena'; (b) 'Boat'; (c) 'Jetplane'; (d) 'Man'; (e) 'Airplane'; (f) 'Peppers'; (g) 'Baboon'; (h) 'Tiffany'.

Lena is taken as an example to show the images of each stage obtained when the method proposed is used, as shown in Fig. 6. The experiment shows that the Peak Signal to Noise Ratio (PSNR) value between the original image and the recovery image is $+\infty$, and the Structural Similarity (SSIM) value is 1. Both of them prove that the proposed method can reverse completely, so the receiver can obtain the original image without loss. Next, the performance of the proposed method is analyzed in terms of embedding capacity and image security, corresponding to Sect. 4.1 and Sect. 4.2 respectively.

4.1   Embedding Capacity

At present, the Embedding Rate (ER) is mainly used to measure the embedding capacity of the image. To be specific, ER is the number of payload bits per pixel (bpp) that can be embedded in one image.

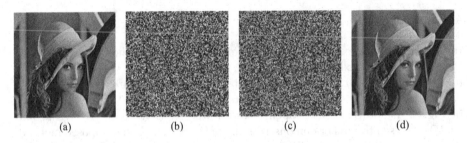

(a)   (b)   (c)   (d)

Fig. 6. Results of applying our method to *Lena* image when $n = 4$: (a) original image; (b) encrypted image; (c) marked encrypted image; (d) recovery image.

Gray Images. The corresponding ER with different block sizes n on eight classic gray images is shown in Table 1. It is evident that the ER of each image is the highest when $n = 3 \times 3$. The ER gradually decreases when the block size n increases. It indicates that the larger the block size, the weaker the correlation between pixels in the block. Furthermore, a 2×2 block is too small, resulting in more auxiliary information and less payload.

Table 1. The ER(bpp) for different block size n.

Images	2*2	3*3	4*4	5*5
Lena	2.2804	**2.4950**	2.3722	2.0481
Boat	1.6560	**1.8612**	1.688	1.5069
Jetplane	3.2495	**3.4704**	3.3458	3.1653
Man	1.9574	**2.1417**	2.1143	1.8349
Airplane	2.5768	**2.7807**	2.6573	2.4397
Peppers	2.2504	**2.4231**	2.3414	2.0097
Baboon	0.7435	**0.9976**	0.9845	0.5356
Tiffany	2.6402	**2.7769**	2.7342	2.4832

The maximum ER of the proposed method is compared with several excellent existing methods, as shown in Table 2. In each method, the maximum ER is selected. Obviously, the proposed method performs better than other methods in embedding capacity. Specifically, the maximum ER of the proposed method on eight test images is about 0.2 bpp higher than that of the baseline method [8] on average and is also better than the advanced method [5].

Image Datasets. In order to further analyze the performance of our proposed method, three open image datasets BOSSBase, BOWS-2, and UCID, are also tested. The results are shown in Table 3. The average ER of the proposed method in these three datasets reaches 2.8726 bpp, 2.5823 bpp, and 2.7298 bpp, respectively, which is about 0.16 bpp higher than [8] on average. It indicates that the proposed scheme has broader applicability than [8].

Table 2. The maximum ER(bpp) in different methods.

Images	[14]	[27]	[8]	[5]	Proposed Method
Lena	1.6592	1.9942	2.3018	2.4553	**2.4950**
Boat	1.3428	1.5763	1.7853	1.8021	**1.8612**
Jetplane	–	–	3.0916	3.3945	**3.4704**
Man	–	–	2.0654	2.1268	**2.1417**
Airplane	1.3892	2.4316	2.5227	2.7728	**2.7807**
Peppers	1.7345	2.1385	2.2743	2.1848	**2.4231**
Baboon	–	–	0.9201	0.9934	**0.9976**
Tiffany	–	–	2.5216	2.7533	**2.7769**

Table 3. Average, maximum, and minimum ER(bpp) comparison in different datasets: BOSSbase, BOWS-2, and UCID.

Scheme	Database	Minimum	Maximum	Average
[8]'s Scheme	BOSSBase	0.0322	5.7476	2.6965
	BOWS-2	0.2834	5.6842	2.4385
	UCID	0.0313	5.7034	2.5634
Proposed Scheme	BOSSBase	**0.0645**	**5.9962**	**2.8726**
	BOWS-2	**0.3228**	**5.9043**	**2.5823**
	UCID	**0.0512**	**5.9408**	**2.7298**

4.2 Security Analysis

The security of RDHEI has attracted wide attention in recent years. To prove the safety of the image in the proposed method, image pixel correlation is analysed in this section.

Image pixel correlation reflects the correlation degree of adjacent pixel values in an image. A good image encryption algorithm needs to make the correlation coefficients of adjacent pixels approach 0 in horizontal, vertical, and diagonal directions. For the *Lena* image, the correlation coefficients of adjacent pixels of encrypted images obtained by the proposed method are compared with [8], and the results are shown in Table 4. The correlation coefficients of the proposed method in three directions are all lower than [8], indicating that the proposed method performs better in image security.

Table 4. Correlation coefficients analysis.

Images	Horizontal	Vertical	Diagonal
Original Image	0.9726	0.9861	0.9752
Encrypted Image using [8]'s Scheme	0.0751	0.0973	0.0849
Encrypted Image using Proposed Scheme	**0.0514**	**0.0757**	**0.0703**

5 Conclusion

In this paper, an efficient RDHEI method based on the MGAC mechanism was proposed, which could better use the correlation of adjacent bit planes. In addition, an encryption algorithm based on a hyper-chaotic system was used to obtain a more random key. Experimental results showed that the proposed method not only improved the embedding performance but also enhanced the security of the image. Meanwhile, the whole method was completely reversible.

Future work will include how to improve the performance of the proposed method. For example, the running efficiency of the algorithm can be increased, and the running time can be shortened. Moreover, other novel room reservation methods can be explored to improve the embedding performance. In addition, we will consider applying the proposed method to color images to meet the demands of the big data era.

Acknowledgements. This work is supported by the Science & Technology project (4411700474, 4411500476). If there is any question, please contact the corresponding author: Shiqun Yin, qqqq-qiong@163.com.

References

1. Alattar, A.M.: Reversible watermark using the difference expansion of a generalized integer transform. IEEE Trans. Image Process. **13**(8), 1147–1156 (2004)
2. Barton, J.M.: Method and apparatus for embedding authentication information within digital data. United States Patent, 5 646 997 (1997)
3. Cao, X., Du, L., Wei, X., Meng, D., Guo, X.: High capacity reversible data hiding in encrypted images by patch-level sparse representation. IEEE Trans. Cybern. **46**(5), 1132–1143 (2015)
4. Chen, K., Chang, C.C.: High-capacity reversible data hiding in encrypted images based on extended run-length coding and block-based msb plane rearrangement. J. Vis. Commun. Image Represent. **58**, 334–344 (2019)
5. Chen, S., Chang, C.C.: Reversible data hiding in encrypted images using block-based adaptive msbs prediction. J. Inf. Secur. Appl. **69**, 103297 (2022)
6. Chen, Y.C., Shiu, C.W., Horng, G.: Encrypted signal-based reversible data hiding with public key cryptosystem. J. Visual Commun. Image Represent. **25**(5), 1164–1170 (2014)
7. Fridrich, J., Goljan, M., Du, R.: Invertible authentication. In: Security and Watermarking of Multimedia Contents III, vol. 4314, pp. 197–208. SPIE (2001)
8. Han, Z., Guohua, C.: Reversible data hiding in encrypted image with local-correlation-based classification and adaptive encoding strategy. Signal Process. **205**, 108847 (2023)
9. Hu, G., Kou, W., Peng, J., et al.: A novel image encryption algorithm based on cellular neural networks hyper chaotic system. In: 2018 IEEE 4th International Conference on Computer and Communications (ICCC), pp. 1878–1882. IEEE (2018)
10. Huang, F., Huang, J., Shi, Y.Q.: New framework for reversible data hiding in encrypted domain. IEEE Trans. Inf. Forensics Secur. **11**(12), 2777–2789 (2016)
11. Kumar, S., Gupta, A., Walia, G.S.: Reversible data hiding: a contemporary survey of state-of-the-art, opportunities and challenges. Appl. Intell., 1–34 (2022)

12. Liu, Z.L., Pun, C.M.: Reversible data hiding in encrypted images using chunk encryption and redundancy matrix representation. IEEE Trans. Depend. Secure Comput. **19**(2), 1382–1394 (2020)
13. Ma, K., Zhang, W., Zhao, X., Yu, N., Li, F.: Reversible data hiding in encrypted images by reserving room before encryption. IEEE Trans. Inf. Forensics Secur. **8**(3), 553–562 (2013)
14. Ma, S., Li, X., Xiao, M., Ma, B., Zhao, Y.: Fast expansion-bins-determination for multiple histograms modification based reversible data hiding. IEEE Signal Process. Lett. **29**, 662–666 (2022)
15. Ni, Z., Shi, Y.Q., Ansari, N., Su, W.: Reversible data hiding. IEEE Trans. Circ. Syst. Video Technol. **16**(3), 354–362 (2006)
16. Shi, Y.Q., Li, X., Zhang, X., Wu, H.T., Ma, B.: Reversible data hiding: advances in the past two decades. IEEE Access **4**, 3210–3237 (2016)
17. Shih, F.Y.: Digital Watermarking and Steganography: Fundamentals and Techniques. CRC Press, Boca Raton (2017)
18. Tian, J.: Reversible watermarking by difference expansion. In: Proceedings of Workshop on Multimedia and Security, vol. 19. ACM, Juan-les-Pins (2002)
19. Tsai, P., Hu, Y.C., Yeh, H.L.: Reversible image hiding scheme using predictive coding and histogram shifting. Signal Process. **89**(6), 1129–1143 (2009)
20. Wang, Y., Cai, Z., He, W.: High capacity reversible data hiding in encrypted image based on intra-block lossless compression. IEEE Trans. Multimedia **23**, 1466–1473 (2020)
21. Xiao, D., Xiang, Y., Zheng, H., Wang, Y.: Separable reversible data hiding in encrypted image based on pixel value ordering and additive homomorphism. J. Visual Commun. Image Represent. **45**, 1–10 (2017)
22. Yin, Z., Luo, B., Hong, W.: Separable and error-free reversible data hiding in encrypted image with high payload. Sci. World J. **2014** (2014)
23. Yin, Z., Peng, Y., Xiang, Y.: Reversible data hiding in encrypted images based on pixel prediction and bit-plane compression. IEEE Trans. Depend. Secure Comput. **19**(2), 992–1002 (2020)
24. Yin, Z., Xiang, Y., Zhang, X.: Reversible data hiding in encrypted images based on multi-msb prediction and huffman coding. IEEE Trans. Multimedia **22**(4), 874–884 (2019)
25. Zhang, W., Wang, H., Hou, D., Yu, N.: Reversible data hiding in encrypted images by reversible image transformation. IEEE Trans. Multimedia **18**(8), 1469–1479 (2016)
26. Zhang, X.: Reversible data hiding in encrypted image. IEEE Signal Process. Lett. **18**(4), 255–258 (2011)
27. Zhang, Y., Luo, W.: Vector-based efficient data hiding in encrypted images via multi-msb replacement. IEEE Trans. Circ. Syst. Video Technol. **32**(11), 7359–7372 (2022)
28. Zhou, Y., Bao, L., Chen, C.P.: Image encryption using a new parametric switching chaotic system. Signal Process. **93**(11), 3039–3052 (2013)

Enhanced Entity Interaction Modeling for Multi-Modal Entity Alignment

Jinxu Li, Qian Zhou, Wei Chen, and Lei Zhao[(✉)]

School of Compute Science and Technology, Soochow University, Suzhou, China
jxlia@stu.suda.edu.cn, {qzhou0,robertchen,zhaol}@suda.edu.cn

Abstract. Multi-modal Entity Alignment (MMEA) aims to find equivalent entities across different multi-modal knowledge graphs (MMKGs). Most existing methods focus on how to encode or fuse information from different modalities effectively, without considering the critical interactions between entities, especially those between an entity and its neighbors within each modality. To fill the gap, we propose a novel model namely **E**nhanced Entity **I**nteraction Modeling for Multi-modal **E**ntity **A**lignment (EIEA). Specifically, we first utilize multiple separate pretrained models to acquire single-modal data based entities' embeddings. Then, the module Enhanced Entity Representation (EER) is designed to mine interactions between entities and their neighborhoods, and facilitate effective multi-modal embedding fusion using a weighting mechanism. Finally, through contrastive learning, we ensure that the aligned entities have higher similarity than non-aligned ones within each modality. The extensive experiments demonstrate that EIEA outperforms the state-of-the-art baselines on three benchmark datasets.

Keywords: Entity Alignment · Multi-modal Knowledge Graph · Enhanced Entity Interaction · Contrastive Learning · Multi-modal Fusion

1 Introduction

Knowledge graphs (KGs) such as Freebase and DBpedia, are composed of factual triplets, where entities are connected by various relations. They have been widely used in many applications such as question answering and recommendation [23]. Recently, the multi-modal knowledge graphs (MMKGs) such as MMKG and Richpedia [9] have been introduced, which incorporate images as a visual modality on top of traditional KGs to enhance KG-based applications. However, MMKGs often suffer from low coverage and incompleteness. To address this issue, the task of multi-modal entity alignment (MMEA) is proposed to integrate multiple MMKGs into a unified knowledge graph, thereby increasing the knowledge coverage by linking entities that refer to the same real-world identity.

The above-mentioned task has attracted significant attention in recent years, owing to its immense significance. Many efforts have been devoted to it, and previous MMEA studies [2,3,5,9,10] have demonstrated that incorporating visual

© The Author(s), under exclusive license to Springer Nature Switzerland AG 2023
Z. Jin et al. (Eds.): KSEM 2023, LNAI 14118, pp. 214–227, 2023.
https://doi.org/10.1007/978-3-031-40286-9_18

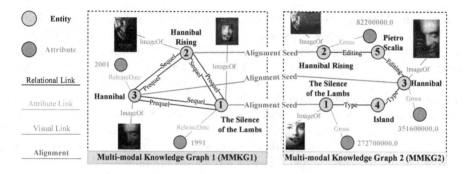

Fig. 1. An example of MMEA between MMKG1 and MMKG2.

information (e.g., images) in modeling can improve the performance of entity alignment. Despite the significant contributions made by these studies, they mainly focus on how to effectively encode or fuse information from different modalities, such as utilizing different MMKG embedding methods or designing an efficient cross-modal fusion paradigm (e.g., connecting single-modal representations directly or learning modality-level weights for fusion). They ignore the crucial interactions between entities, particularly the interactions between an entity and its neighbors within each modality. Incorporating such information can significantly enhance the representational ability of an entity's embedding [20], thereby enhancing the effectiveness of MMEA. Additionally, most of these methods only consider graph structure, text, and images, while neglecting videos that are important supplementary information for MMEA.

Intuitively, dividing the original MMKG into multiple KGs based on modality can allow us to further explore the interactions between entities. A toy example is illustrated in Fig. 1, based on which we detailedly analyze the shortcomings of existing work in modeling the interactions between entities, from two different perspectives. 1) From the perspective of graph structure, the embeddings of graph structure are obtained by using Graph neural networks (GNNs) to aggregate the one-hop neighbors of entities in existing work. As shown in Fig. 1, the three nodes in MMKG1 are closely adjacent, and each node can obtain significant information from others with GNNs. However, in MMKG2, node 2 cannot receive such information from node 1 with existing methods, which makes node 2 in two MMKGs cannot obtain similar embeddings for alignment, thus long-range node interactions are not non-negligible [20]. 2) From the perspective of relation/attribute, the equivalent entities usually share similar relations and attributes in KGs [21]. In previous EA studies, the alignment signal [12] from an entity's discriminative relations and attributes is only reserved for the entity itself, which has not been utilized while embedding its neighbors and other nodes that are important to it. To utilize the alignment signal effectively, we model the short-range and long-range node interactions simultaneously in this work.

To address aforementioned problems effectively, we propose a novel model namely Enhanced Entity Interaction Modeling for Multi-modal Entity Alignment (EIEA), which consists of three modules: 1) Multi-modal Knowledge

Embedding (MMKE), 2) Enhanced Entity Representation (EER), and 3) Multi-modal Contrastive Representation Learning (MMCRL). Specifically, in MMKE, we first leverage multiple separate pre-trained models to obtain entity-related single-modal representation for graph structure, relation, attribute, image, and video. Then, the module EER is designed to enhance an entity's representation, where a mixed block attention is introduced to model pairwise entity-node interactions, and a new fusion strategy is developed to fuse multi-modal embeddings. Finally, the module MMCRL is used to ensure that the aligned entities in each modality have higher similarity than unaligned ones, and the gaps between embedding distributions across different modalities are minimized.

Overall, the contributions can be summarized as follows. 1) In this paper, we further improve the performance of existing work on MMEA by enhancing the entity representation. 2) We propose a novel model called EIEA, which embeds information from different modalities into a unified vector space, where the interactions between entities are modeled by a mixed block attention, the intra-modal and inter-modal relationships are explored by contrastive learning. 3) The extensive experiments are conducted on three real-world datasets and the results demonstrate the superiority of the proposed model.

The paper is organized as follows. Section 2 discusses the related works. Section 3 gives the problem definition. Section 4 introduces our proposed model. Experimental results are reported in Sect. 5. Finally, Sect. 6 concludes our work.

2   Related Work

The related works can be roughly divided into Entity Alignment (EA) and Multi-modal Entity Alignment (MMEA). Specifically, EA aims to discover equivalent entities from different KGs to facilitate knowledge fusion, mainly including translation-based and GNNs-based methods. The former approaches [4,13,16] typically embed entities into a unified and low-dimensional vector space with translation-based knowledge graph embedding models and measure the similarity between entity embeddings. The latter methods [8,15,19,22,24] obtain the representations of entities by utilizing graph neural networks to model the global information of the graph. Although these studies have achieved promising results, they cannot be directly extended to multi-modal data.

Multi-modal Entity Alignment (MMEA). The task has attracted increasing attention with the construction of many MMKGs [10,11]. Similar to the task of EA on single-modal KGs, MMEA aims to identify equivalent entities from different MMKGs by effectively integrating multi-modal attributes such as text, images, and videos. Various approaches have been proposed, such as PoE [11], which considers aligned links between entities as SameAs relations to perform link prediction, and [2] proposes a common space to fuse multi-modal representations. EVA [10] leverages visual similarity to create an initial seed dictionary and uses an adaptive weighting mechanism to fuse multi-modal features, while MSNEA [3] integrates visual features and adopts multi-modal contrast learning. MCLEA [9] explores intra-modal relations and inter-modal interactions via contrastive learning, reducing the gaps between modalities for each entity. Despite the significant efforts made by these studies, they mainly focus on designing effective cross-modal fusion paradigms and ignore pairwise entity-node interactions, which is crucial for enhancing the representational ability of entities and improving the performance of MMEA.

3 Problem Definition

In this section, we give the definitions of multi-modal knowledge graph (MMKG) and multi-modal entity alignment (MMEA) as follows.

Definition 1. MMKG. *A MMKG is formalized as $KG = (E, R, A, P, V, T_r)$, where $e_i \in E$, $r_i \in R$, $a_i \in A$, $p_i \in P$, and $v_i \in V$, they denote an entity, a relation, an attribute, an image, and a video respectively, and $(e_i, r_k, e_j) \in T_r$ is a relation triple.*

Definition 2. MMEA. *Given two MMKGs $KG_1 = (E_1, R_1, A_1, P_1, V_1, T_{r_1})$ and $KG_2 = (E_2, R_2, A_2, P_2, V_2, T_{r_2})$, the goal of MMEA is to find a function Ψ to identify a set of entity pairs $H = \{(e_i^1, e_j^2) | e_i^1 \equiv e_j^2, e_i^1 \in E_1, e_j^2 \in E_2\}$ based on $\mathcal{S} \subset H$ and the multi-modal features in two MMKGs, such as attributes, images and videos. Here, $\equiv$ denotes that two entities are equivalent in the real world, and $\mathcal{S}$ is a set of few annotations.*

4 Proposed Method

Observed from Fig. 2, the proposed model EIEA consists of three modules: i.e., Multi-modal Knowledge Embedding (MMKE), Enhanced Entity Representation (EER), and Multi-modal Contrastive Representation Learning (MMCRL), and the details of them are introduced as follows.

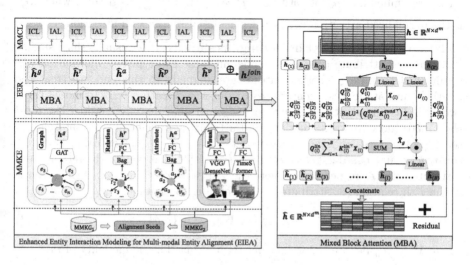

Fig. 2. Overview of the proposed model EIEA

4.1 Multi-modal Knowledge Embedding

In MMKGs, entities usually have various information, such as graph structure, relation, attribute, and visual feature. To capture the unique characteristics of each modality, several encoders are utilized to obtain the representations.

Graph Structure Embedding. To extract the structural features of entities in MMKGs, we aggregate information from entities' neighbors using Graph Attention Network (GAT) [17]. Formally, we first construct a homogeneous graph $\mathcal{G} = (\mathcal{V}, \mathcal{E})$ based on T_r. In detail, each node $\mathcal{V}_i \in \mathcal{V}$ denotes an entity e_i and if there exists a triple (e_i, r_k, e_j) in T_r, $\mathcal{E}$ includes two edges: $(\mathcal{V}_i, \mathcal{V}_j)$ and $(\mathcal{V}_j, \mathcal{V}_i)$. Then, given an entity e_i, we generate its one-hop neighbors $\mathcal{N}_i$ with self-loop based on $\mathcal{G}$. For each entity e_i, the neighbor aggregating process is defined as:

$$h_i^g = \text{ReLU}(\sum\nolimits_{j \in \mathcal{N}_i} \alpha_{ij} h_j^g) \tag{1}$$

where $h_i^g, h_j^g \in \mathbb{R}^d$ are the hidden states of entities e_i and e_j, d is the hidden dimension, $\text{ReLU}(\cdot)$ denotes the ReLU nonlinearity, and α_{ij} is the importance of entity e_j to entity e_i, expressed as:

$$\alpha_{ij} = \frac{\exp(\text{LeakyReLU}(\mathbf{a}^\top [\mathbf{W}h_i^g \oplus \mathbf{W}h_j^g]))}{\sum_{u \in \mathcal{N}_i} \exp(\text{LeakyReLU}(\mathbf{a}^\top [\mathbf{W}h_i^g \oplus \mathbf{W}h_u^g]))} \tag{2}$$

where $\mathbf{W} \in \mathbb{R}^{d \times d}$ denotes a diagonal weight matrix for reducing the amount of calculation [8], $\mathbf{a} \in \mathbb{R}^{2d}$ is a learnable weight parameter, $\oplus$ represents a column concatenation operation, and $\text{LeakyReLU}(\cdot)$ is the LeakyReLU nonlinearity. To stabilize the self-attention learning [17], we perform parallel independent attention with $K = 2$ heads in Eq. (1) and concatenate these features to obtain the structure embedding h_i^g of entity e_i: $h_i^g = \overset{K}{\underset{k=1}{\oplus}} \text{ReLU}(\sum_{j \in \mathcal{N}_i} \alpha_{ij}^k h_j^g)$, where α_{ij}^k is the normalized attention coefficient calculated by the k-th attention.

Relation and Attribute Embedding. As aligned entities usually share similar relations and attribute types [21], modeling these two types of information will facilitate determining whether entities are aligned. To this end, we treat the relations and attributes of entities as bag-of-words features [21] to model these two modalities explicitly. Without loss of generality, we only consider the top-l ($l = 1000$) most frequent relations and attributes. Specifically, for the relation set $\{r_1, r_2, \cdots, r_l\}$ and the attribute set $\{a_1, a_2, \cdots, a_l\}$ of entity $e_i \in E$, we construct count-based x-hot vectors $f_i^r, f_i^a \in \mathbb{R}^{1 \times l}$ that denote the relation and attribute features respectively, where the j-th term of f_i^r (or f_i^a) is the count x of the j-th relation (or attribute) corresponding to entity e_i.

$$h_i^m = \mathbf{W}_m f_i^m + \mathbf{b}_m, \ m \in \{r, a\} \tag{3}$$

where $\mathbf{W}_m, \mathbf{b}_m$ denote the weight matrix and bias for the modality of m.

Visual Embedding. Without loss of generality, the equivalent entities tend to exhibit greater visual similarity than unaligned ones, i.e., the visual features can be used to enhance the effectiveness of entity alignment to a certain extent. In this subsection, we use pre-trained visual models (PVMs) such as VGG16 [14], TimeSformer [1], and DenseNet [7] to learn image and video embeddings. Specifically, we first feed the image p_i (or keyframes sampled from video v_i) of entity e_i into VGG16 (or TimeSformer). Then we take the output before the last fully connected layer and apply a linear transformation to obtain the image embedding h_i^p (or video embedding h_i^v) for e_i, i.e., $h_i^m = \mathbf{W}_m \mathrm{PVM}(m_i) + \mathbf{b}_m$, $m \in \{p, v\}$, where $\mathrm{PVM}(\cdot)$ is a pre-trained model, such as TimeSformer.

4.2 Enhanced Entity Representation

After obtaining the set of multi-modal feature embeddings $\{h^g, h^r, h^a, h^p, h^v\}$, where h^g is a matrix with each row denoting the representation of an entity learned from graph structure, we present the module Enhanced Entity Representation (EER) including two components: Mixed Block Attention (MBA) and Multi-modal Fusion (MMF), and the details of them are as follows.

Mixed Block Attention (MBA). As emphasized in Sect. 1, exploring pairwise interactions between any pair of entities within each modality, especially between an entity and its neighbors, is critical. In light of this insight, we take inspiration from Graph Transformer [20] and FLASH [6] to develop the Mixed Block Attention (MBA). This component effectively models an entity's neighborhoods and co-occurrence information, and mines pairwise entity-node interactions to enhance the entity's representation. MBA consists of two stages: *Local Block Self-Attention* and *Global Attention across Blocks*, and the implementation of it is presented below.

Prior to delving into the details of MBA, it is essential to provide the following preparation illustration. To effectively tackle the above-mentioned task and leverage the parallel processing capability of the Transformer-based model, we adopt the following strategy to rank entities within the entity set and bring each entity closer to their neighbors, before the module Multi-modal Knowledge Embedding (MMKE) in Subsect. 4.2. In detail, given a MMKG $KG = (E, R, A, P, V, T_r)$, we assume that E contains N entities. $\mathcal{N}_i$ is the set of one-hop neighbors of the entity numbered ID_i. Specifically, an entity is first randomly selected from E and numbered ID_1. Then, we number the entities in $\mathcal{N}_1$ starting with ID_2. Next, the operation is repeated for all remaining entities in E according to $\{\mathcal{N}_2, \mathcal{N}_3, \cdots\}$. Notably, if an entity has been numbered in $\mathcal{N}_i$, it cannot be numbered again in $\mathcal{N}_j$ $(i < j)$. Finally, we obtain the set of entity number $\mathcal{ID} = \{ID_1, \cdots, ID_N\}$, where the embedding of the entity numbered ID_i is the i-th element in h, and $h \in \{h^g, h^r, h^a, h^p, h^v\}$ denotes the embedding matrix learned from a certain type of modal information.

In what follows, for the single-modal embedding matrix h, we first divide it into B non-overlapping blocks with a given size c, where the value of c is determined by the statistical distribution of entity neighborhood sizes. Then, for the i-th block $h_{(i)} \subset h$, it is transformed through an affine transformation (i.e., linear mapping with activation function) to obtain $U_{(i)}$, $X_{(i)}$, and $Z_{(i)}$:

$$U_{(i)} = \phi_u(h_{(i)}\mathbf{W}_u), \quad X_{(i)} = \phi_x(h_{(i)}\mathbf{W}_x) \in \mathbb{R}^{c \times t} \tag{4}$$

$$Z_{(i)} = \phi_z(\boldsymbol{h}_{(i)}\mathbf{W}_z) \in \mathbb{R}^{c \times s} \tag{5}$$

where $\mathbf{W}_u$, $\mathbf{W}_x$, $\mathbf{W}_z$ are trainable dense matrices, t denotes the expanded inter-mediate size, s is the dimension of hidden layer, and $\phi(\cdot)$ is an element-wise activation function. Finally, four types of attention heads $Q_{(i)}^{quad}$, $K_{(i)}^{quad}$, $Q_{(i)}^{lin}$, $K_{(i)}^{lin}$ are produced from $Z_{(i)}$ by applying per-dim scaling and offset [6]. Based on these four attention heads, we design the following two stages.

Local Block Self-attention. This stage is designed to capture short-range interactions between entities, that is, interactions between an entity and its neighbors. A local quadratic attention [6] is independently introduced to each block that serves as a head, and the formulation of it is given as follows:

$$\hat{\boldsymbol{X}}_{(i)}^{quad} = \frac{1}{cs}\text{ReLU}^2\left(\boldsymbol{Q}_{(i)}^{quad}\boldsymbol{K}_{(i)}^{quad\top}\right)\boldsymbol{X}_{(i)} \tag{6}$$

where $\hat{\boldsymbol{X}}_{(i)}^{quad}$ is the output of *Local Block Self-Attention.*

Global Attention Across Blocks. The goal of this stage is to consider sparse, long-range interactions between entities across different blocks. Detailedly, we introduce a global linear attention mechanism that can efficiently handle long sequences and reduce the complexity to linear, as demonstrated by FLASH [6] and Linformer [18]. Based on the global linear attention mechanism, this stage is formulated as follows:

$$\hat{\boldsymbol{X}}_{(i)}^{lin} = \frac{1}{N}\boldsymbol{Q}_{(i)}^{lin}\left(\sum_{j=1}^{B}\boldsymbol{K}_{(j)}^{lin\top}\boldsymbol{X}_{(j)}\right) \tag{7}$$

where $\hat{\boldsymbol{X}}_{(i)}^{lin}$ is the output of *Global Attention across Blocks.*

In the immediate aftermath, $\hat{\boldsymbol{X}}_{(i)}^{quad}$ and $\hat{\boldsymbol{X}}_{(i)}^{lin}$ are first added together and then fed into Gated Attention Unit [6] for post-attentional projection to obtain the output of the i-th block $\hat{\boldsymbol{h}}_{(i)}$: $\hat{\boldsymbol{h}}_{(i)} = (\boldsymbol{U}_{(i)} \odot (\hat{\boldsymbol{X}}_{(i)}^{quad} + \hat{\boldsymbol{X}}_{(i)}^{lin}))\mathbf{W}$. After obtaining the output of B blocks $\{\hat{\boldsymbol{h}}_{(1)}, \cdots, \hat{\boldsymbol{h}}_{(i)}, \cdots, \hat{\boldsymbol{h}}_{(B)}\}$, we utilize the row concatenation operation $\|$ and an adaptive weight long-range residual connection to obtain the final enhanced entity representations $\hat{\boldsymbol{h}}$, i.e., $\hat{\boldsymbol{h}} = w_1(\hat{\boldsymbol{h}}_{(i)})\|_{i=1}^{B} + w_2\boldsymbol{h}$, where w_1 and w_2 are trainable weight parameters. Note that since MBA is implemented in each modality, we obtain a set of enhanced entity representations $F = \{\hat{\boldsymbol{h}}^g, \hat{\boldsymbol{h}}^r, \hat{\boldsymbol{h}}^a, \hat{\boldsymbol{h}}^p, \hat{\boldsymbol{h}}^v\}$.

Multi-modal Fusion (MMF). To facilitate effective multi-modal embedding fusion, the Multi-modal Fusion (MMF) component is designed based on a weighting mechanism and the enhanced entity representations. Specifically, given a MMKG corresponding to $F = \{\hat{\boldsymbol{h}}^g, \hat{\boldsymbol{h}}^r, \hat{\boldsymbol{h}}^a, \hat{\boldsymbol{h}}^p, \hat{\boldsymbol{h}}^v\}$, we first L2-normalize the enhanced entity representations for each modality in F, and then obtain the joint embedding $\boldsymbol{h}_i^{join}$ via a trainable weighted connection, i.e.,

$$\boldsymbol{h}_i^{join} = \bigoplus_{m \in \mathcal{M}=\{g,r,a,p,v\}} \left[\frac{\exp(w_m)}{\sum_{j \in \mathcal{M}}\exp(w_j)}\hat{\boldsymbol{h}}_i^m\right] \tag{8}$$

where w_m is a trainable attention weight of modality m.

4.3   Multi-modal Contrastive Learning

Inspired by previous work [9], we develop the module Multi-modal Contrastive Learning (MMCL), including Intra-modal Contrastive Loss (ICL) and Inter-modal Alignment Loss (IAL). Specifically, ICL aims at maximizing the intra-modal interactions, i.e., maintaining higher similarity for aligned entities than non-aligned ones within each modality. IAL is to minimize the inter-modal gaps, i.e., reducing the differences between embedding distributions across different modalities caused by encoders.

Intra-modal Contrastive Loss (ICL). According to the 1-to-1 alignment assumption [16], we consider all entity pairs in S as positive samples. In detail, given any entity pair (e_i^1, e_j^2), the positive sample set of e_i^1 is defined as $\mathcal{T}_i = \{e_j^2 | e_j^2 \in E_2\}$, and the negative sample set of it is defined as $\mathcal{F}_i = \{e_o^1 | \forall e_o^1 \in E_1, o \neq i\} \cup \{e_o^2 | \forall e_o^2 \in E_2, o \neq j\}$. Overall, the alignment probability distribution of modality m for each positive pair (e_i^1, e_j^2) is define as follows:

$$\mathcal{P}_m(e_i^1, e_j^2) = \frac{\epsilon_m(e_i^1, e_j^2)}{\epsilon_m(e_i^1, e_j^2) + \sum_{e_o^* \in \mathcal{F}_i} \epsilon_m(e_i^1, e_o^*)} \tag{9}$$

where $\epsilon(e_i, e_j) = exp(\hat{h}_i^{m\top} \hat{h}_j^m / \tau_1)$, embeddings in $\hat{h}^m$ are L2-normalized and τ_1 is a temperature hyper-parameter. In addition, to consider bidirectional alignment, we extend the loss objective of modality m from Eq. (9) as follows:

$$\mathcal{L}_m^{\text{ICL}} = -\frac{1}{2}\log\left(\mathcal{P}_m(e_i^1, e_j^2) + \mathcal{P}_m(e_j^2, e_i^1)\right) \tag{10}$$

Inter-modal Alignment Loss (IAL). As clarified in previous work [9], incorporating multi-modal features in joint embeddings can transfer other modality information to single-modal embeddings as supplementary information, thus reducing the gaps between the distribution of embeddings across different modalities. To achieve this, an inter-modal alignment loss is designed to minimize the bidirectional KL divergence on the alignment probability distribution between joint and single-modal embeddings, i.e.,

$$\mathcal{L}_m^{\text{IAL}} = \frac{1}{2}\left(\text{KL}(\mathcal{P}_{join}'(e_i^1, e_j^2) \| \mathcal{P}_m'(e_i^1, e_j^2)) + \text{KL}(\mathcal{P}_{join}'(e_j^2, e_i^1) \| \mathcal{P}_m'(e_j^2, e_i^1))\right) \tag{11}$$

where $\mathcal{P}_{join}'(\cdot)$ and $\mathcal{P}_m'(\cdot)$ represent the alignment probability distributions of the joint and single-modal embeddings of modality m respectively, calculated based on Eq. (9) with setting the temperature parameter to τ_2. Furthermore, we only back-propagate $\mathcal{P}_m'(e_i^1, e_j^2)$ and $\mathcal{P}_m'(e_j^2, e_i^1)$ as knowledge distillation [9].

4.4   Training Objective

The overall loss of EIEA is expressed as follows:

$$\mathcal{L} = \mathcal{L}_{join}^{\text{ICL}} + \sum_{m \in \mathcal{M}} \alpha_m \mathcal{L}_m^{\text{ICL}} + \sum_{m \in \mathcal{M}} \beta_m \mathcal{L}_m^{\text{IAL}} \tag{12}$$

where $\mathcal{M} = \{g, r, a, p, v\}$, $\mathcal{L}_{join}^{ICL}$ denotes the ICL operated on joint embeddings, and α_m and β_m are hyper-parameters that balance the importance of losses. To automatically learn the above hyper-parameters during training, we treat the MMEA task as a multi-task learning paradigm and then design a multi-task loss function by maximizing the Gaussian likelihood with task-dependent uncertainty, inspired by [9]. Hence, the loss in Eq. (12) can be rewritten as:

$$\mathcal{L} = \mathcal{L}_{join}^{ICL} + \sum_{m \in \mathcal{M}} \left(\frac{1}{\alpha_m^2} \mathcal{L}_m^{ICL} + \frac{1}{\beta_m^2} \mathcal{L}_m^{IAL} + \log \alpha_m + \log \beta_m \right) \quad (13)$$

Last but not least, the bi-directional iterative strategy in [10] is applied to iteratively add new aligned seeds during training. In the inference, the cosine similarity metric is utilized to calculate the similarity between joint embeddings of entities to determine their counterparts.

5   Experiment

5.1   Experiment Setting

Datasets. We conduct experiments on two publicly available datasets, FB15K-DB15K/YAGO15K provided by MMKG [11] and an individual dataset Baidu-Douban. Table 1 presents the statistics of these datasets. In cases where an entity lacks an image or a video, EIEA assigns a random vector [10] to represent the missing modality. In experiments, we divide the ground truth alignment seeds into training and testing sets, following a ratio of 2:8, 5:5, and 8:2 for each dataset [2]. We adopt Hits@n (n = 1, 5, 10), MRR (Mean Reciprocal Rank ↑), and MR (Mean Rank ↓) as the evaluation metrics for all models.

Table 1. Statistics of all datasets.(Ent.: Entity, Rel.: Relation, Att.: Attributes, Rel tr.: Relation Triple, Att tr.: Attribute Triple, Img.: Image, Vid.: Video)

Dataset	#Ent.	#Rel.	#Att.	#Rel tr.	#Att tr.	#Img.	#Vid.	#Seed
FB15K	14,951	1,345	116	592,213	29,395	13,444	–	–
DB15K	12,842	279	225	89,197	48,080	12,837	–	12,846
YAGO15K	15,404	32	7	122,886	23,532	11,194	–	11,199
Baidu	8,720	10	3	13,986	1,879	2,905	435	–
Douban	16,467	10	11	32,202	8,637	3,355	472	5,177

Baselines. To evaluate the effectiveness of EIEA, we select 12 state-of-the-art EA methods as baselines for comparison, which can be divided into two categories: 1) *Traditional EA methods*, including structure-based methods and auxiliary-enhanced methods, such as MTransE [4], GCN-Align [19], SEA [13], HyperKA [15], RAGA [24], and RAC [22]. 2) *Multi-modal methods*, which combine multi-modal features to generate entity representations, including PoE [11], MEA [2], HMEA [5], EVA [10], MSNEA [3], and MCLEA [9].

Implementation Details. To ensure a fair comparison, we use the best hyper-parameters reported in literature for all baselines and set the entity representation dimension to 300. For standardizing visual embeddings, we employ VGG16

[14] as the PVM for processing images in FB15K-DB15K/YAGO15K and use DenseNet [7] and TimeSformer [1] for processing images and videos in Baidu-Douban, respectively. Our model utilizes a two-layer GAT [17] with a dropout rate dr of 0.1 for each layer. The model is trained for 1000 epochs, with the last 500 epochs being iterative learning. The learning rate lr for the AdamW optimizer is set to 5×10^{-4}, and the batch size is set to 3500. The block size c and query/key dimensions are set to 400, 300, and 300, respectively. The hyper-parameters τ_1 and τ_2 are set to 0.1 and 4.0, respectively.

5.2 Performance Comparison

Table 2 and Table 3 present the performance comparison of EIEA with different baselines on different datasets. The best results are marked **in bold**, with the second-best results underlined, and "Improv.%" indicates the relative improvement of EIEA over the best baseline [9].

Table 2. Experimental results of EA methods with 20% alignment seeds on MMKG. Hits@n (H@n) and MRR are expressed as percentages, while MR takes a positive value.

Method	FB15K-DB15K					FB15K-YAGO15K				
	H@1	H@5	H@10	MRR	MR	H@1	H@5	H@10	MRR	MR
MTransE	0.41	1.63	2.7	5.06	215.23	0.33	0.93	1.62	4.24	322.15
GCN-Align	6.64	15.57	21.25	7.9	809.31	4.88	12.77	17.64	8.9	758.31
SEA	16.97	33.46	42.51	25.5	191.90	14.08	28.69	37.15	21.8	207.24
HyperKA	14.45	30.92	39.51	24.3	254.43	11.48	24.74	33.24	42.1	189.32
RAGA	8.84	19.16	26.05	14.3	432.34	6.23	15.81	21.41	12.3	354.32
RAC	18.89	29.36	41.47	26.5	501.51	13.23	26	31.6	19.6	548.03
PoE	12.0	–	25.6	16.7	–	10.9	–	24.1	15.4	–
MEA	26.48	45.13	54.1	35.7	124.81	23.39	39.76	48	31.7	147.44
HMEA	12.7	–	36.9	–	–	10.5	–	31.3	–	–
EVA	12.13	27.22	34.91	19.8	430.94	8.78	19.67	26.22	14.6	560.19
MSNEA	28.3	47.06	56.63	36.5	189.31	26.73	45.27	53.16	35.7	215.58
MCLEA	45.27	66.9	71.9	54.7	109.37	39.5	58.3	65.4	47.9	142.86
EIEA	**57.43**	**74.28**	**79.26**	**65.2**	**98.2**	**49.55**	**66.91**	**72.68**	**57.5**	**84.99**
Improv.%	26.9	11.0	10.2	19.2	10.22	25.4	14.8	11.1	20.0	40.5

Table 2 reports the performance of all methods trained with 20% alignment seeds on FB15K-DB15K/YG15K. Overall, EIEA achieves the best performance on all evaluation metrics. Specifically, we have the following observations. Firstly, on both datasets, Hits@1 and MRR are improved by at least 25.4% and 19.2%, respectively, while MR is reduced by at least 10.22%, demonstrating the effectiveness of our proposed model. Secondly, most multi-modal methods achieve better results than single-modal approaches, further suggesting the importance of utilizing multi-modal knowledge for entity alignment. Thirdly, compared to all existing MMEA methods, EIEA has performance improvement, indicating the importance of enhancing the interactions between entities.

Table 3. Experiment results with different ratios of alignment seeds on Baidu-Douban

Method	20%			50%			80%		
	H@1	H@10	MRR	H@1	H@10	MRR	H@1	H@10	MRR
MEA	31.7	61.54	42.6	49.17	81.26	51.9	61.2	86.87	71.7
EVA	33.82	62.29	44.0	58.99	86.91	72.2	76.41	88.17	75.1
MSNEA	19.28	35.92	25.7	45.17	61.26	51.9	63.9	80.89	69.5
MCLEA	<u>40.86</u>	<u>67.79</u>	<u>55.2</u>	<u>62.4</u>	<u>86.96</u>	<u>75.0</u>	<u>77.08</u>	<u>90.88</u>	<u>85.2</u>
EIEA	**47.36**	**73.83**	**57.5**	**69.19**	**91.67**	**78.4**	**83.76**	**95.61**	**89.1**
Improv. %	15.9	8.9	4.2	10.9	5.4	4.5	8.7	5.2	4.6

To verify the scalability of EIEA from the perspective of modality and the effectiveness of EIEA in dealing with sparse data, we conduct experiments on dataset Baidu-Douban, and the results are reported in Table 3. Overall, EIEA performs best in all evaluation metrics, mainly because the contrastive learning can effectively reduce the modality gap in entity embeddings and avoid the excessive impact of sparse data. Furthermore, we observe a sharp drop in the performance of MSNEA, possibly due to it relies on visual features for representation learning, while the visual data on Baidu-Douban are extremely sparse.

Table 4. Experiment results of ablation study on three datasets.

	Methods	FB15K-DB15K			FB15k-YAGO15K			Baidu-Douban		
		H@1	H@10	MRR	H@1	H@10	MRR	H@1	H@10	MRR
	EIEA	**57.43**	**79.26**	**65.2**	**49.55**	**72.68**	**57.5**	**47.36**	**73.83**	**57.5**
Modalities	w/o structure	47.44	74.19	56.8	40.94	68.03	50.1	39.31	69.41	50.6
	w/o relation	51.32	76.82	60.2	44.28	70.44	53.2	42.32	71.56	53.1
	w/o attribute	54.62	78.85	62.4	47.13	72.30	55.1	45.02	73.47	55.2
	w/o image	56.98	79.14	64.5	49.20	72.61	56.9	46.51	73.61	56.3
	w/o video	-	-	-	-	-	-	47.03	73.68	56.9
Training	w/o MBA	45.27	72.21	55.2	39.2	64.71	47.1	37.32	67.26	48.6
	w/o ICL	47.22	73.36	56.3	41.74	68.27	51.5	39.12	68.79	49.9
	w/o IAL	56.4	78.61	63.6	48.15	72.06	56.1	46.52	73.84	56.4
	w/o iter.strategy	52.16	77.12	60.3	45.01	70.72	53.2	43.01	71.84	53.2
	w/o uncertainty	53.16	77.78	61.9	45.97	71.32	54.5	43.89	72.51	54.5

5.3   Ablation Study

The results of ablation study are presented in Table 4. 1) Removing different modalities has varying degrees of impact on performance, with the graph structure and relation having the most significant impact, while other modalities have less contributions to EIEA. 2) We investigate various training strategies in EIEA. Removing MBA and ICL from EIEA leads to a significant performance decrease, indicating the importance of MBA in enhancing entity's representation and ICL in maintaining the proximity of aligned entities. IAL learns the interdependence between different modalities, contributing to the model. Training EIEA without the iterative strategy or replacing the uncertainty mechanism with uniform weights (i.e., *w/o* uncertainty) also leads to decreased performance.

5.4 Parameter Analysis

Seed Sensitivity. To evaluate the sensitivity of these EA methods to pre-aligned entities, we divide 20%, 50%, and 80% of the pre-aligned entity pairs into the training set S following the existing work [2,11]. Figure 3 and Table 3 detail the comparison results of all models with different alignment seed ratios on three datasets. The experimental results demonstrate that many methods perform poorly when only 20% of training seeds are utilized. With the increase of the ratio of training seeds, methods like SEA, HyperKA, and MEA gradually improve their performance because they rely too much on pre-aligned seeds. On the contrary, MTransE, GCN-Align, and EVA are still impractical due to the simple network structure. In contrast, EIEA has no strong dependence on pre-aligned entities and can utilize the smallest number of alignment seeds to obtain effective entity representation and achieve excellent performance.

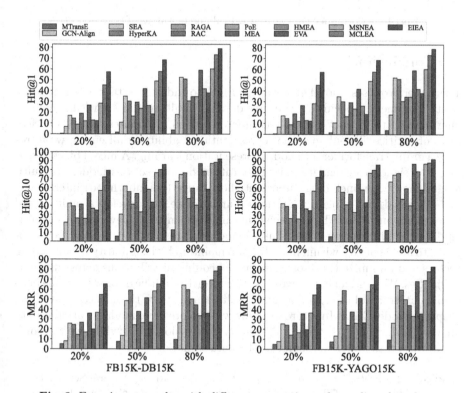

Fig. 3. Experiment results with different proportions of pre-aligned seeds

Impacts of Parameters c, lr and dr. We study the effects of the parameters block size c, learning rate lr and dropout rate dp on FB15K-DB15K, as shown in Fig. 4. We adjust the parameter c from 50 to 1000 and the model achieves the best performance at $c = 400$. Observed from Fig. 4(a), EIEA is not very sensitive to the block size because the important neighborhoods of the entities are mostly distributed in the range of $[100, 1000]$, with the most frequent interval being $[300, 500]$. The best performance is achieved when the learning rate is set to 0.0005 in Fig. 4(b). The lr that is too large may lead to issues such as overfitting, while the lr that is too small may lead to underfitting. Additionally, the dropout rate dr of our model is searched from 0.0 to 0.5. The results show that ignoring a certain rate of node features will achieve better results.

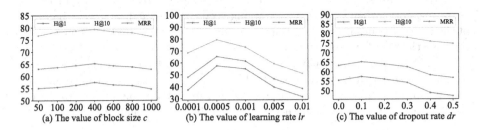

Fig. 4. Performance comparison with different values of c, lr and dr

6 Conclusion

This paper proposes a novel model called EIEA to address the task of multi-modal entity alignment. Specifically, we first design a multi-modal knowledge embedding module to extract graph structures, relations, attributes, and visual features of entities. To enhance the representational ability of an entity, we introduce a graph transformer into node representation learning. A mixed block attention is designed to calculate pairwise entity-node interactions hidden in multi-modal knowledge, including important short-range (neighborhood) interactions and neglected long-range interactions. Furthermore, we develop a multi-modal fusion component based on a weighting mechanism to achieve effective multi-modal embedding fusion. Then, a multi-modal contrastive learning module is proposed to align entities within modalities to maintain high similarity in embedding vectors and minimize the gaps between embedding distributions across different modalities. We conduct extensive experiments on two public datasets and one individual dataset, and the experimental results demonstrate the effectiveness of our proposed model EIEA. In future work, we will explore more modality attributes to improve performance, such as audio, entity description. Meanwhile, we will solve the MMEA task under the sparse modal data scenario.

Acknowledgments.. This work is supported by the National Natural Science Foundation of China No. 62272332, the Major Program of the Natural Science Foundation of Jiangsu Higher Education Institutions of China No. 22KJA520006.

References

1. Bertasius, G., Wang, H., et al.: Is space-time attention all you need for video understanding? In: ICML, pp. 813–824 (2021)
2. Chen, L., Li, Z., et al.: MMEA: entity alignment for multi-modal knowledge graph. In: KSEM, pp. 134–147 (2020)
3. Chen, L., Li, Z., et al.: Multi-modal Siamese Network for Entity Alignment. In: KDD, pp. 118–126 (2022)
4. Chen, M., Tian, Y., et al.: Multilingual knowledge graph embeddings for cross-lingual knowledge alignment. In: IJCAI, pp. 1511–1517 (2017)
5. Guo, H., Tang, J., et al.: Multi-modal entity alignment in hyperbolic space. Neurocomputing **461**, 598–607 (2021)
6. Hua, W., Dai, Z., et al.: Transformer quality in linear time. In: ICML, pp. 9099–9117 (2022)
7. Huang, G., Liu, Z., et al.: Densely connected convolutional networks. In: CVPR, pp. 2261–2269 (2017)
8. Li, C., Cao, Y., et al.: Semi-supervised entity alignment via joint knowledge embedding model and cross-graph model. In: EMNLP-IJCNLP, pp. 2723–2732 (2019)
9. Lin, Z., Zhang, Z., et al.: Multi-modal contrastive representation learning for entity alignment. In: COLING, pp. 2572–2584 (2022)
10. Liu, F., Chen, M., et al.: Visual pivoting for (unsupervised) entity alignment. In: AAAI, pp. 4257–4266 (2021)
11. Liu, Y., Li, H., Garcia-Duran, A., Niepert, M., Onoro-Rubio, D., Rosenblum, D.S.: MMKG: multi-modal knowledge graphs. In: Hitzler, P., et al. (eds.) ESWC 2019. LNCS, vol. 11503, pp. 459–474. Springer, Cham (2019). https://doi.org/10.1007/978-3-030-21348-0_30
12. Liu, Z., Cao, Y., et al.: Exploring and evaluating attributes, values, and structures for entity alignment. In: EMNLP, pp. 6355–6364 (2020)
13. Pei, S., Yu, L., et al.: Semi-supervised entity alignment via knowledge graph embedding with awareness of degree difference. In: WWW, pp. 3130–3136 (2019)
14. Simonyan, K., Zisserman, A.: Very deep convolutional networks for large-scale image recognition. In: ICLR (2015)
15. Sun, Z., Chen, M., et al.: Knowledge association with hyperbolic knowledge graph embeddings. In: EMNLP, pp. 5704–5716 (2020)
16. Sun, Z., Hu, W., et al.: Bootstrapping entity alignment with knowledge graph embedding. In: IJCAI, pp. 4396–4402 (2018)
17. Velickovic, P., Cucurull, G., et al.: Graph attention networks. In: ICLR (2018)
18. Wang, S., Li, B.Z., et al.: Linformer: self-attention with linear complexity. CoRR abs/2006.04768 (2020)
19. Wang, Z., Lv, Q., et al.: Cross-lingual knowledge graph alignment via graph convolutional networks. In: EMNLP, pp. 349–357 (2018)
20. Wu, Z., Jain, P., et al.: Representing long-range context for graph neural networks with global attention. In: NeurIPS, pp. 13266–13279 (2021)
21. Yang, H., Zou, Y., et al.: Aligning cross-lingual entities with multi-aspect information. In: EMNLP-IJCNLP, pp. 4430–4440 (2019)
22. Zeng, W., Zhao, X., et al.: Reinforced active entity alignment. In: CIKM, pp. 2477–2486 (2021)
23. Zhang, R., Trisedya, B.D., et al.: A benchmark and comprehensive survey on knowledge graph entity alignment via representation learning. VLDB J. **31**(5), 1143–1168 (2022)
24. Zhu, R., Ma, M., et al.: RAGA: relation-aware graph attention networks for global entity alignment. In: PAKDD, pp. 501–513 (2021)

Monte Carlo Medical Volume Rendering Denoising via Auxiliary Feature Guided Self-attention and Convolution Integrated

Guodong Zhang$^{(\boxtimes)}$ ⓘ, Wenliang Zhang, and Jihang Duan

School of Computer Science, Shenyang Aerospace University,
Shenyang 110136, China
zhanggd@sau.edu.cn

Abstract. Medical volume rendering with advanced illumination models using Monte Carlo path tracing for realistic scientific visualization has been applied in medical education and other fields widely. However it takes several hours to produce high-quality rendering results. In this paper, we proposed an auxiliary feature guided self-attention and convolution integrated network (AFGACmix) to obtain approximately high-quality rendering results with denoising from low-sampled medical volume rendering images. The AFGACmix is a weighted mixture of self-attention and convolution in the auxiliary feature guided transformer module, which can better extract the local detail information in the auxiliary features and noisy images. In order to improve the accuracy of image reconstruction, we extract the normal, albedo and depth auxiliary features from the medical volume data. We also added the high frequency error norm to the loss function compensates to improve the quality of image details. The experimental results on different sampling rate datasets show that our method performs better on RMSE, PSNR, 1-SSIM and can reduce the noise effectively than other methods. Finally, we verified the effectiveness of our method through ablation experiments.

Keywords: Volume rendering · Monte Carlo denoising · Transformer · Self-attention · Ray tracing

1 Introduction

Monte Carlo denoising can be divided into surface denoising and volume denoising depending on the medium. For surface denoising, some studies proposed convolution-based methods such as parameter prediction networks [5] and kernel prediction networks [1], but they perform poorly when dealing with images with complex structures and backgrounds. Yu et al. [9] proposed AFGSA (Auxiliary Feature Guided Self-Attention) network based on self-attention [8] to extract global information, which outperformed the other networks, but it cannot make full use of local information. In addition, the surface denoising network require auxiliary features such as normal, albedo to assist the network.

In volume denoising, surface networks cannot be applied directly due to the differences in data structure between them. Hofmann et al. [4] used customized

© The Author(s), under exclusive license to Springer Nature Switzerland AG 2023
Z. Jin et al. (Eds.): KSEM 2023, LNAI 14118, pp. 228–236, 2023.
https://doi.org/10.1007/978-3-031-40286-9_19

auxiliary features like color of scattering events to apply surface network for medical volume rendering, helping produce high-quality results from noisy images. However, these features are complex, contain noise and lack universality.

To solve these problems, we propose the AFGACmix (auxiliary feature guided self-attention and convolution Integrated) network for low-sampled medical volume rendering denoising. Pan et al. [6] proposed the concept of integration of convolution and self-attention for image classification and object detection, the results showed that the mixed model outperformed convolution or self-attention alone. In this paper, We introduce it to Monte Carlo denoising. The main contributions of this paper are three-fold:

(1) We proposed the AFGACmix network which uses a weighted mixture of self-attention and convolution in transformer to extract more local details from auxiliary features and noisy images. (2) We designed a process to generate auxiliary features from volume. They can help network better understand image structure and improve reconstruction accuracy. (3) Add high-frequency error norm to the loss function. By penalizing errors in high-frequency components of reconstructed image, it can reduce visible artifacts and improve image quality.

2 Methodology

Our network is adversarial. The generator includes multi-scale feature extractor, transformer module and decoder, using auxiliary features and noisy images as input. The discriminator uses VGG [7] structure and be trained with the generated images and ground-truth. Figure 1 shows the workflow.

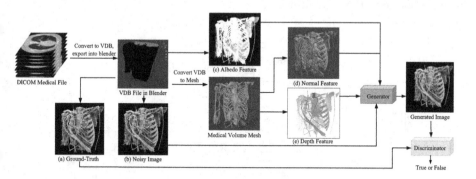

Fig. 1. The overall workflow of medical volume rendering denoising with AFGACmix

Medical Volume to Mesh and Auxiliary Feature Extraction. We convert medical DICOM files to VDB (Virtual Data Block) using 3Dslicer or Paraview. To create surface geometry and generate depth and normal from volume, we use VolumetoMesh node in blender with the marching cubes algorithm to convert it into meshes. Normal, depth and albedo can help the network understand shape, distance and material, recover detail information and avoid mistaking

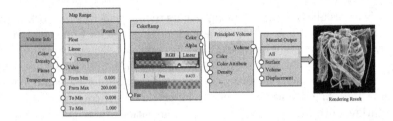

Fig. 2. Implementation of transfer function, node setup and rendering result in blender

noise for detail. Volume has no texture and material, and mesh can only be used to generate normal and depth. We use the Denoising Albedo channel as albedo, which separates areas with low contrast and rich details, allowing for accurate denoising of the image. The feature result is shown in Fig. 1(c)(d)(e).

Medical Volume Transfer Function Implement in Blender. The transfer function maps density to color. It is implemented differently in various software, but the calculation method is similar. We uses blender to implement it, as shown in Fig. 2. "Volume Info" provides density information, "Map Range" normalize it to [0, 1]. "ColorRamp" maps values to colors, then display the result.

2.1 Network Architecture

The generator in Fig. 3 uses a multi-scale feature extractor and 5 transformer blocks to process the input. The decoder produces an output image that is evaluated by the discriminator. Block self-attention can reduce computation and memory usage in the generator.

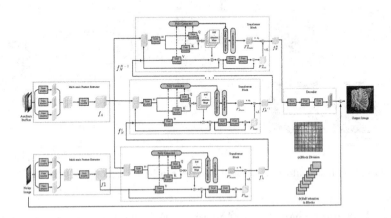

Fig. 3. Generator of medical volume rendering denoising via AFGACmix

Multi-scale Feature Extractor. Multi-scale feature extractor uses three different kernel sizes (1×1, 3×3, 5×5) to extract features from various spatial scales, thereby allowing self-attention to discover more valuable information. The features obtained from noisy image and auxiliary feature is defined as f_N^0, f_A.

Transformer Modules. Transformer modules are used to extract more features. Depth, normal, and albedo have clearer edges than noisy images, making them suitable for computing attention scores. f_A is only used to calculate Q and K in self-attention, while V is the noisy image's pixel values and is unaffected by the auxiliary features. We use the transformer module guided by auxiliary features with a weighted mixture of self-attention and convolution. It can capture more local details in auxiliary features and noisy images. Figure 4 shows that after self-attention and convolution, Q, K, and V produce two outputs: $F_{N\,conv}^i$ is convolution output, $F_{N\,att}^i$ is self-attention output, $F_{N\,att}^i$ is defined as:

$$F_{N\,att}^i = \mathrm{Softmax}\left(\frac{QK^T}{\sqrt{d_k}}\right)V \tag{1}$$

In Eq. (1), $Q = W_Q(f_N^{i-1}; f_A)$, $K = W_K(f_N^{i-1}; f_A)$, $V = W_V(f_N^{i-1})$. In Fig. 3, $F_{N\,att}^i$ and $F_{N\,conv}^i$ are added together to produce the integrated output f_N^i, α_i and β_i are the weights, which are controlled by training. It is defined as:

$$f_N^i = \alpha_i F_{N\,att}^i + \beta_i F_{N\,conv}^i \tag{2}$$

Decoder. After 5 transformer, f_N^5 is obtained, use a simple decoder consisting of three 3×3 convolutional layers to transform features into images.

Discriminator. The discriminator use VGG's structure. Figure 4 shows that a vector is created after convolution and downsampling, which is then transformed into a score between 0–1 to indicate the probability of the image being real. "Conv k1c256" refers to a convolutional layer with 256 1×1 kernels, the other definitions are the same as this. All convolutional layers use "reflect" padding and "1" stride, without normalization in Fig. 3 and Fig. 4.

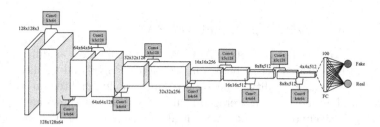

Fig. 4. Discriminator of medical volume rendering denoising via AFGACmix

2.2 Loss Function

We combines hfen (high-frequency error norm) with Rec (pixel reconstruction) loss and Adv (adversarial) loss to generate a new loss function, it is defined as:

$$L = \lambda_{rec}L_{rec} + \lambda_{adv}L_{adv} + \lambda_{hfen}L_{hfen} \tag{3}$$

λ_{rec}, λ_{adv}, and λ_{hfen} are hyperparameters that control the weights. Rec loss is defined as the L1 distance between the generated image and ground-truth, and the WGAN-GP [3] loss is used to define Adv loss. These two terms for AFGACmix are the same as AFGSA, and specific formulas can be found in [9]. For simplicity, we omit them in the paper. hfen loss [2] can penalize errors in the high-frequency portion of the reconstructed image to improve detail quality, it is defined as:

$$L_{hfen} = \frac{1}{N} \sum_{i}^{N} \left| \nabla \hat{I}_i - \nabla I_{gti} \right| \tag{4}$$

N represents the total number of pixels in the image, ∇ is gradient operator, $\hat{I}_i$ and I_{gti} is the value of the i-th pixel in generated image and ground-truth.

3 Evaluation

We compare with Nvidia's OptiX denoising and AFGSA, the results showed that our method can effectively reduce noise. Due to the lack of a standard medical volume rendering dataset, we create a dataset using blender. The dataset has 36 shots with noisy images and three auxiliary features along with ground-truth. The noisy images were rendered at various Spp (Samples per pixel), the ground-truth was rendered at 4096 Spp. Each shot has an 800×800 image, which is divided into 128×128 images. The dataset includes around 50000 noisy images, the same number of ground-truth and auxiliary features. The algorithm randomly selects 95% for training and 5% for validation.

The transformer blocks number was set 5 and it was run on a NVIDIA TITAN XP GPU with 12 GB. The adam optimizer was used with initial learning rate 10^{-4} that was halved every 3 epochs, totally 24 epochs. The batch size was set 2. The loss function weights were set $\lambda_{rec} = 0.9$, $\lambda_{hfen} = 0.1$, $\lambda_{adv} = 5 \times 10^{-3}$. We training at 4, 8, 16, 32, and 128Spp. We use RMSE, PSNR, and 1-SSIM as evaluation metrics. They can provide a comprehensive evaluation for denoising.

3.1 Comparison with OptiX and AFGSA

Table 1 shows the results of OptiX, AFGSA and our method at different Spp. Smaller RMSE indicates better performance, higher PSNR and smaller 1-SSIM indicate better image quality. The best results are highlighted in bold and underlined and all metrics are averaged results. Our method shows good performance and effectively reduces noise in medical volume rendering. The comparison between AFGSA and AFGACmix is listed in Fig. 5.

Figure 6 compare our method with OptiX and AFGSA at different Spp. It shows denoising results for different methods, including OptiX (without auxiliary feature), OptiX+A (using albedo), OptiX+A+N (using albedo and normal), AFGSA (only using Rec loss), AFGSA+hfen (using Rec+hfen loss), AFGACmix (only using Rec loss), and AFGACmix+hfen (using Rec+hfen loss). The red marking indicates a magnified area. The ground-truth and noisy image are also displayed, PSNR and 1-SSIM are listed right each image.

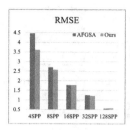 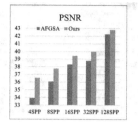 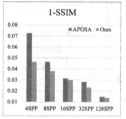

Fig. 5. RMSE, PSNR, 1-SSIM comparison between AFGSA and AFGACmix

Table 1. Denoising results with OpitX, AFGSA and our proposed AFGACmix.

Spp	Metrics	OpitX	OpitX+A	OpitX+A+N	AFGSA	Ours
4Spp	RMSE $(10^{-3})\downarrow$	8.07	7.014	6.783	4.463	**3.605**
	PSNR↑	28.8179	29.4143	29.4567	33.9174	**36.5426**
	1-SSIM↓	0.1585	0.1207	0.1062	0.0725	**0.0463**
8Spp	RMSE $(10^{-3})\downarrow$	5.051	4.494	4.491	2.686	**2.565**
	PSNR↑	30.7995	31.2698	31.3891	36.0777	**37.7512**
	1-SSIM↓	0.12482	0.0849	0.0682	0.0463	**0.0379**
16Spp	RMSE $(10^{-3})\downarrow$	3.338	3.098	3.046	1.779	**1.775**
	PSNR↑	32.565	32.895	33.0357	38.281	**39.4016**
	1-SSIM↓	0.0993	0.0666	0.0489	0.0313	**0.0299**
32Spp	RMSE $(10^{-3})\downarrow$	2.119	2.118	2.043	1.253	**1.223**
	PSNR↑	34.4951	34.5893	34.7434	38.7612	**39.9741**
	1-SSIM↓	0.0764	0.0492	0.0351	0.0283	**0.0232**
128Spp	RMSE $(10^{-3})\downarrow$	1.031	0.982	0.913	**0.561**	0.581
	PSNR↑	37.6397	37.889	38.0013	42.2363	**42.8091**
	1-SSIM↓	0.0537	0.0292	0.0199	0.0148	**0.0138**

3.2 Ablation Experiment

To verify ACmix (self-attention and convolution integrated) and hfen loss separately, we designed ablation experiments. The experiments tested the denoising results of AFGSA ($\lambda_{rec} = 1.0$), AFGSA+hfen ($\lambda_{rec} = 0.9$, $\lambda_{hfen} = 0.1$), AFGACmix ($\lambda_{rec} = 1.0$), and AFGACmix+hfen ($\lambda_{rec} = 0.9$, $\lambda_{hfen} = 0.1$). λ_{adv} = 5×10^{-3} in all tests. Table 2 shows the results. The values in the table are the average of the training data from the 19–24 epoch. The best results are highlighted in bold and underlined. In most cases, AFGACmix+hfen performs better than other methods with higher PSNR and lower 1-SSIM. It shows that ACmix is effective, and significantly improve reconstruction results in most cases, It maintain image structure and perceptual quality increasing PSNR and 1-SSIM but may decreasing RMSE, indicating there is still room for improvement in preserving detailed information. It also shows that adding hfen loss can get better results, not only preserving detailed in images with lower RMSE and higher PSNR, but also improving the overall structure with lower 1-SSIM.

234   G. Zhang et al.

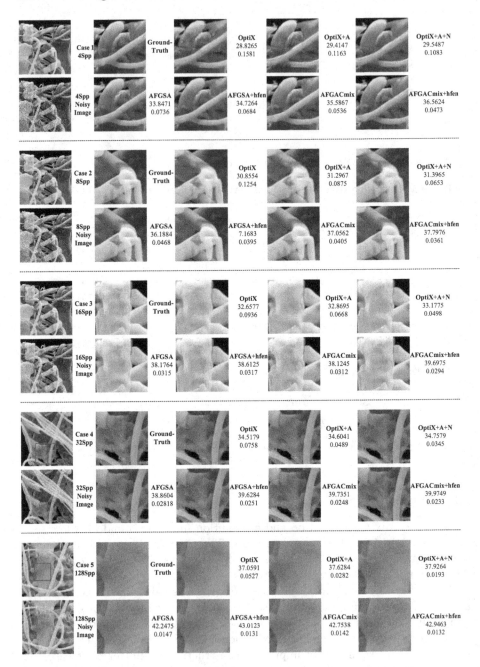

Fig. 6. 4Spp, 8Spp, 16Spp, 32Spp, 128Spp image denoising results evaluation

Table 2. Evaluation of ablation experiment results.

Spp	Metrics	AFGSA	AFGSA+hfen	AFGACmix	AFGACmix+hfen
4Spp	RMSE $(10^{-3})\downarrow$	4.459	4.118	3.701	**3.603**
	PSNR↑	33.8537	34.6553	35.3629	**36.5215**
	1-SSIM↓	0.0721	0.0681	0.0524	**0.0461**
8Spp	RMSE $(10^{-3})\downarrow$	2.673	**2.457**	2.691	2.559
	PSNR↑	35.9812	37.1777	37.0513	**37.7382**
	1-SSIM↓	0.0458	0.0386	0.0402	**0.0381**
16Spp	RMSE $(10^{-3})\downarrow$	1.765	**1.686**	1.825	1.784
	PSNR↑	38.1873	38.6895	38.1511	**39.3857**
	1-SSIM↓	0.031	0.0317	0.0312	**0.0305**
32Spp	RMSE $(10^{-3})\downarrow$	1.249	**1.137**	1.283	1.226
	PSNR↑	38.6283	39.7012	39.7521	**39.9532**
	1-SSIM↓	0.028	0.0246	0.0245	**0.0235**
128Spp	RMSE $(10^{-3})\downarrow$	0.559	**0.5**	0.591	0.585
	PSNR↑	42.2134	**43.0284**	42.679	42.7895
	1-SSIM↓	0.0145	**0.0129**	0.0141	0.014

4 Conclusion and Future Work

In this paper, we designed a process to generate auxiliary features from medical volume. Meanwhile, we proposed the AFGACmix network and added the high-frequency error norm to loss function for medical volume rendering denoising. The experimental results show that our method can denoise effectively. In the future, we will expand the dataset and apply our method to more scenarios.

References

1. Bako, S., et al.: Kernel-predicting convolutional networks for denoising Monte Carlo renderings. ACM Trans. Graph. **36**(4), 97:1–97:14 (2017)
2. Chaitanya, C.R.A., et al.: Interactive reconstruction of Monte Carlo image sequences using a recurrent denoising autoencoder. ACM Trans. Graph. (TOG) **36**(4), 1–12 (2017)
3. Gulrajani, I., Ahmed, F., Arjovsky, M., Dumoulin, V., Courville, A.C.: Improved training of Wasserstein GANs. In: Advances in Neural Information Processing Systems, vol. 30 (2017)
4. Hofmann, N., Martschinke, J., Engel, K., Stamminger, M.: Neural denoising for path tracing of medical volumetric data. Proc. ACM Comput. Graph. Interact. Tech. **3**(2), 1–18 (2020)
5. Kalantari, N.K., Bako, S., Sen, P.: A machine learning approach for filtering Monte Carlo noise. ACM Trans. Graph. **34**(4), 1–12 (2015)

6. Pan, X., et al.: On the integration of self-attention and convolution. In: Proceedings of the IEEE/CVF Conference on Computer Vision and Pattern Recognition, pp. 815–825 (2022)
7. Simonyan, K., Zisserman, A.: Very deep convolutional networks for large-scale image recognition. arXiv preprint arXiv:1409.1556 (2014)
8. Vaswani, A., et al.: Attention is all you need. In: Advances in Neural Information Processing Systems, vol. 30 (2017)
9. Yu, J., Nie, Y., Long, C., Xu, W., Zhang, Q., Li, G.: Monte Carlo denoising via auxiliary feature guided self-attention. ACM Trans. Graph. **40**(6), 1–13 (2021)

View Distribution Alignment with Progressive Adversarial Learning for UAV Visual Geo-Localization

Cuiwei Liu, Jiahao Liu, Huaijun Qiu$^{(\boxtimes)}$, Zhaokui Li, and Xiangbin Shi

School of Computer Science, Shenyang Aerospace University, Shenyang, China
{liucuiwei,lzk,sxb}@sau.edu.cn, 20220071@email.sau.edu.cn

Abstract. Unmanned Aerial Vehicle (UAV) visual geo-localization aims to match images of the same geographic target captured from different views, i.e., the UAV view and the satellite view. It is very challenging due to the large appearance differences in UAV-satellite image pairs. Previous works map images captured by UAVs and satellites to a shared feature space and employ a classification framework to learn location-dependent features while neglecting the overall distribution shift between the UAV view and the satellite view. In this paper, we address these limitations by introducing distribution alignment of the two views to shorten their distance in a common space. Specifically, we propose an end-to-end network, called PVDA (Progressive View Distribution Alignment). During training, feature encoder, location classifier, and view discriminator are jointly optimized by a novel progressive adversarial learning strategy. Competition between feature encoder and view discriminator prompts both of them to be stronger. It turns out that the adversarial learning is progressively emphasized until UAV-view images are indistinguishable from satellite-view images. As a result, the proposed PVDA becomes powerful in learning location-dependent yet view-invariant features with good scalability towards unseen images of new locations. Compared to the state-of-the-art methods, the proposed PVDA requires less inference time but has achieved superior performance on the University-1652 dataset.

Keywords: UAV visual geo-localization · UAV view · satellite view · distribution alignment · adversarial learning

This work was supported in part by the National Natural Science Foundation of China under Grant No. 62171295, and in part by the Liaoning Provincial Natural Science Foundation under Grant No. 2021-MS-266, and in part by the Applied Basic Research Project of Liaoning Province under Grant 2023JH2/101300204, and in part by the Shenyang Science and Technology Innovation Program for Young and Middle-aged Scientists under Grant No. RC210427.

© The Author(s), under exclusive license to Springer Nature Switzerland AG 2023
Z. Jin et al. (Eds.): KSEM 2023, LNAI 14118, pp. 237–248, 2023.
https://doi.org/10.1007/978-3-031-40286-9_20

1   Introduction

Cross-view geo-localization task is to acquire the real-world geographic position of a given image by retrieving the most relevant images in a geo-tagged reference database captured from another view, e.g., the satellite view. Such technologies have attracted great attention since they are particularly useful in practical applications, such as autonomous driving [1], augmented reality [2], and mobile robots [3]. Cross-view geo-localization was first presented to address ground-to-aerial geo-localization task [4–7], which matches a ground-view query image against aerial-view reference images with geo-tags. Recently, some works [8] consider the UAV visual geo-localization problem as bidirectional cross-view matching between UAV-view images and satellite-view images. Specifically, UAV-to-satellite image matching achieves UAV-view target localization in GPS-denied situations by comparing a UAV-view query with a collection of geo-tagged satellite-view images. Conversely, satellite-to-UAV image matching navigates the UAV back to a target place in the satellite-view image by searching for the most similar UAV-view images in the flight historic record.

UAV visual geo-localization is essentially a cross-view scene image retrieval task based on the characteristics of the geographic target with its surroundings, such as neighbor houses, roads, and trees. The variations in viewpoint, height, and seasons lead to large appearance differences in UAV-satellite image pairs and pose great challenges for accurate image matching. The mainstream methods utilize a classifier of different geographic locations as a proxy to train a common feature space for images captured by UAVs and satellites, then the learned space is used at inference to extract descriptors for image retrieval. Early studies [8,9] extract global features from the whole image, while more appealing works [10–13] take spatial or semantic contextual patterns into consideration and learn local features for part matching. However, the above works [8–10,12,13] neglect the significant appearance gap between UAV-view images and satellite-view images, leading to inferior image retrieval performance when applying the learned feature space to unseen images of new locations. Some recent cross-view geo-localization methods for ground-to-aerial geo-localization [14–17] and UAV visual geo-localization [18] employ cross-view image synthesis techniques as data augmentation to explicitly transform images from one view to another view before feature extraction. Although such data augmentation techniques narrows down the gap between query and reference images, they require a two-step procedure for image retrieval and put an extra burden on computation time as well as resources for practical applications.

Unlike previous works, we handle the domain shift problem between UAV-view images and satellite-view images by performing distribution alignment of these two views in a common feature space to narrow the gap between them. We propose an end-to-end network, called PVDA (Progressive View Distribution Alignment), which pulls UAV-view images and satellite-view images of the same location together considering both view distribution alignment and location classification. We introduce a view discriminator to determine whether an image was captured by a UAV or a satellite. A novel progressive adversarial learning strategy is designed to jointly optimize the feature encoder, the location classifier and the view discriminator in a unified framework. The feature encoder is optimized under the guidance of the location classifier while trying to fool the view discriminator into regarding UAV-view images as satellite-view images and vice versa. It is increasingly hard to deceive the view discriminator over time since competition between the feature encoder and the view discriminator prompts both of them to be stronger. To solve this problem, the proposed learning strategy progressively emphasizes the task of confusing the view discriminator and simulates a warm restart of the learning rate to adapt to the fine-tuned objective.

The main contributions are summarized as follows: (1) We propose a new UAV visual geo-localization method PVDA, which performs view distribution alignment as well as location classification in an adversarial learning framework to close the domain gap between UAV-view images and satellite-view images. (2) We develop a novel progressive adversarial learning strategy, in which the feature encoder is continuously promoted in competition with the view discriminator and able to generate location-dependent yet view-invariant features for training images as well as unseen images of new locations.

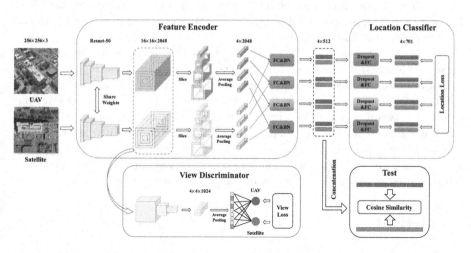

Fig. 1. Overall framework of our method. In this exemplar, a feature encoder, a 701-way location classifier, and a 2-way view discriminator are trained on images of 701 buildings. The feature encoder takes images resized to $256 \times 256 \times 3$ as input and outputs four 512-dimensional vectors for each image.

2 Related Works

The main stream in the research for UAV-satellite geo-localization is based on the location classification framework. Zheng et al. [8] first formulated the UAV-satellite geo-localization and presented the University-1652 benchmark including multi-view images of different buildings. They viewed each location as one class and employed a two-branch CNN to learn a classification model. Ding et al. [9] considered the imbalance of UAV-view and satellite-view images and presented a Location Classification Matching (LCM) method. They tried to learn a location-dependent feature space and implemented the cross-view matching of images from unseen locations via feature similarity ranking. Wang et al. [10] devised a Local Pattern Network (LPN) where a set of location classifiers are trained on part-level features generated by a square-ring feature partition strategy. Compared to early studies [8,9] using global features of the whole image, LPN explores spatial contextual information around the geographic target and achieves more accurate part matching. Lin et al. [11] jointly performed feature learning and key-point detection to pay more attention on salient regions. The above methods [8–11] map UAV-view and satellite-view images into a common feature space and search for the classification boundaries among locations, while neglecting the gap between the UAV view and satellite view.

Tian et al. [18] synthesized several vertical view images for a UAV-view image and then employed LPN to match the new synthetic UAV-view images against satellite-view images for geo-localization. Although their method can decrease the viewpoint variations between the UAV view and satellite view, extra perspective projection transformation is introduced in the cross-view image matching. Zhuang et al. [12] added a multi-scale block attention mechanism into LPN for reinforcing salient features in local regions and applied the KL loss to enhance the similarity between paired UAV-view and satellite-view images. Dai et al. [13] presented a transformer-based model which achieves automatic region segmentation to obtain part-level features and utilizes the triplet loss for feature alignment. Different from the above two methods [12,13] that focus on closing the distance between paired UAV-view and satellite-view images, our method performs global distribution alignment of the UAV view and satellite view to reduce the domain gap between them. With the proposed progressive adversarial learning strategy, we can learn a location-dependent yet view-invariant feature space, which is crucial to matching cross-view images of unseen locations.

3 Method

As shown in Fig. 1, the proposed PVDA incorporates a feature encoder, a location classifier, and a view discriminator that learns to determine whether an image was captured by a UAV or a satellite. The three modules are jointly optimized with a novel progressive adversarial learning strategy, where the location classifier guides the feature encoder to produce location-dependent features while competition between the feature encoder and the view discriminator enables distribution alignment of the two views. During training, the three modules are constructed on a training dataset D containing M UAV-view images $\{(x_i^{\mathrm{u}}, y_i^{\mathrm{u}})\}_{i=1:M}$ and N satellite-view images $\{(x_j^{\mathrm{s}}, y_j^{\mathrm{s}})\}_{j=1:N}$ of C geographic locations, where $y_i^{\mathrm{u}}, y_j^{\mathrm{s}} \in \{1, 2, ..., C\}$ denote the location labels of the i-th UAV-view image and the j-th satellite-view image, respectively.

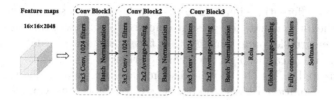

Fig. 2. Architecture of the view discriminator.

3.1 Architecture of the Proposed PVDA

Feature Encoder. ResNet-50 [19] is adopted as the backbone network to extract CNN features from input images. Following the previous work [10], we learn a common backbone network for UAV-view and satellite-view images since they have similar patterns. The feature maps produced by ResNet-50 are divided into multiple parts with a square-ring partition strategy [10] to separately aggregate information of the central geographic target and contextual information of surroundings. This strategy explicitly enhances the consistency of local features of images in the same location and performs well against rotation variation as demonstrated in the previous works [10,12,18]. Specifically, the original feature maps are partitioned into four parts, each of which is aggregated to a feature vector with an average-pooling layer. Next, each feature vector is sent to fully connected layers and batch normalization layers for further refinement. Note that four branches are developed corresponding to four parts segmented by the square-ring partition strategy, so that the feature encoder can better learn the characteristics of different regions. Finally, part-level features $\{g_{i,l}^{u}\}_{l=1:4}$ and $\{g_{j,l}^{s}\}_{l=1:4}$ are generated for the UAV-view image x_i^u and the satellite-view image x_j^s, respectively.

Location Classifier. A four-branch classifier [10] is constructed to separate images captured at different locations based on part-level embeddings. Concretely, embedding vectors $\{g_{i,l}^{u}\}_{i=1:M}$ and $\{g_{j,l}^{s}\}_{j=1:N}$ are sent to the l-th branch including a dropout layer and a fully connected layer with softmax operation to predict their probability distributions $\{p_{i,l}^{u}\}_{i=1:M}$ and $\{p_{j,l}^{s}\}_{j=1:N}$. To evaluate the loss of location classification, we accumulate the cross-entropy between the location labels and the predicted probability distribution of each part. This procedure can be formulated by

$$\ell^{L} = - \sum_{i=1:M} \sum_{l=1:4} \log p_{i,l}^{u}(y_i^u) - \sum_{j=1:N} \sum_{l=1:4} \log p_{j,l}^{s}(y_j^s), \qquad (1)$$

where $p_{i,l}^{u}(y_i^u)$ denotes the probability of the ground-truth location of image x_i^u and $p_{j,l}^{s}(y_j^s)$ indicates the probability of the ground-truth location of image x_j^s.

View Discriminator. We construct the view discriminator on the intermediate feature maps output by ResNet-50 rather than the part-level embedding vectors. The main reason is that spatial details in the intermediate feature maps are critical to differentiate between UAV-view images and satellite-view images. Moreover, the intermediate features are enforced to be view-invariant by the progressive adversarial learning strategy, then the subsequent part-level embeddings derived from them can also get such characteristics.

As illustrated in Fig. 2, the view discriminator first refines the feature maps with three convolutional blocks (denoted as Conv Block 1 to Conv Block 3) followed by the ReLU nonlinearity. Convolutional layers in Conv Block 2 and Conv Block 3 are equipped with spatial pooling to reduce the resolution of produced feature maps. The view discriminator ends with a global average pooling layer for aggregating spatial information and a two-way fully connected layer with softmax for view prediction. Given feature maps f_i^{u} of a UAV-view image x_i^{u}, the view discriminator outputs a 2D vector $q_i^{\mathrm{u}} = [q_{i,1}^{\mathrm{u}}, q_{i,2}^{\mathrm{u}}]$ indicating the probabilities that the input belongs to the UAV view and the satellite view, respectively. Similarly, a 2D probability vector $q_j^{\mathrm{s}} = [q_{j,1}^{\mathrm{s}}, q_{j,2}^{\mathrm{s}}]$ is generated for a satellite-view image x_j^{s}. The loss to train the view discriminator is the cross-entropy between the output probabilities and the ground-truth view labels formulated as

$$\ell^{\mathrm{V}} = - \sum_{i=1:M} \log q_{i,1}^{\mathrm{u}} - \sum_{j=1:N} \log q_{j,2}^{\mathrm{s}}, \qquad (2)$$

where $q_{i,1}^{\mathrm{u}}$ is the predicted probability of the UAV view for a UAV-view image and $q_{j,2}^{\mathrm{s}}$ denotes the probability of the satellite view for a satellite-view image.

3.2 Progressive Adversarial Learning Strategy

The location classifier aims to separate images of different locations and the view discriminator determines whether an input is from the UAV view or the satellite view. It is clear that the feature encoder agrees with the location classifier on generating location-dependent features, yet it must fool the view discriminator so as to produce view-invariant features. Therefore, we introduce an adversarial loss ℓ^{A} between the feature encoder and the view discriminator.

$$\ell^{\mathrm{A}} = - \sum_{i=1:M} \log q_{i,2}^{\mathrm{u}} - \sum_{j=1:N} \log q_{j,1}^{\mathrm{s}}, \qquad (3)$$

where $q_{i,2}^{\mathrm{u}}$ and $q_{j,1}^{\mathrm{s}}$ are probabilities predicted by the view discriminator. To be specific, $q_{i,2}^{\mathrm{u}}$ stands for the probability of the satellite view for a UAV-view image, and $q_{j,1}^{\mathrm{s}}$ denotes the probability of the UAV view for a satellite-view image. Obviously, the adversarial loss ℓ^{A} calculates the cross-entropy between the output probability distributions and view labels opposite to the ground-truth labels so that the generated features can deceive the view discriminator into regarding UAV-view images as satellite-view images and vice versa.

During training, the three modules are iteratively optimized in the following two steps. First, the feature encoder and the location classifier are fixed and the view discriminator is optimized with the objective function defined in Eq. 2. Second, we freeze the parameters of the view discriminator and update the feature encoder together with the location classifier by an optimization objective

ℓ^{FL}, which is a weighted combination of the location classification loss ℓ^L and an adversarial loss ℓ^A. More specifically,

$$\ell^{FL} = \ell^L + \alpha \cdot \ell^A, \qquad (4)$$

where α is a weight balancing the two optimization objectives.

In the early stage of training, the three modules cannot fit the training data well, so minimizing the location classification loss ℓ^L is just as important as the adversarial loss ℓ^A. With the continuous update of parameters, they are getting stronger, so it is easier to achieve location classification but harder for the feature encoder to deceive the view discriminator. Inspired by these observations, the proposed progressive adversarial learning strategy gradually puts the emphasis on optimizing the adversarial loss ℓ^A by increasing the weight α in Eq. 4 in regular intervals. Motivated by the work [20], we integrate the warm restart technique that periodically restarts and decays the learning rate into the proposed progressive adversarial learning strategy. Especially, the learning rate is restarted whenever the weight of the adversarial loss is increased. This learning mechanism enables fast gradient descent with a big learning rate when the optimization objective in Eq. 4 is fine-tuned by the increasing weight and employs a small learning rate to approach an optimum.

3.3 Cross-View Image Matching

Once the feature encoder is learned, it is evaluated on cross-view image retrieval tasks with query/gallery data captured at new locations. The classifier cannot predict unseen locations of query/gallery images since they have their own location label space independent to the training images. Nonetheless, we can match a query image against candidate images in the gallery by comparing their embeddings in the learned feature space. Specifically, a query image is sent to the feature encoder to acquire part-level embedding vectors, which are then concatenated to form the query representation. Likewise, we can get the representation of a candidate image by concatenating its part-level embedding vectors produced by the feature encoder. The final retrieval results are derived from the ranking of feature similarity measured by the cosine similarity.

4 Experiments

4.1 Dataset and Experimental Settings

We employ the large-scale University-1652 dataset to evaluate our method on two tasks, i.e., UAV-to-satellite image matching for UAV-view target localization and satellite-to-UAV image matching for UAV navigation. This dataset consists of images of 1,652 buildings from 72 universities and provides one geo-tagged satellite-view image and 54 UAV-view images for each building. The UAV-view images were captured in a simulation flight, and there exist large scale variations as well as rotation variations in this dataset. All the buildings are divided into two

244   C. Liu et al.

Table 1. Cross-view image matching accuracy of different methods.

Method	256 × 256				384 × 384			
	UAV-to-satellite		Satellite-to-UAV		UAV-to-satellite		Satellite-to-UAV	
	Recall@1	AP	Recall@1	AP	Recall@1	AP	Recall@1	AP
Zheng et al. [8]	58.49%	63.31%	71.18%	58.74%	62.99%	67.69%	75.75%	62.09%
LCM [9]	–	–	–	–	66.65%	70.82%	79.89%	65.38%
LPN [10]	75.93%	79.14%	86.45%	74.79%	78.02%	80.99%	86.16%	76.56%
USAM [11]	77.60%	80.55%	86.59%	75.96%	–	–	–	–
PCL [18]	79.47%	83.63%	87.69%	78.51%	81.63%	85.46%	89.73%	80.84%
MSBA [12]	82.33%	84.78%	90.58%	81.61%	86.61%	88.55%	92.15%	84.45%
FSRA [13]	82.25%	84.82%	87.87%	81.53%	84.82%	87.03%	87.59%	83.37%
PVDA	82.73%	85.19%	92.30%	82.48%	87.34%	89.26%	93.72%	86.04%

parts: 701 buildings from 33 universities for training and 951 buildings from the rest 39 universities for testing. For UAV-to-satellite image matching, there are 37,855 UAV-view queries and 951 satellite-view candidates including 701 true-matched images and 250 distractors. For satellite-to-UAV image matching, we have 701 satellite-view queries and 51,355 UAV-view candidates including 37,855 true-matched images and 13,500 distractors. Following the previous work [8], we employ Recall@K and average precision (AP) as evaluation metrics.

ResNet-50 is employed as the backbone of the feature encoder and initialized with the pre-trained weights on ImageNet [21]. We take the feature maps produced by the fifth convolution block as image representations and remove the down-sampling operation in the fifth convolution block to retain more details. The feature encoder and the location classifier are learned with an SGD optimizer and the view discriminator is learned with an Adam optimizer. The parameter α in Eq. 4 is initialized to 0.9 and increased by 0.1 every 140 epochs. We set the initial learning rate to 0.001, 0.01, 0.01, and 0.002 for ResNet-50, the rest layers in the feature encoder, the location classifier, and the view discriminator, respectively. The learning rate is decayed by multiplying 0.8 after 60 epochs and 120 epochs, and reset to the initial value whenever α is increased.

4.2   Experimental Results

Comparison to the State-of-the-Arts. The proposed PVDA is compared with the existing UAV visual geo-localization methods and the results of using two input image sizes (i.e., 256 and 384) are shown in Table 1. ResNet-50 is employed as the backbone in CNN-based methods [8–12,18], while FSRA [13] takes the Vision Transformer [22] as the backbone. All the comparison methods pre-train their backbones on ImageNet [21].

As shown in Table 1, the proposed PVDA performs better than the other methods on both UAV-to-satellite image matching and satellite-to-UAV image matching using two image sizes. Specifically, our method significantly outperforms methods [8,9] using global image features. LPN [10], PCL [18], and our method adopt the same feature encoder and location classifier. The difference is that PCL [18] adopts UAV-to-satellite image synthesis as data augmentation while our method

Table 2. UAV-view target localization accuracy with multiple queries.

Method	256 × 256			384 × 384		
	UAV-to-satellite			UAV-to-satellite		
	Recall@1	Recall@5	AP	Recall@1	Recall@5	AP
Zheng et al. [8]	69.33%	86.73%	73.14%	–	–	–
LCM [9]	–	–	–	77.89%	91.30%	81.05%
PVDA (Single-query)	82.73%	93.60%	85.19%	87.34%	95.78%	89.26%
PVDA (Multi-query)	92.01%	98.00%	93.30%	95.29%	98.43%	95.99%

carries out distribution alignment of UAV-view images and satellite-view images in an adversarial learning framework. In comparison to LPN [10] and PCL [18], our method has achieved superior performance, which demonstrates the effectiveness of our learning framework. USAM [11] and MSBA [12] are also based on LPN [10]. The former forces the feature encoder to focus on salient regions by embedding two attention modules in ResNet-50, while the latter incorporates both global features and local features. FSRA [13] adopts a transformer-based backbone, which is stronger than ResNet-50. Nonetheless, our method still achieves better performance than USAM [11], MSBA [12], and FSRA [13]. It is worth noting that the inference time of our method is the same as that of LPN [10]. However, PCL [18], USAM [11], MSBA [12], and FSRA [13] need more memory usage and longer inference time due to image synthesis [18] or the more complex network structure [11–13]. Therefore, our method is very competitive in real-world applications considering the limitation on computing resources and time.

Multi-query Image Matching. In the above experiments, the models take a single UAV-view image as query and return a ranking list of candidate satellite-view images in the UAV-view target localization task. Due to the fact that the UAV may capture multiple images of one geographic target from different viewpoints and heights in the flight, it is natural to localize the target under a multi-query setting. To this end, we conduct experiments under two image sizes to investigate the effectiveness of using multiple UAV-view images as queries. Particularly, we retrieve the most relevant satellite-view image in the gallery according to the average of features of 54 UAV-view queries. Experimental results shown in Table 2 verify that more accurate target localization can be achieved by integrating multiple queries into a more comprehensive description. The improvements on AP are 8.11% and 6.73% for image sizes 256 × 256 and 384 × 384, respectively. Compared with other geo-localization methods [8,9], our method also performs best under the multi-query setting, which further demonstrates the superiority of our method.

Visualization of UAV Visual Geo-Localization Results. Some cross-view image retrieval results of the proposed method on the UAV-view target localization task and the UAV navigation task are visualized in Fig. 3 and Fig. 4, respectively. Input images are resized to 256 × 256. In the UAV-view target localization task, there is only one true-matched satellite-view image in the gallery for each UAV-view query. As shown in Fig. 3, our method can correctly retrieve

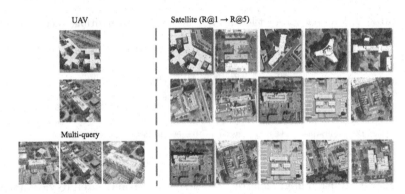

Fig. 3. Top-5 retrieved satellite-view images in the UAV-view target localization task. The first and second rows display the matching results with a single query, while the third row employs multiple UAV-view images as queries. The true-matched satellite-view images are annotated with green borders. (Color figure online)

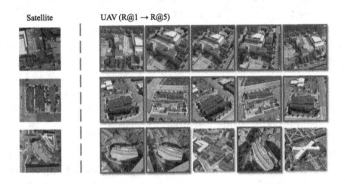

Fig. 4. Top-5 retrieved UAV-view images in the UAV navigation task. The true-matched UAV-view images are annotated with green borders. (Color figure online)

the satellite-view image for the first query though there exist distinct appearance variations between the UAV-satellite image pair. The second row displays a failure case where some irrelevant surroundings of the target building (e.g., the long road on the right top of the query image) interfere with the image matching. When multiple UAV-view images are used as queries, our method can extract more accurate representations of this target and recall the true-matched satellite-view image in top-1 as shown in the third row. In the UAV navigation task, there are multiple true-matched UAV-view images in the gallery for each satellite-view query. As shown in Fig. 4, our method is able to recall UAV-view images of the target building even in large viewpoint and scale variations.

4.3 Ablation Studies

To further study whether the proposed progressive adversarial learning strategy is beneficial to parameter optimization, we design two baseline strategies for

Table 3. Comparison of image matching accuracy between our method and baselines.

Method	UAV-to-satellite		Satellite-to-UAV	
	Recall@1	AP	Recall@1	AP
constant α, w/ warm restart	82.00%	84.55%	91.73%	81.96%
increasing α, w/o warm restart	81.54%	84.09%	92.30%	81.05%
increasing α, w/ warm restart (Ours)	82.73%	85.19%	92.30%	82.48%

comparison. The first baseline adopts a constant weight α (see Eq. 4) and period-ically restarts the learning rate, so the adversarial loss will not be progressively emphasized over time. The second baseline utilizes an increasing weight α like the proposed learning strategy, but doesn't simulate warm restart of the learning rate when weight α is increased. To be specific, the learning rate is initialized in accordance with our learning strategy and decayed by multiplying 0.8 after executing 140, 280, and 420 epochs. As shown in Table 3, the proposed progres-sive adversarial learning strategy outperforms the first baseline by progressively emphasizing the adversarial loss over time. In comparison to the second baseline, our method also achieves superior performance with periodic warm restart of the learning rate. These observations reveal that the proposed progressive adversar-ial learning strategy is effective in parameter optimization and the warm restart scheme works well with the evolving objective of adversarial learning.

5 Conclusion

In this paper, we have presented an end-to-end learning framework to allevi-ate the distribution shift between UAV-view images and satellite-view images in UAV visual geo-localization. A novel progressive adversarial learning strategy is developed to perform view distribution alignment and location classification in a common feature space. By doing this, our method can learn location-dependent yet view-invariant features and thus achieves better performance than the exist-ing methods on the large-scale University-1652 dataset.

References

1. Wilson, D., Alshaabi, T., Van Oort, C., Zhang, X., Nelson, J., Wshah, S.: Object tracking and geo-localization from street images. Remote Sens. **14**(11), 1–26 (2022)
2. Erra, U., Capece, N.: Engineering an advanced geo-location augmented reality framework for smart mobile devices. J. Ambient. Intell. Humaniz. Comput. **10**(1), 255–265 (2019)
3. Senlet, T., Elgammal, A.: Satellite image based precise robot localization on side-walks. In: IEEE International Conference on Robotics and Automation, pp. 2647–2653 (2012)

4. Lin, T.Y., Cui, Y., Belongie, S., Hays, J.: Learning deep representations for ground-to-aerial geolocalization. In: Proceedings of the IEEE Conference on Computer Vision and Pattern Recognition, pp. 5007–5015 (2015)
5. Zhai, M., Bessinger, Z., Workman, S., Jacobs, N.: Predicting ground-level scene layout from aerial imagery. In: Proceedings of the IEEE Conference on Computer Vision and Pattern Recognition, pp. 867–875 (2017)
6. Tian, Y., Chen, C., Shah, M.: Cross-view image matching for geo-localization in urban environments. In: Proceedings of the IEEE Conference on Computer Vision and Pattern Recognition, pp. 3608–3616 (2017)
7. Liu, L., Li, H.: Lending orientation to neural networks for cross-view geo-localization. In: Proceedings of the IEEE/CVF Conference on Computer Vision and Pattern Recognition, pp. 5624–5633 (2019)
8. Zheng, Z., Wei, Y., Yang, Y.: University-1652: a multi-view multi-source benchmark for drone-based geo-localization. In: Proceedings of the 28th ACM International Conference on Multimedia, pp. 1395–1403 (2020)
9. Ding, L., Zhou, J., Meng, L., Long, Z.: A practical cross-view image matching method between UAV and satellite for UAV-based geo-localization. Remote Sens. **13**(47), 1–20 (2021)
10. Wang, T., et al.: Each part matters: local patterns facilitate cross-view geo-localization. IEEE Trans. Circ. Syst. Video Technol. **32**(2), 867–879 (2021)
11. Lin, J., et al.: Joint representation learning and keypoint detection for cross-view geo-localization. IEEE Trans. Image Process. **31**, 3780–3792 (2022)
12. Zhuang, J., Dai, M., Chen, X., Zheng, E.: A faster and more effective cross-view matching method of UAV and satellite images for UAV geolocalization. Remote Sens. **13**(3979), 1–16 (2021)
13. Dai, M., Hu, J., Zhuang, J., Zheng, E.: A transformer-based feature segmentation and region alignment method for UAV-view geo-localization. IEEE Trans. Circ. Syst. Video Technol. **32**(7), 4376–4389 (2022)
14. Regmi, K., Shah, M.: Bridging the domain gap for ground-to-aerial image matching. In: Proceedings of the IEEE/CVF Conference on Computer Vision (2019)
15. Shi, Y., Liu, L., Yu, X., Li, H.: Spatial-aware feature aggregation for cross-view image based geo-localization. In: 33rd Conference on Neural Information Processing Systems (2019)
16. Guo, Y., Choi, M., Li, K., Boussaid, F.: Soft exemplar highlighting for cross-view image-based geo-localization. IEEE Trans. Image Process. **31**, 2094–2105 (2022)
17. Zhang, X., et al.: SSA-Net: spatial scale attention network for image-based geo-localization. IEEE Geosci. Remote Sens. Lett. **19**, 1–5 (2022)
18. Tian, X., Shao, J., Ouyang, D., Shen, H.T.: UAV-satellite view synthesis for cross-view geo-localization. IEEE Trans. Circ. Syst. Video Technol. **32**(7), 4804–4815 (2022)
19. He, K., Zhang, X., Ren, S., Sun, J.: Deep residual learning for image recognition. In: Proceedings of the IEEE/CVF Conference on Computer Vision and Pattern Recognition, pp. 770–778 (2016)
20. Loshchilov, I., Hutter, F.: SGDR: stochastic gradient descent with warm restarts. arXiv e-prints (2016)
21. Deng, J., Dong, W., Socher, R., Li, L.J., Li, K., Fei-Fei, L.: ImageNet: a large-scale hierarchical image database. In: Proceedings of the IEEE/CVF Conference on Computer Vision and Pattern Recognition, pp. 248–255. IEEE (2009)
22. Dosovitskiy, A., et al.: An image is worth 16 × 16 words: transformers for image recognition at scale. In: International Conference on Learning Representations (2021)

Hbay: Predicting Human Mobility
via Hyperspherical Bayesian Learning

Li Huang[1,2], Kai Liu[1], Chaoran Liu[1], Qiang Gao[1,2(✉)], Xiao Zhou[1], and Guisong Liu[1,2]

[1] The Complex Laboratory of New Finance and Economics, Southwestern University of Finance and Economics, Chengdu, Sichuan, China
qianggao@swufe.edu.cn
[2] Kash Institute of Electronics and Information Industry, Kashgar, Xinjiang, China

Abstract. Accurate human mobility prediction is an essential but critical task in location-based services. Although existing deep learning solutions such as deep recurrent neural networks have remarkable achievements for this task, The diversity of check-in preferences and the sparsity of trajectory representations still prevent us from effectively capturing the richness of human mobility intentions and patterns. To this end, this study introduces a novel Hyperspherical Bayesian learning approach for mobility prediction problem, i.e., HBay. As a generative model, HBay considers multiple contextual semantics underlying check-ins to maximize human diverse preferences and encodes human trajectories in a latent space to mimic complex mobility patterns. In contrast to traditional generative models, HBay operates the latent variables derived from human trajectories in the hyperspherical space to avoid the concern of posterior collapse. In addition, HBay couples with an attentive layer to capture human long-term check-in preferences. The experimental results conducted on four real-world datasets demonstrate our HBay significantly outperforms the state-of-the-art baselines.

Keywords: human mobility · representation learning · varitional inference · hyperspherical space · attention mechanism

1 Introduction

The proliferation of smart mobile devices enables large-scale human footprints, which allows us to become familiar with human movement signals or patterns and accordingly stimulate the emergence of various downstream location-based applications [1,2]. One of the most popular tasks in location-based services is predicting the near-future movement of humans by mining their vast historical trajectories, also known as mobility (or next POI) prediction [3–5].

Traditional solutions for mobility prediction mainly rely on pattern-based or data-driven methods [6,7]. For instance, using Markov-based [8] or matrix factorization (MF)-based methods [9] to model successive check-in preferences.

© The Author(s), under exclusive license to Springer Nature Switzerland AG 2023
Z. Jin et al. (Eds.): KSEM 2023, LNAI 14118, pp. 249–262, 2023.
https://doi.org/10.1007/978-3-031-40286-9_21

Recently, most researchers turn to take efforts in deep learning methods to capture human sequential dynamics. Deep recurrent neural networks (RNNs) are widely favored for their excellent performance to model sequential dependencies [10,11]. For example, DeepMove devises an RNN-based method to learn the sequential dynamics from each user's historical trajectories, yielding higher gains on mobility prediction [10]. Zhang et al [12] employ an LSTM-based layer to study human current trajectories jointly with a self-attention layer to encode human long-term check-in behaviors.

Despite the promising results of these approaches, we consider that two major challenges remain in the effective distillation of human mobility regularities: (1) **Diversity of check-in preferences:** While most mobility prediction solutions consider the spatial and (or) temporal preferences underlying historical check-ins to facilitate the learning of human transitional regularities [4,10], other factors, such as activity interest and long-term visiting interest, are critical to understanding human diverse mobility preferences. Especially, the uncertainty behind transitional regularities is under-explored. Besides, efficiently exploring human distinct long-term check-in preferences is a positive signal to improve the ability of their future moving intents, as human historical trajectories are extremely longer than their current movements and contain richer individual check-in preferences. (2) **Sparsity of trajectory representations:** Existing methods typically build a discriminative model [3,12] directly to bridge the interactive gap between the past trajectories and possible target POIs to visit. However, they fail to fully explore the complex distribution of diverse trajectories. Recent generative models, such as Variational Auto-Encoder (VAE) [13], provide an opportunity to promote the representation ability regarding different trajectories. But these models are usually conditioned on simple multivariate Gaussian assumptions and suffer from the collapse problem during the posterior approximation, leading to poor trajectory representations.

In this work, we present a novel framework that targets inferring human next POI with Hyperspherical Bayesian learning, called HBay. It first considers multiple contexts underlying each check-in including consecutive interaction, temporal information, and activity semantics. More importantly, we built a POI graph to generate more synthetic trajectories reflecting human diverse moving intentions, with the aim of mitigating uncertainty in transitional patterns. Next, HBay as a generative model strives to encode human trajectories in a hyperspherical space to explore human complex mobility patterns as well as avoid the concern of posterior collapse problem. Whereafter it fine-tunes itself for mobility prediction with respect to the optimal generative model, associating with an attention layer, which efficiently captures human long-term check-in preferences. In sum, the main contributions of this study include:

- The proposed HBay considers multiple contextual semantics underlying human check-ins. Especially, it builds a graph-based structure to capture more uncertain transitional regularities.
- A novel probabilistic generative mechanism in HBay is devised to encode trajectories into hyperspherical space rather than simple Gaussian assump-

tion, aiming to promote the capture of the underlying real distribution from narrow human trajectories. Besides, HBay also employs an attentive layer to capture human long-term check-in preferences for the purpose of boosting the downstream mobility prediction.
- The extensive experiments conducted on four real-world datasets demonstrate that the proposed HBay can better infer human moving intentions compared to existing several representative baselines.

2 Related Work

Recently, most researchers assume that the users' future intents are positively affected by their recent visits or check-ins, whereby they employ deep neural networks to explore human transitional regularities from their massive historical trajectories. Particularly, RNNs, such as LSTM [14] and GRU [15], become one of the hot settlements for mobility prediction, as they can explore human sequential dynamics or dependencies on diverse check-in behaviors [3,10,12,16]. For example, ST-RNN [3] inspired by text classification solutions incorporates dynamic spatial-temporal preferences into vanilla RNNs, yielding promising results for mobility prediction. ATST-LSTM [17] considers the different contributions of each POI and the spatiotemporal contextual information from a given trajectory and proposes an LSTM-based model to predict a user's next POI. In addition, The current researches also indicate that incorporating human long-term check-ins enables higher gains in scratching the inherent preference of human transitional patterns. For instance, DeepMove [10] incorporates each user's historical check-in preferences to enhance the distillation of human mobility learning. CFPRec [12] employs a self-attention network to capture user past preferences from long-term visiting dependencies.

In practice, recent studies also demonstrate that exploring multifarious human check-in semantics (interests) and complex distribution behind massive trajectories is crucial for downstream mobility prediction. First, capturing multiple semantics underlying visited POIs can significantly enhance the performance of downstream tasks. Existing methods, such as those presented in [18] and [19], primarily focus on modeling the sequential patterns of POI sequences, with limited attention to the intrinsic interests surrounding each POI. This oversight neglects the complex interactions between POIs. Second, current mobility pattern learning methods invest considerable effort in mining historical trajectory information, striving to learn as much representative information as possible from the narrow trajectory data. Approaches like LSPL [20] and PLSPL [21] address this challenge by learning long-term interests and employing LSTM models for trajectory representation learning. VANext [4] follows a data-driven manner that considers the transitional semantics from the observed trajectories and devises a variational attention method inspired by the generative model to distill the check-in preferences from users' entire historical trajectories. However, we consider that they still face a serious sparsity problem due to the narrow trajectory data. Also, the complex distribution behind a large number of trajectories is difficult to explore, yielding a small margin of gain in mobility prediction.

3   Methodology

3.1   Problem Definition (Mobility Prediction)

Let a triplet $p = \langle id, lo, la \rangle$ denote a POI reported by the location-based system, where id, lo, and la represent the POI id, longitude, and latitude, respectively. Let T denote a trajectory that includes a set of time-ordered POIs, i.e., $T = \{p_1, p_2, \cdots, p_n\}$. And each p_i is associated with a visiting time t_i. Let $\mathcal{T}$ represent a user's entire historical trajectory. Given a user's recently visited trajectory T and his/her historical trajectory $\mathcal{T}$, our goal is to build a model $\mathcal{F}(T, \mathcal{T})$ that can predict the next POI p_{n+1}.

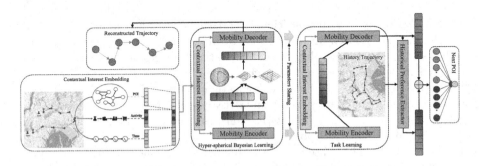

Fig. 1. The framework of HBay.

3.2   Architecture Design

As shown in Fig. 1, HBay mainly consists of four components: (1) *Contextual Interest Embedding*, which aims to capture multiple contextual interests behind check-in behaviors; (2) *Mobility Encoder*, which explores the sequential dynamics behind human trajectories; (3) *Mobility Decoder*, which aims to reconstruct trajectories over latent variables that are generated by our hyperspherical Bayesian learning. In our context, the mobility decoder also plays the role of making downstream mobility prediction; (4) *Historical Preference Extractor*, which aims to incorporate human long-term preferences regarding check-in behaviors. We present each component in detail.

Contextual Interest Embedding. It aims to incorporate three fundamental but critical contextual interests underlying human check-in behaviors, including:

- *POI Embedding:* We first build a POI graph derived from the collected trajectories, where we treat each distinct POI as the graph node and build an edge between two consecutive POIs. Then, we employ the popular node2vec [22] toolkit to generate massive synthetic trajectories for the purpose of alleviating the uncertainty or unobserved transitional regularities. Finally, we generate each POI embedding (e.g., e_τ^p) by maximizing the probability of its occurrence from the surrounding POIs.

- *Time Embedding:* Following previous studies [5,12], we discretize all times-tamps into n_t time slots and map each timestamp into a corresponding time slot. Then, we randomly sample a low-dimensional embedding from multivariate Gaussian to represent each slot, e.g., e_τ^t refers to the embedding of time slot τ. We set n_t to 48, primarily seeking to uncover human daily patterns.
- *Activity Embedding:* As each POI is associated with a specific category that is a textual description of the POI function, we incorporate such information to expose human potential activity behaviors. In our study, we use a similar embedding manner as time embedding and encode each category into a low-dimensional space. For instance, given a category of POI p_τ, e.g., c, we also randomly generate a dense embedding e_τ^c from multivariate Gaussian.

Mobility Encoder. Given a user's short-term trajectory $T = \{p_1, p_2, \cdots, p_n\}$, the mobility encoder employs the popular GRU to capture the sequential dynamics underlying it as the user's short-term trajectory is extremely shorter than his/her long-term trajectory. Since we have obtained each POI's semantic representation, we first transform each discrete POI into a dense representation. Additionally, we also should incorporate the associated temporal and category semantics of each POI. For example, given a POI p_τ in T, we have:

$$c_\tau = \tanh\left(\left[e_\tau^p \oplus e_\tau^t \oplus e_\tau^c\right] W_c + b_c\right), \tag{1}$$

where $\oplus$ is the concatenation operation, $W_c \in \mathbb{R}^{d \times d'}$ and $b_c \in \mathbb{R}^{d'}$ are learnable parameters, and tanh is the Tanh activation function. Next, we use the GRU cell to obtain the hidden state h_τ^e regarding c_τ, which can be described as follows,

$$h_\tau^e = \text{GRU}_{enc}\left(c_\tau, h_{\tau-1}^e\right), \tag{2}$$

thus, we can obtain each POI's hidden state, i.e., $\{h_1^e, h_2^e, \cdots, h_n^e\}$.

Mobility Decoder. The mobility decoder is to reconstruct the input trajectory over its latent variable, e.g., z. And it has a similar network structure as the mobility encoder, which can be summarized as follows,

$$h_\tau^d = \text{GRU}_{dec}\left(c_\tau, h_{\tau-1}^d, z\right), \tag{3}$$

where initial hidden state z is the latent variable, learning by Hyperspherical Bayesian module, which is introduced later.

Historical Preference Extractor. It is vital to efficiently extract human long-term preferences from their historical trajectories. To this end, we use a simple attention network with positional encoding to extract human long-term preferences. Given a user's entire historical trajectory $\mathcal{T}$, we first transform it into a dense representation T through our contextual interest embedding, and then we use the positional embedding to preserve the original structure of T, which can be summarized as follows,

$$T' = T + \Theta(T), \tag{4}$$

where $\Theta(\boldsymbol{T})$ is the position embedding. Next, we use the additive attention mechanism [23,24] to correlate a user's short-term trajectory and his/her entire historical trajectory for the purpose of extracting the individual check-in preference. Specifically, We treat each component in $\boldsymbol{T}'$, e.g., $\boldsymbol{T}'_k$ as the key while the last hidden state (e.g., $\boldsymbol{h}_n^d$) of mobility decoder as the query to measure the

$$\boldsymbol{g}_{n,k} = \tanh(\boldsymbol{W}_h \boldsymbol{h}_n^d + \boldsymbol{W}_{T'} \boldsymbol{T}'_k + \boldsymbol{b}_g), \tag{5}$$

$$a_{n,k} = \frac{\exp\left(\boldsymbol{W}_a \boldsymbol{g}_{n,k} + \boldsymbol{b}_a\right)}{\sum_{j=1}^{|\boldsymbol{T}'|} \exp\left(\boldsymbol{W}_a \boldsymbol{g}_{n,j} + \boldsymbol{b}_a\right)}. \tag{6}$$

Herein, the parameter matrices are $\boldsymbol{W}_h \in \mathbb{R}^{d_{model} \times d_q}$, $\boldsymbol{W}_{T'} \in \mathbb{R}^{d_{model} \times d_k}$, $\boldsymbol{W}_a \in \mathbb{R}^{d_k \times 1}$. In this work we employ h parallel attention heads. For each of these, we use $d_q = d_k = d_{model}/h$. Also, $\boldsymbol{b}_g$ and $\boldsymbol{b}_a$ are trainable parameters. After measuring the contribution of each POI in $\boldsymbol{T}'$, we use the sum operation to formulate the final output by:

$$o_n = \sum_{k=1}^{|\boldsymbol{T}'|} a_{n,k} \boldsymbol{T}'_k. \tag{7}$$

3.3 Learning Pipeline

The training pipeline of HBay contains two procedures. It first employs the mobility encoder and decoder to explore the complex distribution behind massive trajectories via hyperspherical Bayesian learning. Then, it is coupled with a historical preference extractor to fine-tune the model for mobility prediction.

Hyperspherical Bayesian Learning. As one of the most popular generative models, VAE [13] has drawn widespread attention as it enables the learning of discrete samples as well as its generation ability. The standard VAE consists of an encoder and a decoder, where the encoder is to parameterize the approximate posterior $q_\phi(\boldsymbol{z}|x)$ and the decoder takes the role of reconstructing the input x from the latent variable $\boldsymbol{z}$. Hence, the marginal likelihood $p(x)$ can be derived by maximizing the Evidence Lower BOund (ELBO), which is summarized as follows:

$$\log p_\theta(x) \geq \mathbb{E}_{\boldsymbol{z} \sim q_\phi(\boldsymbol{z}|x)} \left[\log p_\theta(x|\boldsymbol{z})\right] - \mathbb{KL}\left[q_\phi(\boldsymbol{z}|x) \| p(\boldsymbol{z})\right], \tag{8}$$

where $p_\theta(x|\boldsymbol{z})$ is a likelihood function parameterized by θ, $p(\boldsymbol{z})$ is a prior assumption, and $\mathbb{KL}$ denotes the KL divergence. In practice, the goal of Eq. (8) is to minimize the reconstruction loss of input x and minimize the divergence between the posterior $q_\phi(\boldsymbol{z}|x)$ and the prior $p(\boldsymbol{z})$.

Recall recent generative models on mobility learning, they usually assume that the prior follows a multivariate Gaussian, i.e., $p(\boldsymbol{z}) \sim \mathcal{N}(\boldsymbol{0}, \boldsymbol{I})$. Due to the existence of the posterior collapse problem, we manipulate the latent variables in the hyperspherical space. Inspired by recent studies [25–27], we assume the latent variables are sampled from the von Mises-Fisher (vMF) distribution [28,29] rather than the simple Gaussian assumption. vMF is the maximum-entropy distribution on the surface of a $(d-1)$-dimensional hypersphere $(\mathbb{S}^{d-1})$, where the sampled variables lie on the surface of the unit sphere. More specifically, vMF is parameterized by two factors, i.e., a direction vector $\boldsymbol{\mu}$ with $||\boldsymbol{\mu}||^2 = 1$ and an isotropic concentration parameter $\kappa \geq 0$. $\boldsymbol{\mu}$ is to determine the mean value in the distribution and κ determines the spread of the probability mass around the mean. As such, the pdf for an d-dimensional unit vector $\boldsymbol{z}$ can be defined as follows:

$$\mathcal{F}_d(\boldsymbol{z}; \boldsymbol{\mu}, \kappa) = \mathcal{C}_d(\kappa) \exp\left(\kappa \boldsymbol{\mu}^T \boldsymbol{z}\right), \mathcal{C}_d(\kappa) \quad = \frac{\kappa^{d/2-1}}{(2\pi)^{d/2} I_{d/2-1}(\kappa)}, \qquad (9)$$

where $\boldsymbol{z}, \boldsymbol{\mu} \in \mathbb{S}^{d-1}$ (or $\in \mathbb{R}^d$) and $I_{d/2-1}$ refers to the modified Bessel function of the first kind at order radius. $\mathcal{C}_d(\kappa)$ is the normalizing constant. Especially, the vMF distribution will degenerate to a uniform distribution over the hypersphere independent of $\boldsymbol{\mu}$ when $\kappa = 0$. For simplicity, in our implementation, we assume that the prior $p(\boldsymbol{z})$ in VAE follows the uniform distribution $vMF(\cdot; \kappa = 0)$. Correspondingly, we assume that the posterior $q_\phi(\boldsymbol{z}|x)$ follows $vMF(\boldsymbol{z}; \boldsymbol{\mu}, \kappa)$. Hence, we can modify the second term of Eq. (8) as follows:

$$\begin{aligned}
\mathbb{KL}[q(\boldsymbol{z}; \boldsymbol{\mu}, \kappa) \| p(\boldsymbol{z})] &= \int_{\mathbb{S}^{d-1}} q(\boldsymbol{z}; \boldsymbol{\mu}, \kappa) \log \frac{q(\boldsymbol{z}; \boldsymbol{\mu}, \kappa)}{p(\boldsymbol{z})} d\boldsymbol{z} \\
&= \int_{\mathbb{S}^{d-1}} q(\boldsymbol{z}; \boldsymbol{\mu}, \kappa) \left(\log \mathcal{C}_d(\kappa) + \kappa \boldsymbol{\mu}^T \boldsymbol{z} - \log p(\boldsymbol{z})\right) d\boldsymbol{z} \\
&= \kappa \boldsymbol{\mu} \mathbb{E}_q[\boldsymbol{z}] + \log \mathcal{C}_d(\kappa) - \log \left(\frac{2\left(\pi^{d/2}\right)}{\Gamma(d/2)}\right)^{-1} \\
&= \kappa \frac{I_{d/2}(\kappa)}{I_{d/2-1}(\kappa)} + \left(\frac{d}{2} - 1\right) \log \kappa - \frac{d}{2} \log(2\pi) - \log I_{d/2-1}(\kappa) \\
&\quad + \frac{d}{2} \log \pi + \log 2 - \log \Gamma\left(\frac{d}{2}\right).
\end{aligned}$$

$$(10)$$

Herein, κ will be fixed in model optimization. As such, we can observe that the optimization of Eq. (10) will not suffer the posterior collapse problem since it does not condition on $\boldsymbol{\mu}$.

In our context, we treat the mobility encoder as the posterior $q(\boldsymbol{z}|T)$ while the Mobility Decoder takes the role of reconstructing the input trajectory T. Specifically, we first employ the Mobility Encoder to generate trajectory representation $\boldsymbol{h}_n^e$ and set $\boldsymbol{\mu} = \boldsymbol{h}_n^e$. Then, we use the Wood algorithm[30] to sample latent variable $\boldsymbol{z}$ from the vMF distribution by adding a uniform noise, which can be summarized as follows,

$$\mathcal{A}(\boldsymbol{v}') = \min\left[10^{-9}, \exp\left(\kappa\left(\boldsymbol{v}' \cdot \boldsymbol{\mu} - 1\right)\right)\right], \boldsymbol{v}' = \boldsymbol{v}/||\boldsymbol{v}||, \qquad (11)$$

where $\boldsymbol{v}$ is a randomly sampled vector $\boldsymbol{v} \sim \mathcal{N}(\boldsymbol{0}, \boldsymbol{I})$, $\boldsymbol{v}'$ is a vector normalized to $\boldsymbol{v}$, tangent to the hypersphere at $\boldsymbol{\mu}$. After obtaining the reception probability $\mathcal{A}(\boldsymbol{v}')$, we randomly use a variable x sampled from uniform distribution $x \sim \mathcal{U}(0, 1)$ to determine the final latent variable z. Specifically, if $x \leq \mathcal{A}(v')$, then accept v' as latent variable z, otherwise, we regenerate the vector v. In sum, the objective of hyperspherical Bayesian learning can be summarized as follows,

$$\mathcal{L}_H = -\mathbb{E}_{z \sim q_\phi(z|T)}\left[\log p_\theta(T|z)\right] + \mathbb{KL}[q_\phi(z; \mu, \kappa) \| p(z)]. \tag{12}$$

Task Learning. Now we turn to use the pre-trained model to boost the downstream mobility prediction task. To be specific, we first make the parameters in the pre-trained model unchangeable. Then, we use the historical preference extractor to produce the historical preference representation o_n. In contrast to previous studies [4,10], we use the last state (i.e., h_n^d) of the mobility decoder and o_n to predict the user's next POI, which can be denoted as follows,

$$\tilde{p}_{n+1} = \text{Softmax}([h_n^d \oplus o_n]W_f + b_f), \tag{13}$$

where W_f and b_f are trainable parameters. Correspondingly, the objective of mobility prediction for trajectory T can be expressed as:

$$\mathcal{L}_T = -p_{n+1} \log\left(\tilde{p}_{n+1}\right), \tag{14}$$

where p_{n+1} is the one-hot distribution of POI p_{n+1}.

4   Evaluation

Datasets. We evaluate our HBay on four widely used location-based datasets, where Tokyo and New York are derived from Foursquare while Los Angles and Houston are extracted from Gowalla. For each dataset, we remove POIs with fewer than 8 visits. We first concatenate each user's historical footprints to formulate his/her historical trajectory. And then, we divide each trajectory into sub-trajectories for mobility pattern learning, where each of them is generated within 24 h. Finally, we select 80% of the sub-trajectories of each user as the training set and the rest as the test set. The details are illustrated in Table 1.

Table 1. Statistics of the datasets.

City	Users	POIs	Check-ins	Trajectories
Tokyo	2102	6789	240056	60365
New York	990	4211	79006	23252
Los Angeles	2346	8676	195231	61542
Houston	1351	6994	121502	37514

Baselines. To comprehensively evaluate our approach, we compare HBay with recent popular solutions, including: **GRU** [15] is a benchmarking RNN model that uses the GRU cell to capture the sequential dependencies underlying massive trajectories. **ST-RNN** [3] is also a popular RNN-based approach for the next POI prediction task, where the spatial-temporal semantics underlying trajectories are incorporated. **HST-LSTM** [31] aims at exploring human diverse behavioral regularities in an end-to-end manner through spatial-temporal LSTM. **DeepMove** [10] uses an attention-based RNN to consider both human recent sequential behaviors and long-term check-in preferences. **VANext** [4] is the first generative model for next POI prediction, where the variational attention module is devised to correlate human short-term and long-term check-in behaviors. **MobTCast** [5] extends the Transformer architecture to understand human mobility in an end-to-end manner. Notably, we remove the Social Context Extractor in MobTCast as the social ties in our context are not available. **CFPRec** [12] employs an LSTM layer to capture human current trajectories while using self-attention to explore human long-term check-ins.

Metric Protocols and Implementations. We follow most of the recent studies [4, 5, 10] and strictly select three commonly used metrics to evaluate the model performance of our method and the baselines, including ACC@K, area under the ROC curve (AUC), and mean average precision (MAP). In our experiments, we report the different testing results of $K = 1, 5$. We implement our HBay as well as the baselines in Python using the PyTorch library. All approaches are accelerated by one NVIDIA GeForce-RTX-3090. Additionally, we choose Adam to train all deep learning methods. In Hyperspherical Bayesian Learning, the learning rate is initialized as 0.005, we set the scaling coefficient κ to 16 and the dimension of z to 128. In Task Learning, the learning rate is initialized with 5e-4. The dropout rate is set as 0.5, and the batch size is 128. Besides, the dimensions of POI, time, and category are set as 256 and the hidden size of the GRU network is set to 512.

Performance Comparisons. Table 2 reports the performance of different approaches on four datasets, where the best is highlighted in **bold** and the second is underlined. Specifically, we have the following observations:

We can find that ST-RNN does not provide us with competitive scores compared to GRU, even though ST-RNN takes into account spatial and temporal constraints. The rationale behind it is that the sparsity of check-in data severely affects the refinement of semantic contexts, such as geographical distance. In contrast, HST-LSTM combines spatial and temporal factors with a gate mechanism that can largely improve the capture of human mobility patterns. As for DeepMove and VANext, They both attempt to combine the recent trajectory with the historical trajectory to accurately discover the individual moving periodicity, which results in higher gains. Furthermore, VANext is the first generative method that models human trajectories using Gaussian assumptions. As a result, it outperforms DeepMove as it alleviates the inherent uncertainty of human mobility by Bayesian learning. MobTCast is a Transformer-based approach that uses self-attention to study the interaction signals between POIs in a given trajectory. The results of MobTCast indicate that considering multiple semantic contexts does help to discover users' future check-in intentions. CFPRec employs an LSTM layer to capture human short-term trajectories while using self-attention to explore human long-term check-ins, and the results show that long-term trajectories are useful to explore users' check-in preferences.

In sum, our proposed HBay significantly outperforms the compared methods by a large margin in four cities. For instance, For ACC@1 and MAP, the gains of HBay are on average 13.73% and 25.44% higher than the optimal baseline, respectively. This observation demonstrates that HBay using Hyperspherical Bayesian Learning enables the capture of human diverse mobility patterns, as well as our proposed Contextual Interest Embedding.

Table 2. Performance comparisons on four cities.

Method	Tokyo				New York			
	ACC@1	ACC@5	AUC	MAP	ACC@1	ACC@5	AUC	MAP
GRU	13.11	27.88	88.01	7.36	15.37	31.73	81.40	8.59
ST-RNN	13.38	29.20	89.82	7.41	13.50	32.86	81.91	8.20
HST-LSTM	18.70	39.14	90.66	9.82	17.48	42.77	86.25	8.53
DeepMove	19.92	40.61	90.47	12.21	21.56	45.09	87.30	13.06
VANext	20.21	44.49	91.30	12.36	22.54	51.26	89.30	14.02
MobTCast	19.58	43.41	89.95	11.67	22.37	54.31	88.59	14.03
CFPRec	20.18	46.32	92.29	12.15	24.21	56.73	91.68	16.14
HBay	**23.15**	**48.83**	**94.12**	**15.63**	**27.45**	**58.31**	**93.09**	**19.50**

Method	Los Angeles				Houston			
	ACC@1	ACC@5	AUC	MAP	ACC@1	ACC@5	AUC	MAP
GRU	10.11	19.05	78.07	4.97	10.74	18.01	80.47	5.99
ST-RNN	10.01	19.30	80.48	5.11	11.33	20.21	82.34	6.88
HST-LSTM	12.01	23.97	82.57	5.29	13.41	22.86	82.58	6.58
DeepMove	13.31	25.73	82.41	7.26	14.13	24.59	83.29	8.46
VANext	14.36	27.91	86.22	7.73	14.88	26.78	86.06	8.31
MobTCast	14.30	28.62	83.41	7.65	15.40	28.27	83.87	8.66
CFPRec	15.06	30.91	87.67	8.18	16.55	31.25	87.78	9.75
HBay	**17.64**	**33.54**	**91.05**	**10.68**	**18.14**	**32.75**	**90.51**	**12.12**

Ablation Study. To scrutinize the contribution of different components of HBay, we compare its variants from two aspects. Specifically, we derive the variants as follows: *HBay-Base* is a basic model that removes Hyperspherical Bayesian Learning and replaces our graph-based POI embedding with a random POI embedding. *HBay w/o H* is using only the standard VAE instead of Hyperspherical Bayesian Learning as a pre-training. *HBay w/o G* is removing only the graph-based embedding and using random for POI embedding instead.

Figure 2 illustrates the performance of variants in four cities. First, we can find that removing any module brings a significant performance degradation, which suggests that all three modules in our HBay are beneficial for enhancing POI prediction. Second, HBay-Base performs worse than HBay w/o H on all cities, suggesting that extracting data by pre-training and then fine-tuning the training is useful for discovering human movement patterns. Meanwhile, HBay w/o H is worse than HBay indicating that the Hyperspherical Bayesian Learning is superior to the standard VAE as pre-training. Third, HBay w/o G does

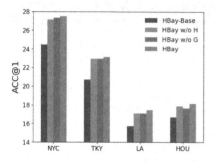
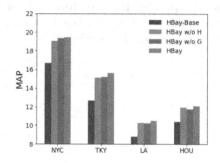

Fig. 2. Visualization of ablation study.

not perform as well as HBay, proving that our proposed POI embedding is an effective module that provides promising representations for task inference.

Figure 3 illustrates how the constraint of a small KL diver divergence diminishes after a certain number of training epochs when using the standard VAE, resulting in posterior collapse. As shown in Fig. 3(a), the distribution of trajectory points does not conform to a single Gaussian distribution. Our solution circumvents this issue by employing a hyperspherical distribution and introduces a scaling factor. This is demonstrated in Fig. 3(b), where trajectory points are uniformly distributed and more closely adhere to a Gaussian distribution.

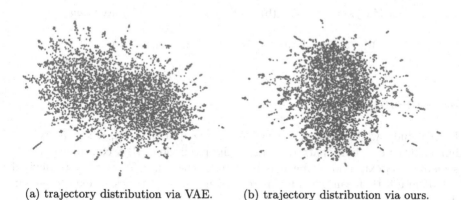

(a) trajectory distribution via VAE.   (b) trajectory distribution via ours.

Fig. 3. Visualization of trajectory distribution.

Robustness Analysis. In the end, we investigate the impacts of key hyperparameters in our HBay, i.e., the embedding size of POI, the hidden size of the GRU cell, and the dimensionality in the attention layer of the Historical Preference Extractor. As shown in Fig. 4 and Fig 5, we can find HBay is not sensitive to the embedding size. To make a trade-off between model complexity and efficiency, we set the embedding size to 256. As for the hidden size of GRU cell, we observe that HBay performs better as the dimension of hidden size increases but stabilizes after 512. For dimensionality in the attention layer, we find that HBay performs the best when it is 128.

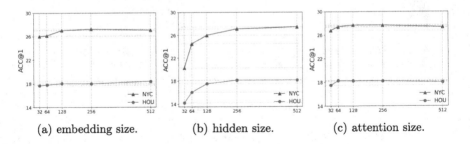

(a) embedding size.   (b) hidden size.   (c) attention size.

Fig. 4. Visualization of robustness analysis on $ACC@1$.

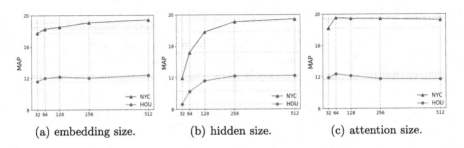

(a) embedding size.   (b) hidden size.   (c) attention size.

Fig. 5. Visualization of robustness analysis on MAP.

5   Conclusion

In this study, we introduced a novel generative approach, i.e., HBay, to explore human diverse mobility patterns for mobility prediction. HBay considers multiple semantic contexts underlying massive human check-ins. Especially, we devised a POI graph that can generate more reasonable trajectories to expose human diverse but unobserved mobility patterns. Moreover, HBay as a new generative model can address the posterior collapse problem. To the best of our knowledge, HBay is the first work that learns human mobility in a hyperspherical space. In addition, we presented an additive attention module to extract human long-term check-in preferences. The experimental results conducted on four real-world datasets demonstrate higher gains on mobility prediction tasks compared to several baselines. In the future, we consider employing a unified graph model to capture more interactive dynamics underlying human check-ins.

Acknowledgements. This work was supported by the National Natural Science Foundation of China (Grant No. 62102326), the Natural Science Foundation of Sichuan Province (Grant No. 2023NSFSC1411), the Key Research and Development Project of Sichuan Province (Grant No. 2022YFG0314), and Guanghua Talent Project.

References

1. Atluri, G., Karpatne, A., Kumar, V.: Spatio-temporal data mining: a survey of problems and methods. ACM Comput. Surv. (CSUR) **51**(4), 1–41 (2018)
2. Hamdi, A., et al.: Spatiotemporal data mining: a survey on challenges and open problems. Artif. Intell. Rev. **55**, 1441–1488 (2022). https://doi.org/10.1007/s10462-021-09994-y
3. Liu, Q., Wu, S., Wang, L., Tan, T.: Predicting the next location: a recurrent model with spatial and temporal contexts. In: Proceedings of the AAAI Conference on Artificial Intelligence, vol. 30 (2016)
4. Gao, Q., Zhou, F., Trajcevski, G., Zhang, K., Zhong, T., Zhang, F.: Predicting human mobility via variational attention. In: The World Wide Web Conference, pp. 2750–2756 (2019)
5. Xue, H., Salim, F., Ren, Y., Oliver, N.: MobTCast: Leveraging auxiliary trajectory forecasting for human mobility prediction. Adv. Neural. Inf. Process. Syst. **34**, 30380–30391 (2021)
6. Mathew, W., Raposo, R., Martins, B.: Predicting future locations with hidden Markov models. In: Proceedings of the 2012 ACM Conference on Ubiquitous Computing, pp. 911–918 (2012)
7. Rudenko, A., Palmieri, L., Herman, M., Kitani, K.M., Gavrila, D.M., Arras, K.O.: Human motion trajectory prediction: a survey. Int. J. Robot. Res. **39**(8), 895–935 (2020)
8. Gambs, S., Killijian, M.-O., del Prado Cortez, M.N.: Next place prediction using mobility Markov chains. In: Proceedings of the 1st Workshop on Measurement, Privacy, and Mobility, pp. 1–6 (2012)
9. Cheng, C., Yang, H., Lyu, M.R., King, I.: Where you like to go next: successive point-of-interest recommendation. In: Proceedings of the 23rd International Joint Conference on Artificial Intelligence, IJCAI 2013, pp. 2605–2611. AAAI Press (2013)
10. Feng, J., et al.: DeepMove: predicting human mobility with attentional recurrent networks. In: Proceedings of the 2018 World Wide Web Conference, pp. 1459–1468 (2018)
11. Long, J., Chen, T., Nguyen, Q.V.H., Yin, H.: Decentralized collaborative learning framework for next poi recommendation. ACM Trans. Inf. Syst. **41**(3), 1–25 (2023)
12. Zhang, L., Sun, Z., Wu, Z., Zhang, J., Ong, Y., Qu, X.: Next point-of-interest recommendation with inferring multi-step future preferences. In: Proceedings of the 31st International Joint Conference on Artificial Intelligence (IJCAI), pp. 3751–3757 (2022)
13. Kingma, D.P., Welling, M.: Auto-encoding variational Bayes. arXiv preprint arXiv:1312.6114 (2013)
14. Hochreiter, S., Schmidhuber, J.: Long short-term memory. Neural Comput. **9**(8), 1735–1780 (1997)

15. Cho, K., van Merriënboer Caglar Gulcehre, B., Bahdanau, D., Schwenk, F.B.H., Bengio, Y.: Learning phrase representations using RNN encoder-decoder for statistical machine translation. In: Proceedings of the 2014 Conference on Empirical Methods in Natural Language Processing (EMNLP), pp. 1724–1734 (2014)
16. Luca, M., Barlacchi, G., Lepri, B., Pappalardo, L.: A survey on deep learning for human mobility. ACM Comput. Surv. (CSUR) **55**(1), 1–44 (2021)
17. Huang, L., Ma, Y., Wang, S., Liu, Y.: An attention-based spatiotemporal LSTM network for next poi recommendation. IEEE Trans. Serv. Comput. **14**(6), 1585–1597 (2019)
18. Zhao, S., Chen, X., King, I., Lyu, M.R.: Personalized sequential check-in prediction: beyond geographical and temporal contexts. In: 2018 IEEE International Conference on Multimedia and Expo (ICME), pp. 1–6. IEEE (2018)
19. Liao, J., Liu, T., Liu, M., Wang, J., Wang, Y., Sun, H.: Multi-context integrated deep neural network model for next location prediction. IEEE Access **6**, 21980–21990 (2018)
20. Wu, Y., Li, K., Zhao, G., Qian, X.: Long-and short-term preference learning for next poi recommendation. In: Proceedings of the 28th ACM International Conference on Information and Knowledge Management, pp. 2301–2304 (2019)
21. Yuxia, W., Li, K., Zhao, G., Qian, X.: Personalized long-and short-term preference learning for next poi recommendation. IEEE Trans. Knowl. Data Eng. **34**(4), 1944–1957 (2020)
22. Grover, A., Leskovec, J.: node2vec: scalable feature learning for networks. In: Proceedings of the 22nd ACM SIGKDD International Conference on Knowledge Discovery and Data Mining, pp. 855–864 (2016)
23. Bahdanau, D., Cho, K., Bengio, Y.: Neural machine translation by jointly learning to align and translate. In: Bengio, Y., LeCun, Y. (eds.) 3rd International Conference on Learning Representations, ICLR 2015, Conference Track Proceedings, San Diego, CA, USA, 7–9 May 2015 (2015)
24. Lin, Z., et al.: A structured self-attentive sentence embedding. In: 5th International Conference on Learning Representations, ICLR 2017, Conference Track Proceedings, Toulon, France, 24–26 April 2017. OpenReview.net (2017)
25. Scott, T.R., Gallagher, A.C., Mozer, M.C.: von Mises-Fisher Loss: an exploration of embedding geometries for supervised learning. In Proceedings of the IEEE/CVF International Conference on Computer Vision, pp. 10612–10622 (2021)
26. Xu, J., Durrett, G:. Spherical latent spaces for stable variational autoencoders. In: Proceedings of the 2018 Conference on Empirical Methods in Natural Language Processing, pp. 4503–4513 (2018)
27. Wang, P., et al.: Deep adaptive graph clustering via von Mises-Fisher distributions. ACM Trans. Web (2023, accepted). https://doi.org/10.1145/3580521
28. Mardia, K.V., El-Atoum, S.A.M.: Bayesian inference for the von Mises-Fisher distribution. Biometrika **63**(1), 203–206 (1976)
29. Yang, L., Fan, L., Bouguila, N.: Deep clustering analysis via dual variational autoencoder with spherical latent embeddings. IEEE Trans. Neural Netw. Learn. Syst., 1–10 (2021). https://doi.org/10.1109/TNNLS.2021.3135460
30. Wood, A.T.A.: Simulation of the von Mises Fisher distribution. Commun. Stat. Simul. Comput. **23**(1), 157–164 (1994)
31. Kong, D., Wu, F.: HST-LSTM: a hierarchical spatial-temporal long-short term memory network for location prediction. In: Proceedings of the 27th International Joint Conference on Artificial Intelligence, pp. 2341–2347 (2018)

Spatial-Temporal Diffusion Probabilistic Learning for Crime Prediction

Qiang Gao[1,2] (ID), Hongzhu Fu[1] (ID), Yutao Wei[3] (ID), Li Huang[1,2(✉)] (ID),
Xingmin Liu[1] (ID), and Guisong Liu[1,2] (ID)

[1] The Complex Laboratory of New Finance and Economics, Southwestern University
of Finance and Economics, Chengdu, Sichuan, China
lihuang@swufe.edu.cn
[2] Kash Institute of Electronics and Information Industry, Kashgar,
Xinjiang, China
[3] University of Electronic Science and Technology of China, Chengdu,
Sichuan, China

Abstract. Crime prediction is a critical issue in the field of urban management, as it makes it possible to prevent potential public safety threats.
Previous studies mainly concentrate on exploring the multiple dependencies regarding urban regions and temporal interactions. Nevertheless,
more complex interactive semantics behind crime events remain largely
unexplored. Besides, the sparsity and uncertainty of historical crime data
have not been thoroughly investigated. In this study, we introduce a novel
spatial-temporal diffusion probabilistic learning framework for crime prediction, namely ST-DPL. To be specific, we devise a spatial-temporal
crime encoding module in ST-DPL to handle multiple dependencies covering the temporal, spatial, and crime-type aspects. Then, the designed
crime diffusion probabilistic (CDP) module in ST-DPL plays the role of
generating a more robust behavioral portrayal regarding historical crime
cases for future crime prediction. The experiments conducted on two
real-world datasets demonstrate that ST-DPL outperforms the state-of-
the-art baselines.

Keywords: crime prediction · temporal dependency · spatial
dependency · diffusion model · attentive network

1 Introduction

Accurate crime prediction has become an essential task in the field of urban
safety or management, as various criminal activities, such as robbery and burglary, endanger the daily life of human beings and society. Recent advances in
urban sensing and urban computing offer the opportunity to perceive a wide variety of future urban crimes. Hence, recent researchers are eager to collect crime
cases along with multiple pieces of information such as geographical knowledge
to forecast the occurrences of crimes [1–3].

Early efforts primarily seek to model hand-craft features underlying crime
cases, along with considering the domain-aware expert experience [4,5]. Due

© The Author(s), under exclusive license to Springer Nature Switzerland AG 2023
Z. Jin et al. (Eds.): KSEM 2023, LNAI 14118, pp. 263–275, 2023.
https://doi.org/10.1007/978-3-031-40286-9_22

to the achievement of recent deep learning techniques, recent studies focus on using deep learning approaches to explore temporal dependency and region-aware spatial correlations. For instance, recent attention-based models are capable of capturing spatial-temporal information from high-dimensional crime data. DeepCrime as an attention-based model combines the recurrent neural network (RNN) with an attentive layer that can explore the relevance of crime patterns from previous time slots [2]. Moreover, recent studies have also shown that crime prediction can be categorized as a spatial-temporal prediction problem [6]. As such, [3] introduces a TCP approach that aims at modeling intra-region temporal correlation and inter-region spatial correlation for crime prediction. Besides, the achievement of recent graph neural networks shows that exploring the spatial-temporal interaction on graph structure enables the exposure of higher-order dependencies underlying massive historical crime cases. For instance, Xia et al. present a hypergraph network that incorporates multiple relationships behind the spatial-temporal crime data for crime prediction [7].

Challenges: Despite the fruitful achievements in previous studies, we consider that most of them still confront the following challenges. *(1) Complex Interactive Semantics:* First, the occurrence of crime changes over time, indicating that it is essential to consider the time-aware dependency across crime cases. Second, there may be a relative correlation between different types of crime cases in the same region. For example, violent crimes (e.g., robbery and assault) are more likely to occur simultaneously due to a lack of police resources [6]. Third, existing studies usually consider the geographical correlations behind crime cases while overlooking temporal correlations. The reason is that criminals may split up their missions in different regions. *(2) Sparsity in Crime Representation:* Recent deep learning approaches mainly produce good latent representations from historical crime data. However, the sparsity issue of crime occurrence in different regions results in insufficient representations and prevents us from comprehensively capturing the intricate distribution underlying the crime data. Correspondingly, uncertainty in modeling the distribution of crime data occurs frequently.

Contribution: To this end, we introduce a novel **S**patial-**T**emporal **D**iffusion **P**robabilistic **L**earning framework for crime prediction, namely ST-DPL. In ST-DPL, we first devise a spatial-temporal crime encoding module that primarily seeks to explore time-aware dynamics and region-aware correlations behind historical crime cases, oriented towards temporal, spatial, and crime-type aspects. Next, we introduce a crime diffusion probabilistic module, which serves to generate a more robust behavior portrayal for future crime prediction, alleviating the sparsity concern as well as uncertainty issue during the distribution modeling process. In summary, we make our main contributions as follows:

- We present ST-DPL, a novel generative model for alleviating the sparsity concern and uncertainty problem during crime distribution modeling.
- In ST-DPL, our spatial-temporal crime encoding module considers multiple interactive semantics behind the historical crime cases, which is capable of uncovering both explicit and implicit behavioral relationships to enhance the ability of crime data representations.

– The experiments conducted on two publicly available datasets demonstrate our ST-DPL achieves higher gains compared to the several baselines.

2 Related Work

In general, crime prediction includes conventional crime prediction techniques and crime prediction with hybrid models. Early works on crime mining often use its property of time series to build models [4] and enroll external information to consider the relations between different crime categories, as it is proposed in the traffic field firstly [7,8]. Recently, more relevant crime prediction models focus on exploring complex spatial-temporal information behind crime cases. For example, there exists a crime prediction model that obtains intra-region temporal correlation and inter-region spatial correlation through new spatial-temporal patterns [3]. STtrans [9] proposes a hierarchically structured spatial-temporal transformer network to capture spatial inter-dependencies and temporal dependencies. Besides, DeepCrime [2] is a recurrent framework of crime with an attention mechanism to fuse spatial-temporal correlations. Although the above methods have achieved effective results, they still lack the extraction of richer spatial-temporal information due to the sparsity of crime data.

Meanwhile, crime prediction is actually a sub-problem of the spatial-temporal prediction problem. Thus, numerous spatial-temporal prediction methods are also applicable in the field of crime prediction [10,11]. One ubiquitous solution is training the recurrent neural networks such as STRNN [12] and D-LSTM [13]. Moreover, the attention mechanism is usually used to combine spatial dependency and temporal dependency. For instance, MiST [14] improves the recurrent neural network with an attention mechanism to automatically evaluate the different contributions of correlated regions, time slots, and categories. Furthermore, convolutional neural networks can also be used to fuse latent spatial-temporal information such as STDN [15]. Another solution is making full use of graph neural networks owing to the advancement of their strong relational learning ability. Thereupon, STGCN [16] chooses to build a convolution structure on the spatial graph in order to make full use of spatial information. Xia et al. use the hypergraph network to model multiple relationships behind the spatial-temporal crime cases for crime prediction [7]. Nevertheless, crime prediction from complex crime cases is not trivial, we should consider multiple interactions underlying crime cases. In addition, we also need to alleviate the sparsity concern of historical crime data. To this end, we introduce a novel spatial-temporal diffusion probabilistic learning method for crime prediction.

3 ST-DPL

3.1 Definitions

Following most previous studies [2,6,7], we first divide the entire urban space into R-size equal regions using grid-scale map partitioning. Note that each region

$r \in R$ is the geographical minimum unit for predicting crime occurrence. The raw crime data includes geographic latitude and longitude, timestamp and crime type in the general format $< crimetype, timestamp, latitude, longitude >$. Each crime record is assigned to the appropriate area based on its coordinates. Hence, we can obtain the final three-way crime tensor $\mathbf{X} \in \mathbb{R}^{R \times T \times C}$. Notably, the high-dimensional crime tensor $\mathbf{X}$ contains the spatial-temporal information and crime type information, where R, T and C denote the number of the grid-scale regions, time slots and crime types, respectively. For instance, any entry $\mathbf{X}_{r,t,c}$ denotes the number of urban crime cases with crime type c at region r during the t-th time slot.

Crime Prediction. We formulate the problem of crime prediction as follows: given the historical crime tenor $\mathbf{X} \in \mathbb{R}^{R \times T \times C}$, the goal is to build a model to infer the number of crime cases for each region with different crime types during the next coming time slot $T + 1$, which can be denoted as $\hat{\mathbf{X}}_{T+1} \in \mathbb{R}^{R \times C}$.

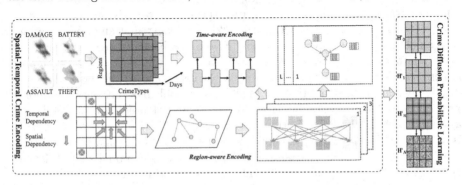

Fig. 1. The architecture of ST-DPL.

3.2 Architecture Overview

Figure 1 shows the general architecture of our proposed ST-DPL. Specifically, it contains two main components, including spatial-temporal crime encoding and crime graph diffusion modules. In spatial-temporal encoding, we devise a recurrent crime network to capture the sequential dynamics regarding the time aspect. In addition, we build a crime graph and employ an attentive mechanism to obtain the spatial and temporal correlations across different regions. In crime graph diffusion, we design a deep graph diffusion model that aims to operate the underlying evolving patterns behind historical crime data in a latent space, along with considering the data sparsity concern. We will detail them next.

3.3 Spatial-Temporal Crime Encoding

Crime Embedding: As a prerequisite, we need to prepare a reasonable representation for each crime type in the context of deep learning. Specifically, given the spatial-temporal crime tensor $\mathbf{X} \in \mathbb{R}^{R \times T \times C}$, we first randomly generate an initial embedding $\mathbf{e}_c \in \mathbb{R}^d$ from Gaussian for each crime type c, where d is the dimensionality. Then, we can prepare the initial representation $\mathbf{e}_{r,t,c} \in \mathbb{R}^d$ that primarily seeks to expose the crime pattern with c-th type at region r during the t-th time slot. Inspired by [7], each $\mathbf{e}_{r,t,c}$ is derived from $\mathbf{e}_c$ along with the spatial and temporal factors, which can be summarized as follows:

$$\mathbf{e}_{r,t,c} = \frac{\mathbf{X}_{r,t,c} - \mu}{\sigma} \cdot \mathbf{e}_c. \tag{1}$$

Herein, μ and σ refer to the mean and standard deviation of the tensor $\mathbf{X}$, respectively, for the purpose of normalization. Then we will get the four-way tensor $\mathbf{E} \in \mathbb{R}^{R \times T \times C \times d}$ as the input for the next component.

Time-Aware Encoding: In order to capture the temporal dependencies (sequential dynamics) regarding the time aspect, we use the vanilla Recurrent Neural Network (RNN) to obtain the hidden state $\mathbf{H}_\tau$ which has the same dimension as each $\mathbf{E}'_\tau \in \mathbf{E}'$, where $\mathbf{E}' \in \mathbb{R}^{RTC \times d}$ is a two-way tensor by merging the original $\mathbf{E}$. As such, modeling $\mathbf{E}'$ enables to explore the complete sequential dynamics behind $\mathbf{E}$. Therefore, the encoding process can be expressed as follows,

$$\mathbf{H}_\tau = \mathbf{S}_\tau \cdot \mathbf{O}, \mathbf{S}_\tau = ReLU\left(\mathbf{E}'_\tau \cdot \mathbf{U} + \mathbf{S}_{\tau-1} \cdot \mathbf{W}\right), \tag{2}$$

where $\mathbf{O}, \mathbf{U}, \mathbf{W} \in \mathbb{R}^{d \times d}$ are trainable parameters and $\mathbf{S}_\tau$ and $\mathbf{S}_{\tau-1}$ are the current and last hidden states, respectively. After the encoding, We will transform all the hidden states into a unified state $\mathbf{H} \in \mathbb{R}^{R \times T \times C \times d}$, which will be the input of the following region-aware encoding.

Region-aware Encoding: As different regions may have interactive correlations regarding different crime types, we first explore the inherent correlation across different regions regarding the crime type aspect. Specifically, we follow routing and self-attention mechanisms [7,9,17] and make information aggregation. For each time slot t, we have:

$$\text{Attn}\left(\mathbf{H}_{i,t,c}, \mathbf{H}_{j,t}\right) = \|_{m=1}^M \sum_{c'=1}^C \gamma_{c,c'}^m \cdot \mathbf{V}^m \mathbf{H}_{j,t,c'}. \tag{3}$$

Herein, $\gamma_{c,c'}^m$ is the attention score between two crime types, which captures the dependency degree between crime type c in the region r_i and crime type c' in the region r_j. $\mathbf{V}^m \in \mathbb{R}^{d/M \times d}$ is the trainable parameters regarding $\mathbf{H}_{j,t,c'}$. In order to provide different views of attention function, in our study multi-head attention is adopted. Hence, $\|$ represents a concatenation operation. Correspondingly, the attention score $\gamma_{c,c'}^m$ can be described as follows,

$$\bar{\gamma}_{c,c'}^m = \frac{\left(\mathbf{Q}^m \mathbf{H}_{i,t,c}\right)^\top \left(\mathbf{K}^m \mathbf{H}_{j,t,c'}\right)}{\sqrt{d/M}}, \tag{4}$$

$$\gamma_{c,c'}^m = \frac{\exp\left(\bar{\gamma}_{c,c'}^m\right)}{\sum_{c'} \exp\left(\bar{\gamma}_{c,c'}^m\right)}, \tag{5}$$

where $\mathbf{Q}^m, \mathbf{K}^m \in \mathbb{R}^{d/M \times d}$ are both trainable parameters in attention mechanism.

To explore spatiotemporal interaction among different regions, we construct a crime graph G and treat each distinct region r as the graph node $v \in V$. Clearly, we can build an edge between the neighboring regions, primarily seeking to preserve the spatial correlations between different regions. In addition, two regions where crimes occur on the same day could also be relatively correlated even if they are distant from each other, as the criminals may take split jobs or even roam between zones. Hence, we also build an edge between such two regions to incorporate the temporal correlation between them. In the end, we use an adjacent matrix A to preserve the above correlations. Formally, given region node v_i and v_j, any $A_{ij} \in E$ can be defined as follows:

$$A_{ij} = \begin{cases} 1, \text{if } v_i \text{ and } v_j \text{ are spatial or temporal neighboring;} \\ 0, \text{ otherwise.} \end{cases} \tag{6}$$

Now we explicitly extract the spatiotemporal correlations between different regions via the built adjacent matrix A, which can be expressed as,

$$\text{Trans}\left(\mathbf{H}_i, \mathbf{H}_j\right) = A'_{i,j} \cdot \text{Attn}\left(\mathbf{H}_i, \mathbf{H}_j\right), \tag{7}$$

where $\text{Trans}(\cdot)$ indicates that information aggregation between the region r_i and its within a fixed time slot t. Besides, $A' = D^{-1/2}AD^{1/2}$ is a normalized adjacent matrix, where D indicates a diagonal (degree) matrix. Finally, to extract the long-distance propagation between regions, the complete message aggregation can be expressed as follows:

$$\mathbf{H}_i^{(l+1)} = ReLU \left(\sum_{j=1}^{R} \text{Trans}\left(\mathbf{H}_i^{(l)}, \mathbf{H}_j^{(l)} \right) \right), \tag{8}$$

where $\mathbf{H}_i^{(l+1)}$ is the crime representation obtained after $l \in L$ iterations.

3.4   Crime Diffusion Probabilistic Learning

So far, we have obtained the contextual tensor $\mathbf{H}^L \in \mathbb{R}^{R \times T \times C \times d}$ that encodes multiple interactive semantics regarding temporal, spatial, and type-aware aspects. We turn to introduce a crime diffusion probabilistic (CDP) module [18,19] to alleviate the sparsity and uncertainty concerns underlying historical crime data. Due to the multiple-way dimension of crime tensor $\mathbf{H}^L$, we first transform $\mathbf{H}^L$ into a two-dimensional matrix $\mathbf{H}' \in \mathbb{R}^{RTC \times d}$, which will not affect the semantic context in terms of region, time slot, and crime type. CDP takes $\mathbf{H}'$ as input and uses a forward Markov chain to sequentially add Gaussian noise in the diffusion process q. Specifically, let $\mathbf{H}'_0 = \mathbf{H}'$, the forward diffusion process can be summarized as follows,

$$q\left(\mathbf{H}'_{1:N} \mid \mathbf{H}'_0\right) := \prod_{n=1}^{N} q\left(\mathbf{H}'_n \mid \mathbf{H}'_{n-1}\right), \tag{9}$$

$$q\left(\mathbf{H}'_n \mid \mathbf{H}'_{n-1}\right) := \mathcal{N}\left(\mathbf{H}'_n; \sqrt{(1-\beta_n)}\mathbf{H}'_{n-1}, \beta_n \mathbf{I}\right), \tag{10}$$

where $\mathbf{H}'_n$ is the noise crime data for n-th iteration in the process of adding noise and β_n is a hyperparameter (i.e., forward process variance) of n-th iteration. In this study, $\{\beta_n\}_1^N$ will be set to an arithmetic sequence in the interval $[0,1]$, satisfying $\beta_1 < \beta_2 < \cdots < \beta_N$. When n $= 1$, $\beta = 0$ while $\beta = 1$ when $n = N$.

After the diffusion process is completed, the denoising process $p_\theta(\mathbf{H}'_{N:0})$, which is the same as the diffusion process, can be represented by a reverse Markov diffusion process p_θ. The process can be summarized as follows,

$$p_\theta\left(\mathbf{H}'_{N:0}\right) := p\left(\mathbf{H}'_N\right) \prod_{n=1}^N p_\theta\left(\mathbf{H}'_{n-1} \mid \mathbf{H}'_n\right), \tag{11}$$

$$p\left(\mathbf{H}'_N\right) = \mathcal{N}\left(\mathbf{H}'_N; \mathbf{0}, \mathbf{I}\right), \tag{12}$$

$$p_\theta\left(\mathbf{H}'_{n-1} \mid \mathbf{H}'_n\right) = \mathcal{N}\left(\mathbf{H}'_{n-1}; \boldsymbol{\mu}_\theta(\mathbf{H}'_n, n), \boldsymbol{\epsilon}_\theta(\mathbf{H}'_n, n)\right), \tag{13}$$

Herein, $\boldsymbol{\mu}_\theta$ and ϵ_θ are learnable mean and variance functions at diffusion step n, respectively. In this way, we can finally obtain the target $\mathbf{H}^{new} \in \mathbb{R}^{R \times T \times C \times d}$ for prediction, where $\mathbf{H}^{new}$ is the output tensor obtained by the reverse diffusion process p_θ. As such, CDP is able to generate $\mathbf{H}^{new}$ with uncertainty instead of using $\mathbf{H}'_0$ (i.e., $\mathbf{H}'$) directly, which makes the model training more robust. Notably, CDP adopts the maximum likelihood function $p_\theta(\mathbf{H}'_0)$ as the target function. In sum, the variational upper bound operation is performed on it based on variational inference to maximize the optimization objective:

$$
\begin{aligned}
\log p_\theta\left(\mathbf{H}'_0\right) &= \log \int p_\theta\left(\mathbf{H}'_{0:N}\right) d\mathbf{H}'_{1:N} \\
&= \log \int \frac{p_\theta\left(\mathbf{H}'_{0:N}\right) q\left(\mathbf{H}'_{1:N} \mid \mathbf{H}'_0\right)}{q\left(\mathbf{H}'_{1:N} \mid \mathbf{H}'_0\right)} d\mathbf{H}'_{1:N} \\
&\geq \mathbb{E}_{q\left(\mathbf{H}'_{1:N} \mid \mathbf{H}'_0\right)}\left[\log \frac{p_\theta\left(\mathbf{H}'_{0:N}\right)}{q\left(\mathbf{H}'_{1:N} \mid \mathbf{H}'_0\right)}\right].
\end{aligned}
\tag{14}
$$

We also alter the final output $\mathbf{H}^{new}$ to $\mathbf{H}'' \in \mathbb{R}^{R \times T \times C \times d}$ for crime prediction.

3.5 Training and Inference

After we get the target crime tensor $\mathbf{H}''$, our model ST-GPL sums up it along the time slot dimension to obtain the final representation $\boldsymbol{\kappa} \in \mathbb{R}^{R \times C \times d}$. Then, we produce the next time slot's crime result $\hat{\mathbf{X}}_{T+1}$ with the Sigmoid function, which can be expressed as: $\hat{\mathbf{X}}_{r,T+1,c} = \phi\left(\mathbf{W}_c^\top \boldsymbol{\kappa}_{r,c}\right)$. For the crime classification task, ST-GPL minimizes the objective as follows:

$$\mathcal{L} = -\sum_t^T \delta\left(\mathbf{X}_t\right) \log \hat{\mathbf{X}}_t + \bar{\delta}\left(\mathbf{X}_t\right) \log\left(1 - \hat{\mathbf{X}}_t\right) + \lambda \|\boldsymbol{\Theta}\|_2^2 \tag{15}$$

where t is the time slot. $\delta\left(\cdot\right)$ and $\bar{\delta}\left(\cdot\right)$ are element-wise positive and negative indicator functions, respectively [7]. The last term is L_2 regularization and λ denotes the decay weight.

4 Evaluation

We conduct our experiments on two publicly available datasets. And the ablation study and sensitivity analysis are also provided.

Datasets. We evaluate our method on Chicago (CHI) and New York (NYC) City datasets [2,7] from the public platform. And each record is reported as (crime category, timestamp, and geographical coordinates). Table 1 presents the data statistics. In addition, we follow previous studies [7] and split the entire city into multiple no-overlapping regions, where each region with 3km× 3km spatial unit. The time interval is set as one day. We divide each original dataset into training and test datasets with a ratio of 7:1 along with the time interval.

Table 1. The description of urban crime datasets.

Data	NYC-Crimes		Chicago-Crimes	
Time Span	Jan, 2014 to Dec, 2015		Jan, 2016 to Dec, 2017	
Crime Types	Burglary	Robbery	Theft	Battery
Number	31,799	33,453	124,630	99,389
Crime Types	Assault	Larceny	Damage	Assault
Number	40,429	85,899	59,886	37,972

Baselines. We compare ST-GPL with recent representative baselines, including: **ARIMA** [20] is a popular time series analysis model that utilizes the regression algorithm for value prediction. **SVM** [21] transforms non-linear time series data into feature space, and then it can be used to tackle the crime prediction problem. **ST-GCN** [16] proposes to use the spatial convolutional layers with the temporal gated convolutional layers to capture the corresponding spatial and temporal dependencies. **DCRNN** [22] integrates the bidirectional random walks with recurrent neural networks to make the crime prediction with an encoder-decoder structure. **STDN** [15] learns the temporal patterns to capture the time-aware dependence between regions with a flow-gating mechanism and an attentive mechanism. **DeepCrime** [2] utilizes the recurrent neural network to obtain crime representations and then get the aggregative temporal dependency with the attention mechanism. **ST-SHN** [7] explores the sparsity of crime data by hypergraph neural networks and a multi-channel attentive mechanism.

Evaluation Protocols. We adopt three widely used metrics for performance evaluation, including micro-F_1, macro-F_1, and F_1-score [2,7]. Note that we use F_1-score to evaluate the performance regarding each crime type while micro-F_1 and macro-F_1 are used to evaluate the overall performance.

Implementation Details. We employ the Scikit-learn library to implement the machine learning methods while other deep learning methods are based on the Torch library. The hyperparameter settings of ST-DPL are as follows: The learning rate of our ST-DPL is 1e-6 with a 0.96 decay rate. The embedding size of the crime type is 16 for New York and 8 for Chicago. L is set to 2. The number of heads in the attention mechanism is 4.

Overall Performance. Table 2 shows the performance of the ST-DPL and baselines on the NYC and CHI datasets. Overall, ST-DPL achieves the best gains not only in overall performance but also in the performance of any specific crime type, except for the Assault's performance in NYC. For instance, it outperforms all baselines with a 3%–6% average improvement regarding Micro-F_1 and Macro-F_1 metrics. Among the baselines, deep learning models obviously perform better than machine learning and traditional statistical methods. We find that convolutional and recurrent neural networks (e.g., DCRNN) that aggregate significant spatial-temporal dependencies from historical crime cases perform better than traditional techniques such as SVM. Moreover, although DeepCrime, STDN, and ST-SHN utilize attention networks to capture crime cross-category perception patterns, ST-DPL still achieves better results than them, the reason is that these methods do not explicitly consider the complex spatial-temporal dependencies between different types of crime patterns, especially for temporal correlations. Meanwhile, CDP in ST-DPL alleviates the sparsity issue behind the crime data distribution more effectively and enhances the generalization.

Table 2. Overall performance of crime prediction on two datasets.

Method	New York (NYC)					
	Crime Categories				Overall	
	Burglary	Larceny	Robbery	Assault	Micro-F_1	Macro-F_1
ARIMA	0.0046	0.0047	0.0606	0.0655	0.0332	0.0327
SVM	0.0027	0.0108	0.0081	0.0081	0.0075	0.0074
ST-GCN	0.5322	0.5632	0.6027	0.5073	0.5520	0.5514
DCRNN	0.5158	0.6129	0.6007	0.5239	0.5650	0.5633
STDN	0.5139	0.5766	0.5633	0.4921	0.5350	0.5365
DeepCrime	0.4963	0.6129	0.6244	0.5517	0.5727	0.5713
ST-SHN	0.6154	0.5950	0.6880	**0.5593**	0.6154	0.6144
ST-DPL	**0.6424**	**0.7073**	**0.6957**	0.5197	**0.6465**	**0.6413**
Method	Chicago (CHI)					
	Crime Categories				Overall	
	Theft	Battery	Assault	Damage	Micro-F_1	Macro-F_1
ARIMA	0.0869	0.0028	0.0474	0.2595	0.0089	0.0061
SVM	0.0054	0.0032	0.0054	0.0746	0.0081	0.0054
ST-GCN	0.4549	0.5019	0.5628	0.4437	0.4908	0.4895
DCRNN	0.5217	0.5642	0.6105	0.5233	0.5549	0.5559
STDN	0.5232	0.5714	0.5874	0.4712	0.5383	0.5381
DeepCrime	0.4227	0.5549	0.5672	0.5296	0.5186	0.5174
ST-SHN	0.6522	0.6542	0.5816	0.6761	0.6390	0.6410
ST-DPL	**0.7723**	**0.7586**	**0.6577**	**0.7297**	**0.7237**	**0.7296**

Ablation Study. We conduct ablation studies to evaluate the effectiveness of our spatial-temporal diffusion probabilistic learning architecture. We denote a base model as ST-DPL, and we consider three contrast models to form variants: 1) "w/o CDP": ST-DPL without the crime diffusion probabilistic learning component; 2) "w/o RNN": ST-DPL without time-aware encoding; 3) "w/o

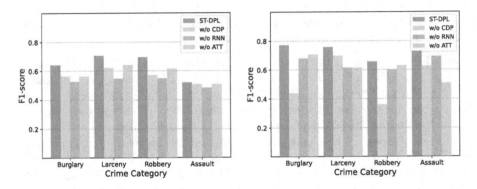

Fig. 2. Evaluation results on NYC.   **Fig. 3.** Evaluation results on CHI.

ATT": ST-DPL without region-aware encoding. As shown in Fig. 2 and Fig. 3, removing each component will confront severe performance degradation, which demonstrates our effectiveness in the module design of ST-DPL. Specifically, w/o RNN performs the worst on the New York dataset, demonstrating that capturing the sequential dynamics behind crime cases does help enhance crime prediction. Moreover, the performance of w/o CDP on the Chicago dataset indicates that the sparsity problem really affects crime inference. This also indirectly reveals the effectiveness of our proposed CDP. Finally, the experimental results of w/o ATT conducted on two datasets indicate capturing the region-aware semantics is a positive effort to improve the model performance. Also, Fig. 4 is one of the inferring results that indicate the probability of whether a crime occurs in NYC at $T + 1$ time slot. We can observe that the neighboring regions have a similar behavioral pattern such as Burglary and Larceny.

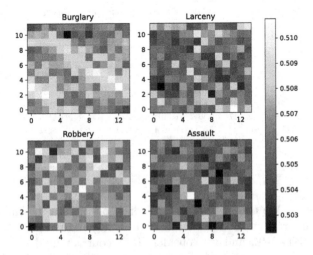

Fig. 4. Inferring results on NYC.

Sensitivity Analysis. To analyze the impact of the key hyperparameters, we evaluate the performance of ST-DPL with different parameter settings. We alter a specific hyperparameter while ensuring that the other hyperparameters are at the default settings. Note that there exist some other hyperparameters that could affect the results, we only perform the impacts of embedding size and spatial range, which could significantly influence the model performance. Figure 5 illustrates the experimental results.

– *Embedding Size.* We vary the dimension of the embedding size from 8 to 48. We can observe that the model performs best when the embedding size is 8 in Chicago and the embedding size is 16 in New York.

– *Iteration L.* In our region-aware encoding, the iteration L influences the information dissemination on the crime scale-region map. We empirically search a series of iterations in the range of $\{1, 2, 3, 4\}$. The experimental results show that the model achieves the best when the spatial range is 2 on both datasets. And using too large a value of L does not provide us with a higher return.

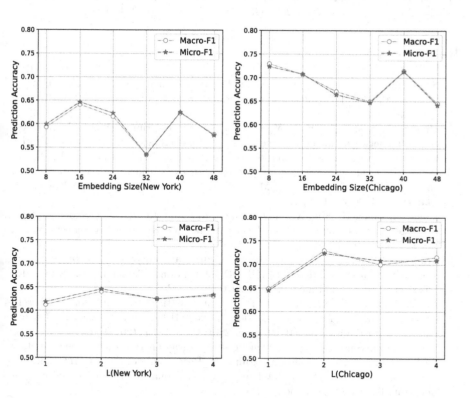

Fig. 5. Sensitivity analysis.

5 Conclusion

In this study, we presented a novel spatial-temporal diffusion probabilistic learning approach for crime prediction, namely ST-DPL. To our knowledge, ST-DPL is the first attempt to investigate the possibility of using diffusion-based models to tackle the crime prediction task. In addition, ST-DPL considers multiple interactive semantics, covering temporal, spatial, and crime-type aspects, which further enhances the ability of crime data representations. The experimental results conducted on two real-world crime datasets demonstrated the higher gains of our proposed ST-DPL compared to several representative baselines. In our future work, we plan to devise a more compact diffusion model to study the complex distribution underlying crime data.

Acknowledgements. This work was supported by the National Natural Science Foundation of China (Grant No.62102326), the Natural Science Foundation of Sichuan Province (Grant No. 2023NSFSC1411), the Key Research and Development Project of Sichuan Province (Grant No. 2022YFG0314), and Guanghua Talent Project.

References

1. Shamsuddin, N.H.M., Ali, N.A., Alwee, R.: An overview on crime prediction methods. In: 2017 6th ICT International Student Project Conference (ICT-ISPC), pp. 1–5. IEEE (2017)
2. Huang, C., Zhang, J., Zheng, Y., Chawla, N.V.: DeepCrime: attentive hierarchical recurrent networks for crime prediction. In: Proceedings of the 27th ACM International Conference on Information and Knowledge Management, October 2018
3. Zhao, X., Tang, J.: Modeling temporal-spatial correlations for crime prediction. In: Proceedings of the 2017 ACM on Conference on Information and Knowledge Management, November 2017
4. Chen, P., Yuan, H., Shu, X.: Forecasting crime using the ARIMA model. In: 2008 5th International Conference on Fuzzy Systems and Knowledge Discovery, vol. 5, pp, 627–630 (2008)
5. Wang, H., Kifer, D., Graif, C., Li, Z.: Crime rate inference with big data. In: Proceedings of the 22nd ACM SIGKDD International Conference on Knowledge Discovery and Data Mining, August 2016
6. Li, Z., Huang, C., Xia, L., Xu, Y., Pei, J.: Spatial-temporal hypergraph self-supervised learning for crime prediction. In: 2022 IEEE 38th International Conference on Data Engineering (ICDE), pp. 2984–2996. IEEE (2022)
7. Xia, L., et al.: Spatial-temporal sequential hypergraph network for crime prediction with dynamic multiplex relation learning. In: Proceedings of the 30th International Joint Conference on Artificial Intelligence. International Joint Conferences on Artificial Intelligence Organization (2021)
8. Wei, H., et al.: PressLight: learning max pressure control to coordinate traffic signals in arterial network. In: Proceedings of the 25th ACM SIGKDD International Conference on Knowledge Discovery & Data Mining, July 2019
9. Wu, X., Huang, C., Zhang, C., Chawla, N.V.: Hierarchically structured transformer networks for fine-grained spatial event forecasting. In: Proceedings of the Web Conference 2020, May 2020

10. Huang, C., Zhang, C., Dai, P., Bo, L.: Deep dynamic fusion network for traffic accident forecasting. In: Proceedings of the 28th ACM International Conference on Information and Knowledge Management, November 2019
11. Liu, J., Li, T., Xie, P., Shengdong, D., Teng, F., Yang, X.: Urban big data fusion based on deep learning: an overview. Inf. Fus. **53**, 123–133 (2019)
12. Liu, Q., Wu, S., Wang, L., Tan, T.: Predicting the next location: a recurrent model with spatial and temporal contexts. In: Proceedings of the AAAI Conference on Artificial Intelligence, June 2022
13. Rose, Y., Li, Y., Shahabi, C., Demiryurek, U., Liu, Y.: A generic approach for extreme condition traffic forecasting. In: Proceedings of the 2017 SIAM International Conference on Data Mining (SDM) (2017)
14. Huang, C., Zhang, C., Zhao, J., Wu, X., Yin, D., Chawla, N.: MiST: a multiview and multimodal spatial-temporal learning framework for citywide abnormal event forecasting. In: The World Wide Web Conference, May 2019
15. Yao, H., Tang, X., Wei, H., Zheng, G., Li, Z.: Revisiting spatial-temporal similarity: a deep learning framework for traffic prediction. In: Proceedings of the AAAI Conference on Artificial Intelligence, pp. 5668–5675, August 2019
16. Yu, B., Yin, H., Zhu, Z.: Spatio-temporal graph convolutional networks: a deep learning framework for traffic forecasting. In: Proceedings of the 27th International Joint Conference on Artificial Intelligence, July 2018
17. Vaswani, A., et al.: Attention is all you need. In: Proceedings of the 31st International Conference on Neural Information Processing Systems, pp. 6000–6010 (2017)
18. Ho, J., Jain, A., Abbeel, P.: Denoising diffusion probabilistic models. In: Advances in Neural Information Processing Systems, vol. 33, pp. 6840–6851 (2020)
19. Croitoru, F.-A., Hondru, V., Ionescu, R.T., Shah, M.: Diffusion models in vision: a survey. IEEE Trans. Pattern Anal. Mach. Intell., 1–20 (2023). https://doi.org/10.1109/TPAMI.2023.3261988
20. Pan, B., Demiryurek, U., Shahabi, C.: Utilizing real-world transportation data for accurate traffic prediction. In: 2012 IEEE 12th International Conference on Data Mining, January 2013
21. Chang, C.-C., Lin, C.-J.: LIBSVM: a library for support vector machines. ACM Trans. Intell. Syst. Technol. **2**, 1–27 (2012)
22. Li, Y., Yu, R., Shahabi, C., Liu, Y.: Diffusion convolutional recurrent neural network: data-driven traffic forecasting. In: 6th International Conference on Learning Representations, ICLR 2018, Conference Track Proceedings, Vancouver, BC, Canada, 30 April–3 May 2018. OpenReview.net (2018)

DBA: An Efficient Approach to Boost Transfer-Based Adversarial Attack Performance Through Information Deletion

Zepeng Fan[1], Peican Zhu[2]($\boxtimes$), Chao Gao[2], Jinbang Hong[1], and Keke Tang[3]($\boxtimes$)

[1] School of Computer Science, Northwestern Polytechnical University (NWPU),
Xi'an 710072, China
zepengf@mail.nwpu.edu.cn

[2] School of Artificial Intelligence, Optics, and Electronics (iOPEN), NWPU,
Xi'an 710072, China
{ericcan,cgao}@nwpu.edu.cn

[3] Cyberspace Institute of Advanced Technology, Guangzhou University,
Guangzhou 510006, China
tangbohutbh@gmail.com

Abstract. In practice, deep learning models are easy to be fooled by input images with subtle perturbations, and those images are called adversarial examples. Regarding one model, the crafted adversarial examples can successfully fool other models with varying architectures but the same task, which is referred to as adversarial transferability. Nevertheless, in practice, it is hard to get information about the model to be attacked, transfer-based adversarial attacks have developed rapidly. Later, different techniques are proposed to promote adversarial transferability. Different from existing input transformation attacks based on spatial transformation, our approach is a novel one on the basis of information deletion. By deleting squares of the input images by channels, we mitigate overfitting on the surrogate model of the adversarial examples and further enhance adversarial transferability. The corresponding performance of our method is superior to the existing input transformation attacks on different models (here, we consider unsecured models and defense ones), as demonstrated by extensive evaluations on ImageNet.

Keywords: Adversarial examples · Transfer-based adversarial attacks · Input transformation · Information deletion · Transferability

1 Introduction

Nowadays, deep learning is becoming a fundamental means for computer vision (CV), thereby efficiently handling tasks including semantic segmentation [1], image classification [2,3], and 3D point clouds classification [4,5]. Although we have made tremendous successes, concerns about the robustness of deep learning models still exist. As revealed by previous works [6], it is easy to deceive deep learning models by injecting some malicious noise into the original clean images,

© The Author(s), under exclusive license to Springer Nature Switzerland AG 2023
Z. Jin et al. (Eds.): KSEM 2023, LNAI 14118, pp. 276–288, 2023.
https://doi.org/10.1007/978-3-031-40286-9_23

which is imperceptible to human beings but might result in wrong prediction by deep learning models. Thus, it is of great significance to enhance the robustness of deep learning models through studying adversarial attacks by revealing their vulnerabilities. By exposing as many vulnerabilities as possible, we can develop defense mechanisms [7] with superior performance to boost the reliability of deep learning models.

Usually, the adversarial attacks are sorted as white-box adversarial attacks, black-box adversarial attacks. Under the white-box scenario [8–10], attackers can gain entire access to the victim model. By acquiring model architecture and parameters, attackers can make direct malicious perturbations to input images that overfit the model. Under the black-box setting [11], attackers can not access any information about the victim model. Therefore, attackers must craft perturbations on the surrogate model to cross the invisible decision boundary of the victim model. Transfer-based adversarial attacks [12–16] belongs to the black-box adversarial attack category. The attackers do not generate perturbations being designed for any specific victim model, but aim to increase the success rates of directly deceiving other unknown models.

Currently, the primary challenge in transfer-based adversarial attacks lies in that the adversarial examples generated often exhibit poor transferability as a result of overfitting to the surrogate model. For the purpose of overcoming the overfitting phenomenon and boosting adversarial transferability, numerous techniques have been developed. Thus, the transfer-based adversarial attacks can be further assorted into three groups, including input transformation attacks, feature-level attacks, and gradient optimization ones.

From an optimization standpoint [14], the adversarial transferability is analogous to the generalization ability of the trained models. Similar to how data augmentation techniques enhance the ability of trained models to generalize, input transformation methods can improve the transferability of adversarial attacks. The majority of existing input transformation attacks are based on spatial transformations. Motivated by the fact that information deletion can alleviate the overfitting phenomenon, we propose an input transformation attack method called DropBlock Attack (DBA) to enhance the adversarial transferability of the adversarial examples. Specifically, for each input image, we randomly delete information at each channel to generate a set of copies. Adversarial perturbations are generated from the average gradient computed over this set of copies. We evaluate the efficacy of our proposed DBA on the widely used ImageNet dataset and compare its performance to that of existing input transformation attacks. Our method exhibits superior transferability in the black-box setting without sacrificing attack performance in the white-box setting. The contributions of this work are listed as:

- In contrast to conventional input transformation attacks, we introduce an attack method based on information deletion, which independently deletes information from the input images by channels.
- By integrating our method with other input transformation techniques, the carefully crafted adversarial examples can achieve better transferability.

- Extensive evaluations on widely used ImageNet have indicated the remarkable superiority of our method, which surpasses current SOTA input transformation attacks by a large margin on the adversarial transferability.

We organize the rest of this paper as follows: Sect. 2 provides some related studies. Section 3 presents a detailed introduction of our approach, i.e., DBA. In Sect. 4, we describe our experimental setups and perform a thorough analysis of the results. We conclude this work in Sect. 5.

2   Related Works

Researchers usually sort adversarial attacks into two categories based on the information available to the attackers, i.e., white-box adversarial attacks and black-box adversarial ones. Studying black-box adversarial attacks, especially transfer-based adversarial attacks, is of great significance in practice. In this study, we primarily concentrate on attack transferability and the corresponding three types of transfer-based adversarial attacks are briefly introduced.

Gradient Optimization Attacks. The pioneering approach, i.e., Fast Gradient Sign Method (FGSM) [8], is first put forward in 2015 which takes advantage of one step gradient to generate adversarial perturbations. Kurakin *et al.* [9] argue that relying on one-step gradients alone to fully exploit perturbations is unhelpful. Instead, they propose I-FGSM, which uses FGSM in small steps for many iterations in the generation process. Subsequently, several iterative variants based on more advanced gradient calculations have been developed. Dong *et al.* [10] propose Momentum I-FGSM (MI-FGSM) by introducing the momentum to I-FGSM, which utilizes the accumulated gradient to escape local optima faster and get more stable disturb direction. Lin *et al.* [14] observe that Nesterov Accelerated Gradient (NAG) achieves better convergence results than momentum during the gradient descent process. Thus they propose NI-FGSM by taking NAG to look ahead which efficiently improves the transferability.

Input Transformations Attacks. Drawing inspiration from data augmentation, researchers have developed several input transformation techniques that can help reduce the overfitting of carefully crafted adversarial examples on surrogate models. Xie *et al.* [12] propose to adopt different input transformations such as random scaling and padding. To overcome overfitting on surrogate models, Dong *et al.* [13] shift the input images to produce diverse translated versions and estimate the global gradient through approximation. Lin *et al.* [14] update the adversarial perturbations by replacing the gradient with the average gradient of some image copies with different scales. Wang *et al.* [17] propose the Admix method, which computes gradient by mixing the target image with images from other classes.

Feature-Level Attacks. In addition to using the output layer to create adversarial examples, some works have noticed that adversarial examples created using intermediate layer features have better transferability. Zhou et al. [18] propose Transferable Adversarial Perturbations (TAP) which crafts adversarial perturbations by directly extending the distance on feature maps between original inputs and adversarial examples. Wang et al. [19] generate adversarial examples by destroying important features on the specific layer according to the feature importance, where feature importance is calculated by gradients of feature maps.

3   Methodology

3.1   Existing Attack Approaches

Firstly, we need to provide some necessary definitions of adversarial attacks. Let x represent a clean input image, y^{true} denote the corresponding true label. Let $f(x)$ be a surrogate model with the loss function $L(x, y^{true})$. The objective of the adversarial attack is to craft an adversarial example x^{adv} corresponding to the input image x that misleads the surrogate model $f(x)$ to produce incorrect predictions, i.e., $f(x^{adv}; \theta) \neq y^{true}$. To maintain consistency with previous works, the l_∞-norm is utilized to limit the discrepancy between x^{adv} and x, i.e., $\|x^{adv} - x\|_\infty \leq \epsilon$, where ϵ is the maximum value of the adversarial perturbations.

Fast Gradient Sign Method (FGSM) [8] first attempt to craft the adversarial perturbations by exploiting the gradient sign with one step:

$$x^{adv} = x + \epsilon \cdot \text{sign}\left(\nabla_x L(x, y^{true})\right) \tag{1}$$

where $\nabla_x L(x, y^{true})$ represents the gradient of loss function w.r.t. the clean input image x.

Iterative FGSM (I-FGSM) [9] modifies the FGSM with one step update into multiple steps with fixed small step size α, which is depicted as:

$$x_0^{adv} = x, \quad x_{t+1}^{adv} = \text{Clip}_x^\epsilon \left\{ x_t^{adv} + \alpha \cdot \text{sign}\left(\nabla_x L\left(x_t^{adv}, y^{true}\right)\right) \right\} \tag{2}$$

where Clip_x^ϵ aims to limit the adversarial perturbations with a clip operation.

Momentum I-FGSM (MI-FGSM) [10] is an extension of the I-FGSM, which incorporates momentum to escape from the local optima and stabilize the update direction. It can be formulated as:

$$g_{t+1} = \mu \cdot g_t + \frac{\nabla_x L\left(x_t^{adv}, y^{true}\right)}{\left\|\nabla_x L\left(x_t^{adv}, y^{true}\right)\right\|_1}$$
$$x_{t+1}^{adv} = \text{Clip}_x^\epsilon \left\{ x_t^{adv} + \alpha \cdot \text{sign}(g_{t+1}) \right\} \tag{3}$$

where $x_0^{adv} = x$ and $g_0 = 0$, μ indicates the decay factor of g_t.

Diverse Inputs Method (DIM) [12] increases the diversity by inserting random resizing and padding into input images with a fixed probability p, and utilizes the diverse inputs to obtain gradient and optimize the generation of perturbations.

Translation-invariant Method (TIM) [13] computes the gradients of a batch of random translated copies to craft more transferable adversarial perturbations. The gradients of translated images are calculated by convolving the original image's gradient with the predefined Gaussian kernel.

Scale-invariant Method (SIM) [14] finds that deep neural networks have scale invariance and similar outputs for the same image at different scales. Therefore, SIM updates the perturbations by computing the average gradient of m replicas of different scales. The updated expression is as follows:

$$\hat{g}_{t+1} = \frac{1}{m} \sum_{i=0}^{m-1} \nabla_{x_t^{adv}} L\left(x_t^{adv}/2^i, y^{true}\right)$$

$$g_{t+1} = \mu \cdot g_t + \frac{\hat{g}_{t+1}}{\|\hat{g}_{t+1}\|_1}$$

$$(4)$$

Admix [17] first generates m_1 mixed images by blending the input image with the images from other categories $(x' \in X')$. Then it applies the SIM to generate m_2 scaled copies of each mixed image. Therefore, the update formula for Admix is given as:

$$\hat{g}_{t+1} = \frac{1}{m_1 \cdot m_2} \sum_{x' \in X'} \sum_{i=0}^{m_2-1} \nabla_{x_t^{adv}} L\left(\left(x_t^{adv} + \eta \cdot (x')\right)/2^i, y^{true}\right)$$

$$g_{t+1} = \mu \cdot g_t + \frac{\hat{g}_{t+1}}{\|\hat{g}_{t+1}\|_1}$$

$$(5)$$

where η indicates the mixing ratio of the images from other categories.

3.2 Proposed Method

Lin *et al.* [14] observed that the process of creating adversarial examples shares similarities with the training of deep learning models. Utilizing input transformations to boost adversarial transferability can be considered as an extended type of data augmentation. We observe that many existing input transformations are

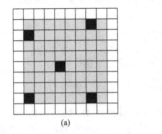
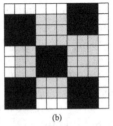

(a)   (b)

Fig. 1. Mask of DropBlock. (a) The center mask with the center points to delete. (b) The final mask M with deleted squares.

based on spatial transformation data augmentation, such as random resizing and padding. Motivated by the success of information deletion techniques in relieving the overfitting phenomenon on deep learning models, we aim to explore an information deletion approach as an input transformation attack method which can further enhance adversarial transferability.

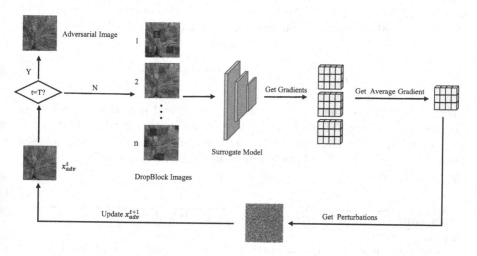

Fig. 2. Overview of DropBlock Attack (DBA).

DropBlock [20] is a regularization method commonly applied to convolutional networks. Through removing certain semantic information by masking consecutive regions of the feature maps, DropBlock can prevent the model from overfitting the training data and improve its generalization capability. Vary from the original method, we want to apply DropBlock directly on the input images rather than the feature maps to diversify the input image. Specifically, we generate different masks and apply them to the input image to create a set of DropBlock images, then compute the average gradient to update the perturbations. Utilizing the average gradient of diverse DropBlock images allows the perturbation not to overfit the surrogate model which improves its transferability. Encouraged by this analysis, we propose DropBlock Attack (DBA) to boost the adversarial transferability.

$$\gamma = \frac{(1 - prob)\,(H \times W)}{(square\_size^2)\,(H - square\_size + 1) \times (W - square\_size + 1)} \quad (6)$$

Let x be an input image with the size (C, H, W). Our goal is to generate a mask $M = (square\_size, prob)$ to delete information of the input image x. Here, $square\_size$ is the length of the deleted squares, and $prob$ is the parameter that controls the keep proportion of each channel. First, we calculate a parameter γ by

Eq. (6) to generate a center mask that follows a distribution of $Bernoulli\ (\gamma)$ with size $(C, H-square\_size+1, W-square\_size+1)$, which determines the number of the deleted squares. Then, we pad the center mask to the size of (C, H, W), and expand each center point to a square with the size of $square\_size$ to obtain the final mask M (see Fig. 1). For each channel, we generate the corresponding mask separately. Later, we apply the generated masks on the input image to craft a set of DropBlock images. Similar to previous works, we use the average gradient of those DropBlock images to optimize the perturbations, which is provided as:

$$\hat{g}_{t+1} = \frac{1}{n \cdot m} \sum_{j=0}^{n-1} \sum_{i=0}^{m-1} \nabla_{x_t^{adv}} L \left(DBA \left(x_t^{adv} \right) / 2^i, y^{true} \right) \tag{7}$$

where n denotes the number of DropBlock images and m is the corresponding number of scaled copies for each DropBlock image. Note that when $n = 0$, DBA degenerates into the traditional SIM. The overall schematic of our proposed DBA is shown in Fig. 2. Algorithm 1 summarizes the DBA being integrated with MI-FGSM.

Algorithm 1. The schematic of our proposed DBA Method.

Input:
A surrogate model f with loss function L, a clean example x with true label y^{true}, the maximum perturbations size ϵ, the number of iterations T, the momentum decay factor μ, the length of the deleted square $square\_size$, the keep proportion of each channel $prob$, the number of DropBlock images n and scaled copies m;

Output:
An adversarial example x^{adv}
1: $\alpha = \epsilon/T$; $g_0 = 0$; $\hat{g}_0 = 0$; $x_0^{adv} = x$
2: **for** $t = 0 \rightarrow T - 1$ **do**
3:     Generate a set of DropBlock images.
4:     Obtain the gradient $\hat{g}_{t+1}$ with regard to x^{adv} by Eq. (7).
5:     Calculate momentum g_{t+1}:

$$g_{t+1} = \mu \cdot g_t + \frac{\hat{g}_{t+1}}{\|\hat{g}_{t+1}\|_1}$$

6:     Update x_{t+1}^{adv}:

$$x_{t+1}^{adv} = x_t^{adv} + \alpha \cdot \text{sign}\left(g_{t+1} \right)$$

7: **end for**
8: $x^{adv} = x_T^{adv}$
9: **return** x^{adv}.

---

4 Experiment

4.1 Experimental Settings

Dataset. In terms of the selected experimental dataset, we use 1000 images provided by Wang *et al.* [17] which are randomly selected from the ILSVRC 2012 validation set [21] within different categories. We resize all the selected images to $299 \times 299 \times 3$ aiming to ensure that they can be accurately classified by the victim models.

Victim Models. For the purpose of assessing the adversarial transferability, we select seven popular models as victim models. Among them, Inception-v3 (Inc-v3) [22], Inception-v4 (Inc-v4) [23], Inception-Resnet-v2 (IncRes-v2) [23], and Resnet-v2-101 (Res-101) [24] are four unsecured models. The other three are defense ones, including Inc-v3$_{ens3}$ (ensemble of 3 Inc-v3 models), Inc-v3$_{ens4}$ (ensemble of 4 Inc-v3 models), and IncRes-v2$_{ens}$ (ensemble of 3 IncRes-v2 models) [25].

Compared Attacks. Four competitive input transformation attacks are chosen as baselines, including DIM, TIM, SIM, and Admix. In addition, we consider the integrated versions of these attacks to show the superiority of our proposed DBA method, namely SIM-DI-TI, Admix-DI-TI, and DBA-DI-TI.

Parameter. For the parameter settings of the selected comparison attacks, we adopt the settings in [17] with the maximum value of perturbations $\epsilon = 16$, the attack iterations $T = 10$, and the step size for each iteration is assigned to $\alpha = 1.6$. The decay factor μ for MI-FGSM is set to 1.0. The transformation probability p for DIM is set to 0.5. We adopt a 7×7 Gaussian kernel for TIM. The number of scaled copies m is set to 5 for SIM. We set the number of mixture images m_1 to 3 and the mixing ratio η to 0.2 for Admix. For our proposed DBA, we set the *square_size* = 50, *prob* = 0.9, $m = 5$ and $n = 20$.

4.2 Comparison of Single Input Transformation Attack

First, we test the performance of our DBA method and other input transformation attacks, including DIM, TIM, SIM, and Admix. We craft adversarial examples on four unsecured surrogate models and test the transferability on seven different victim models, respectively. The attack success rates (the error rates of the victim model on the adversarial examples) are adopted to measure the transferability. We report the results in Table 1. Rows represent surrogate models and columns represent victim models.

As revealed by the results, we can find that among the five input transformation attacks, DIM performs the worst in terms of transferability to defense models, but performs better than TIM on unsecured models. SIM and Admix have better transferability to both unsecured and defense models than DIM and

TIM, and Admix performs better than SIM. However, our DBA method significantly outperforms the existing four competitive attacks. For instance, when we adopt Inc-v3 as the surrogate model, the performance of DBA is 14.5% higher than SIM and 6.5% higher than Admix on average. Furthermore, the adversarial examples being crafted on IncRes-v2 with DBA achieve a success rate of 65.8% when attacking the Inc-v3$_{ens4}$, while SIM and Admix only have success rates of 48.3% and 56.7%, respectively.

Table 1. Success rates (%) derived by applying single input transformation attack on seven victim models. Four models are adopted to craft adversarial examples, i.e., Inc-v3, Inc-v4, IncRes-v2 and Res-101. The best performance is in bold.

Surrogate Model	Method	Inc-v3	Inc-v4	IncRes-v2	Res-101	Inc-v3$_{ens3}$	Inc-v3$_{ens4}$	IncRes-v2$_{ens}$
Inc-v3	DIM	99.0	64.3	60.9	53.2	19.9	18.3	9.3
	TIM	**100.0**	48.8	43.6	39.5	24.8	21.3	13.2
	SIM	**100.0**	69.4	67.3	62.7	32.5	30.7	17.3
	Admix	**100.0**	82.6	80.9	75.2	39.0	39.2	19.2
	DBA	**100.0**	**90.1**	**87.6**	**84.0**	**48.6**	**47.7**	**23.8**
Inc-v4	DIM	72.9	97.4	65.1	56.5	20.2	21.1	11.6
	TIM	58.6	99.6	46.5	42.3	26.2	23.4	17.2
	SIM	80.6	99.6	74.2	68.8	47.8	44.8	29.1
	Admix	87.8	99.4	83.2	78.0	55.9	50.4	33.7
	DBA	**94.9**	**100.0**	**91.2**	**88.2**	**64.8**	**59.9**	**37.6**
IncRes-v2	DIM	70.1	63.4	93.5	58.7	30.9	23.9	17.7
	TIM	62.2	55.4	97.4	50.5	32.8	27.6	23.3
	SIM	84.7	81.1	99.0	76.4	56.3	48.3	42.8
	Admix	89.9	87.5	99.1	81.9	64.2	56.7	50.0
	DBA	**95.9**	**93.0**	**99.8**	**90.2**	**71.5**	**65.8**	**54.7**
Res-101	DIM	75.8	69.5	70.0	98.0	35.7	31.6	19.9
	TIM	59.3	52.1	51.8	99.3	35.4	31.3	23.1
	SIM	75.2	68.9	69.0	99.7	43.7	38.5	26.3
	Admix	85.4	80.8	79.6	99.7	51.0	45.3	30.9
	DBA	**87.8**	**84.5**	**84.9**	**100.0**	**57.5**	**52.5**	**33.4**

4.3   Comparison of Integrated Input Transformation Attack

Previous work [14] has proved that input transformation attacks can be integrated to further boost transferability. First, we integrate DIM and TIM into DI-TI. Then we combine it with SIM, Admix, and DBA to obtain more competitive attack performance, i.e., SIM-DI-TI, Admix-DI-TI, and DBA-DI-TI. Similarly, we test the performance of these attacks on seven models, and the corresponding performance is provided in Table 2.

It can be seen that the transferability of SIM and Admix is further improved after integrating with TIM and DIM, while our DBA still outperforms integrated attack algorithms in terms of transferability. When using Inc-v4 as the

Table 2. Success rates (%) obtained by applying integrated input transformation attack on seven victim models. Four models are adopted to craft adversarial examples, i.e., Inc-v3, Inc-v4, IncRes-v2 and Res-101. The best performance is in bold.

Surrogate Model	Method	Inc-v3	Inc-v4	IncRes-v2	Res-101	Inc-v3$_{ens3}$	Inc-v3$_{ens4}$	IncRes-v2$_{ens}$
Inc-v3	SIM-DI-TI	99.1	83.6	80.8	76.7	65.2	63.3	46.5
	Admix-DI-TI	99.9	89.0	87.0	83.1	72.2	71.1	52.4
	DBA-DI-TI	**100.0**	**95.5**	**94.2**	**91.5**	**83.2**	**80.6**	**60.8**
Inc-v4	SIM-DI-TI	87.9	98.7	83.0	77.7	72.4	68.2	57.5
	Admix-DI-TI	90.4	99.0	87.3	82.0	75.3	71.9	61.6
	DBA-DI-TI	**96.7**	**99.9**	**94.5**	**91.0**	**86.3**	**83.3**	**71.5**
IncRes-v2	SIM-DI-TI	88.8	86.8	97.8	83.9	78.7	74.2	72.3
	Admix-DI-TI	90.1	89.6	97.7	85.9	82.0	78.0	76.3
	DBA-DI-TI	**96.9**	**94.7**	**99.7**	**93.9**	**89.9**	**86.2**	**84.3**
Res-101	SIM-DI-TI	84.7	82.2	84.8	99.0	75.8	73.5	63.4
	Admix-DI-TI	91.0	87.7	89.2	99.9	81.1	77.4	70.1
	DBA-DI-TI	**93.8**	**91.9**	**92.4**	**100**	**86.6**	**83.9**	**73.0**

surrogate model, the average attack success rate of DBA-DI-TI is 89.0%, while the corresponding values for SIM-DI-TI and Admix-DI-TI are 77.9% and 81.1%, respectively. When we adopt IncRes-v2 to craft adversarial examples, the performance of DBA-DI-TI is 7.9%–12.0% higher SIM-DI-TI and 5.1%–8.2% higher than Admix-DI-TI. The best performance is achieved by combining our proposed approach with other input transformation attacks.

4.4 Parameter Analysis

For fair comparison, we adopt $m = 5$ which is consistent with the settings in SIM [14]. Furthermore, we establish comprehensive ablation studies to investigate contributions of varying hyper-parameters (i.e., *square_size*, *prob*, and *n*) to the adversarial transferability of our proposed DBA method. In these ablation studies, we adopt Inc-v3 as surrogate model, while the remaining models are regarded as victim ones to be attacked.

Varying the Length of Deleted Square. We test the sensitivity of *square_size* on the adversarial transferability. We adopt the following settings of *prob* = 0.9 and *n* = 20, then gradually increase the value of *square_size*; the corresponding performance is presented in Fig. 3(a). As revealed, we find that the attack success rates increase gradually when the *square_size* is smaller than 50. When the *square_size* is larger than 50, the corresponding average attack success rates will decrease slightly. Therefore, we set *square_size* to 50 here to ensure better average performance.

Varying the Keep Proportion of Each Channel. In addition, we also tune the keep proportion of each channel to investigate its impact on the adversarial

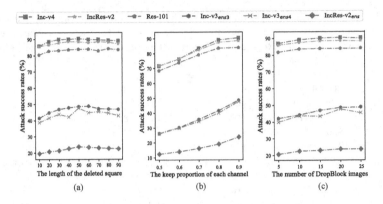

Fig. 3. Attack success rates (%) of DBA on other six victim models (a) varying the length of the deleted square *square_size*, (b) varying the keep proportion of each channel *prob*, (c) varying the number of DropBlock images *n*. The adversarial examples are crafted via Inc-v3.

example's transferability. We set *square_size* = 50 and $n = 20$, then adjust *prob* from 0.5 to 0.9. As indicated in Fig. 3(b), the attack success rates continuously keep improving as *prob* increases. The highest attack success rates are obtained when *prob* = 0.9. This indicates that the information of the original image should not be removed overmuch, as this would not be conducive to finding the correct attack direction.

Varying the Number of DropBlock Images. Furthermore, we measure the adversarial transferability by altering the number of DropBlock images. We fix *square_size* = 50 and *prob* = 0.9. As shown in Fig. 3(c), as n increases, the performance gradually increases. However, when n continues to increase, the improvement in attack success rates is limited. Furthermore, the adoption of a larger n will also incur an increase in the overall time overhead. Considering the equilibrium between complexity and transferability, we ultimately set $n = 20$.

5   Conclusion

In this work, we propose the DropBlock Attack (DBA) based on information deletion to craft adversarial examples with boosted transferability. Specially, we first create a batch of DropBlock images through deleting information on the input images by channels. The generated DropBlock images are then utilized to calculate the average gradient which guides the update process of adversarial perturbations. Later, we compare the adversarial transferability of our method with other advanced input transformation ones by conducting extensive experiments. As revealed, the adversarial transferability of our proposed method is superior to considered state-of-the-art baselines. Notably, our method can also be integrated with other input transformation attacks. We hope our method based on information deletion can provide some valuable help in investigating the security of machine learning techniques.

Acknowledgement. This work was supported by the National Key R&D Program of China (No. 2020AAA0107704), National Natural Science Foundation of China (Nos. 62073263, 61976181, 62102105, 62261136549), Guangdong Basic and Applied Basic Research Foundation (Nos. 2020A1515110997, 2022A1515011501), Technological Innovation Team of Shaanxi Province (No. 2020TD-013).

References

1. Chen, L.C., Papandreou, G., Kokkinos, I., Murphy, K., Yuille, A.L.: Deeplab: semantic image segmentation with deep convolutional nets, atrous convolution, and fully connected crfs. IEEE Trans. Pattern Anal. Mach. Intell. 40(4), 834–848 (2017)
2. He, K., Zhang, X., Ren, S., Sun, J.: Identity mappings in deep residual networks. In: Proceedings of European Conference on Computer Vision (ECCV), pp. 630–645. Amsterdam (2016)
3. Tang, K., et al.: Decision fusion networks for image classification. IEEE Trans. Neural Netw. Learn. Syst. (2022)
4. Tang, K., et al.: Rethinking perturbation directions for imperceptible adversarial attacks on point clouds. IEEE Internet of Things J. **10**(6), 5158–5169 (2022)
5. Tang, K., et al.: NormalAttack: Curvature-aware shape deformation along normals for imperceptible point cloud attack. Secur. Commun. Netw. **2022** (2022)
6. Szegedy, C., et al.: Intriguing properties of neural networks. In: International Conference on Learning Representations (ICLR). Banff (2014)
7. Guo, S., Li, X., Zhu, P., Mu, Z.: ADS-detector: an attention-based dual stream adversarial example detection method. Knowl.-Based Syst. **265**, 110388 (2023)
8. Goodfellow, I. J., Shlens J., and Szegedy, C.: Explaining and harnessing adversarial examples. In: Proceedings of International Conference on Learning Representations (ICLR). San Diego (2015)
9. Kurakin, A., Goodfellow, I., Bengio, S.: Adversarial examples in the physical world. arXiv preprint arXiv:1607.02533. (2016)
10. Dong, Y., et al.: Boosting adversarial attacks with momentum. In Proceedings of the IEEE Conference on Computer Vision and Pattern Recognition (CVPR), pp. 9185–9193. IEEE, Salt Lake City (2018)
11. Ilyas, A., Engstrom, L., Athalye, A., Lin, J.: Black-box adversarial attacks with limited queries and information. In: International Conference on Machine Learning (PMLR), pp. 2137–2146. Stockholm (2018)
12. Xie, C., et al.: Improving transferability of adversarial examples with input diversity. In: Proceedings of the IEEE Conference on Computer Vision and Pattern Recognition (CVPR), pp. 2730–2739. IEEE, Long Beach (2019)
13. Dong, Y., Pang, T., Su, H., Zhu, J.: Evading defenses to transferable adversarial examples by translation-invariant attacks. In: Proceedings of the IEEE Conference on Computer Vision and Pattern Recognition (CVPR), pp. 4312–4321. IEEE, Long Beach (2019)
14. Lin, J., Song, C., He, K., Wang, L., Hopcroft, J. E.: Nesterov accelerated gradient and scale invariance for adversarial attacks. In: International Conference on Learning Representations(ICLR). New Orleans (2019)

15. Hong, J., Tang, K., Gao, C., Wang, S., Guo, S., Zhu, P.: GM-Attack: Improving the transferability of adversarial attacks. In: Proceedings of Knowledge Science, Engineering and Management (KSEM), pp. 489–500. Springer, Singapore (2022). https://doi.org/10.1007/978-3-031-10989-8_39

16. Zhu, P., Hong, J., Li, X., Tang, K., Wang, Z.: SGMA: A novel adversarial attack approach with improved transferability. Complex Intell. Syst., pp. 1–13 (2023)

17. Wang, X., He, X., Wang, J., He Kun.: Admix: Enhancing the transferability of adversarial attacks. In: Proceedings of the IEEE International Conference on Computer Vision, pp. 16158–16167. IEEE, Montreal (2021)

18. Zhou, W., et al.: Transferable adversarial perturbations. In: Proceedings of the European Conference on Computer Vision (ECCV), pp. 452–467. Munich (2018)

19. Wang, Z., Guo, H., Zhang, Z., Liu, W., Qin, Z., Ren, K.: Feature importance-aware transferable adversarial attacks. In: Proceedings of the IEEE International Conference on Computer Vision (ICCV), pp. 7639–7648 IEEE, Montreal (2021)

20. Ghiasi, G., Lin, T.Y., Le, Q. V.: DropBlock: A regularization method for convolutional networks. In: Proceedings of the International Conference on Neural Information Processing Systems (NeurIPS), pp. 10750–10760. Red Hook (2018)

21. Russakovsky, O., et al.: Imagenet large scale visual recognition challenge. Int. J. Comput. Vision **115**(3), 211–252 (2015)

22. Szegedy, C., Vanhoucke, V., Ioffe S., Shlens J., Wojna Z.: Rethinking the inception architecture for computer vision. In: Proceedings of IEEE Conference on Computer Vision and Pattern Recognition (CVPR), pp. 2818–2826. IEEE, Las Vegas (2016)

23. Szegedy, C., Ioffe, S., Vanhoucke, V., Alemi, A. A.: Inception-v4, inception-resnet and the impact of residual connections on learning. In: Proceedings of AAAI Conference on Artificial Intelligence, pp. 4278–4284. San Francisco (2017)

24. He, K., Zhang, X., Ren, S., Sun, J.: Deep residual learning for image recognition. In: Proceedings of the IEEE Conference on Computer Vision and Pattern Recognition (CVPR), pp. 770–778. IEEE, Las Vegas (2016)

25. Tramèr, F., Kurakin, A., Papernot, N., Goodfellow, I., Boneh, D., McDaniel, P.: Ensemble adversarial training: Attacks and defenses. In: International Conference on Learning Representations (ICLR). Vancouver (2018)

A Graph Partitioning Algorithm Based on Graph Structure and Label Propagation for Citation Network Prediction

Weiting Xi[1,2], Hui He[1], Junyu Gu[2,3], Jue Wang[2,3(✉)] (ID), Tiechui Yao[2,3] (ID), and Zhiqiang Liang[2]

[1] North China Electric Power University, Beijing, China
[2] Computer Network Information Center, Chinese Academy of Sciences, Beijing, China
wangjue@sccas.cn
[3] University of Chinese Academy of Sciences, Beijing, China

Abstract. With the development of deep learning and artificial intelligence technologies, Graph Neural Network (GNN) has become a popular research topic in recent years. As the scale of graph data continues to increase, training massive graph data with GNN is still challenging. Distributed GNN training has become an ideal solution. However, most real-world large-scale graph data exhibit power-law distribution characteristics. Existing graph partitioning algorithms are unable to partition graphs with computation load balancing for distributed GNN training yet. This paper proposes a graph partitioning algorithm based on multi-level partitioning that considers the degree information of the graph structure, label propagation, and migration. We verified the applicability of the proposed algorithm using citation network datasets. The experimental results demonstrate that the algorithm improves the load balancing level of subgraph partitioning. Furthermore, we verified in distributed GNN training that the algorithm has a better effect on graph partitioning than that of traditional graph partitioning algorithms. Compared to non-distributed GNN training, distributed GNN training based on the graph partitioning algorithm presented in this paper can achieve better acceleration while maintaining prediction accuracy.

Keywords: Graph partition · Citation network · Distributed graph neural network · Multi-level partition · Label propagation

1 Introduction

Graph is a fundamental structure in computer science that represents many relationships in the real world. In recent years, with the rapid development of big data, such as citation networks, social networks, and biochemical networks, have increased in size. However, processing and computing large-scale graphs still requires a lot of storage and computing resources. And most of these

© The Author(s), under exclusive license to Springer Nature Switzerland AG 2023
Z. Jin et al. (Eds.): KSEM 2023, LNAI 14118, pp. 289–300, 2023.
https://doi.org/10.1007/978-3-031-40286-9_24

datasets cannot be executed on a single computer. One of the approaches to solve this problem is to partition [11] the large graph into multiple balanced parts, and ensure less communication between subgraphs while preserving the graph's structural information as much as possible.

Training with a distributed graph neural network (GNN) first requires solving the graph partitioning problem, which is an NP-hard problem. Currently, there are mainly two mainstream graph partitioning methods: Vertex-cut [7] and Edge-cut [2], as shown in Fig. 1. The Kernighan-Lin (KL) [4] algorithm is a heuristic-based graph partitioning algorithm. Karypis proposed a multi-level graph partitioning framework Metis [3]. Common multi-level graph partitioning methods include Metis and Scotch [9] . And the partitioning method of these multilevel graph partitioning algorithms is vertex-cut. These commonly used graph partitioning algorithms work well for structured graphs like circuit diagrams and grid maps, but their effectiveness is not ideal for real-world graphs with power-law distribution characteristics, such as social networks and citation networks. Therefore, a graph partitioning algorithm that is effective for power-law distributed graphs in the real world is worth exploring.

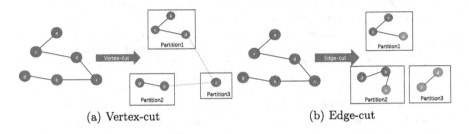

(a) Vertex-cut   (b) Edge-cut

Fig. 1. Two strategies of graph partitioning

This paper takes the citation network datasets as an example. The citation network has the characteristic of power-law distribution, which makes common graph partition algorithms do not have good load balancing effects on citation network datasets. Therefore, the commonly used graph partitioning algorithms do not perform well on citation network datasets, and the load balancing of subgraphs can also become a bottleneck for distributed GNN training.

To address the aforementioned issues, this paper proposes a graph partitioning algorithm framework that includes Metis graph partitioning, the degree multi-level graph partition (DMP) algorithm that considers graph information, and the label propagation and migration-based DMP graph partitioning (DMP-LP) algorithm for power-law citation network datasets to accelerate distributed GNN training.

Our contributions are summarized as follows:

1. We propose a GNN training framework that embeds several commonly used graph partitioning algorithm, such as the Metis multi-level graph partitioning algorithm, and proposed algorithms which include the DMP algorithm that

considers graph information, and the DMP-LP algorithm which incorporates label propagation and migration. The results of the graph partitioning algorithm are applied to distributed GNN training.

2. We propose a multi-level graph partitioning algorithm based on label propagation and migration that considers graph structure for citation network datasets with power-law distribution characteristics. This algorithm combines the degree information with the Metis multi-level graph partitioning algorithm and uses label propagation to adjust the subgraphs after label migration to improve the load balancing level of the partitioned subgraphs.

3. We conducted distributed GNN training on the citation network datasets based on the graph partitioning algorithm proposed in this paper. The experiments show that, compared with non-distributed training, the algorithm mentioned in the paper has a better acceleration effect on training time while maintaining prediction accuracy as much as possible. This work provides a useful guideline for training large-scale graph data on GNN.

2 Related Work

An ideal partitioning algorithm [18] can effectively improve the performance of distributed graph processing which should follow two principles: 1) to make the partitioning computation load as balanced as possible; 2) to minimize communication between partitioned subgraphs.

The Kernighan-Lin (KL) algorithm is a heuristic-based graph partition algorithm [4]. It assumes that the graph nodes have equal weights, which firstly performs bipartite partition and multiple iterations to re-partition. When the size of the graph data is large, the bipartitioning process requires a lot of resources and time. So it is not suitable for larger scale graphs. Multi-level graph partitioning first coarsens the graph to a much smaller size before partitioning, which saves a lot of time compared to directly partitioning the large graph. The flowchart of multi-level graph partitioning algorithm is shown in Fig. 2 which involve three steps: coarsening, initial partitioning, and refinement. This algorithm makes the large graph size acceptable by coarsening steps, and then partitions the coarsened graph into multiple sub-graphs through the initial partition. Afterwards, the sub-graph information is restored through refinement steps. However, the coarsened sub-graph cannot contain all the graph information, and the partitioned sub-graphs may have a large difference in edge numbers due to the degrees of different vertices are different. Especially for some graph data exhibiting power-law distribution characteristics like social networks and citation networks.

The label propagation algorithm (LPA) [16] is a semi-supervised learning algorithm widely used for community detection on large-scale graphs with approximately linear time complexity of $O(k*E)$. LPA assigns a unique label to each node on the graph and randomly selects a starting node for propagation with the process is shown in Fig. 2. All nodes change their label information based on their neighbors' when the algorithm traverses the entire graph. Through multiple iterations, LPA considers that each label should be the same as that

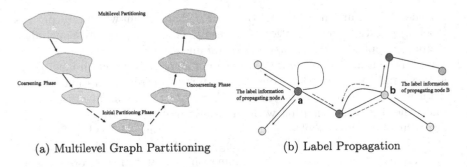

(a) Multilevel Graph Partitioning   (b) Label Propagation

Fig. 2. Graph partitioning algorithms

of its majority neighbors. Ugander et al. [14] inspired by LPA and proposed the label propagation algorithm based on community mining to solve the problem of graph partitioning. Rahimain [12] designed JA-BE-JA algorithm which spread label information with neighbors and randomly exchanged labels with other vertices to prevent local optima.

Currently, there are many studies on distributed GNN , and many distributed systems have embedded some graph partitioning algorithms. For example, Md V et al. proposed the DistGNN training framework and embedded the Libra graph partitioning algorithm [8], but in the actual partitioning process, the high vertex replication ratio of the Libra partitioned subgraph results in a large amount of communication between subgraphs during distributed GNN training, which affects the training time and effectiveness. Zheng D et al. proposed its parallel version DistDGL based on the existing GNN training library DGL and embedded the Metis graph partitioning algorithm on this basis [19]. However, due to the poor performance of Metis partitioning for power-law distribution graph data, DistDGL is not ideal for training on large-scale power-law graphs such as Facebook social networks and ogbn-papers 100 m.

3   GNN Training Framework for Citation Network

3.1   GNN Training Framework

We proposes a GNN training framework that incorporates several kinds of graph partitioning algorithms. These algorithms include the commonly used multilevel graph partitioning algorithm metis algorithm, the DMP algorithm which considers the degree information of the graph structure on this basis, and the DMP-LP algorithm which incorporates label propagation and migration. The specific introduction of these algorithms is shown in Sect. 3.2. For the citation network datasets, the proposed GNN training framework first employs the graph partitioning algorithm to partition the datasets into subgraphs before conducting distributed GNN training on these partitioned subgraphs. The diagram depicting the structure of the specific GNN training framework can be found in Fig. 3.

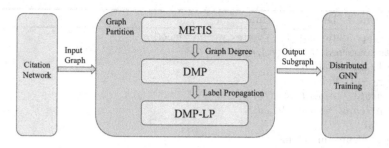

Fig. 3. Distributed GNN training framework

3.2 Graph Partition Algorithm for Citation Network

The citation network datasets processed in this paper mostly has the characteristics of power-law distribution. The nodes with a large degree of power-law distribution account for a small proportion, while the nodes with a small degree account for the vast majority. This is reflected in the citation network datasets, where some well-known papers are cited by most other relevant papers, so the degree of the paper is high, while some other papers are not discovered or cited by other papers, so the degree is small. When using Metis for initial partitioning, the load balance will not be effective due to the large difference in vertex degree. The algorithm proposed in this paper first adds the vertex degree as a weight indicator into the process of Metis multilevel graph partitioning, so that Metis can consider the degree information of vertices during the partitioning process. This algorithm is referred to as DMP algorithm in this paper.

Based on the DMP algorithm, this paper proposes a DMP-LP algorithm which incorporates label propagation and migration. And it consists of three stages: label propagation stage, subgraph label identification stage, and label migration stage. The DMP-LP algorithm first performs label propagation on the citation network, and at the end of the LPA, a certain number of partitions are formed, which have the following two characteristics: 1) inconsistent size, 2) all vertices within a partition have the same label. Given these characteristics of the partitions, we can assume that vertices with the same label have a closer Euclidean distance, which means that papers represented by vertices with the same label in the citation network are more likely to belong to the same category of papers and have closer citation relationships. The algorithm in this paper moves subgraphs based on vertices with the same label, improving the balance of points and edges between subgraphs, which can reflect load balancing effect of partitioning subgraphs.

The DMP algorithm is based on the Metis multi-level graph partitioning algorithm, which views vertex degree as vertex weight. The algorithm consists of three stages: coarsening, initial partitioning, and refinement. Let the citation network graph data be denoted as $G = (V, E)$ and the initial number of vertices in the graph be denoted as v_0. The DMP algorithm is shown in algorithm 1. Lines 1 to 5 are the initialization of the algorithm 1. in algorithm 1, vertex degree

Algorithm 1. DMP algorithm

---

input: graph_data= $G(v_0, e_0)$,vertex_weight=$vwgt[]$
output: coarsen_data=$G_m(v_m, e_m)$
1: step1 : initialization
2: **for** $v_0 \rightarrow G(V, E)$ **do**
3:     $vwgt[v_0] \leftarrow getdegree(v_0)$
4:     $match[v_0] \leftarrow unmatched$
5: **end for**
6: step2 : Coarse matching
7: **for** $v_0 \rightarrow G(V, E)$ **do**
8:     **if** $match[v_0] == unmatched$ **then**
9:         **for** $v_1 \rightarrow getadj[v_0]$ **do**
10:             **if** $match[v_1] == unmatched$ **then**
11:                 **if** $vwgt[v_0] + vwgt[v_1] <= maxvwgt[0]$ **then**
12:                     $macthed(v_0, v_1)$
13:                     $match[v_0] \leftarrow matched$
14:                     $match[v_1] \leftarrow matched$
15:                 **end if**
16:             **end if**
17:         **end for**
18:     **end if**
19: **end for**

---

information is obtained during the initialization phase and used for the next step. Lines 6 to 19 are the coarsening phase, in the coarsening stage, algorithm 1 uses the method of random matching. After m iterations, the number of vertices and edges in the graph data are denoted as v_m, e_m, respectively. Algorithm 1 adds degree information in the coarsening stage to improve the partitioning effect of power law distribution graphs. We only introduce algorithm 1 in the coarsening stage where we have modified in the DMP algorithm.

Based on the partitioning of the DMP algorithm, we consider using the idea of label propagation and migration to further improve the partitioning effect which is called DMP-LP algorithm. The DMP-LP algorithm is shown in algorithm 2. Lines 1 to 4 initialize the graph labels, and Lines 5 to 11 propagate the labels of the vertices in the graph. Algorithm 2 iterates multiple times until each vertex label returns its maximum label of first-order neighbors, and then stops iterating to obtain the label information of each vertex. The time complexity of algorithm 2 is O(k*E), where k represents the number of iterations, and E is the number of edges in the graph. Lines 12 to 22 determine which labels will be moved between the partitioned subgraphs and use labels as the basic unit for inter-subgraph migration to further improve the load balancing effect of the partitioned subgraphs.

Algorithm 2. DMP-LP algorithm

---

input: graph_data=$G(v_0, e_0)$, sub_graph=$G_i(v_i, e_i)$,$i \in (1, k)$, part=k
output: after_sub_graph=$G_i'(v_i', e_i')$, $i \in (1, k)$
 1: step1 : label propagation
 2: **for** $v_0 \to G(V, E)$ **do**
 3:     $label[v_0] = v_0$
 4: **end for**
 5: **for** $v_0 \to G(V, E)$ **do**
 6:     **if** $label[v_0] == max\_adj\_label(v_0)$ **then**
 7:         *continue*
 8:     **else**
 9:         $label[v_0] \leftarrow max\_adj\_label(v_0)$
10:     **end if**
11: **end for**
12: step2 : label Reading and Migration
13: $avg\_edge = \sum_{i=1}^{k} e_i/k$
14: **for** $i \to k$ **do**
15:     $get\_label\_number(G(v_i, e_i))$
16:     **if** $e_i > avg\_edge$ **then**
17:         $imgratelabel \leftarrow label$
18:         $e_i = e_i - get\_label\_number[]$
19:     **else**
20:         $G(v_i, e_i) \leftarrow imgratelabel$
21:     **end if**
22: **end for**

---

4 Experiments

4.1 Datasets

The citation network datasets used in this experiment are Cora, CiteSeer, and PubMed [13]. The Cora dataset contains 2708 papers, and there are 5429 edges representing citation relationships between papers. The dimensions of features are 1433. The CiteSeer dataset divides commonly used papers into six categories and contains 3312 vertices and 4723 edges. The feature dimension of Citeseer is 3703. The PubMed dataset includes 19717 scientific publications about diabetes from the PubMed database which have 44338 edges and 500 features. The features of these datasets include title, keywords, abstract, and cited references, etc. of the papers.

4.2 Evaluation Indicators

Several evaluation metrics are proposed in this paper to evaluate the partitioning effectiveness,1) Vertex Ratio, 2) Edge Ratio. Vertex Ratio refers to the multiple ratio between the maximum and minimum vertices of a subgraph obtained by partitioning using the graph partitioning algorithm. Edge Ratio refers to the multiple ratio between the edges of the maximum and minimum vertices of a subgraph obtained by partitioning using the graph partitioning algorithm. The larger the Vertex Ratio or Edge Ratio, the greater the difference in the number of vertices or edges between the partitioned subgraphs. The smaller these two indicators, the more balanced the load is considered to be for the graph partitioning algorithm.

$$VertexRatio = \frac{Max\_Subgraph\_G(v_i)}{Min\_Subgraph\_G(v_i)} \tag{1}$$

$$EdgeRatio = \frac{Max\_Subgraph\_G(e_i)}{Min\_Subgraph\_G(e_i)} \tag{2}$$

4.3   Experimental Setting

In the experiments, the datasets are first partitioned. By comparing the point and edge balance indicators of the initial Metis multi-level partitioning algorithm, the DMP algorithm, and DMP-LP algorithm, the load balancing effects of various partitioning algorithms are compared. Subsequently, the partitioned subgraphs are trained using distributed GNNs in a distributed cluster environment. By verifying the accuracy of paper prediction classification of each partitioned subgraph under distributed training, the possibility of the proposed algorithm for distributed training of large-scale graph data is validated. The numerical calculations in this study are carried out on the ORISE Supercomputer. The ORISE Supercomputer has thousands of nodes, and each computing node of the supercomputing system is equipped with 4 accelerator cards(DCU) to support computation and training.

4.4   Results and Analysis

Graph Partition. For different datasets, we use graph partitioning algorithms to partition different partitions for distributed GNN training. As can be seen, Table 1 shows the partitioning of the three graph partitioning algorithms on citation network datasets. With regard to Metis partitioning, Metis initial partitioning is a graph partitioning method based on point partitioning, which has good point balance on each citation network dataset. For example, the Vertex Ratio of the Metis graph partitioning algorithm in the cora dataset for 2 partitions is 1.001 and for the Citeseer dataset for 2 partitions, it is 1.006. The number of sub-graph vertices partitioned by the Metis partitioning algorithm can be approximately considered equal, but the degree of edge balance of each sub-graph is not ideal. Regarding the partitioning of the DMP algorithm, it can be seen that this algorithm improves the load balance of edges well, while the load balance of vertices increases slightly but still within an acceptable range. This is because graph partitioning is an NP-hard problem, and if one wants to ensure that both vertices and edges have a degree of load, it is necessary to duplicate nodes or increase or decrease the edge cut information, which will inevitably increase the communication between subgraphs and affect the subsequent process of distributed GNN training. Regarding DMP-LP algorithm, it can be seen that this algorithm has better edge balance compared to Metis partitioning and a certain degree of improvement in vertex balance and edge balance compared to DMP algorithm.

Distributed GNN Training. We compare against the same baseline methods as in GCN [5], label propagation (LP) [20], semi-supervised embedding (SemiEmb) [15], manifold regularization (ManiReg) [1] and skip-gram based graph embeddings (DeepWalk) [10]. And we conducted a control experiment by running non-distributed gcn training on our own machine.

Table 1. Result of the graph partitioning algorithm on the citation network

Dataset	Graph Partitioning Algorithm	Part	Vertex Ratio	Edge Ratio
Cora	Metis	2	1.001	1.205
		4	1	1.495
	DMP	2	1.178	1.011
		4	1.421	1.055
	DMP-LP	2	**1.129**	**1.008**
		4	**1.272**	**1.037**
Citeseer	Metis	2	1.006	1.306
		4	1.012	2.144
	DMP	2	1.285	1.003
		4	1.678	1.119
	DMP-LP	2	**1.005**	**1.074**
		4	**1.322**	**1.096**
Pubmed	Metis	2	1.001	1.169
		4	1.001	1.825
		8	1.002	2.052
	DMP	2	1.183	1.001
		4	1.673	1.042
		8	2.115	1.235
	DMP-LP	2	**1.142**	**1.001**
		4	**1.375**	**1.011**
		8	**1.786**	**1.031**

Table 2 presents partial experimental results of the baseline and our method on citation network data in this paper. The values represent the classification accuracy of each method on the citation network data's paper nodes. It can be seen that compared with traditional methods, GCN has a better performance on node classification accuracy. Therefore, we compares with GCN method. Based on the graph partitioning algorithm proposed in this paper, the distributed GNN training shows good performance on various citation network datasets.

Table 2. Summary of results in terms of classification accuracy (%)

Method	Citeseer	Cora	Pubmed
ManiReg [1]	60.1	59.5	70.7
SemiEmb [15]	59.6	59.0	71.1
LP [20]	45.3	68.0	63.0
DeepWalk [10]	43.2	67.2	65.3
ICA [6]	69.1	75.1	73.9
Planetoid [17]	64.7	75.7	77.2
GCN [5]	67.9	80.1	78.9
GCN(DCU)	62.1	75.4	74.8
Distributed GCN(Metis)	64.76	76.3	78.48
Distributed GCN(DMP-LP)	**66.56**	**77.15**	**79.6**

Compared with the prediction accuracy reported in the GCN paper, For example, take the Pubmed dataset, our algorithm's prediction accuracy is 79.6%, while the accuracy reported in the GCN paper is 78.9%, and the training accuracy is only 0.7% higher than that of the GCN paper. Compared with running non-distributed GCN on our machine, it can be seen that under the same distributed GNN training parameters, for example, takethe Cora dataset, the node prediction accuracy under our algorithm is 77.15%, while the accuracy of non-distributed GCN is 75.4%, and the training accuracy increases by 1.75%.

Table 3 shows the comparison of training time among the graph partitioning algorithms on distributed GCN used in this paper and the training time of non-distributed GCN. Taking the cora dataset with 2 partitions as an example, the training time using non-distributed GCN on our machine is 9.643 ms, and the training time using DMP-LP graph partitioning algorithm for distributed training is 8.368 ms. The improvement compared to the non-distributed GCN is about 11.62%. It can be seen that the training time in the GCN paper differs greatly from the time spent running non-distributed GCN on our machine, which is due to we use the sparse matrix multiplication to aggregate node features on distributed GCN. For citation network datasets, training time does not vary significantly between more partitions and fewer partitions. This is because the datasets size is relatively small, and communication occupies a larger proportion than graph partitioning in distributed GCN training. As the data size increases, the number of nodes trained in the distributed training will have a greater impact on the acceleration of the distributed GCN training.

By comparing and analyzing the prediction accuracy and training time of the citation network datasets, apparently, using the proposed algorithm for distributed GNN training has a good acceleration effect while maintaining node prediction accuracy as much as possible. Moreover, as the data scale increases, the acceleration effect becomes more significant. This provides the possibility of using the proposed graph partitioning algorithm for distributed training of large-scale graph data. By comparing the subgraphs using the initial partitioning of

Table 3. Comparsion of training time among different algorithms(ms)

Dataset	Part	GCN(DCU)	Metis	DMP-LP
Cora	2	9.643	8.441	8.297
Cora	4	9.643	9.145	8.368
Citeseer	2	10.503	8.462	8.348
Citeseer	4	10.503	8.162	7.927
Pubmed	2	28.198	19.217	19.317
Pubmed	4	28.198	19.008	17.792
Pubmed	8	28.198	17.661	18.121

Metis and the subgraphs using DMP-LP algorithm for distributed GCN training, it is clear that compared to the initial partitioning of Metis, our algorithm improves the node prediction accuracy by 1.8% for Cora, 0.85% for Citeseer, and 1.12% for Pubmed, respectively. This indicates that our proposed algorithm has better partitioning results for distributed training.

5 Conclusions

In this paper, we first added vertex degree information as a partitioning metric based on the Metis multilevel graph partitioning algorithm, proposed the DMP algorithm. And we incorporated the idea of label propagation and migration to propose the DMP-LP algorithm. The experiments have shown that the DMP-LP algorithm has better load balancing. Based on the partitioning, we conducted distributed GCN training and demonstrated that compared to non-distributed GCN, our proposed method has better acceleration while ensuring node prediction accuracy to a certain extent. We also proved that compared to the initial partitioning of Metis, our algorithm has better node prediction accuracy for distributed GCN, which further confirms the better partitioning effect of our proposed algorithm.

Acknowledgement. This work was supported by National Key R&D Program of China (No. 2021ZD0110403). We would like to thank the MindSpore team for their support.

References

1. Belkin, M., Niyogi, P., Sindhwani, V.: Manifold regularization: a geometric framework for learning from labeled and unlabeled examples. J. Mach. Learn. Res. 7(11) (2006)
2. Gonzalez, J.E., Low, Y., Gu, H., Bickson, D., Guestrin, C.: Powergraph: distributed graph-parallel computation on natural graphs. In: Presented as Part of the 10th Symposium on Operating Systems Design and Implementation, no. 12, pp. 17–30 (2012)

3. Karypis, G.: Metis: unstructured graph partitioning and sparse matrix ordering system. Technical report (1997)
4. Kernighan, B.W., Lin, S.: An efficient heuristic procedure for partitioning graphs. Bell Syst. Tech. J. **49**(2), 291–307 (1970)
5. Kipf, T.N., Welling, M.: Semi-supervised classification with graph convolutional networks. arXiv preprint arXiv:1609.02907 (2016)
6. Lu, Q., Getoor, L.: Link-based text classification. Grobelnik et al. [62]
7. Malewicz, G., et al.: Pregel: a system for large-scale graph processing. In: Proceedings of the 2010 ACM SIGMOD International Conference on Management of Data, pp. 135–146 (2010)
8. Md, V., et al.: Distgnn: scalable distributed training for large-scale graph neural networks. In: Proceedings of the International Conference for High Performance Computing, Networking, Storage and Analysis, pp. 1–14 (2021)
9. Cois Pellegrini, F., Roman, J.: Scotch: a software package for static mapping by dual recursive bipartitioning of process and architecture graphs? (1996)
10. Perozzi, B., Al-Rfou, R., Skiena, S.: Deepwalk: online learning of social representations. In: Proceedings of the 20th ACM SIGKDD International Conference on Knowledge Discovery and Data Mining, pp. 701–710 (2014)
11. Priyadarshi, A., Kochut, K.J.: Partkg2vec: embedding of partitioned knowledge graphs. In: Proceedings of the Knowledge Science, Engineering and Management: 15th International Conference, KSEM 2022, Singapore, 6–8 August 2022, Part II, pp. 359–370. Springer, Cham (2022). https://doi.org/10.1007/978-3-031-10986-7_29
12. Rahimian, F., Payberah, A.H., Girdzijauskas, S., Jelasity, M., Haridi, S.: Ja-be-ja: a distributed algorithm for balanced graph partitioning. In: 2013 IEEE 7th International Conference on Self-Adaptive and Self-Organizing Systems, pp. 51–60. IEEE (2013)
13. Sen, P., Namata, G., Bilgic, M., Getoor, L., Galligher, B., Eliassi-Rad, T.: Collective classification in network data. AI Magazine **29**(3), 93–93 (2008)
14. Ugander, J., Backstrom, L.: Balanced label propagation for partitioning massive graphs. In: Proceedings of the Sixth ACM International Conference on Web Search and Data Mining, pp. 507–516 (2013)
15. Weston, J., Ratle, F., Collobert, R.: Deep learning via semi-supervised embedding. In: Proceedings of the 25th International Conference on Machine Learning, pp. 1168–1175 (2008)
16. Xiaojin, Z., Zoubin, G.: Learning from labeled and unlabeled data with label propagation. In: Tech. Rep., Technical Report CMU-CALD-02-107. Carnegie Mellon University (2002)
17. Yang, Z., Cohen, W., Salakhudinov, R.: Revisiting semi-supervised learning with graph embeddings. In: International Conference on Machine Learning, pp. 40–48. PMLR (2016)
18. Zhang, J.: A new k-multiple-means clustering method. In: Proceedings of the 15th International Conference on Knowledge Science, Engineering and Management (KSEM 2022), Singapore, 6–8 August 2022, Part II, pp. 621–632. Springer, Cham (2022). https://doi.org/10.1007/978-3-031-10986-7_50
19. Zheng, D., et al.: Distdgl: distributed graph neural network training for billion-scale graphs. In: 2020 IEEE/ACM 10th Workshop on Irregular Applications: Architectures and Algorithms (IA3), pp. 36–44. IEEE (2020)
20. Zhu, X., Ghahramani, Z., Lafferty, J.D.: Semi-supervised learning using gaussian fields and harmonic functions. In: Proceedings of the 20th International Conference on Machine learning (ICML-03), pp. 912–919 (2003)

Hybrid Heterogeneous Graph Neural Networks for Fund Performance Prediction

Siyuan Hao[1], Le Dai[1], Le Zhang[2(✉)], Shengming Zhang[3], Chao Wang[4],
Chuan Qin[5], and Hui Xiong[6(✉)]

[1] University of Science and Technology of China, Hefei, China
{hao794249121,dl123}@mail.ustc.edu.cn
[2] Business Intelligence Lab, Baidu Research, Beijing, China
zhangle0202@gmail.com
[3] Rutgers University, New Jersey, USA
shengming.zhang@rutgers.edu
[4] Guangzhou HKUST Fok Ying Tung Research Institute, The Hong Kong University
of Science and Technology (Guangzhou), Guangzhou, China
[5] PBC School of Finance, Tsinghua University, Beijing, China
[6] The Hong Kong University of Science and Technology (Guangzhou),
Guangzhou, China
xionghui@ust.hk

Abstract. Fund performance prediction aims to evaluate the performance of financial funds. It is of great interest to financial investors to achieve high returns while maintaining sustainable fund development. Existing studies primarily focus on analyzing the performance of individual fund managers using empirical analysis based on statistics, with limited attention given to leveraging social connections between managers and the latent characteristics of the fund learned from various financial market information for fund performance appraisal. In this paper, we propose to develop Hybrid Heterogeneous Graph Neural Networks for Fund Performance Prediction with Market Awareness. Specifically, we aim to build a heterogeneous fund information network to measure the social relationships between fund managers and the influence of funds on the investment relationship of stocks. Given the challenges of heterogeneous graph neural networks in dealing with relationship fusion of different types, we have designed a hybrid approach that combines heterogeneous graph embedding and tensor factorization to fuse two different sources of information over the heterogeneous fund information network. Furthermore, we incorporate a market-aware scheme, which combines static fund representation with dynamic market trends, to capture the dynamic factors of the market and enhance the accuracy of fund performance prediction. We conduct extensive experiments on real fund market datasets to confirm the effectiveness of our proposed framework, and the investment simulation shows that our approach can achieve higher returns compared to the baselines.

Keywords: Fund Performance Prediction · Graph Representation Learning · Hybrid Heterogeneous Graph · Tensor Factorization

© The Author(s), under exclusive license to Springer Nature Switzerland AG 2023
Z. Jin et al. (Eds.): KSEM 2023, LNAI 14118, pp. 301–317, 2023.
https://doi.org/10.1007/978-3-031-40286-9_25

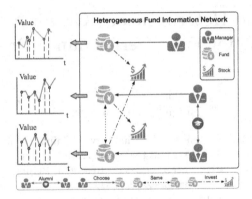

Fig. 1. An example of Heterogeneous Fund Information Network. Social connection between managers represented in the network is important for fund performance.

1   Introduction

In finance, while the stock market traditionally receives the most attention, mutual funds have emerged as a dynamic and significant pricing institution due to the increasing diversification of trading methods on the financial network. Accurate prediction of fund performance not only helps investors achieve high returns but also promotes the healthy development of the fund trading market. Many studies rely on traditional statistical methods and consider explicit information characteristics of the fund itself to predict performance. Prior research has primarily focused on a single fund manager's impact on the funds they manage, as the manager is responsible for the portfolio and overall operations [1–3]. However, alumni relationships serve as an important means for fund managers to close the gap between them, leading to a convergence of investment decisions among managers, creating a positive feedback loop, amplifying market fluctuations, and ultimately impacting the performance of the fund. As illustrated in Fig. 1, for example, the managers, who share alumni connections, invest in the same funds, and these funds exhibit similar trends. But the investment direction of the fund, managed by a manager without any alumni relationship, is noticeably different from the other two.

So, we are eager to construct the Heterogeneous Fund Information Network, which encompasses all the information, as illustrated in Fig. 1. Although Heterogeneous Graph Neural Network (HGNN) seems promising for our task, we encountered two key challenges when trying to apply existing HGNN directly. Firstly, in our heterogeneous fund information network, there are quantitative relationships that traditional HGNN may not effectively capture. Secondly, previous studies on heterogeneous graphs have mainly focused on binary relationships, such as indicating whether two funds belong to the same class, while our network has more complex relationships. These challenges require us to consider factors such as data type, value range, semantics, etc., to better capture the relative significance of knowledge from two distant sources [4–6]. In the field of fund trading, the type of market can have different effects on various funds. However, existing Hybrid

Heterogeneous Graph Neural Networks (HGNN) may not accurately capture the dynamic characteristics of the market, which is critical for precise fund performance prediction. To address these challenges, we propose a Hybrid Heterogeneous Graph Neural Network for Fund Performance Prediction with Market Awareness (MFP). Our model fuses two different sources of information in the Heterogeneous Fund Information Network using a hybrid approach that combines Heterogeneous Graph Embedding and Tensor Factorization. We also incorporate a market-aware scheme to simulate the dynamic factors of the fund market. We evaluate our model on four real datasets corresponding to different market categories and our MFP framework outperforms existing fund prediction models on various evaluation metrics, confirming its superiority. Moreover, our investment simulation results show that our model consistently achieves higher returns compared to the baselines over a long-term period. We also conduct additional analysis to investigate the effects of different components in our framework and perform case studies to explain the impact of fund market factors on fund trends.

In summary, the contributions of our work include:

- We propose a novel framework called MFP to address the issue of fund performance prediction. In comparison to traditional fund prediction setups, our framework incorporates the social relationships between fund managers and the semi-annual fund portfolio. Specifically focusing on their impact on the fund trend.
- To address the limitations of HGNN and extract internal representations of funds, we have developed a Heterogeneous Graph Embedding Module and a Tensor Factorization Module based on the social graph of fund managers and the management-investment three-dimensional tensor, which are derived from the heterogeneous fund information network we have constructed. Additionally, we have introduced a Fund-Market Fusion Module to simulate dynamic fund market trends by combining static fund representations with fund macro features and dynamic features. This integrated approach enables us to achieve fund performance prediction by leveraging both macro and dynamic features of funds.
- We performed comprehensive experiments on fund portfolio datasets collected from semi-annual reports of mutual funds across various financial markets. The results and analysis confirm the validity and rationality of our framework, and shed light on the factors that influence the fund market.

2   Related Work

2.1   Fund Investment

The construction of a fund performance prediction framework often focuses on the fund itself, fund managers, and fund companies, aiming to depict the characteristic indicators of the influence mechanism on fund performance. The goal is to facilitate adjustments to fund performance and ultimately achieve the purpose of prediction [1]. First, we begin by describing the characteristic indicators of the fund from its own dimension, which includes the fund's net capital flow, fund size, fund turnover rate, and other relevant factors [7]. What's more, from the perspective of the fund manager, their professional experience is also a crucial factor in assessing their effectiveness on one hand [8]. On the other hand, fund managers may alter their investment choices based on informal gatherings, such as dinners, and receive sound advice from alumni, executives, and friends. Additionally, there are studies that examine the relationship between venture capital networks and investment performance from a network perspective [8]. For forecasting fund performance models, it is generally a two-stage or three-stage DEA network, or TM model and HM model [1]. This form of research has certain limitations in predicting fund performance, it may not fully account for the social relationships among fund managers and their individual abilities. Furthermore, it often only considers the explicit characteristics of the fund, neglecting the impact of both the fund market and the fund's inherent attributes.

2.2 Heterogeneous Graph Embedding

Heterogeneous graphs consist of diverse types of entities and relationships. The goal of heterogeneous graph embedding is to learn representations in a low-dimensional space [9]. Given the diverse information present in the nodes and edges of a heterogeneous graph, there are various embedding methods used for heterogeneous graphs. Some methods, based on link relationships, aim to capture the heterogeneity of the graph by closely modeling the relationships between nodes, some researchers utilize the meta-path method to conduct random walks on a heterogeneous graph, generating sequences of heterogeneous nodes with rich semantics [10, 11, 32]. While the heterogeneity of a heterogeneous graph allows it to effectively represent the relationships between different categories, there are still numerous challenges in heterogeneous graph embedding. For instance, efficiently and effectively preserving these complex structures in heterogeneous graph embedding poses a significant challenge. Currently, only a few studies have explored meta-path structure [10] in this context. In a heterogeneous graph, the attributes of different nodes and edges carry different meanings, posing a challenge in effectively integrating the attributes of neighbors during heterogeneous graph embedding [9].

2.3 Tensor Factorization

Tensor factorization can be regarded as a generalization of matrix factorization in general. Without losing its generality, we can understand that it is similar to matrix factorization for matrices with more than two dimensions. There exist many tensor factorization methods, for example, CANDECOMP/PARAFAC decomposition [12] factorizes a tensor into a sum of component rank-one tensors, and Tucker decomposition [13, 29] is a form of higher-order PCA, decomposing a tensor into a core tensor multiplied (or transformed) by a matrix along each mode. In addition, tensor factorization arises in many machine learning applications, such as knowledge base modeling [14, 30], and learning graphical models [15, 31]. In our model, we design a tensor factorization module to extract the internal representations of the fund.

3   Problem Definition

The heterogeneous fund information network can be defined as graph $G = (\mathcal{V}, \mathcal{E})$, where $\mathcal{V}$ denotes an object set and $\mathcal{E}$ denotes a link set, and is also associated with a node type mapping function $\phi : \mathcal{V} \to \mathcal{A}$ and a link type mapping function $\psi : \mathcal{E} \to \mathcal{R}$. $\mathcal{A}$ and $\mathcal{R}$ denote the sets of predefined object types and link types, where $|\mathcal{A}| + |\mathcal{R}| > 2$. χ_t^d means the relevant dynamic feature of the fund on the day t (such as the daily accumulated net value and net unit value of the fund). $r_t^m, m \in \{m_g, m_h\}$ means the dynamic change of the fund market to which different funds belong. Our target is to predict fund performance r_{t+1}:

$$[G, \chi_t^d, r_t^m] \xrightarrow{f} r_{t+1}. \tag{1}$$

where r_{t+1} is the daily fluctuation of the fund, which is determined by comparing the latest trading price (or closing price) of the current trading day with the closing price of the previous trading day, typically expressed as a percentage.

4   Framework

Figure 2 shows the illustration of our framework. The blue, orange and green nodes in the heterogeneous fund information network represent managers, funds and stocks. The constructed heterogeneous fund information network G is divided into two parts: the manager social subgraph G_{sub} and the investment management tensor $\mathbf{T}$. After Heterogeneous Graph Embedding and Tensor Factorization respectively, the fund internal representation $\mathbf{e}_f$ is obtained by fusion. In the fund-market integration module, the static $\mathbf{e}_f$ is used to simulate the dynamic trend of the market and is integrated with it to obtain the fund macro feature χ^f. Finally, χ^f is combined with the provided fund dynamic feature χ^d to complete the fund performance prediction.

4.1   Heterogeneous Graph Embedding

Fund managers play a crucial role in determining the performance of a fund. Additionally, the social relationships among fund managers can also impact their own fund portfolio strategies, leading to potential convergence or alignment effects [27]. In order to underscore the effect of fund managers' contacts in person on the investment pool, we extract a Manager Social Subgraph denoted as G_{sub} from the heterogeneous fund information network, only constructed by the "Alumni" relationship between the managers, the "Choose" relationship between the managers and the "Same" relationship between the funds. We draw inspiration from previous research methods [5] to design the Fund-Information Encoder and Manager-Fund Attention mechanisms in order to obtain the representation of the fund denoted as $\mathbf{e}_g$. Specifically, in the Fund-Information Encoder, we transform the original features of fund nodes and fund manager nodes denoted as h_j, where h_j represents the original feature of fund j, using a feature transformation matrix denoted as $\mathbf{M}_{f_j}$. This projection allows us to map the features of

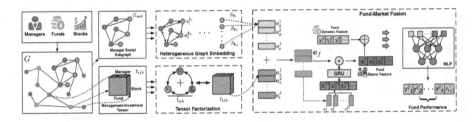

Fig. 2. MFP model architecture.

different types of funds or fund managers into a unified feature space, resulting in the updated fund feature denoted as h'_j, that is: $h'_j = \mathbf{M}_{f_j} \cdot h_j$. To capture the weight or importance of different funds and fund managers, we employ a self-attention mechanism [17], which allows us to encode the information of fund nodes. Through a softmax operation, we obtain the weight coefficients that represent the significance of each fund's feature. This enables us to dynamically assign different weights to different funds and fund managers based on their respective contributions, facilitating effective information encoding.

$$q^{\Phi}_{ij} = \text{ReLU}\left(a^T_{\Phi} \cdot \text{Concat}\left(h'_i, h'_j\right)\right), \quad \alpha^{\Phi}_{ij} = \text{softmax}_j\left(q^{\Phi}_{ij}\right) = \frac{exp\left(q^{\Phi}_{ij}\right)}{\sum exp\left(q^{\Phi}_{ij}\right)}. \quad (2)$$

where Φ [16] means the meta-path between fund pair (i, j), a^T_{Φ} and ReLU denotes the fund-information encoder vector and the activation function, respectively.

Furthermore, prior to obtaining the meta-path based embedding of fund node j, we apply multi-head attention [5] to selectively attend to information from different representation subspaces at various locations. This is achieved through:

$$\mathbf{e}^{\Phi}_j = \text{Concat}\left(\sum_{j \in \mathcal{N}^{\Phi}_j} \alpha^{\Phi^1}_{ij} \cdot h'_j, \cdots, \sum_{j \in \mathcal{N}^{\Phi}_j} \alpha^{\Phi^{K_t}}_{ij} \cdot h'_j\right). \quad (3)$$

where K_t is the times we repeat the fund-information encoder, and $\mathcal{N}^{\Phi}_j$ is the set of nodes which connect with node j via meta-path Φ, and the node's neighbors includes itself.

As the manager social subgraph G_{sub} comprises various types of nodes, including funds and fund managers, as well as different types of edges such as "Alumni", "Same" and "Choose" as mentioned previously, we have designed the Manager-Fund Attention mechanism to integrate the embeddings of different types of connections. Specifically, we obtain the weights β_{Φ_j} associated with different meta-paths Φ_j through the following process:

$$\omega_{\Phi_p} = \frac{1}{|\mathcal{V}|} \sum_{j \in \mathcal{V}} \mathbf{d}^T \cdot \tanh\left(\mathbf{W} \cdot \mathbf{e}^{\Phi_p}_j + \mathbf{b}\right), \quad \beta_{\Phi_j} = \frac{exp\left(\omega_{\Phi_p}\right)}{\sum_{p=1}^{P} exp\left(\omega_{\Phi_p}\right)}. \quad (4)$$

where ω_{Φ_p} is calculated by Eq. 4, in which $\mathbf{d}$ is our module vector, $\mathbf{W}$ is the weight matrix, $\mathbf{b}$ is the bias vector and $\Phi_p \in \{\Phi_1, \Phi_2, \cdots, \Phi_P\}$. Finally, we attain the fund j embedding with the learned weights as coefficients as follows:

$$\mathbf{e}_g^j = \sum_{p=1}^{P} \beta_{\Phi_p} \cdot \mathbf{e}_{\Phi_p}. \tag{5}$$

4.2   Tensor Factorization Module

Previous studies utilize matrix factorization methods to extract intrinsic representations of funds from fund portfolios [18]. However, it is important to note that during the same time period, multiple fund managers may choose the same fund, and there is not always a one-to-one correspondence between fund managers and funds. In fact, the composition of a fund portfolio is determined by various factors, including the personal ability of the fund manager, the type and attributes of the fund, and the stocks in the portfolio. Therefore, we also construct a three-dimensional tensor, the management-investment tensor $\mathbf{T} \in \mathbb{R}^{I \times J \times K}$ from the heterogeneous fund information network, in which I, J, K respectively indicates the set of fund managers, funds and stocks in the fund portfolio, Each $t_{ijk} \in \mathbf{T}$ represents the proportion of the stock k in the fund j held by the fund manager i if the fund manager holds the fund; If he does not hold then t_{ijk} is assigned the value 0. Taking into consideration the sparsity of our tensor and the high computational complexity of existing methods, we follow the previous approaches [19], decompose the Management-Investment Tensor into three latent vectors: $\mathbf{U}$, $\mathbf{V}$, and $\mathbf{Z}$. These vectors respectively represent the fund managers' preferences, the intrinsic characteristics of the funds, and the internal properties of the stocks. For each element $\hat{t}_{ijk}$ in the estimated tensor $\hat{\mathbf{T}}$ of the Management-Investment Tensor $\mathbf{T}$, we compute it as follows:

$$\hat{t}_{ijk} = \mathbf{U}_i^T \mathbf{V}_j + \mathbf{U}_i^T \mathbf{Z}_k + \mathbf{V}_j^T \mathbf{Z}_k, \tag{6}$$

where $\mathbf{U}_i$, $\mathbf{V}_j$ and $\mathbf{Z}_k$ denote the latent vector of fund manager i, fund j and stock k and $\mathbf{U}_i^T \mathbf{V}_j$, $\mathbf{U}_i^T \mathbf{Z}_k$ and $\mathbf{V}_j^T \mathbf{Z}_k$ is corresponding to the latent interaction between the fund manager and fund, the fund manager and stock, the fund and stock, respectively. To quantify the disparity between the ground truth and the prediction of each element in the management-investment tensor, we utilize the Mean Square Error (MSE) as our evaluation metric. The loss incurred in learning the investment representation of funds through Tensor Factorization can be expressed as:

$$\mathcal{L}_T = \sum_{(i,j,k)} \left\| t_{ijk} - \hat{t}_{ijk} \right\|^2 = \sum_{(i,j,k)} \left\| t_{ijk} - \left(\mathbf{U}_i^T \mathbf{V}_j + \mathbf{U}_i^T \mathbf{Z}_k + \mathbf{V}_j^T \mathbf{Z}_k \right) \right\|^2. \tag{7}$$

Through the gradient descent algorithm, we can solve and obtain the fund investment representation vector $\mathbf{e}_t = \mathbf{V}$.

4.3   Fund-Market Fusion

Considering the variations in fund attributes and in order to mitigate algorithmic complexity, we proceed with the Embedding Fusion as the next step: $\mathbf{e}_f = \mathbf{e}_g + \mathbf{e}_t$, so that we can get the fund internal representation $\mathbf{e}_f$. Directly linking the internal representation of the fund, denoted as $\mathbf{e}_f$, with the dynamic features of the fund, denoted as χ^d, may not be sufficiently convincing as a method to evaluate fund performance. This approach could potentially overlook the impact of macro factors on the funds. However, directly incorporating dynamic changes in the fund market may appear to disrupt the linkage between macro factors (i.e., fund market) and micro variables (i.e., fund internal representation). Influenced by previous research [18], we propose a novel approach to provide a more accurate description of the fund market. We redefine the fund market feature as the average of the top-K_f funds from different fund types that exhibit the closest correlation with the changes in their respective fund markets, with K_f being defined as the market simulation factor. To elaborate further, let $j = 1, 2, ..., N_g$ denote the different fund classes, e_f^j and r_t^j represent the corresponding fund representation and fund performance on day t, respectively. r_t^m signifies the market movement of the specific type of fund on the day t. Based on this, the fund market feature χ_t^m can be expressed as follows:

$$d_j = |r_t^j - r_t^m| \quad (j = 1, \cdots, N_g), \chi_t^m = \frac{1}{K_f} \sum_{j=1}^{K_f} \mathbf{e}_f^j \quad \left(d_1 < \cdots < d_{K_f} < \cdots \right),$$
(8)

where d_j means the degree of similarity between the performance of a single fund j and the fund market movement r_t^m on the day t.

Furthermore, taking into account the time lag associated with market impact, we utilize the Gated Recurrent Unit (GRU) [21] to incorporate the fund market factors from multiple past trading days. GRU is a model capable of capturing long-term dependencies in the fund market trend χ^m. The calculation formula is as follows:

$$\hat{\chi}_t^m = \text{GRU}\left(\chi_1^m, \chi_2^m, \cdots, \chi_j^m \right) \ (j < t).$$
(9)

where $\hat{\chi}_t^m$ is the predicted value of χ^m at the day t, which stands for the predicted fund market factor. Finally, we fuse the obtained fund market factor $\hat{\chi}_t^m$ with the internal representation of the fund $\mathbf{e}_f$, so as to obtain the macro feature of the fund χ_t^f, the calculation method is: $\chi_t^f = \hat{\chi}_t^m \cdot \mathbf{e}_f^T$, where $\mathbf{e}_f^T$ means the fund internal representation's transpose.

4.4   Fund Performance Prediction

To achieve a more comprehensive prediction of fund performance, we incorporate the fund dynamic feature χ_t^d. Subsequently, for different categories of funds, we combine the fund dynamic feature χ_t^d with the corresponding macro feature of the fund, denoted as χ_t^f, to predict the fund performance:

$$\hat{r}_{t+1} = \text{MLP}\left(\text{Concat}\left[\chi_t^f, \chi_t^d\right]\right), \tag{10}$$

where $\hat{r}_{t+1}$ denotes the predicted fund performance at the day $t+1$. So the loss function of the prediction can be written as:

$$\mathcal{L}_R = \|\hat{r}_{t+1} - r_{t+1}\|^2, \tag{11}$$

r_t means the ground-truth fund performance at the day $t+1$. By incorporating the loss function $\mathcal{L}_T$, which was designed in Sect. 4.2, with L_2 regularization, we obtain the ultimate loss function for the model:

$$\mathcal{L} = \mathcal{L}_R + \lambda_T \mathcal{L}_T + \lambda_\Theta \|\Theta\|^2. \tag{12}$$

where λ_T and λ_Θ are the different regularization parameters and Θ represents all of the parameters in our framework. As for the final loss $\mathcal{L}$ we leverage the stochastic gradient descent (Adam) algorithm to optimize our MFP framework.

5   Experiments

In this section, we implement our market-aware hybrid heterogeneous graph neural network for predicting fund performance through a series of comprehensive experiments. Our objective is to address the following research questions using the experimental results: **RQ1:** How effective is our model compared with the existing mainstream financial market forecasting model? **RQ2:** Can our model get a higher return on investment in the investment simulation on the real dataset? **RQ3:** How does each component of our framework contribute to the prediction task? **RQ4:** How do different market simulation factors affect the model performance? **RQ5:** How to prove the validity of our model from the perspective of fund managers?

Table 1. Statistics of the datasets.

Bull Market				Bear Market			
Time	Managers	Funds	Stocks	Time	Managers	Funds	Stocks
2018-06-30	654	1405	4918	2021-06-30	865	1946	5334
2018-12-31	658	1295	5138	2021-12-31	927	2215	5824

5.1   Data Collection and Preprocessing

We gather comprehensive resume information of fund managers in the financial trading market and to provide a more comprehensive analysis of the bull and bear markets in the financial market and various funds, our collected fund portfolio data and market mainly encompasses two types of funds: Shares Fund and Hybrid Fund, along with their respective semi-annual reports for 2018 and 2021. The selection of these specific years is based on verifiable economic facts and statements. Notably, the official inclusion of China A-shares in the MSCI (Morgan Stanley Capital International) Index serves as evidence of 2018 being a bull market, while we identify 2021 as a minor bear market due to the epidemic's impact. For each market segment, we utilize the daily change in the total net asset value of the fund market as an indicator of the fund market trend. Moreover, we also collect additional initial features of the fund, such as fund establishment years and fund establishment scale, as supplementary data. The length of our dynamic time series data is determined based on the effective trading days over a six-month period, which amounts to 120 days. Table 1 presents details regarding our manager social graph, including the number of fund managers, funds, and stocks, after applying filters to the semi-annual mutual fund portfolio reports.

5.2   Experimental Setting

Evaluation Metrics. In order to better show the error effect of our model on fund performance prediction, we use three standard evaluation metrics related to regression problems, which are **Mean Absolute Error (MAE)**, **Root Mean Squared Error (RMSE)** and **Median Absolute Error (MedAE)**. Among them, MAE means the mean value of absolute error between labels and predictions; RMSE means the root of the median of squared error between labels and predictions, and MedAE is the median of absolute error between labels and predictions. Lower values of these three evaluation metrics indicate better performance. All experiments were repeated five times and the results were averaged.

Baseline Methods. Due to the limited previous research on fund performance prediction, we here mainly adopt the methods commonly used in stock prediction tasks and the latest method of combining graph and time series as baselines. The details of these baselines are as follows:

- **ARIMA** [22]: ARIMA uses historical time series information to predict the future trend, and this model has been used to predict stock prices in the early years.
- **LSTM** [23]: This model is a widely used neural network in the scenarios of many time series prediction problems.
- **Transformer** [17]: This model is the first sequence transduction model based entirely on attention, replacing the recurrent layers most commonly used in encoder-decoder architectures with multi-headed self-attention.
- **IMTR** [18]: IMTR is a model that uses the algorithm of matrix factorization to obtain the static representation of stocks, and here we use its method to obtain the internal representation of funds.
- **Multi-GCGRU** [28] A model comprises graph convolutional network (GCN) and gated recurrent unit (GRU) to predict stock movement.

- **LSTM-RGCN** [24]: LSTM-RGCN uses the graph convolution model to simulate the transmission of information in the network structure on heterogeneous graph networks and to predict the overnight movement in stock market.
- **HG-GNN** [25]: The core idea of this model is to transform heterogeneous graph into homogeneous graph to obtain the fund representation, which can better capture the interaction between different objects for downstream prediction.
- **Ahead** [26]: Ahead is a spatiotemporal model, which designs an attentive heterogeneous graph embedding to obtain representations of nodes, and further leverages them to enhance the performance of the time series prediction task.

Hyper-Parameters Setup. In the fund-information encoder section, the long attention K_t to be 4, the module vector $\mathbf{d}$ to be 64, and the dropout of attention to be 0.6 in the manager-fund attention module. The embedding dimension between the heterogeneous graph embedding module and tensor factorization has been set to 16 for consistency. Building upon previous research on fund prediction, we have chosen to set the value of K_f to 15, as it best captures the dynamics of the fund market. In the optimization phase, we have set the parameter λ_T to 5×10^{-2} and λ_Θ to 10^{-2}, with a learning rate of 10^{-2} and a mini-batch size of 128. The training epoch is set at 30.

5.3 Models' Performance Comparison (RQ1)

We conduct experiments using the models mentioned in the previous section, along with our own model, on various datasets that represent diverse fund market conditions, as discussed in Sect. 5.1. Table 2 presents the performance results of various models based on different evaluation metrics. It is evident that our proposed model, MFP, consistently achieves lower performance results compared to other baseline models across different evaluation indicators. Notably, among the compared time series prediction models, ARIMA performs the poorest, followed by LSTM, Transformer. The overall performance of graph neural network-based

Table 2. The experimental results of different models in different stock markets on fund performance prediction.

Model	2018-06-30			2018-12-31			2021-06-30			2021-12-31		
	MAE	RMSE	MedAE	MAE	RMSE	MedAE	MAE	RMSE	MedAE	MAE	RMSE	MedAE
ARIMA [22]	0.1696	0.2174	0.1087	0.1595	0.2216	0.1258	0.1420	0.1911	0.1143	0.1439	0.1930	0.1146
LSTM [23]	0.1611	0.2090	0.0964	0.1581	0.2179	0.1052	0.1380	0.1905	0.1025	0.1389	0.1907	0.1067
Transformer [17]	0.1551	0.2138	0.0878	0.1487	0.2176	0.0823	0.1258	0.1928	0.0844	0.1317	0.2052	0.0836
IMTR [18]	0.0920	0.1061	0.0881	0.0873	0.1098	0.0629	0.0975	0.1213	0.0715	0.1100	0.1355	0.0822
Multi-GCGRU [28]	0.0881	0.0987	0.0656	0.0795	0.0953	0.0692	0.0893	0.0877	0.0635	0.0998	0.1232	0.0555
LSTM-RGCN [24]	0.0821	0.0900	0.0576	0.0881	0.1094	0.0555	0.0799	0.0716	0.0688	0.0971	0.1186	0.0507
HG-GNN [25]	0.0978	0.0892	0.0357	0.0800	0.1014	**0.0307**	0.0943	0.0777	0.0790	0.0957	0.1445	0.0531
Ahead [26]	0.0827	0.0880	0.0385	0.0872	0.1069	0.0352	0.0868	0.0862	0.0522	0.0815	0.1156	0.0568
MFP	**0.0793**	**0.0660**	**0.0233**	**0.0538**	**0.0711**	0.0391	**0.0604**	**0.0670**	**0.0503**	**0.0621**	**0.0803**	**0.0475**

models, such as Multi-GCGRU, LSTM-RGCN, HG-GNN, and Ahead, is superior to that of time series models that solely rely on the dynamic features of the fund itself. Among them, Ahead demonstrates the best overall performance, with HG-GNN showing better performance in terms of MedAE. Multi-GCGRU performs the poorest among the four, highlighting the advantage of our model over HGNN in heterogeneous graph representation. The performance of IMTR, which employs matrix factorization, is better than that of a simple time series model, but falls short of the model that incorporates heterogeneous graph neural network. In general, our model MFP, which combines the method of heterogeneous graph neural network with tensor factorization, exhibits the most favorable performance compared to other models.

5.4 Fund Investment Simulation (RQ2)

We employ various models to evaluate the relevant data of funds across different markets, in order to further validate the effectiveness of our framework. Prior to this, we standardize the investment simulation process. Following the principle set at the outset of the investment simulation, our simulations are conducted on a daily basis. Based on the predictions generated by different models, we invest in the top-K funds and hold these funds for a one-day period. Disregarding transaction fees, the entire profit from the previous day is reinvested in the next day's investment. Figure 3 illustrates the simulated investment forecast results of our model, as well as other models, across various stock market conditions, with K set to 20 in this case. Our model MFP demonstrates superior

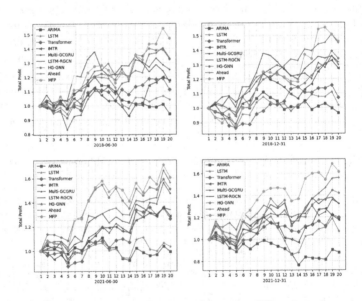

Fig. 3. The total return curve of different models under different stock market quotation ($K = 20$).

Table 3. The experimental results of different model parts.

Model	2018-06-30			2018-12-31			2021-06-30			2021-12-31		
	MAE	RMSE	MedAE	MAE	RMSE	MedAE	MAE	RMSE	MedAE	MAE	RMSE	MedAE
MFP-HGE	0.0817	0.0702	0.0260	0.0572	0.0723	0.0403	0.0618	0.0730	0.0543	0.0686	0.0855	0.0446
MFP-HGE$_{sub}$	0.0924	0.0821	0.0285	0.0585	0.0789	0.0421	0.0653	0.0779	0.0652	0.0696	0.0871	0.0422
MFP-FC	0.0849	0.0725	0.0276	0.0598	0.0744	0.0418	0.0694	0.0803	0.0642	0.0651	0.0857	0.0431
MFP-TF	**0.0727**	**0.0648**	0.0252	0.0597	0.0760	0.0396	0.0676	0.0735	**0.0454**	0.0674	0.0821	**0.0400**
MFP	0.0793	0.0660	**0.0233**	**0.0538**	**0.0711**	**0.0391**	**0.0604**	**0.0670**	0.0503	**0.0621**	**0.0803**	0.0475

performance in terms of long-term return on investment, outperforming other models in both favorable stock market conditions (bull market) and challenging stock market conditions (bear market), as evidenced by consistently achieving the highest returns on three different datasets. Similar to the findings in Sect. 5.1, the model employing heterogeneous graph neural networks also outperforms the time series models in simulated investment, with Ahead exhibiting the best performance among the graph neural networks, further highlighting the advantages of attention mechanisms. On the other hand, traditional time series models like ARIMA and LSTM show comparatively poorer performance.

5.5 Ablation Study (RQ3)

In order to verify the effect of "Hybrid" in our model, we directly adopt the heterogeneous graph embedding method to obtain fund representation (MFP-HGE) for the originally constructed heterogeneous fund information network as one case of the ablation study. Three other cases are as follows: By excluding the fund market part of the model, which means that a direct concatenate between fund representations and fund dynamic features (MFP-FC) mentioned in Sect. 4.3; Only the heterogeneous graph embedding module is used for the manager social subgraph (MFP-HGE$_{sub}$) and only the tensor factorization part of the model (MFP-TF).

Table 3 shows the results of the ablation experiment. Obviously, the effect of using the whole graph (MFP-HGE) is stronger than the effect of the subgraph (MFP-HGE$_{sub}$), but it is not as good as our model (MFP). The effect of directly connecting the fund dynamic features and the fund internal representations (MFP-FC) is not satisfactory. In different financial market environments, the evaluation index is almost the worst. On the other hand, compared with MFP-TF and MFP-HGE, the effect of MFP-TF is better than MFP-HGE, which further illustrates the importance and correctness of our combination of HGNN and tensor factorization instead of simply constructing the heterogeneous fund information network.

5.6 Fund Market Factor Analysis (RQ4)

In the fund-market fusion module of our model, we determine the trend of the fund market by selecting the average representative of the top K_f funds whose

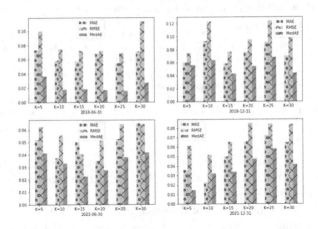

Fig. 4. The effect of our model MFP under different K_f values.

daily returns and types are most similar to the market trend. To comprehensively evaluate the model's performance with different values of K_f, we conduct experiments to assess its effectiveness. Specifically, we set the market simulation factor K_f within the range of $\{5, 10, 15, 20, 25, 30\}$.

Figure 4 illustrates the model's performance under different K_f values.

The results indicate that when K_f is set to 15, the model performs optimally in terms of the three evaluation metrics on the first dataset, and maintains a consistently low level of performance on other datasets as well. Moreover, models with values of K_f closer to 15 outperform those with larger or smaller values. Notably, for high values of K_f, such as 30, the overall model performance is relatively poorer across all four datasets. These findings support our previous selection of K_f in the comparative experiments.

5.7   Case Study (RQ5)

Previous research has demonstrated that fund managers with alumni connections often exhibit similar behavior in selecting funds, which can result in a "herding effect". To confirm this, we incorporate the alumni relationship of managers when constructing the heterogeneous fund information network and the manager social subgraph. We employ the t-distributed Stochastic Neighbor Embedding (t-SNE) algorithm to reduce the dimensionality of the embedded representations which extracted from the embedded representations of fund managers from four selected schools using the trained model. The results visualized in Fig. 5 is evident that the embedded representations of fund managers with alumni ties are clustered, while there is a clear distinction among the embedded representations of managers from different schools. This finding further corroborates the influence of alumni relations on managers' fund selection.

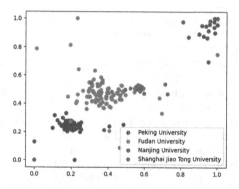

Fig. 5. Experimental results of t-SNE for manager embedding with different alumni relationships.

6 Conclusion

In this paper, we propose a market-aware hybrid heterogeneous graph neural network for fund performance prediction, MFP, whose main idea is to solve the challenges of HGNN and mine the dynamic characteristics of the fund market to achieve the correct prediction and prediction of the fund performance. In our research, we have divided a heterogeneous fund information network into two distinct components, namely the manager social graph and the management-investment tensor. Our proposed framework takes into consideration the social relationships between fund managers and the fund portfolio, and incorporates two specialized modules designed to extract and analyze the fund embeddings and fund investment representations. Furthermore, a fund-market fusion module combines static fund representations with dynamic market features, culminating in the task of predicting fund performance. Experimental results obtained from various real-world fund market data showcase the effectiveness of our proposed framework. Additionally, investment simulation results indicate that our MFP framework outperforms other approaches, yielding higher investment returns.

Acknowledgements. This work was supported by the Foshan HKUST Projects (FSUST21-FYTRI01A, FSUST21-FYTRI02A).

References

1. Galagedera, D., Roshdi, I., Fukuyama, H., Zhu, J.: A new network DEA model for mutual fund performance appraisal: an application to US equity mutual funds. Omega **77**, 168–179 (2018)
2. Middleton, K.L.W.: Becoming entrepreneurial: gaining legitimacy in the nascent phase. Int. J. Entrep. Behav. Res. (2013)
3. Qian, G., Wu, Y., Xu, M.: Multiple change-points detection by empirical Bayesian information criteria and Gibbs sampling induced stochastic search. Appl. Math. Model. **72**, 202–216 (2019)

4. Schlichtkrull, M., Kipf, T., Bloem, P., Berg, R., Titov, I., Welling, M.: Modeling relational data with graph convolutional networks. In: European Semantic Web Conference, pp. 593–607 (2018)
5. Wang, X., et al.: Heterogeneous graph attention network. In: The World Wide Web Conference, pp. 2022–2032 (2019)
6. Yun, S., Jeong, M., Kim, R., Kang, J., Kim, H.: Graph transformer networks. Adv. Neural Inf. Process. Syst. **32** (2019)
7. Elton, E., Gruber, M., Blake, C.: Fundamental economic variables, expected returns, and bond fund performance. J. Financ. **50**, 1229–1256 (1995)
8. Hochberg, Y., Ljungqvist, A., Lu, Y.: Whom you know matters: venture capital networks and investment performance. J. Financ. **62**, 251–301 (2007)
9. Wang, X., Bo, D., Shi, C., Fan, S., Ye, Y., Philip, S.: A survey on heterogeneous graph embedding: methods, techniques, applications and sources. IEEE Trans. Big Data (2022)
10. Dong, Y., Chawla, N., Swami, A.: metapath2vec: scalable representation learning for heterogeneous networks. In: Proceedings of the 23rd ACM SIGKDD International Conference on Knowledge Discovery and Data Mining, pp. 135–144 (2017)
11. Hussein, R., Yang, D., Cudré-Mauroux, P.: Are meta-paths necessary? Revisiting heterogeneous graph embeddings. In: Proceedings of the 27th ACM International Conference on Information and Knowledge Management, pp. 437–446 (2018)
12. Kiers, H.: Towards a standardized notation and terminology in multiway analysis. J. Chemomet. J. Chemomet. Soc. **14**, 105–122 (2000)
13. Kolda, T., Bader, B.: Tensor decompositions and applications. SIAM Rev. **51**, 455–500 (2009)
14. Nickel, M., Tresp, V., Kriegel, H.: A three-way model for collective learning on multi-relational data. ICML (2011)
15. Halpern, Y., Sontag, D.: Unsupervised learning of noisy-or Bayesian networks. In: Proceedings of the Twenty-Ninth Conference on Uncertainty in Artificial Intelligence, pp. 272–281 (2013)
16. Sun, Y., Han, J.: Mining heterogeneous information networks: principles and methodologies. Synth. Lect. Data Mining Knowl. Discov. **3**, 1–159 (2012)
17. Vaswani, A., et al.: Attention is all you need. Adv. Neural Inf. Process. Syst. **30** (2017)
18. Chen, C., Zhao, L., Bian, J., Xing, C., Liu, T.: Investment behaviors can tell what inside: exploring stock intrinsic properties for stock trend prediction. In: Proceedings of the 25th ACM SIGKDD International Conference on Knowledge Discovery and Data Mining, pp. 2376–2384 (2019)
19. Liu, Q., Wu, H., Ye, Y., Zhao, H., Liu, C., Du, D.: Patent litigation prediction: a convolutional tensor factorization approach. In: IJCAI, pp. 5052–5059 (2018)
20. Deng, Y., Bao, F., Kong, Y., Ren, Z., Dai, Q.: Deep direct reinforcement learning for financial signal representation and trading. IEEE Trans. Neural Netw. Learn. Syst. **28**, 653–664 (2016)
21. Cho, K., et al.: Learning phrase representations using RNN encoder-decoder for statistical machine translation. In: EMNLP (2014)
22. Brown, R.: Smoothing, Forecasting and Prediction of Discrete Time Series. Courier Corporation (2004)
23. Nelson, D., Pereira, A., De Oliveira, R.: Stock market's price movement prediction with LSTM neural networks. In: 2017 International Joint Conference On Neural Networks (IJCNN), pp. 1419–1426 (2017)

24. Li, W., Bao, R., Harimoto, K., Chen, D., Xu, J., Su, Q.: Modeling the stock relation with graph network for overnight stock movement prediction. IJCAI **20**, 4541–4547 (2020)
25. Pang, Y., et al.: Heterogeneous global graph neural networks for personalized session-based recommendation. In: Proceedings of the Fifteenth ACM International Conference on Web Search and Data Mining, pp. 775–783 (2022)
26. Zhang, L., et al.: Attentive heterogeneous graph embedding for job mobility prediction. In: Proceedings of the 27th ACM SIGKDD Conference on Knowledge Discovery and Data Mining, pp. 2192–2201 (2021)
27. Lin, J., Wang, F., Wei, L.: Alumni social networks and hedge fund performance: evidence from China. Int. Rev. Financ. Anal. **78**, 101931 (2021)
28. Ye, J., Zhao, J., Ye, K., Xu, C.: Multi-graph convolutional network for relationship-driven stock movement prediction. In: 2020 25th International Conference on Pattern Recognition (ICPR), pp. 6702–6709 (2021)
29. Wang, C., et al.: Personalized and explainable employee training course recommendations: a Bayesian variational approach. ACM Trans. Inf. Syst. **40**, 1–32 (2021)
30. Wang, C., Zhu, H., Zhu, C., Qin, C., Xiong, H.: SetRank: a setwise Bayesian approach for collaborative ranking from implicit feedback. In: AAAI, pp. 6127–6136 (2020)
31. Qin, C., et al.: Duerquiz: a personalized question recommender system for intelligent job interview. In: Proceedings of the 25th ACM SIGKDD International Conference on Knowledge Discovery and Data Mining, pp. 2165–2173 (2019)
32. Qin, C., et al.: An enhanced neural network approach to person-job fit in talent recruitment. ACM Trans. Inf. Syst. **38**, 1–33 (2020)

WGCN: A Novel Wavelet Graph Neural Network for Metro Ridership Prediction

Junjie Tang, Junhao Zhang, Juncheng Jin, and Zehui Qu$^{(\boxtimes)}$

College of Computer and Information Science, Southwest University,
Chongqing, China
{swu645867768,superblack,arieldong522}@email.swu.edu.cn,
quzehui@swu.edu.cn

Abstract. Metro ridership prediction is a significant and difficult task in intelligent urban transportation systems due to the unique traffic pattern of each station, the implicit transfer of ridership, and the sparse connectivity of the metro network. Existing methods mostly use auxiliary information for modeling, which increases the difficulty of data collection and the complexity of the model. Given the power of the wavelet transform in capturing complex information, we incorporate wavelet analysis into deep learning networks and propose a gated learnable wavelet filter module, it can fully excavate the spatio-temporal correlations without the graph. Meanwhile, a flow-aware K-order graph convolution network is designed to mine the connections of stations in topology by mixing weights and a K-order adjacency matrix. Based on these two modules, we propose a novel wavelet graph neural network: WGCN, which stacks them to capture spatio-temporal correlations from multiple scales. A large number of experiments on two real-world datasets demonstrate the superiority of the proposed model, which outperforms the state-of-the-art models on multiple metrics.

Keywords: Ridership prediction · Graph convolution network · Wavelet neural network · Spatial-temporal data · Deep learning

1 Introduce

Metro plays a pivotal role in modern cities. With the development of smart cities, many researchers have turned their attention to intelligent rail transit. Improving the effectiveness and quality of metro ridership prediction can better provide a reference for metro scheduling [7], managing dense passenger flow as well as providing more convenient travel plans for passengers [13,15].

Metro ridership prediction is a spatio-temporal forecasting task. For each station, its signal is temporal data, but for the whole rail transit system, the stations constitute an undirected graph, so it contains spatial information too. Several methods have been proposed for accurately forecasting metro ridership, early researchers used machine learning models such as ARIMA [16] to forecast ridership, but these models usually model individual stations and ignore

© The Author(s), under exclusive license to Springer Nature Switzerland AG 2023
Z. Jin et al. (Eds.): KSEM 2023, LNAI 14118, pp. 318–330, 2023.
https://doi.org/10.1007/978-3-031-40286-9_26

the connections between stations. Not long after that, CNN-based and RNN-based models [18,26] are proposed to capture the spatio-temporal correlations. Nevertheless, these methods do not make full use of the graph structure and RNN-based models have a high computational time. Recently GNN-based models have become the SOTA model for solving this problem. Due to the sparsity of the metro network, GNN-based models do not work well on physical graphs only and usually need additional data such as OD matrix [2], DO matrix, and physical distance [20] to build auxiliary graphs to help modeling, which undoubtedly increases the difficulty of data acquisition and the complexity of the model.

To solve these problems, we apply wavelet transform to deep learning and propose a wavelet neural network: Wavelet Graph Convolution Network (WGCN). Wavelet transform is a powerful feature extraction tool, it decomposes the original signal to obtain approximation coefficients and detail coefficients. The approximation coefficients capture the overall trends of the signal, while the detail coefficients capture local variations or fine-grained information. Wavelet transform has been widely used in the past for sequence analysis. However, there has been limited exploration into combining this powerful technique with deep learning models to enhance spatio-temporal prediction. In WGCN, we design a gated learnable wavelet filter module to capture spatio-temporal correlations, it utilizes two learnable wavelet filters to capture global information from the temporal dimension and the spatial dimension respectively, and later fuse them by a gated unit. Meanwhile, considering the dynamic connections and sparse topology of the graph, we design a flow-aware K-order GCN which uses the K-order adjacency matrix and two kinds of weights for graph convolution. It can alleviate the graph sparsity problem effectively and dynamically adjust the edge weights according to the past ridership. The contributions of this paper are summarized as follows:

1) We design a gated learnable wavelet filter module to capture the spatio-temporal correlations of metro ridership.
2) A multilayer wavelet graph convolution network WGCN is proposed for metro ridership prediction. It integrates the gated learnable wavelet filter module and flow-aware K-order GCN, which can mine spatio-temporal correlations from multiple scales.
3) Extensive experiments on two real-world datasets demonstrate the effectiveness of the proposed model and show that WGCN outperforms the current state-of-the-art approaches.

2 Related Work

2.1 Traffic Flow Forecasting

Early traffic flow prediction mainly relied on machine learning methods [14, 16,21], which only used temporal information from individual stations for prediction, then CNN-based and RNN-based models started to be widely used in traffic flow forecasting, DeepST [27] used CNN to extract features on spatial heat maps, ACFM [12] designed a convolutional LSTM network based on attention mechanism to predict spatial weights, ConvLSTM [18] mined spatio-temporal dependence by integrating CNN and LSTM, these methods generally ignored the topology structure of the graph. The latest research findings are GCN-based models, GraphWaveNet [22] captures spatial and temporal dependencies utilizing adaptive GCN and dilation convolution respectively. DCRNN [11] incorporates GCN into LSTM to achieve simultaneous convolution of spatio-temporal information.

Specifically for metro ridership forecasting, DEASeq2Seq [10] utilizes attention to model station-level ridership. DeepPF [26] combine multiple sources of data to forecast metro ridership. STGCNNmetro [9] constructs a deep structure composed of GCNs to capture distant spatio-temporal dependencies at the city-wide level. PVCGN [2] further extends the GCN structure by constructing virtual graphs to capture deep connections between nodes. GCN-SUBLSTM [3] combines GCN and LSTM to capture spatio-temporal correlations. DSTHGCN [20] constructs a dynamic spatio-temporal hypergraph to achieve node-level prediction. STDGRL [23] uses a dynamic graph relationship learning module to capture the dynamic connections between nodes.

2.2 Wavelet Neural Network

Wavelet neural network is an algorithm that integrates wavelet analysis into deep learning. WT-ANN [8] utilizes discrete wavelet transform and MLP for forecasting water temperature. IPSO-WNN [4] optimizes wavelet neural network with an improved particle swarm optimization algorithm to forecast traffic flow. WCNN [6] complements missing information by wavelet transform and combines CNN to perform multi-resolution analysis of images. Wavelet-SVM [19] combines wavelet analysis and SVM to predict subway passenger flow. GWNN [24] uses graph wavelet transform instead of graph Fourier transform to speed up the operation speed. GWGR [5] utilize graph wavelet to extract spatial features. It can be found that most current wavelet analysis methods for spatial modeling are based on graph wavelet. Compared with our method, it relies on the original graph structure and lacks flexibility.

3 Preliminaries

3.1 Problem Definition

We can define the metro network as an undirected graph $\mathcal{G} = (V, E)$, where $|V| = N$ denotes the set of metro stations and E denotes the set of edges. For the metro ridership of station i observed at time step t we can define it as $X_{i,t} \in \mathbb{R}^C$, where C denotes different types of data, here we focus on the passenger counts of inflow and outflow, so $C = 2$. The data of the whole metro network observed in the past T time steps can be expressed as $X_{\mathcal{G}} = [X_1, X_2, \cdots, X_N] \in \mathbb{R}^{N \times T \times C}$.

Given the past T time steps of metro ridership defined above, our goal is to learn a function f to predict future metro ridership for P time steps, so we can define the problem as:

$$[X_1, \cdots, X_N] \xrightarrow{f} [\hat{X}_1, \cdots, \hat{X}_N] \tag{1}$$

where $\hat{X}_i \in \mathbb{R}^{P \times C}$.

3.2   Discrete Wavelet Transform

Discrete wavelet transform(DWT) is widely used in feature extraction which can provide information about the behavior of a signal in the time-frequency domain [1]. The DWT decomposes a vector to its approximate and detail coefficients by a low pass filter g and a high pass filter h [17]. In the j-th level, it can be described as:

$$
\begin{aligned}
x_{j,L}[n] &= \sum_k x_{j-1,L}[k]g[2n-k] \\
x_{j,H}[n] &= \sum_k x_{j-1,L}[k]h[2n-k]
\end{aligned}
\tag{2}
$$

where $x_{i,L}[n]$ is the n-element of approximate coefficients in the i-level ($x_{0,L}[n] = x[n]$), $x_{j,L}$ and $x_{j,H}$ are approximate coefficients and detail coefficients, respectively. The set $\{x_{1,H}, x_{2,H}, \cdots, x_{J,H}, x_{J,L}\}$ is the J-level DWT results of x .Also, we can reconstruct the original signal by inverse discrete wavelet transform(IDWT):

$$x_{j-1,L}[k] = \sum_n (x_{j,L}[n] \cdot g[2n-k]) + \sum_n (x_{j,H}[n] \cdot h[2n-k]) \tag{3}$$

4   Methodology

In this section, we will introduce the proposed model Wavelet Graph Neural Network (WGCN). Its overall structure is shown in Fig. 2(a), it consists of three parts: (1) embedding layer: transforming various types of raw data into a unified feature space; (2) multi-scale information extraction layer: Mining spatio-temporal correlations from multiple scales; (3) output layer: making predictions.

4.1   Embedding Layer

Data Embedding. To reduce the dimension of the data and speed up the inferring, we first flatten X_i to a one-dimensional vector $X_i' \in \mathbb{R}^{TC}$, then its dimension is transformed to d to represent the mixed information by a fully connected neural network:

$$DE_i = W^d X_i' + b^d \tag{4}$$

where W^d and b^d are the feature transform matrix and bias of data embedding.

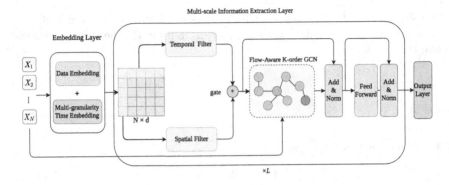

Fig. 1. The overall architecture of the proposed WGCN.

Multi-granularity Time Embedding. In each prediction, the input sequences are observed from the same day. Considering the obvious periodicity of metro ridership, we design a multi-granularity time embedding, it contains two parts: (1) large granularity time information: the day-of-month and the day-of-week; (2) specific time information: the hour-of-day and the minute-of-hour for each time step. We concatenate them together to obtain the original time vector $T_i \in \mathbb{R}^{2+2T}$. Similarly, we apply a MLP to transform it:

$$TE_i = W^t T_i + b^t \tag{5}$$

where TE_i is the multi-granularity time embedding of station i, W^t and b^t are the feature transform matrix and bias of multi-granularity time embedding.

Finally, we add up these two embeddings to obtain the final embedding of node i in the input sequence:

$$E_i = DE_i + TE_i \tag{6}$$

where $E_i \in \mathbb{R}^d$ and the complete sequence can be expressed as $E = [E_1, \cdots, E_N] \in \mathbb{R}^{N \times d}$.

4.2 Multi-scale Information Extraction Layer

Based on the embedding layer, we design a multi-scale information extraction layer composed of a stack of L identical layers. There are three modules in each layer: a gated learnable wavelet filter module, a flow-aware K-order GCN module, and a feedforward neural network. The input of the i-th layer can be represented as $H^{(i)}(H^{(0)} = E \in \mathbb{R}^{N \times d})$.

Gated Learnable Wavelet Filter Module. Considering the complex spatio-temporal correlations in metro ridership, a generic learnable wavelet filter is designed to extract signal characteristics, its structure is shown in Fig. 2(a). Specifically, we utilize a temporal filter to mine the temporal features of each

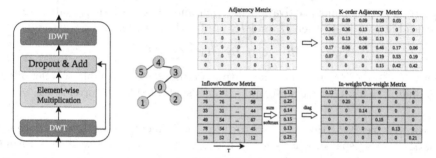

(a) Learnable wavelet filter

(b) Illustration of K-order adjacency matrix and weight matrixs of flow-aware K-order GCN($K = 2$)

Fig. 2. Details of each module in WGCN.

node from the temporal dimension and a spatial filter to mine the spatial correlations through each temporal feature from the spatial dimension.

Take the temporal filter as an example, we perform a J-level discrete wavelet transform on the input data along the temporal dimension and transform the matrix to the wavelet domain:

$$(M_0, \cdots, M_J) = \mathcal{W}_t(H^{(i)}) \tag{7}$$

where $\mathcal{W}_t$ denotes the J-level discrete wavelet transform in the temporal dimension, $M_i(i = 0, \cdots, J - 1)$ and M_J denote the detail coefficients and approximation coefficients, they represent the details variations and the overall trend in the temporal information respectively, and then we define a matrix W_j^n to compute its hadamard product with M_j as follows:

$$\hat{M}_j = W_j^n \odot M_j \quad j = 0, \cdots, J \tag{8}$$

where $\odot$ denotes the element-wise multiplication, W_j^n is a learnable matrix that adaptively optimizes the parameters according to our task, $\hat{M}_j$ represents the matrix filtered in the wavelet domain. After dropout and residual connection, we utilize IDWT to transform the matrix back into the time domain:

$$H_t = \mathcal{W}_t^{-1}(\hat{M}_0, \cdots, \hat{M}_J) \in \mathbb{R}^{N \times d} \tag{9}$$

H_t is the filtered matrix on the temporal dimension, the noise in the data is reduced effectively and the temporal feature is extracted.

In the same way, we can implement the spatial filter to obtain the matrix H_s filtered in the spatial dimension, which captures the features of the nodes on each temporal feature without the graph.

Next, we use a gated neural network to fuse them to obtain a hybrid representation of spatio-temporal correlations, specifically, we used a fully connected neural network to calculate the weights:

$$Q = \sigma(W^g H^{(i)} + b^g) \tag{10}$$

where σ is the sigmoid activation function and Q is the weight matrix taking values between [0–1], then H_t and H_s are fused by the following equation:

$$H_1 = Q \odot H_t + (1 - Q) \odot H_s \tag{11}$$

here $H_1 \in \mathbb{R}^{N \times d}$ represents the output of the gated learnable wavelet filter module, which filters out noise and extracts spatio-temporal correlations.

Flow-Aware K-Order GCN Module. For a metro network, its adjacency matrix is very sparse, what's more, a station with more inflow should output more information while a station with more outflow should receive more information. Based on these ideas, we propose a flow-aware K-order GCN module. It uses a K-order adjacency matrix A^k as the static weight and expands the receptive field:

$$A^k = softmax((A^1)^k) \tag{12}$$

here $A^1 = I + A$ and softmax only processes non-zero data to normalize A^k. In addition, we design two diagonal matrices based on the ridership to adjust the weight of edges dynamically:

$$D = Diag(softmax(sum(X))) \tag{13}$$

where the sum represents the summation of X by category, and $Diag$ denotes the generation of the diagonal matrices. $D \in \mathbb{R}^{2 \times N \times N}$, where D_0 denotes the in-weight matrix and D_1 denotes the out-weight matrix, Fig. 2(b) is a demonstration of an example. Then the graph convolution network is calculated as:

$$H_2 = \sigma(D_1 A^k D_0 H_1 W^l + b^l) \tag{14}$$

where σ is the ReLU activation function. $W^l \in \mathbb{R}^{d \times d}$ and b^l are the learnable feature transform matrix and bias.

Feedforward Neural Network. Finally, we utilize a feedforward neural network to enhance the expressiveness of the model. It contains two fully connected neural networks with GELU as the activation function:

$$H_3 = GELU(H_2 W^1 + b^1)W^2 + b^2 \tag{15}$$

where the dimension of the input and output is d and the inner dimension d_{ff} is $2d$.

4.3   Prediction and Model Optimization

Output Layer. After obtaining the hybrid spatio-temporal representation of the nodes through the multi-scale information extraction layer, we use a fully connected neural network to make predictions for future P steps in category c:

$$Z^c = HW^c + b^c \tag{16}$$

where $H \in \mathbb{R}^{N \times d}$ is the output of the multi-scale information extraction layer and $Z^c \in \mathbb{R}^{N \times P}$. The prediction result $\hat{X}$ is concatenated by $Z^c (c \in C)$.

Model Optimization. We choose MAE(mean absolute error) with L2 regularization to train WGCN:

$$\mathcal{L}(\Theta) = \frac{1}{N \times K} \sum_{n=1}^{N} \sum_{t=1}^{K} |X_{n,t} - \hat{X}_{n,t}| + \lambda \cdot \|\Theta\| \qquad (17)$$

where Θ represents the set of all trainable parameters in WGCN and λ controls the penalty strength of L2 regularization.

5   Experiments

Extensive experiments are performed to evaluate the performance of WGCN for metro ridership prediction. In this section, we first describe two datasets used for evaluation and the implementation details of the proposed model, then we compare WGCN with several basic and advanced models, and further ablation experiments demonstrate the effectiveness of each proposed module. Finally, we investigate the influence of hyperparameters on WGCN.

5.1   Experiments Settings

Dataset Description. The experiments are conducted on two real-world and widely used datasets: SHMetro dataset and HZMetro dataset [2]. Table 1 summarizes the basic statistics of the two datasets. For each dataset, we choose the period of 5:30-23:30 for the experiments and split the data into 15-min time slices, so 72 time steps will be generated per day. We forecast the next $P = 4$ steps based on the past $T = 4$ steps. Meanwhile, Z-score normalization is applied to the data to obtain more stable training. Following the universal setting, in HZMetro, we use the first 18 d for training, 2 d for validation, and the last 4 d for testing. In SHMetro, we use the time range from July 1 to August 31 for training, and September 1 to September 9 for validation, the data from the remaining days are used for testing.

Table 1. Statistics of the datasets.

Dataset	City	#Station	#Edge	Time Range	Time Interval
HZMetro	Hangzhou	80	84	1/1/2019-1/25/2019	15 min
SHMetro	Shanghai	288	335	7/1/2016-9/30/2016	15 min

Baseline. Nine basic and advanced baseline models are compared with the proposed model WGCN to demonstrate its advantages, including HA, a seasonal prediction model. LSTM, long short-term memory model. GCN, graph convolutional neural network. DCRNN, diffusion convolutional recurrent neural network.

Table 2. Performance comparisons on HZMetro and SHMetro.The best and second-best results are highlighted in boldface and underlined respectively.

MODEL	HZMetro			SHMetro		
	MAE	MAPE	RMSE	MAE	MAPE	RMSE
HA	36.24	19.51%	63.98	47.45	31.28%	136.50
LSTM	24.97	16.75%	43.71	25.11	23.36%	51.65
GCN	28.15	19.82%	51.51	27.55	27.23%	55.57
DCRNN	25.6	15.91%	45.05	26.01	18.97%	52.42
STGCN	27.48	14.58%	51.63	28.87	20.57%	62.30
GraphWaveNet	25.49	16.67%	45.19	27.92	22.31%	57.50
STDGRL	24.44	22.58%	42.01	25.02	22.25%	51.61
PVCGN	23.79	14.36%	<u>40.17</u>	24.77	<u>17.67%</u>	<u>50.02</u>
GCN-SUBLSTM	<u>23.29</u>	<u>14.32%</u>	41.96	<u>24.35</u>	18.30%	50.86
ours	**22.27**	**13.79%**	**36.74**	**23.94**	**16.96%**	**47.50**
#improvement	4.37%	3.70%	8.53%	1.68%	4.01%	5.03%

STGCN [25], spatio-temporal graph convolutional networks.GraphWaveNet [22]. STDGRL [23]. GCN-SBULSTM [20], a graph convolutional stacked bidirectional unidirectional-LSTM model. PVCGN [2] physical-virtual collaboration graph network. For each baseline, we use the results provided by the authors.

Implementation Details. Our proposed model WGCN is implemented with PyTorch. We train the model using RAdam with a learning rate of 1e-4. The wavelet function is chosen from {Haar, Daubechies, Symlets, Coiflets}, they will generate different g and h. The level J is set as 5 and embedding size d is fixed to 256. The number of the multi-scale information extraction layer L is chosen from {2,3,4,5}. The number of K is searched in {1,3,5,7,9,11,13}. Batch normalization and early stop are used to avoid overfitting. We employ a variety of evaluation metrics, including mean absolute error (MAE), root mean square error (RMSE), and mean absolute percentage error (MAPE).

5.2 Experiments Result

Overall Performance. Table 2 shows the results of full-scale experiments on the HZMetro and SHMetro datasets. We can see that HA has the worst performance on these datasets. Commonly used spatio-temporal models(e.g., DCRNN, STGCN, GraphWaveNet) also do not work well on metro ridership prediction due to the sparse graphs and small datasets. Surprisingly, LSTM obtains a MAE of 24.97 on HZMetro and 25.11 on SHMetro, which outperforms most of the models. PVCGN and GCN-SUBLSTM also show competitive performance with the help of auxiliary graph modeling. Compared with baselines, WGCN outperforms the current SOTA model on all metrics in all datasets. The largest improvement is seen in RMSE, which has an improvement of 8.53% in HZMetor. It means the model is more sensitive to large data and can predict the overall trend more accurately. Compared to the SHMetro, the model improves more significantly in HZMetro, indicating that WGCN is better adapted to small sample tasks and has strong resistance to overfitting.

We also visualize the prediction results of inflow by WGCN and PVCGN at three stations, as shown in Fig. 3, WGCN can fit the ground-truth well. Compared with PVCGN, WGCN can better capture the overall trend and detailed transformation in ridership, especially when there is sudden high flow (e.g., morning peak and evening peak), as shown in Fig. 3(b) and Fig. 3(c), WGCN performs a better prediction.

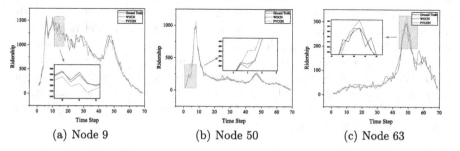

Fig. 3. Comparison prediction values of inflow on three stations of HZMetro.

Ablation Study. Ablation experiments are conducted in HZMetro to verify the effectiveness of the proposed modules, To be specific, WGCN, WGCN-TE, WGCN-GCN, WGCN-TF, and WGCN-SF denote the complete model, WGCN without multi-granularity time embedding, WGCN without flow-aware K-order GCN, WGCN without temporal filter and WGCN without spatial filter respectively. The results in Table 3 show that multi-granularity time embedding can help the model to capture periodic temporal information, which has the greatest improvement on the model, and the temporal filter and spatial filter modules has the greatest impact on the RMSE because the wavelet decomposition is better at capturing subtle changes to the data. Flow-aware K-order GCN also can increase the accuracy of prediction.

Hyperparameters Analysis. In addition, we investigated the influence of hyperparameters on the performance of the model. Different wavelet functions have different emphases on feature extraction, which has a significant impact on the performance of WGCM, as shown in Fig. 4(a). Dmeyer and Biorthogonal perform poorly and can not extract spatio-temporal correlations well. The

Table 3. Ablation study result on HZMetro.

model	MAE	MAPE	RMSE
WGCN	22.27	13.79%	36.74
WGCN-TE	24.02	15.21%	40.64
WGCN-SF	23.76	14.71%	40.69
WGCN-TF	23.49	14.39%	39.61
WGCN-GCN	22.56	14.36%	36.89

best-performing wavelet is Symlets, which outperforms other wavelets in several metrics.

The number of order K determines the receptive field of each node in the graph, as shown in Fig. 4(b), with the increase of K the model performance gradually improves, and when $K = 5$, the model achieves the best results at HZMetro. As K continues to increase, the model performance gradually stabilizes in an interval because of over-smoothing. Thanks to the two kinds of weight adjustment mechanisms of flow-aware and the K-order adjacency matrix, we can effectively alleviate this problem. Even if the value of K is already large it does not cause a significant decline in accuracy.

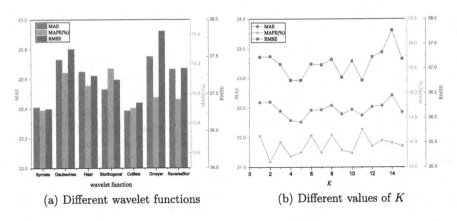

(a) Different wavelet functions   (b) Different values of K

Fig. 4. Comparison of predicting performance under different hyperparameters.

6   Conclusion

In this paper, we proposed a novel model WGCN for predicting metro ridership by integrating wavelet transform and deep learning techniques. WGCN can fully represent temporal information through data embedding and multi-granularity time embedding. In addition, the multi-scale information extraction layer consisting of the gated learnable wavelet filter module and flow-aware K-order graph convolution network help to excavate the spatio-temporal correlations at the global scale and the topological structure, respectively. Extensive experiments on real-world datasets also demonstrate the effectiveness and robustness of WGCN. WGCN also shows the feasibility of solving other spatio-temporal prediction problems.

References

1. Abda, Zaki, Chettih, Mohamed, Zerouali, Bilel: Assessment of neuro-fuzzy approach based different wavelet families for daily flow rates forecasting. Model. Earth Syst. Environ. **7**(3), 1523–1538 (2020). https://doi.org/10.1007/s40808-020-00855-1
2. Chen, J., Liu, L., Wu, H., Zhen, J., Lin, L.: Physical-virtual collaboration modeling for intra- and inter-station metro ridership prediction. Trans. Intell. Transp. Sys. **23**(4), 3377–3391 (2022)
3. Chen, P., Fu, X., Wang, X.: A graph convolutional stacked bidirectional unidirectional-lstm neural network for metro ridership prediction. IEEE Trans. Intell. Transp. Syst. **99**, 1–13 (2021)
4. Chen, Q., Song, Y., Zhao, J.: Short-term traffic flow prediction based on improved wavelet neural network. Neural Comput. Appl. **33**, 8181–8190 (2021)
5. Cui, Z., Ke, R., Pu, Z., Ma, X., Wang, Y.: Learning traffic as a graph: a gated graph wavelet recurrent neural network for network-scale traffic prediction. Transp. Res. Part C: Emerg. Technol. **115**, 102620 (2020)
6. Fujieda, S., Takayama, K., Hachisuka, T.: Wavelet convolutional neural networks. arXiv preprint arXiv:1805.08620 (2018)
7. Gong, Y., Li, Z., Zhang, J., Liu, W., Zheng, Y.: Online spatio-temporal crowd flow distribution prediction for complex metro system. IEEE Trans. Knowl. Data Eng. **99**, 1–1 (2020)
8. Graf, R., Zhu, S., Sivakumar, B.: Forecasting river water temperature time series using a wavelet-neural network hybrid modelling approach. J. Hydrol. **578**, 124115 (2019)
9. Han, W., Ren, J., Gao, Chen, G.: Predicting station-level short-term passenger flow in a citywide metro network using spatiotemporal graph convolutional neural networks. Int. J. Geo-Inform. **8**(6), 243 (2019)
10. Huang, H., Mao, J., Lu, W., Hu, G., Liu, L.: Deaseq2seq: an attention based sequence to sequence model for short-term metro passenger flow prediction within decomposition-ensemble strategy. Transport. Res. Part C: Emerg. Technol. **146**, 103965 (2023)
11. Li, Y., Yu, R., Shahabi, C., Liu, Y.: Diffusion convolutional recurrent neural network: Data-driven traffic forecasting. In: ICLR (2018)
12. Liu, L., Zhang, R., Peng, J., Li, G., Liang, L.: Attentive crowd flow machines. ACM (2018)
13. Luo, M., Yu, S.: Traffic route planning in partially observable environment using actions group representation. In: Knowledge Science, Engineering and Management, pp. 101–113 (2021)
14. Makridakis, S., Hibon, M.: Arma models and the box-jenkins methodology. J. Forecast. **16**(3), 147–163 (1997)

15. Shang, S., Chen, L., Wei, Z., Jensen, C.S., Wen, J.R., Kalnis, P.: Collective travel planning in spatial networks. IEEE Trans. Knowl. Data Eng. 28(5), 1–1 (2016)
16. Shekhar, S., Williams, B.: Adaptive seasonal time series models for forecasting short-term traffic flow. Transport. Res. Record J. Transport. Res. Board 2024(2024), 116–125 (2007)
17. Shensa, M., J.: The discrete wavelet transform: wedding the a trous and mallat algorithms. Signal Process., IEEE Trans. 40(10), 2464–2482 (1992)
18. Shi, X., Chen, Z., Wang, H., Yeung, D.Y., Wong, W.K., Woo, W.C.: Convolutional lstm network: A machine learning approach for precipitation nowcasting. MIT Press (2015)
19. Sun, Y., Leng, B., Guan, W.: A novel wavelet-SVM short-time passenger flow prediction in Beijing subway system. Neurocomputing 166, 109–121 (2015)
20. Wang, J., Zhang, Y., Wei, Y., Hu, Y., Piao, X., Yin, B.: Metro passenger flow prediction via dynamic hypergraph convolution networks. IEEE Trans. Intell. Transport. Syst. 22(12), 7891–7903 (2021)
21. Wu, C.H., Ho, J.M., Lee, D.T.: Travel-time prediction with support vector regression. IEEE Trans. Intell. Transp. Syst. 5(4), 276–281 (2004)
22. Wu, Z., Pan, S., Long, G., Jiang, J., Zhang, C.: Graph wavenet for deep spatial-temporal graph modeling. In: IJCAI-19 (2019)
23. Xie, P., et al.: Spatio-temporal dynamic graph relation learning for urban metro flow prediction. IEEE Trans. Knowl. Data Eng. 1–12 (2023)
24. Xu, B., Shen, H., Cao, Q., Qiu, Y., Cheng, X.: Graph wavelet neural network. arXiv preprint arXiv:1904.07785 (2019)
25. Yu, B., Yin, H., Zhu, Z.: Spatio-temporal graph convolutional networks: A deep learning framework for traffic forecasting. In: Proceedings of the 27th International Joint Conference on Artificial Intelligence, pp. 3634–3640 (2018)
26. Zhang, J., Chen, F., Cui, Z., Guo, Y., Zhu, Y.: Deep learning architecture for short-term passenger flow forecasting in urban rail transit. IEEE Trans. Intell. Transport. Syst. 99, 1–11 (2020)
27. Zhang, J., Zheng, Y., Qi, D., Li, R., Yi, X.: Dnn-based prediction model for spatio-temporal data. In: Proceedings of the 24th ACM SIGSPATIAL International Conference on Advances in Geographic Information Systems, pp. 1–4 (2016)

GMiRec: A Multi-image Visual Recommendation Model Based on a Gated Neural Network

Caihong Mu[1] 🄯, Xin Tang[1], Jiashen Luo[1(✉)], and Yi Liu[2] 🄯

[1] Key Laboratory of Intelligent Perception and Image Understanding of Ministry of Education, Collaborative Innovation Center of Quantum Information of Shaanxi Province, School of Artificial Intelligence, Xidian University, Xi'an 710071, China
`caihongm@mail.xidian.edu.cn`, {`xxintang,`
`jiashenluo`}`@stu.xidian.edu.cn`
[2] School of Electronic Engineering, Xidian University, Xi'an 710071, China
`yiliu@xidian.edu.cn`

Abstract. Making use of visual perception in recommender systems is becoming more and more important. In the existing visual recommendation models (VRMs), the visual features of items are usually extracted based on the pre-trained convolutional neural network, and then combined with the non-visual features modeling to complete the prediction of users' interest. There are two challenges in this field so far. First, most VRMs are developed around single-image items, and how to more effectively mine the visual features of multi-image items is seldom considered. Second, most models do not consider the distribution difference between the training datasets of the pre-trained model and the datasets for recommendation when extracting visual features based on the pre-training model, which may deepen the gap in the convolutional neural network's understanding of image semantics on datasets. To address the above challenges, a Multi-image Visual Recommendation Model based on a Gated Neural Network (GMiRec) is proposed. It performs different forms of pooling operations on the visual features of multi-image items and uses the feed-forward neural network to realize the fusion of the multi-image visual information. In addition, a gated neural network taking item categories as input is designed to achieve supervised dimensionality reduction on the item visual features, which alleviates the problem of semantic gap. Experiments conducted on the Amazon datasets show that the proposed model is significantly improved compared with the existing models.

Keywords: Recommender Systems · Visual Information · Gated Neural Networks

1 Introduction

As an information filtering system, the recommender system (RS) [1] plays an increasingly important role in assisting users to find an item that matches their interest from massive data. Modern RSs mainly use the interaction data between users and items to

© The Author(s), under exclusive license to Springer Nature Switzerland AG 2023
Z. Jin et al. (Eds.): KSEM 2023, LNAI 14118, pp. 331–342, 2023.
https://doi.org/10.1007/978-3-031-40286-9_27

provide users with personalized recommendation services. For example, in the Item-to-Item Collaborative Filtering (ItemCF) [2] model first proposed by Amazon, targeted marketing services are achieved by recommending items similar to the user's historical purchases. The Matrix Factorization (MF) [3] model proposed by Koren et al. maps users and items to the factor space that reflects their latent semantic information, and then uses the dot product between users and items to capture users' interest in items. As a basic and effective model, MF has derived many variants in subsequent development, such as [4, 5]. With the widespread use of deep learning technology, collaborative filtering models based on neural network including [6, 7], etc. have emerged. However, the recommendation models mentioned above still cannot deal with the data sparsity problem in RSs very well. According to the survey in [8], the observable interaction data in reality usually accounts for less than 5%, the small proportion of available data will also exacerbate the long tail and cold start problems in RSs to a certain extent.

An effective way to alleviate data sparsity is to utilize auxiliary information, which contains additional clues about user-item interactions, such as image information. Benefited from the development of modern communication technology, more and more items on the Internet begin to use images as part of the content display. As the most intuitive information carrier among content descriptions of items, images play an important role in attracting users to further understand the items. Research by JD's business growth team [9] has shown that many ads achieve higher Click-Through Rates (CTR) simply by switching to more appealing images. As a special form for people to understand the world, aesthetics exists in people's daily life, it is becoming more and more important to predict users' interest and improve the user experience based on visual perception. Nowadays, the use of CNNs [10, 11, 24] to extract features from item images has become increasingly mature, which has led to a number of excellent results on recommendation with visual features of items in RSs. For example, some visual recommendation models (VRMs) were applied to online advertising [9, 12, 13]. In the fashion RS, existing works [14–18] aim to explore users' visual interest preferences on fashion related items, where the visual features of the items are firstly trained through a pre-trained CNN, and then combined with other contextual information for modeling. In addition to the research works above, there are still many works on recommendation modeling based on item visual features, such as movie [19, 20], news [21], picture [22], and art recommendation [23].

However, there still are unresolved challenges. In the previous VRMs, visual feature extraction was basically based on a single image of an item. Even for multi-image items, the key image (the first image of the item display page) of the item is used as a representation of the appearance, intuitively resulting in incomplete utilization of item image information. In addition, due to the difference in the understanding of image information between people and machines, the problem of "semantic gap" arises. In most VRMs, the pre-training datasets of CNN and the target recommendation datasets are often not consistent, which will undoubtedly further deepen the semantic gap. To overcome the above challenges, in this paper, we propose a Multi-image Visual Recommendation Model based on a Gated Neural Network (GMiRec) for the task of personalized ranking on implicit feedback datasets. Our main contributions include:

- A multi-image visual fusion network is built to mine visual features of multi-item images. Since the multi-image information of an item often includes descriptions of the item from different views, the method we proposed can effectively reduce the loss of the visual information of the item at source.
- A gated neural network (GateNN) is proposed to extract more accurate visual features of items by combining the category information of items with visual information, thereby alleviating the problem of semantic gap in image understanding.
- Empirical results on three large real-world datasets, *Baby*, *Boys & Girls* and *Men & Women* from Amazon demonstrate that our models are able to outperform the state-of-the-art models significantly, both in all- and cold-start settings.

2 Notations

Let $U = \{u_1, u_2, ..., u_n\}$ and $I = \{i_1, i_2, ..., i_m\}$ denote the set of users and items respectively, each user u is associated with an item set I_u^+ for which u has provided explicit positive feedback. Additionally, there are $t_i (t_i \geq 1)$ images available for each item $i \in I$. Our goal is to generate for each user u a personalized ranking over items (i.e., $I \backslash I_u^+$) with which the user u has not yet interacted.

Fig. 1. Different styles or display views of items with the same ID.

3 Our Model

3.1 Multi-image Information Fusion Network

As shown in Fig. 1, in most e-commerce scenarios, items with the same ID may contain multiple images of different styles, and items of the same style may contain the images in different views. To fully mine the visual features of items, we propose a Multi-image Information Fusion Network (MIIFN) as shown in the yellow region of Fig. 2, which includes three steps: visual feature extraction, feature pooling, and feature dimension reduction.

Visual Feature Extraction: We extract visual features of items based on a pre-trained CNN architecture called MobileNet-v2 [24]. It extracts the visual features with 1280 dimensions, which saves more memory space compared to the models [10, 11] extracting features with 4096 dimensions, and the performance of which is not inferior.

Feature Pooling: For each item i, we feed the t_i images belonging to item i into the pre-trained CNN model. On the output layer of the CNN model, there is a D-dimensional visual feature vector denoted as $f \in \mathbb{R}^D$ for each image. Therefore, the visual feature matrix of item i containing t_i images can be expressed as $\mathbf{F}_i \in \mathbb{R}^{t_i \times D}$.

The number of images contained in different items may be different. To ensure that the feature dimensions of the input model are consistent, the visual feature matrix $\mathbf{F}_i$ are processed as follows:

$$f_i^{\text{avg}} = \text{AvgPool}(\mathbf{F}_i) \tag{1}$$

$$f_i^{\text{max}} = \text{MaxPool}(\mathbf{F}_i) \tag{2}$$

where $f_i^{\text{avg}} \in \mathbb{R}^D$ and $f_i^{\text{max}} \in \mathbb{R}^D$ denotes the results of the visual feature matrix of item i after Average and Max pooling [25], respectively.

Then, the pooled visual vectors are concatenated as:

$$x_i = \text{Concatenate}\left(\left[f_i^{\text{avg}} \cdot f_i^{\text{max}}\right]\right) \tag{3}$$

Feature Dimension Reduction: The pooled visual features still have the problem of high spatial dimension. For each item i, we use a two-layer feed-forward neural network to achieve dimension reduction of high-dimensional visual features. Then, we take the low-dimensional visual features $\theta_i \in \mathbb{R}^d$ of item i as follows:

$$\theta_i = \varphi(\mathbf{W}_2\varphi(\mathbf{W}_1 x_i + b_1) + b_2) \tag{4}$$

where $\mathbf{W}_1 \in \mathbb{R}^{D \times 512}$ and $\mathbf{W}_2 \in \mathbb{R}^{512 \times d}$ are weight matrixes, b_1 and b_2 are bias terms, $\varphi(\cdot)$ is a nonlinear activation function named ReLU.

3.2 Gated Neural Network

People's observation of item images is based on the semantic understanding of the objects described by the images, rather than the underlying visual features of the images. There is often a huge difference between the low-level visual features automatically extracted by computers and the high-level semantic features understood by people, thus resulting in the "semantic gap" [26] problem. In visual recommendation, the inconsistency in data distribution between the training set of pre-trained CNN and the target recommendation set may deepen the semantic gap. If a predictive model is directly built on the underlying features, it will lead to excessive requirements on the capabilities of the predictive model.

With the representation that reflects the high-level features of the data, the subsequent machine learning models can be built easier. In general, the category of an item contains the description of the image, and the image reflects the category characteristics of the item. To extract visual features that are more in line with the image description, we design a GateNN using item categories as the feature input. Then, the GateNN is combined with the feed-forward neural network to achieve supervised dimension reduction of visual features.

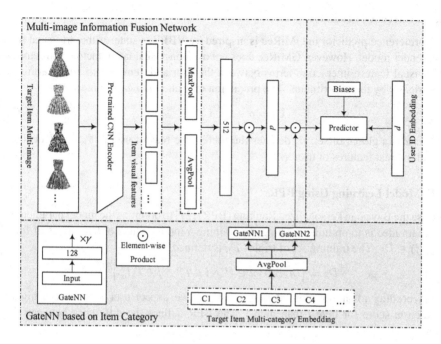

Fig. 2. The framework of GMiRec.

As shown in Fig. 2, GateNN is also a two-layer feed-forward neural network. The output of the l-th GateNN is as follows:

$$g_i^l = \gamma \times \text{Sigmoid}\left(\mathbf{W}_2^l \text{ReLU}\left(\mathbf{W}_1^l c_i + b_1^l\right) + b_2^l\right) \tag{5}$$

where $\mathbf{W}_1^l \in \mathbb{R}^{d \times 128}$ and $\mathbf{W}_2^l \in \mathbb{R}^{128 \times d_l}$ are weight matrixes, b_1^l and b_2^l are bias terms. The activation function $\text{ReLU}(x) = \max(0, x)$, $\text{Sigmoid}(x) = 1/(1 + \exp(-x))$. γ is a hyperparameter which is set as 3. $c_i \in \mathbb{R}^d$ is the category feature of item i, which is trainable. If the item i contains n_i categories, the original category feature will be represented as $C_i \in \mathbb{R}^{n_i \times d}$, and c_i is obtained by averaging the n_i elements in each column of C_i, which shows a better effect than using maximum or weighted sum operation.

Then, we get the element-wise product of the output vector of the l-th GateNN and the output vector of the l-th layer of the feed-forward neural network. We can obtain a new visual feature $\theta_i^{\text{new}} \in \mathbb{R}^d$ of item i as follows:

$$\theta_i^{\text{new}} = \sigma\left(\mathbf{W}_2\sigma(\mathbf{W}_1 x_i + b_1) \odot g_i^1 + b_2\right) \odot g_i^2 \tag{6}$$

where $g_i^1 \in \mathbb{R}^{512}$ and $g_i^2 \in \mathbb{R}^d$ represent the output of the 1-th and 2-th GateNN respectively, and they share the same input c_i but different model parameters.

Through GateNN, we achieve the fusion of item category features and visual features, alleviating the semantic gap caused by the differences in data distribution. Besides, the value range of each element in vector g_i^1 and g_i^2 is $(0, \gamma)$, which leads to the enhancement of important features and the weakening of redundant features.

3.3 Preference Predictor

The preference predictor in GMiRec is inspired by VBPR, a state-of-the-art visual rec-ommender model. However, GMiRec does not use non-visual latent factors and remove non-visual feature interaction terms between the user and item, which are determined empirically by the experiments. The prediction of u on item i can be made by:

$$\hat{x}_{ui} = \alpha + \beta_u + \boldsymbol{\theta}_u^T \boldsymbol{\theta}_i^{\text{new}} \tag{7}$$

where α is a global offset, β_u denotes the preference bias of user u, $\boldsymbol{\theta}_u \in \mathbb{R}^d$ denotes visual interest features of user u.

3.4 Model Learning Using BPR

We use the Bayesian Personalized Ranking (BPR) [27] to optimize the model parameters, the main idea is to optimize rankings by training a model which orders triples of form $(u, i, j) \in \mathcal{D}_S$. The training set of triples $\mathcal{D}_S$ is defined as:

$$\mathcal{D}_S = \left\{ (u, i, j) \mid u \in U \wedge i \in I_u^+ \wedge j \in I \backslash I_u^+ \right\} \tag{8}$$

According to the previous definition of $\hat{x}_{ui}$, we expect user u to have a higher prediction score for item i than item j. The BPR defines the difference between the scores

$$\hat{x}_{uij} = \hat{x}_{ui} - \hat{x}_{uj} \tag{9}$$

The model parameters are learned by optimizing the following objective function

$$\underset{\Theta}{\text{argmax}} \ \log \sigma \left(\hat{x}_{uij} \right) - \lambda_\Theta |\Theta|^2 \tag{10}$$

where $\sigma(\cdot)$ is the sigmoid function, Θ means all parameters of model, and λ_Θ is a regularization hyperparameter.

Finally, the model parameters Θ are updated based on gradient ascent as follows:

$$\Theta \leftarrow \Theta + \eta \cdot \left(\sigma \left(-\hat{x}_{uij} \right) \frac{\partial \hat{x}_{uij}}{\partial \Theta} - \lambda_\Theta \Theta \right) \tag{11}$$

where η is the learning rate.

4 Experiments

4.1 Datasets

The experiments of this paper and related comparative methods are all done on the dataset *Clothing Shoes and Jewelry* from *Amazon Review Data* [28]. We further divide the *Clothing Shoes and Jewelry* dataset into sub-datasets. As shown in Table 1, it contains the relevant information of the three sub-datasets respectively. We discard users with consumption records less than 5 and the related interactions by referring to the settings in [9, 14, 16, 18]. All VRMs use the MobileNet-v2 to extract visual features. For other models that need a key image, the average pooling result of the item multi-image visual features is used as the input.

For each user in the datasets, the last interaction data is used as the test set, the penultimate interaction data is used as the verification set, and the remaining data are all used as the training set $\mathcal{P}_u$. All models will use the validation set $\mathcal{V}_u$ to debug model parameters, and compare their performance indicators on the test set $\mathcal{T}_u$.

Table 1. Dataset statistics (after preprocessing)

Dataset	#users	#items	#feedback	#Sparsity
Amazon Baby	7950	15516	55831	99.95%
Amazon Boys & Girls	27667	49158	204024	99.98%
Amazon Men & Women	64846	122278	482367	99.99%

4.2 Evaluation Metrics

All models are evaluated on $\mathcal{T}_u$ with the widely used Area Under the Roc Curve (AUC):

$$\text{AUC} = \frac{1}{|U|} \sum_u \frac{1}{|E(u)|} \sum_{(i,j) \in E(u)} \delta\left(\hat{x}_{ui} > \hat{x}_{uj}\right) \qquad (12)$$

where the indicator function $\delta(\cdot)$ returns 1 if condition is met, and 0 otherwise. The set of evaluation pairs for user u is defined as:

$$E(u) = \{(i,j) \mid (u,i) \in \mathcal{T}_u \wedge (u,j) \notin (\mathcal{P}_u \cup \mathcal{V}_u \cup \mathcal{T}_u)\} \qquad (13)$$

In all cases, we searched for the optimal hyperparameters through validation set $\mathcal{V}$ and report performance on test set $\mathcal{T}$.

4.3 Baselines

To verify the effectiveness of GMiRec, we compare it with the following baselines:

- **Random (RAND)**: A random strategy is used to recommend items to all users.
- **MF-BPR** [3]: It is a Matrix Factorization model based on BPR and tailored to learn from implicit feedback.
- **NeuMF** [6]: It is a neural collaborative filtering model that consists of Generalized Matrix Factorization (GMF) module and Multi-layer Perceptron (MLP) module.
- **VisRank** [29]: It is a similarity retrieval method based on visual features. The visual features corresponding to the items that the user has interacted with are averaged to obtain the user's visual vector representation.
- **VNPR** [30]: It is a VRM based on Neural Personalized Ranking (NPR) model. NPR is a personalized pairwise ranking model over implicit feedback datasets.
- **VBPR** [14]: It is a state-of-the-art VRM based on BPR Optimization. The visual features interaction is additionally introduced.

- **DeepStyle** [15]: It is a VRM that subtracts categorical information from visual features of items generated by CNN.
- **TVBPR** [16]: It is a VBPR-based VRM with dynamic evolution, which captures fashion and user taste temporal shifts.
- **VNPR-C**: It is a VNPR-based VRM which incorporates the category interest of users and the category features of items by using the element-wise product.
- **VBPR-C:** It is a VBPR-based VRM which incorporates the category interest of users and the category features of items by using the inner product.
- **GMiRec**: It is a multi-image VRM based on GateNN proposed in this paper.

4.4 Performance Comparison

We evaluate the performance of all models on the test set, and the evaluation settings include two types: **All-Items** and **Cold-Items**. All-Items does not distinguish between popular items and cold-start items, which helps to reflect the recommended performance of the model from an overall perspective. Cold-Items only performs performance evaluation on cold-start items with less than 5 purchases, which focuses on measuring the recommendation effect of the model in cold-start scenarios.

For the sake of fairness, all models are tuned to obtain the optimal parameters on the validation set. The main parameters of different models include vector dimension, learning rate, regularization hyperparameter, etc. The selection of the optimal parameters of each model is carried out independently, we just specify the value range of all parameters, and then use the automatic machine learning tool NNI [31] to complete the selection. In addition, when each model is evaluated on the test set, the new training set will be composed of the original training set and the verification set, and Adam [32] is used for model optimization learning during the training process. We perform the experiments 5 times independently on each model and then calculate the average results. The final experimental results are shown in Table 2 and Table 3.

Table 2 shows the average AUC values of all models achieved on three datasets for **All-Items**. The main findings from Table 2 are summarized as follows:

1. The AUC indicators of MF-BPR and NeuMF are both higher than 0.7 due to the use of interaction data between users and items, but they are inferior to VBPR and VNPR, which add visual interaction items between users and items. VBPR achieved an average AUC improvement of 2.94% over MF-BPR on the three datasets.
2. Compared with VNPR and VBPR, VNPR-C and VBPR-C achieved an average AUC improvement of 1.77% and 2.34%, respectively. DeepStyle uses category information to extract more pure style features of items, which gets better results than VNPR-C. TVBPR captures visual temporal dynamics by introducing time factors, which has better performance than the common VRM such as VBPR.
3. GMiRec outperforms other VRMs due to the user of MIIFN and GateNN. The results of Table 2 demonstrate that the GMiRec model can extract more advanced visual semantic features, thereby improving the accuracy of the user's interest prediction.

Table 3 shows the average AUC values of all models achieved on three datasets for **Cold-Items**. The main findings from Table 3 are summarized as follows:

1. The AUC of MF-BPR and NeuMF on Cold-Items is lower than the RAND. The main reason is that cold-start items have insufficient features expression learning due to the small number of interactions, and their interaction scores with users will be lower than popular items and basically the same as other cold-start items.
2. VRMs are significantly better than other non-visual models in the performance of Cold-Items. The AUC of DeepStyle is further improved due to the use of item category features. TVBPR makes no improvement on AUC compared with other VRMs, indicating that the time factor is ineffective in cold start scenario.
3. GMiRec also achieves the best results on three datasets with Cold-Items, demonstrating the superiority of GMiRec in solving the item cold-start problem.

Table 2. AUC on test set $\mathcal{T}$ (**All-Items**). The global best results are in bold font and the second-best ones are underlined.

Model	Baby	Boys & Girls	Men & Women
RAND	0.5000 ± 0.0000	0.5000 ± 0.0000	0.5000 ± 0.0000
MF-BPR	0.7206 ± 0.0014	0.7525 ± 0.0009	0.7491 ± 0.0006
NeuMF	0.7240 ± 0.0071	0.7520 ± 0.0048	0.7543 ± 0.0044
VisRank	0.7211 ± 0.0016	0.7185 ± 0.0003	0.7084 ± 0.0001
VNPR	0.7472 ± 0.0006	0.7627 ± 0.0022	0.7519 ± 0.0006
VBPR	0.7669 ± 0.0011	0.7662 ± 0.0023	0.7774 ± 0.0030
DeepStyle	0.7646 ± 0.0030	0.7816 ± 0.0017	0.8054 ± 0.0017
TVBPR	<u>0.7892 ± 0.0035</u>	0.7817 ± 0.0026	0.7668 ± 0.0010
VNPR-C	0.7675 ± 0.0027	0.7719 ± 0.0155	0.7756 ± 0.0006
VBPR-C	0.7778 ± 0.0051	<u>0.7926 ± 0.0020</u>	<u>0.8102 ± 0.0022</u>
GMiRec	**0.8187 ± 0.0030**	**0.8335 ± 0.0031**	**0.8487 ± 0.0022**

4.5 Ablation Study

The better performance of GMiRec mainly results from the use of a MIIFN and GateNN. To verify their effectiveness, we remove the GateNN in GMiRec and generate a variant of GMiRec (named as MiRec), and compare VBPR with MiRec and GMiRec. VBPR is a VRM only using a key image, but multiple images of the item are used here.

Figure 3 shows the experimental results of three models on three datasets. The results on both **All-Items** and **Cold-Items** show the similar trend: GMiRec > MiRec > VBPR. Compared to VBPR, MiRec achieves better performance, which does not use item ID feature but benefits from the use of the MIIFN. GMiRec extracts higher-level item semantic features through GateNN, greatly improving the model's prediction of user interest preferences, which can be observed in the comparison with MiRec.

Table 3. AUC on test set $\mathcal{T}$ (**Cold-Items**). The global best results are in bold font and the second-best ones are underlined.

Method	Baby	Boys & Girls	Men & Women
RAND	0.5000 ± 0.0000	0.5000 ± 0.0000	0.5000 ± 0.0000
MF-BPR	0.4331 ± 0.0027	0.4154 ± 0.0020	0.4334 ± 0.0010
NeuMF	0.4706 ± 0.0036	0.4185 ± 0.0189	0.4997 ± 0.0087
VisRank	0.6612 ± 0.0021	0.6551 ± 0.0008	0.6397 ± 0.0005
VNPR	0.6721 ± 0.0018	0.6479 ± 0.0023	0.6916 ± 0.0008
VBPR	0.6625 ± 0.0034	0.6515 ± 0.0056	0.6906 ± 0.0026
DeepStyle	0.6790 ± 0.0007	0.6841 ± 0.0035	0.7159 ± 0.0019
TVBPR	0.6821 ± 0.0059	0.6638 ± 0.0070	0.6839 ± 0.0012
VNPR-C	<u>0.7044 ± 0.0020</u>	0.6840 ± 0.0062	<u>0.7184 ± 0.0008</u>
VBPR-C	0.6786 ± 0.0058	<u>0.6978 ± 0.0020</u>	0.7148 ± 0.0011
GMiRec	**0.7228 ± 0.0049**	**0.7381 ± 0.0019**	**0.7541 ± 0.0008**

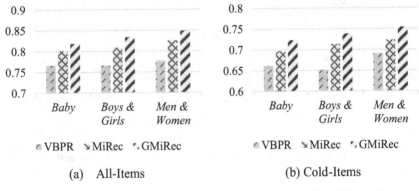

(a)   All-Items

(b)   Cold-Items

Fig. 3. The AUC comparison of VBPR, MiRec, and GMiRec on three different datasets.

5   Conclusion

In this paper, we propose a Multi-image Visual Recommendation Model based on a Gated Neural Network (GMiRec) for mining the multi-image visual features of items and users' interest preferences. GMiRec realizes the extraction and dimensionality reduction of the visual features of multi-image items through the multi-image information fusion network, reducing the loss of item visual information at source. The design of the gated neural network (GateNN) skillfully integrates the visual features and category features of items, providing higher-level semantic features for subsequent modeling, which is of great help to alleviate the semantic gap problem. Further study is needed for datasets that are less sensitive to visual interest. In addition, when the category features of an item are sparse, GateNN may not be able to learn the distribution of visual features of the item well, which may be solved from the perspective of text semantics in our further research.

Acknowledgement. This work was supported by the National Natural Science Foundation of China (Nos. 62077038, 61672405, 62176196 and 62271374).

References

1. Zhang, S., Yao, L., Sun, A., et al.: Deep learning based recommender system: a survey and new perspectives. ACM Comput. Surv. **52**(1), 1–38 (2019)
2. Linden, G., Smith, B., York, J.: Item-to-item collaborative filtering. IEEE Internet Comput. **7**(1), 76–80 (2003)
3. Koren, Y., Bell, R., Volinsky, C.: Matrix factorization techniques for recommender systems. Computer **42**(8), 30–37 (2009)
4. Koren, Y.: Factor in the neighbors: scalable and accurate collaborative filtering. ACM Trans. Knowl. Discov. Data **4**(1), 1–24 (2010)
5. Pan, R., Zhou, Y., Cao, B., et al.: One-class collaborative filtering. In: 8th IEEE International Conference on Data Mining, pp. 502–511. IEEE, Piscataway (2008)
6. He, X., Liao, L., Zhang, H., et al.: Neural collaborative filtering. In: 26th International Conference on World Wide Web Companion, pp.173–182. ACM, New York (2017)
7. He, X., Du, X., Wang, X., et al.: Outer product-based neural collaborative filtering. In: 27th International Joint Conference on Artificial Intelligence, pp. 2227–2233. ACM, New York (2018)
8. Truong, Q., Salah, A., Lauw, H.: Multi-modal recommender systems: hands-on exploration. In: 15th ACM Conference on Recommender Systems, pp. 834–837. ACM, New York (2021)
9. Liu, H., Lu, J., Yang, H., et al.: Category-specific CNN for visual-aware CTR prediction at JD. Com. In: 26th ACM SIGKDD International Conference on Knowledge Discovery & Data Mining, pp. 2686–2696. ACM, New York (2020)
10. Krizhevsky, A., Sutskever, I., Hinton, G.: Imagenet classification with deep convolutional neural networks. Commun. ACM **60**(6), 84–90 (2017)
11. He, K., Zhang, X., Ren, S., et al.: Deep residual learning for image recognition. In: 13th IEEE Conference on Computer Vision and Pattern Recognition, pp. 770–778. IEEE, Piscataway (2016)
12. Mo, K., Liu, B., Xiao, L., Li, Y., Jiang, J.: Image feature learning for cold start problem in display advertising. In: 24th International Conference on Artificial Intelligence, pp. 3728–3734. IJCAI, Buenos Aires Argentina (2015)
13. Zhao, Z., Li, L., Zhang, B., et al.: What you look matters? Offline evaluation of advertising creatives for cold-start problem. In: 28th ACM International Conference on Information and Knowledge Management, pp. 2605–2613. ACM, New York (2019)
14. He, R., Mcauley, J.: VBPR: visual Bayesian personalized ranking from implicit feed-back. In: 16th AAAI Conference on Artificial Intelligence, pp. 144–150. AAAI, Menlo Park (2016)
15. Liu, Q., Wu, S., Wang, L.: Deepstyle: learning user preferences for visual recommendation. In: 40th International ACM SIGIR Conference on Research and Development in Information Retrieval, pp. 841–844. ACM, New York (2017)
16. He, R., Mcauley, J.: Ups and downs: modeling the visual evolution of fashion trends with one-class collaborative filtering. In: 25th International Conference on World Wide Web, pp. 507–517. WWW, Switzerland (2016)

17. Yu, W., Zhang, H., He, X., et al.: Aesthetic-based clothing recommendation. In: 18th World Wide Web Conference, pp. 649–658. WWW, Switzerland (2018)
18. Yu, W., et al.: Visually aware recommendation with aesthetic features. VLDB J. **30**(4), 495–513 (2021). https://doi.org/10.1007/s00778-021-00651-y
19. Zhang, F., Yuan, N., Lian, D., et al.: Collaborative knowledge base embedding for recommender systems. In: 22nd ACM SIGKDD International Conference on Knowledge Discovery and Data Mining, pp. 353–362. ACM, New York (2016)
20. Chen, X., Zhao, P., Liu, Y., et al.: Exploiting visual contents in posters and still frames for movie recommendation. IEEE Access **6**, 68874–68881 (2018)
21. Wu, C., Wu, F., Qi, T., et al.: MM-Rec: visiolinguistic model empowered multimodal news recommendation. In: 45th International ACM SIGIR Conference on Research and Development in Information Retrieval, pp. 2560–2564. ACM, New York (2022)
22. Lei, C., Liu, D., Li, W., et al.: Comparative deep learning of hybrid representations for image recommendations. In: 13th Conference on Computer Vision and Pattern Recognition, pp. 2545–2553. IEEE, Piscataway (2016)
23. Yilma, B., Leiva, L.: CuratorNet: visually-aware recommendation of art images. In: 23rd Conference on Human Factors in Computing Systems, pp. 1–17. ACM, New York (2023)
24. Sandler, M., Howard, A., Zhu, M., et al.: MobileNetV2: inverted residuals and linear bottlenecks. In: 15th IEEE Conference on Computer Vision and Pattern Recognition, pp. 4510–1520. IEEE, Piscataway (2018)
25. Boureau, Y., Ponce, J., LeCun, Y.: A theoretical analysis of feature pooling in visual recognition, pp. 111–118. Omnipress, United States (2010)
26. Hein, A.: Identification and bridging of semantic gaps in the context of multi-domain engineering. In: 2010 Forum on Philosophy, Engineering & Technology, pp. 57–58 (2010)
27. Rendle, S., Feudenthaler, C., Ganther, Z., et al.: BPR: Bayesian personalized ranking from implicit feedback. In: 25th Conference on Uncertainty in Artificial Intelligence, pp. 452–461. ACM, New York (2009)
28. Ni, J., Li, J., McAuley, J.: Justifying recommendations using distantly-labeled reviews and fine-grained aspects. In: Proceedings of the 2019 Conference on Empirical Methods in Natural Language Processing and the 9th International Joint Conference on Natural Language Processing, pp. 188–197. ACL, Stroudsburg (2019)
29. Jonathan, O.: Product recommendation based on visual similarity. https://www.kaggle.com/code/jonathanoheix/product-recommendation-based-on-visual-similarity. Accessed 1 Feb 2023
30. Niu, W., Ccaverlee, J., Lu, H.: Neural personalized ranking for image recommendation. In: 8th ACM International Conference on Web Search and Data Mining. ACM, New York (2018)
31. Microsoft. Neural Network Intelligence. http://github.com/Microsoft/nni. Accessed 1 Feb 2023
32. Kingma, D.P., Ba, J.: Adam: a method for stochastic optimization. arXiv preprint arXiv:1412.6980 (2014)

Semi-supervised Entity Alignment via Noisy Student-Based Self Training

Yihe Liu and Yuanfei Dai[✉]

College of Computer and Information Engineering, Nanjing Tech University,
Nanjing 211816, China
daiyuanfei@njtech.edu.cn

Abstract. Knowledge graph is a structured data model that captures the relationships between entities in the real world. Entity alignment (EA) has drawn significant attention in recent years as a potential means of identifying corresponding entities across different knowledge graphs. Although knowledge graph embedding-based entity alignment methods have recently obtained significant progress, the shortage of training data remains a severe challenge. Conventional approaches have attempted to solve this issue through semi-supervised learning but still suffer from the negative impacts of entity alignment. To resolute the above issues, we propose a semi-supervised framework with Noisy Student-based self training Entity Alignment named NSEA. Our framework proposes a new noisy student self-training strategy for obtaining diverse entity alignment pairs, and we also design an adaptive alignment selector to infer reliable entity pairs. Through extensive experiments on benchmark datasets, we demonstrate that our method outperforms most existing models in terms of accuracy and efficiency, highlighting its usefulness for large-scale and diverse knowledge graphs with insufficient annotated data.

Keywords: Entity alignment model · Noisy student training · Semi-supervised learning

1 Introduction

Entity alignment is a fundamental task in knowledge graph research, aiming to match entities from multiple knowledge graphs that refer to the same real-world object. In recent years, embedding-based entity alignments such as MTransE [2], AlignE [8] and SEA [6] have made great progress and are widely applied in many applications, including recommendation systems [4,13] and knowledge fusion [1,16]. These models transform entities in the knowledge graph into low-dimensional vector representations to obtain the similarities between two entities from different knowledge graphs in semantic space. The embedding-based entity

This work is in part supported by the National Natural Science Foundation of China under Grant 62202221, and the Natural Science Foundation of Jiangsu Province under Grant BK20220331.

© The Author(s), under exclusive license to Springer Nature Switzerland AG 2023
Z. Jin et al. (Eds.): KSEM 2023, LNAI 14118, pp. 343–354, 2023.
https://doi.org/10.1007/978-3-031-40286-9_28

alignments can resolve the issue of symbolic heterogeneity between knowledge graphs and accomplish the entity alignment task.

However, in practice, annotating datasets for entity alignment is often an expensive and time-consuming task that requires specialist annotation. Thus, many studies have drawn considerable attention to semi-supervised learning to address the problem of insufficient data such as BooTEA [7], IPtransE [17], and CycTEA [15]. The main idea of semi-supervised learning is to improve the performance of a model by iteratively training to make full use of unlabeled data.

Unfortunately, some traditional semi-supervised learning methods may not effectively trackle the existing challenges of entity alignment. These challenges can be summarized as follows: (1) **Inefficient utilization of pseudo-labeling data.** To obtain more realistic and plausible pseudo-labeled data, it is often necessary to set a higher confidence threshold to minimize the risk of noisy data. However, this strategy may result in disregarding a substantial amount of data, which may contain valuable pseudo-labels and semantic information to enhance the performance of the entity alignment model. (2) **Negative impacts of noisy data.** Noisy data can compromise the integrity of the training samples, thereby reducing the accuracy of the entity alignment model in determining entity pairs between different knowledge graphs. Consequently, filtering and re-labeling the noisy data are essential steps in obtaining a robust and effective entity alignment model.(3) **Biased alignment selection.** Semi-supervised approaches often rely on predicted high-confidence alignments to bootstrap themselves. However, such alignments may receive more training in subsequent iterations, leading to a biased alignment selection in favor of the same, supposedly more reliable alignments. Retraining the entity alignment model with existing knowledge can improve performance to some extent, but the benefits of doing so are limited.

To address these issues, we propose semi-supervised entity alignment framework with noisy student-based self training named NSEA. First, we train a teacher aligner using labeled data to infer and filter potential entity alignments. We then feed both labeled and pseudo-labeled data to the student model to train a more robust model that can leverage more reliable training data. The training process is conducted iteratively to extract as many aligned entity pairs as possible. Our contributions are summarized as follows:

- We propose a new semi-supervised framework for entity alignment. It employs noisy-student as the overall training framework and enables iteratively self-train a robust and effective entity alignment model based on a small amount of labeled data.
- To ensure the quality of pseudo labeled data, we introduce a self-adaptive threshold adjustment strategy. At the early stage of iterations, high thresholds allow the aligner to obtain higher quality training samples, thus gradually building a reliable EA model; In the later stages of the iterative process, the model's discriminative ability tends to become more refined. Therefore, a relatively low threshold can be employed to obtain more new samples.
- We conducted detailed experimental analysis on eight benchmark datasets and confirmed that the framework proposed in this paper can effectively filter

and relabel noisy data, significantly improving the performance of the EA model. The ability of the model is also verified in terms of generalisability as well as stability

2 Related Work

Knowledge Graph Embedding Model. The knowledge graph embedding model transform entities and relationships in the knowledge graph into low-dimensional vector representations to capture the semantic information between them. It can be divided into two main categories: translation model and rotation model. The translation model TransE portrayed the relationship between entities as a translation from the head entity to the tail entity. Subsequent studies, such as TransR [5], and TransH [11], used diverse projection strategies for enhancing TransE's performance. The rotation models RotatE [10] subsequently suggested defining each relationship as a rotation from the source entity to the target entity in the complex vector space. This enables the models to model and infer various relationship patterns such as symmetry or asymmetry, inversion, and composition.

Embedding-Based Entity Alignment. The assumption for structure-based entity alignment is that similar entities should have similar relational structures. Early research such as MTransE [2] relied on the TransE model to learn the entity embedding and define some transitions between the embeddings of aligned entities. With the rise of graph neural networks(GNN), some entity alignment models such as Alinet [8] and GCN-AlignE [12] utilized various GNNs for neighborhood structure learning and alignment learning. GCN-AlignE interpreted the semantic information of the knowledge graph by training GCNs to embed entities of each language into a unified vector space

However, the above traditional methods based on supervised learning are affected by the number of training samples and cannot achieve good results in practical applications, so researchers have proposed to apply semi-supervised learning(IPtransE [17], BootEA [7]). IPtransE [17] introduced an iterative alignment model that utilized translation and linear transformation models. This model mapped entities to a unified representation space by aligning translations, linear transformations, and shared parameters under the joint embedding framework. BootEA [7] suggested a substitution strategy based on bootstrapping to counter error accumulation during the iterative alignment process. However, such approaches were also limited by the error-propagation issue of noisy data. Therefore, we aim to design an approach that filters more reliable entity alignment as training data through dynamic threshold based on noisy student.

3 Method

In this article, as shown in Fig. 1, we propose a self-adaptive thresholding method based on the noisy student framework to address the noise accumulation and

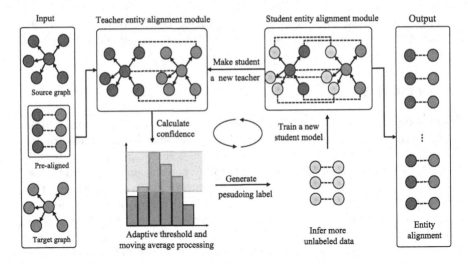

Fig. 1. The structure of proposed NSEA.

error propagation during the training process of semi-supervised learning. To begin, we train a basic teacher entity alignment module using labeled data. Besides, we use the teacher model to discover hidden entity pairs. Moreover, we dynamically filter pseudo-labeled samples by obtaining a suitable threshold through adaptive thresholding and sliding smoothing techniques. Then we feed labeled and pseudo-labeled data to train a more robust and effective student model. Finally, we iterate the process by putting back the student as a teacher to generate new pseudo labels and train a new student.

3.1   Problem Formulation

A knowledge graph can be defined as a set of triples $KG = (h, r, t)$, where h and r represent entities and relations respectively, and $t \subseteq h \times r \times h$. To accomplish the entity alignment task, we split the two knowledge graphs into the source $KG_1 = (h_1, r_1, t_1)$ and target $KG_2 = (h_2, r_2, t_2)$, with the intention to find $A = \{(e_1, e_2) \mid e_1 \equiv e_2, e_1 \in KG_1, e_2 \in KG_2\}$, where $\equiv$ represents equivocation between e_1 and e_2, Given $A_{train} \subseteq A$ as the prior alignment (training data) and $U = \{\tilde{e}_1 \mid \tilde{e}_1 \in KG_1\}$ as the unaligned data in the source knowledge graph. Our task aims to find the most similar entity with $\tilde{e}_1$ from the target graph. The formula for calculating similarity is as follows:

$$e_2 = \underset{e_2' \in KG_2}{\arg\max}\ sim(e_1, e_2'), \tag{1}$$

$$\mathrm{sim}\,(e_1, e_2) = \frac{e_1 \cdot e_2}{\|e_1\| \cdot \|e_2\|}, \tag{2}$$

where $sim(e_1, e_2)$ is the cosine distance between e_1 and e_2, $\|\cdot\|$ represents the L_1 or L_2 norm of a vector, e_2 denotes the entity in the target graph that is most similar to e_1.

3.2 Noisy Student

Recently, many semi-supervised learning methods have struggled to effectively utilize data and handle noisy data. In this paper, we propose a noisy student [14] strategy to deal with potential noisy data. The noisy student strategy builds upon the concept of self-training and distillation, with the use of equal student models and adding noise to the student during learning.

Labeled data are first utilized to train a teacher model θ^t with standard cross entropy loss. We then use the teacher model θ^t to generate pseudo labels on unlabeled entities A_{train} and the loss of teacher model is:

$$L_{tea} = \frac{1}{n} \sum_{i=1}^{n} l(e_{2i}, f^{noised}(e_{1i}, \theta^t)), \tag{3}$$

where e_{1i} and e_{2i} denote the i−th entities from KG_1 and KG_2, n is num of labeled data and function f is the aligned entity of e_1 peridcted by model θ^t. Then a student model is trained by minimizing its combined cross entropy loss on both labeled entities and unlabeled entities. Finally, we iterate the training process by putting back the student as a teacher to generate new pseudo labels and train a new student. For m unlabeled data, the loss of student model is:

$$L_{stu} = \frac{1}{n} \sum_{i=1}^{n} l(e_{2i}, f^{noised}(e_{1i}, \theta^t)) + \frac{1}{m} \sum_{i=1}^{m} l(\tilde{e_{2i}}, f^{noised}(\tilde{e_{1i}}, \theta^t)). \tag{4}$$

3.3 Adaptive Dynamic Similarity Propagator

To leverage unlabeled data for entity alignment, we apply an entity alignment model to predict the similarity between entities in the source and target knowledge graphs. If the similarity between two entities exceeds a given threshold, they are labeled as a potential match pair. However, the matching capability of the same EA model for entity pairs varies across different training stages. At the early stages of training, the model's performance is relatively low, thus requiring a higher threshold to filter high-quality samples. As the model becomes progressively optimized, a lower threshold can be gradually accepted. Therefore, a fixed threshold may not be suitable for all training stages, so we propose a self-adaptive similarity threshold ϵ_t that adjusts the model's learning ability.

$$\epsilon_t = \alpha \times \Phi(t) - \beta \times \frac{t}{T_{max}}, \tag{5}$$

$$\Phi(t) = \min \left\{ 1, \frac{count_{t-1}}{count_t} \right\}, \tag{6}$$

where ϵ_t is the similarity threshold for the current round, α and β are the parameters that control the threshold, t denotes the current iteration, and T_{max} reperesents the maximum number of iterations. The term $\Phi(t)$ adapts the threshold based on the performance of the model on the unlabeled data in the previous iteration. If the performance has improved, the threshold will decrease, allowing more pseudo-labeled pairs to be generated. Conversely, if the performance has decreased, the threshold will increase to filter out less reliable pseudo-labeled pairs. $count_t$ computed as follows:

$$count_t = \sum_{i=1}^{N} \mathbb{1}\left(\mathrm{sim}(x_i, y_i) > \epsilon_{t-1}\right). \tag{7}$$

Here, N is the number of entities in the unlabeled data. The formula for the similarity threshold in our previous section heavily influences the determination of entity alignment. If the $count_{t-1}$ is much smaller than $count_t$, there is a significant risk of integrating numerous low-confidence entity pairs into the model during the iterative training process, which can have adverse effects on the overall performance of the model.

To address this issue, we also propose a moving average process to restrict extreme variations in the similarity threshold and enhance the fidelity of the pseudo-labeled data. Moving average function is applied to correct low thresholds into an acceptable interval. The formula for the similarity threshold ϵ_t after applying the convolution kernel is:

$$\epsilon_t = \begin{cases} \sum_{k=1}^{K} w[k] * \epsilon_{t-k+1}, & \epsilon_t < \lambda, \\ \epsilon_t, & \epsilon_t >= \lambda, \end{cases} \tag{8}$$

where w is the selected convolution kernel, and K is its length. The Moving average function helps to ensure that the similarity threshold remains in the acceptable range, thereby preventing the incorporation of too many low-confidence or noisy entity pairs in the model.

3.4   Training Strategy

In this study, we adopt RotatE as the task model. RotatE defines relations as rotational transformations in a complex space, from head to tail entities, under the assumption that entities and relations satisfy the equation $\mathbf{h} \circ \mathbf{r} = \mathbf{t}$ and $|\mathbf{r}| = 1$. The score function d of Rotate is expressed as:

$$d_r(\mathbf{h}, \mathbf{t}) = -\|\mathbf{h} \circ \mathbf{r} - \mathbf{t}\|, \tag{9}$$

where the score function d represents the alignment score function of the entity $\mathbf{h}$ and $\mathbf{t}$ under the rotation relation $\mathbf{r}$, and the $\|\cdot\|$ refers to the L_1 parmetrization and the loss is:

$$L = -\log \sigma\left(\gamma - d_r(\mathbf{h}, \mathbf{t})\right) - \sum_{i=1}^{n} p\left(h_i', r, t_i'\right) \log \sigma\left(d_r\left(\mathbf{h}_i', \mathbf{t}_i'\right) - \gamma\right), \tag{10}$$

$$p\left(h'_j, r, t'_j \mid \{(h_i, r_i, t_i)\}\right) = \frac{\exp \vartheta d_r\left(\mathbf{h}'_j, \mathbf{t}'_j\right)}{\sum_i \exp \vartheta d_r\left(\mathbf{h}'_i, \mathbf{t}'_i\right)}, \tag{11}$$

where $p(h, r, t)$ represents the probability of negative sampling, the loss L donates cross-entropy after positive and negative sampling, ϑ and γ are coefficients set before and σ is the sigmoid function.

Therefore, our framework algorithm is shown algorithm1: we initialize an entity alignment model as a teacher model. Then we filter potential alignment pairs with the teacher model via Eq. 1 and Eq. 2. Besides, we update the threshold ϵ_t through Eq. 5, Eq. 6, Eq. 7 for next round and fix it via Eq. 8 if it is lower than acceptable range. Finally, a student entity alignment model is trained for a new round of training.

Algorithm 1: The framework based on noisy student self-learning for entity alignment.

Data: $A_{train} = \{(x_m, y_m) : m \in (1, \ldots, M)\}, \mathcal{U} = \{u_n : n \in (1, \ldots, N)\},$
$KG_1 = (h_1, r_1, t_1), KG_2 = (h_2, r_2, t_2), n$ represents max iteration
times.(M prior alignment pairs, N unlabeled data)

Result: Alignment entity pairs

1 **Initialize** teacher entity alignment model.
2 **while** $i = 1$ **to** n **do**
3   **for** $j \leftarrow 1$ **to** N **do**
4 | Filter potential entity alignment pairs via Eq.1 and Eq.2
5   **end**
6   Compute ϵ_t via Eq.5, Eq.6, Eq.7; // Calculate the similarity
       threshold of the current round.
7   **if** $\epsilon_t < \lambda$ **then**
8 | Fix ϵ_t via Eq.8 ;
9   **end**
10   **for** $i = 1$ **to** m **do**
11 | $\mathcal{L}^i_{t_n} = \mathcal{L}_{stu}(x^i; \theta)$; // Update the model by minimizing $\mathcal{L}_{t_n}$ with
       student entity alignment model.
12   **end**
13     $h_\theta \leftarrow \nabla_\theta \frac{1}{m} \sum_{i=1}^m \mathcal{L}_{t_n}$;
14     $\theta \leftarrow \theta - \alpha_n \cdot \text{Adagrad}(\theta, h_\theta)$;
15 **end**

---

4 Experiment

In this section, we will verify the performance of our framework using a benchmark dataset. Additionally, we will demonstrate the effectiveness, generalization, and robustness of our model through various experiments.

4.1 Dataset and Settings

Datasets. We use the benchmark dataset provided by OpenEA [9] as our experimental data sampling real-world KGs DBpedia, Wikidata and YAGO to simulate real-world semantic situations. Our dataset is made up of four subsets:

two cross-lingual datasets (English-to-French and English-to-German), and two same-language datasets that connect different knowledge graphs (DBpedia-to-Wikidata and DBpedia-to-YAGO), each consisting of 15K and 100K pairs of reference entity alignments. To conform to OpenEA's partitioning method, 20% of the data is allocated for training, 10% for validation, and 70% for testing and validation and testing sets are treated as unlabeled data, ensuring a labeled to unlabeled data ratio of 1:4.

Implementation Details. In the experiment, we select RotatE as the teacher model and set the initial values of the hyperparameters α and β to 0.9 and 0.1, respectively. Additionally, we apply a convolution kernel of $[1, 1, 2.85]$ for moving average processing to fix a low threshold. Then we follow the experimental procedures described in OpenEA and employ a five-fold cross-validation method to train our model, ensuring fairness and accuracy of the results. To facilitate verification and comparison of model performance, we utilize evaluation metrics such as Hits@1, Hits@5(Hits@n means top-n Hit Ratio), and MRR(Mean Reciprocal Rank), where higher scores indicate better performance.

Baselines. In this study, we select some automated entity alignment models for comparison. These include four structure-based entity alignment models (MtransE [2], AlignE [7], and RSN4EA [3]), two semi-supervised entity alignment models (BootEA [7] and IPTransE [17]), and two graph neural network entity alignment models (GCN-Align [12] and Alinet [8]). Additionally, we include the CycTEA [15] model for comparison performing well currently.

4.2   Experimental Results

After comparing our model with all baseline models, we obtained the following entity alignment results on 15K and 100K datasets. As shown in Tables 1 and 2:

– Our model outperforms other models, particularly on EN-DE-15K, D-W-15K, D-Y-15K, EN-DE-100K, and D-Y-100K datasets, where its performance is significantly superior.It also exhibits strong performance on the remaining four datasets. In comparison to the aforementioned methods, our framework demonstrates a percentage improvement ranging from 10.5% to 18.6% on the 15K dataset and 9.6% to 10% on the 100K dataset. Even when compared to CycTEA, which employs multiple aligners, our model achieves a performance advantage of 0.2% and 2.3% on the EN-DE-15K and D-W-15K datasets respectively. Additionally, on the 100K dataset, our model outperforms CycTEA by 3% and 14.3% on the EN-DE-100K and D-Y-100K datasets.
– We find that the performance of the Rotate model is outstanding on the D-Y-15K dataset. This means RotatE has already explained semantic information of this knowledge graph. That is why our framework do not bring much improvement on D-Y-15K.

Table 1. Entity alignment results on a 15K dataset. Using red bold to indicate the best performing model and blue bold to indicate the second.

	EN-FR-15K			EN-DE-15K			D-W-15K			D-Y-15K		
	Hits@1	Hits@5	MRR	Hits@1	Hits@5	MRR	Hits@1	Hits@5	MRR	Hits@1	Hits@5	MRR
MTransE	0.247	0.467	0.351	0.307	0.518	0.407	0.259	0.461	0.354	0.463	0.675	0.559
BootEA	**0.507**	0.718	**0.603**	0.675	0.820	0.740	0.572	0.744	0.649	0.739	0.849	0.788
AlignE	0.357	0.611	0.473	0.552	0.741	0.638	0.406	0.627	0.506	0.551	0.743	0.636
IPTransE	0.169	0.320	0.243	0.350	0.515	0.430	0.232	0.380	0.303	0.313	0.456	0.378
RSN4EA	0.393	0.595	0.487	0.587	0.752	0.662	0.441	0.615	0.521	0.514	0.655	0.580
AliNet	0.364	0.597	0.467	0.604	0.759	0.673	0.440	0.628	0.522	0.559	0.690	0.617
GCN-Align	0.338	0.589	0.451	0.481	0.679	0.571	0.364	0.580	0.461	0.465	0.626	0.536
CycTEA	0.622	0.814	0.708	**0.756**	0.892	**0.816**	**0.686**	**0.838**	**0.753**	**0.777**	**0.871**	**0.820**
NSEA	0.444	**0.748**	0.580	0.764	**0.881**	0.818	0.690	0.872	0.770	0.964	0.988	0.974

Table 2. Entity alignment results on a 100K dataset. Using red bold to indicate the best performing model and blue bold to indicate the second.

	EN-FR-100K			EN-DE-100K			D-W-100K			D-Y-100K		
	Hits@1	Hits@5	MRR	Hits@1	Hits@5	MRR	Hits@1	Hits@5	MRR	Hits@1	Hits@5	MRR
MTransE	0.138	0.261	0.202	0.140	0.264	0.204	0.210	0.358	0.282	0.244	0.414	0.328
BootEA	**0.389**	0.561	**0.474**	0.518	0.673	0.592	0.516	0.685	0.594	**0.703**	**0.827**	**0.761**
AlignE	0.294	0.483	0.388	0.423	0.593	0.505	0.385	0.587	0.478	0.617	0.776	0.691
IPTransE	0.158	0.277	0.219	0.226	0.357	0.292	0.221	0.352	0.285	0.396	0.558	0.474
RSN4EA	0.293	0.452	0.371	0.430	0.570	0.497	0.384	0.533	0.454	0.620	0.769	0.688
AliNet	0.266	0.444	0.348	0.405	0.546	0.471	0.369	0.535	0.444	0.626	0.772	0.692
GCN-Align	0.230	0.412	0.319	0.317	0.485	0.399	0.324	0.507	0.409	0.528	0.695	0.605
CycTEA	0.442	0.627	0.530	**0.560**	**0.709**	**0.630**	0.566	**0.732**	0.641	0.667	0.810	0.732
NSEA	0.352	**0.585**	0.462	0.577	0.728	0.649	**0.512**	0.767	**0.602**	0.792	0.889	0.837

- From the experimental results, we can see that our model's performance is very close to the CycTEA model, which is better than other models. This is because we both use noise filtering and relabeling strategies. However, the difference is that their model requires three agents to vote, so they need to train three aligners at the same time, which requires relatively high computing resources and also consumes a lot of time. However, our model accelerate the ability to obtain high-quality data through mutual learning between the teacher and the student and the adaptive threshold method.
- On the 100K dataset, most models did not perform well due to more complex Knowledge graph structures and a larger alignment space. However, our model still show good performance, proving that our model has good robustness, effectiveness, and generalization ability.

4.3 Ablation Experiments

Effecctiveness of Components in NSEA. In this study, we evaluate the effectiveness of each component in NSEA by testing the following variants: (1) NSEA(FT) uses a fixed similarity threshold α to propagate label information to unlabeled data. (2) NSEA(-MS) utilizes adaptive similarity without a smoothing function to select unaligned entity pairs.

Table 3. Hits@1 and MRR of different frameworks on 15K datasets.

	EN-DE		D-W	
	Hits@1	MRR	Hits@1	MRR
BooTEA	0.675	0.740	0.572	0.649
CycTEA	0.756	0.816	0.686	0.753
NSEA(FT)	0.745	0.803	0.595	0.678
NSEA(-MS)	0.731	0.790	0.645	0.735
NSEA	**0.764**	**0.818**	**0.690**	**0.770**

Table 3 displays the components and the semi-supervised learning performance on EN-DE and D-W with 15K. NSEA is the best-performing method with better results than NSEA(FT) and NSEA(-MS), with a performance increase of 3.5% to 13.5%. Our model accepts more entity pair data compared to NSEA(FT) and gained higher quality pseudo-labels compared to NSEA(-MS). These results confirm the effectiveness of all of our framework's components. Through experiments, it has been demonstrated that both the FT and MS components can effectively improve the model's ability to filter noise and relabel data and verify the effectiveness of two components.

Impacts of Different Noisy Radio. The original ratio of labeled data to unlabeled data is 1:4. To investigate the impact of different ratios of labeled data on the model performance, we design the following experiments. Figure 2 illustrates the performance of the model in terms of Hit@1, Hits@5, and MRR with varying ratios of labeled and unlabelled data. The experimental results from EN-DE and D-W 15K datasets show that increasing the ratio of unlabelled data (from 1:1 to 1:2 to 1:4) leads to a gradual improvement in model performance, particularly in terms of MRR and Hits@5. This indicates that the model becomes better equipped to accurately align corresponding entities across knowledge graphs with an increased amount of unlabeled data.

Robustness of NSEA. We evaluate our model's tolerance to data by adjusting the training data ratio, as shown in Fig. 3. Specifically, we examine the model's performance on the EN-DE-15K and D-W-15K datasets with 10%, 15%, and 20% training data. The Alinet(semi) model represents a semi-supervised learning method based on Alinet that utilizes self-training. Our analysis reveals that RS4NA and AlignE are significantly impacted by the data volume, while our model's performance remained relatively stable across various data settings. Therefore, our model exhibits robustness as it is relatively insensitive to the training data volume.

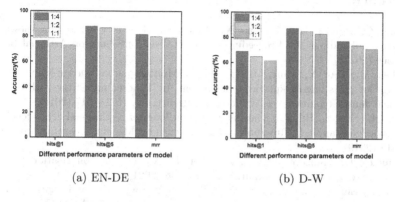

(a) EN-DE   (b) D-W

Fig. 2. Different ratio between labeled data and unlabeled data.

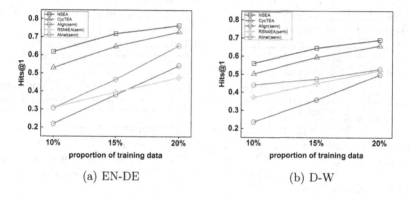

(a) EN-DE   (b) D-W

Fig. 3. Hits@1 w.r.t different proportions of training data.

5 Conclusion

In this paper, we propose a new semi-supervised entity alignment framework
with noisy student-based self training named NSEA to unleash the potential of
unlabeled data. We employ an adaptive threshold adjustment method to obtain
more reliable data and accelerate our training process in order to enhance the
performance of the knowledge graph embedding model. Experimental results
demonstrate that our framework surpasses most semi-supervised learning methods in entity alignment. Moreover, our approach is not limited to the domain
of entity alignment, it can also be applied to natural language processing suffer-
ing from insufficient annotated data. In summary, our framework is capable of
addressing the entity alignment problem.

References

1. Cao, Z., Xu, Q., Yang, Z., Cao, X., Huang, Q.: Geometry interaction knowledge graph embeddings. In: Proceedings of the AAAI Conference on Artificial Intelligence (2022)
2. Chen, M., Tian, Y., Yang, M., Zaniolo, C.: Multilingual knowledge graph embeddings for cross-lingual knowledge alignment. In: Proceedings of the 26th International Joint Conference on Artificial Intelligence, pp. 1511–1517 (2017)
3. Guo, L., Sun, Z., Hu, W.: Learning to exploit long-term relational dependencies in knowledge graphs. In: International Conference on Machine Learning, pp. 2505–2514 (2019)
4. Jannach, D., Manzoor, A., Cai, W., Chen, L.: A survey on conversational recommender systems. ACM Comput. Surv. 5, 1–36 (2021)
5. Lin, Y., Liu, Z., Sun, M., Liu, Y., Zhu, X.: Learning entity and relation embeddings for knowledge graph completion. In: Proceedings of the AAAI Conference on Artificial Intelligence (2015)
6. Pei, S., Yu, L., Hoehndorf, R., Zhang, X.: Semi-supervised entity alignment via knowledge graph embedding with awareness of degree difference. In: The World Wide Web Conference, pp. 3130–3136 (2019)
7. Sun, Z., Hu, W., Zhang, Q., Qu, Y.: Bootstrapping entity alignment with knowledge graph embedding. In: Proceedings of the 27th International Joint Conference on Artificial Intelligence, pp. 4396–4402 (2018)
8. Sun, Z., et al.: Knowledge graph alignment network with gated multi-hop neighborhood aggregation. In: Proceedings of the AAAI Conference on Artificial Intelligence, pp. 222–229 (2020)
9. Sun, Z., et al.: A benchmarking study of embedding-based entity alignment for knowledge graphs. In: Proceedings of the VLDB Endowment, pp. 2326–2340 (2020)
10. Sun, Z., Deng, Z.H., Nie, J.Y., Tang, J.: Rotate: Knowledge graph embedding by relational rotation in complex space. In: International Conference on Learning Representations (2019)
11. Wang, Z., Zhang, J., Feng, J., Chen, Z.: Knowledge graph embedding by translating on hyperplanes. In: Proceedings of the AAAI Conference on Artificial Intelligence (2014)
12. Wang, Z., Lv, Q., Lan, X., Zhang, Y.: Cross-lingual knowledge graph alignment via graph convolutional networks. In: Proceedings of the 2018 Conference on Empirical Methods in Natural Language Processing, pp. 349–357 (2018)
13. Wu, S., Sun, F., Zhang, W., Xie, X., Cui, B.: Graph neural networks in recommender systems: a survey. ACM Computing Surveys, pp. 1–37 (2022)
14. Xie, Q., Luong, M.T., Hovy, E., Le, Q.V.: Self-training with noisy student improves imagenet classification. In: Proceedings of the IEEE/CVF Conference on Computer Vision and Pattern Recognition, pp. 10687–10698 (2020)
15. Xin, K., et al.: Ensemble semi-supervised entity alignment via cycle-teaching. In: Proceedings of the AAAI Conference on Artificial Intelligence, pp. 4281–4289 (2022)
16. Zhao, X., Jia, Y., Li, A., Jiang, R., Song, Y.: Multi-source knowledge fusion: a survey. World Wide Web 23(4), 2567–2592 (2020). https://doi.org/10.1007/s11280-020-00811-0
17. Zhu, H., Xie, R., Liu, Z., Sun, M.: Iterative entity alignment via joint knowledge embeddings. In: IJCAI, pp. 4258–4264 (2017)

Modeling Chinese Ancient Book Catalog

Linxu Wang[1,2], Jun Wang[1,2](✉), and Tong Wei[1,2]

[1] Department of Information Management, Peking University, Beijing, China
{wanglinxu,junwang,weitong}@pku.edu.cn
[2] The Research Center for Digital Humanities at Peking University, Peking
University, Beijing, China

Abstract. Chinese ancient book catalogs are a unique type of Chinese ancient books, which are essential resources for Chinese humanities research. They are distinguished by their systematic arrangement and provision of organization, classification, review, and generalization of ancient books. However, the lack of knowledge bases that support the discovery and representation of knowledge interrelationships poses a significant challenge for utilizing these catalogs. Identifying, extracting, standardizing, and analyzing the entities and relationships in Chinese ancient book catalogs remains difficult. Ontology can serve as a potent tool for facilitating knowledge discovery and representation, addressing the organization of catalog resources in the digital environment. This paper develops the CABC ontology, which aims to formally represent the concepts present in Chinese ancient book catalogs. By drawing on academic tradition and research needs in this area, the CABC ontology offers a reference conceptual model and opens new avenues for comprehending Chinese ancient books, thereby expanding the application scope of traditional Chinese ancient book catalogs. This study provides a powerful tool for knowledge organization and retrieval, empowering scholars to explore and analyze knowledge interrelationships in Chinese ancient culture, humanities, and history with greater ease.

Keywords: Ontology · Chinese ancient book · Chinese ancient book catalog · Digital humanities · protégé

1 Introduction

Chinese ancient books are witnesses to history and provide foundations for the study of ancient Chinese culture, humanities, history, society, and other related fields. Among the various types of Chinese ancient books, the Chinese ancient book catalog (CABC) stands out as a systematically arranged list of Chinese ancient books. It serves as a means of screening and collecting ancient books within specific periods, while also providing organization, classification, review, and generalization of these works. Originating in China in 26 BC, the CABC has

Supported by the NSFC project *The Construction of the Knowledge Graph for the History of Chinese Confucianism* (Grant No. 72010107003).

© The Author(s), under exclusive license to Springer Nature Switzerland AG 2023
Z. Jin et al. (Eds.): KSEM 2023, LNAI 14118, pp. 355–367, 2023.
https://doi.org/10.1007/978-3-031-40286-9_29

remained a fundamental resource for scholars' learning and research endeavors throughout history. Scholars engage with the contents of these books, study their classification and generalization methods, and utilize them as valuable indexing tools.

The progress of information technology and the availability of large-scale databases have led to a paradigm shift in the research methods employed by humanities scholars. Retrieval has emerged as an additional approach for utilizing the CABC, offering convenience, rapidity, and efficiency. However, recent developments in digital humanities and international Sinology research have resulted in an increased demand for digital resources related to the CABC. Scholars now seek more than just permanent data preservation and information retrieval; they aim for deep processing and knowledge discovery [1]. Particularly, the discovery and representation of interconnected knowledge have emerged as a new area for using CABC information resources. This shift holds significant potential for advancing research in the fields of Chinese ancient culture, humanities, and history.

Research that relies on knowledge associations necessitates a comprehensive analysis of ancient book catalogs, involving transforming CABC information into quantifiable entities and their analyzable relationships, including people, works, time, location, relationships, events, and more. By quantifying, relating, analyzing, and interpreting these entities and relationships, catalog information can be transformed into valuable historical evidence. However, the current lack of datasets supporting this type of research poses a significant challenge. This limitation makes it challenging to identify, extract, standardize, and analyze the entities and relationships contained within the catalog.

Ontology, as a formal and explicit specification of shared concepts, is an effective method for representing and modeling knowledge. It can translate information resources into machine-readable knowledge, provide rich data "schemas" based on terms, improve data application [2], and support the construction of semantically enhanced knowledge bases. Ontology can also serve as a framework for knowledge organization and retrieval, allowing scholars to easily search for and explore the relationships between different concepts and entities in the CABC. Thus, ontology can serve as a powerful tool to enable knowledge discovery and representation and can meet the needs of humanities scholars for CABC resources in the digital environment.

This paper utilizes ontology to systematically model the Chinese ancient book catalog, providing a comprehensive description of the knowledge system and relationships between entities within the catalogs. The ontology model transforms information entities in ancient book catalogs into quantifiable, traceable, and interpretable historical evidence, establishing a shared framework for understanding and representing CABC and supporting the semantic organization of CABC information resources. This study offers two primary contributions. Firstly, the Chinese Ancient Book Catalog Ontology integrates the academic tradition and research needs of CABC, provides a reference conceptual model, and restructures the humanities research framework for tracing the origins and observing the evolution of Chinese ancient books. Secondly, the ontology model offers a new approach to understanding Chinese ancient books and expands the application scope of traditional CABC. By providing a machine-readable and semantically rich representation of CABC, this study offers a powerful tool for knowledge organization and retrieval, enabling scholars to more easily explore and analyze the interrelation of knowledge in Chinese ancient culture, humanities, and history.

This paper utilizes ontology to systematically model the Chinese ancient book catalog, offering a comprehensive depiction of the knowledge system and relationships between entities within the catalogs. The ontology model establishes a shared framework for understanding and representing the CABC, supporting the semantic organization of CABC information resources. This study makes two primary contributions. Firstly, the Chinese Ancient Book Catalog Ontology integrates the academic tradition and research requirements of the CABC, providing a reference conceptual model. It restructures the humanities research framework by tracing the origins and observing the evolution of Chinese ancient books. Secondly, the ontology model introduces a new approach to understanding Chinese ancient books and expands the application scope of the traditional CABC. By offering a machine-readable and semantically rich representation of the CABC, this study provides a powerful tool for knowledge organization and retrieval. And it enables scholars to explore and analyze the relations of knowledge in Chinese ancient books easily.

2   Foundation of Research

2.1   Brief Introduction of CABC

Chinese ancient books encompass books that were written and printed in China before 1912, and among them, the ancient book catalog holds a significant position. The Chinese ancient book catalog (CABC) is a distinct type of book that was specifically created to organize and safeguard these literary treasures. Serving as a crucial resource for studying the history and evolution of Chinese literature and culture, the CABC remains indispensable for contemporary researchers and scholars.

Table 1 summarizes the key contents of the CABC. The top three entries, labeled No.1, No.2, and No.3, represent the core elements of the CABC and have established themselves as academic traditions and disciplines. On the other hand, entries No.4, No.5, and No.6 comprise valuable information for current research and study, often overlooked in various projects focused on organizing CABC information resources.

The number of CABCs is extensive, with hundreds of thousands of ancient books included in its collection. Given this vastness, this paper has chosen a representative CABC as the data source. Specifically, the research data domain focuses on *The National Rare Ancient Book Directory* (*The NRAB Directory*), which stands as a notable achievement in the organization and cataloging of ancient books over the past two decades.

Table 1. The key contents in the Chinese ancient book catalog.

No.	Content
1	A collected **book's title, volume, authors, language, and other basic information**. Besides, the CABC usually provides a **brief introduction of the authors**, including their names (ancient Chinese people usually have more than two names), dynasties, hometowns, and etc
2	**The essential details of a collected book's edition**, including temporal information, document type, and publishing method. Notably, ancient Chinese books were published using a diverse array of methods, which can be categorized into handwriting, engraving, printing, and rubbing, among others. These numerous publishing techniques, numbering over a dozen, play a significant role in understanding the history of Chinese printing and publishing methods, as well as their development over time
3	**The classification** of the collected book. It reflects changes in knowledge production and organization over time and provides valuable insights into intellectual trends and developments
4	**Physical characteristics** of a collected book, including layout design, lines per page, and color. These factors not only shed light on the production methods employed in creating the books but also provide insights into the cultural and aesthetic values of the era. Furthermore, these details can assist scholars in gaining a deeper understanding of the historical context of books and the intended audience
5	**Contextual information** about a collected book includes details about its historical background and dissemination process. This information can be obtained from external sources, such as the vocabulary of the dynasty (a kind of term of temporal entity) and the taxonomy of the office, as well as the seals of book collectors
6	Information regarding the **current location** of a collected book, especially in relation to specific collectors or collection institutions. Knowing the current whereabouts of the collected books allows researchers to plan visits, request access, or collaborate with the respective collectors to delve deeper into the contents of these valuable resources

2.2   Description About Data Resource

The NRAB Directory is an officially approved catalog of valuable ancient books in China. It has undergone six nationwide collections and reviews, resulting in a listing of over 13,026 ancient books. Unlike other catalogs that aim for a broad and comprehensive collection, *The NRAB Directory* has a specific objective of condensing Chinese culture and transmitting classic Chinese books. Through the organization and categorization of these precious and representative ancient books across various dimensions, valuable insights can be gained into the evolution of Chinese civilization from 221 B.C. to 1912 A A.D.

In *The NRAB Directory*, book descriptions are provided in unstructured text, typically comprising less than one hundred words. Despite their brevity, these descriptions contain a wealth of information, such as edition descriptions, responsible behavior records, and features of layout, as shown in Fig. 1. However, without domain knowledge and external data, it is challenging to fully discover and present the rich information in *The NRAB Directory*.

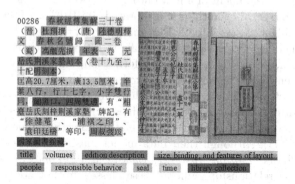

Fig. 1. An example of a book entry in *The NRAB Directory*.

3   Objective

The goal of the paper is to construct an open ontology in a W3C standard to represent the knowledge of the Chinese ancient book catalog. The ontology aims to formally represent the information in the catalog, including the traditional understanding of book organization as outlined in No.1, No.2, and No.3 in Table 1, as well as additional knowledge that requires further marking and annotation as described in No.4, No.5, and No.6 in Table 1.

4   State of the Art

Ontology, originally developed in philosophy, has been extended to various other fields due to the rapid development of computer science. The definition of ontology encompasses four layers of meaning: conceptual model, explicit specification, formal, and shared [3]. The use of ontology enables the creation of structured and standardized knowledge representation systems that can facilitate data integration, knowledge sharing, and knowledge discovery.

Some ontologies target semantically published documents, including books, and journal articles, employing web and web technologies to enhance those documents, enrich their meaning, and facilitate their automatic discovery [4]. Two of them provide the basis for our research, including Fabio (the FRBR-aligned Bibliographic Ontology) [5] and BIBFRAME 2.x [6]. They present a general understanding of published documents and provide common description frameworks including vocabularies and ontologies.

Moreover, some efforts have been made to construct explicit ontologies for ancient books, identifying and linking related concepts. These studies provide controlled vocabularies with precise and formal descriptions of terminologies and classification schemes [7,8].

Chen's study [9] aimed to explore the potential reuse and extension of BIBFRAME 2.0 for Chinese rare books (a kind of Chinese ancient books), resulting in the development of a new ontology called the **Chinese Rare Book Ontology (CRBO)**. The authors incorporated 20 BIBFRAME classes and four external vocabulary classes into CRBO, and designed two new classes. Additionally, CRBO includes new properties specific to Chinese ancient books, such as page decoration, layout design, taboo information, and seal information. The ontology was employed to develop a linked open dataset for the Fu Ssu-Nien Library at Academia Sinica. The Shanghai Library has designed an **ancient book data model** aiming to cover all Chinese ancient books, including the lost books [10], to support the evidence-based platform for the Chinese ancient book union catalogs [11]. Although their data model consists of nine classes, including *Resource, Work, Edition, Instance, Classification, Time, Place, Agent,* and *Annotation*, the relationships among these classes are not adequately emphasized, with the majority of relations focusing on the concept of Work. OuYang et al. proposed a **Large-scale Chinese Ancient Books Framework** based on web crawling or scraping data and constructed a knowledge graph [12,13], with a focus on four classes: *Work, Person, Version,* and *Place*, along with the relations around *Work*. Additionally, there are some data models designed for particular types of books, like Tang Poetry [14] and chronological biography [15].

In conclusion, ontology is a critical approach for representing information about Chinese ancient books and serves as the basis for knowledge bases and service-oriented information systems. While it is widely acknowledged that differentiating the concept of an Ancient Book is essential and valuable, there has been limited research on its subclasses and their relationships. Despite various case studies demonstrating the potential and advantages of organizing knowledge in the utilization of ancient texts, the lack of systematic data organization and the supplementation of background knowledge makes it difficult to intuitively comprehend the inherent logic of ancient texts. As a result, this inconvenience hampers the ability of ordinary users to understand and learn about ancient knowledge.

5   The Procedure of Ontology Design and Construction

The construction of ontologies typically follows a lifecycle consisting of several stages [16] and covers methods, techniques, and design principles. This paper adopts the procedures that involve four phases [17] and makes some adjustments.

The first stage involves analyzing the domain and determining its scope. In this paper, the focus is on the Chinese ancient book catalog (CABC) and entities in its content, including different states of a Chinese ancient book, editions, and responsible behaviors. The primary objective is to describe and represent the contents outlined in Table 1.

The second stage of ontology development involves identifying terms and objects, as well as defining the concepts and relationships of the ontology. In this paper, the main data source used is *The NRAB Directory*, from which the terms and objects in the records of *The NRAB Directory* are selected. Additionally, a high-level conceptual framework is constructed based on domain knowledge of cataloging and classical philology to define concepts and their properties. The essential characteristics of Chinese ancient books are identified by considering the general understanding of a document provided by FRBR and BIBFRAME 2.x. The concept of a Chinese ancient book is then divided into three states: work, edition, and item. Subsequently, the ontology is iteratively refined and expanded based on *The NRAB Directory* to enrich ontology's properties. The core classes and the objective properties that link these classes are illustrated in Fig. 2.

The fourth stage involves formalizing the ontology using a standard ontology language. This paper uses Protégé, an open-source ontology editor, to create and edit the ontology. CABC ontology includes 34 classes, 24 object properties, 8 data properties, and 242 logical axioms.

Finally, the last stage involves evaluating and validating the ontology, which will be discussed in Sect. 7.

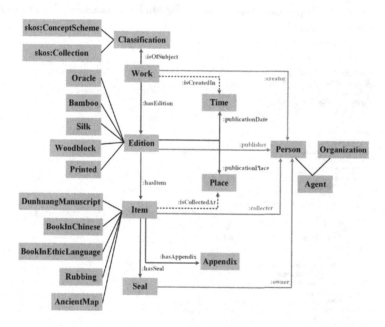

Fig. 2. The framework of classes in CABC ontology.

6   The CABC Ontology (Chinese Ancient Book Catalog Ontology)

6.1   Class

The CABC ontology primarily focuses on Chinese ancient books, while also encompassing other concepts such as Classification, Seal, Agent, and others (as shown in Fig. 2).

The core of the CABC ontology is the Ancient Book class, which includes three subclasses representing different states of the Chinese ancient book: as a creative work, as an expression, and as an accessible item, namely *Work, Edition*, and *Item*. Each state is further expandable in the CABC ontology, as illustrated on the left side of Fig. 3.

This study aims to identify concepts related to these classes by focusing on their essential characteristics. Specifically, the concept of an *Edition* can be defined by three aspects.

– Firstly, the carrier of an edition is an important factor, which includes tortoise armor, animal bones, silks, bamboo slips, wood chips, and paper. To further expand the Edition class, the CABC ontology incorporates this distinction and defines six types of classic editions for ancient books (as depicted on the left side of Fig. 3).

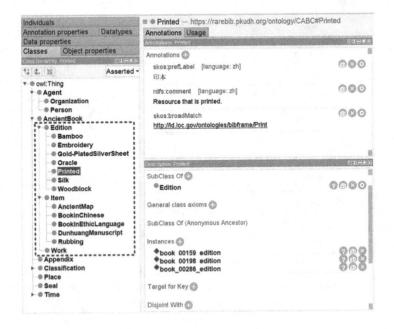

Fig. 3. The Ancient Book class.

– Secondly, the way to express a version, or how the text was recorded, is another important factor, and there are three approaches: writing, carving, and printing.
– Lastly, for paper-based ancient books, the printing process is a crucial factor. The printing process involves the use of molds, and different combinations of molds and recording methods can result in various types of editions. These combinations are defined as subclasses of *Classification,* and the different types are represented as instances of the *EditionCollection* class.

The concept of an *Item* can be defined by the terms selected from *The NRAB Directory* which includes the most representative collection in mainland China.

6.2 Property

There were 24 object properties, which are listed in Table 2.

Table 2. The object properties.

Object Properties	Domain	Range
creator	Work	Person
contributor	Work	Person
hasEdition	Work	Edition
hasPartOf	Work	Work
isOfSubject	Work	Classification
carver	Edition	Person
printer	Edition	Person
publisher	Edition	Person
carvingDate	Edition	DateTime
printDate	Edition	Time
publicationDate	Edition	Time
publicationPlace	Edition	Place
hasItem	Edition	Item
isOfEdition	Edition	EditionCollection
formerCollector	Item	Person
formerReviewer	Item	Person
collectionInstitution	Item	Organization
cre collectionPlace	Item	Place
hasAppendix	Item	Appendix
hasSeal	Item	Seal
location	Organization	Place
owner	Seal	Agent
birthYear	Person	DateTime
deathYear	Person	DateTime
dynasty	Person	Dynasty

Data properties include *isFoundAt, title, language, layout, banKou, banKuang, banXin, hangGe,* and *layoutSize.* Among them, the last five properties aim to describe the physical characteristics of the *Edition.*

6.3   Annotation

Annotations allow to enrich the description of the ontology and thus facilitate its understanding and reuse. The RDFS, DC, and SKOS vocabularies are used to express metadata and the linguistic dimension associated with a concept (*dc:publisher, dc:license, dc:creator, skos:prefLabel, skos:altLabel, skos:definition, rdfs:comment*) as well as to express linking and mapping to external resources (*rdfs:seeAlso, skos:broadMatch*).

7   Evaluation

Evaluation is the last stage of building ontology, whose goal is *to assess the quality and correctness of the obtained ontology* [18]. In this paper, OOPS! [19], OntoMetrics [20] were adopted to evaluate the CABC ontology.

When we submitted the CABC ontology to OOPS!, it only detected minor pitfalls, which are not problems. When we submitted the CABC ontology to OntoMetrics, Table 3 shows the result of schema metrics and knowledge base metrics about ontology clarity and conciseness.

Table 3. The CABC ontology advanced metrics.

Metric	Value
Attribute richness	0.257143
Inheritance richness	0.8
Relationship richness	0.605634
Class/relation ratio	0.492958
Average population	1.628571

- The **attribute richness** is premised on the belief that the more attributes a class possesses, the more information the ontology can provide. Since the CABC ontology primarily focuses on attributes related to *Work, Edition,* and *Item,* disregarding attributes of other classes that are not relevant to ancient books, such as *Person, Organization, Place, Time,* etc.
- The **inheritance richness** (IR) reflects the average number of subclasses per class, indicating the distribution of information across different levels of the inheritance tree. The CABC ontology has a high IR, suggesting a broad coverage of general knowledge with a relatively low level of detail. Given the vast time span and the substantial quantity of Chinese ancient books, it is

challenging to include all the intricacies in the ontology. Therefore, the focus of the CABC ontology is on generic descriptions and practical applications like bibliographic control and data curation.

- The CABC ontology, with its focus on Chinese ancient books, may not exhibit a high diversity of relation types compared to ontologies covering broader domains. However, it is still crucial to ensure that the ontology adequately represents the **relationship richness** between classes. The **class relation ratio** metric depends on the ontology's size, making it challenging to make a general statement about its performance without considering specific details. As the ontology evolves and more properties are added to the classes, there is potential for an improvement in the diversity of relation types and the class relation ratio.

- The **average population** of instances is an indicator of the number of instances. However, in the case of the CABC ontology developed in this paper, the main focus is on modeling the catalog of Chinese ancient books rather than creating a comprehensive knowledge base. As a result, only a few instances are provided as examples, and the average population of instances is not a significant metric for this particular ontology.

Compared to other ancient book ontologies, the CABC ontology offers a more distinct hierarchical categorization of ancient book concepts, considering their layered relationships. Furthermore, the scope of the CABC ontology is well-defined, primarily focusing on organizing the existing ancient books listed in *The National Rare Ancient Book Directory*. This aspect makes it applicable and relevant to other authoritative ancient book organization initiatives.

8   Conclusion

This paper introduces the CABC ontology, which serves as a formal representation of the concepts found in Chinese ancient book catalogs (CABCs). The CABC ontology comprises 34 classes, including top-level classes such as *Work, Edition, Item, Classification, Seal, Agent, Time*, and *Place*. These classes are constructed based on a conceptual framework that integrates domain knowledge from cataloging and classical philology, using terminology primarily sourced from *The National Rare Ancient Book Directory*.

The CABC ontology encompasses six types of information extracted from CABCs, encompassing responsible behaviors of agents involved in book creation, edition details, content classification, physical layout characteristics, contextual information, and collection institutions. By identifying essential concepts related to Chinese ancient books and leveraging the general document understanding provided by FRBR and BIBFRAME, the CABC ontology aims to offer a comprehensive understanding of a Chinese ancient book in its various states, including as a creative work, an expression, and an accessible item. Moreover, the CABC ontology employs objective properties to establish connections between the subclasses of Ancient Book (*Work, Edition, Item*) and other classes, thus enabling a semantic description of CABC.

The CABC ontology is publicly available at: https://github.com/yisanLX/CABC-ontology.

In our future work, we would like to enrich our work by developing a multilingual e-dictionary for our ontology. The multilingual e-dictionary will provide a user-friendly entry point to access our outcome. Another issue that deserves to be researched is that is there a common method or process or workflow to identify essential characteristics of abstract concepts. It will be a methodological discussion.

References

1. Zhao, W.: Transformation and Transcendence of Humanities Research in the Digital Age ——Digital Humanities in China. Exploration and Free Views, pp. 191–206+232-233 (2021)
2. Kendall, E.F., McGuinness, D.L.: Ontology engineering. Synthesis Lectures on the Semantic Web: Theory and Technology 9(1), i–102 (2019), publisher: Morgan and Claypool Publishers
3. Gruber, T.R.: A translation approach to portable ontology specifications. Knowl. Acquis. **5**(2), 199–220 (1993)
4. Peroni, S., Shotton, D.: FaBiO and CiTO: ontologies for describing bibliographic resources and citations. J. Web Semantics **17**, 33–43 (2012)
5. Peroni, S., Shotton, D.: FaBiO, the FRBR-aligned Bibliographic Ontology (Feb 2019). https://sparontologies.github.io/fabio/current/fabio.html
6. BIBFRAME - Bibliographic Framework Initiative (Library of Congress). https://www.loc.gov/bibframe/
7. Castañé, G.G., Xiong, H., Dong, D., Morrison, J.P.: An ontology for heterogeneous resources management interoperability and HPC in the cloud. Futur. Gener. Comput. Syst. **88**, 373–384 (2018)
8. Bouyerbou, H., Bechkoum, K., Lepage, R.: Geographic ontology for major disasters: methodology and implementation. Int. J. Disaster Risk Reduction **34**, 232–242 (2019)
9. Chen, S.: BIBFRAME Reuse and Extension for Linked Data of Chinese Rare Books in the Context of Digital Humanities. In: Conference Proceedings of Dialogue between Libraries and Digital Humanities, pp. 202–220. Taipei (Jul 2021)
10. Xia, C., Lin, H., Zhao, W.: Designing a data m odel of chinese ancient books for evidencebased practice. J. Libr. Sci. China **43**(6), 16–34 (2017)
11. Shanghai Library: An Ancient Book Ontology Based on BibFrame Vocabulary (2014). https://gj.library.sh.cn/ontology/view
12. OuYang, J.: Visual analysis and exploration of ancient texts for digital humanities research. J. Libr. Sci. China **42**(2), 66–80 (2016)
13. OuYang, J., Liang, Z., Ren, S.: Research on the construction of knowledge graph of large-scale Chineses ancient books. Libr. Inform. Serv. **65**(5), 126–135 (2021)
14. Zhou, L., Hong, L., Gap, Z.: Construction of knowledge graph of Chinese tang poetry and design of intelligent knowledge services. Libr. Inform. Serv. **63**(2), 24–33 (2019)
15. Wei, T., et al.: WebGIS approach of entity-oriented search to visualize historical and cultural events. Digital Sch. Humanit. **37**(3), 868–879 (2022)
16. Fernández-López, M., Gómez-Pérez, A., Juristo, N.: Methontology: from ontological art towards ontological engineering (1997)

17. Bravo, M., Hoyos Reyes, L.F., Reyes Ortiz, J.A., Bravo, M., Hoyos Reyes, L.F., Reyes Ortiz, J.A.: Methodology for ontology design and construction. Contaduría y administración 64(4) (Dec 2019), publisher: Facultad de Contaduría y Administración, UNAM
18. Sabou, M., Fernandez, M.: Ontology (Network) evaluation. In: Suárez-Figueroa, M.C., Gómez-Pérez, A., Motta, E., Gangemi, A. (eds.) Ontology Engineering in a Networked World, pp. 193–212. Springer, Heidelberg (2012). https://doi.org/10.1007/978-3-642-24794-1_9
19. Poveda-Villalón, M., Gómez-Pérez, A., Suárez-Figueroa, M.C.: OOPS! (OntOlogy Pitfall Scanner!): an on-line tool for ontology evaluation. Int. J. Semantic Web Inform. Syst. **10**(2), 7–34 (2014)
20. Lantow, B.: OntoMetrics: Putting Metrics into Use for Ontology Evaluation. In: Proceedings of the 8th International Joint Conference on Knowledge Discovery, Knowledge Engineering and Knowledge Management, pp. 186–191. SCITEPRESS - Science and and Technology Publications, Porto, Portugal (2016)

Joint Extraction of Nested Entities and Relations Based on Multi-task Learning

Jing Wan$^{(\boxtimes)}$, Chunyu Qin, and Jing Yang

Beijing University of Chemical Technology, Beijing 100029, China
{wanj,2020210463,2018200801}@mail.buct.edu.cn

Abstract. Nested named entity recognition and relation extraction are two crucial tasks in information extraction. Traditional systems often treat them as separate, sequential tasks, which can lead to error propagation. To mitigate this issue, we present a joint extraction model for nested named entities and relations based on a two-level structure, which facilitates joint learning of these subtasks through parameter sharing. Initially, we employ a hierarchical network to identify nested entities. Then, to extract relationships between the nested entities identified at different layers, we introduce multiple rounds of hierarchical relation extraction, creating a dual-dynamic hierarchical network structure. Moreover, as there is a current lack of suitable tagging schemes, we propose a novel tagging scheme grounded in a hierarchical structure. Utilizing this approach, we relabel three datasets: Genia, KBP, and NYT. Experimental results indicate that our proposed joint extraction model significantly outperforms traditional methods in both tasks.

Keywords: Nested named entity recognition · Relation extraction · Multi-task learning · Parameter sharing · Annotation strategy

1 Introduction

Nested named entity recognition (NNER) and relation extraction (RE) are two fundamental tasks in information extraction. These tasks play a vital role in downstream applications such as information retrieval, question answering, and recommender systems within the field of natural language processing [1].

Traditional approaches to entity and relation extraction employ a pipelined method, treating named entity recognition (NER) and relation extraction as distinct, independent tasks [2,3]. Although separately training the models simplifies the tasks, it overlooks the inherent interdependencies between the two subtasks. Consequently, errors in entity recognition may propagate to relation extraction [4]. Moreover, this approach disregards the internal associations between entities and relationships.

In contrast to pipelined methods, joint extraction models employ an end-to-end approach to address both tasks simultaneously, effectively integrating information from entities and relations while fully utilizing the associations between

© The Author(s), under exclusive license to Springer Nature Switzerland AG 2023
Z. Jin et al. (Eds.): KSEM 2023, LNAI 14118, pp. 368–382, 2023.
https://doi.org/10.1007/978-3-031-40286-9_30

the tasks [5]. Joint extraction of entities and relations entails the concurrent identification of entities within the text and the semantic relations between them. Figure 1 presents two examples. Sentence (a) contains three entities: United States, Biden, and Apple Inc. A "Country-President" relation (a predefined relation type) exists between "United States" and "Biden", but no relationship is present between other entity pairs in the sentence. Consequently, the final extraction result is United States, country president, Biden. Sentence (b) demonstrates nested entity and relation extraction, where the entity "third president of the United States" encompasses the inner nested named entity "United States", and a "Country-President" relation exists between the two entities.

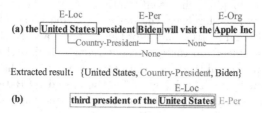

Extracted result: {United States, Country-President, Biden}

Fig. 1. Two examples of named entity and relations extraction.

Recent research on joint models has predominantly concentrated on two aspects: parameter sharing and tagging schemes. The former involves sharing the encoding layer while addressing independent tasks through a distinct decoding layer [6]. Although parameter sharing can effectively tackle the end-to-end modeling challenges of NER and RE, it fails to identify nested entities when used exclusively. The latter approach utilizes a tagging scheme capable of tagging entities and relations simultaneously, using the label as output for joint training [7]. However, the model overlooks the impact of information associated with both tasks by merely innovating the tagging scheme.

In the task of nested named entity relationship extraction, we encounter two primary challenges: 1) The nested structure of entities complicates the extraction of these entities and their relationships. 2) The information exchange between entity recognition and relation extraction can enhance extraction performance, yet the associated information is not fully exploited. Consequently, this study introduces a combination of parameter sharing and tagging scheme, forming a joint extraction model for nested entities and relations grounded in a two-level structure. Specifically, we employ a hierarchical network to identify nested entities. To extract the relationships between cross-layer entities, multiple rounds of hierarchical relation extractions are incorporated, resulting in a dual-dynamic hierarchical network structure. The model leverages parameter sharing to achieve joint learning for nested named entity recognition and relation extraction. Concurrently, a tagging scheme is devised based on a hierarchical structure to efficiently address the relation labeling of cross-layer entities.

The primary contributions of this paper are as follows:

(1) We propose a joint extraction model for nested named entities and relations, based on a two-level structure. The model employs parameter sharing to facilitate joint learning for nested named entity recognition and relation extraction tasks. Initially, a dual-dynamic hierarchical network structure is designed to identify nested entities. Building upon this, the model conducts multiple rounds of hierarchical relation extraction, effectively discerning relationships between nested entities identified by different layers.

(2) We introduce a tagging scheme founded on a hierarchical structure, defining the extraction of nested named entities and relations as a sequence labeling problem. This tagging scheme efficiently addresses the relation labeling of cross-layer entities. Moreover, the devised tagging scheme is applied to update the entity and relation labels of Genia, KBP, and NYT datasets.

(3) We perform experiments on three datasets: refined Genia, KBP, and NYT. These experiments reveal that the joint extraction model enhances the performance of both tasks. The F1-score for the nested NER task shows an average improvement of 4.3%, while the relation extraction task exhibits an average improvement of 2% in the F1-score.

2   Related Work

Information extraction underpins downstream tasks such as information retrieval, question answering, and recommender systems. Entity and relation extraction are vital components, with significant research implications. Currently, pipelined methods and joint learning models are the primary frameworks for entity and relation extraction.

The pipelined approach addresses named entity recognition (NER) and relation extraction as distinct tasks, training models independently. Classic NER models, like Hidden Markov Models (HMM) [8], treat NER as a sequence labeling problem. Recently, deep learning-based neural networks have demonstrated strong NER performance [9,10]. For nested NER, various models have been proposed, including boundary assembling [11], state transitions [12], dynamic layer stacking with bidirectional long short-term memory (Bi-LSTM) and conditional random field (CRF) [13], entity enumeration and classification [14], pyramid models [15], BiFlaG with two subgraph modules [16], NER as machine reading comprehension (MRC) [17], and a two-stage entity identifier [18]. Relation extraction models are categorized into rule- and template-based [19,20], feature engineering-based [21,22], and deep learning-based methods [5,23–25]. Although the pipelined approach is straightforward, errors in entity recognition may adversely affect relationship classification performance. Additionally, it disregards the association between subtasks, leading to information loss and diminished extraction efficacy.

Joint models tackle both tasks with a single model, enhancing results through parameter sharing and tagging schemes. In joint extraction models based on parameter sharing, various methods have been proposed. Zheng et al. integrated neural networks for NER using Bi-LSTM and relation classification with LSTM and convolutional neural network (CNN) [26]. Wang et al. transformed joint tasks into directed graphs [27]. Fu et al. introduced a weighted joint model using a graph convolutional network (GCN) [28]. Nayak and Ng suggested encoder-decoder approaches [29]. This method reduces error accumulation and exploits task relationships but cannot address nested entity recognition. In joint extraction models based on tagging schemes, Kate et al. proposed a compactly encoded graph [30]. Miwa et al. used tables for labeling entities and relations [31]. Dai et al. labeled entities by query word position and adopted a position-attention mechanism [32]. Wang et al. combined tags of entities and relationships in a unified label space [33]. However, these annotation strategies overlook subtask correlations.

The proposed method combines parameter sharing and a novel tagging scheme, linking subtasks and addressing nested entity identification. A dual-dynamic hierarchical network structure is employed, extracting cross-layer entity relations after identifying nested entities through the hierarchical structure.

3 Method

3.1 Problem Definition

This study treats both nested named entity recognition and relation extraction as sequence labeling problems. Given that the context sequence $S = \{w_1, w_2, \ldots, w_n\}$, n is the number of words in the sequence, w_i is the i-th word in the sequence, and the maximum level of nested named entities contained in the sequence is N.

The result of nested named entity recognition is $NR = \{\{TE_1^1, TE_1^2, \ldots, TE_1^n\}, \ldots, \{TE_N^1, TE_N^2, \ldots, TE_N^n\}\}$. The result of the relation extraction is $RR = \{\{TR_{11}^1, TR_{11}^2, \ldots, TR_{11}^n\}, \{TR_{21}^1, TR_{21}^2, \ldots, TR_{21}^n\}, \ldots, \{TR_{N1}^1, TR_{N1}^2, \ldots, TR_{N1}^n\} \ldots, \{TR_{NN}^1, TR_{NN}^2, \ldots, TR_{NN}^n\}\}$, where TE_i^j is the label of the word w_j in the i-th NER layer, and TR_{km}^j is the label of word w_j in the m-th layer of the k-th round relation extraction.

3.2 Model

The joint extraction model of nested entities and relations based on a two-level structure (JE-NNER-TL), proposed in this paper, comprises a hybrid word embedding layer, a dynamic multi-layer nested named entity recognition, a parameter sharing layer, and a multi-round hierarchical relations extraction module. This framework is illustrated in Fig. 2.

Embedding Layer. A hybrid word embedding layer is utilized to derive the word representation of the input context sequence. For the i-th word w_i, the hybrid word embedding includes character-level embedding c_i, basic word embedding j_i, and BERT-based word embedding b_i. The character-level embedding adopts Bi-LSTM to capture the orthographic and morphological features

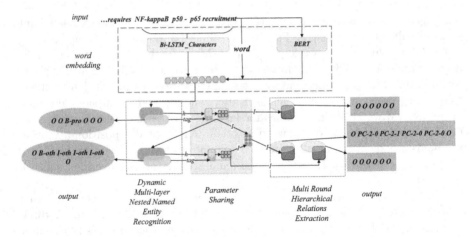

Fig. 2. Based on the two-level structure nested named entity and relationship joint extraction model.

of words. The basic word embedding obtains the co-occurrence matrix through word frequency statistics and subsequently employs SVD to reduce dimensionality and derive basic word semantic information. The BERT-based word embedding passes through the BERT model to obtain richer semantic information on the training corpus. The mixed word embedding e_i of word w_i is formulated in Eqs. (1) and (2), where the basic word embedding j_i and the BERT-based word embedding b_i are combined to derive the word-level embedding h_i, where W_1 and W_2 are the weight matrices.

$$h_i = W_1 * j_i + W_2 * b_i \tag{1}$$

$$e_i = [c_i; h_i] \tag{2}$$

Dynamic Multi-Layer Nested Named Entity Recognition and Multi-Round Hierarchical Relations Extraction. The two-layer network proposed in this study comprises a dynamic multi-layer nested named entity recognition (DM-NNER) module and a multi-round hierarchical relations extraction (MR-HRE) module. DM-NNER is composed of a multilayer basic network that dynamically stacks the basic network according onto the actual number of nested layers. The basic NER layer adopts the structures of Bi-LSTM and CRF. The model result for the word at time t, denoted as h_t, is obtained by concatenating the forward and backward hidden states as shown in Eq. (3).

$$h_t = \left[h_t^f; h_t^b\right] \tag{3}$$

where h_t^f represents the forward hidden state of the word at time t, and h_t^b represents the backward hidden state of the word at time t.

Inspired by the model proposed by Ju et al. (2018) [13], DM-NNER dynamically determines whether to continue stacking the basic network. The model stacks the next basic layer when the current layer has identified entities, and then these identified entities are sent to the next layer to recognize the external entities. If the current layer does not identify a valid entity, the stacking of the network is stopped. The input of the first basic network is derived from the hybrid embedding layer, while the inputs of the other base layers come from the previous basic network. The output of the LSTM layer is combined with the result of the CRF layer to form inter-layer word features. Then, we average the inter-layer word features of the more fine-grained entities that have been currently identified to obtain region features. The features and recognition results are fed into the next basic network and parameter sharing layer. The model fully utilizes the encoded information of the inner entities, to extract outer entities in an inside-to-outside manner until no outer entities remain to extract.

Inter-layer word features: This study adopts inter-layer word features to make the lower basic network provide richer information for the upper network. The model vectorizes the label obtained from the CRF layer and merges it with the last hidden state of the LSTM layer to obtain the inter-layer word features. The inter-layer word feature $L_{k,k+1}^i$ is calculated as shown in Eq. (4).

$$L_{k,k+1}^i = \left[h_k^i; tag_k^i\right] \tag{4}$$

where $L_{k,k+1}^i$ represents the inter-layer word feature of word w_i from the k-th to the $k+1$-th basic network; h_k^i represents the output of word w_i from the LSTM layer in the k-th basic network; and tag_k^i is the tag representation of word w_i from the CRF layer in the k-th basic network. The label representation is generated by Label Embedding.

Region features: In stacking the $k+1$-th basic network on top of the k-th layer, the aim is to extract coarse-grained entities. The model weights the inter-layer word features of each word in the entities that have been identified by the k-th layer to obtain the region features and then inputs them into the $k+1$-th layer to help identify more coarse-grained entities. Through a large amount of data analysis of nested named entities, it is found that in some fields, when some fixed words are used as the end of the entity, it is helpful to determine the entity type, as there may be nesting. For example, 82% of the entities ending with the word "chain" in the Genia data set are of type "pro" or "nucl" and 65% are nested entities. Therefore, different weights are assigned to retain important information regarding these tail words. The region feature fusion is given by Eq. (5).

$$Y_{k,k+1}^i = \alpha \left(\frac{1}{l-1} \sum_{i=start}^{start+l-2} L_{k,k+1}^i\right) + (1-\alpha) L_{k,k+1}^{start+l-1} \tag{5}$$

where $Y_{k,k+1}^i$ represents the region feature of the j-th entity recognized by the k-th layer; l represents the length of the j-th entity recognized by the k-th basic network; $start$ denotes the starting position of the j-th entity recognized by the k-th basic network; and α represents the weight of other words in the entity except for the tail word. If the area is a non-entity, the inter-layer representation remains without region feature fusion.

The result of a single NER base layer passes through the parameter sharing layer and is input to the RE module, which extracts the relations between a single NER layer or two different layers. Corresponding to the hierarchy-based NER model, the MR-HRE needs to traverse and match all NER base layers. Therefore, in this work, a two-level hierarchy was used to extract the relations of all identified entities, as shown in Fig. 2. The basic network of the MR-HRE module adopts an LSTMd-CRF structure. LSTMd [7] is an improved LSTM.

Given a sentence $S = \{w_1, w_2, \ldots, w_n\}$ with N levels of nested entities, the DM-NNER module contains N entity recognition base layers. Whenever the i-th NER base layer recognizes the result, the i-th round of RE is started. Each round of RE includes i basic relation extraction layers (LSTMd-CRF), including an RE base layer for entities of the single NER layer and $i-1$ layers for entities detected in distinct NER layers. Thus, the whole model ends with a DM-NNER including N entity recognition basic layers, and the MR-HRE includes $1 + 2 + \ldots + N$ relation extraction layers.

Parameter Sharing Layer. For an entity set $E = \{q_1, q_2, \ldots, q_N\}$ with N entities identified by the DM-NNER module. For the entities q_i and q_j in E, if they hold a relation R, there are two situations for q_i and q_j : 1) Both entities are from the k-th NER base layer; 2) The entity q_i comes from the k-th layer, and q_j comes from the p-th layer. For the relation extraction of these two cases, the model adopts parameter sharing.

Case 1: The model merges the inter-layer word feature $L_{k,k+1}^i$ and the region feature $Y_{k,k+1}^i$ of word w_i in the k-th NER basic network and inputs it to the RE module. The calculation of the vector I_i fed into the RE module is given by Eq. (6).

Case 2: The model merges the inter-layer word feature $L_{k,k+1}^i$ and region feature $Y_{k,k+1}^i$ of the word w_i in the k-th NER base layer with the inter-layer word feature $L_{p,p+1}^i$ and region feature $Y_{p,p+1}^i$ of the word w_i in the p-th NER base layer and inputs result into the relation recognition module. The calculation of the vector $I_{k,p}^i$ fed into the RE module is shown in Eqs. (7), (8), (9), (10).

$$I_i = \begin{cases} L_{k,k+1}^i, & w_i^k \text{ not entity} \\ (1 - \beta) L_{k,k+1}^i + \beta Y_{k,k+1}^i, & w_i^k \in j \end{cases} \tag{6}$$

$$I_{k,p}^i = L_{k,k+1}^i + L_{p,p+1}^i, \quad w_i^p, w_i^k \text{ not entity} \tag{7}$$

$$I_{k,p}^i = (1 - \beta) L_{k,k+1}^i + \beta Y_{k,k+1}^i + L_{p,p+1}^i, \\ w_i^k \in j, w_i^p \text{ not entity} \tag{8}$$

$$I_{k,p}^i = L_{k,k+1}^i + (1 - \beta) L_{p,p+1}^i + \beta Y_{p,p+1}^i, \\ w_i^k \text{ not entity}, w_i^p \in q \tag{9}$$

$$I_{k,p}^i = (1 - \beta) L_{k,k+1}^i + \beta Y_{k,k+1}^i + (1 - \beta) L_{p,p+1}^i \\ + \beta Y_{p,p+1}^i, \ w_i^k \in j, w_i^p \in q \tag{10}$$

where $L^i_{k,k+1}$ is the inter-layer word feature of word w_i in the k-th base layer, $w^k_i \in j$ represents the word w_i as the constituent word of the j-th entity recognized by the k-th base layer, and $Y^i_{k,k+1}$ is the region feature of the j-th entity recognized by the k-th base layer, β denotes the proportion of region features in the fusion representation.

3.3 The Tagging Scheme

This study defines relation extraction as a sequence labeling problem. Based on the hierarchical recognition of nested named entities, the head and tail entities involved in the relations may cross layers. Here, a new tagging scheme is proposed based on the cross-layer features of the entities. The label formats proposed in this article include "$R - T_a - T_b$" and "$R - T_c$," where "$R - T_a - T_b$" is used for labeling relation of cross-layer entity, and "$R - T_c$" is used for labeling relation of the same-layer entity. The specific meaning can be explained as follows:

(1) R represents a specific relation type, and its value is determined by the specific corpus. For example, in the biomedical field, common relations types include "Protein-Component", "Equiv", "Subunit-Complex", and so on.
(2) $R - T_a - T_b$ is the label of the relations between the i-th layer and the k-th ($k < i$) layer entities. The value range of "T_a" and "T_b" is 0, 1, 2. "T_a" represents the role (head entity or tail entity) of the i-th layer entity in the relations, and "T_b" represents the role of the k-th layer entity in the relations. The specific values of "T_a" and "T_b" are shown in Table 1.
(3) $R - T_c$ is the label of the relationship between the entities of the i-th layer. The value of "T_c" can be either 1 or 2. The specific meanings are listed in Table 1.

Table 1. Value meanings of "T_a, T_b, T_c" in the hierarchical labeling strategy.

	1	2	3
T_a	The entity that the word belongs to in the i-th layer is the head entity of relation R.	The entity that the word belongs to in the i-th layer is the tail entity of relation R.	The word does not belong to the entity in the i-th layer or the entity it belongs to has nothing to do with relation R
T_b	The entity that the word belongs to in the k-th layer is the head entity of relation R.	The entity that the word belongs to in the k-th layer is the tail entity of relation R.	The word does not belong to the entity in the k-th layer, or the entity it belongs to has nothing to do with relation R
T_c	The entity that the word belongs to in the i-th layer is the head entity of relation R.	The entity that the word belongs to in the i-th layer is the tail entity of relation R.	

For an input sequence of length n, the number of nested named entity levels is N, and there are $n * \sum_{i=1}^{N} i$ labels in the $\sum_{i=1}^{N} i$ relation extraction layer.

4 Experiments

4.1 Datasets

The three commonly used datasets used to conduct the experiments are Genia, KBP, and NYT. The source data of the three datasets are analyzed and processed to expand the number of nested named entities, and the three datasets were annotated using a hierarchical tagging and relation tagging scheme. Specifically, we combine the token annotation set and relation label set in Genia corpus into a joint set. The proportion of the nested entities in the dataset before and after processing are listed in Table 2. The generated Genia joint set contains five entity types for a total of 110 K, and three relation types for a total of 50 K. The processed KBP contains five entity types with a total number of 142 K and seven relation types with a total number of 134 K. NYT contains three entity types with a total number of 800 K and nine relation types with a total number of 100 K.

Table 2. The proportion of nested entities in the dataset.

Dataset		Percentage of nested entities		Percentage of nested relationships (relations involving nested entities)	
		Before	After	Before	After
Genia	Token annotation set	21.56%	35.26%	——	——
	Relation label set	19.76%	24.37%	11.76%	13.65%
	Joint data set	——	33.74%	——	13.65%
KBP	——	19.21%	22.75%	19.52%	21.63%
NYT	——	18.07%	18.63%	9.39%	11.74%

4.2 Parameter Settings

In the experiment, all words are represented by pretrained BERT word embedding in the hybrid word embedding layer. The BERT training parameters are adjusted according to the sequence size and number of words involved in the different datasets. Details are presented in Table 3. The character-level embedding vector dimension in this model is 300; the basic word embedding vector dimension is 200; the BERT-based word embedding vector dimension is 1024; and the label representation dimension is 50. The initial training learning rate is set to 0.0001. The parameters adjusted for the dataset are listed in Table 3. The dropout is used to avoid overfitting and it is set to 0.5. Our model training adopts the five-fold crossover method, and the results are the average of the five experimental results.

4.3 Evaluation

This paper adopts the exact-match evaluation method [34]. The prediction result is considered correct only when the predicted label of the entire entity perfectly

Table 3. Model parameters of different datasets.

Dataset	Bert		Our model	
	Maximum sequence length	Batch size	Epoch size	Batch size
Genia	200	50	30	10
KBP	150	35	20	10
NYT	120	20	20	15

matches the correct label. Similarly, for the prediction results of relation extraction, only when the relation type and labels of the head and tail entities are correct, the relation is considered to be extracted correctly. The commonly used evaluation indicators for entity recognition and relation extraction are precision, recall, and F1 score. Precision represents the proportion of correct instances in the prediction result; recall represents the proportion of all entities or relations in the dataset that are predicted; and the F1 score is used as the primary evaluation metric. The calculations are presented in Eqs. (11), (12), and (13).

$$precision = a/b \qquad (11)$$

$$recall = a/c \qquad (12)$$

$$F_1 = 2 * precision * recall/(precision + recall) \qquad (13)$$

where a represents the total number of entities or relations that are correctly classified; b represents the total number of predicted entities or relations of a certain type; and c represents the number of entities or relations of a certain type in the dataset.

4.4 Baselines

We compare our method with several extraction methods: NLM [13], Pyramid [15], JoinM [7], CoType [35], JointM-P [32], and JointM-G [27]. Among them, NLM and Pyramid serve as benchmarks for nested entity recognition results. JointM-P and JointM-G are utilized for comparing relationship extraction results. JoinM and CoType provide a basis for comparison in both nested entity recognition and relationship extraction. All models adhere to the original paper's settings and are tested on this study's dataset.

4.5 Results and Analysis

Overall Results. The entity recognition effects of the proposed model and the four baseline models (NLM model, Pyramid model, JoinM model, and CoType model) on the Genia, KBP, and NYT datasets are shown in Table 4. The RE experimental results of this model and the JointM-P, JointM-G, JoinM, and CoType models on the three datasets are shown in Table 5. It is observed that, among the three datasets, the proposed model achieves the best F1 score on the entity recognition task, regardless of whether it is comparing the single-task models or joint models. In the model based on the hierarchical structure, compared with the NLM and Pyramid models, the proposed model shows 2.11% and 0.31% improvement on the Genia joint set, 3% and 1.12% improvement on the KBP dataset, and 3.55% and 0.33% improvement on the NYT dataset, respectively. The single-task models NLM and Pyramid do not consider relational information and lose some semantic features. In the joint model, compared with the JoinM and the CoType models, the proposed model shows an improvement of 8.6% and 38.2% on the KBP dataset and an improvement of 45.7% and 39.2% on the NYT dataset, respectively. The JoinM and CoType models cannot solve the problem of identifying nested named entities, resulting in poor entity recognition performance. These two models can only recognize entities within relations and have low efficiency in recognizing entities without relations. The proposed model has a more significant effect on entity recognition on the NYT dataset because a large amount of entity information is involved in the None relation in the NYT set. This comparative experiment illustrates the advantages of our model over the baseline method of NER. In Table 5, it is observed that the proposed model has the best effect on both the Genia joint set and KBP datasets. The effect on the NYT dataset is second only to that of the directed graph model JointM-G. Our model can address the relation extraction of nested entities, so it provides more advantages to the Genia joint set, where nested entity relations account for a larger proportion. Therefore, the model benefits solving relation-extraction tasks involving nested named entities.

Table 4. Entity recognition results of each model.

Model	Genia joint set			KBP			NYT		
	P(%)	R(%)	F1(%)	P(%)	R(%)	F1(%)	P(%)	R(%)	F1(%)
NLM	65.377	58.517	61.757	73.935	70.574	72.215	89.389	90.197	89.791
Pyramid	62.385	64.762	63.551	80.716	67.981	73.804	93.283	92.751	93.016
JoinM	41.379	44.444	42.857	64.912	68.519	66.667	55.556	41.667	47.617
CoType	–	–	–	41.277	33.564	37.023	54.199	54.058	54.129
Our	67.637	58.787	**63.860**	78.049	72.587	**75.219**	93.772	92.916	**93.342**

Table 5. The performance of the model on the task of relation extraction.

Model	Genia joint set			KBP			NYT		
	P(%)	R(%)	F1(%)	P(%)	R(%)	F1(%)	P(%)	R(%)	F1(%)
JoinM	46.655	31.247	37.428	55.575	45.868	50.257	53.185	40.378	45.905
JointM-G	54.225	41.530	47.036	71.718	57.590	63.882	80.822	68.445	**74.121**
CoType	54.478	43.948	48.650	71.338	54.763	61.961	69.970	63.487	66.571
JointM-P	46.655	31.247	37.428	50.400	36.628	42.424	52.663	50.377	51.495
Ours	59.176	50.448	**54.464**	64.901	70.335	**67.509**	72.030	69.617	70.803

Ablation Study. To further analyze the effect of each part of the proposed model, an ablation experiment was designed. The impact on NER is shown in Table 6, and the impact on RE is shown in Table 7. Ours[-X] indicates that the model removes module X, and Ours[Full] is the complete model. Ours[-tag] means that the model removes the tag embedding of the inter-layer word feature in the parameter sharing layer. The information input to the k+1-th NER base layer and the input to the k-th round of the relation extraction layer do not contain label information. Ours[-reg] indicates that the model will cancel the weight of the entity tail word in the region feature and only average it. Ours[-Join] indicates that the model does not integrate inter-layer word features and region features, and directly inputs inter-layer word features into the relation extraction layer. Ours[-rel-Jion] indicates that the relation extraction module is removed from the complete model. The fusion process of word features and region features between layers is canceled in the parameter sharing layer.

It is also observed that BERT has the most significant impact on the results of NER and RE in the word embedding layer because the BERT model is capable of learning semantics. The BERT model can perform entity recognition alone, and adding it to the proposed model can result in a more noticeable improvement. The improvements in basic word embedding and character-level embedding are

Table 6. The influence of each part of the model on the effect of the nested named entity recognition (The value in the table is F1 score).

Model	Genia joint set	KBP	NYT
Our[-BERT]	60.775	67.273	81.719
Our[-Char]	62.287	72.155	89.791
Our[-word]	63.177	74.300	89.335
Ours[-tag]	60.948	73.544	91.212
Ours[-reg]	60.456	73.764	91.914
Our[-rel-Jion]	62.610	73.684	92.203
Our[Full]	63.860	75.219	93.342

Table 7. The influence of each part of the model on the effect of the relation extraction task (The value in the table is F1 score).

Model	Genia joint set	KBP	NYT
Our[-BERT]	51.324	66.131	69.078
Our[-Char]	53.646	66.854	70.429
Our[-word]	54.203	67.470	71.007
Ours[-tag]	50.302	64.865	67.630
Ours[-reg]	53.636	66.667	68.058
Our[-Jion]	52.016	67.009	68.387
Our[Full]	54.464	67.509	70.803

appreciable. Character-level embedding captures the morphological features of words and provides rich information. Corresponding changes can be made to character-level embedding according to different languages of the corpus. For example, the representation of radicals can be used in the Chinese corpus to achieve similar results. The label information and region features were proven to be very useful for NER in the three datasets. However, in the KBP and NYT datasets, the label information is more remarkable than the region features, and region features in Genia are more significant than the label information. Through dataset analysis, it was determined that region features favored more domain data and nested named entities, and the biomedical domain had more prominent tail word features than the general domain. Therefore, the fusion of region features significantly affects nested named entity recognition.

5 Conclusion

In this study, we adopt the concept of multi-task learning to address the problem of nested named entity recognition and relation extraction. We propose a joint model for nested named entity and relation extraction based on a two-tiered structure. Concurrently, we introduce a hierarchy-based tagging scheme for relation labeling of nested named entities. The experimental results reveal that the joint extraction model presented in this study exhibits superior recognition capability compared to the single-task model for nested named entity recognition and outperforms other joint models in detecting entities. Additionally, the proposed model surpasses other models in handling relation extraction involving nested named entities. Although the method presented in this paper enhances the effectiveness of nested named entity recognition, the identification of nested entities remains reliant on the first-layer nested entity recognition module. Consequently, more fine-grained entities may go unrecognized. In future, we plan to incorporate a reverse hierarchical extraction module to extract fine-grained nested entities.

References

1. Li, J., Sun, A., Han, J., Li, C.: A survey on deep learning for named entity recognition. IEEE. TKDE **34**(1), 50–70 (2022)
2. Limsopatham, N., Collier, N.H.: Bidirectional LSTM for named entity recognition in twitter messages. In: COLING, pp. 145–152 (2016)
3. Wang, L., Cao, Z., Melo, G.D., Liu, Z.: Relation classification via multi-level attention CNNs. In: ACL, pp. 1298–130 (2016)
4. Li, Q., Ji, H.: Incremental joint extraction of entity mentions and relations. In: ACL, pp. 402–412 (2014)
5. Miwa, M., Bansal, M.: End-to-end relation extraction using LSTMs on sequences and tree structures. In: ACL, pp. 1105–1116 (2016)
6. Zhang, M., Yue, Z., Fu, G.: End-to-end neural relation extraction with global optimization. In: EMNLP, pp. 1730–1740 (2017)
7. Zheng, S., Wang, F., Bao, H., Hao, Y., Zhou, P., Xu, B.: Joint extraction of entities and relations based on a novel tagging scheme. In: ACL, pp. 1227–1236 (2017)

8. Hiemstra, D.: Nymble: a high performance learning name-finder. In: ANLP, pp. 194–201 (1997)
9. Kong, L., Dyer, C., Smith, N.A.: Segmental recurrent neural networks. In: ICLR (2016)
10. Chiu, J., Nichols, E.: Named entity recognition with bidirectional LSTM-CNNs. TACL **4**, 357–370 (2016)
11. Chen, Y., Zheng, Q., Chen, P.: A boundary assembling method for Chinese entity-mention recognition. IEEE Intell. Syst. **30**(6), 50–58 (2015)
12. Wang, B., Lu, W., Wang, Y., Jin, H.: A neural transition-based model for nested mention recognition. In: EMNLP, pp. 1011–1017 (2018)
13. Ju, M., Miwa, M., Ananiadou, S.: A neural layered model for nested named entity recognition. In: NAACL, pp. 1446–1459 (2018)
14. Sohrab, M.G., Miwa, M.: Deep exhaustive model for nested named entity recognition. In: EMNLP, pp. 2843–2849 (2018)
15. Wang, J., Shou, L., Chen, K., Chen, G.: Pyramid: a layered model for nested named entity recognition. In: ACL, pp. 5918–5928 (2020)
16. Luo, Y., Zhao, H.: Bipartite flat-graph network for nested named entity recognition. In: ACL, pp. 6408–6418 (2020)
17. Li, X., Feng, J., Meng, Y., Han, Q., Wu, F., Li, J.: A unified MRC framework for named entity recognition. In: ACL, pp. 5849–5859 (2020)
18. Shen, Y., Ma, X., Tan, Z., Zhang, S., Wang, W., Lu, W.: Locate and label: a two-stage identifier for nested named entity recognition. In: ACL, pp. 2782–2794 (2021)
19. Chapman, W.W., Bridewell, W., Hanbury, P., Cooper, G.F., Buchanan, B.G.: A simple algorithm for identifying negated findings and diseases in discharge summaries. J. Biomed. Inform. **34**(5), 301–310 (2001)
20. Sohn, S., Wu, S., Chute, C.G.: Dependency parser-based negation detection in clinical narratives. In: Proceedings of the 2012 AMIA Joint Summits on Translational Science Proceedings, pp. 1–8. (2012)
21. Bunescu, R., Mooney, R.J.: Subsequence kernels for relation extraction. In: NIPS, pp. 171–178 (2005)
22. Jing, J., Zhai, C.X.: A systematic exploration of the feature space for relation extraction. In: NAACL, pp. 113–120 (2007)
23. Santos, C.N.D., Xiang, B., Zhou, B.: Classifying relations by ranking with convolutional neural networks. In: ACL-IJCNLP, pp. 626–634 (2015)
24. Ji, G., Liu, K., He, S., Zhao, J.: Distant supervision for relation extraction with sentence-level attention and entity descriptions. In: AAAI, pp. 3060–3066 (2017)
25. Chen, T., Shi, H., Tang, S., Chen, Z., Wu, F., Zhuang, Y.: CIL: contrastive instance learning framework for distantly supervised relation extraction. In: ACL-IJCNLP, pp. 6191–6200 (2021)
26. Zheng, S., et al.: Joint entity and relation extraction based on a hybrid neural network. Neurocomputing **257**, 59–66 (2017)
27. Wang, S., Yue, Z., Che, W., Liu, T.: Joint extraction of entities and relations based on a novel graph scheme. In: IJCAI, pp. 4461–4467 (2018)
28. Fu, T.J., Li, P.H., Ma, W.Y.: GraphRel: modeling text as relational graphs for joint entity and relation extraction. In: ACL, pp. 1409–1418 (2019)
29. Nayak, T., Ng, H.T.: Effective modeling of encoder-decoder architecture for joint entity and relation extraction. In: AAAI, pp. 8528–8535 (2020)
30. Kate, R., Mooney, R.: Joint entity and relation extraction using card-pyramid parsing. In: CoNLL, pp. 203–212 (2010)

31. Miwa, M., Sasaki, Y.: Modeling joint entity and relation extraction with table representation. In: EMNLP, pp. 1858–1869 (2014)
32. Dai, D., Xiao, X., Lyu, Y., Dou, S., She, Q., Wang, H.: Joint extraction of entities and overlapping relations using position-attentive sequence labeling. In: AAAI, pp. 6300–6308 (2019)
33. Wang, Y., Sun, C., Wu, Y., Zhou, H., Li, L., Yan, J.: UNIRE: a unified label space for entity relation extraction. In: ACL-IJCNLP, pp. 220–231 (2021)
34. Sang, E.F., De Meulder, F.: Introduction to the CoNLL-2003 shared task: language-independent named entity recognition. In: CoNLL, pp. 142–147 (2003)
35. Xiang, R., et al.: CoType: joint extraction of typed entities and relations with knowledge bases. In: WWW, pp. 1015–1024 (2017)

A Grasping System with Structured Light 3D Machine Vision Guided Strategy Optimization

Jinhui Lin[1], Haohuai Liu[2], Lingxi Peng[1(✉)], Xuebing Luo[1], Ziyan Ke[1], Zhiwen Yu[3], and Ke Ding[4]

[1] School of Mechanical and Electrical Engineering, Guangzhou University,
Guangzhou 510006, China
manplx@163.com

[2] Analysis and Test Center, Guangzhou University, Guangzhou 510006, China

[3] School of Computer Science and Engineering, South China University of Technology,
Guangzhou 510650, Guangdong, China

[4] CNC Equipment Cooperative Innovation Institute, Foshan Nanhai Guangdong Technology
University, Foshan 528225, Guangdong, China

Abstract. In scenarios such as automated sorting in logistics warehouses, automated assembly on industrial production lines, and transportation of rescue tasks and items, it is necessary to quickly grasp and place objects. Although existing methods can achieve simple object grabbing and placement, when selecting specific objects for grabbing, the grabbing strategy is usually based on the priority of the target object recognition matching score, and the grabbing strategy is relatively single. This paper introduces a robot grabbing system based on the optimization of structured light 3D imaging machine vision guidance strategy. First, the pose of all grabbing objects in the scene is estimated, and the optimal grabbing sequence is calculated, so as to achieve rapid classified grabbing and placement of sorted objects. First, the objects in the scene are scanned by a structured light camera, and the captured objects are modeled. Secondly, the optimized point-to-point feature matching algorithm is used to estimate the pose of scene objects and obtain item pose information. Finally, the robot plans the optimal order of grasping objects based on the optimized Monte Carlo tree search algorithm. This grabbing strategy can consider the distance of the grabbing path and the relevant weights of the matching score before conducting the operation.

Keywords: structured light · point-to-point feature · pose estimation · Monte Carlo tree search · object grasping and placing

The paper is supported by the Tertiary Education Scientific research project of Guangzhou Municipal Education Bureau under grant No. 202235165.

© The Author(s), under exclusive license to Springer Nature Switzerland AG 2023
Z. Jin et al. (Eds.): KSEM 2023, LNAI 14118, pp. 383–395, 2023.
https://doi.org/10.1007/978-3-031-40286-9_31

1 Introduction

Sorting items is a common application in manufacturing and logistics, and robots are widely used for this purpose. They can efficiently handle warehouse items, reducing labor costs and improving management efficiency. However, current visual robot grasping methods have drawbacks. Firstly, environmental factors in warehouses, such as lighting conditions, can affect the performance of visual-guided robots and distort images. Secondly, robots may struggle with grasping accuracy, especially for irregularly shaped items. Lastly, there is a need for flexible grasping strategies that consider factors like item types, quantities, and locations in the warehouse. Vision-based robots perform three tasks during the grasping process: target localization, target pose estimation, and grasping estimation [1].

Point-to-point features have been effective for pose estimation. The viewpoint feature histogram, proposed in [2], allows for low-cost and real-time object pose recognition. In [3], a method based on point-to-point features improves the recognition accuracy and efficiency of free 3D objects in point clouds. Building on this, [4] proposes a stable observation point pair feature-based object recognition and pose estimation method, utilizing stable and distinctive features. [5] enhances the PPF algorithm by incorporating normal clustering and efficient downsampling using equivalent angular units.

Grasping estimation involves 2D planar grasping and 6DoF grasping. In 2D planar grasping, the robotic arm descends vertically and performs a single-angle grasp, which is well-suited for industrial applications. Once the object's pose is determined, it can be directly grasped. [6] introduces an end-to-end learning architecture for acquiring object properties and operations, enhancing the adaptability of grasping based on object attributes. 6DoF grasping allows for evaluating grasping position and quality, with different grasping poses for different objects, providing greater flexibility. In [7], the Monte Carlo tree search method [8] is used to approximate the optimal selection, achieving object recognition solely through the end tactile sensor. [9] generates a collision-free path for the robotic arm within a confined space, enabling obstacle avoidance grasping of the object.

After estimating the grasping pose, the robotic arm proceeds to move to the object's location and perform the grasp. There are also selection strategies for determining the grasping order. To address large-scale target sorting tasks and transportation costs, [10] proposes a single-step greedy pushing or grasping algorithm that improves the spatial strategy for optimal proximity grasping. In [11], a greedy strategy with iterative local search techniques is utilized for large-scale multi-object reordering tasks, avoiding local minima and enhancing grasping outcomes in reordering planning problems. [12] introduces a color-aware method that dynamically selects motion paths based on input signals, enabling quick adaptation of robot operations to changing working conditions. [13] designs an optimal initial grasping strategy that predicts collisions based on the grasped object, minimizing impact force and maximizing grasping trajectory safety. Similar to the predictive approach mentioned earlier, [14] precomputes potential collisions during offline planning and prioritizes grasping collision-free targets.

In this paper, a 3D machine vision guided grasping system using structured light technology is proposed, and the grasping strategy is optimized. Compared to the existing system, the following improvements have been made. Firstly, the structured light camera offers anti-interference capability in low-light indoor scenes and has a lower cost than laser scanners, facilitating easier deployment [15]. By scanning objects with the camera, enabling direct model creation. Secondly, an optimized point-to-point feature matching algorithm accurately matches scene objects and provides precise pose estimation. Thirdly, the MCTS method comprehensively evaluates pose information, spatial distances, and targets in the scene, enabling optimal decision-making for grasping strategy. Fourthly, the algorithm's effectiveness is evaluated based on object recognition performance and overall grasping and placing time.

2 Background

This section provides an overview of the mathematical methods used in structured light imaging principle, camera calibration, and point-to-point feature extraction.

2.1 Structured Light Imaging

The structured light camera is a type of active illumination 3D imaging device which comprises a projector and a 2D camera. The operational mechanism of structured light technology is depicted in Fig. 1.

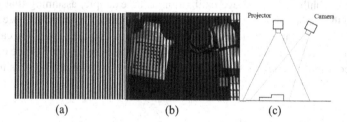

Fig. 1. (a) Structured light stripes, (b) Scene structured light scanning, (c) Structure Light Principle.

The structured light camera utilizes a projector to project coded light onto the object surface. By analyzing the deformation of the grating and calculating the phase difference, the depth information of the object is obtained. Structured light technology offers several advantages: it actively projects coded light and is not affected by low light conditions. Additionally, it ensures high accuracy and fast imaging speed, meeting the requirements of most tasks [16].

2.2 Camera Calibration

The transformation relationship in the calibration process of stereo cameras is achieved through Eq. 1.

$$Z_C \begin{bmatrix} u \\ v \\ 1 \end{bmatrix} = \begin{bmatrix} f_x & 0 & u_0 & 0 \\ 0 & f_y & v_0 & 0 \\ 0 & 0 & 1 & 0 \end{bmatrix} \begin{bmatrix} R & T \\ \vec{0} & 1 \end{bmatrix} \begin{bmatrix} X_W \\ Y_W \\ Z_W \\ 1 \end{bmatrix} = M_1 M_2 \tilde{X}_W = M \tilde{X}_W \quad (1)$$

M_1 is completely determined by f_x, f_y, u_0 and v_0, which are only related to the camera structure and are therefore called internal parameters. The position of the camera in the world coordinate system determines the value of M_2, and is therefore called external parameters. M is a 3×4 matrix called the projection matrix. The internal and external parameter matrices can be obtained through Zhang's calibration method [17]. Stereo calibration is a prerequisite for robot hand-eye calibration, which can be divided into two modes: eye-on-hand and eye-outside-hand (Fig. 2).

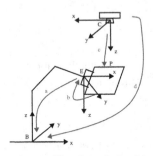

Fig. 2. Hand-eye calibration relationship diagram.

Taking exophthalmic hand eye calibration as an example, assuming that the pose matrix a of the robot's end effector in the reference coordinate system, the pose matrix b of the camera in the calibration board coordinate system, and the pose of the calibration board in the reference coordinate system are known, the pose matrix c of the camera in the robot coordinate system is solved. Their transformation relationship is as follows:

$$a_1 \times c \times b_1 = a_2 \times c \times b_2 \tag{2}$$

The transformation is as follows:

$$\left(a_1 \times a_2^{-1}\right) \times c = c \times \left(b_1^{-1} \times b_2\right) \tag{3}$$

This is equivalent to:

$$A \times X = X \times B \tag{4}$$

Common methods for solving this Equation include the two-step method [18], which uses Kronecker product and singular value decomposition [19].

2.3 Point Pair Feature Extraction

Complete the coarse matching process based on the point-to-point feature definition proposed by Drost [3]. Point to point feature (PPF) is defined as formula 5, and finally, the iterative nearest point (ICP) algorithm [20] is used to complete fine matching:

$$F(m_1, m_2) = (\|d_2\|, \angle(n_1, d), \angle(n_2, d), \angle(n_1, n_2)) \tag{5}$$

3 3D Machine Vision Guided Grasping System

This paper studies a structured light 3D machine vision guided grabbing system, and selects the grabbing object according to the optimized grabbing strategy (Figs. 3 and 4).

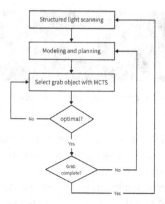

Fig. 3. Flowchart of 3D machine vision guided grasping system.

3.1 Construction of Work Platform

The hardware construction of the system platform designed in this paper is shown in Fig. 5.

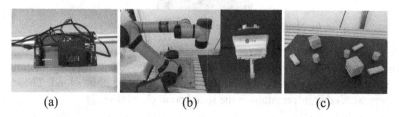

(a)   (b)   (c)

Fig. 4. (a) Structured light camera, (b) Robot and gripper, (c) Experimental scene.

In Fig. 6(a), the structured light camera is positioned above the robot, outside its workspace, to capture the scene and acquire point cloud data for object recognition. The robot's end-effector is equipped with an OnRobot VGC10 suction gripper for grasping and releasing target objects. The experimental scene includes multiple diverse objects, allowing for the simulation of various scenarios for object grasping selection.

3.2 Object Modeling and Planning

This system can capture objects without prior knowledge of the complete model of the object. First, we use a structured light camera to scan the object and obtain its surface

388   J. Lin et al.

point cloud data, which can be used as a model for subsequent scene object matching. Secondly, filter and ROI process the newly obtained point cloud, retaining only the point cloud information of the captured object. Then, repeat the modeling process for all the objects that need to be mastered.

Fig. 5. Obtain object point cloud models one by one.

After modeling all grasping objects, the point pair features of the scene point cloud objects to be matched are obtained by calculating $F(m_1, m_2)$ using Eq. (5). Subsequently, the hash table is searched, and the result is voted upon. However, there are optimization areas in this algorithm [5]. When calculating the surface normal vector as a feature of the point cloud surface, point clouds with fewer points may be included in the surface of point clouds with more points, resulting in recognition errors as depicted in Fig. 8.

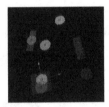

Fig. 6. Matching circular objects inside rectangular objects.

We obtain a 2D image from the camera, then map the edge pixel coordinates of the 2D image to the position of the depth map, and calculate the point cloud. These point clouds represent edge information in the scene point cloud (Fig. 7).

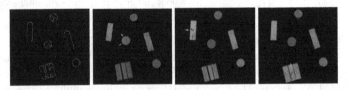

Fig. 7. Scene point cloud edge and the output result after the matching.

This step can be extended to recognize objects of any shape, reducing the number of calculated point-to-point features and improving recognition speed. The specific implementation process is outlined in Algorithm 1.

Algorithm 1: Extract 2D edge features and map to 3D point cloud indices.

Input: Scene point cloud *scence*; Scene 2D image *image*; Depth map *depth*.

Output: Edge feature index array *index*.

1 | Perform preprocessing on the *image*;
2 | Perform edge segmentation on the preprocessed image to obtain an edge feature image *edges*;
3 | Declare a point cloud format variable *cloud_edge* for edge feature indexing;
4 | **for** *edges.rows* **do**
5 | **for** *edges.cols* **do**
6 | **If** *depth(rows, cols)* exists **then**
7 | *cloud_edge* ← *depth(rows, cols)*;
8 | **end if**
9 | **end for**
10 | **end for**
11 | Filtering out point clouds that are too far away using *kdtree* algorithm;
12 | Obtaining the edge contour of the point cloud;
13 | *Return*

3.3 Grasping Strategy Using MCTS Algorithm

By considering the voting score, grasping target pose p_1 target placement pose p_2, and known robot pose P, a more effective grasping strategy can be devised. This approach prioritizes decision-making for candidate targets, avoiding the selection based solely on individual attributes like spatial distance and voting score. Utilizing the Monte Carlo Tree Search (MCTS) principle, we can define the following approach.

1. Selection. The pose information of the root serves as the root node, while the target with the highest obtained score, which requires grasping, is considered an unexplored child node *node'*. The tree is recursively traversed downward through the child nodes.
2. Expanding the child node involves the following steps. The pose information of the target placement is considered a child node (*node'*) of the current node, and the unexplored node can be simulated.
3. Simulate the selected node. Calculate Euclidean distance based on grasping and placing two points.

Evaluate the grasping value of the node by synthesizing the matching *score* and other factors. At this point, we can define a heuristic function UCB1 [21, 22] (Upper Confidence Bounds) to evaluate the quality of the simulation results. The UCB formula is as follows:

$$UCB1_j = \vec{x}_j + \sqrt{\frac{2 \ln n}{n_j}}, j = 1, \ldots, K \tag{6}$$

where $\bar{x}_j$ is the estimated value of the node $\bar{x}_j \in [0, 1]$; n_j is the number of times the node has been visited; and n is the total number of times its parent node has been visited. By setting the number of algorithm runs under certain conditions, when $UCB1_{max}$ is reached, $\bar{x}_{max}$ is updated [23].

4. Backpropagation is used to update the *node'* information. The value obtained from simulating the child node is updated to the state of the current node, and then this process is recursively applied to all the parent nodes.
5. All child nodes of the root *node* repeat the above process until the predeter. Mined search count or time limit is reached.
6. Finally, the best grasp target is selected based on the value of the node's state, and the grasping process is executed.

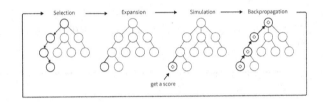

Fig. 8. MCTS Algorithm Grasping Strategy Process.

4   Experiments

The experimental setup of this system is composed of the contents shown in Fig. 5. The visual detection system includes a structured light camera, an Intel(R) Core(TM) i5-9400F CPU, a NVIDIA GeForce GTX 1650 computer. The experimental subjects consist of three objects, namely long wooden blocks, cylinders, and cubes. The average number of points in the model point cloud is approximately 3000.

We compared the improved PPF algorithm with other PPF algorithms and obtained the results shown in Table 1 and Table 2.

Table 1. RMSE of matching different objects.

Methods	PPF	FPFH [24] + SAC [25]	FPFH + SAC + Edge	PPF + Edge	PPF + 2D Edge (Ours)
Pane	5.456 e−01	3.286 e−05	4.409 e−04	5.824 e−03	4.474 e−02
Diamond	8.501 e−01	2.945 e−04	1.906 e−03	3.211 e−03	1.331 e−02
Cylinder	3.051 e−01	1.229 e−04	3.780 e−01	3.904 e−01	3.586 e−01

Table 2. Average matching time of point pair features for rectangular, cubic, and spherical objects using different algorithms.

Methods	PPF	FPFH + SAC	FPFH + SAC + Edge	PPF + Edge	PPF + 2D Edge (Ours)
Pane	6252 ms	6846 ms	126 ms	30 ms	5 ms
Diamond	8247 ms	9620 ms	753 ms	67 ms	9 ms
Cylinder	3870 ms	2270 ms	79 ms	42 ms	9 ms

Our algorithm performs well in the experiment, as evidenced by the comparison of RMSE values in Table 1 and matching times in Table 2. It successfully matches point-to-point features within a short time frame without compromising target recognition and centroid grasping. Equation (7) shows the RMSE formula used for evaluation. By utilizing an optimized grasping strategy, we comprehensively assess the distance, matching score, and other pertinent information of the grasping target. This approach leads to improved decision sequences and enhances the efficiency of the recognition and grasping process.

$$RMSE = \sqrt{\frac{1}{m} \sum_{i=1}^{m} (\hat{y}_i - y_i)^2} \tag{7}$$

In Fig. 9, the matching score and Z-axis height of the grasping pose identified before the grasp are shown, as well as the height of the camera to the object, which is measured in millimeters *mm*.

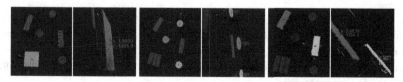

Fig. 9. Grasping object voting score and grasping pose depth.

Table 3 shows the position information of each object obtained through pose estimation, as well as the scores obtained after matching.

According to Eq. (6), the spatial distance between all corresponding object positions and placement positions can be obtained, as shown in Table 4.

Table 3. The position information and score information of the robot, rectangular block, block, and circular block in space.

Initial Position	X	Y	Z	Score
Robot	360.267	−118.867	412.772	
Pane 1	−408.033	111.327	1337.901	0.9979
Pane 2	−282.721	182.547	1354.193	0.8836
Cylinder 1	−378.093	203.625	1327.572	0.9763
Cylinder 2	−326.193	123.535	1297.554	0.9620
Cylinder 3	−405.351	30.452	1314.852	0.9526
Diamond	−295.809	36.624	1305.918	1.000

Table 4. Distances and scores of rectangular prism, cube, and cylinder to their respective placement positions.

Initial Position	Distance (mm)	Score
Pane 1	317.065 m	0.9979
Pane 2	184.977	0.8836
Cylinder 1	278.846	0.9763
Cylinder 2	234.9	0.9620
Cylinder 3	340.203	0.9526
Diamond	317.548	1.000

Table 4 presents the calculation of distance scores per unit, representing the probability of winning each decision. Following the MCTS decision-making process, objects chosen in the previous round are excluded from the subsequent rounds. The simulation yielded the following effects:

First round of decision: *Pane 2, Cylinder 2* win; Second round of decision: *Cylinder 1, Diamond* win; Third round of decision: *Pane 1* wins; Therefore, the order of grasping is *Pane 2, Cylinder 2, Cylinder 1, Diamond* and *Pane 1*. The algorithmic flow of the program is as follows.

Algorithm 2 Grasping Decision Flow.

Input: Winning probability *means*.

Output:Grasping object *target*.

1	Input the array of winning probabilities *means*;
2	Output objects with high probabilities first, based on the average value *avg* of all elements in the *means* array;
3	**If** $avg < means$ **then**
4	$Reward[i] + 1$;
5	**end if**
6	$Counts[i] = Counts[i] + 1$;
7	**for** $means.size$ **do**
8	$Reward[i] = (Reward[i] * 1.0) / Counts[i]$;
9	$decValues[i] = Reward[i] + sqrt\ ((2.0 * log(t) / Counts[i]))$;
10	**end for**
11	$selected = Max(decValues)$;
12	**If** $avg < means[selected]$ **then**
13	$Reward[selected] + 1$;
14	**end if**
15	$Counts[selected] + 1$;
16	*Return*

Fig. 10. Grasping process.

In the experiment, the robot was able to perform grasping and placing tasks using 3D machine vision, and make grasping decisions according to the calculated grasping strategy (Fig. 10).

5 Conclusion

This paper explores an optimized strategy guided by structured-light 3D machine vision, aimed at swiftly recognizing target objects in a scene and enhancing grasping efficiency. A refined point-pair feature matching algorithm is introduced, which effectively distinguishes objects with diverse appearances and accelerates the matching process. Additionally, a grasping strategy based on MCTS is proposed to make decisions regarding the status of all objects in the scene and determine the optimal grasping order. The feasibility of the proposed method is verified through experiments involving objects of varying shapes and appearances.

References

1. Du, S.: Vision-based robotic grasping from object localization, object pose estimation to grasp estimation for parallel grippers: a review. Artif. Intell. Rev. Int. Sci. Eng. J. **54**(3) (2021)
2. Rusu, R.B., Bradski, G.R., Thibaux, R., et al.: Fast 3D recognition and pose using the viewpoint feature histogram. In: 2010 IEEE/RSJ International Conference on Intelligent Robots and Systems, 18–22 October 2010, Taipei, Taiwan. IEEE (2010)
3. Drost, B., Ulrich, M., Navab, N., et al.: Model globally, match locally: efficient and robust 3D object recognition. IEEE (2010)
4. Wang, H., Wang, H., Zhuang, C.: 6D pose estimation from point cloud using an improved point pair features method. In: International Conference on Control, Automation and Robotics. IEEE (2021)
5. Yang, Y., Liu, Y., Liang, H., et al.: Attribute-based robotic grasping with one-grasp adaptation (2021)
6. Zhang, G., Jia, S., Zeng, D., et al.: Object detection and grabbing based on machine vision for service robot. In: 2018 IEEE 9th Annual Information Technology, Electronics and Mobile Communication Conference (IEMCON). IEEE (2018)
7. Zhang, M.M., Atanasov, N., et al.: Active end-effector pose selection for tactile object recognition through monte Carlo tree search. In: IEEE International Conference on Intelligent Robots and Systems (2017)
8. Browne, C.B., Powley, E., Whitehouse, D., et al.: A survey of monte Carlo tree search methods. IEEE Trans. Comput. Intell. AI Games **4**(1), 1–43 (2012)
9. Zagoruyko, S., Labbé, Y., Kalevatykh, I., et al.: Monte-Carlo tree search for efficient visually guided rearrangement planning (2019)
10. Kang, M., Kee, H., Kim, J., Oh, S.: Grasp planning for occluded objects in a confined space with lateral view using monte Carlo tree search. In: 2022 IEEE/RSJ International Conference on Intelligent Robots and Systems (IROS), Kyoto, Japan, pp. 10921–10926 (2022). https://doi.org/10.1109/IROS47612.2022.9981069
11. Pan, Z., Hauser, K.: Decision making in joint push-grasp action space for large-scale object sorting (2020)
12. Cai, L., Liu, Y., et al.: Color recognition and dynamic decision-making model of 6 axis of industrial robot based on embedded system
13. Mavrakis, N., Amir, M., Stolkin, R.: Safe robotic grasping: minimum impact-force grasp selection. In: 2017 IEEE/RSJ International Conference on Intelligent Robots and Systems (IROS). IEEE (2017)
14. Nieuwenhuisen, M., Droeschel, D., Holz, D., et al.: Mobile bin picking with an anthropomorphic service robot. IEEE (2013)
15. Huang, E., Jia, Z., Mason. M.T.: Large-scale multi-object rearrangement. In: 2019 International Conference on Robotics and Automation (ICRA) (2019)
16. Geng, J.: Structured light 3D surface imaging: a tutorial. Adv. Opt. Photon. **3**(2), 128–160 (2011)
17. Zhang, Z.: Flexible camera calibration by viewing a plane from unknown orientations. In: Seventh IEEE International Conference on Computer Vision. IEEE (1999)
18. Tsai, R.Y., Lenz, R.K.: A new technique for fully autonomous and efficient 3D robotics hand/eye calibration. IEEE Trans. Robot. Autom. **5**(3), 345–358 (1989)

19. Shah, M.: Solving the robot-world/hand-eye calibration problem using the Kronecker product. ASME J. Mech. Rob. **5**(3), 031007 (2013)
20. Zhang, Z.: Iterative point matching for registration of free-form curves and surfaces. Int. J. Comput. Vis. **13**(2), 119–152 (1994)
21. Kocsis, L., Szepesvári, C.: Bandit based monte-carlo planning. In: Fürnkranz, J., Scheffer, T., Spiliopoulou, M. (eds.) ECML 2006. LNCS (LNAI), vol. 4212, pp. 282–293. Springer, Heidelberg (2006). https://doi.org/10.1007/11871842_29
22. Kocsis, L., Szepesvári, C., Willemson, J.: Improved Monte-Carlo Search. University Tartu (2013)
23. Auer, P., Cesa-Bianchi, N., Fischer, P.: Finite-time analysis of the multiarmed bandit problem. Mach. Learn. **47**, 235–325 (2002)
24. Rusu, R.B., Blodow, N., Beetz, M.: Fast point feature histograms (FPFH) for 3D registration. In: IEEE International Conference on Robotics & Automation. IEEE (2009)
25. Buch, G., Kraft, D., Kämäräinen, J.-K., Petersen, H.G., Krüger, N.: Pose estimation using local structure-specific shape and appearance context. In: International Conference on Robotics and Automation (ICRA) (2013)

A Cognitive Knowledge Enriched Joint Framework for Social Emotion and Cause Mining

Xinglin Xiao[1,2], Yuan Tian[1,2], Yin Luo[3], and Wenji Mao[1,2(✉)]

[1] School of Artificial Intelligence, University of Chinese Academy of Sciences,
Beijing, China

[2] MAIS, Institute of Automation, Chinese Academy of Sciences, Beijing, China
{xiaoxinglin2018,tianyuan2021,wenji.mao}@ia.ac.cn

[3] Beijing Wenge Technology Co., Ltd., Beijing, China
yin.luo@wenge.com

Abstract. Social emotion mining and its cause identification are important tasks in Web-based social media analysis and text mining with many domain applications, which focus on analyzing the emotions evoked to the reader and their corresponding causes. Previously, they are conducted as separate tasks. Based on the cognitive emotion theory, there is a deep coupling relationship between social emotion and its cause identification. In this paper, we propose a cognitive knowledge enriched joint framework (JointPSEC) for predicting social emotion and its causes. Specifically, we formulate the rules based on the cognitive emotion model and utilize this knowledge together with the lexicon-based knowledge to improve emotion-clause relation learning for social emotion mining. Meanwhile, we utilize the predicted emotion to enhance dimension-clause relation learning for cause identification. Our method is mediated by cognitive knowledge to mutually facilitate the joint prediction task. Experimental results on the benchmark dataset verify the effectiveness of our framework.

Keywords: Social emotion and cause mining · Cognitive knowledge · Emotion-dimension correspondence · Joint learning

1 Introduction

Social emotion refers to the emotion evoked to the reader by a textual document [8,9]. Different from the classical sentiment analysis focusing on analyzing the author's sentiments expressed in text [1], social emotion mining is conducted from the reader's perspective [12]. Social emotion cause identification aims at mining the causes of social emotion evoked to the reader. Social emotion and its causes mining can help to understand people's feelings and possible responses to external events, and explain the elicited public emotions based on textual descriptions. Thus it is an important task in Web-based social media analysis and text mining, and support a variety of potential applications such as public opinion mining, news recommendation and government decision-making.

© The Author(s), under exclusive license to Springer Nature Switzerland AG 2023
Z. Jin et al. (Eds.): KSEM 2023, LNAI 14118, pp. 396–405, 2023.
https://doi.org/10.1007/978-3-031-40286-9_32

Previous work on social emotion mining mainly adopts word-based, topic-based and neural network-based method [8,9] to learn text representations. In contrast, social emotion cause identification was rarely explored in previous research. Our previous work [12] proposed the social emotion cause identification (SECI) task, and developed a computational method CogEES to tackle this new task. However, CogEES needs to specify the elicited social emotion in advance so as to predict its cause clauses, which greatly hinders the practical applications of SECI. Moreover, as identified by the cognitive emotion theory [6], there is deep cognitive association between emotions and its antecedents. Yet this deep coupling relationship between social emotion and its cause identification has not been explored in previous research.

In this paper, we propose a cognitive knowledge enriched **Joint** framework for **P**redicting **S**ocial **E**motion and its **C**auses (**JointPSEC**). Our framework utilizes emotional dimension information identified in the cognitive structure of emotions (OCC) model [6] to enhance document-level social emotion mining and clause-level cause identification. For social emotion mining, we formulate the OCC rules and utilize this knowledge together with the lexicon-based knowledge to improve emotion-clause relation learning. For social emotion cause identification, we establish the correspondence between emotional dimensions and clauses, and use the predicted emotion to enhance dimension-clause relation learning. The two components are jointly trained and mediated by cognitive knowledge to mutually facilitate the joint prediction of social emotion and its causes.

The main contributions of our work are as follows:

- We first propose a cognitive knowledge enriched joint framework for social emotion and cause mining, which leverages the emotion-dimension correspondence and linguistic relation informed by cognitive emotion model to mutually facilitate the two tasks.
- Our method learns emotion-clause relation and dimension-clause relation for predicting social emotion and its causes respectively, and relies on cognitive knowledge to jointly enhance relation representation learning.
- Experimental results on the benchmark dataset demonstrate that our method achieves the SOTA performances on each individual task, verifying the effectiveness of our method.

2   Related Work

2.1   Cognitive Emotion Model

In cognitive psychology, the antecedents and consequences of emotions are well studied under cognitive appraisal theories. Among them, the cognitive structure of emotions model (i.e. the OCC model) proposed by Ortony et al. [6] is a prominent theory for computational modeling of emotion. In the OCC model, each emotion type is triggered under certain conditions, which are represented as appraisal variables that characterize different emotional dimensions with dimensional values. Desirability, praise/blame-worthiness and likelihood are the three key emotional dimensions to derive certain major emotions. *Desirability* is related to the goals of agents, with desirable or undesirable value. *Praise/blame-worthiness* is related to the standards of actions, with praiseworthy or blameworthy value. The dimensional value of likelihood is certain by default. The combination of different emotional dimensions and their values can further elicit diverse social emotions, such as *anger*, *gratitude*, *reproach* and *admiration*. (e.g. a desirable event to self-agent leads to *joy*, while an undesirable event caused by the blameworthy act of other-agent leads to *anger*). The OCC model provides the cognitive foundation for social emotion and its cause identification.

2.2   Social Emotion Mining and Its Cause Identification

Social emotion mining aims to predict the elicited public sentiments evoked by a textual document from the reader's perspective. Early work on social emotion mining typically employs word-based methods [3] or topic model-based methods [7]. Recent work mainly adopts neural network-based approaches to learn text representations [8,9]. Wang et al. [8] incorporated sentence syntactic dependency and topic information into the neural network. To further improve text representations, they integrated semantic and topic features into a self-attention network [9]. However, mining the causes of social emotion was rarely explored in previous work.

Another line of work is Emotion cause extraction (ECE), which is closely related to identifying the causes of social emotion. ECE aims to extract the cause clauses of the author's sentiments in text, based on the explicitly expressed emotion word. Early work on ECE mainly adopts rule-based methods [4] and machine learning methods [1] to extract causes for certain emotions. Recent work employs deep learning based methods [2,10,11]. Xiao et al. [11] used attention networks to capture clause/emotion-oriented features from clauses. Xia et al. [10] proposed a Transformer based hierarchical network to model the interrelations between the clauses. Hu et al. [2] further adopted GCN to fuse the inter-clause semantic and structural information for emotion cause extraction.

Different from the above studies on ECE, our previous work [12] first proposed social emotion cause identification (SECI) as an important task, and built the computational method CogEES and benchmark dataset for this task. However, as CogEES is purely designed for SECI, it needs to specify the elicited social emotion from text in advance so as to predict its cause clauses. This largely hinders the application of SECI in realistic setting. Moreover, as it is identified by the OCC model, there is a deep cognitive correspondence between emotions and appraisal variables (i.e. emotional dimensions with dimensional values), which capture the causal factors of social emotion. So far, this deep coupling relationship between emotion and its cause has been neglected in previous research, which we shall address in this paper.

3   Joint Prediction Method

The joint prediction task is defined as follows. Given a document D consisting of N clauses $\{c_i\}_{i=1}^{N}$, where c_i is the i-th clause comprising words $\{w_j^i\}_{j=1}^{|c_i|}$, the

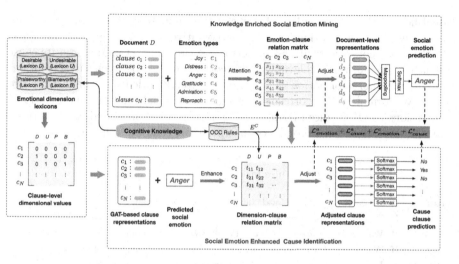

Fig. 1. Overview of the cognitive knowledge enriched joint framework JointPSEC.

goal of the joint prediction task is to identify the social emotion type e evoked to the reader by D and its corresponding cause clause(s) $\{c_j^e\}_{j=1}^L$ in D that elicit e, where e belongs to the set of social emotion types $\{e_j\}_{j=1}^K$.

Figure 1 gives the overview of our joint framework JointPSEC. It consists of two main components, knowledge enriched social emotion mining and social emotion enhanced cause identification. Cognitive knowledge, including emotion-dimension correspondence (i.e. OCC rules) and lexicon-based dimension-clause relation (i.e. EDLs), interacts with the two components and enhances the clause-level and document-level relation learning to mutually support the joint task.

3.1 GAT-Based Clause Representation Learning

To obtain the embeddings of clauses incorporated with inter-clause relations, we take the clauses of a document as the nodes in a fully-connceted graph and adopt the Graph Attention Network (GAT) for clause representation learning.

For the initial representations $\{s_j^i\}_{j=1}^{|c_i|}$ of words $\{w_j^i\}_{j=1}^{|c_i|}$ in clause c_i, which was acquired by combining word embeddings and dimensional information of words [12], we use word-level and clause-level bi-LSTM to encode them into the hidden clause representations $\{h_i^{(0)}\}_{i=1}^N$. We then construct a fully-connected clause graph $\mathcal{G}$ with all the clauses as nodes, and apply a GAT network on $\mathcal{G}$ with the stacked graph attention layers to aggregate the features of neighbor clauses [12]. Finally, the output of the GAT is the clause representations $\{h_i^c\}_{i=1}^N$.

3.2 Representations of Cognitive Knowledge

Since the elicited social emotions are not explicitly or implicitly expressed in text, the underlying cognitive process and variable values of emotions identified by the OCC model is beneficial to the analysis of social emotion and its causes. This information is utilized as cognitive knowledge in our framework. As there is a coupling relationship between social emotion mining and its cause identification, our method leverages this correspondence between social emotions and dimensional information as the intermediated knowledge to connect the two tasks. We formulate this correspondence between social emotions and emotional dimensions as OCC rules in Table 1. These rules are represented in the form of emotion-dimension correspondence matrix in our computational method.

Table 1. The OCC rules for emotion-dimension correspondence.

Rule 1:	**If** Desirability=$desirable$ **and** Likelihood=$certain$ **Then** Emotion=Joy
Rule 2:	**If** Desirability=$undesirable$ **and** Likelihood=$certain$ **Then** Emotion=$Distress$
Rule 3:	**If** Worthiness=$praiseworthy$ **and** Perspective=$other$ **Then** Emotion=$Admiration$
Rule 4:	**If** Worthiness=$blameworthy$ **and** Perspective=$other$ **Then** Emotion=$Reproach$
Rule 5:	**If** Desirability=$desirable$ **and** {Worthiness=$praiseworthy$ **and** Perspective=$other$} **Then** Emotion=$Gratitude$
Rule 6:	**If** Desirability=$undesirable$ **and** {Worthiness=$blameworthy$ **and** Perspective=$other$} **Then** Emotion=$Anger$

According to the OCC rules, we can obtain the emotion-dimension correspondence matrix $E^C \in \mathbb{R}^{K \times 4}$ between social emotions and four emotional dimension values $\{v_1, v_2, v_3, v_4\}$, whose element $\alpha_{i,j}^C$ is defined as follows: If the emotion e_i is related to the dimension value v_j, then $\alpha_{i,j}^C = 1$; otherwise, $\alpha_{i,j}^C = 0$.

Another cognitive knowledge is the correspondence between emotional dimensions and linguistic expressions in text, which is used to bridge the gap between the causal analysis and social emotions and clause-level linguistic manifestation of dimensional values. To this end, we rely on the emotional dimension lexicons (EDLs) [12], which establish the correspondence between word/phrase expressions and emotional dimension values identified by the OCC model.

The EDLs is comprised of the lexicons for $desirable$ (D), $undesirable$ (U), $praiseworthy$ (P) and $blameworthy$ (B). Based on the EDLs, we can obtain clause-level dimensional values between clauses and four dimensional values, which can be formulated as the dimension-clause relation matrix $D^R \in \mathbb{R}^{N \times 4}$ (conflict cases are detected and cleaned up), whose element $\alpha_{i,j}^R$ is defined as follows: If the clause c_i contains words with the dimension value v_j, then $\alpha_{i,j}^R = 1$; otherwise, $\alpha_{i,j}^R = 0$.

3.3   Knowledge Enriched Social Emotion Mining

To mine the social emotion of a document, we first utilize the correspondence between social emotions and clauses to learn the emotion-clause relation matrix, and then utilize the OCC rules and EDLs to adjust the emotion-clause relation matrix. Finally, we aggregate the clause representations to form the emotion-oriented document representations for social emotion prediction.

The representations of social emotion type words are denoted as $\boldsymbol{H}^e = \{\boldsymbol{h}_i^e\}_{i=1}^K \in \mathbb{R}^{K \times d}$. We first obtain the original emotion-clause relation matrix $\boldsymbol{S}^R \in \mathbb{R}^{K \times N}$, which represents the weighted correlations between social emotions and clauses based on textual inputs. It is formulated as:

$$s_{i,j} = \exp(\boldsymbol{h}_i^e \cdot \boldsymbol{h}_j^c) / \sum\nolimits_{j=1}^N \exp(\boldsymbol{h}_i^e \cdot \boldsymbol{h}_j^c), \tag{1}$$

where $s_{i,j}$ is the correspondence value between the i-th emotion and the j-th clause.

We further get the emotion-clause relation matrix $\boldsymbol{E}^R \in \mathbb{R}^{K \times N}$ between social emotions and clauses, which is calculated as:

$$\boldsymbol{E}^R = \boldsymbol{E}^C \boldsymbol{D}^{R'} \in \mathbb{R}^{K \times N}, \tag{2}$$

where $\boldsymbol{D}^{R'}$ denotes the transpose of matrix $\boldsymbol{D}^R$.

To force the document-level representations to focus on the clauses with corresponding emotion types indicated by $\boldsymbol{E}^R$, we define the adjustment loss $\mathcal{L}_{emotion}^a$ as the following:

$$\mathcal{L}_{emotion}^a = \| \boldsymbol{S}^R - \boldsymbol{E}^R \|_F, \tag{3}$$

where $\| \cdot \|_F$ denotes the Frobenius norm.

Finally, we compute the emotion-oriented document representations $\boldsymbol{V}^e = \{v_1^e, v_2^e, \ldots, v_K^e\} \in \mathbb{R}^{K \times d}$ with the weighted average of clause representations according to the emotion-clause relation matrix $\boldsymbol{S}^R$:

$$v_i^e = \sum\nolimits_{j=1}^N s_{i,j} \boldsymbol{h}_j^c, \quad i \in [1, K], \tag{4}$$

where $v_i^e \in \boldsymbol{R}^d$ is the emotion-oriented document representation of i-th social emotion. We then transform $\boldsymbol{V}^e$ to a vector $\boldsymbol{v}^e \in \boldsymbol{R}^d$ by a max-pooling function, and feed it into a linear layer for social emotion classification:

$$\hat{\boldsymbol{y}}_e = \text{Softmax}(\sigma(\boldsymbol{W}_e \boldsymbol{v}^e + \boldsymbol{b}_e))), \quad k_e = \arg\max(\hat{\boldsymbol{y}}_e) \tag{5}$$

where $\sigma(\cdot)$ is the activation function ReLU, $\boldsymbol{W}_e \in \boldsymbol{R}^{K \times d}$ and $\boldsymbol{b}_e \in \boldsymbol{R}^K$ are the learnable parameters, and k_e is the index of predicted social emotion. The loss function for social emotion prediction is computed by cross-entropy function:

$$\mathcal{L}_{emotion}^c = -\boldsymbol{y}_e^T \log \hat{\boldsymbol{y}}_e, \tag{6}$$

where $\boldsymbol{y}_e \in \boldsymbol{R}^K$ is the one-hot ground truth label vector for the social emotion.

3.4 Social Emotion Enhanced Cause Identification

After the prediction of social emotion, to identify social emotion cause enhanced by the predicted emotion, we first add the predicted emotion to the establishment of the original dimension-clause relation. We then use the clause-level dimensional values to adjust the dimension-clause relation matrix. Finally, we apply the adjusted clause representations to the prediction of cause clauses.

Initially, we construct the original dimension-clause relation matrix $\boldsymbol{T}^R \in \mathbb{R}^{N \times 4}$ between clauses and emotional dimension values:

$$t_{i,j} = \exp(\boldsymbol{h}_i^c \cdot \boldsymbol{W}_j^d) / \sum\nolimits_{j=1}^4 \exp(\boldsymbol{h}_i^c \cdot \boldsymbol{W}_j^d), \tag{7}$$

where $t_{i,j}$ is the correspondence value of the i-th clause and the j-th dimensional value in $\boldsymbol{T}^R$, and $\boldsymbol{W}_j^d$ is a trainable vector denoting the jth dimensional value.

We further enhance the relation between clauses and dimensional values using the result of social emotion prediction. Given a predicted emotion e_k, we compute the adjusted dimension-clause relation matrix $\widetilde{\boldsymbol{T}}^R \in \mathbb{R}^{N \times 4}$ with normalization:

$$\boldsymbol{T}^e = \sum\nolimits_{i=1}^4 (\boldsymbol{D}^R(:,i))' \boldsymbol{E}^C(k,:), \quad \widetilde{\boldsymbol{T}}^R = \boldsymbol{T}^R + \boldsymbol{T}^e, \tag{8}$$

where k is the index of predicted social emotion in the stage of social emotion prediction, $\boldsymbol{D}^R(:,i) \in \mathbb{R}^{1 \times N}$ performs the column extraction to form the relation vector between clauses and the i-th dimensional value, and $\boldsymbol{E}^C(k,:) \in \mathbb{R}^{1 \times 4}$ performs the row extraction to form the correspondence vector between social emotion e_k and emotional dimension values.

To force the adjusted clause representations to focus on the corresponding dimensional information of clauses indicated by $\boldsymbol{D}^R$, we define the adjustment loss $\mathcal{L}_{clause}^a$ as the following:

$$\mathcal{L}_{clause}^a = \| \widetilde{\boldsymbol{T}}^R - \boldsymbol{D}^R \|_F . \tag{9}$$

Finally, we feed the dimension-adjusted clause representations into a linear layer for social emotion clause prediction:

$$\hat{\boldsymbol{y}}_c^i = \text{Softmax}(\sigma(\boldsymbol{W}_c \boldsymbol{h}_i^c + \boldsymbol{b}_c))), i \in [1, N], \tag{10}$$

where $\hat{\boldsymbol{y}}_c^i$ is the predicted probability distribution of clause c_i on being cause clause or not, $\boldsymbol{W}_c \in \boldsymbol{R}^{2 \times d}$ and $\boldsymbol{b}_c \in \boldsymbol{R}^2$ are the trainable parameters. The loss function for social emotion prediction is computed by cross-entropy function:

$$\mathcal{L}_{clause}^c = -\sum\nolimits_{i=1}^N (\boldsymbol{y}_c^i)^T \log \hat{\boldsymbol{y}}_c^i, \tag{11}$$

where $\boldsymbol{y}_c^i$ is the one-hot ground truth label vector of i-th clause.

3.5   Joint Learning Objective

To leverage the interrelation between social emotion prediction and social emotion cause identification connected by the OCC cognitive knowledge, we jointly train two tasks in our framework with the final loss $\mathcal{L}$:

$$\mathcal{L} = \lambda_e \mathcal{L}_{emotion}^a + \lambda_c \mathcal{L}_{cause}^a + \mathcal{L}_{emotion}^c + \mathcal{L}_{cause}^c, \tag{12}$$

where λ_e and λ_c are balanced hyper-parameters.

4 Experiments

4.1 The Dataset and Experimental Setup

We evaluate our method on the SECI benchmark dataset [12], which is the only dataset for social emotion cause identification. For experimental setup, the dimension of word embeddings and the size of the hidden states of BiLSTM and GAT are set to 30. We build GAT with two graph attention layers and the dropout rate of each layer is set to 0.15. We train our method with 32 batch size and 10^{-3} learning rate. The hyper-parameters λ_e and λ_c are set to 10^{-2}.

4.2 Comparative Methods

As our proposed JointPSEC is the first to jointly predict social emotion and its causes, we select the representative methods from the individual tasks of social emotion mining and emotion cause extraction for comparison. Comparative methods for social emotion mining include ATTBiLSTM [5], GatedDRGT [8] and TESAN [9]. ATTBiLSTM is a basic network based on attention mechanism and Bi-LSTM. GatedDRGT and TESAN are the current SOTA social emotion mining methods. For social emotion cause identification, we compare our method with the only related method CogEES [12], as well as the representative methods [2,10,11] in the closely related ECE (i.e. emotion cause extraction) task including COMV [11], RTNN [10] and FSS-GCN [2]. Note that CogEES uses additional emotion information for cause prediction. As this information should not be used for joint prediction tasks, we remove it for fair comparison.

Table 2. Results of comparative methods and our method on SECI benchmark.

Task	Method	P	R	F_1
Social emotion mining	ATTBiLSTM [5]	0.640	0.635	0.637
	GatedDRGT [8]	0.662	0.650	0.656
	TESAN [9]	**0.677**	0.654	0.665
	JointPSEC	0.676	**0.671**	**0.673**
Social emotion cause identification	COMV [11]	0.639	0.614	0.626
	RTHN [10]	0.654	0.630	0.641
	FSS-GCN [2]	0.658	0.641	0.649
	CogEES [12]	0.661	0.646	0.653
	JointPSEC	**0.680**	**0.677**	**0.678**

4.3 Experimental Results

Main Results. The upper part of Table 2 gives the results of comparative methods for social emotion mining. ATTBiLSTM encodes a text via BiLSTM and emotion type attention, which cannot capture enough document-level information. As GatedDRGT incorporates topic information into document representation learning, it achieves better performance than ATTBiLSTM. TESAN further combines both syntactic dependency and topic information into representation learning, thus achieves better performance than GatedDRGT. From the lower part of Table 2, we can see that CogEES achieves better performance than emotion cause extraction methods COMV, RTHN and FSS-GCN for social emotion cause identification. The results also show that JointPSEC achieves 2.6% performance gain on F_1 value compared to that of CogEES. In general, the experimental results demonstrate the effectiveness of our JointPSEC for both social emotion mining and its cause identification.

Table 3. Results of the ablation study on our method.

Method	Social emotion mining			Cause identification		
	P	R	F_1	P	R	F_1
JointPSEC (full model)	0.676	0.671	0.673	0.680	0.677	0.678
$- T^e$ (w/o predicted emotion)	0.674	0.670	0.672	0.678	0.676	0.677
$- \mathcal{L}_{emotion}^{a}$ (w/o emotion-clause adjust.)	0.665	0.661	0.663	0.677	0.674	0.675
$- \mathcal{L}_{cause}^{a}$ (w/o dimension-clause adjust.)	0.670	0.667	0.668	0.675	0.670	0.672
$- \mathcal{L}_{emotion}^{a} - \mathcal{L}_{cause}^{a}$ (w/o emotion-clause and dimension-clause adjust.)	0.662	0.654	0.658	0.665	0.642	0.653

Ablation Study. We further test the design of each component in JointPSEC, using its four variations. Removing the predicted social emotion information from the adjusted dimension-clause relation matrix in social emotion cause identification (i.e. $- T^e$); Removing the emotion-clause adjustment in social emotion mining, which is equivalent to removing the adjustment loss $\mathcal{L}_{emotion}^{a}$ (i.e. $- \mathcal{L}_{emotion}^{a}$); Removing the dimension-clause adjustment in cause identification, which is equivalent to removing the adjustment loss $\mathcal{L}_{cause}^{a}$ (i.e. $- \mathcal{L}_{cause}^{a}$); Removing the cognitive knowledge from our method, including both emotion-clause adjustment and dimension-clause adjustment, which is equivalent to removing both adjustment losses $\mathcal{L}_{emotion}^{a}$ and $\mathcal{L}_{cause}^{a}$ (i.e. $- \mathcal{L}_{emotion}^{a} - \mathcal{L}_{cause}^{a}$).

We can see from Table 3, removing the predicted social emotion results in 0.1% performance drop of F_1 value on both social emotion mining and cause identification. Removing emotion-clause adjustment in social emotion mining or removing dimension-clause adjustment in cause identification leads to considerable performance drop of F_1 values on both tasks (ranging from 0.3% to 1.0%). Finally, removing the cognitive knowledge has the most significant impact on both tasks, leading to 1.5% and 2.5% performance drop of F_1 values on social emotion mining and cause identification, respectively. The results of the ablation study further verify the effectiveness of model design in our joint framework.

5   Conclusion

We propose a cognitive knowledge enriched framework JointPSEC for jointly predicting social emotion and its causes. Our method utilizes the cognitive knowl-

edge about the correspondences between social emotions, dimensional information and lexicon expressions for the mutual facilitation of both tasks. Experimental results demonstrate the effectiveness of our method for the joint prediction.

Acknowledgements. This work is supported by the Ministry of Science and Technology of China under Grant #2022YFB2703302, NNSFC under Grants #11832001
and #62206287, and Beijing Nova Program Z201100006820085 from Beijing Municipal
Science and Technology Commission.

References

1. Gui, L., Wu, D., Xu, R., Lu, Q., Zhou, Y.: Event-driven emotion cause extraction
   with corpus construction. In: Proceedings of the Conference on Empirical Methods
   in Natural Language Processing, pp. 1639–1649 (2016)
2. Hu, G., Lu, G., Zhao, Y.: FSS-GCN: a graph convolutional networks with fusion
   of semantic and structure for emotion cause analysis. Knowl.-Based Syst. **212**,
   106584–106594 (2021)
3. Katz, P., Singleton, M., Wicentowski, R.: SWAT-MP: the SemEval-2007 systems
   for task 5 and task 14. In: Proceedings of the International Workshop on Semantic
   Evaluations, pp. 308–313 (2007)
4. Lee, S. Y. M., Chen, Y., Li, S., Huang, C.-R.: Emotion cause events: corpus construction and analysis. In: Proceedings of the International Conference on Language Resources and Evaluation, pp. 1121–1128 (2010)
5. Li, Y., Caragea, C.: Multi-task stance detection with sentiment and stance lexicons.
   In: Proceedings of the Conference on Empirical Methods in Natural Language Processing and the International Joint Conference on Natural Language Processing,
   pp. 6299–6305 (2019)
6. Ortony, A., Clore, G. L., Collins, A.: The cognitive structure of emotions. Cambridge University Press, Cambridge (1990)
7. Rao, Y.: Contextual sentiment topic model for adaptive social emotion classification. IEEE Intell. Syst. **31**(1), 41–47 (2016)
8. Wang, C., Wang, B., Xiang, W., Xu, M.: Encoding syntactic dependency and
   topical information for social emotion classification. In: Proceedings of the International ACM SIGIR Conference on Research and Development in Information
   Retrieval, pp. 881–884 (2019)
9. Wang, C., Wang, B.: An end-to-end topic-enhanced self-attention network for
   social emotion classification. In: Proceedings of the Web Conference, pp. 2210–
   2219 (2020)
10. Xia, R., Zhang, M., Ding, Z.: RTHN: a RNN-transformer hierarchical network for
    emotion cause extraction. In: Proceedings of the International Joint Conference on
    Artificial Intelligence, pp. 5285–5292 (2019)
11. Xiao, X., Wei, P., Mao, W., Wang, L.: Context-aware multi-view attention networks
    for emotion cause extraction. In: Proceedings of the IEEE International Conference
    on Intelligence and Security Informatics, pp. 128–133 (2019)
12. Xiao, X., Mao, W., Sun, Y., Zeng, D.: A cognitive emotion model enhanced sequen-
    tial method for social emotion cause identification. Inf. Process. Manag. **60**(3),
    103305 (2023)

TKSP: Long-Term Stance Prediction for Social Media Users by Fusing Time Series Features and Event Dynamic Evolution Knowledge

Zijian Zhou, Shuoyu Hu, Kai Yang, and Haizhou Wang[✉]

School of Cyber Science and Engineering, Sichuan University, Chengdu, China
{2020141530063,2020141530110,2020141530041}@stu.scu.edu.cn,
whzh.nc@scu.edu.cn

Abstract. The rise of social media has led to an increasing number of public discussion on hot topics. People always like to express their stances by posting tweets on social media. Mining stance information contained in text is significantly important for researchers to conduct analysis of public opinion, which makes the issue of stance detection as one of the hot research problems. In recent years, user-level stance detection has become a hot research topic in the field of stance detection, while fewer researches have been conducted on predicting users' stances. The current studies are mainly about short-term prediction of users' stances. **To the best of our knowledge, this paper is the first research work to conduct long-term stance prediction for social media users.** Specifically, this paper first builds a large-scale Chinese dataset for long-term prediction of social media users' stances. Subsequently, we propose a method of mining event dynamic evolution knowledge to improve the prediction performance. Finally, we construct a model fusing **T**ime series features and event dynamic evolution **K**nowledge for long-term **S**tance **P**rediction (TKSP). The experimental results demonstrate that our model outperforms other state-of-the-art models on the problem of long-term stance prediction for social media users.

Keywords: Stance detection · Social media · Time series features · Knowledge fusion · Deep learning

1 Introduction

In recent years, with the development of the Internet, social media has become a significant part of people's daily lives. More and more users are expressing their opinions on social media platforms such as Twitter and Weibo. The massive amount of text in social media contain users' stances for various social events. Mining stance information contained in text is significant important for researchers to conduct analysis of public opinion. In such a case, stance detection has become one of the hot research issues in the field of natural language processing. Stance detection is the task of automatically determining whether

© The Author(s), under exclusive license to Springer Nature Switzerland AG 2023
Z. Jin et al. (Eds.): KSEM 2023, LNAI 14118, pp. 406–421, 2023.
https://doi.org/10.1007/978-3-031-40286-9_33

the text's author is in favor, against, or neutral towards a statement or targeted event, person, organization, government policy, movement, etc. [4].

However, the stances of users are not constant. They may change over time and as social events continuously evolve, which makes long-term stance prediction for users difficult. Conducting long-term stance prediction for users is beneficial for companies or governments to make informed decisions, which may bring immeasurable rewards. In such a case, it is necessary to conduct long-term stance prediction for social media users.

The traditional stance detection problem tends to detect the stance contained text, which has achieved excellent results with various machine learning and deep learning methods [5,7,8,10,19,24]. More and more researchers are now focusing on the user-level stance detection problem [3,6,17].

Stance prediction is a new direction of stance detection research, which aims to predict the future stance of a user on a certain topic. Current user stance prediction studies are mainly about short-term stance prediction for users [12, 13,15]. They model the user posting behavior to predict the stance attitude contained in one or several future tweets, which are called short-term stance prediction. But there is a lack of work in long-term stance prediction for users.

Compared to traditional stance prediction, the research challenges of long-term stance prediction of social media users are as follows: (1) There is no publicly available dataset for long-term stance prediction for social media users. (2) Existing studies on stance prediction do not consider the influence on users brought by the evolution of events. (3) The existing stance prediction models oriented to users are mainly for short-term predictions, which are not suitable for the problem of long-term stance prediction. Therefore, a model for long-term stance prediction is needed.

In order to address the above challenges, this paper builds and publishes a benchmark dataset, proposes a model fusing time series features and event dynamic evolution knowledge for long-term stance prediction (TKSP). Specifically, we first collect and build a large-scale dataset from Sina Weibo, named SP-Dataset. After that, we propose a method of mining event dynamic evolution knowledge to improve the prediction performance of users' stances. Finally, this paper constructs a model for long-term stance prediction of social media users by fusing time series features and event dynamic evolution knowledge. The main contributions of this paper are summarized as follows:

- We construct the first large-scale Chinese dataset oriented to the problem for long-term stance prediction of social media users.
- We propose an innovative method of mining event dynamic evolution knowledge to improve the prediction performance of users' stances.
- To the best of our knowledge, we are the first to propose a model TKSP oriented to the problem of long-term stance prediction for social media users.

2   Related Work

The current work on stance detection is mainly divided into text-level stance detection and user-level stance detection. The stance prediction problem is completely a new research direction in the field of stance detection.

2.1   Text-Level Stance Detection

So far, researches in the field of stance detection are mainly about text-level stance detection. Machine learning and deep learning methods have been widely used in the research field. Majumder et al. [5] used a memory neural network to model inter-aspect dependencies and the network showed effectiveness in classifying multifaceted sentences. Hardalov et al. [8] proposed a cross-linguistic stance detection method based on sentiment pre-training. Xu et al. [9] used two feature selection strategies (top k-based selection and leave-out k-based selection) to generate the optimal feature set.

At present, more mature results have been achieved in the text-level stance detection research.

2.2   User-Level Stance Detection

User-level stance detection research has evolved rapidly in recent years. Darwish et al. [3] proposed an efficient unsupervised framework for detecting Twitter users' stances on controversial topics. Samih et al. [6] improved user-level stance detection by representing tweets using contextual embeddings that capture the potential meaning of words in context. Williams et al. [17] proposed a highly efficient Twitter Stance Propagation Algorithm (TSPA) for detecting user-level stance on Twitter that leverages the social networks of Twitter users.

Currently, user-level stance detection research is continuing to make progress.

2.3   Stance Prediction

Stance prediction is a new direction for stance detection research. Chen et al. [11] use temporally ordered tweets for stance prediction by introducing an attention layer to weight the importance of a user's previous tweets, current tweets, and neighboring tweets. They also used an LSTM layer to capture historical influences from past eras. Fang et al. [13] proposed a multi-task learning model that exploits a large amount of textual information in existing datasets to improve stance prediction. Zhou et al. [15] used recurrent neural networks to model each user's posting behavior on Twitter and used an attention mechanism to merge neighbors' topic-related contexts into attention signals for user-level stance prediction.

Currently, stance prediction works are focused on short-term prediction of users' stances (e.g., predicting the stance of the user's next tweet or next few tweets), but such prediction results do not reflect users' stance attitudes in a certain time period in the future. A small number of existing studies consider the influence of users' historical tweets on their future stances, but these works do not use the time-series features contained in historical tweets to achieve long-term prediction of users' stances. There are also no studies that consider introducing event dynamic evolution knowledge into stance prediction work.

3   Methodology

In this section, we will introduce our method of long-term stance prediction for social media users that fuses time series features and event dynamic evolution knowledge.

3.1   Dataset Construction

Currently, Sina Weibo[1] is one of the largest Chinese social platforms in the world, and hundreds of millions of users post their tweets on Sina Weibo every day. In our study, we choose Sina Weibo to collect historical tweets from different users to construct our dataset. We chose three events "Russia's special military operation against Ukraine", "Chatbot ChatGPT" and "The movie *Full River Red*" as the objects of data collection. In the specific labeling process of the dataset, we labeled the tweets with a supportive attitude as "1", the tweets with a neutral attitude as "0", and the tweets with an opposing attitude as "–1". After rigorous manual annotation, our dataset contains a total of 949 users and 58,310 tweets. We name the dataset as SP-Dataset. The dataset is now publicly available[2] and its specific information is shown in Table 1.

Table 1. Dataset statistics

Topics	Number of users	Number of tweets	Period	Examples
俄罗斯对乌克兰 的特别军事行动 (Russia's special military operation against Ukraine)	425	44,419	2022.3.1- 2023.3.31	战争残酷无情，昔日兄弟还是早日 坐下和谈吧。(The war is merciless. Let the old brothers sit down and talk soon.) label=0 见到入侵的俄军就打，绝不要手下 留情！(If you see invading Russian troops, fight them. Show no mercy!) label=-1
聊天机器人模型 ChatGPT(Chatbot ChatGPT)	241	5,845	2022.12.1 -2023.4.7	个性化定制版ChatGPT？ 这个厉 害了。(Personalized customized ChatGPT? This is amazing.) label=1 ChatGPT能让百度少一点竞价广告 。(ChatGPT can allow Baidu to offer fewer ads through bidding.) label=0
电影《满江红》(The movie *Full River Red*)	283	8,046	2022.5.17- 2023.4.7	满江红真的好厉害呀！！！单日4.6 亿。(The movie *Full River Red* is really good! It made 460 million yuan in a single day.) label=1 欢喜传媒上市公司公告，《满江红》 盈利12亿。(Huanxi media company announced that *Full River Red* made a profit of 1.2 billion yuan.) label=0

---

[1] https://weibo.com/.
[2] https://github.com/yiyepianzhounc/TKSP.

3.2   Prediction Model

As shown in Fig. 1, we propose a model for stance prediction of social media users that incorporates time series features and event dynamic evolution knowledge. This model contains five parts, which are named pre-processing module, stance detection module, calculation of stance scores, the mining of event dynamic evolution knowledge and prediction module. The details of each part are as follows.

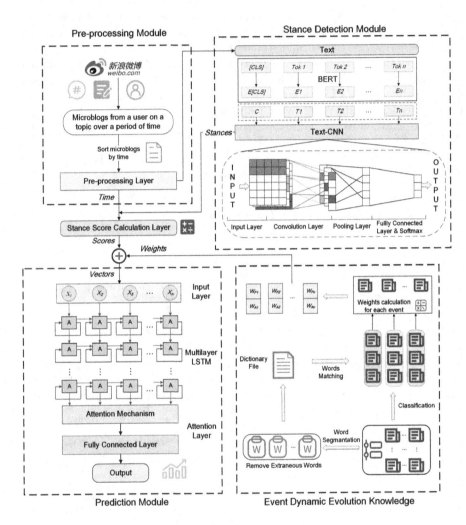

Fig. 1. TKSP model structure

Pre-processing Module. In the pre-processing module, we pre-process the user's historical tweets. First, we collect a user's historical tweets from Sina Weibo. Then these tweets will be arranged in chronological order and fed into the pre-processing layer. In the pre-processing layer, the text content is processed through text normalization, text cleaning, word segmentation, word cleaning, and word normalization. The pre-processed tweets will be used as input to the stance detection module.

Stance Detection Module. We first input the pre-processed tweets from a user into the pre-trained Chinese BERT model [1] to get their vector representations. The output vectors go through convolutional neural networks for further feature extraction. As for the CNN module, we choose the Text-CNN model [20], which can help BERT with classification tasks of specific topics. By connecting the CNN structures, the BERT model is fed into the CNN model as an embedding layer for further learning. Based on the original semantic information combined with the text information of the topic, CNN structure is used for convolutional pooling to extract the semantic features of the target topic. And then the classifier is trained and classified according to these features to finally achieve the classification of stances under the target topic.

The loss function for the training process uses the cross-entropy. The parameter optimizer used to train the model uses the Adam optimizer [21]. The loss function is defined as follows:

$$Loss = -\sum_{i=1}^{N}\sum_{j=1}^{C} y_j^i \log p_j^i \qquad (1)$$

where y_j^i indicates the true label of the ith sample, C is the number of categories of stance labels and N is the total number of samples. The model is trained iteratively using this loss function until convergence.

Calculation of Stance Scores. The stance of a user in a certain time window cannot be simply characterized as "favor", "neutral", or "against", we propose a stance-scoring mechanism based on the number of tweets and stance of each tweet. For a given user, we will get the stance of each historical tweet according to the stance detection module. And these tweets are arranged in chronological order and divided according to the specific time window (In all the experiments, the size of the time windows is forty-eight hours). The procedure for stance score calculation of a given user is elaborated in Algorithm 1.

After the above process, we can get the user's stance score for each time window. If the score is higher than 0 and the higher the score is, the more supportive to the topic the user is during this time window. If the score is less than 0 and the lower the score is, the more opposed to the topic the user is during this time window. If the score is equal to 0, the user is neutral during this time window. The stance-scoring mechanism can help us reasonably evaluate the degree of users' inclinations, which will be beneficial to our prediction work based on time series.

Algorithm 1. Stance scores calculation

Input :

   N_f, The number of tweets with a favorable stance in the each time window

   N_n, The number of tweets with a neutral stance in the each time window

   N_o, The number of tweets with an opposing stance in the each time window

   f_s, Square root of arithmetic calculation function f_t, Inverse tangent function

Output :

   S_s, Stance scores of the user

1: // n is the number of time windows

2: **for** i in n **do**

3:    $A_i = \frac{\pi}{2} - f_t(\frac{n_i}{f_i - o_i}), f_i \in N_f, n_i \in N_n, o_i \in N_o$; //Calculate intermediate variables

4: **end for**

5: **for** i in n **do**

6:    $P_i = f_s(f_i + n_i + o_i), f_i \in N_f, n_i \in N_n, o_i \in N_o$; //Calculate intermediate variables

7: **end for**

8: **for** i in n **do**

9:    $s_i = P_i \times A_i$ //Calculate stance score in each time window

10: **end for**

11: **return** $S_s = \{s_1; s_2; ...; s_n\}$

The Mining of Event Dynamic Evolution Knowledge. In this part, we consider the influence on users brought by the dynamic evolution of topic events. We collect breaking news that occurred during the dynamic evolution of topic events from news websites[3]. We generate two weights, W_F and W_A for each news. W_F indicates the weight of the news that makes the user's stance favorable. W_A indicates the weight of the news that makes the user's stance unfavorable. Specifically, for a given topic, we first perform word segmentation on the news we collected. After that, we remove the words that are not related to the change of stance. Then we assign three levels of scores (1, 2, 3) to the remaining words. If a word has a higher score, it will exert a greater impact on users. Then we form a dictionary with these words and their corresponding scores. Finally, we manually divide all the news into three categories: news that is favorable to supporters, news that is favorable to opponents, news that is neutral. The procedure for weights calculation of each news is elaborated in Algorithm 2.

After the above process, we get values of W_F and W_A for each news, while each news has its time node of occurrence. We generate three-dimensional vectors by fusing the user's stance score in each time window and weights for the news at the corresponding time node. The three-dimensional vector corresponding to the nth time window is $\boldsymbol{X_n} = (S_n, W_F(n), W_A(n))$. S_n is the stance score in the nth time window; $W_F(n)$ and $W_A(n)$ denote the value of W_F and W_A for news that occurred in the nth time window. If none of the collected news occurred during a time window, we set both the value of the W_F and W_A to 0.

---

[3] https://www.sohu.com/a/645326473_121425542, https://zhuanlan.zhihu.com/p/615712600, https://www.sohu.com/a/635606929_120546417.

Algorithm 2. Weight calculation

Input :

    n_s, News that is favorable to supporters

    n_o, News that is favorable to opponents

    n_n, News that is neutral

    s_d, The score for each word in the dictionary

    f_m, Word match function

    f_c, Total score calculation function

Output :

    W_n, Weights for each news;

 1: // *news* is the news for which we calculate the weights

 2: **if** $news \in n_n$ **then**

 3:    $W_F = 0$

 4:    $W_A = 0$

 5: **end if**

 6: **if** $news \in n_s$ **then**

 7:    $W_F = f_c(f_m(news), s_d)$ //Calculate the value of W_F

 8:    $W_A = 0$

 9: **end if**

10: **if** $news \in n_o$ **then**

11:    $W_F = 0$

12:    $W_A = f_c(f_m(news), s_d)$ //Calculate the value of W_A

13: **end if**

14: **return** $W_n = (W_F, W_A)$

Prediction Module. In this part, we input three-dimensional vectors that we get from previous modules and time information into the prediction module. The prediction module first consists of a multilayer LSTM. The data are processed in the LSTM [14] structural unit in the following order: Forget gate f_t discard unwanted information:

$$f_t = \sigma(W_f \times [h_{t-1}, X_t] + b_f) \tag{2}$$

Input Gate i_t determines the data that needs to be updated:

$$i_t = \sigma(W_i \times [h_{t-1}, X_t] + b_i) \tag{3}$$

Outputs the updated data through the output gate O_t:

$$O_t = tanh(W_O \times [h_{t-1}, X_t] + b_O) \tag{4}$$

Update cell status C_t :

$$C_t = C_{t-1} \odot f_t + i_t \odot O_t \tag{5}$$

Determine the value of the output at the current moment:

$$h_t = \sigma(W_O \times [h_{t-1}, X_t] + b_O) \odot \tanh(C_t) \tag{6}$$

where X_t is the input at moment t, h_{t-1} and h_t are the outputs at moments $t-1$ and t, C_{t-1} and C_t are the cell states at moments $t-1$ and t. The W_f, W_i, W_O, b_f, b_i and b_O are the weights. The σ denotes the activation function sigmoid.

A multilayer LSTM structure is used in our model, which consists of multiple sets of LSTM cells stacked together. The cell state C_t and the hidden state h_t of each LSTM layer are used as input for the next LSTM layer. The use of multi-layer LSTM structure helps to improve the prediction performance.

The output of the last LSTM hidden layer is fed to the attention layer for further processing. The attention mechanism can improve the effect of important time steps in the LSTM, thus further reducing prediction errors of the model. The output vector of the LSTM hidden layer is used as the input of the attention layer, which is trained by a fully connected layer. And then the output of the full connection layer is normalized using the softmax function to obtain the assigned weight of each hidden layer vector. The weight size indicates the importance of the hidden state at each time step for the prediction result. The weight training process is as follows:

$$S_i = tanh(W h_i + b_i) \tag{7}$$

$$\alpha_i = softmax(S_i) \tag{8}$$

$$C_i = \sum_{i=0}^{k} \alpha_i h_i \tag{9}$$

where h_i is the output of the last LSTM hidden layer; S_i is the score of the output of each hidden layer; α_i is the weighting factor; C_i is the result after weighted summation, and $softmax$ is the activation function.

The final output specifies a prediction time step of O_t. So the final part outputs O_t steps of the prediction results.

4   Experiments

In this section, we evaluate the performance of our proposed model. First, we describe the experimental setup in our work. Then, we illustrate the superiority of our model compared to the baseline models. After that, the effects of different modules in the model are examined by the ablation experiment. Finally, we tested the performance of our model at different proportions of training data through early detection experiment.

4.1   Experimental Settings

The dataset used in our experiments is SP-Dataset that we collected and constructed from Weibo platform. In our work, all experiments were undertook on a workstation equipped with Intel Xeon Platinum 8255C CPU and NVIDIA Tesla T4 with 32 GB of memory.

In following experiments, we divide our tweet data into training, validation and test sets in the ratio of 6: 2: 2. These data are used for training and testing in the stance detection module. In the prediction module, for each user, we use the first 80% of the user's data for training and the last 20% for testing.

4.2   Baseline Model Comparison Experiment

To demonstrate the effectiveness of our TKSP model, we tested our model and seven other baselines on the constructed SP-Dataset. Our study is divided into two parts: stance detection and stance prediction, so we select seven popular model combinations. In the specific experiment, we randomly select 30 users from the total of 949 users to conduct the experiment. The evaluation metrics of the experiment are MAE and RMSE of original data and MAE and RMSE of the first-order difference of original data.

We present the average, maximum and minimum values of the experimental results of the 30 users. The experimental results are shown in Table 2. The results show that our model outperforms these advanced models in terms of MAE and RMSE of original data and MAE and RMSE of the first-order difference of original data, which indicates that the prediction performance of our model is better. In the test of our TKSP model, we present the prediction results for six randomly selected users (we call them User 1, User 2, User 3, User 4, User 5 and User 6) as a display, which are shown in Fig. 2. From the prediction results, we can find that User 5 has significantly better prediction results than other users. This is because the stance scores of User 5 change much less than that of other users. The stance scores of User 5 tend to be stable within a smaller interval. Therefore, User 5 can achieve better prediction results.

Table 2. Results of the baseline model comparison experiment

Metrics		Models							
		ARIMA [16]	RF [25]	ANN [23]	CNN [26]	GRU [16]	BiLSTM [18]	LSTM [18]	TTSF (ours)
MAE	AVG	0.4737	0.4115	0.4562	0.4500	0.4484	0.4484	0.3838	**0.3432**
	MAX	0.8171	0.6442	0.7903	0.7935	0.7944	0.7912	0.5658	**0.5141**
	MIN	0.1420	0.1452	0.1483	0.1464	0.1455	0.1458	0.1468	**0.1380**
RMSE	AVG	0.5648	0.4791	0.5382	0.5038	0.5009	0.4998	0.4546	**0.4230**
	MAX	0.9081	0.7235	0.9665	0.8829	0.9044	0.8801	0.6230	**0.5537**
	MIN	0.1873	0.1897	0.1865	0.1862	0.1852	0.1861	0.1864	**0.1784**
MAE of FOD	AVG	0.4559	0.4639	0.4044	0.3931	0.3952	0.3930	0.4032	**0.3819**
	MAX	0.5677	0.5388	0.5337	0.5016	0.5028	0.5024	0.5011	**0.4832**
	MIN	0.2670	0.2838	0.2544	0.2556	0.2541	0.2550	0.2556	**0.2501**
RMSE of FOD	AVG	0.4732	0.5490	0.4696	0.4458	0.4478	0.4570	0.4497	**0.4371**
	MAX	0.5574	0.6489	0.6079	0.5628	0.5636	0.5625	0.5622	**0.5460**
	MIN	0.2852	0.2873	0.2839	0.2856	0.2859	0.2867	0.2854	**0.2793**

1. Due to the limitation of the table size, we use "MAE of FOD" and "RMSE of FOD" instead of the MAE and RMSE of the first-order difference of the original data in the table.
2. The baseline models we use in the table are combinations with the BERT model. Due to space limitations, we do not show theirs full names.

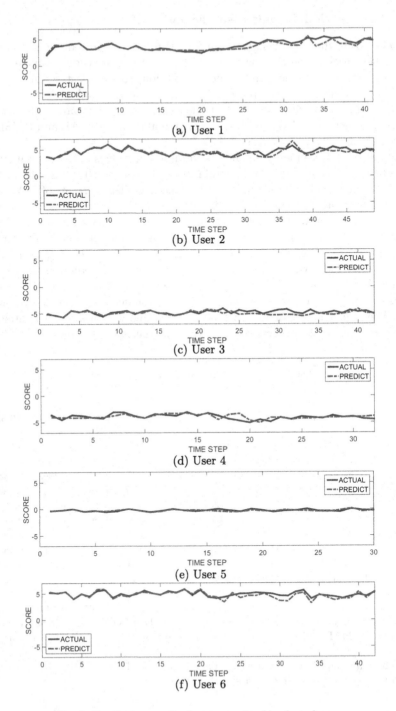

Fig. 2. Prediction results for six randomly selected users

4.3   Ablation Experiment

Our proposed TKSP model combines text features, event dynamic evolution knowledge, and attention mechanism. We examine the contribution of each block to the model through this experiment. Specifically, the use of ablation features is shown in Table 3, where **K** denotes the event dynamic evolution knowledge, **A** denotes the attention mechanism and "/" means "without". We use the same metrics in the baseline experiment as the evaluation metrics of the experiments and use the average of the experimental results of 30 users that are randomly selected from 949 users as the demonstration. The experimental results are shown in Fig. 3. The results show that each block plays an important role in our model, and the ablation of any block weakens the prediction effect of the model. Evidently, our proposed blocks can effectively help the model predict stance scores of users.

Table 3. Settings of ablation experiment

Module set	Categories of modules included
TKSP	Text features, Event dynamic evolution knowledge, Attention mechanism
TKSP/**K**	Text features, Attention mechanism
TKSP/**A**	Text features, Event dynamic evolution knowledge
TKSP/**K&A**	Text features

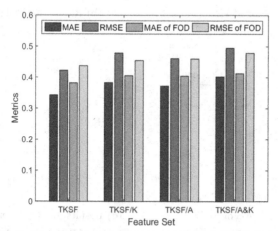

* Due to the limitation of the image size, we use "MAE of FOD" and "RMSE of FOD" instead of the MAE and RMSE of the first-order difference of the original data in the figure.

Fig. 3. Results of ablation experiment

4.4   Early Detection Experiment

In the above experiments, we use 80% of the user data to train and predict the other 20% of the user data. In the early detection experiment, we reduce the proportion of our training data to varying degrees and compare the prediction performance of our model with other baseline models. We use the same metrics in the baseline experiment as the evaluation metrics of the experiments. We use the average of the experiment results of 30 users that are randomly selected from 949 users as the demonstration. The experimental results are shown in Fig. 4. Experimental results show that our model outperforms other baseline models in the vast majority of cases. In addition to this, the overall decrease in the prediction performance of our model is not as significant as other models.

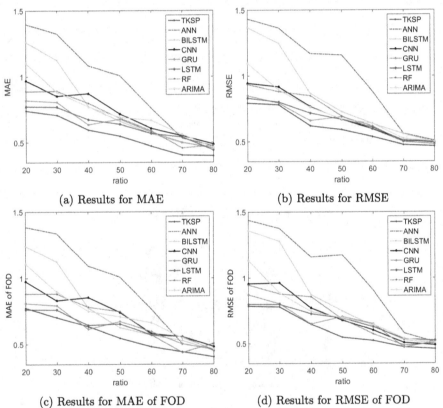

(a) Results for MAE   (b) Results for RMSE

(c) Results for MAE of FOD   (d) Results for RMSE of FOD

* Due to the limitation of the image size, we use "MAE of FOD" and "RMSE of FOD" instead of the MAE and RMSE of the first-order difference of the original data in the figure.

Fig. 4. Results of early detection experiment

5 Conclusion

In this paper, we construct the first SP-Dataset for the long-term stance prediction problem for social media users. In the problem of long-term stance prediction for social media users, we utilize historical tweets of users, time series features and event dynamic evolution knowledge to construct a new model TKSP. Experimental results on our SP-Dataset show that our model can effectively achieve the long-term stance prediction for social media users and our method outperforms other state-of-art models. In the future, we will try to incorporate images and videos from social media users' tweets into our research to achieve a more comprehensive analysis of users' stances.

Acknowledgements. This work is supported by the Key Research and Development Program of Science and Technology Department of Sichuan Province under grant No. 2023YFG0145. In addition, this work is also partially supported by the National Key Research and Development Program of China under grant No. 2022YFC3303101, the Key Research and Development Program of Science and Technology Department of Sichuan Province (nos. 2020YFS0575, 2021YFG0159, 2021KJT0012-2021YFS0067), Sichuan University and Yibin Municipal People's Government University and City Strategic Cooperation Special Fund Project (No. 2020CDYB-29), and Science and Technology Plan Transfer Payment Project of Sichuan Province (No. 2021ZYSF007).

References

1. Cui, Y., Che, W., Liu, T., et al.: Pre-training with whole word masking for Chinese bert. IEEE/ACM Trans. Audio Speech Lang. Process. **29**, 3504–3514 (2021)
2. Al Dayel, A., Magdy, W.: Stance detection on social media: state of the art and trends. Inf. Process. Manag. **58**(4), 102597 (2021)
3. Darwish, K., Stefanov, P., Aupetit, M., et al.: Unsupervised user stance detection on twitter. In: Proceedings of the 14th International AAAI Conference on Web and Social Media, pp. 141–152 (2020)
4. Mohammad, S.M., Sobhani, P., Kiritchenko, S.,: Stance and sentiment in tweets. ACM Trans. Internet Technol. **17**(3), 26:1–26:23 (2017)
5. Majumder, N., Poria, S., Gelbukh, A., et al.: IARM: inter-aspect relation modeling with memory networks in aspect-based sentiment analysis. In: Proceedings of the 11th Conference on Empirical Methods in Natural Language Processing, pp. 3402–3411 (2018)
6. Samih, Y., Darwish, K.: A few topical tweets are enough for effective user stance detection. In: Proceedings of the 16th Conference of the European Chapter of the Association for Computational Linguistics: Main Volume, pp. 2637–2646 (2021)
7. Umer, M., Imtiaz, Z., Ullah, S., et al.: Fake news stance detection using deep learning architecture (CNN-LSTM). IEEE Access **8**, 156695–156706 (2020)
8. Hardalov, M., Arora, A., Nakov, P., et al.: Few-shot cross-lingual stance detection with sentiment-based pre-training. In: Proceedings of the 14th AAAI Conference on Artificial Intelligence, pp. 10729–10737 (2022)

9. Xu, J., Zheng, S., Shi, J., et al.: Ensemble of feature sets and classification methods for stance detection. In Proceedings of 5th CCF Conference on Natural Language Processing and Chinese Computing, pp 679–688 (2016)
10. Wang, Z., Huang, Y., He, B., et al.: TDDF: HFMD outpatients prediction based on time series decomposition and heterogenous data fusion. In: Proceedings of the 15th Conference on Advanced Data Mining and Applications, pp. 658–667 (2019)
11. Chen, C., Wang, Z., Li, W.: Tracking dynamics of opinion behaviors with a content-based sequential opinion influence model. IEEE Trans. Affect. Comput. **11**(4), 627–639 (2018)
12. Dong, R., Sun, Y., Wang, L., et al.: Weakly-guided user stance prediction via joint modeling of content and social interaction. In: Proceedings of the 26th ACM on Conference on Information and Knowledge Management, pp. 1249–1258 (2017)
13. Fang, W., Nadeem, M., Mohtarami, M., et al.: Neural multi-task learning for stance prediction. In: Proceedings of the 2nd Workshop on Fact Extraction and Verification, pp. 13–19 (2019)
14. Hochreiter, S., Schmidhuber, J.: Long short-term Memory. Neural Comput. **9**(8), 1735–1780 (1997)
15. Zhou, L., He, Y., Zhou, D.: Neural opinion dynamics model for the prediction of user-level stance dynamics. Inf. Process. Manag. **57**(2), 102031 (2020)
16. Yamak, P. T., Yujian, L., Gadosey, P. K.: A comparison between ARIMA, LSTM, and GRU for time series forecasting. In: Proceedings of the 2nd International Conference on Algorithms, Computing and Artificial Intelligence, pp. 49–55 (2019)
17. Williams, E. M., Carley, K. M.: TSPA: efficient target-stance detection on twitter. In: Proceedings of the 13th IEEE/ACM International Conference on Advances in Social Networks Analysis and Mining, pp. 242–246 (2022)
18. Siami-Namini, S., Tavakoli, N., Namin, A. S.: The performance of LSTM and BiLSTM in forecasting time series. In: Proceedings of the 7th IEEE International Conference on Big Data, pp. 3285–3292 (2019)
19. Wei, P., Mao, W., Chen, G.: A topic-aware reinforced model for weakly supervised stance detection. In: Proceedings of the 13th AAAI Conference on Artificial Intelligence, pp. 7249–7256 (2019)
20. Zhang, Y., Wallace, B.: A sensitivity analysis of (and practitioners' guide to) convolutional neural networks for sentence classification. arXiv preprint arXiv:https://arxiv.org/abs/1510.03820 (2015)
21. Kingma, D.P., Ba, J.: Adam: a method for stochastic optimization. arXiv preprint arXiv:https://arxiv.org/abs/1412.6980 (2012)
22. Zhou, H., Zhang, S., Peng, J., et al.: Informer: beyond efficient transformer for long sequence time-series forecasting. In: Proceedings of the 15th AAAI Conference on Artificial Intelligence, pp. 11106–11115 (2021)
23. Aras, S., Kocakoç, İD.: A new model selection strategy in time series forecasting with artificial neural networks: IHTS. Neurocomputing **174**, 974–987 (2016)
24. Kobbe, J., Hulpus, I., Stuckenschmidt, H.: Unsupervised stance detection for arguments from consequences. In: Proceedings of the 11th Conference on Empirical Methods in Natural Language Processing, pp. 50–60 (2020)
25. Cutler, A., Cutler, D.R., Stevens, J.R.: Random forests. Ensemble Mach. Learn. Methods Appl., 157–175 (2012)
26. Wang, K., Li, K., Zhou, L., et al.: Multiple convolutional neural networks for multivariate time series prediction. Neurocomputing **360**, 107–119 (2019)
27. Cai, Y., Wang, H., Ye, H., et al.: Depression detection on online social network with multivariate time series feature of user depressive symptoms. Expert Syst. Appl., 119538 (2023)

28. Li, Y., Zhu, Z., Kong, D., Han, H., et al.: EA-LSTM: evolutionary attention-based LSTM for time series prediction. Knowl.-Based Syst. **181**, 104785 (2019)
29. Wang, W., Liu, W., Chen, H.: Information granules-based BP neural network for long-term prediction of time series. IEEE Trans. Fuzzy Syst. **29**(10), 2975–2987 (2020)

A Cross-Document Coreference Resolution Approach to Low-Resource Languages

Nathanon Theptakob[1], Thititorn Seneewong Na Ayutthaya[1], Chanatip Saetia[1], Tawunrat Chalothorn[1], and Pakpoom Buabthong[1,2(✉)] [iD]

[1] Kasikorn Business-Technology Group, Nonthaburi, Thailand
{o_nathanon.t,thititorn.s,chanatip.sae,tawunrat.c}@kbtg.tech
[2] Nakhon Ratchasima Rajabhat University, Nakhon Ratchasima, Thailand
pakpoom.b@nrru.ac.th

Abstract. Coreference resolution is an important area of research in natural language processing that deals with the task of identifying and grouping all the expressions in a text that refer to the same entity. This work presents a system to improve and develop a coreference resolution model for Thai language, based on the existing English clustering-based model. Specifically, we introduce a method to convert Thai text into ECB + -equivalent datasets, which can be used as benchmark for the Thai language. This paper follows an existing model trained for English coreference resolution which uses agglomerative clustering to segment clusters of coreference entities across document. The model trained and evaluated using our data achieves the best CoNLL F1 score of 72.87. Finally, we present a comparative study of the effect of manual and automatic span extractors on Thai language model performance. The results of our study indicate that our proposed pipeline, which utilizes the fine-tuned longformer model as the encoder, offers a viable alternative to more complex and resource-intensive methods. Our work also suggests that the use of existing NER and entity recognizer models can help automate span annotation prior to the subsequent conference clustering module. This study offers a potential framework for the construction of coreference resolution models in other low-resource languages.

Keywords: Coreference resolution · Entity alignment · Cross-document relation extraction · Knowledge graph construction · Clustering

1 Introduction

Nowadays, the amount of text data being produced surpasses the human capacity to handle it manually. One of the common approaches to efficiently utilize the information is to create a knowledge graph (KG) that stores the relational data from the text. Identifying the entity is a crucial step in constructing a KG. However, natural language often refers to an entity by multiple terms. Neglecting these variations can result in an excessive number of entities in the KG, subsequently deminishing its inferencial capacity [1] To solve this problem, coreference resolution step is needed to group entities or noun

© The Author(s), under exclusive license to Springer Nature Switzerland AG 2023
Z. Jin et al. (Eds.): KSEM 2023, LNAI 14118, pp. 422–431, 2023.
https://doi.org/10.1007/978-3-031-40286-9_34

spans that indicate the same entity in input text together [2]. This task can facilitate downstream tasks such as recommendation system [3] or question answering [4] by helping the agent traverse through the graph more efficiently. Depending on the location of the entities, different approaches may be required. Within-document coreference resolution pertains to entities found in a single document, which is frequently employed in question-answering and document retrieval systems. Cross-document coreference resolution, on the other hand, involves entities scattered among multiple documents and is more intricate. In the latter case, approaches that rely on word distance are ineffective, while those that focus on semantics are more adventageous.

Although cross-document coreference resolution model has been developed using various design choices for widely used languages, such as English, models that can handle languages with less resources, especially Thai, are not yet well developed. Herein, we propose a system to improve and develop a coreference resolution model for Thai, based on the existing English clustering-based model [5]. The three main contributions of this research are as follows:

- **Thai string annotation:** we introduce a method to convert Thai text into ECB + -equivalent datasets, which can be used as benchmark for coreference resolution for Thai language.
- **Thai coreference resolution model:** we introduce an approach to coreference resolution for Thai language based on a language-independent algorithm using external data.
- **Automatic span detection experiment:** we further present a comparative study of the effect of manual and automatic span extractors on Thai coreference resolution model performance.

2 Related Works

2.1 Sub-systems of Coreference Resolution Models

Coreference resolution models have been developed with various techniques and design ideas. According to [6], a coreference resolution system can generally be separated into 5 following sub-systems:

Model decides the main framework of the task. Other subsequent components are designed according to the model. There are three main model approaches as follows:

Graph-based model represents spans along with their contexts as graph elements and predict coreference between spans by applying graph algorithms. Rahimian et al. studied this approach by using community detection algorithm on entity-location graph to discover coreference spans topologically [7].

Probabilistic model calculates probability in which spans are in coreference with statistical model. Culotta et al. applied this approach by designing a heuristic algorithm based on Markov Chain Mont Carlo to search for coreference spans, provided with various features about each span [8].

Clustering-based model, in which each span is grouped in an unsupervised manner. Baron et al. proposed this approach using agglomerative clustering on feature vectors of spans, grouping spans together on meeting of certain conditions [9].

Entity resolution determines which region of the text contains spans. This task can be done manually using human annotation or automatically using name-entity recognition (NER), noun resolution, or entity detection modules available in a wide range of languages.

Context representation represents the spans along with its context as vectors, generally by language models such as BERT or its variations.

Similarity computation calculates similarity measures between the context vectors, typically using cosine distance or other built-in similarity scores.

Coreference decision predicts the likelyhood of the spans being in the same coreferencing cluster.

These approaches to coreference resolution resulted in different advantages and disadvantages, which can affect design choices of models with specific purposes. For example, certain methods of similarity computation may require an external data source. For example, Wikitology generates a context vector of a span by comparing it to Wikipedia pages, resulting in a pre-calculated word similarity profile in the similarity computation step that can boost the performance of the model [10]. However, Wikipedia data are only considered available in some high-resource languages, making this approach not easily transferrable to other low-resource languages.

More recent work has combined multiple model frameworks to improve the overall performance. Xue et al. integrates graph-based with probabilistic model during the coreference decision step by modeling relation between spans as a graph and performing coreference resolution by calculating the affinity score of each span pair using a language model [11].

2.2 Dataset and Evaluation Metrics

The ECB+ dataset, which is an extension to the existing EventCorefBank (ECB) dataset [12], is used in this study for English coreference benchmark. Briefly, the ECB+ dataset consists of 502 documents among 43 topics, each representing news with connectible events and entities. This dataset was constructed from Internet-sourced news with the manually annotated spans and coreferences. Similar Internet-sourced news, as well as internal corporate documents in banking domain, written in Thai were used to construct the Thai coreference resolution dataset in this work. A CoNLL F1 score introduced in 2016 [13] is used to compare the coreference resolution performance of each model.

Document 1

หลังจากที่ทีมชาติอาร์เจนตินาชวลสุดไทยชนะทีมชาติฝรั่งเศส 4-2 หลังเสมอใน 120 นาที กัปตันทีมชาติอย่าง ลิโอเนล เมสซี ถูกยกย่องให้เป็นตำนานของอาร์เจนตินา

(After Argentina national team won a shootout against France national team with the score of 4-2 after the draw at 120-minute, Lionel Messi, as national team captain, was praised as Argentina's legend)

Document 2

ลิโอเนล เมสซี ยอดดาวเตะอาร์เจนตินาโพสต์โซเชียลมีเดียส่วนตัวเพื่อขอบคุณแฟน ๆ

(Lionel Messi, the Argentina national team star posted on personal social media to thank his fans)

Fig. 1. Thai coreference resolution

3 Methods

For coreference resolution in Thai, the existing tools are restricted to within-document resolution, such as Thai dependency parsers and Thai anaphora resolution system [14]. This work therefore focuses on outlining how to develop the dataset, training and evaluating the cross-document resolution models.

3.1 Thai String Annotation

The example of Thai coreference resolution is shown in Fig. 1 with its respective English translation. To annotate Thai strings, the overall procedure is summarized in Fig. 2. First, a set of Thai articles were grouped by topics, given by the news providers, to increase the likelihood of cross-document coreference entity appearance.

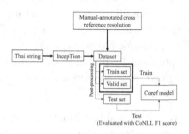

Fig. 2. Thai string annotation procedure

Each article was tokenized using 'crfcut' algorithm implemented in PyThaiNLP [15], a package in which Thai language NLP algorithms are collected, then fed to INCEp-TION [16], an accessible GUI annotation tool that has been modified to handle Thai characters and tokens to perform within-document coreference annotation. To standard-ize this annotation procedure, we have provided a guideline[1] covering span selection and performing within-document coreference annotation. To annotate cross-document coreferences, annotated entities with cross-document coreferences were manually anno-tated without any tools. Then, annotated within-document and cross-document coref-erences were combined together to create a complete dataset in CoNLL 2012 format (.conll) using Python scripts. Afterwards, the dataset will then be separated into training, validation, and testing set to train and evaluate the model.

3.2 Thai Coreference Resolution Model

In this research, we extend the existing model proposed by Catan et al. [5] because the model does not rely on features other than the embedding of the string, making it more robust when applying to other languages. The model utilizes RoBERTa-large to vectorize the word in ECB+ dataset, then uses agglomerative clustering to segment clusters of coreference entities both within and across documents. Coreference resolution was later

---

[1] https://github.com/pbuabthong/thai-coreference-resolution.

performed by chaining together a classification model with a clustering model. Firstly, a classification model is used to predict the coreference probability of all possible pairs of the entity spans. Then, the predicted pairs are forwarded to the clustering model to generate clusters of coreference entities. Our Thai coreference resolution model is based primarily by this approach. According to the 5 sub-systems of coreference resolution [6], our Thai coreference resolution model is designed as follows:

1. Model is designed using an agglomerative clustering framework since this method would require less resources compared to other feature extraction modules such as graph-based or probability-based.
2. Entity resolution is performed manually.
3. Context representation is done using a compatible Thai language model. Models with transformers approach are favored due to the ability to encode contexts along with the meaning of each span.
4. Similarity computation is derived by the classification and clustering of span pairs. Similarity is quantified by the classification model that measures the probability in which each pair of spans is in the same conference instance. Then, the agglomerative clustering algorithm will be performed to generate clusters of coreference spans.
5. Coreference decision is optimized by training and hyperparameter tuning of both classification and clustering part of the coreference resolution model. The best model was selected according to CoNLL F1 score.

Benchmarking Dataset. To create a Thai benchmarking dataset for this research, 160 documents, consist of 16 documents from 10 topics each of news, occurring in the late 2022 written in Thai, are downloaded from various Thai news sources. These documents are annotated and processed into a coreference resolution benchmarking dataset called "TH2022News" using the aforementioned guideline. Documents in each topic in TH2022News dataset are separated into training set, validation set, and testing set by 12:2:2 ratio.

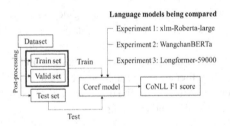

Fig. 3. Language model comparative experiments

Model Training and Evaluation. To create Thai coreference resolution model, a model studied in [5] is modified to be compatible with Thai language. Three language models, xlm-RoBERTa-large [17] (a multilanguage version of RoBERTa-large), Wangchan-BERTa [18] (a popular Thai language model trained with Thai news), and a fine-tuned longformer model specially trained for entity extraction from financial text, are selected and tested as context representation module of the model. This experiment schematics is shown in Fig. 3.

The language models will encode each annotated word along with its context, transforming them to vectors. Then, the classification and the clustering component, collectively called "pairwise model", was trained to calculate pairwise similarity measurement as well as agglomerative clustering to the recognized spans. The best hyperparameters were tuned with a grid search of 50 combinations of data slice to optimize the conference cluster cutoff threshold. Each model is then evaluated with CoNLL F1 score.

3.3   Automatic Span Detection Experiment

According to the ECB + and TH2022News dataset generation method, the presence of spans and their coreferences, both within- and cross-document were annotated by humans. Here an alternative automatic method, which does not fully require manual annotation, is suggested as a means to scale this process. In this experiment, automatic span detectors are used to extract all possible spans, which are then passed along to the Thai coreference resolution model. After the coreference resolution model assigns the spans to their respective coreference cluster, the spans that do not belong to any cluster are then removed.

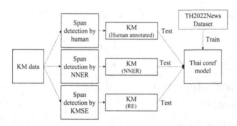

Fig. 4. Diagram of automatic span recognizer experiment

For this experiment, another dataset generated from 42 Thai finance-related documents (called KM), was introduced to study domain-specific coreference entities. The raw text data was annotated and processed with the same method as TH2022News.

Figure 4 outlines the schematics for data preparation in this experiment. Other than human annotation, Thai Nested Named Entity Recognition (Thai-NNER) [19] — a Nested Named Entity Recognition (NNER) that can detect entities nested in each other and a generative relation extraction method based on Deepstruct [20] are used on KM as spans detectors. Spans detected by these two methods are then processed into benchmarking datasets which result in another 2 datasets called KM (NNER) and KM (RE), respectively. Since these two methods cannot connect coreference spans on their own, both within-document and cross-document coreference annotation will be done by detecting entities with the exact same name, namely, any spans with the exact same name will be considered coreference anywhere on any document. Since the amount of KM raw data available is considered too small to train the model, all 42 documents in the KM datasets are used as the testing set, while the primary coreference resolution model is still trained using the fine-tuned longformer with the TH2022News dataset. The details of the Thai dataset presented here can be found in Table 1.

4 Results

4.1 Thai String Annotation

Thai strings from 2 sources are annotated according to the guideline. Then, two datasets, TH2022News and KM (Human annotated) are generated using the aforementioned method. Table 1 shows the number of documents, words, and coreference spans for each dataset.

Table 1. Thai datasets used in this work

Dataset	Documents	Words	Coreferences
TH2022News	160	19,404	1,411
KM	42	13,315	1,347

Table 2. Performance of Thai coreference resolution model

Dataset	Dev CoNLL F1	Test CoNLL F1
ECB + (RoBERTa-large) [5]	N/A	73.1
TH2022News (xlm-RoBERTa-large) [17]	63.70	64.11
TH2022News (WangchanBERTa) [18]	69.61	69.49
TH2022News (Fine-tuned longformer)	74.43	72.89

4.2 Thai Coreference Resolution Model

From the result shown in Table 2, the model trained with fine-tuned longformer achieves the best performance compared to the other two language models with CoNLL F1 score on the test set at 72.89, comparable to 73.1 test set performance of the English coreference resolution model. In the time used to train and test perspective (not shown in the table), fine-tuned longformer model also takes relatively less time to train and predict compared with bigger models such as xlm-RoBERTa-large. From the performance and efficiency of the model, fine-tuned longformer is chosen as the best language model for Thai coreference resolution. Notably, using this model, when dropping the number of topics from 10 to 3 topics, the CoNLL F1 score increases to 75.13.

4.3   Automatic Span Detection Experiment

In comparison of Thai coreference resolution model performance with various span detection methods, the results are shown in Table 3. It is shown that the model trained with a variation of KM data works best when compared with solution of that specific variation. For example, the model trained with KM (Human annotated) achieves the highest at 49.31 CoNLL F1 score when compared with KM (Human annotated) solution, but achieves much lower score compared with other variation solutions. For example, the KM (Human annotated) trained model achieves near zero score compared with KM (NNER) or KM (RE) solution.

Table 3. Results of automatic span detection experiment

Dataset	Compared with human annotation	Compared with NNER annotation	Compared with RE annotation
KM (Human annotated)	49.31	0.16	0.01
KM (NNER)	0.06	16.70	0.00
KM (RE)	0.00	0.00	63.63

5   Discussions

5.1   Performance of the Model

It is shown that Thai coreference resolution model trained using fine-tuned longformer achieves comparable score to English coreference resolution model. However, this experiment uses only one dataset as a benchmark, TH2022News. In one of the experiments comparing the performance of Thai coreference resolution model using the cut down TH2022News to 3 topics to the original 10 topics TH2022News, it is shown that the model trained with 3 topics TH2022News achieve even higher score than model trained with 10 topics TH2022News. From this experiment, dataset seems to have major impact on the model. Details of the features affecting the model are still unknown and should be further investigated.

Moreover, a factor directly affecting coreference resolution decisions is the encoding algorithm provided by chosen language model. Compared with English, there are only a few language models that support Thai language, especially in specific fields. This fact becomes limiting factor of developing Thai coreference resolution with this approach. To tackle this problem, the language model can be fine-tuned beforehand with more Thai data to increase its performance to distinguish between spans.

From the span detection experiment, the human-annotated dataset performs well compared to its own solution but still lower than the domain specific automatic KM (RE) datasets. This suggests the performance of the model is not entirely dependent on the quality of the annotation, but rather on the specific characteristics of the data used for training and the way these features are extracted. This also allows for decoupling between span recognition and the coreference clustering model in other low-resource languages. For example, for the language that currently only has capacity for fundamental tasks, such as POS tagging or NER, one could use these existing models to extract all possible entities and focus the effort to develop or fine-tune the coreference clustering module. In this way, the clustering module would essentially aid in screening the non-relevant entities by assigning them to non-clustering groups.

5.2 Model Improvements

Data Problem. In this work, TH2022News, which are collected from news are used as training data while KM, our main testing data is financial data. The drop in performance may be accounted from out-of-domain problem the model face when transferring from news domain to financial domain. Moreover, while training the model with TH2022News can prove that this approach can result in feasible Thai coreference resolution model, more data should result in better generalization. Training and evaluating the model with large amount of data should be further investigated.

Other Coreference Resolution Algorithms. It is shown that clustering-based without external data approach works well with Thai data. However, it is found that the classification model that predicts the probability of pairwise coreference between two entities spans has a high rate of false negatives, resulting in frequent events of two spans that are actually a coreference pair being dropped from coreference candidate. This miscalculation accounts for more than half of the missing prediction of the model. To compensate for this problem, another approach that has less restriction of holding on to the spans may be favored.

5.3 Accessibility Improvements

To result in better accessibility of the model, it is recommended to integrate coreference resolution model to other Natural Language Processing algorithms such as NER or Entity Linking. Automating coreference resolution can also be extended to automated knowledge management systems such as KMQA.

6 Conclusion

The results of our study indicate that the clustering-based coreference resolution algorithm presented here can be effectively applied to Thai language with comparable performance to similar models trained in English. Additionally, our proposed pipeline, which utilizes the fine-tuned longformer model as the encoder, offers a viable alternative to more complex and resource-intensive methods. Our work also suggests that the use of existing NER and entity recognizer models can help automate span annotation prior to the subsequent conference clustering module. This work provides possible outline to develop coreference resolution model in other low-resource languages. Nevertheless, further investigation into the impact of dataset quality and other features affecting model performance is likely required for each specific language.

References

1. Wang, T., Li, H.: Coreference resolution improves educational knowledge graph construction. In: ICKG (2020)
2. Sukthanker, R., Poria, S., Cambria, E., Thirunavukarasu, R.: Anaphora and coreference resolution: a review. Inform. Fusion **59**, 139–162 (2020)
3. Deng, Y.: Recommender systems based on graph embedding techniques: a review. IEEE Access (2022)
4. Khongcharoen, W., Saetia, C., Chalothorn, T., Buabthong, P.: Question answering over knowledge graphs for thai retail banking products. In: iSAI-NLP. IEEE (2022)
5. Cattan, A., Eirew, A., Stanovsky, G., Joshi, M.,Dagan, I.: Cross-document coreference resolution over predicted mentions. In: ACL (2021)
6. Keshtkaran, A., Yuhaniz, S.S., Ibrahim, S.: An overview of cross-document coreference resolution. In: IConDA (2017)
7. Rahimian, F., Girdzijauskas, S., Haridi, S.: Parallel community detection for cross-document coreference. In: IEEE WI (2014)
8. Culotta, A., Wick, M., McCallum, A.: First-order probabilistic models for coreference resolution. In: ACL (2007)
9. Baron, A., Freedman, M.: Who is who and what is what: experiments in cross-document co-reference. In: EMNLP (2008)
10. Syed, Z. S., Finin, T., Joshi, A.: Wikitology: using wikipedia as an ontology. In: ICAART (2008)
11. Xue, Z., Li, R., Dai, Q., Jiang, Z.: CorefDRE: document-level relation extraction with coreference resolution. In: KSEM (2022)
12. Cybulska, P.V.A.: Using a sledgehammer to crack a nut? Lexical diversity and event coreference resolution. In: LREC (2014)
13. Moosavi, N.S., Strube, M.: Which coreference evaluation metric do you trust? a proposal for a link-based entity aware metric. In ACL (2016)
14. Kongwan, A., Kamaruddin, S.S., Ahmad, F.K.: anaphora resolution in Thai EDU segmentation. J. Comput. Sci. **18**, 306–315 (2022)
15. Phatthiyaphaibun, W., Chaovavanich, K., Polpanumas, C., Suriyawongkul, A., Lowphansirikul, L., Chormai, P.: PyThaiNLP: thai natural language processing in python. Zenodo (2016). https://doi.org/10.5281/zenodo.3519354
16. Klie, J.-C., Bugert, M., Boullosa, B., de Castilho, R.E., Gurevych, I.: The inception platform: machine-assisted and knowledge-oriented interactive annotation. In: COLING (2018)
17. Conneau, A., Khandelwal, K., Goyal, N., Chaudhary, V., Wenzek, G., Guzmán, F., et al: unsupervised cross-lingual representation learning at scale. In: ACL (2019)
18. Lowphansirikul, L., Polpanumas, C., Jantrakulchai, N., Nutanong, S.: WangchanBERTa: Pretraining transformer-based Thai Language Models, arXiv: 2101.09635 (2021)
19. Buaphet, W., Udomcharoenchaikit, C., Limkonchotiwat, P., Rutherford, A., Nutanong, S.: Thai nested named entity recognition corpus. In: ACL (2022)
20. Wang, C., Liu, X., Chen, Z., Hong, H., Tang, J., Song, D.: DeepStruct: pretraining of language models for structure prediction. In: ACL (2022)
21. Liu, Y., Ott, M., Goyal, N., Du, J., Joshi, M., Chen, D., et al.: RoBERTa: A Robustly Optimized BERT Pretraining Approach. arXiv: 1907.11692 (2019)

Network Flow Based IoT Anomaly Detection Using Graph Neural Network

Chongbo Wei[1,2], Gaogang Xie[3], and Zulong Diao[1,4]([✉])

[1] Institute of Computing Technology, Chinese Academy of Sciences, Beijing, China
`{weichongbo,diaozulong}@ict.ac.cn`
[2] University of Chinese Academy of Sciences, Beijing, China
[3] Computer Network Information Center, Chinese Academy of Sciences, Beijing, China
`xie@cnic.cn`
[4] Purple Mountain Laboratories, Nanjing, China

Abstract. Deep learning-based traffic anomaly detection methods are usually fed with high-dimensional statistical features. The greatest challenges are how to detect complex inter-feature relationships and localize and explain anomalies that deviate from these relationships. However, existing methods do not explicitly learn the structure of existing relationships between traffic features or use them to predict the expected behavior of traffic. In this work, we propose a network flow-based IoT anomaly detection approach. It extracts traffic features in different channels as time series. Then a graph neural network combined with a structure learning approach is used to learn relationships between features, which allows users to deduce the root cause of a detected anomaly. We build a real IoT environment and deploy our method on a gateway (simulated with Raspberry PI). The experiment results show that our method has excellent accuracy for detecting anomaly activities and localizes and explains these deviations.

Keywords: Deep learning · Anomaly detection · Internet-of-things · Network flow · Graph neural network

1 Introduction

Internet of Things (IoT) devices have been more widely used over the years. As predicted by Cisco [3], there could be more than 29 billion by the end of 2023. While the IoT brings convenience to our work and life, it also introduces risks. The devices exposed to the Internet are vulnerable to attackers due to their own security flaws and users' misuse, which bring great threat to cyber-security due to their large volume. Therefore, it is crucial to block the propagation of malicious traffic at IoT edge.

A common security system used to secure networks is a traffic anomaly detection system (ADS). Deploying it in the local network can prevent malicious traffic from spreading early. Conventionally, it is deployed at a single point where it

© The Author(s), under exclusive license to Springer Nature Switzerland AG 2023
Z. Jin et al. (Eds.): KSEM 2023, LNAI 14118, pp. 432–445, 2023.
https://doi.org/10.1007/978-3-031-40286-9_35

can monitor the traffic entering and leaving the local network. One approach to achieve this goal is to embed it directly into gateways or router devices.

Over the last decade, many traffic anomaly detection methods have been proposed. One popular approach is to use deep learning (DL) model to perform intrusion detection. Their capability of learning complex patterns and behaviors makes them a suitable solution to classify network traffic as being either normal. DL does not necessarily need feature engineering as they can obtain optimal features automatically from raw data. In recent days, DL architecture has performed well in solving many cyber security problems such as botnet detection [16], malware detection [15], etc.

Therefore, traffic anomaly detection methods based on DL have been increasingly proposed. Deep learning-based techniques have enabled improvements in anomaly detection in high-dimensional datasets. For instance, Autoencoders (AE) are a popular approach for anomaly detection which uses reconstruction error as an outlier score. More recently, Generative Adversarial Networks (GANs) [8] and LSTM-based approaches [12] have also reported promising performance for multivariate anomaly detection. Typically, they take the statistical features of packet headers on flow-level as input data. However, their performance is weak for both capturing complex inter-feature relationships and localizing and explaining deviations of anomalies. This limits their ability to detect and explain deviations from such relationships when anomalous events occur.

How do we take full advantage of the complex relationships between traffic features? First, extract traffic features as time series. The network behavior of an IoT device is usually regular and periodic, which means its traffic features are predictable. Moreover, contextual information in time series are important to distinguishing between two similar network flows. And then, graph neural networks (GNNs) have shown success in modelling graph-structured data. These include graph convolution networks (GCNs) [7], graph attention networks (GATs) [14] and multi-relational approaches [13]. However, applying them to traffic anomaly detection requires overcoming two main challenges. Firstly, different features have very different behaviors. However, typical GNNs use the same model parameters to model the behavior of each node. Secondly, the graph edges (i.e., relationships between features) are initially unknown, and have to be learned along with our model, while GNNs typically treat the graph as an input.

In this work, we propose our novel IoT traffic anomaly detection approach, which characterizes activities of network flow with multi-dimensional time series, and learns relationships between features as a graph, and then identifies and explains deviations in anomalies from the learned patterns. Our method involves two main components: 1) **Feature Extractor**, which extracts features from the arriving packets in an efficient online manner, and then uses embedding vectors to flexibly capture the unique characteristics of each feature. 2) **GNN-based Anomaly Detector**, which learns the relationships between pairs of features, and encodes them as edges in a graph. Then learns to predict the future behavior over its neighboring features in the graph. Finally, identifies and explains deviations from the learned feature relationships in the graph.

In summary, the contributions of this paper as follows:

- We propose a novel method for characterizing activities of IoT traffic, which treat features in dynamic windows as multi-dimensional time series. We also demonstrate how to capture them in an efficient online manner.
- We apply a GNN-base anomaly detector to improve the detection performance and interpretability of anomalies.
- We build an experimental environment composed of real IoT devices and deploy our novel approach on a Raspberry PI. The results demonstrate that our approach detects anomalies more accurately and helps to explain them by comparing the predicted and actual behavior on characterizations.

The rest of the paper is organized as follows: Sect. 2 provide a background on IoT traffic anomaly detection and GNN. Section 3 presents our approach and its entire pipeline. Section 4 presents experimental results in terms of detection performance and run-time performance. In Sect. 5 we present our conclusion.

2 Background

2.1 Cyber Attacks for IoT Nework

The smart home is a typical small IoT network. There are some Iot devices including smart switches, cameras, etc., which are connected through one or more wireless access points and access the Internet through a gateway. Unfortunately, such networks are vulnerable to various attacks due to user misuse or their security flaws. As demonstrated in Fig. 1, ① an attacker scans IoT devices exposed on the Internet and try to gain control of them; ② once a device is compromised, it executes attack commands from the attacker, such as Distributed Denial of Service (DDoS) attacks, spam mail, etc.

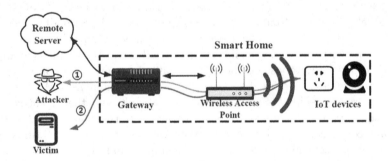

Fig. 1. An instance of attack on a single IoT network.

2.2   Traffic Anomaly Detection for IoT Nework

The anomaly detection system based on network traffic determines whether the connection is secure by communication traffic between devices. In general, as demonstrated in Fig. 2, an traffic anomaly detection system is composed of the following components:

- Packet Capturer: Acquires the raw packet.
- Packet Parser: Parses raw packets to obtain the meta information.
- Feature Extractor: Extracts features from the arriving packets. These features describe the recent network activity of a device.
- Anomaly Detector : Determines whether the traffic is malicious according to extracted features.

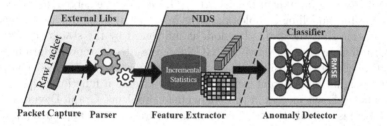

Fig. 2. A framework of DL-based traffic aomaly detection system.

There are many external libraries for packet fcapture and parser, such as shark [9]. Researchers focus on the feature extractor and anomaly detector to improve perfermance.

One popular approach is to embed such a detection system into the gateway device where it can monitor the traffic entering and leaving the local network [10,16]. The famous Kitsune [10] and the latest work [16] all use autoencoders as anomaly detectors. As demonstrated in Fig. 3, they capture the traffic characteristics within the most recent time window as input to AE, and then use autoencoders to learn the pattern of normal traffic.

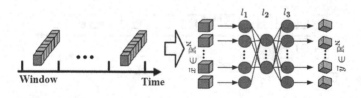

Fig. 3. An instance of AE-based traffic aomaly detection system. All feature instances are independent for AE.

The reconstruction error is used to distinguish between benign and malicious traffic. It can be computed by taking root mean squared error (RMSE) between $\vec{x}$ and the reconstructed output $\vec{y}$. The RMSE between two vectors is defined as

$$RMSE(\vec{x}, \vec{y}) = \sqrt{\frac{\sum_{i=1}^{k}(x_i - y_i)^2}{k}} \qquad (1)$$

where k is the dimensionality of the input vectors.

However, the most serious drawbacks to this approach are that 1) contextual information for each time window is ignored, and 2) no localization and explanation for RMSE value about anomaly is provided.

2.3 Graph Neural Networks

In recent years, graph neural networks (GNNs) have emerged as successful approaches for modelling complex patterns in graph-structured data. In general, GNNs assume that the state of a node is influenced by the states of its neighbors. Graph Convolution Networks (GCNs) aggregate the representations of its one-step neighbors [7]. And then graph attention networks (GANs) computes different weights for different neighbors by an attention function [14]. Related variants have shown success in time-dependent problems. Graph Deviation Network (GDN) is a novel attention-based graph neural network approach [4], which learns a graph of relationships between sensors, and detects deviations from these patterns.

3 Methodology

3.1 Problem Statement

On a simple network device such as a gateway, we monitor the traffic entering and leaving the local network as an infinite packets sequence $P = \{p_1, p_2, \cdots\}$. There are multiple communication channels from devices among the packets, and some may be malicious.

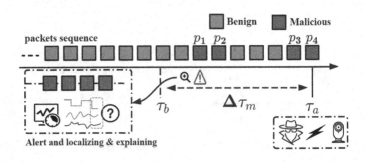

Fig. 4. An illustration of our anomaly detection work.

Our goal is to 1) detect the malicious channels by characterizing traffic within the latest time window $\Delta\tau_m$, and 2) localize and explain the deviations in characteristics. As demonstrated in Fig. 4, when the packet p_4 arrived, we find a malicious channels composed of $\{p_1, p_2, p_3, p_4\}$ in $[\tau_b, \tau_a]$.

3.2 Overview

We propose a novel traffic anomaly detection framework, as showed in Fig. 5. As the contributions of this paper, we discuss how the Feature Extractor (FE) and Anomaly Detector (AD) components work in greater detail.

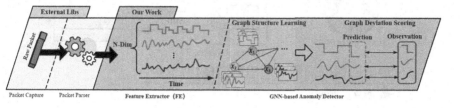

Fig. 5. The framework of our traffic anomaly detection approach.

3.3 Feature Extractor (FE)

The feature extraction component receives meta information of the packets and extracts features that are used to implicitly describe the current status of the local network. The statistics related to count and bandwidth of packets are significant in most anomaly detection works. Therefore, we propose characteristic set as Table 1. We aggregate packets into three communication channels: (1) originating from or sending to a certain IP (denoted **IP**), (2) sent between a couple of IPs (denoted **Channel**), and (3) sent between a TCP/UDP Socket (denoted **Socket**).

Table 1. The statistics extracted from a sequence of packet length

Aggregated by	Statistics	#Features	Common Features (CF)
IP	CF, #Channel, #Socket	8	# (inbound, outbound) μ (inbound, outbound) σ (inbound, outbound)
Channel	CF, #Socket	7	
Socket	CF	6	

Extract Traffic Features as Time Series. In order to extract features of the sequence, we save the meta information of the recent packets within a time window $\Delta\tau_m$ in a buffer, and extract features from the packet sequence in a dynamically maintained manner, as shown in Fig. 6. The framework has an O(1) complexity because the collection of feature instances is maintained in a hash table.

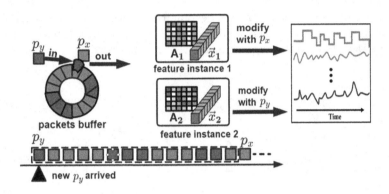

Fig. 6. An illustration of FE. When a new packet p_y arrives, we put meta information of p_y into the packet buffer, and discard p_x if it is out of time window Δ_τ or the buffer is full. Meanwhile, we modify feature instances that are related to p_x and p_y.

We will now present how to calculate these statistic features with O(1) complexity. Let $S_k = \{a_1, a_2, a_3, \cdots, a_k\}$ be a sequence where $a_i \in \mathbb{N}^+$. For example, it is a sequence of packet length of inbound traffic in a communication channel. The current dynamically maintained datas are $(N_{S_k}, LS_{S_k}, \sigma^2_{S_k})$, where N_{S_k}, LS_{S_k} and $\sigma^2_{S_k}$ are the number, linear sum, and variance of S_k. The current calculations for statistics are $\mu_{S_k} = \frac{LS_{S_k}}{N_{S_k}}$, $\sigma_{S_k} = \sqrt{\sigma^2_{S_k}}$. The update procedure for inserting a_{k+1} into S_k are

$$N_{S_{k+1}} = N_{S_k} + 1 \tag{2}$$

$$LS_{S_{k+1}} = LS_{S_k} + a_{k+1} \tag{3}$$

$$\mu_{S_{k+1}} = \mu_{S_k} + \frac{a_{k+1} - \mu_{S_k}}{N_{S_k} + 1} \tag{4}$$

$$\sigma^2_{k+1} = \sigma^2_k + \frac{(a_{k+1} - \mu_k)(a_{k+1} - \mu_{k+1}) - \sigma^2_k}{N_{S_k} + 1} \tag{5}$$

When a packet p_x leaves the buffer, the feature instance related to p_x is sent to the TF component for detection. One optimization is that the feature instance related to $p_{x'}$ will not be detected when $p_{x'}$ leaves the buffer, if $p_{x'}$ is in buffer now and belong to the same socket as p_x. The update procedure for deleting a_k from S_k can also be derived easily according to the adding procedure and will not be detailed described here.

Feature Embedding. Features of different dimensions can be related in complex ways. Hence, we would want to represent each dimension in a flexible way that captures the different 'factors' underlying its behavior in a multidimensional way. We representing each dimension by an **embedding vector** $\vec{v}_i \in \mathbb{R}^d$, for $i \in \{1, 2, \cdots, N\}$. These embeddings are initialized randomly and then trained along with the rest of the model.

The similarity between these embeddings $\vec{v}_i$ indicates simisimilarity of behaviors. These embeddings will be used in structure learning to determine which features are related to one another, and perform attention over neighbors.

3.4 GNN-Bsed Anomaly Detector

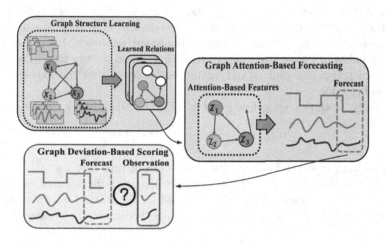

Fig. 7. GNN-based anomaly detector.

This component receives traffic features that are treated as time series of embeddings, and detects and localizes anomalies. To do this, three important procedures are used, which are demonstrated in Fig. 7. We discuss each process briefly below.

Graph Structure Learning. A directed graph is used to learn the relationships between characteristic dimensions in the form of a graph structure, whose nodes represent dimensions and whose edges represent dependency relationships between them. An adjacency matrix A is used to represent this directed graph, where A_{ij} represents the presence of a directed edge from node i to node j.

Formally, for dimension $i \in \{1, 2, \cdots, N\}$, we compute the similarity between node i's embedembedding vector and other node $j \in \{1, 2, \cdots, N\}\backslash\{i\}$:

$$e_{ji} = \frac{\mathbf{v}_i^\top \mathbf{v}_j}{\|\mathbf{v}_i\| \cdot \|\mathbf{v}_j\|} \tag{6}$$

Then, we will define our graph attention-based model which makes use of this learned adjacency matrix A:

$$A_{ji} = 1\{j \in \text{TopK}(\{e_{ki}\})\} \tag{7}$$

where TopK denotes the indices of top-k values among its input. The value of k can be chosen by the user according to the desired sparsity level.

Graph Attention-Based Forecasting. To tell us which dimensions of traffic features are deviating from normal behavior and how they are deviating from normal behavior, we use a forecasting-based approach. It forecasts the expected behavior of each feature at each time based on the past. Therefore, the administrator can understand anomalies by comparing the expected and observed behavior.

Formally, at time t, we define input $\mathbf{x}^{(t)} \in \mathbb{R}^{N \times w}$ based on a sliding window of size w.

$$\mathbf{x}^{(t)} := \left[\mathbf{s}^{(t-w)}, \mathbf{s}^{(t-w+1)}, \cdots, \mathbf{s}^{(t-1)} \right] \tag{8}$$

The target output is the feature data at the current time tick, i.e. $\mathbf{s}^{(t)}$.

To capture the relationships between dimensions of traffic features, we extract a node's information with its neighbors based on the learned graph structure. To do this, node i's aggregated representation z_i is computed as follows:

$$z_i^{(t)} = \text{ReLU}\left(\alpha_{i,i} \mathbf{W}_i^{(t)} + \sum_{j \in \mathcal{N}(i)} \alpha_{i,j} \mathbf{W} \mathbf{x}_j^{(t)} \right) \tag{9}$$

where $\mathcal{N}(i) = \{j | A_{ji} > 0\}$ is the set of neighbors of node i obtained from the learned adjacency matrix A, $\mathbf{W} \in \mathbb{R}^{d \times w}$ is a trainable weight matrix which applies a shared linear transformation to every node, and $\alpha_{i,i}$ are attention coefficients.

Then, For each $z_i^{(t)}$, we element-wise multiply (denoted $\circ$) it with the corresponding time series embedding $\mathbf{v}_i$, and use the results across all nodes as the input of stacked fully-connected layers with output dimensionality N, to predict $\mathbf{s}_i^{(t)}$

$$\hat{\mathbf{s}}^{(t)} = f_\theta \left(\left[\mathbf{v}_1 \circ z_1^{(t)}, \cdots, \mathbf{v}_N \circ z_N^{(t)} \right] \right), \tag{10}$$

and we use the Mean Squared Error between the predicted output $\hat{\mathbf{s}}^{(t)}$ and the observed data $\mathbf{s}^{(t)}$.

Graph Deviation Scoring. To detect and explain anomalies from these learned relationships, we compute individual anomalousness scores for each node, and also combine them into a single anomalousness score for each time tick. The anomalousness score compares the expected behavior at time t to the observed behavior, computing an error value Err at time t and dimension (node) i:

$$\text{Err}_i(t) = \left| \text{s}_i^{(t)} - \hat{\text{s}}_i^{(t)} \right| \tag{11}$$

Deviation values of different characteristic dimensions may have very different scales. Therefore, we perform a robust normalization of the error values of each dimension.

$$a_i(t) = \frac{\text{Err}_i(t) - \widetilde{\mu}_i}{\widetilde{\sigma}_i}, \tag{12}$$

where $\widetilde{\mu}_i$ and $\widetilde{\sigma}_i$ are the median and inter-quartile range across time ticks of the $\text{Err}_i(t)$ values respectively.

Then, to compute the overall anomalousness at time tick t, we aggregate over dimensions using the max function:

$$A(t) = \max_i a_i(t) \tag{13}$$

Finally, we label a time tick t as an anomaly if $A_s(t)$ exceeds a fixed threshold. In this work, we set the threshold as the max of $A_s(t)$ over the benign traffic in train data.

4   Evaluation

In this section, we evaluate the performance of our approach. As the baselines, we present the comparison to the state-of-the-art methods for IoT traffic anomaly detection called Kitsune[10] and LiMNet [5].

4.1   Datasets

We built a real IoT network (pictured in Fig. 8) and deployed the proposed method on a Raspberry PI for performing benchmarks. The PI was connected to the switch to monitor traffic crossing the switch.

We deployed two open-source IoT botnets, BASHLITE [1] and Mirai [2] in our network, and captured botnet data during "spreading" and "C&C communication" phases over one month. The open datas MedBIoT [6] and IoT-23 [11] are also used. They are collected from a medium-sized network with several physical IoT devices and many virtual devices.

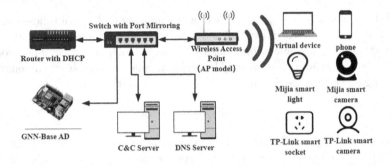

Fig. 8. The network topologies used in the experiments.

4.2 Experimental Setup

We performed benchmarks on a Raspberry PI 4B. The experiments were coded in Python 3.7.9 and Pytorch 1.12.0, and were executed on a single core. The models are trained using the Adam optimizer with learning rate 1×10^{-3}. We use embedding vectors with length of 16, k with 8 and hidden layers of 16 neurons. The window size w is set as 5.

4.3 Detection Performance

Table 2 compares the detection performance between our approach and the two famous approaches. *Kitsune* uses an ensemble of ANN model called autoencoder, and *LiMNet* uses recurrent neural networks (RNNs) with a novel cell. We test them with the optimal setting mentioned in thier work. The results show that our approach obtains excellent performance in all metrics.

Table 2. Detection performance

Approach	Prec(%)	Rec(%)	F1(%)
Kitsune	91.2	96.3	93.7
LiMNet	81.9	93.3	87.2
Ours	**98.4**	**99.7**	**99.0**

4.4 Interpretability

We now interpret embeddings and graph structure learned. The relationship between traffic features is reflected in embedding vectors. The similarity in this embedding space indicates similarity between the features.

According to the experience, our feature set can be divided into 7 categories, including $|\{\#, \mu, \sigma\}| \times |\{inbound, outbound\}|$ and others. To validate this, we visualize the model's embedding vectors using t-SNE. As shown in Fig. 9, we

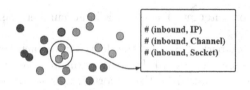

Fig. 9. A t-SNE plot of the embeddings vector.

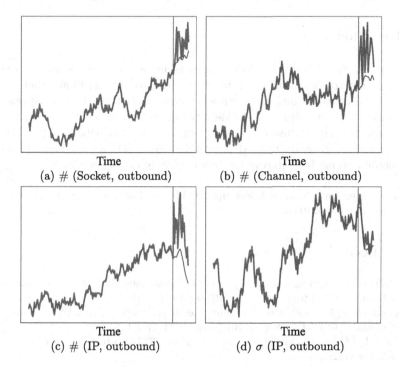

Fig. 10. Comparing expected and observed data helps to explain the anomaly. The predicted data is colored as green and observed data is colored as red. The attack period is started at cutting line. (Color figure online)

color the nodes using 7 colors corresponding to 7 categories. The result verifies the effectiveness of the learned feature representations in reflecting the localized features' similarity.

Moreover, the attention weights further indicate the importance of each feature's (node) neighbors.

4.5   Localizing and Explaining Anomalies

We conduct a case study involving an anomaly with a known cause: an IoT device compromised by Botnet spreads virus. Its major approach is scanning for vulnerable devices on Internet. Therefore, a large number of scanning packets are sent.

During this attack period, we plot the deviation of each feature dimension, some of which are shown in Fig. 10. It clearly indicates the deviation and tells us that the deviation is caused by the abnormal number of outbound packets depicted in subgraphs (a), (b) and (c), not the variance of packet length depicted in subgraphs (d).

5   Conclusion

In this work, we proposed our GNN-based traffic anomaly detection approach, which extracts traffic features in different channels as time series and then uses a graph neural network combined with a structure learning to learn relationships between features. It helps users to identify and localize anomalies, as well as to understand how the anomaly deviates from the expected behavior. We demonstrate its performance in a real IoT network. Future work can consider additional architectures to further improve the practicality of the approach.

Acknowledgement. This work was supported by the National Natural Science Foundation of China No.62102397.

References

1. Angrishi, K.: Turning internet of things (iot) into internet of vulnerabilities (iov): Iot botnets. arXiv preprint arXiv:1702.03681 (2017)
2. Antonakakis, M., et al.: Understanding the mirai botnet. In: 26th USENIX security symposium (USENIX Security 2017), pp. 1093–1110 (2017)
3. Cisco, U.: Cisco annual internet report (2018–2023) white paper. San Jose, CA, USA, Cisco (2020)
4. Deng, A., Hooi, B.: Graph neural network-based anomaly detection in multivariate time series. In: Proceedings of the AAAI Conference on Artificial Intelligence, vol. 35, pp. 4027–4035 (2021)
5. Giaretta, L., Lekssays, A., Carminati, B., Ferrari, E., Girdzijauskas, Š: LiMNet: early-stage detection of iot botnets with lightweight memory networks. In: Bertino, E., Shulman, H., Waidner, M. (eds.) ESORICS 2021. LNCS, vol. 12972, pp. 605–625. Springer, Cham (2021). https://doi.org/10.1007/978-3-030-88418-5_29
6. Guerra-Manzanares, A., Medina-Galindo, J., Bahsi, H., Nõmm, S.: Medbiot: Generation of an iot botnet dataset in a medium-sized iot network. In: ICISSP, pp. 207–218 (2020)
7. Kipf, T.N., Welling, M.: Semi-supervised classification with graph convolutional networks. arXiv preprint arXiv:1609.02907 (2016)
8. Li, D., Chen, D., Jin, B., Shi, L., Goh, J., Ng, S.-K.: MAD-GAN: multivariate anomaly detection for time series data with generative adversarial networks. In: Tetko, I.V., Kůrková, V., Karpov, P., Theis, F. (eds.) ICANN 2019. LNCS, vol. 11730, pp. 703–716. Springer, Cham (2019). https://doi.org/10.1007/978-3-030-30490-4_56

9. Merino, B.: Instant traffic analysis with Tshark how-to. Packt Publishing Ltd. (2013)
10. Mirsky, Y., Doitshman, T., Elovici, Y., Shabtai, A.: Kitsune: an ensemble of autoencoders for online network intrusion detection. arXiv preprint arXiv:1802.09089 (2018)
11. Parmisano, A., Garcia, S., Erquiaga, M.J.: A labeled dataset with malicious and benign iot network traffic. Praha, Czech Republic, Stratosphere Laboratory (2020)
12. Qin, Y., Song, D., Chen, H., Cheng, W., Jiang, G., Cottrell, G.: A dual-stage attention-based recurrent neural network for time series prediction. arXiv preprint arXiv:1704.02971 (2017)
13. Schlichtkrull, M., Kipf, T.N., Bloem, P., van den Berg, R., Titov, I., Welling, M.: Modeling relational data with graph convolutional networks. In: Gangemi, A., et al. (eds.) ESWC 2018. LNCS, vol. 10843, pp. 593–607. Springer, Cham (2018). https://doi.org/10.1007/978-3-319-93417-4_38
14. Veličković, P., Cucurull, G., Casanova, A., Romero, A., Lio, P., Bengio, Y.: Graph attention networks. arXiv preprint arXiv:1710.10903 (2017)
15. Vinayakumar, R., Alazab, M., Jolfaei, A., Soman, K., Poornachandran, P.: Ransomware triage using deep learning: twitter as a case study. In: 2019 Cybersecurity and Cyberforensics Conference (CCC), pp. 67–73. IEEE (2019)
16. Wei, C., Xie, G., Diao, Z.: A lightweight deep learning framework for botnet detecting at the iot edge. Comput. Sec., 103195 (2023)

Disentangled Multi-factor Graph Neural Network for Non-coding RNA-Drug Resistance Association Prediction

Hui Li[1,2], Miaomiao Sun[1], Kuisheng Chen[1(✉)], and Zhenfeng Zhu[2(✉)]

[1] Department of Pathology, The First Affiliated Hospital of Zhengzhou University, Henan Key Laboratory for Tumor Pathology, Zhengzhou 450052, China
{miaomiaosun,kuishengchen}@zzu.edu.cn
[2] School of Computer and Artificial Intelligence, Zhengzhou University, Zhengzhou 450001, China
iezfzhu@zzu.edu.cn

Abstract. Identifying ncRNA-drug resistance associations (NDRAs) can contribute to disease treatment and drug discovery. Currently, graph neural network (GNN)-based methods have shown promising results in this task. However, they fail to recognize the latent factors underneath associations, which may limit their performance. To address this issue, we propose a novel Disentangled Multi-factor Graph Neural Network (DMGNN) for predicting potential NDRAs. In DMGNN, we attribute the formation of associations to multiple factors and dynamically construct factor-aware graphs. Then, we learn factor-aware representations at each factor channel and employ an independence constraint module to ensure that different factor-aware representations contain different semantics. Finally, we obtain disentangled multi-factor representations for prediction by concatenating factor-aware representations. Extensive experiments on three real-world datasets demonstrate that DMGNN outperforms other state-of-the-art methods. Futhermore, case studies show the effectiveness of DMGNN in predicting potential NDRAs.

Keywords: ncRNA-drug resistance association · Disentangled learning · Graph neural network · Multi-factor representations

1 Introduction

Non-coding RNAs (ncRNAs) refer to RNA molecules that are transcribed from the genome but do not encode proteins. ncRNAs such as long ncRNAs (lncRNAs), microRNAs (miRNAs), and circular RNAs (circRNAs) are essential in gene regulatory pathways. Chemotherapy, one of the main treatments for cancer, is widely used in clinical practice. Unfortunately, many patients develop drug resistance during chemotherapy, which leads to recurrence and metastasis of cancer cells, resulting in treatment failure. Numerous studies have shown that treatment resistance in cancer is associated with mutations in the cellular genome [1]. Genomic instability may alter the tumor phenotype, leading to

© The Author(s), under exclusive license to Springer Nature Switzerland AG 2023
Z. Jin et al. (Eds.): KSEM 2023, LNAI 14118, pp. 446–457, 2023.
https://doi.org/10.1007/978-3-031-40286-9_36

drug resistance. This implies that abnormal expression of ncRNAs is not only associated with diseases, but also promotes drug resistance in cancer cells. For example, low expression of miRNA miR-27a is the cause of cisplatin resistance in bladder cancer [2]. Therefore, figuring out the mechanisms of drug resistance at the molecular level can help drug discovery and cancer treatment.

In recent years, many computational methods have been proposed one after another. They can be broadly classified into two categories: machine learning-based methods [3] and graph neural network (GNN)-based methods [4–7]. Despite the effectiveness, traditional machine learning-based methods neglect to exploit topological information. Actually, numerous studies have shown that topological information is beneficial for biomedical link prediction tasks [8,9]. Inspired by successful application of GNNs in various domains [10–12], GNN-based methods have become mainstream in the ncRNA-drug resistance association (NDRA) prediction task. Their core idea is to learn latent and informative representations of ncRNAs and drugs in the ncRNA-drug resistance association graph, which are then used for the subsequent prediction task [4].

Although GNN-based methods have achieved enormous success, they all assume that the mechanisms of drug resistance mediated by ncRNAs are uniform, ignoring the fact that the mechanisms are multifaceted. In fact, drug resistance can be divided into intrinsic resistance and acquired resistance according to the time point when it occurs, which are caused by different mechanisms [13]. These mechanisms often coexist, contribute to tumor progression, and are driven by complex molecular regulatory mechanisms [1]. In this paper, we refer to these mechanisms as *latent factors*. By directly using edges of the ncRNA-drug bipartite graph without distinguishing these latent factors, some fine-grained and valuable information will be inevitably lost. More precisely, this practice fails to comprehensively characterize the impact of ncRNAs on drug resistance production, which leads to suboptimal performance. Therefore, it is highly desired to develop a prediction method that can capture the fine-grained latent factors.

While the idea is promising, two challenges still remain: (i) *How to effectively separate latent factors from the ncRNA-drug bipartite graph?* Although ncRNAs have been identified as mediators of drug resistance, their regulatory mechanisms for drug resistance are not directly observed. Thus, the proposed method needs to automatically discover these factors. Moreover, latent factors should be as different from each other as possible, so that they contain less redundancy and more semantics. (ii) *How to adaptively learn node representations by leveraging GNN and multiple latent factors?* Different drug resistance may be caused by different latent factors. It remains a challenge to learn informative node representations using GNN while making full use of multiple latent factors.

To address the above challenges, we propose a novel Disentangled Multi-factor Graph Neural Network (DMGNN[1]) for predicting NDRAs. As shown in Fig. 1, DMGNN consists of five key components. Specifically, we first randomly initialize the multi-factor representations of nodes and utilize these representations to construct factor-aware graphs. Then, we perform message passing on the

---

[1] Code and datasets will be available at http://github.com/ai4slab/DMGNN.

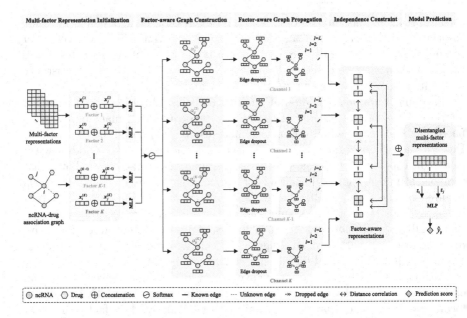

Fig. 1. An illustration of DMGNN model architecture.

graphs to learn factor-aware representations. In this process, an edge dropout strategy is used to increase the randomness and diversity of factor-aware graphs. Next, we apply independence constraint to make the different factor-aware representations to be different from each other, i.e., to enrich their semantic information. Finally, we concatenate these factor-aware representations to obtain the final disentangled multi-factor representations for prediction.

Overall, our main contributions are as follows:

- We propose a novel model called DMGNN, which can efficiently predict NDRAs by disentangling and leveraging multiple latent factors that contribute to association formation.
- We construct factor-aware graphs instead of directly using the ncRNA-drug bipartite graph to learn more expressive node representations. Furthermore, independence constraint is used to ensure that learned disentangled multi-factor representations contain more semantics.
- We conduct extensive experiments on three benchmark datasets, showing superiority over recent state-of-the-art methods. Moreover, case studies on two drugs demonstrate that DMGNN can effectively identify novel NDRAs.

2   Preliminaries

Definition 1 (*ncRNA-drug Association Graph*). Suppose we have M ncRNAs and N drugs. Let $\mathcal{R} = \{r_1, r_2, \ldots, r_M\}$ and $\mathcal{D} = \{d_1, d_2, \ldots, d_N\}$ denote the ncRNA set and the drug set, respectively. Known NDRAs can be represented by an association matrix $\boldsymbol{Y} \in \mathbb{R}^{M \times N}$, whose element $y_{ij} = 1$ if ncRNA r_i is associated with drug d_j, and $y_{ij} = 0$ otherwise. Moreover, a ncRNA-drug association graph $\mathcal{G} = (\mathcal{V}, \mathcal{E})$ can be constructed based on $\boldsymbol{Y}$, where the edges reflect the relationship between ncRNAs and drug resistance. Note that $\mathcal{V} = \mathcal{R} \cup \mathcal{D}$ and $\mathcal{E}$ denote the node set and the edge set, respectively.

Problem Formulation. In this paper, the ncRNA-drug resistance association prediction task is formulated as a binary classification problem. Given $\mathcal{G}$, for each unknown ncRNA-drug pair (r_i, d_j) in the graph, we aim to predict whether there is an association between them.

3 Methodology

3.1 Multi-factor Representation Initialization

We assume that the NDA graph $\mathcal{G}$ is driven by K latent factors. Different factors capture distinct semantics and reflect potential interaction mechanisms between ncRNAs and drugs. So, we intend to disentangle the representation of each node into K chunks, where each chunk is associated with a latent factor. To this end, we adopt random initialization to initialize K embedding matrices $\boldsymbol{X} = \left\{ \boldsymbol{X}^{(1)}, \boldsymbol{X}^{(2)}, \ldots, \boldsymbol{X}^{(K)} \right\}$. Note that these matrices are different from each other to ensure the difference among factors before starting training. More formally, for each node $v_i \in \mathcal{V}$, its initial representation $\boldsymbol{x}_i \in \mathbb{R}^{1 \times (K \times D)}$ is as follows:

$$\boldsymbol{x}_i = \left[\boldsymbol{x}_i^{(1)}, \boldsymbol{x}_i^{(2)}, \ldots, \boldsymbol{x}_i^{(K)} \right] \tag{1}$$

where chunk representation $\boldsymbol{x}_i^{(k)} \in \mathbb{R}^{1 \times D}$ is taken from the i-th row of $\boldsymbol{X}^{(k)} \in \mathbb{R}^{(M+N) \times D}$, describing the characteristics of node v_i at the k-th factor. We refer to $\boldsymbol{x}_i^{(k)}$ as the representation of node v_i in the k-th factor channel.

3.2 Factor-Aware Graph Construction

Corresponding to K factors, we disentangle the edges into K channels to dynamically construct factor-aware graphs $\left\{ \mathcal{G}^{(k)} \right\}_{k=1}^{K}$. Each factor-aware graph reflects the probability that different edges are connected under the corresponding factor. To reduce computational complexity and avoid introducing noise, we only calculate the edge existence probability of connected node pairs in G. Specifically, for each edge $e_{ij} = (v_i, v_j) \in \mathcal{E}$, we first compute the probability that factor k influences the edge existence as follows:

$$p_{ij}^{(k)} = \sigma_2 \left(\boldsymbol{W}_2^{(k)} \sigma_1 \left(\boldsymbol{W}_1^{(k)} \left(\boldsymbol{x}_i^{(k)} \parallel \boldsymbol{x}_j^{(k)} \right) \right) \right) \tag{2}$$

where $\boldsymbol{W}_1^{(k)}$ and $\boldsymbol{W}_2^{(k)}$ are trainable parameters of the k-th channel regarding factor k. $\sigma_1(\cdot)$ is a ReLU function, $\sigma_2(\cdot)$ is a sigmoid function, and $\parallel$ is the concatenation operation. $x_i^{(k)}$ and $x_j^{(k)}$ are the representations of nodes v_i and v_j. $p_{ij}^{(k)}$ reveals how factor k attributes to the linkage of between v_i and v_j. To obtain the distribution over K latent factors, we then normalize the probability via the softmax function. Note that $\alpha_{ij}^{(k)}$ satisfies $\sum_{k=1}^{K}\left(\alpha_{ij}^{(k)}\right) = 1$. Finally, we can construct the weighted factor-aware graph $\mathcal{G}^{(k)}$ corresponding to factor k, whose adjacency matrix $A^{(k)}$ consists of elements $\left\{\alpha_{ij}^{(k)} \mid (v_i, v_j) \in \mathcal{E}\right\}$.

3.3   Factor-Aware Graph Propagation

Each channel k has a factor-aware embedding matrix $X^{(k)}$ and a factor-aware graph $\mathcal{G}^{(k)}$. Within individual factor channel, we aim to leverage topological information to make the factor-aware node representations more discriminative. Thus, we employ the message passing paradigm to iteratively aggregate neighborhood information in each channel. The propagation rule is defined as follows:

$$h_i^{(k,l)} = \sigma\left(W^{(k,l)}h_i^{(k,l-1)} + \sum_{j\in\mathcal{N}_{(i)}}\left(\alpha_{ij}^{(k)}W^{(k,l)}h_j^{(k,l-1)}\right)\right) \tag{3}$$

where $\sigma(\cdot)$ is a ReLU function. $W^{(k,l)}$ is the parameter matrix of l-th layer in the k-th channel. $h_i^{(k,l-1)}$ is the representation of l-th layer obtained by node v_i at the k-th channel, and $h_i^{(k,0)} = x_i^{(k)}$. $\mathcal{N}_{(i)}$ represents the neighbors of node v_i.

Notably, in each training epoch, we randomly discard a certain percentage of edges in $\mathcal{G}^{(k)}$ using an edge dropout strategy. This strategy not only increases the randomness and diversity of the factor-aware graph, but also reduces the risk of over-fitting of the model. In addition, it avoids the inherent over-smoothing problem in GNNs to some extent as the edge connections become more sparse.

After L iterations, to enhance the representation power of nodes, we first obtain the factor-aware representation of node v_i at the k-th channel by summing the representations of different layers:

$$z_i^{(k)} = h_i^{(k,0)} + h_i^{(k,1)} + \cdots + h_i^{(k,L)} \tag{4}$$

Then, learned factor-aware representations can be denoted as $\left\{Z^{(k)}\right\}_{k=1}^{K}$, where $Z^{(k)} = \left[z_1^{(k)}, z_2^{(k)}, \ldots, z_{M+N}^{(k)}\right]^{\mathsf{T}} \in \mathbb{R}^{(M+N)\times D}$ and $\cdot^{\mathsf{T}}$ denotes the transposition operation. Finally, for each node v_i, we get the final disentangled multi-factor representations $z_i \in \mathbb{R}^{1\times(K\times D)}$ as follows: $z_i = \left[z_i^{(1)}, z_i^{(2)}, \ldots, z_i^{(K)}\right]$.

3.4   Independence Constraint

In Sect. 3.1, we generate initial multi-factor representations via random initialization. However, such approach may lead to redundancy among multi-factor representations. To avoid this problem, we adopt distance correlation [14] as a regularizer to enhance the independence of any pair of node representations in the disentangled multi-factor representations. The coefficient is 0 if the two representations are independent. The regularization loss is calculated as follows:

$$\mathcal{L}_{\text{IC}} = \sum_{k=1}^{K} \sum_{k'=k+1}^{K} dCor\left(\boldsymbol{Z}^{(k)}, \boldsymbol{Z}^{(k')}\right) \tag{5}$$

$$dCor\left(\boldsymbol{Z}^{(k)}, \boldsymbol{Z}^{(k')}\right) = \frac{dCov\left(\boldsymbol{Z}^{(k)}, \boldsymbol{Z}^{(k')}\right)}{\sqrt{dVar\left(\boldsymbol{Z}^{(k)}\right) dVar\left(\boldsymbol{Z}^{(k')}\right)}} \tag{6}$$

where $dCov\left(\cdot\right)$ represents the distance covariance between two representations. $dVar\left(\cdot\right)$ represents the distance variance of each representations.

3.5 Model Prediction

After obtaining the disentangled representations of all nodes, for ncRNA r_i and drug d_j, we can obtain their representations $\boldsymbol{z}_i$ and $\boldsymbol{z}_j$, respectively. Then, we employ MLP to get the prediction score between r_i and d_j as follows:

$$\hat{y}_{ij} = \sigma(\text{MLP}\left(\boldsymbol{z}_i \parallel \boldsymbol{z}_j\right)) \tag{7}$$

where $\sigma(\cdot)$ is a sigmoid activation function.

3.6 Model Optimization

We employ the binary cross-entropy loss to optimize the model parameters.

$$\mathcal{L}_{\text{BCE}} = - \sum_{(i,j)\in\boldsymbol{Y}^+\cup\boldsymbol{Y}^-} y_{ij} \log \hat{y}_{ij} + (1 - y_{ij}) \log\left(1 - \hat{y}_{ij}\right) \tag{8}$$

where $\boldsymbol{Y}^+$ and $\boldsymbol{Y}^-$ denote positive and negative samples, respectively. If the pair $(r_i, d_j) \in \boldsymbol{Y}^+$ then the ground truth $y_{ij} = 1$, otherwise $y_{ij} = 0$.

To disentangle the learned multi-factor representations when optimizing the model, we jointly optimize the association prediction and independence constraint losses using a multi-task training strategy. Formally, the total loss is:

$$\mathcal{L} = \mathcal{L}_{\text{BCE}} + \beta\mathcal{L}_{\text{IC}} \tag{9}$$

where β is used to control the strength of the independence constraint.

4 Experiments and Results

4.1 Datasets

To evaluate the effectiveness of DMGNN, we adopt three benchmark datasets for experiments. These datasets were collected from previous studies and contain different entities and association types. The dataset statistics are summarized in Table 1. For each dataset, we consider known associations as positive samples and randomly select the same number of unknown associations as negative samples.

Table 1. Statistics of three benchmark datasets.

Dataset	ncRNA Category	#ncRNAs	#Drugs	#Associations	Sparsity (%)
DB1 [4,15]	miRNA	754	106	3,338	95.82
DB2 [5,7]	lncRNA, miRNA	625	121	2,693	96.44
DB3 [6,16]	miRNA	445	145	2,091	96.76

4.2 Baselines

We compare our proposed DMGNN with several state-of-the-art methods:

- **KATZHMDA** [17] first calculates the Gaussian interaction profile kernel similarity of microbes and diseases separately, and then uses KATZ measure to predict potential associations between them.
- **DMFCDA** [18] applies deep matrix factorization to infer circRNA-disease associations.
- **GAEMDA** [19] adopts graph auto-encoder to identify potential miRNA-disease associations.
- **GANLDA** [20] utilizes graph attention networks to predict lncRNA-disease associations.
- **GCMDR** [4] is the first method to introduce GCNs to predict miRNA-drug resistance associations.
- **LRGCPND** [5] designs a linear residual graph convolution to predict potential associations between ncRNAs and drug resistance.
- **PDSM-LGCN** [6] introduces a light graph convolution neural network to predict miRNA-drug resistance associations.
- **GSLRDA** [7] integrates self-supervised learning and light graph convolution neural network to predict NDRAs.
- **GATv2** [21] is the latest variant of GAT that uses dynamic attention instead of static attention.

4.3 Experimental Settings

Following the settings in [5–7], we apply five-fold cross-validation (5-fold CV) to evaluate the performance of DMGNN. To alleviate the randomness, we repeat all experiments 10 times to get the average results. During the evaluation, We use the area under the receiver operating characteristic (ROC) curve (AUC) and area under the precision-recall (PR) curve (AUPR) as major evaluation metrics. For DMGNN, we employ the Adam optimizer to train it. In terms of hyperparameters, we determine the optimal parameter settings by grid search. To be more specific, the number of layers L is searched in $\{1, 2, 3, 4\}$, the embedding size of each channel D is varying in $\{8, 16, 32, 64\}$, and the number of factors K is tuned in $\{2, 3, 4, 5\}$.

Table 2. Performance comparison of DMGNN with nine baselines on benchmark datasets under 5-fold CV (mean±std%). Note that he best result and the runner-up in each column are marked in **bold** and <u>underlined</u>, respectively.

Model	DB1		DB2		DB3	
	AUC	AUPR	AUC	AUPR	AUC	AUPR
KATZHMDA	85.00±1.74	86.49±0.41	85.51±0.91	85.91±1.32	83.63±0.54	84.76±0.57
DMFCDA	86.25±2.80	87.13±1.17	86.99±0.87	86.47±1.82	84.85±0.56	84.77±0.13
GAEMDA	88.23±0.26	89.67±0.14	88.24±0.69	88.80±1.05	86.05±1.91	87.82±1.19
GANLDA	90.50±0.90	89.58±1.88	89.15±2.01	87.93±3.21	87.00±1.46	87.63±1.55
GCMDR	88.74±0.77	88.68±1.13	89.30±1.16	89.04±1.32	87.55±1.86	88.43±1.30
LRGCPND	91.26±0.96	90.99±0.95	89.75±0.22	90.57±0.40	88.58±0.64	90.06±0.36
PDSM-LGCN	90.38±0.79	91.22±0.53	89.33±0.42	89.20±0.59	88.50±0.79	88.89±0.56
GSLRDA	91.05±0.50	<u>91.61±0.73</u>	<u>90.70±0.72</u>	<u>91.81±0.93</u>	<u>88.96±0.84</u>	<u>90.34±0.64</u>
GATv2	<u>91.64±0.58</u>	91.31±0.50	90.08±0.93	89.06±0.87	88.09±0.86	88.42±1.34
DMGNN	**93.44±0.43**	**92.59±0.77**	**91.69±0.80**	**91.86±0.33**	**90.88±0.62**	**91.15±0.94**

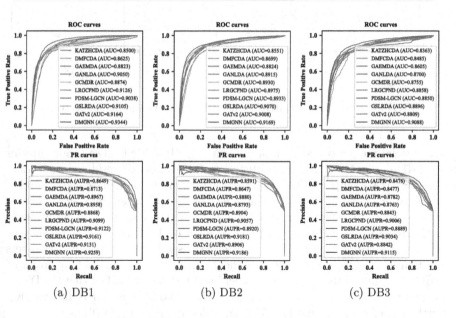

(a) DB1   (b) DB2   (c) DB3

Fig. 2. ROC and PR curves on three benchmark datasets.

4.4 Performance Comparison

The experimental results of DMGNN and nine baselines on three benchmark datasets are presented in Table 2. Furthermore, we plot the ROC and PR curves, as shown in Fig. 2. Based on these results, we can make the following observations: (1) Compared with KATZHMDA and DMFCDA, GNN-based methods obtain better performance, which indicates that topological information

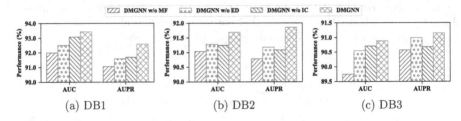

Fig. 3. Performance of DMGNN and its variants on three benchmark datasets.

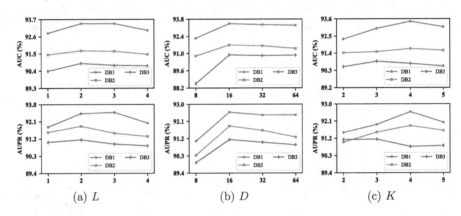

Fig. 4. Performance of DMGNN under different hyperparameter settings.

is beneficial for performance improvement. (2) LRGCPND always outperforms GAEMDA and GCMDR, indicating the effectiveness of residual connection. (3) GSLRDA is superior to other GNN-based methods in most cases, probably because self-supervised learning makes use of unlabeled data and enhances the representation power of nodes. (4) GATv2 achieves comparable performance to GSLRDA on DB1, but inferior to GSLRDA on DB2 and DB3. This may be because the use of attention mechanisms brings a large number of parameters and limited training data makes it difficult to optimize them. (5) Our proposed DMGNN significantly outperforms other baselines due to the fact that the Disentangled multi-factor representations learned by DMGNN are more informative. Furthermore, it shows that DMGNN can effectively predict NDRAs.

4.5   Ablation Study

In this section, we perform ablation studies to validate the effectiveness of different components in DMGNN. Among them, DMGNN w/o MF implies that DMGNN does not disentangle the multi-factor representations. DMGNN w/o ED means that DMGNN removes the edge dropout strategy. DMGNN w/o IC represents that DMGNN removes the independence constraint. As shown in Fig. 3, DMGNN clearly outperforms its variants on all three benchmark datasets. In particular, among the three variants, DMGNN w/o MF performs the worst.

Table 3. Top 10 ncRNAs related to Cisplatin resistance and Doxorubicin resistance predicted by DMGNN.

Cisplatin			Doxorubicin		
Rank	ncRNA	PubMed	Rank	ncRNA	PubMed
1	miR-181a	24183997	1	miR-21	21820606
2	miR-125b	29416757	2	miR-181a	24335172
3	miR-21	28789414	3	GAS5	27878359
4	GAS5	28686971	4	miR-125b	26966351
5	miR-128a	29186980	5	miR-221	28677788
6	miR-146a	29702190	6	miR-145	27487127
7	miR-221	29876362	7	miR-193a	25542424
8	miR-100	24559685	8	miR-22-3p	–
9	miR-222	25474084	9	miR-128a	–
10	ANRIL	29176691	10	let-7a	25669981

These results validate that learning disentangled multi-factor representations is effective in improving the performance of the model.

4.6 Hyperparameter Sensitivity Analysis

In this section, we investigate the effect of different hyperparameter settings on DMGNN, as shown in Fig. 4.

Effect of the number of layers L. The performance of DMGNN first increases and then decreases as L increases. The possible reason for this is that the known NDRAs are few and sparse, and capturing 2- or 3-order neighborhood information is sufficient for this task. Thus, $L = 3$ is appropriate for DB1, and L defaults to 2 for the other datasets.

Effect of the embedding size of each channel D. We observe that there is a significant performance improvement when D grows from 8 to 16. When D continues to increase, the performance remains stable or slightly decreases. These results suggest that $D = 16$ is a good choice in most cases.

Effect of the number of latent factors K. The performance of DMGNN first improves and then decreases as K increases. This is due to the increase in K leading to an increase in model parameters, which are difficult to optimize with limited training data. Therefore, the optimal value of K on DB1 and DB2 is 4, while on DB3 it is 3.

4.7 Case Study

We also conduct case studies on DB2 to further show the ability of DMGNN in predicting novel NDRAs. Following previous studies [5,7], for a specific drug, we remove known ncRNAs while retaining only one ncRNA associated with it.

We consider these removed associations as novel associations. Then, we train the model using all the processed data and predict all ncRNAs that may be associated with this drug. Finally, we sort the prediction results and select the top 10 most likely ncRNAs to check whether the removed ncRNAs are recovered as well as confirmed by PubMed.

Here we use two common chemotherapeutic drugs, Cisplatin and Doxorubicin, as examples. They are used to treat a variety of cancers, and drug resistance often leads to a reduction in their chemotherapeutic efficacy. As shown in Table 3, 10 and 8 of the top 10 predictions of Cisplatin and Doxorubicin can be confirmed, respectively. For example, Chen et al. [22] found that miR-181a targets PRKCD to increase chemotherapy resistance to Cisplatin in human cervical squamous carcinoma. These results suggest that DMGNN is effective in identifying novel NDRAs.

5 Conclusion

In this paper, we propose a novel model called DMGNN for predicting NDRAs, which aims to improve performance by learning disentangled multi-factor representations. First, DMGNN adaptively constructs factor-aware graphs and learns factor-aware representations based on them. Then, an edge dropout strategy increases the randomness and diversity of factor-aware graphs, and independence constraint ensures that the factor-aware representations are independent of each other. Finally, disentangled multi-factor representations are obtained by concatenating factor-aware representations, which contain rich semantic information. Extensive experiments demonstrate the superior performance of DMGNN compared with other state-of-the-art methods, and further case studies validate it as a powerful tool to predict proteial NDRAs.

Acknowledgements. This work was supported by the National Natural Science Foundation of China (Grant No. 82070222, 81873455) and the Training Program for Young and Middle-aged Health Science and Technology Innovation Leaders in Henan Province (Grant No. YXKC2022015).

References

1. Vasan, N., Baselga, J., Hyman, D.M.: A view on drug resistance in cancer. Nature **575**(7782), 299–309 (2019)
2. Drayton, R.M., et al.: Reduced expression of miRNA-27a modulates cisplatin resistance in bladder cancer by targeting the cystine/glutamate exchanger SLC7A11Cisplatin resistance in bladder cancer. Clin. Cancer Res. **20**(7), 1990–2000 (2014)
3. Deepthi, K., Jereesh, A.: An ensemble approach based on multi-source information to predict drug-miRNA associations via convolutional neural networks. IEEE Access **9**, 38331–38341 (2021)
4. Huang, Y.A., Hu, P., Chan, K.C., You, Z.H.: Graph convolution for predicting associations between miRNA and drug resistance. Bioinformatics **36**(3), 851–858 (2020)

5. Li, Y., Wang, R., Zhang, S., Xu, H., Deng, L.: LRGCPND: predicting associations between ncRNA and drug resistance via linear residual graph convolution. Int. J. Molecul. Sci. **22**(19), 10508 (2021)
6. Deng, L., Fan, Z., Xu, H., Yu, S.: PDSM-LGCN: Prediction of drug sensitivity associated microRNAs via light graph convolution neural network. Methods **205**, 106–113 (2022)
7. Zheng, J., Qian, Y., He, J., Kang, Z., Deng, L.: Graph neural network with self-supervised learning for noncoding RNA-drug resistance association prediction. J. Chem. Inf. Model. **62**(15), 3676–3684 (2022)
8. Lou, Z., Cheng, Z., Li, H., Teng, Z., Liu, Y., Tian, Z.: Predicting miRNA-disease associations via learning multimodal networks and fusing mixed neighborhood information. Brief. Bioinform. **23**(5) (2022)
9. Li, H., Wu, B., Sun, M., Ye, Y., Zhu, Z., Chen, K.: Multi-view graph neural network with cascaded attention for lncRNA-miRNA interaction prediction. Knowl. Based Syst. **268**, 110492 (2023)
10. Wu, B., He, X., Wu, L., Zhang, X., Ye, Y.: Graph-augmented co-attention model for socio-sequential recommendation. IEEE Trans. Syst. Man Cybernet. Syst. (2023)
11. Wu, B., Zhong, L., Ye, Y.: Graph-augmented social translation model for next-item recommendation. IEEE Trans. Indust. Inform. (2023)
12. Wu, B., Zhong, L., Li, H., Ye, Y.: Efficient complementary graph convolutional network without negative sampling for item recommendation. Knowl. Based Syst. **256**, 109758 (2022)
13. Chen, B., Dragomir, M.P., Yang, C., Li, Q., Horst, D., Calin, G.A.: Targeting non-coding RNAs to overcome cancer therapy resistance. Signal Transduct. Target. Therapy **7**(1), 1–20 (2022)
14. Székely, G.J., Rizzo, M.L.: Brownian distance covariance. Annal. Appl. Statist. **3**(4), 1236–1265 (2009)
15. Niu, Y., Song, C., Gong, Y., Zhang, W.: MiRNA-drug resistance association prediction through the attentive multimodal graph convolutional network. Front. Pharmacol. **12** (2022)
16. Yu, S., Xu, H., Li, Y., Liu, D., Deng, L.: LGCMDS: predicting miRNA-drug sensitivity based on light graph convolution network. In: 2021 IEEE International Conference on Bioinformatics and Biomedicine (BIBM), pp. 217–222. IEEE (2021)
17. Chen, X., Huang, Y.A., You, Z.H., Yan, G.Y., Wang, X.S.: A novel approach based on KATZ measure to predict associations of human microbiota with non-infectious diseases. Bioinformatics **33**(5), 733–739 (2017)
18. Lu, C., Zeng, M., Zhang, F., Wu, F.X., Li, M., Wang, J.: Deep matrix factorization improves prediction of human circRNA-disease associations. IEEE J. Biomed. Health Inform. **25**(3), 891–899 (2021)
19. Li, Z., Li, J., Nie, R., You, Z.H., Bao, W.: A graph auto-encoder model for miRNA-disease associations prediction. Brief. Bioinform. **22**(4) (2021)
20. Lan, W., Wu, X., Chen, Q., Peng, W., Wang, J., Chen, Y.P.: GANLDA: graph attention network for lncRNA-disease associations prediction. Neurocomputing **469**, 384–393 (2022)
21. Brody, S., Alon, U., Yahav, E.: How attentive are graph attention networks? arXiv preprint arXiv:2105.14491 (2022)
22. Chen, Y., Ke, G., Han, D., Liang, S., Yang, G., Wu, X.: MicroRNA-181a enhances the chemoresistance of human cervical squamous cell carcinoma to cisplatin by targeting PRKCD. Exp. Cell Res. **320**(1), 12–20 (2014)

Author Index

© The Editor(s) (if applicable) and The Author(s), under exclusive license
to Springer Nature Switzerland AG 2023
Z. Jin et al. (Eds.): KSEM 2023, LNAI 14118, pp. 459–461, 2023.
https://doi.org/10.1007/978-3-031-40286-9

Printed in the United States
by Baker & Taylor Publisher Services

Printed in the United States
by Baker & Taylor Publisher Services